FULGENCIO BATISTA

FULGENCIO BATISTA

From Revolutionary to Strongman

FRANK ARGOTE-FREYRE

RUTGERS UNIVERSITY PRESS
NEW BRUNSWICK, NEW JERSEY, AND LONDON

A British Cataloging-in-Publication record for this book is available
from the British Library

All photographs are courtesy of Fulgencio Rubén Batista Godínez,
private collection, Coral Gables, Florida.

Library of Congress Cataloging-in-Publication Data

Argote-Freyre, Frank.
    Fulgencio Batista / Frank Argote-Freyre.
        p. cm.
    Includes bibliographical references and index.
    ISBN-13: 978-0-8135-3701-6 (hardcover : alk. paper)
    ISBN-13: 978-0-8135-3702-3 (pbk. : alk. paper)
1. Batista y Zaldívar, Fulgencio, 1901–1973. 2. Cuba—
History—1933–1959. 3. Presidents—Cuba—Biography. I. Title.

F1787.5.B27A74 2006
972.9106′3—dc22
                                                    2005011245

For Pita and Mom,
my first inspirations.

For my wife, Caridad,
my inspiration of today.

For my children, Amanda and Andrew,
my greatest inspirations.

CONTENTS

PREFACE

Fulgencio Batista, and for that matter most of Cuban history prior to the Revolution of 1959, is lost in the historical mists. There was a Cuba prior to Fidel Castro and the Marxist Revolution, and this study seeks to rediscover it. Batista dominated Cuban politics from the period between 1933 and 1959 in the same way Fidel Castro dominates Cuba today, and has done for more than the past four decades. This work attempts to accurately represent Batista.

These are my scholarly aims, but my motivations are more than historical. A large part of the motivation to write this book comes from a desire to know my family and the Cuba they lived in prior to the revolution. My father emigrated to the United States in 1955, during the period that Batista ruled Cuba, when one of his close friends in the railroad labor movement died under mysterious circumstances. The island was awash in revolution and revolutionaries, and he chose to emigrate to avoid becoming the next mysterious victim. In the aftermath of the revolution's triumph, many of my relatives, some Castro supporters and others opponents, fled into exile. Some family members remained loyal to the revolution and decided to stay. Family conversations often centered on the Cuba prior to the revolution, so in many ways this book is one of self-discovery. In the process of uncovering the historical Batista, I have sought to uncover something about the world of my father and his brothers and sisters. It is a journey that I hope will interest readers.

I chose Batista as my subject because his failures and achievements played out on a grand scale in the Cuba of the 1930s, 1940s, and 1950s, and even

at this late date there is no scholarly biography of the second-most controversial and important figure in modern Cuban history. In spite of his
importance, he remains a stick-figure caricature defined by his enemies, a
poster boy for a failed dictatorship, fleeing in disgrace in the middle of the
night on January 1, 1959. The stereotypes are well known: pawn of the U.S.
government, right-hand man to the Mob, iron-fisted dictator. There is some
truth to these clichés, but they are superficial truths that barely scratch the
surface of his multifaceted political career. This book, the first installment
of a two-volume biography of Batista, aims to look at his life with all its
complexities. It attempts to use Batista as an interpretive prism to review an
entire era—the republican period (1933–1959) of Cuban history—relatively
ignored by scholars until recently.

Many Batistas

The Batista most often written about is the dictator of the 1950s. His dramatic coup of March 10, 1952, the subsequent revolutionary struggle against
him, and the transformative events of 1959 receive the bulk of scholarly
attention. But the Batista of the 1930s and 1940s is not the Batista of the
1950s, no more than the Fidel Castro of the 1960s is the same as the political figure of the early twenty-first century. To treat the many Batistas as a
single character is to distort and impoverish the historical record. The tendency among scholars has been to transplant the dictator of the 1950s back
into the 1930s and 1940s. Put another way, the trend is to view his earlier
actions as motivated by the same pressures, principles, and factors. Batista
has been reduced to a cardboard cutout in a historical play in which the
only outcome can be revolution. But, there was little of the predictable in
the period covered by this work, which includes a worldwide economic
depression, the beginnings of World War II, and in Cuba, the Revolution of
1933, the expansion of the middle class, and the gradual development of
democratic institutions. It was a Cuba emerging from a period of pervasive
and overt domination by the United States (1902–1933), best symbolized by
the hated Platt Amendment, a codicil to the Cuban Constitution of 1901 that
permitted the United States to intervene in Cuban affairs when its interests
were imperiled. It was a Cuba with a growing sense of nationalism—a Cuba
forged, at least in part, by a new relationship of both conflict and cooperation with the United States. The historical Batista, who played a key role in
the abrogation of the Platt Amendment, was an embodiment of that new
relationship and the period that followed. Cuba was not the same in the

1930s as it was in the 1950s, so why should we believe that the political actors and forces were the same?

This volume will focus on two of the many Batistas, the revolutionary leader in the period 1933–1934 and the strongman of 1934–1939. Throughout the 1930s, Batista saw himself, as did many others, as the leader of one faction of a revolutionary movement. He saw himself as inside the Revolution of 1933, not outside of it. Even after toppling President Ramón Grau San Martín and effectively ending the revolution, Batista laid claim to and defended the most far-reaching reforms enacted by the "Government of the One Hundred Days" (actually 134 days), from September 4, 1933, until January 15, 1934. The mantle of revolutionary leadership would be contested ground between Batista and Grau, and remains so to this day for their aging and dying followers in Miami. For the Batista of the period between 1934 and 1939, I have chosen the word "strongman" rather than "dictator," to describe him, because it was a term frequently applied at the time, and it better reflects the historical reality of the period. Batista was the "strong man" if you will, but his commands were by no means the only ones that carried weight in Cuba. In fact, during this period he was as much a political boss as he was a military leader. In order to remain in power, Batista carefully, and repeatedly, crafted political compromises between his military commanders and then argued the position to a volatile and ever-changing coalition of civilian and political leaders. He was a military strongman who was required to operate within a civilian institutional framework.

The rocky relationship between Cuba and the United States is another important theme of this study. Rather than toadying to the United States, the Batista of the 1930s was an irritant to his northern neighbor. The historical evidence points to a leader seeking greater economic and political independence for Cuba but grappling with the fact that the island's export-based economy, revolving around sugar, relied heavily on trade and investment with the United States. Nevertheless, Batista repeatedly challenged his powerful trading partner, displaying a strong reformist streak in his political agenda. Beginning in 1936, he launched the first nationwide effort to eradicate illiteracy. A few years later, he made an alliance with the Cuban Communists in an effort to secure his election to the presidency. This is the same Batista who strictly enforced employment laws reducing the number of U.S. nationals allowed to work in Cuba. The worldwide contest between fascism and communism and the shadow cast by World War II gave Batista more political space to confront the U.S. government and extract more concessions than might have been the case otherwise. All of this is to say that the relationship between Batista and Washington cannot be simplified by the stereotypes so often foisted on us.

These observations are not intended to minimize the enormous influence the United States had over Batista and Cuban affairs. The United States maintained a neocolonial relationship with Cuba throughout the period, and its influence was corrosive to Cuban institutions. Even under Franklin Roosevelt's Good Neighbor policy, of which nonintervention was a keystone, the United States attempted to interfere in every conceivable way, small and large. U.S. officials connived with Batista and his allies to rig the presidential elections of 1936, they threatened economic embargoes on a regular basis when displeased with the Cuban government, and the unspoken threat of military intervention was always present. But the Cubans pushed back. There has been a tendency, again in the aftermath of 1959, to suggest that the United States always got its way. Nothing could be further from the truth.

History should be a living thing, not some dusty tome lying dead and dormant on a bookshelf. It must be reinterpreted by new generations in light of new information and perspectives. Today, more than forty-seven years have passed since Fidel Castro and the revolutionary government took power. Yet, several generations have failed, in large part, to reinterpret Batista and the republican era. For many, the stakes are too important to permit a dialogue. The intent of this book is to contribute to that long-delayed reinterpretation of Batista and the period. It is time to search for the historical Batista rather than continue to live with the cartoon figure that we have inherited.

CURRENT BIOGRAPHICAL LITERATURE

The existing literature on Batista does little to clear up the confusion over his legacy. Most of the biographies were written by friends and associates and border on hero worship. No revolutionary scholar has deigned to write a biography of Batista. The best-known work remains *A Sergeant Named Batista,* an obsequious book written by Associated Press journalist Edmund Chester. A friend of Batista, Chester wrote his book in the aftermath of the coup of March 10, 1952 (it was published in 1954). It paints a Lincolnesque portrait of a man destined to rule Cuba. At times it is difficult to know whether in fact the book was written by Chester or by Batista. Years later in exile, Batista quotes page after page of Chester's book verbatim in his own writings and acknowledges that Chester's account is based on information he provided the author.

The origin of Chester's book merits additional attention, because much of it appears to be a translation of an earlier study by Raúl Acosta Rubio entitled *Ensayo biográfico Batista: Reportaje histórico*, published in 1943. A number of sentences are reproduced almost word-for-word and concept-for-concept in Chester's work. The laudatory tone is consistent in both. Here again, a personal link exists between author and subject. Acosta Rubio was a political aide to Batista, and the stories related in his book seem to be first-hand accounts of events. Neither the work of Chester nor that of Acosta Rubio contains any footnotes. Both appear to be clumsy attempts by Batista and his associates to portray him as a great man in the tradition of Latin American biographical writing. Also published in 1943 was the first of two Batista biographies written by Ulpiano Vega Cobiellas entitled *La personalidad y la obra del General Fulgencio Batista Zaldívar*. Twelve years later, he updated it and released it as *Batista y Cuba: Crónica política y realizaciones*. Vega Cobiellas distances himself a bit more from his subject than does Chester or Acosta Rubio, but still there is little effort at critical analysis. Both versions are spirited defenses of the Batista record, and neither has footnotes. These four works, coupled with the writings and speeches of Batista and Arístides Sosa de Quesada, the intellectual voice of the Cuban military, best represent the pro-Batista literature dealing with his early career.

In opposition to this is an avalanche of books and articles written by the student leaders of the Revolution of 1933, which attribute every possible crime to Batista. Although Batista controlled most of the weapons in the 1930s, the students and senior officers he ousted from power controlled the pens, and they used them to great effect. Their politically motivated attacks, sometimes exaggerated, led in turn to an exaggerated defense of Batista by his allies. There can be no doubt who won the image war. Batista's depiction as a dictator and opportunist was carefully drawn by his early critics and then adopted wholesale by the revolutionary government of the 1960s.

In the immediate aftermath of the Cuban Revolution of 1959, Batista and a few die-hard supporters attempted to defend his second regime and explain its downfall. Batista went on a book-writing spree, publishing six books in the five years between 1959 and 1964. The works utilize a broad range of statistics and measurements to illustrate the achievements of the 1950s Batista regime. But Batista makes no effort in these books to view his life in its totality. Family members say he was writing an autobiography at the time of his death in 1973, but it was never published, and they have declined to release excerpts. A few loyal supporters tried to defend the Batista record, but these works were polemical rather than scholarly. Every few years, a work or two from an aging Batista follower is published in Miami, but apart from some in the Cuban exile community, few read them.

After the 1959 revolution, even more than in the earlier period, Batista's defense was drowned out by his opponents' incessant attacks. In addition to depicting him as a murderer and assassin, supporters of the revolution sought to humiliate him in every possible way, from parading his sick brother, Hermelindo, through the streets and having him declare himself in favor of the revolution to revealing, in newspaper reports about Batista's country home, Kuquine, how many shoes and sports coats he owned. Batista's own discredited rise to power via a military coup on March 10, 1952, invalidating a democratic constitution he helped draft, further weakened any defense of his government and delayed a rational assessment of his career. Events quickly eclipsed Batista's relevancy, as Cuba turned to socialism and the Bay of Pigs invasion was followed by the Cuban Missile Crisis. The importance of placing Batista and his era in historical context was overshadowed. It remains unfinished business to this day.

DUELING INTERPRETATIONS

For many years interpretations of the period have been held hostage by polarized political views. Scholars within Cuba denigrate and minimize earlier political figures as lackeys of the United States and big-business monopolies, and with the triumph of the revolution, irrelevant. This interpretation serves Fidel Castro and the revolutionary government very well, because it debases prerevolutionary leaders, with a few choice exceptions, and sets Castro apart as the spiritual heir to independence leader José Martí. Batista and his representation as a historical figure is central to the revolution's depiction of its victory. The more sinister and nefarious the portrayal of Batista, the more glorious the triumph of the revolution. The more devalued the republican era, the more enhanced the revolution. When I visited Cuba in 1999, the official interpretation of the period was on display at the Museo de la Revolución (the former Presidential Palace) in which Batista was given a special place of shame—*el rincón de los cretinos* (the cretins' corner)—along with former U.S. Presidents Ronald Reagan and George Bush Sr. In the exhibit, the ills of the republican period were elaborately detailed, leaving the impression that everything was made right by the revolution. This is the sort of ideological straitjacket that scholars residing in Cuba must wear. To even mildly challenge this interpretation is to go against one of the central tenets of the revolution, and as a result few revolutionary scholars write of the period, and if they do, they dare not stray from the official interpretation.

A major reassessment of the era is likely once the treasure trove of Cuban government documents becomes available to scholars. But the climate of

political correctness in Havana creates practical problems for scholars seeking to gain access to these records. In order to see some collections, I was
asked to provide sample chapters, a political litmus test to which I was unwilling to submit. Fortunately, I was able to supplement my limited access
to official government documents with an extensive review of several Cuban
newspaper collections in the United States. There is also page upon page
of Cuban government records, interview materials, memos of conversations,
and personal interviews with Batista in archival collections in the United
States. Many Batista supporters and opponents eventually fled to the United
States, and so for the past five years I have conducted a series of oral history interviews and corresponded with family members, surviving officials
of the Batista government, and political adversaries.

The eldest son of the former ruler, Fulgencio Rubén Batista Godínez, was
gracious enough to provide me with access to some of his personal documents, even though he realized this work would be unfavorable to his father
in countless ways. He asked me to specifically note that neither he, nor his
family, is endorsing the content and conclusions contained herein. Some will
view with a critical eye my extensive use of records and oral history interviews provided by the Batista family. With this thought in mind, I viewed
such information with a historian's natural skepticism, as I did my other
sources. Whenever possible in this biography, differing interpretations and
contradictory evidence are provided in order to give readers the opportunity to decide which version of events seems most plausible. In the end,
shining a light on the information provided by the Batista family is one of
this work's most important contributions to the historical record. In addition to the oral history interviews, the Batista family gave me access to some
of Fulgencio Batista's letters, excerpts from his diary, and to rare photos and
memorabilia. They withheld access to some documents, specifically his diary,
because of privacy issues, and one can only hope that with time they will
see the wisdom of releasing that information as well. There are encouraging signs. A few months before the publication of this book, the Batista family donated a collection of documents to the University of Miami.

Another invaluable source was the Sumner Welles collection at the
Franklin D. Roosevelt Library in Hyde Park, New York. This is an archive
rich with historical value, which was made available to the public just over
a decade ago. The letters between Assistant Secretary of State Welles and the
U.S. Ambassadors to Cuba Jefferson Caffery, J. Butler Wright, and George
Messersmith reveal many of the behind-the-scenes machinations of Batista
and the respective ambassadors. The importance of this collection cannot be
overstated. Although Caffery, ambassador from 1933 to 1937, burned all of his

important correspondence, Welles never threw any letters away. This voluminous correspondence opens a revealing door onto the period. Many of the letters I have used here have never before appeared in a scholarly work.

The Cuban community in exile likewise presents a historian of the period with a set of formidable challenges. Many of the voices from Miami and Union City, New Jersey, idealize the republican period. They speak and write of it as a time of lightness before the darkness fell on Cuba. Any critique of the era that in any way justifies or explains the emergence of Fidel Castro and the revolutionary government is dismissed as procommunist.

As a result of these hardened political positions, there is no substantive, ongoing, scholarly dialogue between the two sides. This becomes apparent in glancing at many of the bibliographies of scholarly works produced on the island and in the United States. Each side ignores the scholarship and firsthand accounts of the other. This book attempts to incorporate the findings of all sides, regardless of their political perspective. It seeks a fair and critical assessment of the man and the period. Some will disagree with the balance struck by this work. Let the debate rage.

ACKNOWLEDGMENTS

Most authors wait until the end of the acknowledgments to praise their families; I want to do that right up front. Without my wife, Caridad, there would be no book. In the years I have been at war with this extensive research project, she has kept me and our two children, Amanda, age ten, and Andrew, age six, afloat—emotionally, psychologically, and financially. She has read more drafts of this work than any human being should have to. My children inspire me to write, and it is always with a sense of making them proud of their father and their past that I put pen to paper (or keystroke to word processor). Amanda, who loves to write herself, helped me with the titles for chapters 11 and 12. Andrew and Amanda encouraged me by frequently asking, "How many pages did you write today, Daddy?" My mother, Carmen Argote Pérez, and grandmother, Pita (Asunción Pérez de Argote), always believed in me. They were my first inspirations. My father, George Freyre, and uncle, Fernando Freyre, worked as conductors in Cuba and shared their stories about life on the railroad and provided insight into Batista's early years as a brakeman. Besides my own children, I hope that my niece and nephews, my godchildren, and the little ones who brighten our family life will look on this work with familial pride and realize what is possible with hard work and determination. As I write this I think particularly of Lydia, Leonardo, Alexander, Jonathan, Kelly, Lisa Maria, Anastasia, Michelle, Danielle, Kenny, Ethan, and Tristan. Among the brightest lights was baby Lydia, who graced us with her little smile for just a short time.

My cousins Arthur, María, and Arty and Tío Fernando and Tía Aida and cousin Josefina gave me a place to sleep and fed me during my many research

trips to Miami. My cousin, Ángel García Freyre, accompanied me on a journey of several days to Banes, Holguín, and Cacocum, Cuba, on a tiring research mission. His good humor and Cuban jokes kept us laughing. My aunt
Olga in Camagüey treated me like a king in her home. My in-laws, Tomás
Díaz (Tato) and María Elena Suárez (Tata), and my brother-in-law, Thomas
Díaz Jr. (Tío To), were always there when needed with a kind word and a
helpful act. My cousin Pete traveled the flea market circuit and bought me
whatever he would find on Cuba.

The list of others to whom I owe a debt of friendship and professional
guidance is extensive. Let me start by thanking the members of my dissertation committee at Rutgers University: Mark Wasserman, Luis Martínez-
Fernández, Robert Alexander, Sam Baily, and Gail Triner Besoso. I worked
most closely with Mark and Luis. Mark always believed in the project and
tried his best to nudge me toward the final goal of a completed dissertation.
I often did not listen, and I know this exasperated him, but he never gave
up. For this I am thankful. Luis taught me a great deal about the craft of
historical research and writing. He was gracious enough to include me in
several of his research projects and mentor me through the process. Professor Alexander (I have never presumed to call one of the deans of Latin
American studies Bob) shared with me his extensive oral history collection
and his stories of prerevolutionary Cuba. Sam and Gail inspired me with
the high quality of their historical publications and their dedication to the
field. Robert Whitney offered his suggestions and friendship, as did Danilo
Figueredo.

The Batista family was generous with their time and documents, particularly Fulgencio Rubén Batista Godínez, Mirta Batista Ponsdomenech,
and Jorge Batista Fernández. Several of the people interviewed for this study
have since died, including Santiago Rey Perna, Arístides Sosa de Quesada,
Ramón Grau Alsina, and Antonio Alonso Ávila, but I wish to thank them
posthumously for their cooperation with the research project. Philip F. Dur
graciously shared his stories about Jefferson Caffery. Three very gifted women
in one family—Adrienne Calleja, Marianela Santurio, and Carmen Pizzi
Santurio—were kind enough to share some family letters between Batista
and their beloved relative Enrique Pizzi de Porras, most notably a touching
letter that Batista wrote about his mother, quoted extensively in chapter 1.

It can truly be said that a historian is nothing without a good archivist
and librarian. Fortunately, I encountered many gifted professionals everywhere I went. In Cuba, Araceli García Carranza helped me access the collections at the Biblioteca Nacional José Martí in Havana. At the Roosevelt
Library, Hyde Park, I found a staff eager to help me unlock the secrets of an

era. I wish to particularly thank Raymond J. Teichman, supervisory archivist, and archivists Nancy Snedeker, Alycia J. Vivona, Mark A. Renovitch, Robert H. Parks, Karen Anson, and Dave Bassano. I spent so much time combing over the Sumner Welles papers at Hyde Park that I began receiving invitations to staff parties. I wish to thank the Roosevelt Library for a generous financial award in support of my research.

Rutgers University also provided me with several research fellowships. The staff at the Rutgers History Department, Dawn Ruskai, Mary DeMeo, and Dorothy McGrath are first rate, and they saved me from countless headaches. I would be remiss if I did not mention the generous and constant encouragement of good friends such as Bill and Joan Lopatin. Bill, recently deceased, urged me to complete the work before his death, which, thankfully, I did.

Many others contributed their insights to this work, including Virgilio Blanco Lage, a dear friend and confidante on all things Cuban; Mauricio Font, who shared with me his views on Batista and prerevolutionary Cuba; Ernesto Sagás, a gifted and talented scholar with an amusing sense of humor who helped me with some of the translations; and Humberto García Muñiz, who challenged my assumptions on Batista and the Caribbean. Allan Howard, Mike Gasster, Paul Clemens, John Gillis, and Michael Adas of the Rutgers History Department were always generous with their time. My colleagues at the Puerto Rican and Hispanic Caribbean Studies Department at Rutgers University, Monica Licourt, Carmen Whalen, Pedro Cabán, Asela Laguna Díaz, Larry LaFountain-Stokes, and Astrid Cubano, showered me with encouragement. Jeremy Adelman of Princeton University reviewed drafts of several chapters and provided helpful suggestions. Early in the project, Louis A. Pérez Jr. gave me valuable insights on conducting research in Cuba. Lisandro Pérez and Marifeli Pérez Stable provided helpful criticism on an article drawn from this book. Literary agent Reid Boates provided me with sound advice on marketing the manuscript. Fellow writer Kevin Coyne was generous in sharing his insights on the "writing life." Attorney and friend, Michael Detzky, besides reviewing the contract, urged me to write more and always pleaded with me to "send the next chapter." On the technical side, Cody Richter used his vast knowledge of computers to restore and enhance the political cartoons included in this work.

The editing and production staff at Rutgers University Press deserve my gratitude, especially Director Marlie Wasserman, my friend of many years; Kristi Long and Adi Hovav, who guided the book through the editorial process; Beth Kressel, Michele Gisbert, and Christina Brianik, who contributed to various aspects of the manuscript; and, of course, Beth Gianfagna, my copy editor, who painstakingly worked to make my every sentence a gem. A special mention goes to Production Editor Nicole Manganaro, who took her own time to work on the bibliography of this book and showed great patience with a first-time author.

They all contributed a great deal to this work, but its strengths and weaknesses are uniquely my own.

FULGENCIO BATISTA

CHAPTER 1

END
AND BEGINNING

By the middle of December 1958, Fulgencio Batista knew his days as dictator of Cuba were about to come to an abrupt end. In recent years, he had survived an attack on the Presidential Palace that left several of his personal guards dead and nearly cost him and his wife their lives. He had survived several efforts by trusted military officials to topple him from power, including a naval revolt by forces at the port of Cienfuegos. But most recently, Batista, who had dominated Cuban politics for twenty-five years, had received word from his intelligence operatives that one of his most loyal generals had met on Christmas Eve with rebel leader Fidel Castro.[1] At that meeting a plan to turn over Batista to the rebels was consummated. The result would have been a trial and execution as a war criminal.[2] The master of Cuban Army politics knew the fight was over.

On the afternoon of December 30, Batista told his eldest son, Rubén, to keep the family united throughout the day and to stay where he could be reached at a moment's notice.[3] The plan was to keep up appearances, to make it look as if he was continuing the fight. On the evening of December 31, he invited a group of cabinet ministers to his home at Camp Columbia, the army's principal base in Havana, for "a cup of coffee."[4] The event was intended to be low-key because no one was in a celebratory mood given the recent setbacks on the battlefield. General José Pedraza monitored the battle in the east in Las Villas Province by shortwave radio. To Interior Minister Santiago Rey Perna there was nothing particularly unusual about the gathering, which started shortly after 10 p.m. At the end of the coffee social, Pedraza announced that the "struggle would continue tomorrow."

But in less than five hours, Batista and three airplanes with his family and closest friends and advisers would take off from that same army base.[5] At the age of fifty-eight, Batista would flee into ignominious exile, first to the Dominican Republic, then Portugal, and finally Spain, where he died in 1973. He would never set foot in Cuba or the United States again. Batista left disgraced—his name linked to corruption, brutality, and the U.S. Mafia—and doomed to forever play the villain to Fidel Castro's hero in the revolution's interpretation of history. He spent the last years of his life writing book after book, none of which would garner much attention, in a vain effort to rebuild his image as the "revolutionary leader" of the 1930s who toppled a U.S.-supported government and succeeded in bringing democracy to Cuba. He would always be remembered as the failed dictator who fled in the middle of the night.

Humble Beginnings

There could hardly be a more unlikely candidate to take part in Cuba's national drama than Rubén Fulgencio Batista Zaldívar, who was born to a life of abject poverty on January 16, 1901.[6] He was named for the famous Nicaraguan poet Rubén Darío, then at the height of his popularity, and Saint Fulgentius, a seventh-century Spanish bishop.[7] Batista was the first of four sons born to Belisario Batista Palermo and Carmela Zaldívar González in the Veguitas section of Banes, a small rural community in northeastern Oriente Province.[8] His maternal grandmother, Juana González, was a midwife and helped deliver the baby boy. The Zaldívar family had moved a few years earlier from Aura, a small hamlet about forty miles west of Banes. Batista was baptized a Roman Catholic some months after his birth at a small church in Fray Benito. Most of what is known about Batista's parents comes from second- or thirdhand information passed down by family members, friends, and acquaintances.[9] Carmela Zaldívar was a tender and sweet woman who was very affectionate with her children. She was fifteen when she gave birth to her first child. Carmela was one of three children, but she had lost a brother, Juan, in the Cuban Independence War of 1895–1898. Her younger sister, Cándida, would outlive her and settle in a nearby village. As a boy, Batista formed a very strong attachment to his mother, and years later his eyes would well up with tears as he spoke of her.[10] His mother affectionately nicknamed her oldest son "Beno," a shortened version of Rubén. As a child, it was to her that he turned for love, affection, and comfort.

Belisario Batista, nicknamed "Don Beli," had fought in the Cuban Independence War against Spain under General José Maceo and was reportedly wounded on three occasions. Belisario was a strong man with a slim build, a mustache, and a dark complexion. The elder Batista may have liked to drink, sometimes to excess, and would occasionally stay out all night at parties.[11] Years later, one of Batista's personal secretaries, Raúl Acosta Rubio, said Batista would frequently speak of his mother with "love and pride," but he noticed a reluctance on the part of Batista to speak of his father, surmising that he had little good to say about him. Acosta Rubio probably overstates the point, but clearly, Batista did not have the same affection for his father as he did for his mother. Several others confirm Acosta Rubio's observation that Batista frequently spoke in glowing terms of his mother, while rarely mentioning his father. After his mother's death, he seldom returned to Banes to visit his father, although the difficulty of transportation no doubt contributed to his absence. The relationship between eldest son and father was one of filial duty and respect, but it lacked warmth. As president, Batista dedicated and named a park and library in Banes for his mother.[12] He made no similar gesture to honor his father's memory. Batista did commission a portrait of his father based on his own recollection, since no photographs of Belisario Batista survived, and that painting hung in Batista's Madrid home until his death.[13] It is unlikely he would have commissioned a portrait of his father and hung it in his home if he had detested him.

The relationship with his three brothers, Juan, Hermelindo, and Francisco (Panchín) would be of great significance to Rubén Fulgencio throughout his life. Little is known of their interaction as boys, but a great deal can be discerned from their relationship as adults. Rubén Fulgencio was always the big brother. In his own way, he would try to help each of them and shield them from the adversity of their own lives and the notoriety created by his rise to power. Juan, born in 1905,[14] was closest in age to Rubén, and his death years later of tuberculosis was a traumatic experience for the older brother. Juan would die slowly despite efforts by Rubén Fulgencio to nurse him back to health at his home. Juan's death had a profound impact on the future president and no doubt contributed to Batista's campaign to combat tuberculosis throughout the island. Hermelindo, born in 1906, suffered from bouts of depression and mental instability throughout his life, and Rubén Fulgencio took it upon himself to look after and educate his brother's son, sometimes to his great embarrassment.[15] But his closest bond was with Francisco, his youngest brother, who followed him into politics and whom he shielded from criticism at political cost to himself. Francisco, born in 1911, was only five years old when their mother died.[16] Later in life, Francisco would betray him and make an alliance with his political opponents, but eventually the older brother would forgive him and allow him to rejoin his ruling alliance.

In later years, Fulgencio Batista's political enemies would spread rumors that he was not born in Cuba.[17] One U.S. military attaché speculated that Batista was born in South America.[18] *New York Times* reporter Ruby Hart Phillips, who spent more than two decades in Cuba, was doubtful of Batista's Cuban origins. At one point, Phillips passed on to the U.S. State Department a letter from a Colombian man who claimed to be Batista's father.[19] The question of his place of birth made good fodder for Batista's political enemies, but no serious evidence to back up those claims ever surfaced. The overwhelming evidence from those who lived in Banes in the early 1900s and the testimonies of friends and family members make the claim of a foreign birth highly suspect.

The question of Batista's racial and ethnic origin is a more difficult issue to contend with and was frequently the subject of rumor and innuendo, if not outright debate, throughout his long career. Issues of race and class occasionally surfaced and led to some very public snubs by the Cuban upper classes. Batista frequently acknowledged his humble beginnings, although he rarely discussed his racial and ethnic origins. There are few surviving records from the period, so his antecedents will probably never be fully determined with any precision. In the U.S. media, Batista was often described as a "mulatto" or the "brown dictator." Some thought he might be of Chinese or other Asian extraction. There were even stories that he might be Greek.[20] Volumes have been written in the past decade on the use of race and ethnicity to define the "other" and develop ideologies of control that benefit one group and exclude another. In Latin America that usually translated into an ideology of racial supremacy that privileged Europeans of "pure blood" over Indians, Africans, Chinese, and other racial groups that were deemed inferior.[21]

In a sense, Batista's ethnicity and race were whatever his friends and foes wanted it to be. "His friends called him *el indio* [the Indian], and his enemies called him *el negro* [black man]," recalled his eldest son years later.[22] Over time, the way others chose to racially and ethnically define him evolved as he proved to be more intelligent than some observers expected. When he first saw Batista, U.S. Military Attaché T. N. Gimperling believed he was *achinado*, meaning part Chinese, Indian, and Afro-Cuban. But, as Batista proved himself, Gimperling revised his racial and ethnic profile. "I am very inclined now to believe that Batista is either of Chilean-Indian extraction or of Chilean-Mexican extraction, and not as was first believed, half negro and one-quarter Chinese. I consider the importance of this to be that the Chilean-Indian or the Chilean-Mexican is apt to be more courageous, more sagacious and more crafty than the mixed negro-Chinese-Cuban."[23]

As in other areas of Latin America, the Indians who settled the region hundreds of years before the Spaniards arrived had gained a sort of mythical, magical quality as their numbers and the potential threat they posed declined.[24] To refer to Batista as an *indio* would, in most cases, be a more or less positive reference to the Taino Indians, who predominated in Cuba and in the area around Banes prior to the conquest and who virtually disappeared within fifty years of Columbus's arrival. Identifying Batista as a black man would emphasize his descent from African slaves brought to Cuba to work on the sugar and tobacco plantations in the eighteenth and nineteenth centuries. Race and slavery played an important role in Cuba's two wars of independence and afterward in the Race War of 1912. To refer to Batista as African was to saddle him with all this additional racist baggage and to discredit him among the Cuban elite, particularly those descended from the Spanish and other Europeans.

Batista never raised the race issue publicly and on the rare occasions when it was broached by journalists simply described himself and his parents as "Cuban."[25] It would not have been in his best interests to discuss his racial and ethnic origins given the racial prejudice in Cuba and the United States. His enemies assumed he was Afro-Cuban, and he was frequently depicted as having exaggerated African features in Cuban newspaper cartoons. Any discussion on his part, and certainly any acknowledgment of an African heritage, if he knew of it, would have only provided his enemies with ammunition. Surviving family members say that they themselves are not completely certain of their racial and ethnic origins, although at least one of Batista's grandparents emigrated to Cuba from the Canary Islands.[26] It is quite probable, given the extent of intermarriage in the Banes region and the high number of former African slaves in Oriente Province, that Batista's family was a mixture of Spanish, African, and Indian lineages.

Batista's birthplace, Banes, was completely transformed from a rural backwater to a small and bustling commercial center by the time he reached adolescence. Originally settled by Amerindians and called "Bani," it remained sparsely populated until the twentieth century. By the early 1900s, Banes was a rural community of about five thousand residents consisting of a few scattered rural settlements and neighborhoods with a small, centrally located shopping district that included several pharmacies that served as general stores, as well as a bakery, a watchmaker, two soda factories, three barber shops, five cigar makers, and a few small restaurants. Three doctors and one dentist resided in the town. Photographs from the period reveal a town of narrow streets with several dirt roads and wooden sidewalks.[27] The Batista family moved to a *bohío* in "La Güira," one of Banes' poorer neighborhoods, when their eldest son was only six months old. The walls of a *bohío* are typically made of the bark of palm trees. The roofs consist of carefully interwoven palm leaves. Most have dirt floors and contain no more than one or two rooms. His parents built the tiny home themselves a few months after their oldest son was born, although it is not clear whether they ever had legal title to the land. The Batista home consisted of two rooms, a living room and a bedroom, where the entire family slept. There was no indoor plumbing, so bathroom facilities, often little more than a hole in the ground, were outside, adjacent to the home. For drinking water, the family relied on nearby rivers and ponds, which were often breeding grounds for a variety of diseases. During his childhood, Batista, like many other rural children, suffered frequently from intestinal parasites, which caused diarrhea, dehydration, and stomach cramping.[28]

El Coloso

Belisario Batista was a sugar cane cutter employed by a local contractor (*colono*) that farmed land for the economically and politically powerful United Fruit Company. The company, a U.S. corporation, would dominate Banes and the region for generations to come and provide the young Batista with his first political lessons on the unequal relationship between Cuba and its powerful northern neighbor.

In 1901, the same year Batista was born, United Fruit opened an enormous sugar processing plant, "the Central Boston," on the Bay of Banes. Prior to the opening of the plant the local economy was dominated by several banana plantations established in the 1880s. The largest banana producers and shippers in the region were the Dumois brothers, whose parents were French immigrants from Louisiana. The Dumois brothers built a small railroad, just over three miles long, to transport the bananas from a warehouse in the center of town to the port for shipment to the United States. The Bay of Banes offered a deep harbor for the banana boats, although the entrance is narrow, just seven hundred to one thousand feet wide with a length of about two miles. The Dumois family was able to survive the first years of the Cuban Independence War by flying the French flag over their properties and by paying a tribute to the Cuban rebels. However, in 1896, General Máximo Gómez made a tactical decision to burn the port facilities and the center of Banes to prevent the Spanish from using the town as a base of operations. Witnesses to the event commented that the flames were strikingly "beautiful" because of the wide variety of colors reflected in the sky.[29] The port facilities and banana plantations were abandoned for the rest of the war, and active shipping did not resume on a large scale until the Dumois properties were purchased in 1899 by United Fruit, which operated banana plantations in six countries in Central America and the Caribbean.

United Fruit executives had a different plan for their Cuba properties. After some experimentation with sugar cultivation, company executives decided to forgo banana production in Banes, and construct a sugar processing plant, which would be referred to as *el coloso* (the colossus) by the residents. In the next few years, United Fruit would erect a fence around its port properties, bring in managers from the United States, and construct entire neighborhoods for its workers with separate security, shops and schools. Apart from the plant facilities, the company established its headquarters in the town proper and a brand new neighborhood for its managers and workers. The Barrio Este (East Side), was actually divided into several, separate neighborhoods based on the social status of the residents. The wealthier homes were built to house the North American employees, who made up the managers and high-ranking personnel. They were recognized in the company literature as "first-class Anglo-Saxon employees."[30] Employees from the United States were provided free housing and maid service. There was a less exclusive neighborhood for lower-ranking Cuban managers and technicians and a neighborhood for the workers. The Batista *bohío* was located in the area where many of the low-ranking United Fruit workers lived. The roads were unpaved, and when it rained, the dirt footpaths would become muddy trails. The neighborhood included a large number of Jamaican immigrants, legal and illegal, who like Belisario Batista, worked on United Fruit's sugar plantations. In fact, the Batista home was adjacent to a small street known as Callejón de el Negro (the Black Man's Street).[31] On a typical night, the Jamaican residents of the neighborhood, perhaps to escape the heat inside their homes, could be seen sitting on wooden boxes in the alleyways next to their houses conversing with neighbors. The Jamaicans spoke primarily English, and it is likely that the young Batista was exposed to the language at a very early age. At least one of his closest boyhood friends was Jamaican.[32]

In the early 1900s, United Fruit began a large-scale land purchasing program in the Banes region, which displaced many of the small landowners. The North American corporation used its enormous financial and political clout to undercut the land claims of many of the small farmers of the region.[33] Under Spanish rule, many of the properties had been communal haciendas in which landowners owned a percentage of the property. After independence, Cuban courts were entrusted with dividing the properties based on conflicting claims. United Fruit was frequently awarded the best lands, while the landowners who refused to sell to the company were often awarded the marginal lands furthest away from the center of Banes. United Fruit extended the tiny railroad built by the banana growers so that it criss-crossed its sugar plantations, extending it each time they purchased additional lands. The tiny railroad grew to 79 miles by 1913 and 160 miles by 1927.[34] The population of Banes grew to more than twenty-five thousand by 1917, more than ten times the number of residents in the town at the beginning of the century. By 1909, United Fruit owned two-thirds of the land in Banes and accounted for more than 50 percent of the municipal budget. It was in this environment that Batista grew into adolescence. The local economy was booming, but it was controlled by a foreign corporation that looked down on its Cuban employees. The best jobs, housing, schooling, and medical facilities were set aside for the foreigners, while the Cubans were accorded second-class status. Years later, Batista told a reporter that he remembered that as a boy he and his friends would look with anger and bitterness on the children of the North American employees, who would occasionally ride into their side of town on well-fed ponies wearing immaculate clothing.[35] The Cubans were treated better than the migrant workers, brought at first from Jamaica and then in later years from Haiti, but they were clearly lower in the pecking order than the North Americans.

As a sugar cane cutter, Belisario Batista worked intensively for six months of the year during the *zafra* (sugar harvest), typically from February through August. The work was back-breaking and long during the cutting season, often ten to twelve hours a day, but for the rest of the year employment was scarce. As was typical of United Fruit operations, the elder Batista did not work directly for the company, but for a contractor named Adolfo Coronel. As part of a strategy to reduce labor strife, United Fruit purposely hired out contractors to cut the cane on its land, leaving it to them to organize and pay the work crews.[36] Coronel must have treated Belisario Batista fairly, because years later, after he had retired from the sugar cane business, Fulgencio Batista, then the president of Cuba, purchased a fishing boat for his father's former boss.[37] As a young boy, Batista often took lunch to his father in the cane fields. To supplement the family income in the off-season, Belisario Batista harvested bananas, and his wife sold them at a small, makeshift fruit stand adjacent to their home. The family's economic situation forced the young Batista, at the age of eight, to abandon his primary school education and join his father as a cane cutter.[38]

By all accounts, the young Batista was a dedicated student, and the decision to drop out of public school must have been a difficult one for him. As a consolation, several years later, his parents allowed him to attend the Colegio

"Los Amigos" of Banes, run by the Quakers at night. It is likely that Batista
attended the night school for at least two years, beginning in 1911, although
it is impossible to determine the dates with great precision because most of
his school records have been lost.[39] His parents had mixed feelings about the
time he spent at school. They seldom allowed him to work on his lessons
at home, frequently assigning him chores. Faced with pressing economic
demands, they viewed their oldest son's studies as an indulgence, although
his mother may have been more sympathetic to his desire to get an education than his father.[40] Reading was one of his great passions as a boy and
remained so all his life. On occasion, the young Batista, without the permission of his parents, took part of his savings and bought a book or magazine.
Written materials were rare commodities in rural Cuba, so the acquisition
of an Abraham Lincoln biography by Batista, at the age of thirteen, was a
noteworthy event for the adolescent boy and one he recollected fondly years
later.[41] In his later life, particularly with the media, Batista emphasized his
boyhood interest in the life and writings of Lincoln, perhaps trying to un-
derscore the similarity of their humble origins. As president of Cuba, Batista
prominently displayed a bust of Lincoln in his office.

The young Batista did not dare bring his reading materials to his house,
so he kept them at the home of Ramón Fernández, director of the school's
night classes, a man then in his early fifties, who encouraged his young student to read on a wide variety of topics. Fernández, who died in 1946,
worked as a teacher in Banes for seventy years and was highly regarded by
many of his former students.[42] Batista described him as one of the most
important influences in his life. In his classes, Fernández emphasized history and economics and a thorough knowledge of the writings of Cuban
independence leader José Martí.[43] These interests no doubt influenced the
young Batista, who identified history and geography as his favorite subjects.

Fernández was one of the "native" employees hired by the Quaker missionaries to teach the local children.[44] Even here, the young Batista must
have been aware of the influence of United Fruit and the cultural and economic divide between North Americans and Cubans. The Quaker school
was located in the North American section of Banes, separated from the
workers' village by a small stream. United Fruit invited the Quakers to Banes
even before they opened their sugar plant and funded many of their activities. Few decisions were made by the Quakers without the express approval
of the company. For several years, the Quakers used one of the rooms in
their meeting house to teach their pupils, but growing enrollment made it
evident that they needed a new school. The school, built in large part with
funds provided by United Fruit, opened in September 1911, when Batista,

a boy of ten, was beginning his studies there. Zenas L. Martin, head of the Quaker Mission in Cuba, wrote to his supervisor in Baltimore on January 9, 1911, that "we shall hope to be able to arrange for a school which will thoroughly meet their [United Fruit's] wishes."[45] The two-room schoolhouse was a barracks-style building adjacent to the Quaker meeting house. Each room measured twenty feet by thirty feet and held up to seventy students. Most of the students were Cubans, and they were taught in Spanish, although special classes were given to the children of North American and British families in English.[46] Batista graduated from the Quaker school in the spring of 1913 at the age of twelve with a fourth-grade education. Apart from stenography classes, later in life, it marked the end of his formal education.

The Quakers were an important spiritual influence on the young Batista. For many years, although he did not regularly attend services, Batista identified himself as a Quaker. Batista, baptized a Roman Catholic, was later given the sacrament of confirmation, but the family probably did not attend church services regularly. The Quakers' emphasis on simplicity, humility, and frugality led him to frown on ostentation in public in his early career.[47] The Quakers incorporated religious studies into the curriculum and encouraged their students to attend Sunday school and services, although it is unknown whether Batista participated in church activities as a boy. He did not, however, develop into a deeply spiritual man, although near the end of his life he began to attend Roman Catholic services on a regular basis. For most of his life, he was driven by events of the moment, not thoughts of an afterlife. An aide recalled years later that Batista did not have strongly held religious beliefs and was skeptical about promises of a heaven to come. As president of Cuba, he attended all manner of religious events, but was not a strict adherent to any faith.[48]

At the same time Batista was attending the Quaker school, race relations in Cuba were rapidly deteriorating, and a race war erupted in 1912, centered primarily in Oriente Province.[49] Given his inquisitive nature and love of reading, it is likely that Batista was aware of the events, although his reaction to them is not known. Banes did have a small daily newspaper, *El Pueblo*, which surely covered the events. Race relations in Cuba at the time and throughout most of the period prior to 1959 were cordial, although there was little mixing, particularly among the middle and wealthier classes. Laws were never passed in Cuba codifying segregation, but the races generally segregated themselves. Since the Haitian Revolution, there had been a great fear among Europeanized Cubans, mostly Spanish immigrants, of a black revolt and the eventual "Africanization" of Cuba. Political leaders in the years following independence encouraged immigration from Europe, particularly Spain, and prohibited immigration of those of African ancestry. The Jamaican and Haitian immigrations of the period were primarily illegal.[50]

Afro-Cubans had been among the most loyal supporters of independence and constituted a significant portion of the fighting force. However, in the years after independence the Afro-Cuban population grew dissatisfied with their exclusion from political life and their economic stagnation vis-à-vis the relative prosperity of recent Spanish immigrants. In 1907, several Afro-Cubans formed the Partido Independiente de Color (Independent Party of Color), a move that brought up images of black revolt and separatism. In 1910, legislation was passed outlawing parties based on race, an obvious effort to disband the Afro-Cuban party. The members of the party resisted over the course of several years, and an uprising was planned for May 20, 1912, the tenth anniversary of Cuban independence. The uprising, in which several thousand Afro-Cubans participated, was crushed quickly and violently throughout most of the island, although it persisted for nearly two months in Oriente. The citizens of Banes formed a militia of fifty men to guard against attack by the rebels. Five Afro-Cuban residents of the town were murdered, even though they were not involved in the uprising. One man, a religious healer associated with an African-based faith, was found hanged near the Banes River.[51] President José Miguel Gómez sent five thousand troops to Oriente Province to fight the rebels. To ensure their victory, the United States sent several battleships to the province, including one to the Bay of Nipe, just south of Banes, to protect United Fruit's processing plant there. In the end, three thousand Afro-Cubans were slaughtered in the uprising. It was the first of many violent political uprisings that young Batista lived through and that typified Cuba in the first sixty years after independence.

Apart from the occasional crisis, day-to-day life in Banes was all too predictable for Rubén Fulgencio. It was a daily struggle to maintain a squalid existence, and as the oldest boy, he was expected, more and more as the years went by, to supplement the family's meager income. During the sugar season, most of his days were spent cutting cane with his father. In the off-season he worked at a variety of small jobs in the town, including, at one time or another, a barber's apprentice, picking up scraps of hair, and as a tailor's apprentice.[52] Acosta Rubio tells the story of a young Batista being teased by other boys over his work with the tailor. One day after work, a boy called him "a queer" because he used a needle and thread in his job. The teasing turned into a fistfight, and Rubén Fulgencio went home that night with a black eye. Shortly thereafter he quit the job with the tailor.[53]

Still, in the midst of dire poverty, there were moments of joy and leisure.

Residents of Banes recalled that Batista enjoyed fishing and that he had a penchant for sweets, so that he periodically visited the area pharmacies to indulge that pleasure. Batista's fondest memories centered on the sand and the surf of the beach. Traditionally, the Batista family went on vacation to the beach, probably in the area around the Bay of Banes, between Palm Sunday and Easter Sunday. In his later years, Batista reflected on those family holidays.

> Back in my childhood everything seemed special: the foam created by the waves when they crashed violently against the sand bars; the sound of the waves, sometimes whispery, sometimes grumbling; the breakers, the intimidating reefs . . . everything enchanted me, even the unexpected squall that forced us to row quickly back to land, and the rainbow, about which my father would create legends. And in the midst of those memories, emerges in my memory the figure of my mother—petite, beautiful, tender and caring—her *hicaco* [West Indian cocoa plum] preserves, her seafood stews and a gourd in which she served coffee to my father.
>
> There I see her, young—she died young, upon turning 29—sitting by the edge of the sand, nervous and happy at the same time, anxiously awaiting the arrival of her son on the strong back of the swimming father, who by diving tried to scare her by leaving the boat adrift and the oars floating.[54]

Rubén Fulgencio's childhood came to an abrupt and tragic end in 1916 when his mother died.[55] Family members say she died unexpectedly of an illness before her thirtieth birthday, although the precise cause of death is unknown.[56] Her passing was a crushing blow to the young boy. In the weeks following her death, Belisario moved the family to a local sugar plantation, where the father and his two oldest sons worked in the fields.[57] The move may have been part of an effort by Belisario to take the sons' minds off the loss of their mother. After a short while at the plantation, Rubén Fulgencio was transferred to an office job, where he labored as a bookkeeper and a cane weigher. After the sugar harvest of 1916, Belisario brought his family back to the small *bohío* in La Güira. However, the pain associated with his mother's death manifested itself in a strong desire by Rubén Fulgencio to leave the family home. Perhaps, the absence of her gentle presence led to a strained relationship between father and eldest son.

One version of events has it that the eldest son discussed leaving home with his father, who urged him to "try his luck" in the world at large and to return if things went badly. In another account the boyish Batista asked his father's permission to leave home and was denied. He then took matters into his own hands and ran away, writing home some time later to ask forgiveness.[58] The topic of his leaving was clearly a matter of frequent discussion in the family home, and the younger Batista ultimately left his father little choice in the matter. Years of wandering lay ahead of the fifteen-year-old boy as he made his way out of Banes heading west on foot, occasionally hitching a ride on a cane cart.

CHAPTER 2

RESTLESS ADOLESCENCE

There are many gaps in the story of the next five years of Batista's life. Biographical accounts seldom dedicate more than a few paragraphs to the period between 1916 and April 1921, when he entered the Cuban Army. What survives are sketchy accounts of his travels throughout Oriente Province, working an odd assortment of jobs and finally landing a position at the Ferrocarriles del Norte (Northern Rail Line) in Camagüey Province. Anyone meeting Fulgencio Batista in this period would have considered him an unlikely candidate to become the future leader of Cuba. For part of the time he was homeless, often sleeping at railroad terminals or shipping docks. It was the most desperate period of his life. He was destitute. After his mother's death, his immediate family was fragmented: his younger brothers lived with relatives or friends, while his father continued his work in the cane fields.[1] He contributed to their support by periodically sending them part of his earnings. While working at the railroad, he was nearly killed in a terrible accident that left him hospitalized for several weeks and physically scarred for life. He worked on the railroad at a time of intense labor unrest, although there is no evidence that he participated in any significant way. In his later career, Batista had a seesaw relationship with the labor movement, although he ultimately accepted and supported passage of some of the most important labor legislation of the period.

TRAVELING LIFE

Batista's first stop after leaving Banes was Holguín, a major city thirty-five miles to the west.[2] There he went to live with his mother's sister, Cándida

Zaldívar, and her husband, Alberto Almaguer. While at their home, he worked on an orange farm, picking and packaging fruit.[3] The boy found conditions on the farm intolerable and the bosses abusive. Living under his aunt's roof was emotionally difficult as well because it served as a constant reminder of his mother. Carmela Zaldívar was a frequent topic of conversation at the house, and the constant reminders were a heavy burden. Many years later, Batista told a journalist that it was while he was staying at his aunt and uncle's home that he decided to relinquish the nickname Beno, because it was what his mother always called him.[4] In adulthood he would seldom use his first name, Rubén, preferring to be called Fulgencio. It was as if he was making a conscious and symbolic decision to break with that earlier part of his life. In later visits to Banes, people who knew him as a boy would still refer to him as Beno, but those who knew him after he rose to power seldom addressed him that way.

In the months and years after his mother's death, Batista's younger brothers also went to live, at least periodically, with their aunt and uncle. But Juan and Hermelindo more than likely spent a good deal of the time with their father working in the cane fields or at other side jobs. They were old enough to fend for themselves and remain with their father, whereas their younger brother, Francisco was not. Belisario relied on relatives and neighbors to help raise his youngest son. A Batista family album from the late 1930s contains a photograph of a woman identified only as La Cieguita (the blind woman), who is credited with raising one of the Batista boys, most likely Francisco.[5]

Fulgencio stayed for only a few weeks with his aunt and uncle before he moved on to a small village, known then as San Germán, about nineteen miles southeast of Holguín, where he was hired to help clear land for a sugar plantation.[6] At first he worked as a water boy for the men who were clearing the forests of the area. Sometime thereafter he was promoted to timekeeper for one of the work crews. It is not certain how long he stayed in San Germán, but early in 1917, probably in February or March, in time for the sugar harvest, he returned to Banes to visit his father. The young boy entertained the idea of becoming an independent cane farmer, but the thought of remaining in Banes discouraged him. After what was probably a visit of no more than several weeks, he again began traveling the dusty, dirt roads of Oriente Province.

Northern Oriente is a region of small mountains and foothills rising dramatically from the Atlantic Ocean. The villages and towns of Batista's youth were either located on the coast or were adjacent to sugar plantations or processing plants. Most of the homes were made of wooden planks with strips of zinc or palm leaves serving as roofs. A home of brick and mortar was a

rarity and reserved for the financially well-to-do. The sidewalks consisted of
wooden planks elevated several feet above the dirt streets. Horses, oxcarts,
and carriages were the primary means of transportation. Travel was slow. A
heavy rainstorm could make a dirt road impassable for days. Long rows of
sugar cane fields dominated the landscape outside most of the villages and
towns. Most commerce was related in one way or another to the cane trade.
People either grew and harvested the cane or they transported it, either by
ship or train, on the way to overseas markets. A few years earlier, William
Van Horne, a U.S. railroad tycoon, succeeded in connecting the eastern
provinces of Cuba to the main railroad line from Havana. The train lines
had only recently been extended into Northern Oriente through Holguín
from where the line ran north to the port of Gibara and east to Antilla.[7] As
he traveled across northern Oriente, Batista no doubt took note of the
importance of the rail and shipping industries to the local economy. Moreover, workers in these industries needed to master specialized skills and in
turn could demand greater pay and benefits for their labor. The workers were
frequently unionized, and this strengthened their bargaining power with
management. It was a time of intense union activity. There were a series of
dramatic strikes throughout the period in which the workers won important concessions from the rail companies. It is little wonder then that Batista,
as he made his way around the province, centered his job search on the ports
and railroad towns of the region.

After leaving his father's home for the second time, he traveled to the village of Dumois, about sixteen miles to the south of Banes, a railroad town
where he hoped to land a job. Dumois was a village located at a junction
point between the rail lines that went north to the port city of Antilla and
southeast to Santiago, the country's second-largest city.[8] It is here that he
likely experienced homelessness for the first time. He lived for several weeks
in and around the train station, more often than not sleeping on the floor
or on a wooden bench. He used boxes and sacks to cover himself on chilly
evenings and mornings[9] The wail of a train horn frequently awoke him during the night. He supported himself, at least in part, by running errands for
the railroad men who made their way through the town. When he was not
at the train station, he spent his time at hangouts frequented by the railroad
men, perhaps scrounging meals and playing occasional games of dice or
dominoes. He engaged the men in conversation at every opportunity and
sought to gain information about the Cuba beyond the 150-square-mile
region that had been his entire world up to that point. The young Batista
was fascinated by the railroading life and the promise of travel and escape.

Like sailors, railroad men have a mythology of their own. The work is long, hard, and dangerous, but there is a certain allure to the powerful huff and whistle of the locomotive and the steel tracks winding through the hills and valleys to far-off places. Railroad men stopped, as some still do today, at a different city or town every night. They spent long periods away from their families and frequently established friendships and amorous relationships at different towns along the line. There were restaurants, bars, and lodgings at each stop to serve their needs. It is into this world that the young Batista wished to gain entry. After several weeks in Dumois, he learned from some of the railroad men that there were job opportunities at the port of Antilla. Lacking funds, Batista, in the summer of 1917, convinced one of the train conductors to allow him to ride the thirty-five miles north in the caboose.

Antilla sits on the northern end of the Bay of Nipe, the deepest and widest port in all of Cuba. At first glance, the Bay of Nipe appears to be an ocean onto itself, measuring fourteen miles from north to south and seven and a half miles from east to west. Looking south from the port of Antilla one could barely make out the smokestacks of the Preston Sugar Mill, a United Fruit Company plant, some fifteen miles away at the southern end of the bay. At the time, Antilla was a vibrant and bustling port that served as the major departure point for much of the sugar harvested in eastern Cuba. It was also a major rail center, connected to the rest of the country by the Cuba Railroad Company, whose lines joined further south with the central line that traversed the island. United Fruit's private railway also went through Antilla, bringing sugar north from the Preston plant and passengers and goods south from Banes.

As Batista arrived in Antilla, anxious to find employment, he found soldiers posted all along the rail yard. The workers, predominantly Spanish immigrants, were on strike against the United Fruit Company. Spanish immigrants were an important segment of Antilla's population, and the port town was known as La España Chiquita (Little Spain). The strike evidently stirred up deep passions among the population, and at one point several townsfolk chased a railroad manager into the bay.[10] In an effort to break the strike, the company brought in Cuban-born workers from outside Oriente to run the railroad.[11] Batista immediately received several job offers, but the historical record is unclear about what happened next. Later in life, Batista made it a point to emphasize his respect for the Antilla strike, a story, which if true, could only enhance his reputation with the Cuban labor movement.[12] There is little evidence to prove or disprove Batista's version of events. Acosta Rubio, perhaps more out of vindictiveness than personal knowledge, claims that Batista crossed the picket line. However, in doing so, Acosta Rubio contradicts an earlier written account in which he claims Batista refused to break ranks with the strikers.[13] The historical accounts are further complicated by the fact that Batista did work for a time with United Fruit's railroad, although this was probably many months after the Antilla strike. Whatever the truth might be, Batista did not stay long in Antilla. While there, he considered becoming a seaman, but the idea of riding the rails still captured his imagination and he dropped the idea of going to sea.[14]

Although Batista's interest lay in landing a railroad job, he needed money to support himself, so he returned to the cane fields near the end of the harvest in late summer. The sugar processing plant at Alto Cedro, a village twenty-eight miles southwest of Antilla, was offering higher wages than United Fruit in an effort to attract workers and maximize production.[15] This was the heyday of Cuban sugar production, in response to a worldwide shortage caused by World War I. Sugar prices reached a heady twenty cents a pound, about ten times the prewar price. It was the period of the *vacas gordas* (literally, the fat cows—meaning good economic times).[16] The opportunity to stabilize his finances lured Batista to Alto Cedro where he worked for several weeks. After the harvest, he returned to Holguín and worked with his uncle, and probably lived with his relatives for a time. The two years since his mother's death had been difficult ones for the young boy, and no doubt he sought refuge with his aunt and uncle after many months of insecurity, penury, and homelessness. There can be little doubt of the strong bond he felt for his maternal aunt, her husband, and their children. Years later, after Cándida died, he sought out his old uncle and his cousins after they had moved to the Sierra Maestra to harvest coffee.[17] When he found them, he had them brought to Havana where he provided them with housing and paid to educate his young cousins.[18]

Batista stayed in Holguín for an extended period of time, perhaps up to six months, arriving sometime in the last quarter of 1917. Exactly how he occupied himself there is not known, and official biographies make no mention of the period. Several sources antagonistic to Batista note that he tried to enlist in the army for the first time but was rejected because he was too young.[19] Nonetheless, Batista remained around the army barracks running errands for the soldiers and assisting them in menial chores in exchange for tips and mess hall food. During this informal apprenticeship he earned the nickname *mulato lindo* (the pretty mulatto) from the soldiers. It is possible that Batista omitted these details from his official biographies because the name raises, once again, the specter of race. In the male-dominated politics of the era, it might also be perceived as effeminate with an undercurrent of homosexuality, although the epithet no doubt referred to his fastidious grooming and dress habits, rather than his sexual preference. Race and sexual preference were key weapons in the war of rumor and innuendo that pervaded Cuban politics. To question the manliness of an opponent was perceived as the quickest way to discredit him with the general public. Similar rumors abounded about other prominent officials.[20] However the nickname came about, it was one that would stick with Batista throughout his career.

On the Railroad

In 1918, Batista returned home for a brief time to visit his father and found a job as a brakeman on United Fruit's railway, working on the line between Banes and Antilla.[21] However, he never abandoned his hope of landing a job with a major railroad company, one that traversed the island. Sometime in early 1919, at the age of eighteen, Batista received word that the Ferrocarriles del Norte (Northern Rail Line) in Camagüey, the province to the west of Oriente, was hiring. He made the journey to the city of Camagüey, a distance of about 150 miles, where he tried to arrange an appointment with railroad officials, with little initial success. Again short on funds and with nowhere to stay, Batista befriended an old prostitute and lived with her for a time.[22] Finally, he went one evening to the home of a high-ranking railroad official and implored the man to hire him. Impressed with the young man's enthusiasm and persistence, the official arranged an interview for him. Shortly thereafter, Batista was hired as a brakeman for the railroad company on their cargo line. It was a singular achievement for the young Batista, who for the first time saw that bold action could get immediate results. It was a strategy he would employ again and again throughout his career. Batista was a railroad man not because of any special connection, but as a result of determination and a belief in himself. The railroad job gave him complete financial independence from his family. He never again lived in abject poverty.

It was a happy period in Batista's life. For the first time, he traveled regularly beyond the confines of Northern Oriente. The route to which he was assigned traversed the eastern two-thirds of the island from Santa Clara in the west to Santiago in the east, a distance of 310 miles. Every night he slept at a different stop along the line. He was in constant motion. Years later he would speak glowingly of his months working on the railroad and would turn his travels into a bedtime story for his oldest daughter.[23] Those who knew him in his railroad days remembered him as a friendly *simpático* young man. Even then he had the uncanny ability to listen very carefully to those with whom he spoke and to make them feel as if he was interested in every syllable they uttered. His colleagues on the railroad nicknamed him *el mexicano* (the Mexican) because of his features—narrow dark eyes and jet black hair that they perceived as Indian in origin.[24] By all accounts, he was a bright young man with a broad smile. Photos from the period show him to be immaculately groomed at all times, with every stitch of clothing in its proper place. Even though work on the rails was frequently dirty and grimy, in the photos he always appears to have just stepped out of the shower. This pattern concords with his later career when he was known for changing clothes and showering several times a day. That luxury was unavailable to him on the rails, but his appearance was obviously important to him, even then.

More than anything else, Batista was remembered as someone who spent an inordinate amount of time reading. In their free hours, the railroad men frequently held late-night parties, drinking and womanizing. Batista occasionally attended the parties, but he was remembered more for his abstention. There were some romantic dalliances, but none of much consequence. Those who visited him in his apartment in Camagüey remembered that it was crammed with newspapers, magazines, and books, many of which were highlighted and marked off by Batista, so he could remember particularly cogent points.[25] The young Batista was a voracious reader with a driving desire to learn. He had relatively little money and few connections, but reading and the acquisition of knowledge were ways to level the playing field. The lesson that careful preparation and a thorough understanding could overcome privilege began to resonate, and it drove him to read even more and to educate himself. Throughout his life, Batista was obsessed with getting every detail about a particular issue before making a decision. Aides frequently complained about his indecision. Before striking at a political enemy he waited months and months, then after analyzing every nuance of a situation, he struck unexpectedly and decisively. He would one day own one of the largest private libraries in all of Cuba, and in it he prominently displayed a brakeman's lantern.

Several months after he started working with Ferrocarriles del Norte, Batista suffered a life-threatening injury while working as a conductor trainee.[26] The railroad men frequently walked on top of the moving rail cars to get a better view of the surrounding area and assess any potential hazards. It was also a quick way to get from one end of the train to another. Batista's cargo train was approaching Cacocum, a small rural town in Northern Oriente, a few miles south of Holguín. At the time, Cacocum was little more than a railroad junction point with a few homes surrounding it. The cargo train was slowing down to make way for an approaching passenger train. Batista was running along the top of the cars, trying to reach the front of the train, so that he could turn a switch and prevent the passenger train from derailing. As he crossed from one car to another, the rotting wooden overhang that connected them gave way. Batista fell between the two cars and was nearly crushed by his own train. A piece of his clothing became ensnared in the coupling pin that connected the cars, and he was dragged along beneath them, his right leg scraping against the hard ground.

After he was unhooked, Batista was taken to the home of a local man. The leg wound was sufficiently serious that amputation was considered.[27] He was most likely taken to a local clinic or hospital, possibly in Holguín, until his condition stabilized.[28] After a period of recuperation, the rail company transported him back to Camagüey, where his wound was treated regularly by a doctor and nurse. Years later, Batista credited the attentive care of this black nurse for saving his leg. When he came to power, he tried to find the nurse to reward him, but with no success.[29] Batista stayed out of work for many weeks, and the accident left a permanent scar, a purple discoloration, on his right leg.

The period between 1919 and 1921 was a turbulent one for labor relations in the railroad industry. Rail workers at the Cuba Railroad Company, a competitor of Ferrocarriles del Norte, shut the rail line down in 1918 for nearly a month and secured a significant salary increase.[30] In 1921, the workers again went out on strike after the company tried to take back some of the gains in the wake of a recession caused by the worldwide decline in sugar prices. This strike, which the workers ultimately won, occurred a week after Batista enlisted in the army. There is no record of Batista taking part in labor activity at his own rail line.[31] He never spoke of the railroad labor movement of his youth, and his thoughts on the subject are unknown.[32]

The decision to join the Cuban Army was motivated, like almost everything in his early life, by the desire for economic security and self-improvement. In the army his food and lodging would be provided to him in addition to a modest paycheck. It is also quite likely that Batista was attracted to the educational opportunities offered by the army.[33] Shortly after he joined, Batista entertained the idea of becoming a lawyer and began to read volumes of legal works.[34] He planned to take courses to complete his high school education and then apply to law school. He later dropped his plans for a legal career and chose to study stenography instead, because of the promise for advancement that it offered in the army.[35] As with almost everything involving Batista, his decision to join the army in April 1921 is surrounded by controversy. Batista enlisted in Camagüey and was transferred shortly thereafter to Havana.[36] However, in his original enlistment papers his name appears only as Fulgencio Zaldívar, leading some to speculate that he was never recognized by his father, that in fact he was an illegitimate child.[37] The omission of the name Batista appears to be a clerical error and was addressed in army records when he reenlisted in 1923, a time when he was a private and had no great influence.[38] Batista joined the First Battalion of the Fourth Infantry Company in Havana on April 14, 1921. It would be years before he would rise to leadership in the army. Many years of plodding through the military bureaucracy lay ahead of the twenty-year-old Batista.

The enlistment was a definitive break with his past. He was leaving Banes and Oriente behind for good. Before leaving for Havana he went home again to visit his father and say goodbye to friends and relatives.[39] It would be ten years before he returned to his hometown. He would never see his father again.

CHAPTER 3

SERGEANT STENOGRAPHER

Havana was a bustling metropolis of more than three hundred fifty thousand people when Fulgencio Batista arrived in the spring of 1921. By far the largest city in Cuba, about 15 percent of the island's population lived in the capital and its suburbs.[1] The city, located on Cuba's northwestern coastline, expanded enormously both westward and southward in the decades preceding the Wars of Independence. It originally developed around the entrance to Havana Harbor, with each side defended by a fortification. The famous El Morro stood on the eastern side of the harbor, while the Castillo de la Punta protected the west. Cannons were thus placed on both sides of the harbor, making for a formidable defense. At 9 p.m. every evening a shot was fired from El Morro announcing the closing of the harbor for the night, a custom still followed today.

As with most Spanish colonial municipalities, the heart of the city consisted of a main plaza (Plaza de Armas), a Roman Catholic cathedral, the city hall (Ayuntamiento), a military barracks, and a governor's mansion. But Havana had long outgrown the old Spanish center, known as Habana Vieja, and expanded in the nineteenth century to the west and south. As the city grew, the wealthy moved to the new neighborhoods on the outskirts of the old city, to places like Centro Habana, Víbora, Regla, and Cerro, where they built their mansions. By the time Batista arrived, those neighborhoods were no longer fashionable, and the wealthy had moved yet again, further west to Vedado. Over the next two decades, the wealthy would continue to relocate west and south—to Miramar and Marianao, the latter a suburb of Havana. The mansions of the older neighborhoods were then divided into multifamily dwellings, and it was in these working-class neighborhoods that Batista would live for most of the period from 1921 through 1933, periodically moving from one apartment to another.

Havana would continue its steady growth throughout the 1920s. At the time of Batista's arrival, the famous sea wall, the Malecón, had been under construction for more than twenty years. It would eventually reach eight miles in length and connect Habana Vieja to the new neighborhoods and suburbs to the west that would become playgrounds for wealthy Cubans and North Americans. A new European-style boulevard, Quinta Avenida (Fifth Avenue) was built in the late 1920s from western Havana to the suburbs to make it easier to travel from the center city to the racetrack, casino, and Havana Yacht Club. The contrast between old city and new would become more dramatic with time. The old city was dominated by houses standing wall-to-wall with private, inner courtyards. The new suburbs resembled wealthy North American suburbs with lush, tree-lined boulevards and houses at a considerable distance from each other. Havana was at the center of Cuba's nascent tourism industry and by the end of the decade would be receiving up to eighty thousand visitors a year. The tourism industry and legalized gambling fueled organized crime and government corruption, activities in which Batista would play a major role.[2]

The twenty-year-old Batista must have been awestruck by the sheer movement on the streets of Havana. The capital was crisscrossed by trolley lines; with their seats of wicker and canvas awnings to block out the intense sun, they connected one far-flung end of the city to another. The sights and smells were jolting to the country boy from Banes. Street vendors were everywhere, selling everything from brooms to coal to *croquetas* (croquettes, frequently made of flour, ground ham, and pork). Their cries echoed through the streets. Women often set up small food concessions on the sidewalks in front of their homes to sell to those walking by. Musicians played in the parks dotting Havana and lived on whatever passing patrons wished to contribute. Actors performed impromptu skits, occasionally poking fun at the Afro-Cuban population or recent Spanish immigrants from Galicia or Asturias. The city was alive with theaters—from those catering to the very poor, in which food was frequently hurled from the upper levels, to more refined establishments catering to the wealthy and urbane. Silent movie theaters were commonplace as well, some showing patriotic movies produced by Cuban filmmakers.[3] Batista became quite the theatergoer in Havana, attending classical music concerts and expanding his taste beyond "creole rhythms."[4] He was fond of plays and movies. After he took power, Batista frequently watched the latest films in his study well after midnight to unwind from the activities of the day. Family, close friends, and acquaintances were often invited to these private viewings, which occasionally lasted till dawn. More than one foreign official made note of his peculiar work habits.[5]

CUBAN ARMY

When Batista first entered the army in 1921 he was assigned as a private to the First Battalion, Fourth Infantry Company at Camp Columbia, located to the west on a hill overlooking Havana. Camp Columbia was the seat of army power throughout the island and remained so for the next forty years. Most of the accounts of the period portray Batista as a studious soldier, who in addition to performing his military duties, took mail-order courses in stenography and shorthand from the Metropolitan Institute in New York. He reportedly was given the nickname *el literato* (the literary) by fellow soldiers.[6]

The army that Batista joined numbered around 11,000, of which approximately 720 were officers.[7] It was an institution deeply divided along class lines. The enlisted men were primarily from rural poor families or urban working-class households with little in the way of formal education. The officers, on the other hand, were primarily from upper- and middle-class families, and they were frequently nominated and promoted because of their political connections or their ties to old established families.[8] Dining facilities were segregated, and while sergeants, unlike privates and corporals, were allowed to eat in the officers' dining rooms, they were seated to one side and were not provided with tablecloths. Officers traveled by rail in first-class accommodations, while enlisted men traveled in third class. If an officer entered a theater or orchestra box occupied by an enlisted man, the enlisted man was expected to leave as a sign of deference. The enlisted men often lived in shabby conditions in barracks that were left over from the U.S. occupation at the end of the nineteenth century.[9] Even certain forms of dress were the purview and privilege of the officers, as for example, in the case of riding boots, which enlisted men were forbidden to wear.[10] Although enlisted men were supposed to receive quarterly stipends for uniforms and clothing, those payments were often delayed or never made. In some cases enlisted men were assigned to officers as domestic staff and made to perform household duties.[11] These petty slights and insults were intended to instill a sense of inferiority in the enlisted men.

It was a deeply corrupted institution. It was not unusual for the Cuban treasury to fund more army positions than actually existed, with the extra funds pocketed by high-ranking officers, typically the generals and colonels.[12] One Cuban Army officer noted sarcastically that clothes sold at army stores were considerably more expensive than clothes sold in department stores, noting that a package of ten handkerchiefs at an army store cost more than eight dollars, while in downtown Havana a similar package could be purchased for two dollars and eighty cents.[13] It is not surprising that the contract for army tailor was awarded without competitive bidding and kept in place even after it had expired. The army also controlled the provision of certain goods, such as meat and milk to the general public, and as a result this gave officers and soldiers enormous power over merchants and small businessmen.

The corruption in the army was symptomatic of the pervasive cancer that was commonplace at all levels of government. Each president outdid the next with ever more outlandish corruption schemes. The military frequently played a role in national elections, favoring one candidate over another by means of intimidation or outright fraud. President Alfredo Zayas, who served from 1921 through 1925, was aided in his election bid by widespread military interference.[14] He would go on to bilk the Cuban treasury of millions of dollars, building nonexistent bridges, buying up land at exorbitant prices from political associates, and securing jobs for fourteen family members, most of them in government enterprises. His enemies estimated that he stole between $2 million and $14 million during his administration. The Cuban Congress was no better, frequently awarding inflated contracts for government projects with bribes built in to the overall cost. The newspapers reported the widespread corruption on a day-to-day basis, but the shame factor did little to discourage the pillage of public coffers.[15] Zayas was essentially a transition figure between the Conservative government of General Mario Menocal (1913–1921) and the Liberal administration of Gerardo Machado (1925–1933), which would evolve into a brutal dictatorship in the late 1920s.[16]

It is clear that Batista was uncomfortable with the rules and discipline imposed on him by the army. He was on occasion brought before his sergeant for violating rules regarding sleeping hours in the barracks.[17] He was also troubled by the abuse heaped on the lower-ranking enlisted men by their sergeants.[18] His reservations were such that he decided not to reenlist when his two-year recruitment expired in April 1923. Prior to leaving the army, the young private, twenty-two at the time, enrolled at a small technical school, Colegio San Mario, in an effort to sharpen his stenographic skills. Batista wanted to improve his speed at shorthand as a way to further his professional development. He was learning the Gregg shorthand system, a method by which entire sentences and paragraphs are reduced to a few notations. Mastering the system was an enormous challenge, because it required memorizing hundreds of symbols and transcribing them onto a page at a brisk pace.[19] In later years, practitioners of the system would tout Batista as an example of what one could accomplish by learning shorthand and stenography. One writer noted that Batista was able to transcribe 160 words a minute at his peak. He became a sort of poster boy for stenography, and trade journals and magazines often boasted of his success.[20] He also became an adept typist, taking courses at a number of other schools in the area.[21] Later in life, he would always carry a notebook and pencil with him and take stenographic notes as he saw fit. The technique was not only useful, but it provided him with a degree of privacy and confidentiality, because few people understood the notations. Batista delivered many of his speeches using shorthand notes.[22]

As he became more proficient at stenography and typing, Batista attempted to market his skills outside the army. He was offered a position at a local firm, but when the job fell through, he found himself a civilian with no means of support. He turned to the owner-director of Colegio San Mario, Luis García Díaz, a former army stenographer himself, and succeeded in gaining a position as an instructor in commercial grammar. García Díaz was particularly impressed with his impeccable dress and deep voice.[23] Batista immersed himself in the life of the school, often taking courses on a wide variety of subjects when not teaching classes himself. He studied public speaking and phonetics, courses that would serve him well in the future. However, Batista found life outside the army even more difficult than life within it, and he reenlisted in the Rural Guard at the end of May 1923, after less than two months of civilian life. He was assigned to a desk job at the Fifth Squadron Headquarters in Atarés Fortress in Havana.

Even after he reenlisted, Batista continued his close association with Colegio San Mario, even writing several articles for the school newspaper, using the byline "Rubén."[24] In one of the articles for the *Mercantile Educator*, he attacked the army for reducing the pension of a veteran of the War of Independence. He concluded the article by calling on the "Supreme Creator of the Universe to provide strength to the afflicted veteran."[25] The newspaper article, written in July 1923, marks Batista's first public position regarding a major national issue. A month later, a powerful political coalition organized around the pension issue, made up largely of Independence War veterans. The National Association of Veterans and Patriots quickly expanded its agenda from the pension issue to criticizing the flagrant corruption of the Zayas government. The association ultimately called for the reform and overhaul of the political system. Zayas reacted quickly to the threat posed by the movement, and by the end of the year most of the leaders were imprisoned.

In his article, Batista did nothing more than express concern for the veterans. There is no indication of sympathy for the larger anti-Zayas movement. Still, he took some risk in writing it, because it was critical of the government. Even though he took modest steps to conceal his identity by using only his first name, it would not have been difficult to trace the article had anyone in the army wished to do so. But because the newspaper circulated only among a small community of students and teachers, it probably never even came to the attention of his army superiors. Its insignificance was his protection. A few weeks after his article was published, a photo of Batista was published in the newspaper touting him as a prominent "military leader in the not too distant future."[26] In this period, Batista also wrote other articles under the pseudonym "Nebur" and experimented with poetry and short stories. Although he preserved these early literary writings in his personal archives, he never made them public, because as he put it, they were "very bad." The whereabouts of these writings is uncertain. The articles on issues such as veterans' pensions, however, indicate his growing interest in national politics.[27]

Ironically, less than a year later, in May 1924, Batista was assigned to President Zayas's security team based at the president's farm, Finca María, in the small town of Wajay on the southwestern outskirts of Havana.[28] The assignment was a relatively easy one, because there were many hours when the president was away from the farm in Havana or traveling throughout the island. Batista took advantage of the time, reading through the president's extensive library, so much so that Zayas called him "the bookworm."[29] He would remain on the farm until the end of Zayas's presidential term in May 1925.

The Family

While assigned to the farm, Batista met a young woman strolling along the street in Wajay with a female friend. The woman, Elisa Godínez, twenty-one, with light brown hair and hazel eyes, caught his attention, and Batista began following her and struck up an impromptu conversation.[30] The Wajay assignment was fertile ground for romance between the soldiers and the local women. By coincidence, Elisa's sister, Pastora, was engaged to another officer in the president's security detail, Antonio Bausa, a friend of Batista. The formal introduction of Batista into the Godínez household was made by a corporal attached to the security detail, who was engaged to Elisa's neighbor.[31] Shortly after this chance meeting, Batista began to court Elisa Godínez, and they were married on July 10, 1926. Bausa would marry Pastora and become his brother-in-law.[32]

Like himself, Elisa, was of humble origin. She was born in a small farmhouse in the village of Vereda Nueva in Havana Province to Salustiano Godínez Córdoba and Concepción Gómez y Acosta on December 2, 1904. She was one of nine children, although only five reached adulthood, four girls and one boy. The family moved to Wajay several years after Elisa's birth, because her father found a job at the psychiatric hospital, known then as Mazorra. Salustiano Godínez was a member of the Conservative Party and lost his job when Zayas and the Popular Party (Popularistas) took power in 1921. After losing his job, the family was forced to move in with Elisa's older sister, Josefa, who lived in Calabazar, a village a few miles east of Wajay. Elisa was living with her sister, parents, and a three-year-old son, Félix Valdespino, from a prior relationship, at the time she met Batista.

Elisa Godínez was a typical Cuban housewife of the period. She was responsible for the home, while her husband worked a variety of jobs in order to support the family. She was a woman of few words and preferred to express her affection through attentive acts. She took pains to ensure that the assorted apartments they called home in the first years of their marriage were clean and comfortable for her husband. No matter the time of his arrival, she was there to provide him with dinner and conversation. Their first child, Mirta Caridad, was born in April 1927. They had two more children, Fulgencio Rubén (b. 1933) and Elisa Aleida (b. 1941). Years later, their elder daughter remembered them as a happy, young couple—particularly prior to 1933—who would occasionally spend their free days at the beach or picnicking with friends. These family gatherings became ever more rare in the years to come.

Although he was often away from his children, Fulgencio Batista was a dedicated and loving father. It would be up to Elisa to discipline the children on a day-to-day basis, because after his rise to power, their father was seldom present to handle issues in the home. Sometimes the children would try to circumvent their mother by going to their father, but more often than not, he would tell them to "speak to their mother first."[33] When Elisa could not resolve a problem with the children, they would be marched into their father's office for final judgment. Some of the children (he ultimately had at least nine children with three different women) remember sitting outside their father's office nervously waiting to meet with him. The distance created by his public power seems to have created a feeling of awe and respect even among his offspring. But, more often than not, Batista engaged his children in gentle conversation and tried to persuade them to see the logic of a particular decision made by their mother. They left those meetings relieved and, perhaps, more willing to comply with their mother's decision.[34]

He occasionally interrupted state business to tend to the needs of his children, in one case keeping his cabinet waiting in an adjacent room, while he tried to help one of his daughters cope with homesickness, while she was attending boarding school in the United States.[35] He was a dutiful stepfather to Elisa's first child, Félix, known as Felito, providing for the child's education and making him a part of family events.[36] However, the boy did not move in with Batista and his wife, remaining at his aunt Josefa's house throughout his childhood. Evidently, Elisa's parents became very attached to the boy and asked that he remain with them.[37]

Batista's record as a husband is considerably more mixed. He repeatedly cheated on his first wife throughout their eighteen-year marriage, fathering at least one child out of wedlock. As a young girl, Mirta Batista remembers the army women frequently gathering to gossip and discuss their cheating husbands. The rumors and gossip surrounding her father must have been very painful to Elisa, Mirta recalled, although her mother never spoke of it.[38] Batista recognized a daughter he fathered in the early 1930s with another woman and financially provided for the child, even including her in his last will and testament. However, he made no effort to introduce her to her half-brothers and half-sisters. Cuban women of the period were expected to tolerate their husbands' sexual dalliances with other women.[39] Many years later, Batista began a relationship with a teenage schoolgirl, Marta Fernández Miranda. After seven years as his mistress, she married Batista. Elisa Godínez had been aware of the relationship, but she tolerated it rather than divorce Batista. He served her with divorce papers while she was attending to their elder daughter in the days before the birth of their first grandchild.[40]

However, it would be many years before divorce would divide the Batista-Godínez alliance. In the interim, there were more immediate family problems for Fulgencio Batista. On November 28, 1926, several months after his marriage to Elisa, his oldest brother, Juan Batista, arrived in Havana from Camagüey suffering from tuberculosis, which he probably contracted in the countryside.[41] This was an era when tuberculosis was often fatal. It was a ravaging disease that consumed its victims a bit at a time, gradually making it impossible for them to breathe. As the older brother, Fulgencio was in the best position of anyone in the family, financially, and perhaps emotionally, to cope with his brother's illness. His father, Belisario, and brother, Hermelindo, remained in Banes, working in the cane fields and other odd jobs eking out subsistence. His youngest brother, Francisco, was a boy of fifteen and unprepared for such a daunting task. So it fell to twenty-five-year-old Fulgencio and his wife to cope with his brother's illness.

Juan Batista was only twenty years old when he arrived in Havana. For the first few days, he and his older brother went from one hospital and facil-ity to another searching for a cure and a hospital bed. Although he was gravely ill, the young man "still dreamed of living."[42] In the interim, he lived in a small corner of the family apartment. The lack of facilities became evi-dent as they searched, and Fulgencio came to realize that the only way to save his brother might be to send him overseas to the United States or Europe. However, that option was well beyond the family's means. Finally, there was a glimmer of hope when they were able to secure Juan's admission to the Calixto García Hospital in Havana.

Juan Batista was in the hospital for several weeks and then released in January 1927, perhaps because it was thought the disease was in remission. An excerpt of Fulgencio Batista's diary, provided by his eldest daughter, pro-vides no information about Juan's symptoms. Typically, tuberculosis patients experience fatigue, weight loss, and a pronounced cough, which worsens as the disease progresses. As the condition worsens, the lung is progressively scarred by lesions, and patients cough up substantial amounts of blood.[43] As he saw Juan suffering, the older brother felt a great deal of paternal ten-derness and thought often of his mother and the fact that she was not there to comfort him. His decision to care for Juan was typical of the elder Batis-ta's devotion to family throughout his life. He put himself and his wife, pregnant at the time, at considerable risk by allowing his younger brother to stay with him, because of the highly infectious nature of the disease.

After a month, it must have become evident that Juan Batista was not re-covering, and he was readmitted to the hospital on February 7. He remained there for the next twenty-one months, slowly dying. Years later, Fulgencio Batista recalled that the hospital was more a "warehouse" than a treatment facility, where residents went to learn about the disease.[44] The standard treatment of the era was to isolate patients in special hospitals and prescribe long periods of rest, in addition to a variety of drug therapies, with the hope that their bodies would gain the upper hand over the disease.[45] The treat-ments were not always successful. More than one thousand people died each year in Havana of tuberculosis.[46]

Juan Batista passed away on November 5, 1928. As chance would have it, his older brother was visiting on the morning he died. He remembered Juan hemorrhaging and coughing up large amounts of blood, literally "bathing" him in it.[47] Batista had to borrow money to pay for his brother's funeral. The only people in attendance at the burial were Batista, his wife, and two other relatives.[48]

The slow death of his younger brother by tuberculosis was a difficult blow for Fulgencio Batista. Years later, he described it as the second greatest loss he had ever suffered, after the death of his mother. Once in power, he launched an aggressive campaign against the disease, opening up tuberculosis clinics throughout Cuba and a state-of-the art sanatorium. He also established the Consejo Nacional de Tuberculosis (National Council on Tuberculosis).

Up through the Ranks

On the professional side, Batista continued to use his stenographic and typing skills to advance his army career throughout the 1920s and early 1930s. After President Zayas left office in May 1925, Batista was transferred to the office of the Army Chief of Staff where he was named secretary to Colonel Federico Rasco y Ruiz. In June 1926, he applied for a promotion to corporal stenographer and placed first in competitive examinations, besting forty other applicants.[49] He performed equally well in competitive examinations held in 1928 and received another promotion to sergeant stenographer in August of that year.

However, in the interim between his two promotions, Batista's army career was placed in jeopardy by a drunken brawl that took place at a cabaret on the outskirts of Havana, near Camp Columbia. On that occasion, a fight broke out among a number of civilians and soldiers at the Paris Cabaret, and a formal investigation was ordered by the army. The chief investigator, Major Ovidio Ortega, suspected Batista of taking part in the brawl and was set to arrest him. But his commanding officer, Colonel Rasco y Ruiz vouched for Batista's innocence and blocked the arrest. Batista's official biographers carefully chose their words in describing the incident. Both Chester and Acosta Rubio note that Colonel Rasco y Ruiz told the investigating officer that "Batista never frequents such places."[50] They do not state that Batista was somewhere else on the night of the brawl or that he did not participate in it. Whether Batista was involved in the fight will probably never be known. However, the incident once again highlights the importance of favoritism and cronyism in the Cuban Army. Without Colonel Rasco y Ruiz's intervention Batista would most likely have been arrested and put on trial. Justice was always secondary to personal friendships and politics in the Cuban Army, and it remained so under Batista.[51]

The Batista of the late 1920s and early 1930s was anything but a revolutionary. After surviving the nightclub incident, Batista continued his slow and steady efforts to rise through the ranks of the Cuban Army. The next hurdle, the jump from enlisted man to officer, was the most difficult and often required a push, either by a political ally or events. It is clear that in the late 1920s, Batista still saw stenography as his entrée into the officer corps. In August 1930, Batista, then twenty-nine, applied for permission to form a stenography school within the army, with the idea of providing every major department with one qualified stenographer.[52] As head of the stenography school and responsible for training enlisted men, he hoped to position himself for a first or second lieutenancy. His application was rejected, so his hopes for a promotion were temporarily dashed.

However, Batista did not sit around waiting to be elevated to lieutenant. If he failed to get ahead in the army, he would turn instead to business, and he was in the process of acquiring the necessary skills. While working as an army stenographer, Batista also provided home instruction to a number of students on a variety of topics, including stenography, typing, and business writing, and he taught part-time at Colegio Milanés, a small business school in Havana. If that were not enough, he held a variety of other odd jobs, including selling fruit, eggs, and coal wholesale to vendors, and also managing a farm.[53] Batista was occasionally called on by tenant farmers to intercede on their behalf against unreasonable demands made by government officials. In one case, a farmer was charged with illegally diluting his milk, carrying a dangerous weapon, and falsifying a public document, after he refused to sell his milk to unnamed government agents (perhaps from the military) at below market price. After a series of meetings with local officials and the judge hearing the case, the farmer was acquitted.[54] The story was published in a book of reminiscences by a friend of Batista's and no doubt was intended to compliment him. However, it says more about the level of corruption that pervaded the Cuban Army and public life in general than about Batista's good intentions. It is unlikely that the farmer would have fared as well without the intercession of Batista. The story once again proves the efficacy of the old Cuban adage, "Sin padrino no se bautise" (Without a godfather there is no baptism).

As a result of his ambitious work schedule, money was no problem for Batista in this period. As a first sergeant he made $624 a year, plus an annual sum of $120 for his training as a stenographer. This was in addition to whatever he made in his various side jobs. In fact, he was one of the few sergeants to own his own car, a rare thing even for officers in the early 1930s.[55] It is difficult to pinpoint what transformed the ambitious sergeant stenographer of the 1920s and early 1930s into a revolutionary leader, a man who would topple his superiors. Coups by the officer class are not unusual in Latin America, but to take over the army as an enlisted man is a rarity.[56] Chance certainly played a role. After he was promoted to sergeant in 1928, he was transferred to La Cabaña Fortress, adjacent to Habana Vieja to serve as stenographer there, but a short while later he switched jobs with a colleague and began working at Camp Columbia. At the time it was simply a procedural matter, seemingly of little interest. But the lateral transfer placed Batista at the center of classified information during a period of revolutionary turmoil in the Cuban Army and society. The level of corruption and violence reached a climax in the 1930s, and governments fell in rapid succession. Cuba was at revolution's door, and Batista had access to one of the keys: information. He wielded it effectively to establish military contacts among other sergeants and enlisted men throughout the island.

On a personal level, the circumstances surrounding the death of his father must have left him with a deep antipathy toward the Cuban officer corps. In his diary, Batista noted that he received a letter from his brother, Hermelindo, on February 13, 1931, informing him that their father, Belisario, was gravely ill. At the time, he himself was ill and unable to make the trip to Banes. Upon his recovery, he applied to his superiors for permission to go home to see his father, along with the free rail passage and one hundred dollars that was typically allotted for such emergencies.[57] Belisario Batista died on February 21, 1931, but his son was not given permission to travel until March 2. By the time he arrived in Banes, his father had already been buried. In his diary he notes the "insensitivity" of Lieutenant Rufino Blanco, who made him wait a day for the travel funds and then gave him only forty of the one hundred dollars. Blanco, like most of the other officers, rejected Batista's leadership of the army three years later and was discharged. The delay in processing his request for leave at the time of his father's death left Batista with a bitter aftertaste.

It is, perhaps, no coincidence that shortly thereafter Batista became a member of the ABC, a secret revolutionary society committed to toppling the Cuban government and President Gerardo Machado.[58]

CHAPTER 4

MACHADATO

The political history of Cuba in the early 1930s was written in blood. The struggle between President Gerardo Machado and his political opponents escalated into a daily war of bombings and murder. It reached its climax with the Revolution of 1933 and the toppling of two governments.

In the years between 1925 and 1933, Machado evolved into one of the most reviled Cuban leaders of the twentieth century. The struggle against the *Machadato*, the scornful nickname for the government, fundamentally changed the nature of politics on the island. Machado would be the first dictator to flee the island by plane as the foundations of his power began to crumble. But the struggle led to more far-reaching changes than the removal of one man or government. In an effort to counter Machado's brutal and repressive tactics, secret societies formed throughout the island. The most prominent and effective of these was the ABC, whose membership consisted primarily of middle-class and wealthy professionals. Their politics were considerably more conservative than the other revolutionary organizations, and some later labeled them as fascists. Structurally, the organization was made up of small groups, known as cells, that functioned independently of each other, but with common goals. Only the leader of the cell had contact with other cell leaders, and even in that instance, only with a small number of other leaders. Members' knowledge of participants in the movement was contained to those belonging to the same cell. This structure was intended to stifle efforts by the government to crush the entire movement. Even if several members or leaders were apprehended, the amount of information that could be tortured out of them was limited.

The secret societies initiated an extensive campaign of urban warfare and terror in 1932 to destabilize the government and to show the United States that the Machado administration could no longer protect the extensive business holdings of U.S. companies and individuals. It was the first time that urban warfare was unleashed on a large scale in Cuba. Earlier opposition movements employed the strategy of a mass uprising or revolt with the hope of securing either the support of the Cuban Army or U.S. intervention. Urban warfare took a heavy toll on the Machado government, a lesson that was not lost on future generations of revolutionaries and those who disguised their criminal actions in revolutionary costume. It became a staple of Cuban politics.[1] Prominent Cuban historian Herminio Portell-Vilá in his comprehensive, twentieth-century history of the island noted that the struggle against Machado forever changed the political landscape of Cuba and its people. "Cubans never again returned to being a people who occasionally exploded in anger only to later forget and be inclined to forgive; they would learn to hate, to take vengeance, to practice all forms of violence and justify it in the name of political struggle."[2]

Although it ended in disaster, the Machado administration began in promising fashion in 1925, with an ambitious reform program that promised to clean-up government, protect Cuban industry, and expand the nation's road system. Machado struck a nationalist chord when he called for the abrogation of the Platt Amendment, an odious portion of the Cuban Constitution that permitted the United States to intervene in Cuban affairs when it perceived that its national interests were in jeopardy. Under Machado, work on the Central Highway (Carretera Central), which eventually connected all of Cuba's six provinces along a 710-mile stretch of road, was begun. Construction on the Capitol building in Central Havana (Centro Habana) resumed with the aim of rivaling the Capitol building in Washington, D.C. The government spent $20 million on the Capitol project, even importing a diamond encased in marble to symbolically designate the building as mile marker "zero" of the Central Highway.[3] These public works projects later became the center of a long-standing political controversy because they were financed by $80 million in loans from Chase National Bank. These loans became a symbol of U.S. support for Machado and the subject of years of contention between the two governments. Another key element in Machado's election platform was his pledge to not seek reelection, always a hotly debated issue in Cuban politics, because the keys to power also opened the doors to enormous wealth for the ruling party and its supporters.[4] There were essentially two Machados: the "extravagantly praised" Machado of the 1925–1929 period and the "detested" Machado of 1929–1933.[5]

Several factors conspired to undermine Machado's early popularity, some of his own making and others beyond his control. Machado's own character flaws exacerbated a volatile political situation. The president, born in 1871, was a veteran of the Cuban Independence War, rising to the rank of brigadier general. Like a general, he had little tolerance for dissent and ridicule, and he treated his political opponents as if they were members of an opposing army. Although at times a charming and competent politician, Machado was thoroughly incapable of power sharing with adversaries.

On the financial side, Cuba's economy was in rapid freefall throughout the 1920s with the collapse of the world sugar market. In an effort to boost the price on the world market, Machado curtailed exports and discouraged further sugar cultivation with the hopes of reducing worldwide supply.[6] Cuban sugar production fell from 5 million tons in 1925 to 1.5 million by 1933. The policy increased unemployment among agricultural workers and led to growing discontent as wages were reduced by 75 percent. Cuban exports went down from a value of $353 million in 1925 to $80 million in 1932. The decline in exports led to reduced government spending, which translated into job losses and salary reductions for government workers, although Machado was careful not to cut military pay.[7] The declining economy fanned political passions.

In the first few years of his administration, Machado showed a talent for buying out and subverting his political opponents. By means of graft and coercion he succeeded in forming alliances between his ruling Liberal Party and its two rivals, the Conservative and Popular parties. In the face of dire economic conditions he called for "cooperation" among the parties, an arrangement that ultimately made debate within the government pointless and undermined peaceful political challenges within the system. By early 1926, he succeeded in outlawing the reorganization of the parties and ensured that all his allies were members of Congress, thereby securing control of the legislative branch of government. He sweetened the deal for these representatives by distributing $10 million in graft to his political allies in all three parties.[8] The Congress became a rubber stamp for Machado. The high-ranking officers in the army and navy were not forgotten either. The president guaranteed their loyalty by paying them between $1,000 and $1,500 in monthly "bonuses."[9]

The corruption of the party system was a prologue to what quickly became Machado's ultimate goal: the extension of his term of office. To that end, in June 1927, the president secured passage in Congress of legislation to reform the Cuban Constitution of 1901 by means of a Constitutional Convention. The elections for the convention were a mockery of democracy, since only the parties allied with Machado were allowed to participate. The rigged elections drove established political adversaries such as Carlos Mendieta, a former Liberal Party leader, and former President Mario García Menocal, the longtime Conservative Party leader, out of mainstream politics and toward confrontation with Machado. Mendieta formed his own party, National Union (Unión Nacionalista), to challenge Machado. The members of the Constitutional Convention of 1928 obediently passed everything Machado wanted. The president was allowed to seek reelection later that same year for a new six-year term that would last until May 20, 1935. The office of vice president was abolished, thereby eliminating a logical successor to the president. The delegates also approved the creation of a federal district for Havana and several smaller cities, under the control of the president. The establishment of federal districts allowed Machado to weed out popularly elected political rivals, particularly Havana Mayor Miguel Mariano Gómez, son of the island's second president. The removal of Gómez created another rival, who worked determinedly for Machado's downfall. The president alienated the youth by shutting down the University of Havana and the secondary schools throughout the island after violent antigovernment protests broke out in September 1930. The move backfired because it gave students more time to organize political rallies and establish organizations, such as the Directorio Estudiantil Universitario (DEU), which played a major role in the Revolution of 1933, and Ala Izquierda Estudiantil, a left-wing splinter group of DEU.

Machado's distaste for dissent surfaced early in his administration, but grew alarmingly as he gained more and more power over the country. Just three months after taking power, in August 1925, the murder of newspaperman Armando André, stunned Cuba. André, a follower of Menocal, was murdered as he entered his home, shortly after publishing an article speculating on the president's love life.[10] Machado and his supporters in the secret police (the dreaded *porra*), army, and national police not only set about to oppress the opposition but to terrorize them. He literally fed his enemies to the sharks. In one instance in early 1928, the body of an opponent washed up near Havana Bay missing an arm. The arm was found a few days later inside the stomach of a shark caught by a local fisherman. The arm still had part of the shirt sleeve around the wrist with the initials of the political opponent. These acts of cruelty served no political purpose and in fact galvanized the opposition against Machado.[11]

The violence escalated after the bogus reelection of November 1928. One of the most damaging political murders was that of exiled Communist Party leader Julio Antonio Mella, who was gunned down as he walked the streets of Mexico City on January 10, 1929.[12] A former member of Machado's government later accused the president of sending gunmen to Mexico to kill Mella. The identity of the murderer remains a mystery to this day. Some suggest that Mella may have been assassinated by a fellow Communist as part of an internal party struggle.[13] Whether he was responsible or not, Machado's reputation made him a prime suspect. Mella's death, at the age of twenty-nine, created a hero-martyr that would haunt Machado for the remainder of his administration and beyond. More than seventy-five years after his death, Mella is celebrated in Cuba as a great patriot and visionary, while Machado remains forever reviled, as a murderer and a tyrant.

In the midst of this reign of terror, the United States, which had the right by treaty to intervene, did next to nothing to curtail the violence. U.S. Ambassador to Cuba, Harry F. Guggenheim, known as "Jarrito Guggy" by the Cuban upper class, was perceived by the public-at-large and the political opposition as a Machado supporter. As a result of this perception, the ambassador's efforts at securing a compromise between Machado and his political opponents were totally ineffective. As was a traditional practice of the Cuban political opposition, they privately called for U.S. intervention against Machado, while publicly abhorring U.S. interference. Guggenheim, a businessman with little diplomatic experience, was incapable of handling such a difficult negotiation. Machado was forever promising political reforms to Guggenheim and forever breaking those promises, making "Guggy" appear ineffective.[14] In a tortured effort to explain the failure of the negotiations, Guggenheim wrote several years later that he and the State Department were attempting to implement a policy of noninterference in Cuban affairs in the period from 1929 through 1932. To Cubans, it must have seemed a curious departure. For years, past U.S. administrations interfered in every detail of Cuba's government, from electoral reform to sanitation. But at the very point in which political violence was reaching its apex in Cuba, Guggenheim and the State Department maintained a policy of "absolute impartiality and non-interference."[15] The ambassador blamed the breakdown in his negotiations on the inability of Cubans to "cooperate or compromise"[16]

Failing to secure U.S. intervention against Machado, the political opposition, principally Mendieta and Menocal, both veterans of the Independence War, tried to implement a timeworn strategy: the landing of an invasion force in eastern Cuba with the goal of igniting a national uprising. It was the strategy employed by Cuban independence leader José Martí, and future revolutionaries would repeatedly try to harness its enormous symbolic value to unify opponents of the government in Havana.[17] The Machado opposition raised funds from Cuban exiles in the United States and purchased boats and arms for the expedition. In this case, however, the invasion, planned for mid-August 1931, failed. The Machado government knew it was coming and in anticipation began arresting political leaders, a total of two thousand in all, including Mendieta and Menocal. A series of violent clashes erupted throughout the island in which dozens were killed. Many of the Cuban exiles taking part in the invasion were detained in the United States. The remnants of the Cuban exile force, led by journalist Sergio Carbó and several others, landed in eastern Cuba at the port of Gibara on August 16, but they were battered into submission by the Cuban Army, Navy, and Air Force and surrendered three days later.

In the aftermath of this defeat, the secret societies, led primarily by middle-class professionals and the student organizations, emerged as the primary forces in the struggle against Machado.

BATISTA AND THE ABC

Batista played no role in the early struggle against the Machado government. Even after August 1931, when he joined the ABC, his opposition to the government was cautious and modulated. His decision to join the ABC was probably motivated as much by a desire to survive the chaos of the Machado years as by any driving revolutionary spirit. Members of the armed forces were frequently approached by the political opposition in an effort to foment revolt. If Machado were to be toppled it would be useful, even essential, to have contacts in the anti-Machado movement.

At the time, Batista was assigned as a court stenographer at Camp Columbia and as such was present during the trials of many of Machado's political opponents. By early 1931, military courts were charged with hearing civilian cases involving the political opposition. Batista's unique position inside the courtroom made him valuable as an informant for the ABC, and his cell was dedicated to gathering information about the government and disseminating it to the opposition. Batista regularly provided information to a clandestine radio station that broadcast news against the dictatorship and to opposition newspapers.[18] The information was occasionally used to write political tracts and pamphlets that were distributed through the organization's underground network.[19] The cell included other members of the army, including his best friend at the time, Urbano Soler, a sergeant stenographer, like himself; José Eleuterio Pedraza, a field sergeant; Ramón Cruz Vidal, a private; and perhaps a few others.[20] In addition to his activities in the ABC, Batista began to develop contacts with other anti-Machado groups in late 1931 and early 1932, including the student group, Pro Ley y Justicia (For Law and Justice).[21]

It is possible that Batista was a member of more than one ABC cell given the number of civilians who later claimed to have conspired with him. In the future, his enemies would attempt to minimize his role in the Machado opposition, and while he was not a prominent leader, there is little doubt he was an opponent of the regime.

The seeds of discontent were planted in Batista as a result of years of shabby treatment by some members of the officer corps, most notably at the time of his father's death. No doubt the poor treatment was a frequent topic of conversation among Batista and his army colleagues, both in and out of the ABC. Years later, he recalled the many social slights he and the other enlisted men were forced to endure, such as the requirement that enlisted men and noncommissioned officers (such as sergeants) leave a public place when a senior officer arrived. He bristled at institutionalized efforts to make the enlisted men feel inferior. "The fear in which these enlisted men lived created a mass inferiority complex among them and they moved in a miserable little world of their own," Batista recalled.[22] His grievances were against the military power structure, more so than against the Machado government itself.

Batista was a man who had climbed out of desperate poverty, mastered a professional skill, and clawed his way to the rank of sergeant after ten years in the Cuban Army. He was unimpressed by the "professional" officers, who believed it was their birthright to receive promotions and benefits. Batista was self-educated, and he proved a capable teacher and pupil. He had read more books and knew more of the world than most of his superiors. He believed he was as smart as they—no smarter. Time would prove him correct in that assessment. But in 1931, there was no telling how the struggle with Machado would be resolved. A plan by Batista to restructure the army and topple the government emerged many months later as a result of a series of as yet unforeseen events. His immediate goal was to provide information to the ABC, aid the movement, and survive the Machado dictatorship. A revolutionary plan had not yet formed.

Batista's role as an informant was not without its risks. By early 1932, the cycle of violence was claiming lives on a daily basis. At Machado's political trials, he came into contact with many leaders of the political opposition, primarily prominent defense lawyers. From time to time, he provided them with information helpful to their cases and occasionally met with them outside the courtroom. One of the most significant cases Batista was involved with was the killing of Lt. Enrique Diez Díaz, military commander of Artemisa, a farm town thirty-five miles west of Havana in Pinar del Río Province. Díaz was one of several regional commanders and police chiefs targeted by the ABC as part of its May 1932 bombing campaign, timed to mark the thirtieth anniversary of Cuban independence. Díaz was opening the mail at his military command post on May 21, the day after Cuba's Independence Day, when a parcel bomb exploded, killing him and nearly destroying the post.

Batista was assigned as a stenographer to the case involving four defendants charged with Díaz's murder.[23] Four defense lawyers, including Carlos Manuel de la Cruz, a member of the Cuban House of Representatives who refused to attend congressional sessions because of his opposition to Machado, and Gonzalo Freyre de Andrade, a prominent opposition leader, took part in the case. Batista engaged in friendly and conspiratorial relations with both men.[24] Apart from conspiracies, Batista had worked as a freelance stenographer in de la Cruz's law firm and known him for years.[25] Unfolding events during the trial nearly cost Batista his life. At one point, tensions flared up between de la Cruz and one of the army lawyers prosecuting the case. The argument grew heated, and the officer threatened violence against de la Cruz. Batista jumped to the defense of his friend, reportedly even to the point of nearly drawing his pistol.[26] From that moment on, Batista suspected that an attempt would be made to murder de la Cruz and Freyre de Andrade, so he and Soler agreed to accompany them on a daily basis to the trial and back home again.[27] Batista feared he would be punished, perhaps imprisoned, for his actions in defense of the two lawyers. Several days after the incident involving de la Cruz, on the morning of September 27, 1932, Batista was summoned unexpectedly to present himself at Camp Columbia. Suspecting that his home might be searched, Batista asked Soler to remove and hide compromising documents hidden in his apartment. Batista also told Soler to seek out Freyre de Andrade to represent him in the event that he should be imprisoned. Fortunately for him, the unexpected summons was unrelated to the trial or the conspiracies swirling around the army. At around noon the next day, Soler received word from an intermediary that "El Indio" was okay.[28]

But the danger was far from over for Batista. On the afternoon of September 27, Senate President Clemente Vázquez Bello, a close supporter of Machado, was murdered as he drove along the Malecón. Vázquez Bello, who had just left the Havana Yacht Club still wearing sailing attire, was gunned down by a hail of bullets in broad daylight. The assassins timed the killing perfectly, parking their vehicle at an intersection as the senate president was driving home, and firing point blank into his car. The murder was reminiscent of the Chicago gangland killings of the 1930s: at least fifty-four bullets were removed from the body. In the words of historian Portell-Vilá, the assassination of Vázquez Bello would have "received an A plus grade for efficiency from the gunmen of Chicago."[29] The assassins were never apprehended, but the reprisals by Machado supporters would be swift and brutal.[30] Later that same day, gunmen went to the home of Gonzalo Freyre de Andrade and murdered him and his two brothers in his study. Former Congressman Miguel Ángel Aguiar, a supporter of Menocal, was killed after coming to the door of his home. Ironically, Batista and Soler were scheduled to meet with Freyre de Andrade in his home on the evening of his death. But that coincidence was not the only troubling aspect of the murder: Freyre de Andrade had papers in his home that could compromise Batista and Soler and lead to their arrest. Fortunately for the conspiring sergeants, Freyre de Andrade's documents were removed from the house by members of the Machado opposition in the interval between the assassination and the arrival of police.[31] Immediately after the murder of the Freyre de Andrade brothers, the other three defense lawyers in the Díaz case sought exile and safety in foreign embassies. De la Cruz, who would later serve as a close adviser to Batista, was fortunate to escape with his life. While traveling in his car, de la Cruz heard his death announced on the radio and knew he would have to leave Cuba to prevent it.[32]

Despite the conspiracies swirling around him, Batista was careful to keep his family in the dark. His wife must have suspected his involvement in the anti-Machado movement, because of the occasional hushed conversations in the living room of their Toyo Street apartment in Central Havana.[33] It is unlikely, however, that he confided the full extent of his conspiracies to her. Later on he would share some information with his brother-in-law, Heriberto Godínez (Elisa's brother), but he was never central to the plans. On several occasions, Godínez served as a lookout for meetings held at the Batista home.[34]

Batista's trademarks as a revolutionary were caution and circumspection. He was slow to trust and frequently shared only select bits of information with each conspirator. One of his early fellow conspirators, Ramón Cruz Vidal, remembered that Batista was hesitant to involve other enlisted men in his plans, a task that by default he sometimes left to others.[35] Those involved with Batista frequently felt as if they were at the center of his conspiracies, when in fact they were minor players.[36] He had a talent for conspiracy that stemmed from his ability to calculate the cause and effect of an action with great speed. Batista was seldom precipitous, always searching for the best moment to strike at his enemy.

By 1932, Batista's personal life had taken a turn for the better. The three-year period from 1928 through 1931 had been very cruel indeed. Within that span of time he had lost his brother, Juan, and his father, Belisario. He suffered another near tragedy just five months after his father's death. His youngest brother, Francisco "Panchín" Batista, twenty at the time, appeared to have contracted tuberculosis and traveled from Banes to Havana for treatment. Once again, he faced the grim prospect of watching a younger brother die a slow and painful death. Panchín arrived in Havana in July 1931, and Fulgencio began the search for a health-care facility. The older brother succeeded in getting Panchín admitted to La Esperanza Hospital. Unlike Juan, however, Panchín recovered from his respiratory ailment, which may or may not have been tuberculosis.[37]

Mirta Batista, a four-year-old at the time, remembered that her father spoke to Panchín as if he were another of his children.[38] In later years, Panchín periodically rebelled against his older brother in an effort to emerge from his shadow, a goal he never achieved. When Fulgencio grew impatient with Panchín, the younger brother often found a soothing ally in his sister-in-law, Elisa. She urged her husband to take a softer approach with Panchín. Unlike Fulgencio, perhaps in spite of him, Panchín developed a blunt, hard-hitting political style, with none of the finesse and refinement of his older brother. After the Revolution of 1933, Panchín also joined the army but left after he found it difficult to rise through the ranks, despite family connections. He went on to become mayor of Marianao, a wealthy western suburb of Havana, and governor of Havana Province, forming an alliance with his brother's arch-enemies. This, however, occurred years later. In September 1931, evidently cured of his illness, Panchín decided to return to Banes.

The struggle against Machado wore on throughout 1932 and 1933, and it must have become clear to most political observers that the president could not hold on to power indefinitely or even until the end of his term of office—May 20, 1935. Even high-ranking military officers, concerned about the erosion in popular support for the army, believed that Machado would have to go. In the same month as the murders of Vázquez Bello and the Freyre de Andrade brothers, General Alberto Herrera, chief of the army, told Ambassador Guggenheim that he favored, as part of a political solution, the resignation of Machado before the completion of his term.[39] But power would have to be pried out of Machado's hands one bloody finger at a time. In December 1932, he proclaimed that he would serve out the rest of his term—"not one minute more, not one minute less."[40] Even though his government and reputation were in ruins, reaching the end of his term became a matter of pride for Machado.

ENTER SUMNER WELLES

The violence and brutality of the Machado regime was widely publicized, and there was little public support for the Cuban government in the United

States. Headlines such as "Cuban Misery Groans under Iron-Fist Rule" and "Denies He [Machado] is a Dictator" were commonplace in U.S. newspapers.[41] However, U.S. efforts to mediate a solution to the Cuba crisis were placed on hold until after the 1932 elections and the inauguration of Franklin D. Roosevelt as president in March 1933. Cuba quickly became a test case for Roosevelt's grand plan to improve and reorganize relations with Latin America, the so-called Good Neighbor policy, formally unveiled in April before a meeting of the Pan-American Union. The policy was an effort to build closer economic and political ties with Latin America and move away from the heavy hand of military and political intervention that had characterized the relationship for decades.[42] Shortly thereafter, Roosevelt relieved Guggenheim of his duties and appointed Sumner Welles, a fellow graduate of Groton and Harvard, and recently designated assistant secretary of state, as U.S. ambassador to Cuba.[43] The next few weeks were spent drafting a policy outline and a set of instructions for the new ambassador, which called on Welles to offer "friendly mediation" to the Machado government and the political opposition. Welles was also authorized to negotiate a reciprocal trade agreement aimed at boosting the Cuban economy. A May 1 State Department memo to Welles stated that while the measures could be "construed as measures of intervention" by some, they were in fact intended "to prevent the necessity of intervention."[44]

The State Department could characterize its mission any way it wished, but the perception in Cuba was clear: Welles was on his way to shake things up. When he arrived in Havana on May 7 on a United Fruit Company steamer, Welles was greeted as the political savior of Cuba. He was met at the dock by about 150 well-wishers, a number restricted by police, and the route to his residence at the Hotel Nacional, several miles away, was lined with hundreds more waving their hats and handkerchiefs as he passed in his motorcade. Every major newspaper in Cuba covered the arrival, and it was front-page news for days.[45] Welles was transformed into a media star. His every move, his every utterance was chronicled by the Cuban press. For the next seven months, reporters trailed Welles throughout Havana. If he went to afternoon tea, it was reported in the next day's newspapers. Such attention to a foreign diplomat would be unprecedented in most countries, but this was Cuba, 1933. Welles was arguably the most important and powerful figure in the country.

Welles was an odd celebrity. He was tall, lanky, and reserved and carried himself in a patrician manner with an air of condescension. The ambassador used a walking stick, had a finely clipped mustache, and a receding hairline. Always a bit of a dandy, he moved into the luxurious Hotel Nacional where he reserved four adjoining rooms, which included separate sitting rooms and bedrooms for him and his wife and additional rooms for his valet, a maid, and his personal secretary.[46] Welles seldom answered a question directly. In a country where political bravado, displays of manliness, and military prowess were expected of its political leaders, Welles seemed a strange figure indeed. He became the subject of daily political satire, and his long, serious face and pointy chin were ideal for caricaturists. Throughout the mediation negotiations between Machado and the political opposition, the newspapers frequently took note of his reserved style and what they perceived as the slow progress of the negotiations by depicting him as a tortoise. At other times he was portrayed as a referee, a large fish, a cyclone, and a doctor. In *Diario de la Marina* he was regularly depicted as a chef trying to concoct a dish that would be appetizing to all sides of the Cuban conflict. In one cartoon, Welles, wearing a long apron, approaches a customer and inquires whether he has ordered soup, to which the patron responds, "Yes, but I wanted soup with substance." In another political cartoon, a beak-nosed Welles is driving a two-passenger car named "Mediation," and in the back is a portly woman identified as "Public Opinion." At a crossroads, the woman asks Welles whether they would not arrive more quickly by another route, and Welles responds that "perhaps, but then my car might break down."[47]

Four days after his arrival, Welles presented his diplomatic credentials to President Machado, and the chess match between the two began in earnest. Machado was several pieces down from the start. Welles arrived in Cuba to broker a deal between the government and the opposition, but the principal item upon which the opposition was in agreement was the ouster of the president. The "mediation" negotiations of 1933 can only be fully understood in the context of the dependent relationship between the United States and Cuba. The decision by Machado to negotiate his own departure with a foreign diplomat only makes sense in light of years of overt and covert interference by the United States in every facet of Cuban political and economic life. Machado recognized the right of the United States to interject itself in Cuban affairs, and that put him at an immediate psychological disadvantage. "To pretend that Cuba can distance itself from the United States is a political and economic error in addition to being a historical error," Machado wrote several months after fleeing Cuba.[48] At the same time, Welles was supremely confident that he could cajole, convince, and bully the Cuban government and opposition into reaching an agreement acceptable to the United States. Throughout the negotiations, Welles set deadlines for Machado and implied that direct U.S intervention could follow any failure to proceed as expected. The Cuban political opposition, with the notable exception of the student movement, was equally susceptible to Welles's brand of persuasion, and one after another they declared themselves willing to take part in the negotiations. In doing so, they declared that Welles's involvement was not intervention, because the ambassador would arbitrate differences rather than dictate solutions. The ABC declared in its underground newspaper, *Denuncia*, its "anti-interventionist position," forcefully stating that "Cubans can guide their own destinies." But in the same issue, the secret organization accepted U.S. involvement and "pressure" as part of its strategy to oust Machado.[49]

Machado was mistrustful and apprehensive of Welles from their first meeting on May 11. "Welles has an impassive face and a cold stare and it is difficult to divine his thinking," Machado recalled in his memoirs.[50] Perhaps somewhat intimidated, the government made a key tactical error the next day when Cuban Secretary of State Orestes Ferrara, at a meeting with the ambassador, noted that Machado would resign "if the matter were put to him in the proper manner."[51] Welles's official and personal correspondence from the period indicates that he arrived in Cuba with no immediate plan to seek Machado's resignation. The ambassador certainly envisioned Machado's departure, but the timetable was subject to negotiation. Welles feared that Machado's abrupt departure would lead to chaos and hoped a plan to hold free elections the following year would be acceptable to all parties. By raising the topic, Ferrara placed Machado's departure at the forefront of discussions.[52]

A cornerstone of Welles's plan was the appointment of an "impartial" vice president, who would take power after Machado went on a "leave of absence."[53] As leverage, Welles hoped to use the prospect of a new commercial treaty between the United States and Cuba as an enticement to secure a political settlement. In the midst of the Depression, the ambassador planned to tighten the economic screws on Machado further by privately urging U.S. banks to refrain from renegotiating debt payments until the political negotiations were resolved.[54] Welles wanted a political solution in place by the end of the year that would call for elections sometime in 1934 and require Machado to step down several months before the casting of ballots. Welles was convinced that Machado would accede to this plan because the president "is anxious to find a safe way out."[55] With a "constitutional" solution in place, Welles planned to turn over the embassy to Jefferson Caffery, his successor-in-waiting, and return to Washington to oversee regional Latin America policy.[56]

But Welles and Machado would be denied their smooth transition.

Exit Machado

The mediation process destabilized the Machado regime, which had survived by means of terror. Machado spent the months of June and July slowly
capitulating to Welles's demands on everything from the reassignment of
military personnel to the easing of press censorship and the lifting of martial law. The concessions emboldened the opposition. With each concession
they saw Machado's grip on power loosening. At the end of July, as the mediation proceedings began to consider the transition from Machado to a successor, the Cuban president began to try to wiggle out of the political corner
in which he found himself. One political cartoonist of the period depicted
Machado hopping around on one foot wearing a pair of shoes made by the
"Mediation Shoe Company." Grasping his left foot, an irate Machado squeals,
"These shoes how they squeeze me."[57] Machado took several steps to try to
relieve the pressure. First, he ordered his ambassador in the United States,
Oscar Cintas, to meet with Roosevelt on July 25 to size up his support for
Welles.[58] Second, Machado used the lifting of martial law in Havana the next
day as a pretext to undercut Welles by arguing that his advice was personal
and did not represent U.S policy.[59]

Machado was fighting for more time, but his government was entering its
last days. Two days later, on July 28, Welles produced a letter from Roosevelt
backing the ambassador in the mediation proceedings. Welles had anticipated a possible "crisis" in the negotiations sometime in late July over the
issue of the government's future. Up until late July, he considered it likely
that elections would not be held in Cuba until sometime in 1934, with Machado's resignation preceding the election by at least several months.[60] Shortly
after his public confrontation with Machado, Welles undertook to undermine the tottering government.

As the relationship between Machado and Welles deteriorated, strikes broke
out across the nation, starting with the transportation workers in Havana.
The opposition, principally the ABC, sided with the strikers, and angry clashes
soon erupted. Machado suspected Welles of encouraging labor unrest as
part of an effort to secure his resignation but felt constrained against acting
forcefully: "We knew that the [use of troops] would provide the ambassador
with a pretext to justify the armed intervention of the United States in Cuba."[61]
Ruby Hart Phillips, who several years later would become the principal reporter for the New York Times in Cuba, observed that the Cuban people felt
"cocky with Welles here as moral support."[62] Welles, in fact, did meet with
striking workers and engaged in ongoing discussions with opposition leaders for the next two weeks. The strikes soon turned into a national sit-down.

ESTOS ZAPATOS...

—¡Cómo me aprietan!

This cartoon depicts an agitated President Machado jumping up and down holding his left foot. On the bottom of the shoe is inscribed "Mediation Shoe Co." The yelping Machado shouts about how the shoes "squeeze" him. The cartoon refers to the mounting pressure placed on him by U.S. Ambassador Sumner Welles through the "mediation" process.

All of Cuba waited for and speculated on the hour of Machado's departure. *Diario de la Marina* published a political cartoon on August 3 entitled "Commercial Student" in which a young boy goes up to a street vendor selling suitcases and remarks that the vendor had told him he would be selling a lot of suitcases in August. The vendor responds, "Well my boy keep in mind that the month has just begun."[63]

On August 6, Welles urged Machado to resign as an "act of patriotism" and to avoid U.S. intervention.[64] The next day, a pirate ABC station wrongly broadcast the news that Machado had resigned, and thousands ran onto the streets of Havana to march and celebrate. The tension reached a breaking point in Centro Habana around Central Park and the Capitol building, just a few blocks from the Presidential Palace, and police fired at the crowds, killing seventeen and wounding more than a hundred. It became known as the August Seventh Massacre.[65] The day after the massacre, Welles as mediator presented Machado with a "solution" to the Cuban political crisis, which called on the president to resign. Machado rightly interpreted the plan as an "ultimatum." In a State Department dispatch the next day, Welles suggested that diplomatic recognition of the Machado government be withdrawn, which would force the president to resign "within a very limited period." To seal the deal, Welles advised dispatching two U.S. warships to Havana harbor.[66] Machado suspected Welles of encouraging the opposition by telling them that U.S. troops would be used, if necessary, to oust him. The president also had information that U.S. Military Attaché T. N. Gimperling was visiting Cuban Army installations and encouraging revolt among the junior officers.[67]

Like a drowning man gasping for air, Machado made one final move to save himself: he struck an unlikely alliance with the Communists in an effort to break the general strike. In return for their support in ending the strike, Machado agreed to recognize the Communist Party. The effort was a total failure because the Communists were not in control of the strike.[68] When that gambit backfired, Machado responded to Welles by agreeing to resign at a "future date to be determined" and calling on the United States to renounce the Platt Amendment. As these public negotiations went on, political power was slipping from Machado's grasp. Day by day, former political allies began to abandon him and call for his resignation. Even more ominous, support in the military began to wane. By August 11, Machado had agreed to resign and hand over power to Army Chief of Staff General Alberto Herrera, one of his most ardent supporters, who would act as interim president for a short period of time. The designation of Herrera was reluctantly accepted by the political opposition on the recommendation of Welles.[69]

But many of the officers, uncertain of the ramifications of Machado's resignation on their careers, began to try to influence the process with the hope of weathering the crisis. An army revolt on August 11 was resolved when the soldiers agreed to return to the barracks. However, a faction in the army, led by retired General Julio Sanguily and Colonel Horacio Ferrer, found Herrera an unacceptable candidate and refused to support him. They made their opposition to Herrera known to Welles and the political opposition. Negotiations to find a substitute for Herrera began on the night of August 11 and continued into the early hours of the following day, until Welles's candidate, Carlos Manuel de Céspedes, was accepted by all parties to the negotiations.

Machado viewed the appointment of Céspedes as provisional president as the ambassador's final double cross, believing that Céspedes was "Welles's man."[70] At that moment, however, the former president had little time to ponder breaking events. After submitting his resignation to Congress on the morning of August 12, Machado left the Presidential Palace for the last time around 9:30 a.m. and headed for his farm on the outskirts of Havana. By midday it was clear that his survival depended on a quick departure from the country. An orgy of killing and looting soon broke out throughout the country. In the coming weeks, the homes and businesses of Machado's allies were burned and pillaged. Many of his closest supporters were murdered and their bodies mutilated and paraded through the streets. As Machado and several of his closest advisers drove to the airport to hire a hydroplane to take them to the Bahamas, the former president saw the sky stained red. "It was the homes of the *machadistas* that were smoldering," Machado wrote in his memoirs.[71]

One of the greatest humiliations was reserved for the armed forces, which had been Machado's principal backer. Throughout the anti-Machado struggle, the political opposition leveled some of its harshest criticism at the military for its role in maintaining the dictator and oppressing the people. "The army, which pretends to be apolitical, and a defender of the Constitution, is in fact a political instrument of '*continuismo*' and oppression," the ABC proclaimed in its 1932 manifesto to the Cuban people. The military are a "privileged caste" of "assassins working for a stipend."[72] Public support and confidence in the military was at an all-time low. The close association with Machado was a stain on the institution and made it impossible for it to maintain order in the country in the aftermath of his departure. The struggle in the society-at-large opened enormous fissures within the armed forces as various factions sought to restore the military's credibility. In an effort to save their credibility, the junior officers tried to distance themselves from their superiors. The enlisted men feared they would be scapegoated for following orders and their ranks thinned by the junior officers. Members of the ABC and other revolutionary groups patrolled the streets bringing vengeance on Machado supporters. The police and army looked on helplessly at this lawlessness, fearing any action on their part would further diminish their prestige. Rumors of coups and uprisings swept through the armed forces. The army was leaderless.

As a result of this chaos, a lowly sergeant stenographer would seize power twenty-three days after Machado's resignation.

CHAPTER 5

SERGEANTS'
REVOLT

The government of Carlos Manuel de Céspedes was sickly and weak from the moment it took power.[1] Sumner Welles and the United States had their fingerprints all over the provisional government. On the day Céspedes was sworn in, August 13, 1933, Welles went to congratulate the new president. The embrace between the two men, captured in photos in all the national dailies and weeklies, was awkward. Welles, who stood at well over six feet, towered over Céspedes, who was about six to nine inches shorter. The imbalance in their stature could be seen as a metaphor for the power imbalance between the United States and Cuba.

Céspedes was president, in large part, because of Welles. The ambassador agreed to accept General Herrera as provisional president, but when the Cuban Army declined, he worked hard to promote Céspedes as the compromise candidate. Once in power, Welles did all he could to keep him there by securing quick diplomatic recognition from Washington and proposing a loan to assist the government. As a career diplomat and former ambassador to the United States, Céspedes had strong ties to Washington. A personal friend of Welles, he was eminently acceptable to the Roosevelt administration.[2] Gaining the acceptance of the Cuban people would be far more difficult.

In the days after Machado's abrupt departure, mobs roamed the streets of Havana and other major cities hunting down supporters of the former regime. Radio stations urged residents to "stay in their homes and keep their blinds down."[3] Havana's chief of police, Antonio Aincart, committed suicide after being cornered by an angry crowd. Several days later, his rotting corpse was disinterred and dragged through the streets of the capital. Machado supporters were beaten and gunned down in broad daylight. One man was cornered on the third floor of a Havana building, shot, and then thrown out a window onto the pavement below. The crowd then picked him up, carried him up the stairs, and threw him out the window a second time. Struggling to his knees, the man was kicked in the face and left to die in the street.[4] While driving along the Prado, one of the main streets in central Havana, the ambassador's wife, Mathilda Welles, saw that "a small crowd of men were dragging a Machado suspect on the street, a rope tied to his neck. The victim had been shot and killed that morning."[5] The Cuban press captured and fed on the bloodlust by providing a daily menu of photos of the corpses, beaten and mutilated. Typically, youthful revolutionaries posed with the bloody corpses, smiling and making obscene gestures to mock the dead.[6]

The Presidential Palace was sacked, and participants ran through the streets displaying their "souvenirs," including a water cooler, pillows, chairs, and typewriters.[7] The homes of Machado supporters were looted and destroyed as members of the army and police looked on, occasionally taking part in the activities. Pro-Machado newspapers were firebombed, including *El Heraldo de Cuba* in Havana and *Diario de Cuba* in Santiago. Any link to Machado, no matter how tenuous, was sufficient to justify violence, such as the case of Machado's barber, whose pornographic theater was destroyed by an angry mob. The weekly news magazine, *Carteles*, described the violence as "popular justice" and editorially endorsed it.[8]

The armed forces and police were unable and unwilling to control the mobs, because they themselves were suspect. As the bulwarks of Machado's regime, the military and police were viewed with apprehension and disdain. The slightest suggestion that a soldier or officer had close ties with the disgraced dictator was enough to ensure his arrest.[9] Many police officers abandoned their posts after becoming targets of mob violence. A national debate ensued over how to "purify" the army. By the end of August, the Céspedes government arrested twenty-one officers and fifty soldiers, but no one thought the purification process should stop there.[10] There were rumors that the fifteen thousand–man army would be reduced by several thousand and that salaries would be cut.[11] The ABC, which held several cabinet positions in the Céspedes administration, proposed mandatory military service as an alternative to the volunteer army. With the armed forces in disgrace, factionalism was the order of the day as each segment of the military institution sought to defend its reputation and position. Horacio Ferrer, Céspedes's secretary of war, thought the armed forces were on the verge of "disintegrating" as a result of the schisms created by political currents within the institution.[12] As if the political situation was not volatile enough, Army Chief

of Staff Julio Sanguily, a hero of the anti-Machado movement, was hospitalized with a life-threatening illness on August 14, the day after Céspedes was
sworn in as provisional president.[13]

The political struggle brought to the surface deep-seated class and racial
antagonisms within the armed forces. Up until Machado's forced departure,
the highest-ranking positions in the army had been held by veterans of the
independence wars, men in their fifties and sixties, the so-called, Generation
of 1895.[14] Dissatisfaction with their leadership and the older generation's support of Machado led the junior officers, with the help of Sanguily and Ferrer,
to oust the dictator. Many of the junior officers resented the old veterans for
their lack of formal training and their privileged position in the government.
Many of the junior officers, of course, were themselves the product of privileged backgrounds and political patronage, and a large number were recip-
ients of formal military training in the United States, a benefit denied the
older veterans. There was friction as well between the junior officers and
the sergeants and enlisted men. In contrast to many of the junior officers,
the sergeants and enlisted men consisted, primarily, of men drawn from the
rural and urban poor, including a large number of Afro-Cubans.[15] The junior officers resented a ten-year-old law that required that half their ranks be
filled by enlisted men who had served for at least twenty years and worked
their way up to sergeant, and they spoke openly of repealing it.[16]

In an atmosphere where everyone in the armed forces was suspect, it
came down to which side could lay the blame for Machado's atrocities on
the other and make it stick. The junior officers believed the higher-ranking
officials and the enlisted men who carried out the orders were responsible
for the crimes of the dictatorship. The sergeants and enlisted men blamed
the senior and junior officers for supporting and overseeing the brutal
repression. This was fertile ground upon which Batista could sow seeds of
dissent.

To be sure, Batista's development as a revolutionary was a slow process.
During the last two years of Machado's reign, he labored in the background
gathering information and passing it on to the opposition. There is no evidence that he ever participated in a violent act against the regime or publicly spoke out against it. Still, the experience was formative. It gave him his
first taste of politics, Cuban politics, in which the formation of a new government was merely a prelude to new conspiracies by those left outside the
ruling coalition. He learned how to operate inside the secret society of the
ABC and incorporated the concept of secret cells into his own movement.[17]
In short, he learned the fine art of conspiracy. Batista was not unique in his
conspiratorial ways, by the end of the *Machadato* almost every member of

the armed forces was conspiring with one group or another. The same ambition he showed in the cane fields of Banes, he brought to politics.

The flight of Machado created a completely different environment where anything was possible. In this confusion and chaos, Batista saw an opportunity to bring about fundamental change in the army and promote his own self-interests in the process. Besides personal advancement, Batista's efforts were fueled by genuine anger over slights suffered at the hands of the officers—from the small humiliations that were part of Cuban army life to the incompetence and corruption that delayed him from visiting his infirm father. Rumors of pay cuts and personnel reductions intensified his resentment and that of his fellow conspirators toward the officers. Given his position as sergeant stenographer, Batista was intimately acquainted with the officer corps. He possessed firsthand knowledge of the disarray in the command structure caused by the elimination of some of the senior officers. Army headquarters, located in the Castillo de la Fuerza, next to the Plaza de Armas in Habana Vieja, functioned more like a "revolutionary committee" at this time than a hierarchical center dispatching orders. Members of the public entered as they pleased by simply asserting their status as revolutionaries. As a result, military orders were subject to intense public scrutiny and debate.[18]

For lessons on loyalty, the sergeants and enlisted men needed only to observe the actions of their superiors, who were openly plotting against Céspedes. Just days after the new president was sworn in, several junior officers met with representatives of the Student Directory, which had been left out of the government, to dictate a plan of action for the Céspedes government.[19] There were also reports that officers were going to former President Menocal's ranch, El Chico, to plot the overthrow of the provisional government.[20] Officers were speaking out publicly on government policy on a wide array of issues.

There is considerable historical debate over when Batista began conspiring against the Céspedes government and whether he in fact intended to overthrow the regime or merely reorganize the army. The "Sergeants' Revolt" of September 4, 1933, must be seen in the context of an ongoing set of conspiracies by Batista dating back to 1931. He never stopped conspiring; as the political environment changed, so did his goals. But he did not set out in mid-August with the goal of toppling Céspedes. A series of breaking events eventually pushed him in that direction.[21] In mid-August 1933, the character of the Batista conspiracy was defensive. Survival was the goal in the days immediately following the installation of the provisional government. Batista and his fellow conspirators accurately perceived the junior officers as a threat. Their aim was to blunt the efforts by the officers, to reduce their numbers, cut salaries, and restrict promotions.

A Question of Leadership

The original group of conspirators probably did not exceed fifteen men, although in the aftermath of the revolt, the lure of success led countless others to claim a critical role in the conspiracy. The charter members of the conspiracy would for years to come be identified as La Junta de los Ocho (Junta of the Eight). The debate about numbers is misleading. Each conspirator was recruited separately into the movement, so it is impossible to know precisely who knew what and exactly when they knew it. The Junta of the Eight is more public relations fiction than historical reality. Furthermore, civilians, although not central to the military conspiracy in the early days, possessed knowledge of it. Batista was in contact with numerous civilians, like Ramón Macau[22] and Fernando del Busto,[23] to name just a few. Many of the original members of Batista's ABC cell formed the nucleus of the new group, including Sergeants José Pedraza and Urbano Soler[24] and Private Ramón Cruz Vidal. Shortly after the fall of Machado, this nucleus joined forces with Sergeant Pablo Rodríguez, the best known of the conspirators at the time, owing to his role as president of the Enlisted Men's Club at Camp Columbia, and with Sergeant Manuel López Migoya. Other early conspirators included Sergeants Juan Estévez Maymir and Jaime Mariné, Corporal Ángel Echevarría Salas, and Private Mario Hernández.[25] Several key conspirators, who would be intimately associated with Batista for years to come, such as Lieutenant Francisco Tabernilla, Lieutenant Manuel Benítez, and Sergeant Ignacio Galíndez would not join the conspiracy until days or hours before the coup.

In the early stages of the conspiracy, Batista shared leadership of the movement with Pablo Rodríguez, who was a powerful ally because of his popularity among the enlisted men. As president of the Enlisted Men's Club since 1927, Rodríguez had considerable influence among his colleagues. But, he had his political liabilities as well, because as a president of the club he had taken part in at least one banquet in honor of the disgraced Machado.[26] Sources hostile to Batista portray Rodríguez, in August 1933, as the mastermind of the conspiracy and Batista as a minor player. Ricardo Adam y Silva, who as a deposed captain of the army had every reason to despise Batista, claimed that Batista was accepted by the conspirators as a "secretary," rather than a "man of action," because of his stenographic skills.[27]

Soon after the success of the Sergeants' Revolt, Batista phased Rodríguez out of a leadership role and ultimately forced him from the army. Rodríguez's cause as "mastermind" would be taken up by polemicists desiring to discredit and diminish Batista. Throughout his life, Rodríguez gave a series of interviews promoting himself as the leader of the movement.[28] Batista's allies have in turn taken to attacking Rodríguez. Cruz Vidal remembered Rodríguez as a half-hearted revolutionary, who came to conspiracy meetings "very well dressed, but was always the first to leave."[29] In his later years, in exile in Miami, Cruz Vidal said that Batista's leadership of the movement was never questioned. "He was the one who knew the most."[30] Batista never mentioned Rodríguez in his account of events to biographer Edmund Chester. Political agendas aside, Batista joined forces with Rodríguez in mid-August 1933 because it was in both their interests to do so. Each had been conspiring separately, and a union of forces was a logical step, perhaps facilitated by Sergeant Pedraza, who knew and conspired with both men.[31] Leadership of the movement was up for grabs in mid-August. It would go to the soldier willing to take the greatest risks.

Batista's opportunity for leadership came in the form of a tragedy. Sergeant Miguel Ángel Hernández, who like Batista conspired with the ABC against the Machado government, was tortured and murdered in May by his captors in the military fortress of Atarés.[32] His body was not discovered inside until after Machado fled Cuba, along with the bodies of Félix Alpízar, a student, and Margarito Iglesias, a labor leader.[33] The capture and murder of Hernández transformed him into a revolutionary hero. He was proof positive that not everyone in the military had remained loyal to Machado. But the handling of the Hernández burial, on August 19, by army superiors was thoughtless and insensitive.[34] Instead of sending a delegation of officers to the burial and a military honor guard, the army superiors sent a low-ranking delegation. "In designating a funeral procession for Sergeant Hernández [the high command] kept in mind only his rank, rather than considering that he was an apostle to the cause and that importance ought to be given to his funeral," an officer observed.[35] A wake was held for the three victims, Alpízar, Iglesias, and Hernández, at the University of Havana, and their bodies were then transported to the cemetery in separate funeral processions. The attention of the nation was on the burial, but obviously not the attention of the higher-ups in the army.

The enlisted men, including Batista, reacted strongly to the slight. Batista attended the ceremony that morning, accompanied by Soler, at Havana's spectacular Cementerio de Colón, a necropolis of imposing monuments and burial chambers. In the absence of an officer to deliver a graveside eulogy, the twenty or so enlisted men asked Batista to speak. His first public speech was an angry one. He attacked the officer corps for their absence and declared that the army must be "purged" of Machado supporters. It was the destiny of the enlisted men to cleanse the armed forces. He called for all those in the military who were free of blame to unite. "Together we will overcome. If we do not unite, anarchy will destroy the Republic, and we will lose our rights as a people. Towards that goal I urge you all. It is the best way to honor the memory of Hernández, Iglesias, Alpízar, and of the many others who died defending our liberties."[36]

Anger got the best of Batista at the funeral oration. The thirty-two-year-old sergeant revealed his plans publicly for the first time. It was a "tactical error" and one that Batista openly acknowledged years later.[37] Reports of the menacing nature of the speech reached his superiors, and Batista feared reprisals.[38] But while the speech placed him in greater danger, it also increased his visibility and popularity among the enlisted men and solidified his claim to a leadership role. Just as important, Batista came into contact with key civilian leaders at the funeral, particularly influential journalist Sergio Carbó. Hernández's grave was near the one for Margarito Iglesias, buried just minutes before, and some mourners from that ceremony, leaning against nearby headstones, stayed on to listen to Batista's speech.[39]

It is possible that Batista and Carbó knew each other prior to the burial, but their contacts intensified thereafter. They began a regular exchange of views underscoring their mutual unease about the current political situation. Batista was primarily concerned about deteriorating conditions in the army. Carbó, a leader of the failed invasion of 1931, opposed the Céspedes government because he viewed it as the creation of Sumner Welles and the United States. Clearly affected by the funerals of the three men, Carbó dedicated the next edition of his weekly newspaper, *La Semana*, to the burials. In what became a prophetic headline, he asked on his front page, "¿A qué se espera para empezar la Revolución?" ("What are we waiting for to start the Revolution?"). On the editorial page, he urged students, workers, and soldiers to start the revolution. The newspaper also included a drawing of a student, worker, and soldier marching together in solidarity.[40] The relationship between Carbó and Batista would be critical in the weeks to come. They would hold regular, perhaps daily, conversations on the state of affairs in the military. Batista saw Carbó, a man with great prestige throughout the island, as a key to gaining civilian support for the conspiracy.[41] In the days ahead, Carbó would serve as liaison, facilitator, counselor, promoter, and supervisor to Batista. Carbó was a key link between the sergeants and the student movement.

In the days prior to the funeral, the conspirators met on several occasions to debate and draft a manifesto outlining their goals.[42] Some of the early meetings were held at the quartermaster's office in Camp Columbia, where Rodríguez worked, while others were held at Batista's apartment on the corner of Toyo Street. Batista drafted a document summarizing the major points raised at the meetings, and it was unanimously accepted by the conspirators. The manifesto identified three major points: dignity for the soldiers, respect and consideration, and restitution of benefits. Although vague, the manifesto declared that it was "the duty" of the enlisted men to "rebel" when their dignity was violated. The document addressed the question of restoring dignity to the institution by requiring that all members be treated fairly.[43] The information was circulated among the troops, but Batista and his fellow conspirators wanted to disseminate it to the public.

Efforts to broadcast and publish the manifesto accelerated after the Hernández burial. Over the course of several days, Batista took the manifesto to the ABC and asked them to broadcast it on their radio station, but they declined to do so. Batista attempted through his cell leader, Manuel Martí, to contact the leaders of the ABC to solicit support for the fledgling movement. The ABC leadership took a dim view of the issues raised by the conspirators, fearing their call for greater equality in the military would undermine discipline and foment revolt, consequently imperiling their position of power in the Céspedes government. The rejection by the ABC led to the resignation of Batista and some fellow conspirators from that organization.[44] The manifesto was also rejected by an official of the Cuban Telephone Company's radio station and by Carbó, who described it as "too strong."[45]

Their efforts at publicity clearly indicate that even in late August the conspirators had no intention of overthrowing the government. They sought to reform the armed forces. The enlisted men wanted public support to ameliorate the effects of the army purge, which was set to begin. However, a series of decisions by President Céspedes and Secretary of War Ferrer fed their fears and propelled them on the path to open revolt.

Of great concern to the enlisted men was the appointment on August 29 of retired Colonel Armando Montes to serve as interim army chief of staff in Sanguily's absence. Like the Hernández debacle, the appointment of Montes showed singular insensitivity at a time of great unrest in the armed forces. Montes served as army chief of staff under President Zayas in 1921 during an economic crisis, which forced him to reduce military salaries and eliminate more than two thousand positions. Several years later, as secretary of war, Montes opposed the legislation setting aside 50 percent of all officer postings for sergeants. Batista and the enlisted men saw Montes as a hatchet man appointed to clean house.[46] The appointment of Montes was followed, the very next day, by the recall of five retired colonels to serve on a Special Council of War to hear cases against Machado supporters, a decision that Batista later recalled was viewed negatively by the sergeants.[47]

As a result of such decisions, the movement underwent fundamental change. It evolved from a defensive conspiracy whose goal was to protect the enlisted men to an aggressive conspiracy whose goal was to put military power into their hands. The conspirators no longer were content to sit back and allow others to purge the armed forces; they would do that themselves. The idea of eliminating the officers, or at least some of them, may have been suggested to Batista by Carbó.[48] From a political standpoint, the move made eminent sense. If the sergeants satisfied themselves with measures protecting their rights at the expense of the officers, the leaders of the movement could be subject to retaliation by their superiors at a later, less volatile time. By restructuring the officer corps and providing for ample promotion from below, the conspirators could safeguard their positions. Having made the leap to insubordination, Batista and his fellow enlisted men did not have to travel much further to find themselves in complete revolt against the government.

There was some debate among the conspirators over the scheduled date of the uprising. The journalist, Franco Varona, wrote that the revolt was originally planned for September 15, while Batista recalled the original date as September 8.[49] In any case, the date was advanced to September 4 because of persistent rumors that former President Menocal was preparing to stage his own coup on September 7.[50] Welles also suspected Menocal of plotting against Céspedes: "The presence of General Menocal in Cuba is as always an exceedingly disturbing factor. His insatiable ambition and his unwillingness to recognize that he no longer can count on the support of any but a small group is causing him to attempt to undermine the authority of the government and I am reliably informed that he is trying to promote dissidence among the army officers."[51] The Menocal coup was to be spearheaded by the junior officers, who would reshape the army to their liking. By late August, the question for Batista was not whether to take over the army, but rather who would do it first. "They [the officers] also were preparing a coup which would have been a bloody one due to the diversity of tendencies," Batista later told a newspaper reporter. "This was the reason why we decided to eliminate them from our movement."[52]

The ranks of the conspirators grew significantly, and by the end of the month they were forced to meet in more spacious settings, including several meetings at the Grand (Masonic) Lodge of Cuba and at a military hospital in Camp Columbia.[53] Each participant in the conspiracy was charged with recruiting new members to the cause. The goal was to gain a foothold in every company and military installation. "I chose a man at each post or company and then a second man in whom I had confidence and I continued this way until all that remained was to give the signal that the hour in question had arrived," Batista remembered.[54]

They concentrated their efforts at military installations in and around Havana, the center of military power in the nation. In the days immediately before the revolt they branched out into Matanzas Province, about sixty miles east of Havana, to secure support there. Pedraza traveled to the province on several occasions, the last time with Batista and several others on the night of September 3, hours before the revolt. Ironically, on the way back to Havana, the conspirators passed the motorcade of President Céspedes on his way east to check on recent hurricane damage in Matanzas and Las Villas. One of the conspirators in the car commented that if Céspedes knew what was about to happen he would immediately turn around.[55] The decision to concentrate on Havana and Matanzas made sense from a logistical standpoint, as well as a military one, because it would have taken the better part of two days to drive to the eastern provinces of Las Villas, Camagüey, and Oriente, recruit more conspirators, and then return to Havana. The long absence of any one or two of the conspirators from their military posts for an extended period of time could have fostered suspicion. Telegraph dispatches and telephone conversations were likely to be intercepted. The conspirators waited till the day of the revolt to secure allegiance, often via telegraph or by telephone, from sergeants in the eastern provinces, and they sent representatives on the day of the revolt to the western province of Pinar del Río.[56]

Senior military officers were not oblivious to the upheaval in the armed forces. Reports of unusual meetings among the enlisted men were repeatedly passed on to the higher-ups, but in the midst of the turmoil, they were ignored. Given the breakdown in discipline, the senior commanders chose to tolerate dissent rather than force a confrontation with the enlisted men. The chain of command was in tatters. Five days prior to the coup, a lieutenant, informed of the conspiracy by a civilian contact, asked for permission to break-up a meeting of enlisted men at the Masonic Lodge and arrest the plotters, including the "stenographer from Columbia." Permission was denied, and his superior accused the lieutenant of "giving credence to rumors." Adam y Silva wrote that his concerns were dismissed when at the end of August he reported suspicious meetings among the enlisted men to Lieutenant Colonel José Perdomo, chief of Camp Columbia. Perdomo replied that the sergeants and enlisted men were merely discussing "petitions of little importance."[57] Two days before the revolt, Batista became concerned when he was casually questioned by a captain about unusual activity among the enlisted men.[58] Secretary of War Ferrer ordered a halt to meetings of the enlisted men on August 30, but they persisted.[59] In an effort to squash rumors among the enlisted men that pay cuts and staff reductions were in the works, Ferrer issued a flyer to the troops on September 3 noting that "people with bad intentions" were spreading lies.[60]

Batista and the conspirators used the confusion of the moment to conceal the true purpose of the meetings. In fact, the conspirators dutifully informed and sought the permission of their superiors for a meeting of enlisted men at 11 a.m. on September 4 at the Enlisted Men's Club at Camp Columbia. Pablo Rodríguez, on the night of September 2, was designated by the conspirators to seek permission from Lieutenant Colonel Perdomo for the event, which was granted the next day. On September 3, Batista traveled to Matanzas to secure support from Sergeant Desiderio Sánchez and from Clemente Gómez Sicre of the police department. Upon his return, he attended a meeting of key men from military installations throughout Havana to discuss plans for the following day. In the event they were questioned, they were to give as the "official" reason for the meeting the improvement of living conditions and recreational facilities, including construction of a new beach, for the enlisted men.[61] Batista decided against going home to sleep that night, believing his home was under surveillance, and stayed with a friend.[62] He knew that he was in great danger. Word of the conspiracy had spread throughout the military, and he feared that even the lethargic senior command and the tottering government would soon strike against him and his fellow conspirators.

SEPTEMBER 4, 1933

Suspicions reached the sickbed of Colonel Julio Sanguily, the ailing army chief of staff, on the morning of September 4. On the previous day, several enlisted men informed Captain Mario Torres Menier that there was to be a meeting at the Enlisted Men's Club to pick a new army chief and to purge the military of unwanted members. They further advised the captain that the enlisted men, worried about the reduction of more than three thousand positions and substantial pay cuts, had taken the keys to the storage lockers where the machine guns were kept and had disabled several military planes. Sanguily ordered Torres Menier to attend the meeting and determine what demands the sergeants and enlisted men were making. As a result, Torres Menier was waiting for Batista when he arrived at Camp Columbia on the morning of September 4.[63]

That morning, Batista drove to Camp Columbia with Pedraza, and they stopped for gasoline at the quartermaster's depot at around 10:30 a.m. While there, several enlisted men approached Batista and informed him that Torres Menier was waiting for him in front of the Enlisted Men's Club. The soldiers told Batista that they were prepared to revolt immediately, but that the presence of the captain indicated that a bloody struggle was likely. Batista questioned them on how Torres Menier discovered the plot. One of the men admitted to Batista that he had asked the captain to join the revolt. At this point, the loose-lipped conspirator reportedly handed Batista his pistol and told him, "If you think I am a traitor, shoot me."[64] Batista handed the man, Corporal Juan Capote Fiallo, back his pistol and told him to "consult his conscience." He added, "If you have done wrong, you should be the one to shoot yourself or suffer with remorse." Capote Fiallo declined the invitation and served for many years in Batista's military, although ironically, decades later, he was executed by the Castro government. Batista concluded the discussion with Capote Fiallo by urging his fellow conspirators to be more cautious.

On the spot, Batista developed a plan to deal with the unexpected arrival of Torres Menier. Perhaps fearing arrest, Batista told the enlisted men to follow closely behind him. Batista said he would try to convince Torres Menier to enter the club, at which point they were to circle in behind him, thereby surrounding him. After this brief discussion, Batista proceeded to the club to meet the captain.[65] When he arrived, Batista was sweating profusely and several buttons of his uniform were open, Torres Menier recalled in his memoir. Almost immediately, Batista began saying that he "was not afraid of death, even though he had a daughter and wife." The captain told Batista that he wished to attend the meeting in the club. Torres Menier said he was authorized to disband the meeting, but would not, fearing it would be held clandestinely. Batista recalled saluting the captain and then inviting him to attend.[66]

From Batista's account of events, it is clear that he thought Torres Menier was there to break up the meeting and perhaps order the arrest of the conspirators. Fearing the worst, Batista asked several conspirators to call up allies at military installations throughout Havana and urge them to come to Columbia armed and ready for battle.[67] For his part, Torres Menier was unaware of the severity of the crisis and was there to gather complaints and report them back to Sanguily for action. Torres Menier was operating under the false assumption that an airing of disagreements would resolve the crisis, so throughout the day he kept returning to the club seeking a petition of complaint from the enlisted men. Meanwhile, the conspirators solidified their forces. Years later, Adam y Silva, who entered the meeting as it was under way, wrote that Torres Menier failed to appreciate the "gravity of the case and that he was witnessing the beginning of open sedition."[68]

Once inside the club, Batista stalled for time by introducing all of those with him, waiting until the club filled up with sergeants and enlisted men. Batista spoke first to the crowd of enlisted men, a number that ultimately swelled to more than one thousand. He complained of the treatment that the enlisted men received in the army. He blamed the officers for taking full credit for the overthrow of Machado and the ouster of Herrera. The movement by the enlisted men was not motivated by the possible reduction of salaries and concerns about an empty "stomach," he claimed, but rather by high ideals. Batista again cited the Hernández burial as an example of mistreatment of the enlisted men.[69] The theme of "dignity" for the enlisted men was one that Batista emphasized again and again to stir up the crowd against the officers in general and Torres Menier in particular.[70] Despite his many complaints, Batista asserted, as a ruse to buy more time, that the enlisted men would continue to obey their officers.[71]

Torres Menier blamed the Machado regime and General Herrera for many of the indignities suffered by the enlisted men. He denied that salaries and positions were about to be cut and cited the circular issued by the secretary of war the previous day. Colonel Sanguily, when he recovered from his illness, would address the complaints of the enlisted men. "I tried by all means to demonstrate that his complaints were unfounded; but even if they were true, the only way to express them was through the chain of command, complaining to one's superior, and that I was there representing the chief of the army so that they could give me a petition of their complaints so we could take them into account," Torres Menier told the men.

After several exchanges between Batista and Torres Menier, the crowd of enlisted men, sprinkled with some alarmed officers, began to get unruly. There were chants of "Viva Batista!" and several enlisted men interrupted the proceedings to offer their views on purging the army. At one point, Batista began to speak again and one of his fellow conspirators, Private Mario Hernández, tired of the debate, slammed his hand on a table. Hernández told Batista, "Let us not speak about any more nonsense. Tell him [Torres Menier] the truth of the situation."[72] In the midst of this turmoil, Adam y Silva wrote that Torres Menier appeared more like a "congressman in debate" than a superior officer.[73]

In an effort to defuse the volatile situation, Torres Menier asked Batista and the other enlisted men to present him with a petition of grievances by 3 p.m. and asked them to return to their posts. Batista told the captain that they would draft a petition and present it to him later in the day. The petition request bought the enlisted men several more hours to organize and consolidate their forces. While the senior officers waited for a petition that would never come, the conspirators conspired.[74] Pedraza and Rodríguez were dispatched to Matanzas to oversee the operation there. If there had been any doubt about the movement's leadership, those doubts were dispelled by Batista's daring confrontation with Torres Menier. If Pablo Rodríguez was in fact the leader, he would have stayed in Havana to coordinate the revolt, rather than traveling to Matanzas in a supporting role.

Despite the obvious insubordination by Batista and the enlisted men at the club, barely concealed by a veneer of politeness and correctness, the high command failed to comprehend that they were in the midst of a full-scale revolt. No one bothered to inform Secretary of War Ferrer of the demands by the enlisted men.[75] He found out about the meeting almost by accident when he went to Sanguily's home at 2 p.m. on September 4 to discuss plans to purify the armed forces. While there, Sanguily, laying in his bed, informed Ferrer of the meeting at Columbia. Sanguily said he planned to meet with a delegation of sergeants the next day to discuss the reorganization of the army, a meeting that Ferrer opposed. Sanguily then called Torres Menier, who was in another part of the house, to come in to the bedroom and describe the meeting to Ferrer. The secretary of war was livid after hearing of the events. "Did I not decide in a circular that meetings among military men were strictly prohibited? Then how is it that a large number of officers from Columbia and about 1,000 soldiers decide to meet to publicly debate, face to face, a military matter?"[76] When Torres Menier told him that his participation in the meeting was sanctioned by Sanguily, Ferrer stormed out of the house vowing to resign. "I will not stay among traitors." Ferrer would soon have more to worry about than his battered dignity.

The senior officers, likewise, failed to perceive the threat. After the morning meeting at the club, realizing that it had been sanctioned by Sanguily, they not only did nothing to prevent further discussion, they facilitated it by agreeing to transport enlisted men to Columbia for a second meeting scheduled for 8 p.m. that night at the Enlisted Men's Theater. "It was necessary to exceed all precedents in terms of stupidity and so military trucks and automobiles were made available to transport the 'delegations' to the Columbia assembly," wrote Adam y Silva.[77] Repeated warnings by some of the junior officers to the high command went unheeded throughout the day. U.S. Military Attaché T. N. Gimperling, "hearing of certain rumblings among the enlisted men" visited military headquarters and Columbia and was reassured by the officers that the situation was under control.[78]

Meanwhile, Batista and other members of the conspiracy went from barracks to barracks, installation to installation, preparing key supporters to seize power at the designated hour. At most of the stops, the enlisted men offered their support and accepted Batista's leadership. There was resistance at the First Infantry Battalion, where the first sergeants refused to join the revolt. In response, Batista asked his delegate to the battalion, Corporal Oscar Díaz, to gather together the enlisted men for a meeting to rally support for the movement. Putting forth many of the same arguments he laid out at Columbia, Batista convinced the men to obey Díaz by telling them that the enlisted men already had control of Columbia, even though they did not.[79] In his travels, Batista visited Carbó at his newspaper, informed him of events, and urged him to attend the evening meeting at Columbia and bring civilian supporters. Batista also went to see guerrilla leader Juan Blas Hernández, who for two years had fought a hit-and-run battle with Machado's troops in the eastern provinces of Las Villas and Camagüey with a poorly equipped band of between 150 and 200 men. During the meeting, Hernández agreed to support the Sergeants' Revolt.[80] At some point, Batista had the presence of mind to stop at his apartment with several bodyguards and eat a quick meal. When he arrived, his wife informed him of a radio broadcast announcing a failed conspiracy at Columbia. Batista informed her about the evening meeting at Columbia, and perhaps fearing that his plans might go badly, he gave his wife an amethyst ring and watch to keep for him.[81]

Throughout most of the day, high-ranking government officials remained unaware of the gravity of the situation. President Céspedes, still inspecting hurricane damage in the east, was away from the capital and apparently unaware of what was transpiring.[82] Ferrer, after his disagreeable confrontation with Sanguily, returned to his office. Sometime around 6 p.m., another cabinet official brought a lieutenant to speak with Ferrer about the "subversive movement" at Camp Columbia. The secretary of war telephoned the base and spoke with the commanding officer, who assured him that all was calm. Ferrer later came to believe that the person on the other end of the telephone line was an impostor offering false reassurance.[83] Later in the evening, Ferrer and several other cabinet ministers went to the Presidential Palace to get word on the return of President Céspedes. Ferrer would not be informed of the mutiny until 9 p.m., by which time it was well under way.

Upon his return to Columbia, Batista met again with several of the conspirators, and together they finalized plans for the revolt. At about the same time, Batista was summoned to the office of Commander Antonio Pineda, chief of the Sixth Military District, headquartered at the base, but instead of going immediately he told Pineda's messenger to ask the commander to "forgive him, but that he was occupied at the moment." When Batista finally arrived at district headquarters, Torres Menier was waiting for him and questioned him about the petition of grievances. Batista assured him that they would be ready by that evening. When Torres Menier expressed an interest in attending the 8 p.m. meeting, Batista informed him that officers were not allowed. "The enlisted men's bloc will never be destroyed," Batista told the captain. After the talk with Batista, Torres Menier returned to the aviation corps, which he commanded, and found the enlisted men holding rifles and preparing for a possible attack. When he ordered them to put down their weapons, they refused.[84]

OPEN REVOLT

Hundreds of enlisted men were sitting in the theater when Batista, seated onstage, opened the meeting with a review of grievances against the officers. But he quickly went to the heart of the matter. "From this moment forward, do not obey anyone's orders but mine. First sergeants must immediately take control of their respective military units. If there is no first sergeant, or if he refuses to take command, the senior sergeant must do so. If there is no sergeant, a corporal. If there is no willing corporal, then a soldier, and if not, then a recruit. The units must have someone in command and he must be an enlisted man."[85]

On the question of the officers, Batista urged the enlisted men to treat them with "respect and consideration." The officers must not "interfere," because this is a "movement of enlisted men in which you will get the majority of what you want." At one point, Batista was informed that there were officers in the audience. He asked them to leave, ironically noting that they were prohibited from attending by the high command. No one moved in the audience. At last, he stood and spoke in a loud voice, once again asking the officers to leave and promising to inform them promptly of any decisions made. After this second request, several officers exited the theater.

Batista then urged the enlisted men to return to their units and arm themselves until they received further orders from him. "The military high command is now here." He then asked the sergeants to meet him at an adjacent office where he gave out specific orders and assignments. After securing the services of a typist, Batista began dictating telegrams to enlisted officers throughout the island. In a classic photograph taken the night of the revolt, Batista, his sergeant's stripes visible on both arms, appears surrounded by telephones and telegraph wires, his hair disheveled, simultaneously juggling several conversations. Batista appeared to one eyewitness like the "secretary of a revolutionary committee."[86] The process of communicating with military posts would go on throughout the night. At the same time, Batista and fellow conspirators began contacting civilian leaders with the hopes of garnering support.

There were some uneasy moments throughout the night and the next day. In the easternmost province of Oriente, Batista's order to take over the First Military District was given, by the sergeant receiving it, to the officer in charge. As a result, the officers began to plot their own revolt against the enlisted men. However, when the enlisted men learned of the events in Havana they quickly arrested all of the officers as well as the disloyal sergeant who had received the original order.[87] At La Cabaña, the second-most important military installation in Havana, the enlisted men refused to accept Batista's choice of a leader and threatened a revolt of their own. Batista followed up by appointing his close friend, Urbano Soler, as chief, but he too was rejected. The enlisted men ultimately elected their leader, and Batista, eager to avoid a confrontation, was forced to accept their candidate.[88] Elections took place in other units as well in the days following the revolt.[89]

In the Cuban Navy, a similar process was under way. A delegation from the navy attended the meeting at Columbia, and control of the island's two naval districts was easily secured over the course of the next twenty-four hours. Sergeants and corporals were placed in charge of each ship in the small fleet. The path for a takeover of the navy was cleared in mid-August when members of the sergeants' conspiracy made contact with navy enlisted personnel. Control of the navy fell under Batista's overall leadership. Given the relative power of the army vis-à-vis the navy, it is easy to understand why the sailors would follow the lead of the soldiers. Military power was heavily weighted in favor of the Cuban army with its 10,928 members, while the Navy consisted of 1,368 men and fifteen ships. The ability to secure the quick allegiance of the navy further strengthened the position of Batista and his fellow conspirators. The National Police was less of a factor, because many of the 2,400 members abandoned their posts in the aftermath of Machado's flight. Civilian revolutionaries, allied with Batista, took control of many police stations.[90]

An effort at resistance was made by Secretary of War Ferrer, when at around 9 p.m., in response to reports of an uprising, he went to the First Artillery Battalion, charged with protecting nearby government offices. When he arrived, he found the officers under arrest. The officers told Ferrer that the revolt had "taken them by surprise." A sergeant told Ferrer that the enlisted men would retain control of the installation until "certain matters were resolved." Ferrer ordered the sergeant to bring together the troops, so that he could address them, and he complied. Secretary Ferrer and his military aide, Lieutenant César Lorié, urged the enlisted men to return command to the officers. They warned of possible military intervention by the United States if order was not restored. During a speech to the troops, Lorié persuaded them to chant, "Viva Presidente Céspedes. Viva the army. Viva the officers." However, Ferrer and Lorié could not persuade them to hand power back to the officers. The enlisted men informed Ferrer that they had "made a commitment to Columbia and they did not want to be accused of being traitors. It was futile."[91]

The revolt was now clearly at a crossroads. In the next few hours, Batista and his fellow sergeants would take control over most of the armed forces. Yet it is clear from his speech to the men that Batista was still unsure of what course the revolt would take. The movement was built on the grievances of the enlisted men against the officers. It was devoid of political ideology. In the closing days of August, the decision was made to wrest control of the army from the officers. Once accomplished, Batista and his fellow sergeants found that there was no way to remove the officers and promote themselves without toppling the government. The selection of the officer corps was a political decision. In order to accomplish a restructuring of the armed forces, the conspirators would need to control, or at the very least, exert considerable pressure on the government. To achieve anything less would leave them as potential candidates for the firing squad.

As late as the evening of September 4, Batista was still uncertain of how to channel the revolt. He did not wish to alienate the officer corps, because he fully expected that many, if not most, would return to their commands—thus his emphasis on "respect" for the officers. In his address to the enlisted men that evening, Batista made no mention of the Céspedes government or its removal. There was no talk of a revolution.[92]

The political ideology came later in the evening from Carbó and the Student Directory (Directorio Estudiantil Universitario), whose members began arriving at Camp Columbia shortly after 10:30 p.m. Members from several small political groups, including Pro Ley y Justicia and the ABC Radical (a left-wing splinter group of the ABC) also made their way to Columbia, but they took a backseat in importance to the Directory. It is probable that Batista considered the issue of how far to take the movement on numerous occasions in the days leading up to September 4. But more than likely the decision to oust Céspedes was made that evening in reaction to a chain of events that no one could have foreseen. When Carbó arrived, Batista met with him privately. Several people with secondhand knowledge of the meeting said that Carbó urged Batista to abandon the notion of presenting a petition of grievances to the Céspedes government when he could address those grievances directly by seizing power. The journalist warned the sergeant about the very real likelihood of execution if the officers were to regain control of the army and exhorted him to abandon any effort at cooperation with the officers. Carbó warned of a possible alliance between the officers and the United States.[93] The information fits with Carbo's overall political outlook at the time. He was an outspoken opponent of the Céspedes government and the mediation process that brought it to power. By urging Batista to take the movement a step further, Carbó was advancing his own political agenda.

The students were likewise opposed to the Céspedes government and were one of the few major opposition groups to abstain from the mediation process. At the time of the revolt, Directory members were in fact negotiating with the junior officers in an effort to topple the government. Several Directory members were also aware of the sergeants' plans. "We were simultaneously involved in two parallel military conspiracies," according to one Directory member.

The unfolding logic of events dictated an alliance between the students and the enlisted men. Batista and the other conspirators needed civilian support and a political program to survive. The only major group offering to support the Sergeants' Revolt, with the exception of the Communists, was the student movement. It was a symbiotic relationship. Each had what the other needed. The sergeants had no political program; the Directory did. The students did not have the muscle to take power; the sergeants did. Together they would make a revolution.

Upon arriving at Columbia, Directory members were struck by the movement's lack of a national political agenda. Juan Rubio Padilla recalled that the movement "did not have the least political aim" and compared it to a "union strike." The goal of the Directory members was to determine "how far the soldiers and the NCOs [noncommissioned officers] were disposed to go." Emilio Laurent, a former officer with ties to the Directory, wrote in his memoir that when he arrived at Columbia at 10:30 p.m., all the conversations centered on military issues, specifically complaints against the officers.[94]

A meeting between the sergeants and the students and their supporters began around 11 p.m. with the intention of broadening the movement to include in its objectives the establishment of a new government. The Directory's program, which included the creation of an executive commission of five to rule the country (thereafter known as the pentarchy), was approved near midnight by the enlisted men in attendance.[95] Once the Directory's program was adopted by the military, the students set about establishing the framework of a civilian government in a series of meetings that would go on throughout the night. At those later meetings, Batista was the only military man in attendance. Later in the evening, members of the Communist Party arrived at Columbia and asked to participate, but they were denied entry and thereafter excluded from the movement.

PROCLAMATION AND PENTARCHY

The first order of business was to draft a proclamation setting forth the principles of the new ruling coalition, initially designated La Agrupación Revolucionaria de Cuba. Carbó was chosen to draft a document that was unanimously adopted without discussion and signed by eighteen civilians and one military man, Fulgencio Batista, who was identified in the proclamation as Sergeant and Revolutionary Leader of All the Armed Forces of the Republic (Sargento Jefe Revolucionario de Todas las Fuerzas Armadas de la República). The document declared that the revolutionary movement was composed of the enlisted men and several civilian organizations headed by the Directory.[96] The signatories would dominate Cuban politics for the next three decades and included three future presidents, Ramón Grau San Martín,[97] Carlos Prío Socarrás,[98] and Batista.

It was moderate in tone and clearly intended to placate the United States, by noting that the revolutionary government would "respect all loans and agreements" contracted by the republic. It declared that the Agrupación Revolucionaria would seize the "reins of power as a Provisional Revolutionary Government" because the Céspedes regime was incapable of responding to the "urgent demands of the Revolution." The provisional government would relinquish power after a Constitutional Assembly established a new constitutional government, which would hold power until the general elections. Implied in the proclamation was repudiation of the hated Platt Amendment, which allowed the United States to intervene in Cuba's affairs, and which was part of the 1901 Cuban Constitution. In reference to Cuba's traditional dependence on the United States, the proclamation read: "We have confidence that Cuba will be respected like a *new sovereign Nation* [*Patria*] which goes forth with new vigor into international affairs" (italics mine). Decrees would be dictated with the "force of law." The proclamation was published in every major newspaper in the country the next morning and afternoon.[99]

During the course of the evening and early morning, the Directory set about nominating members to serve on its executive commission, which sought to divide the power of the executive branch of the government among five members. The sergeants backed Carbó, and the Directory agreed to make him one of the five. "I doubt that, without the presence of this factor [military support], the Directory, allowed to select freely, would have selected Carbó, not because we had any particular prejudice against him, but because his relations with the Directory and our knowledge of his political activity would not have moved us to select him," observed Rubio Padilla.[100] Three others, Grau, a professor at the University of Havana and longtime supporter of student political causes; Guillermo Portela, also a member of the university faculty; and attorney Jose M. Irisarri, were selected fairly easily.

But the final selection engendered a good deal of debate. The student-military alliance was but a few hours old, and already a Directory supporter, anticipating tensions with Batista, decided to nominate him to be the fifth pentarch. There would be "less danger to civilian authority if the chief of the revolutionary forces were made a member of the executive commission, where he would have one vote among five," Irisarri wrote a year later, explaining his decision to nominate Batista.[101]

The sergeant-turned-revolutionary-chief declined the nomination, citing his lack of experience and the likelihood that his membership on the commission

The Cuban public did not know what to make of the new "pentarchy," or executive commission, selected by the Student Directory to rule the nation on the night of September 4, 1933. The five-member presidency lasted only six days until Ramón Grau San Martín was selected president. This cartoon takes a whimsical look at the pentarchy and portrays each of the pentarchs as one of the "Dionne Quintuplets" (who were born in this period). Carbó, who eventually promoted Batista to colonel, is the first quintuplet on the left, holding the rattle. Grau is seated next to the toy horse. This caricature was published in *Bohemia* on June 5, 1938.

would hurt chances for international recognition of the government. Perhaps Batista detected a trap in the nomination. Events were fluid. His power base was the military, which was in a state of disarray. To accept an essentially civilian position, even if he remained in the army, might create a power vacuum in the military that a rival could take advantage of. It would also leave him more vulnerable to the political winds of change.[102] The Directory finally selected economist and businessman Porfirio Franca as the final pentarch, a compromise candidate who it was thought would appeal to the more conservative elements of society. From the start, Franca was a nonentity in the government, seldom appearing at meetings, and he resigned three days after his selection (September 8).

Conspiracies were already in the air. The first official order issued by the army listed the new military hierarchy, and at the top of the list was "Fulgencio Batista—Leader of Movement" (Jefe del Movimiento). Listed second was Pablo Rodríguez, who was given command of Camp Columbia. There was no effort to give equal status to Rodríguez, a fact that angered him and some of his supporters. However, Rodríguez declined, for the moment, to challenge Batista for the top spot, citing the importance of unity in the movement. The Batista-Rodríguez rift grew wider and wider as the weeks passed, until they could no longer coexist in the military.[103] On the civilian front, Batista, in the early morning hours of September 5, received a visit from high-ranking members of the ABC. He met with them privately, and during the meeting they urged him to oust the Directory from the movement and adopt the ABC's political program.[104] But they were a few hours too late, Batista had a civilian coalition, and to change partners so soon would only weaken efforts to gain public and international support for the actions of the rebellious sergeants. Ironically, several weeks earlier it was the ABC that had rejected Batista's pleas.

FAREWELL TO CÉSPEDES

The end for the Céspedes government came shortly after noon on September 5, when the pentarchs, accompanied by Batista and a group of several hundred supporters went to the Presidential Palace to meet with the president, just returned from his tour of hurricane damage in the east. There was a sort of dark comedic quality to the meeting. Céspedes, sitting in his office, asked the visitors what they wanted, but at first there was so much noise and commotion among those in attendance that no one could be heard. Finally, there was silence, and Grau addressed the president, "We have come to receive from you the government of the nation."

Céspedes responded with a question: "And who has given you authorization to do this?" After a brief explanation by Grau of the civilian components of the revolutionary coalition, Céspedes doubted whether they were "sufficiently strong to topple a legal government." Grau reportedly smiled and told the president, "The revolutionary junta also includes all the soldiers and sailors of the nation." Seeing the force of Grau's argument, Céspedes agreed to leave the palace, although he never formally resigned. In a brief statement outside the Presidential Palace, Céspedes said he lived up to his "responsibilities" to the nation. "Now others take control of the government. It is now their responsibility before the public and history." In the coming weeks, he repeatedly refused to support efforts by those willing to fight to restore his government.[105]

Céspedes went gently into the night of Cuban history.

CHAPTER 6

REVOLUTION

OF 1933

Taking power was relatively easy. Keeping it would prove much more difficult. The government of the enlisted men and student leaders was surrounded
by powerful enemies. U.S. Ambassador Sumner Welles was personally embarrassed by the removal of Céspedes and would do everything in his
power to undermine the new government. The military officers, humiliated
by the events of September 4, refused to return to their posts and share
power with their former underlings. It was hard for them to imagine that *el
negro Batista*, a *guajiro* (country boy) from Banes was responsible for their
ouster.[1] Their sense of military honor and racial and class superiority posed
an obstacle to negotiation and clouded their perception of the new power
structure. The leaders of the ABC movement, champions of the fight against
Machado, found themselves unceremoniously booted from power. Experts
in the art of urban warfare, it was only a matter of time before they struck
against the new government. The Communists sought to ally themselves with
the students and enlisted men, but their overtures were spurned. Pushed
aside, they promoted ongoing labor unrest throughout the island, particularly on some of the large sugar plantations in the eastern provinces of Camagüey and Oriente, where workers took control of the plantations and mills
and established soviets. Each in time would pose fundamental challenges to
the revolutionary government.

Even more dangerous than the external threats were the dangers from
within. The alliance of students and enlisted men was a study in uneasy con-
trasts from its inception. Batista's followers were primarily men of action
from the poorest segments of society. The leaders of the Sergeants' Revolt,

such as Batista, had a modicum of education and training, but they could hardly be classified as profound thinkers and men of letters. They did, however, control the bulk of the weapons. The students were idealists and ideologues. Men and women with years of academic and political training, they spent hours in meetings, vigorously debating every nuance of political and public policy. Government by debate proved haphazard and unpredictable. Their first attempt at governing, the pentarchy, lasted six days, to be replaced by their handpicked president, Professor Ramón Grau San Martín, the champion of student causes. Their supporters, caught up in the revolutionary frenzy of the moment, armed themselves and formed militias, the most popular being the Ejército Caribe (Army of the Caribbean). They took it upon themselves to patrol the streets and uphold revolutionary edicts as they interpreted them. For the most part, the students were from the middle and upper classes of Cuban society. The marriage of students and soldiers was a troubled one and destined to be short-lived.

The Sergeant and the Ambassador

The Sergeants' Revolt caught U.S. officials by surprise. They believed the officers were incapable of a military coup against Céspedes and did not perceive any threat at all from the enlisted men.[2] What little information the Americans had was largely incorrect. The first dispatches from military intelligence identified the leaders as sergeants "Juan Batista" and Pedro Santana, who was in fact an aide to Carbó. In his dispatch of September 5, military attaché T. N. Gimperling wrote, "This revolutionary movement is extremely radical with strong leanings toward communism." Welles thought the revolt was "fomented by the extreme radical elements." In Pavlovian response, Welles immediately recommended the dispatch of three warships, two to Havana and one to Santiago de Cuba in Oriente. President Roosevelt complied with the request and ordered the ships to Cuba, as well as many others in subsequent days, so that one Cuban cartoonist portrayed the island as a spit of land surrounded by warships with the caption "Isle of the Lost Ships."[3] In an effort to allay concerns of imminent military intervention, Roosevelt held a series of meetings with Latin American diplomats in early September to assure them that the warships were sent to Cuba "for the sole purpose of protecting American lives."[4]

On the day the conspirators took power, both Batista and Grau made separate visits to Welles to court U.S. acceptance of the new government. Batista went to the U.S. Embassy on the morning of September 5, sometime around 11 a.m., and asked the ambassador about the likelihood of formal recognition, but Welles declined to comment. The ambassador then questioned Batista about the steps taken to maintain public order. Although Batista tried to assure him, Welles was unconvinced. "It was made quite plain that no measures whatever had been taken in that sense," Welles wrote. The ambassador concluded the meeting by telling Batista that he would be "glad" to see him at "any time."[5] Grau visited Welles in the evening, sometime after 9 p.m. Again, the ambassador emphasized the importance of protecting the "life

No. 2.

"Isle of the Lost Ships"

(La Semana, September 1933)

This political cartoon, "Isle of the Lost Ships," ran in the popular weekly newspaper *La Semana* in September 1933. It pokes fun at the U.S. decision to surround Cuba with warships after the overthrow of the Céspedes government on September 4, 1933.

and property of American citizens." Grau assured him that the soldiers would maintain order because of their "devotion" to the ideals of the revolution. Welles was unimpressed with Grau and described him as "utterly impractical."[6]

The meeting between Batista and Welles offers a glimpse into Batista's mind-set in the first hours after the revolt. The successful takeover was less than twenty-four hours old, and already he was courting U.S. acceptance. Batista went right to the source of power to seek assurances for his coalition government. Although a political novice, he moved swiftly and deftly in the days to come to preserve his newly acquired power and position. Clearly, the sergeant from Banes had a talent for dissecting, analyzing, and manipulating the sources of political power. He slept little, but he never lost his presence of mind, all the while displaying enormous determination and toughness. One observer noted that Batista was "transformed" during the early weeks of September and that with each crisis he began to realize his "enormous potential."[7]

The first Batista-Welles meeting is equally important because of the significance ascribed to it by some scholars and polemicists. Batista's detractors cite it as the first indication that he was planning to betray the students. Some scholars have chosen to look back on Welles's parting offer to Batista to come and visit again as an indication that a Judas kiss was already in the works. With this initial visit, "Batista began his double game," writes Lionel Soto. It is convenient to look at the outcome of an event and then interpret backward to make everything fit a nice and simple interpretation, but simplicity has its limitations. Ultimately, Batista, to maintain his own power, broke with the students and installed a government more to the liking of the United States and its internal political allies. However, that break came four months later. At the time of his initial visit to the embassy, Welles saw Batista as part of the problem, rather than part of the solution. One conspirator remembered that the initial meeting between Welles and Batista was less than warm. Another recollected that it was "extremely formal with no handshakings or other usual demonstrations of courtesy." Both Grau and Batista were engulfed in a political maelstrom at the time of their first visits to Welles. Unlike the scholars who came after them, they could not see the future. The two visits need to be seen for what they were: efforts to gain acceptance from the United States for the new government.[8] Batista had installed Grau and the other pentarchs just hours before his visit, so it is unlikely that he would have begun to plot against them in such a short time.

State Department records indicate that within hours of the successful revolt, Welles developed a multipronged strategy to undermine the new government.

The threat of intervention and diplomatic nonrecognition formed the cornerstones of his plan. In the first days of the revolt, Welles dangled the possibility of U.S. intervention in front of the opposition parties as part of an effort to encourage dissent. Although the diplomatic records are silent on the issue, Batista recollected many years later that Welles proposed to him the landing of marines in Cuba to "guard North American properties and homes" and that these areas should be declared "neutral zones." Batista, while professing a high regard for the United States, told him the plan was unacceptable. "I told him we would not even consider this formula," Batista contended. "It would be most dangerous for both countries. It would provoke much greater difficulties than those we were now facing. He [Welles] was asking us to acquiesce to military intervention."[9]

Intervention was removed from Welles's arsenal early on as a result of opposition by President Roosevelt and Secretary of State Cordell Hull. But nonrecognition would remain a powerful weapon for the ambassador. He maintained that the United States was carefully pondering the question of diplomatic recognition without interfering in events. For Welles, recognition should be based on stability. Yet he did everything he could to ensure instability. The ambassador's knowledge, sometimes well in advance of antigovernment conspiracies, raises serious questions about his efforts to topple the new government.

As an alternative to the student/soldier government, Welles crafted the notion of a "national unity government," a power-sharing arrangement between the political parties that took part in the mediation proceedings and the student leaders. Welles began meeting with disgruntled Cuban political leaders just hours after the successful revolt. On the evening of September 5, the suggestion that Carlos Mendieta, the aging Independence War veteran, would be an ideal candidate to serve as president of this unity government was made to Welles.[10] The ambassador gave his blessings to efforts by his Cuban political allies to come to a power-sharing agreement with the new government. The pentarchs initially rebuffed the proposal. At first, Welles envisioned the reorganization of the Cuban Army by the deposed officer corps, with order maintained by U.S Marines, but he quickly abandoned that solution.[11]

ANGRY OFFICERS

In his first speech to the nation from the balcony of the Presidential Palace on September 5, Batista made the purging of the armed forces a main priority. The revolt by the enlisted men was necessitated by the presence in the military of "leaders and officers who had stained the uniform and from whom the enlisted men were unwilling to take orders." Batista also outlined a second theme in his speech: namely, that the soldiers were uninterested in "promotion or material gain."[12] In the next few days, the sergeant-turned-revolutionary emphasized those themes again and again, often declaring the willingness of the sergeants and soldiers to return authority to an officer corps cleansed of impurities. "We will return command only to the officers who deserve it," Batista told an Associated Press reporter.[13]

Despite his idealistic pronouncements, Batista never intended to hand power back to the officers. In the coming days, Sergeant Batista presented the officers with a series of power-sharing proposals that he suspected they would refuse. Each new proposal was worse than the previous one and reflected the consolidation of his power within the armed forces. If the officers wished to return, they would do so under his leadership and on an equal footing with many of their former subordinates. In the end, most of the officers chose to reject his offers. The officers wanted to reestablish conditions as they were prior to September 4 and considered the offers made by Batista lacking in "honor and dignity."[14] Of the nine hundred officers in place prior to September 4, only two hundred returned to the armed forces. About three hundred fled, resigned, or were imprisoned. The remaining four hundred decided to resist and made their way to the Hotel Nacional where they would make a final, desperate stand against the government.[15] Even if Batista wished to return power to the officers, his constituency, the enlisted men, would never have allowed it. Each resignation from the officer corps represented an opportunity for advancement. The sergeants and corporals became first and second lieutenants, while privates ascended to the ranks of corporals and sergeants.

Although Batista gave lip service to treating the officer corps with respect and dignity, he rightly distrusted them from the onset of the revolt and took immediate steps to restrict their movements and place them under surveillance. In his memoir, Captain Torres Menier wrote that on the morning of September 5, groups of armed enlisted men began visiting the officers and advising them of orders from the military high command to remain in their homes. Torres Menier received hourly calls at his home "day and night" to check on his whereabouts. On September 6, a circular was distributed to the enlisted men at military posts throughout the island authorizing them to "select" the officers who would be allowed to return to duty. The following day, Batista formally declared the officers "under house arrest" and threatened them with incarceration in a military jail if they did not comply. The officers were forbidden to meet in groups.[16]

Resolution of the dispute with the officers was a high priority for the new government, because an armed conflict between different factions in the military could create a justification for U.S. intervention. Civilian elements in the government facilitated a series of negotiations between Batista and representatives of the officer corps in the days immediately following the revolt. The goal of the government was to defuse the crisis, secure the return of some of the junior officers, and divide the officer corps.[17] During these tense days, Batista sent out contradictory messages about his willingness to step down as chief of the armed forces and to even return to civilian life if that became necessary to heal the rifts within the armed forces. But, his brass knuckles approach to the negotiations reveal his true intentions.[18] In the first negotiating session on September 5, Batista offered to hand over power to two well-respected colonels, but only after the armed forces had been purged by the sergeants and enlisted men. The purge would have left the two colonels surrounded by Batista's followers and left him in a strong position to continue in a prominent military position. This was the best proposal the officers were to receive, and one participant to the negotiations thought it was a legitimate offer by Batista.[19] In the second round of negotiations on the afternoon of September 7, the deal got worse. Under a new proposition by Batista, officers would be allowed to take command of the military districts, but they would be assigned two sergeants, one to oversee administrative decisions and another to approve of personnel decisions. At the top of the command structure would be a sort of pentarchy of the military, a Mixed Military Junta (Junta Militar Mixta), consisting of five members, four officers and one sergeant. These were "taunting offers" aimed at reducing the officers to "figureheads," thought former Secretary of War Horacio Ferrer.[20]

The final effort to secure an agreement came during a tumultuous meeting on the evening of September 7 at the Presidential Palace, a meeting that lasted well into the early morning hours. In a radio broadcast, Commissioner of War Sergio Carbó called the officers to the Presidential Palace to complete the negotiations, a summons that was answered by about two hundred of them. Carbó spent most of the night shuffling between two separate rooms in the palace, one holding the officers and the other Batista and his followers, submitting proposals and counterproposals. The officers began the negotiations by asking that one of them be selected as commander in chief of the army, a proposal that was flatly rejected by the enlisted men. Further tightening the screws on the officers, Batista again proposed a junta of five to run the military, but this time the junta would contain three sergeants and two officers.

For hours, the officers debated a variety of issues, never quite coming to the realization that they would have to accept some sort of power-sharing arrangement. Concerned with their "honor and dignity" they failed to grasp the fact that they were in a weak bargaining position and that it was incumbent on them to secure the best deal possible. The very notion that they were negotiating with their subordinates was distasteful to some. One group of officers said they would return only if they were called back to service by another officer. In one of the most illuminating moments of the negotiations, Carbó suggested that the promotion of Batista to the rank of general would ease those concerns. The offer was flatly rejected by the officers.

Tiring of the role of intermediary, Carbó suggested that the officers appoint a delegation to negotiate directly with Batista. A delegation of six officers, along with Carbó, was then escorted down a hallway lined with bodyguards to where Batista was waiting with several assistants. One of the delegates told Batista that the officers would not return to duty if summoned by a sergeant. Batista responded, "The question would be a simple one if all the officers were decent, such as yourself, but the problem is that the enlisted men trust me. I have brought them to this point. How can they now take orders from those who have not been on their side?" In strikingly honest fashion, Batista admitted that his coalition within the military would collapse if he were to step down as leader.[21]

Again came the refrain from another member of the officers' delegation, that they would not be ruled by a sergeant. Once again, Carbó tried to clarify the situation for them. "Everything is based on the fact that the [officers] have nothing more than discipline on their side, while [Batista] has 15,000 bayonets [on his side]." Another officer suggested the appointment of Batista as commissioner of war. Responding with what by then had become his mantra, Batista told the officers that he "aspired to nothing. I want to continue as a sergeant, moreover, the commissioner of war is Carbó."[22]

The officers' delegation left the meeting with Batista dissatisfied and returned to their colleagues to report the results. Several officers proposed that a vote of confidence in Carbó be taken, but that too was rejected after hours of debate. The sentiment among the officers was that they should not cast votes for their absent comrades. The negotiations broke off without agreement at 4 a.m.

After three days of negotiations, Carbó decided it was time to end the impasse and to promote Batista to the rank of general. Carbó did not act in a vacuum. His decision was made after consultations with members of the Student Directory. No formal meeting of the pentarchs was held on the subject, partly because the five-headed government was already in disarray. Years later, Carbó wrote that his decision was forced on him by the "intransigent attitude" of the officers, who by refusing to return to duty were courting "catastrophe."[23] When Carbó returned to the room where Batista was waiting, he informed him of his decision. Batista's response was curious and revealed the collaborative nature of his relationship with Carbó. Rather than accept the promotion, as would a compliant subordinate, Batista told Carbó that the enlisted men would react negatively to his promotion to the rank of general. The sergeant refused to accept any promotion beyond that of colonel.[24] After a decree was drafted and signed by Carbó promoting Batista for "services rendered to the country in time of war," a military honor guard was assembled. The newly designated colonel and military chief of staff spoke briefly, thanked Carbó, and pledged his support to the government. Batista's promotion was followed quickly by a wave of eighteen other promotions, including many of the original conspirators, to the rank of captain or lieutenant. In all, 527 enlisted men and civilians received promotions within a relatively short time.[25] In this strange way, Batista's leadership was codified and legitimized.

Batista's defenders cite his willingness to relinquish power during the negotiations as testament to a man without ambition seeking only the betterment of Cuba. The sergeant turned colonel promoted this notion of himself as magnanimous and self-sacrificing. "Posterity will analyze the event dispassionately, but it ought to be recorded here that the attitude of the sergeants was a generous one," Batista told biographer Edmund Chester. "It is the only case in history where the victors in a revolution have called in the vanquished in order to deliver the command into their hands."[26] Nothing could be further from the truth. In the days after the Sergeants' Revolt, Batista sought to portray the officers as intransigent by repeatedly, and publicly, asking them to return to duty, knowing full well that the terms he was offering were unacceptable. The only terms the humiliated officers were willing to accept was the restoration of all their colleagues to their prior positions with a provision of amnesty for the sergeants. "The stiff-necked officers refused to accept our terms," Batista recalled years later.[27] The officers adherence to "military discipline and honor" was the sword that Batista used to impale them.

The promotion of Batista to the rank of colonel set the stage for a series of dramatic and violent confrontations with the officer corps. The officers, under surveillance by the enlisted men, began congregating in the luxurious Hotel Nacional, overlooking the Havana sea wall, so they could meet to discuss unfolding events and map a unified strategy. Originally the hotel was chosen because Colonel Sanguily moved there after September 4, so that his son, a doctor at the hotel, could supervise his convalescence. But, if Sanguily sought peace and quiet, his followers would not permit it. After he was transferred to the hotel on September 5, the officers began to visit him there to seek advice on the standoff with the enlisted men. As the negotiations intensified at the palace, the officers started meeting regularly at the hotel, and some began living there. Hours after Batista's promotion on September 8, the officers officially voted to reject him as commander. With that decision, the hotel became the de facto headquarters of the officers' conspiracy.[28] The following day, it was encircled by enlisted men and members of the civilian militias. The scene was set for bloody conflict.

DEMISE OF THE PENTARCHY

The promotion of Batista contributed to the demise of the pentarchy, but it was by no means the only factor. The five-member executive commission was an experiment implemented by the students. It failed miserably because no one knew what to make of it. The public looked "comically" upon the notion that Cuba was ruled by five presidents. Even the pentarchs were confused over their individual roles and responsibilities. There were personal rivalries as each of the pentarchs sought to gain approval and popularity among the students. Franca, uncomfortable with some of the reform measures being discussed, stopped attending government meetings, reducing the pentarchy to a quartet. The experiment also met with resistance from the opposition parties and Ambassador Welles. In negotiations between the new government and the opposition, the elimination of the pentarchy and a return to a presidential system was a central demand. First and foremost, however, the pentarchy failed because it was unwieldy. The five-member commission made up of members with roughly equal power had the effect of converting the executive branch of government into a legislature. In such a body, every decision was subject to a debate among equals, as opposed to the sort of consultation that occurs between a president and a cabinet member. In the midst of chaos, Cuba could ill afford vacillation at the top.[29]

Carbó's appointment of Batista caught the other pentarchs by surprise, because although he consulted with the Student Directory, he did not seek the approval of his fellow chief executives. Pentarchs Portela and Irisarri objected to the promotion because they were not consulted.[30] The issue of Batista's promotion coupled with pressure from the opposition, which following standard practice was meeting regularly with Ambassador Welles, led the Student Directory to grudgingly reconsider the structure of the government. To that end, the students and pentarchs met for ten hours on the evening of September 8 and early morning of September 9 to debate the issue. Concerns over U.S. intervention and the failure of the public to accept the pentarchy as a viable form of government dominated the meeting. Two of the pentarchs, Portela and Irisarri, argued in favor of turning over the government to a coalition of opposition parties (the same parties that were meeting with Welles). They both argued that U.S. intervention was inevitable unless a power-sharing arrangement could be worked out.

Grau was more daring and argued that the "revolution could be saved." He observed that in December the United States and all the countries of Latin America were scheduled to meet in Montevideo, Uruguay, at the Pan-American Conference. "It's true that North American warships surround the island, but Roosevelt will not inaugurate his Good Neighbor policy, on the eve of the Pan-American Conference in Montevideo, by militarily occupying Cuba." In a discourse that probably helped him secure the presidency a day later, Grau spoke eloquently about the need of the pentarchs and senior members of the coalition to stand by the students in their time of crisis. "My responsibility, as a professor, is to counsel and guide my students," Grau said, urging the students to preserve the pentarchy.[31]

Many of the students recognized the inefficiency of the pentarchy but were reluctant to abandon it because it was part of their political program. One of the most forceful voices against the pentarchy was Eduardo Chibás, a fiery student leader who would play an important role in Cuban politics for the next twenty years.[32] Chibás urged fellow students to abandon the pentarchy and revert to a presidential system. "The [pentarchy] is so dead that it smells bad," he observed. Chibás's motion was initially rejected by the students but was ultimately accepted sometime around 6 a.m. on the morning of September 9. In eliminating the pentarchy and reverting to a presidential system, the students hoped to gain some acceptance from the opposition. It was, after all, a concession. They were quick to discover that the objections to the pentarchy were really a pretext and that the real issue was who held power rather than how it was wielded. The demise of the pentarchy was seen by Ambassador Welles as an effort to gain U.S. diplomatic recognition. "It should certainly be considered as a tendency towards a return to normality," he wrote lukewarmly.[33]

At the end of the meeting, it was decided by the students that the four remaining members of the pentarchy (now a tetrarchy) would pick the next president of Cuba. The four men, Irisarri, Carbó, Grau, and Portela, were given a day to interview candidates and make a decision. But, the presidential selection process quickly degenerated into slapstick and burlesque. Several members of the Student Directory suspected that Irisarri and Portela would make a pact with the absent Franca to turn over power to the political opposition. As a result, a meeting of the Directory was called for on the evening of September 9 at the palace, and the students voted to strip the pentarchs of the right to appoint a president. The Student Directory then proceeded to name Grau chief executive.

At the same time, the pentarchs were meeting on another floor of the palace, unaware of the fact that their deliberations were now moot. A commission of three, led by Prío, was then dispatched to inform them that a new president had been selected. After the students interrupted the deliberations of the executive commission, a heated argument ensued between Prío and Portela. The students were asked by Portela to leave, because they were interrupting their "historic mission." Prío responded by announcing that the "vote of confidence" placed in the pentarchs was revoked by the students and that Grau was the new president. Their business abruptly concluded, with the executive commission disbanded. Grau joined the students to map out plans for his inauguration the next day and to discuss the selection of cabinet officers.[34]

Concerns of conspiracy on the part of the students were well-founded. Master plotter Welles reported a series of efforts to oust the students from power in the days immediately prior to the selection of Grau as president. On the evening of September 7, Welles reported to Washington that a meeting between the government and opposition was scheduled. "I am reliably informed that the revolutionary group in control will then turn over the government and I am further advised that President Céspedes will be restored as head of the government." There were also reports that a delegation of sergeants, supposedly speaking for Batista, went to Céspedes to offer to reinstall him as president if Batista were allowed to remain as military chief. The former president reportedly rejected the offer. In the same period, Batista was offered safe passage out of Cuba and a job with United Fruit Company in Central America by someone allegedly representing the United States.[35] Two days later, on September 9 (the same day that the executive commission was to meet to select a new president), Welles wrote of another meeting between the opposition and the government in which it "appears likely" that a compromise on a power-sharing arrangement could be reached. However, he notes, "in view of the attitude of Batista it would not seem as if such solution would afford any very favorable prospect of stability."[36]

Welles clearly had specific knowledge about negotiations between the opposition and elements within the government. A deal to hand over power to a coalition of political parties, principally the ABC and parties loyal to Menocal and Mendieta, was clearly on the table. Was Welles behind these efforts? Was the United Fruit offer to Batista part of a plan to further weaken the government? Was Welles reference to Batista's "attitude" an indirect reference to his rejection of the covert job offer? Was Batista plotting separately to reinstall Céspedes? There is enough tantalizing evidence to pose the questions, but not enough to answer them.

FACTIONS WITHIN THE GRAU GOVERNMENT

In spite of the skullduggery all around him, Ramón Grau San Martín was sworn in as president of Cuba at noon on September 10 on the north balcony of the Presidential Palace. In repudiation of the 1901 Constitution, which included the hated Platt Amendment, he swore his oath before the people rather than before the justices of the Cuban Supreme Court. Two days later, Grau made his first cabinet appointments, most important among them the naming of Antonio Guiteras Holmes as interior minister.[37] Although the Grau government lasted just four months, it ushered in a series of political and social reforms that profoundly changed Cuba.

Three men would try to harness the power of the runaway revolution for their own ends. Grau, Guiteras, and Batista would form three sides of a political triangle vying for control of the movement. Amid the violence, political treachery, shifting alliances, and U.S. interference, each man tried to build a coalition to remain in power. The differences among them were striking, and each appealed to different constituencies. Their struggle would determine the fate of the revolutionary government.[38]

Grau, a medical doctor and university professor, was by nature a reformer. A man who often spoke in riddles, he was the champion of the Student Directory. Possessing great personal courage, six years earlier, Grau had opposed the expulsion from the University of Havana of students opposed to Machado and was imprisoned. His father was a wealthy Spanish merchant who had immigrated from Spain in the nineteenth century. A man of inherited wealth, Grau augmented his finances with a successful medical practice specializing in disorders of the digestive tract. Although financially well off, he fostered a relationship with the poorer classes throughout his long political career. He was the consummate aristocrat with his finely clipped mustache, nicely tailored suits, cultured Spanish, and fencing expertise. A tall and gawky bachelor, Grau made it his business in the macho politics of Cuba to be seen regularly in the company of attractive women. Yet he was also a devoted family man: after his only brother's suicide, he raised his nieces and nephews as if they were his own children, and his sister-in-law, Paulina Alsina de Grau, ran his household. A cunning politician, the forty-six-year-old president preferred to politically undermine his opponents rather than resort to violence.[39]

Grau's base of power was the Student Directory, a loose conglomeration of students constantly bickering over political and personal agendas. For the next four months, the president would try to expand his power base beyond his student followers with little success. The students were mercurial allies— even one decision counter to their expectations could turn them into the most dogged of enemies. In search of political allies, Grau negotiated with the political opposition and considered a wide range of power-sharing alternatives. He also tried to build a relationship with Batista, even though he knew the colonel was negotiating, behind his back, with his political enemies. The president sought to satisfy the cry for greater reforms coming from Guiteras and the left, although at times he was a reluctant revolutionary. In essence, he tried to plot a middle course between the political opposition, beholden to Ambassador Welles, and the socialist agenda of Guiteras, with its appeal to the working class. In the process, Grau sought to distance himself from the Student Directory, ultimately alienating his only base of political support. In the end, while trying to satisfy everyone a little bit, Grau antagonized everyone a great deal. In the final days of his presidency, the students emerged as his fiercest opponents. Borrowing from the popular film, *King Kong*, the students popularized the chant, "King Kong. Que se vaya Ramón" (in English, the much less catchy "King Kong. Let us be rid of Ramón.")

Batista was a man without a defined political agenda. His primary objective was to survive. It is clear that he favored many of the reforms enacted by the revolutionary government, and he never sought to rescind them after removing Grau from power. But, foremost in his mind was to cobble together a government that could endure. As the weeks passed, it became obvious to Batista that the United States would never recognize the Grau government. Without recognition, a cycle of violence and confrontation was inevitable as different political players sought to create a new ruling coalition. In this period, there were several attempts to kill Batista, and he traveled everywhere with armed guards. He was forced to put down a series of bloody uprisings in which hundreds were killed. Without a political resolution, the revolution was likely to devour its children. As Luis Aguilar aptly put it, "[Batista] depended for survival on his capacity to detect rapidly which was the most powerful current and which the most propitious moment for changing his course."[40] The consummate pragmatist, Batista negotiated with any party willing to take part in a power-sharing arrangement, with the caveat that they accept his leadership of the military.[41] He was not so much dedicated to ousting Grau, although their relationship was not the best, as he was to solving the political crisis. In the revolution's aftermath, Batista touted himself as the man who established order. As he viewed it, an accommodation with the United States was part of the political equation.

Guiteras was the most ruthless, idealistic, and violent of the three. Ill-suited to be a politician, Guiteras was incapable of compromise. Any deviation from his agenda was construed by him as antirevolutionary. Born in the United States, in Bala Cynwyd, Pennsylvania, of a Cuban father and American mother, his family returned to Cuba in 1912 when he was six. Although he spent part of his childhood in the United States, Guiteras had a deep and abiding distrust of the land of his birth. A devoted Cuban nationalist and socialist, Guiteras did everything in his power to undermine U.S. influence on the island. No movement or government could claim to be revolutionary if it did not challenge the United States. "We can serve Yanqui imperialism or serve the people, the interests of the two are not compatible," Guiteras said.[42] A pharmacist by profession, Guiteras graduated from the University of Havana in 1927. While at the university, he became a member of the Student Directory and maintained his ties with that organization. He was a member of the underground movement against Machado and was plotting against the Céspedes government when it fell. A man of great courage, Guiteras, was only twenty-seven at the time of his appointment to the cabinet. He was something of an ascetic in his personal habits and was frequently described as the "man with one suit."[43] Tall and thin with reddish brown hair and freckles, he walked with a slightly stooped back and shoulders. Unlike most Cuban politicians, Guiteras was uncomfortable with small talk and spoke very little.[44]

No opponent was too formidable for Guiteras. In his four months as interior minister, he openly challenged the United States by attacking the corporations that dominated Cuban economic life. He was the principal proponent of a series of labor laws, including those establishing an eight-hour work day, a minimum wage, and legislation requiring that Cubans receive preference in hiring. Guiteras challenged the Communists for control of labor and defended a violent crackdown on Party activities.[45] He challenged Batista's dominance of the military by developing a base of support in the navy and courting army leaders. The interior minister tried to unify the civilian-student militias into a "Revolutionary Guard," which could serve as a partial counterweight to the military. Whereas Grau was hesitant to use violence, Guiteras, although he had a boyish face, was eager to kill Batista. He was the author of an elaborate plan to arrest, try, and summarily execute the colonel, a plan that would soon unfold.[46] Guiteras was equally ruthless when it came to attacking enemies outside the revolution. While Batista vacillated about attacking the officers at the Hotel Nacional, Guiteras was a forceful proponent of an assault. He authorized an unsuccessful assassination attempt against prominent opposition leader Carlos Mendieta.[47] Guiteras pushed Grau to take a more confrontational stance with the U.S. Embassy and the political opposition. Some of the labor reforms were enacted despite concerns of the president. Guiteras walked around with his letter of resignation in his pocket and threatened to submit it, if he did not get his way.[48] In the end, he became disillusioned with Grau and was unwilling to fight to keep him in power.

REVOLUTIONARY LEGISLATION

The term "revolution" has been widely misused throughout Cuban history. Dictators and gangsters alike have identified themselves as "revolutionaries" and their self-serving governments and programs as "revolutionary." Rarely have the terms fit.[49] One of those rare true revolutionary moments in Cuban history occurred in the days between September 1933 and January 1934.

The student/soldier government that came to power on September 4 had few ties with the old, established political parties. They repudiated the old politics (*politiquería*) of the Conservative and Liberal Parties. The students were idealists with a nationalist agenda, not politicians. They were unskilled in the ways of compromise, which proved to be both a weakness and a strength. Their emergence at the head of the government came as a result of a fortuitous, almost accidental, alliance with the enlisted men. When they came to power, they had no allegiance to the old political system and owed no favors to those who would dilute their program for change. The students rejected the established *políticos* and their fawning obeisance to the United States.

The soldiers wanted a new command structure, with them at the top, but they also wanted to reform the military and end some of the demeaning practices of the past. Shortly after the new government was installed, Batista moved to modify army regulations to make them more "equitable without distinction of ranks." The practice of using enlisted men as valets and servants in officers' homes was discontinued. Distinctions in the uniforms of officers and soldiers, with the exception of insignias and leggings, were done away with. Clothing allowances were again to be paid to the soldiers. Like the officers, soldiers were to be allowed to buy food and furnishings from the commissaries at cost. Perhaps remembering the incident involving the death of his father, Batista moved to expedite and simplify the furlough process. A review of the military penal code was undertaken with an eye to reducing fines and punishments. The soldiers, drawn primarily from the poor, were sympathetic to economic and social reform. Many of them viewed the military as a vehicle for broad social change, a philosophy that prevailed throughout the rest of the decade. The student/soldier combination was a prescription for revolutionary change.[50]

In its four months in power, the revolutionary government enacted by decree a breathtaking series of laws that profoundly changed Cuban society. On the economic front, the government favored labor, particularly Cuban labor. Workers were granted an eight-hour workday and a minimum wage. A labor ministry was established, and, for the first time, workers were included on the National Labor Arbitration Board. Employers were held responsible for work-related accidents. The government targeted foreign companies by requiring that at least 50 percent of the work force consist of Cuban nationals or in the alternative that 50 percent of salaries go to Cuban workers. Low-paid migrant workers from Haiti and Jamaica, used primarily by the large sugar concerns, were deported in large numbers in an effort to increase Cuban wages and employment.[51] Businesses were forbidden from paying their employees with vouchers that could only be used at company stores. In an effort to battle malnutrition, a school breakfast program was unveiled. First-class postage rates were reduced. Electric rates were slashed by 45 percent in Havana and reduced by lesser amounts throughout the rest of the island. When the workers at the Cuban Electric Company (a subsidiary of a U.S. corporation) went out on strike, the government took over the company.

Events were no less dizzying in the foreign policy arena. The government refused to recognize the hated Platt Amendment, a codicil to the 1901 Constitution that allowed the United States to intervene in Cuban affairs when its fundamental interests were perceived to be in jeopardy. In December, the revolutionary government attacked U.S. intervention throughout the hemisphere at the Seventh Pan-American Conference in Montevideo. The delegation challenged the legitimacy of the Platt Amendment, claiming that it served as "a substitute for annexation" for the United States. In his opening address, Angel Alberto Giraudy, the head of the Cuban delegation, declared that the "Cuban people wish to be free, independent and sovereign, and they aspire and demand to be respected in their desire for free determination." Cuba also spearheaded a resolution opposing the "intervention" by one sovereign state in the affairs of another, which was unanimously passed, approved even by the United States with some reservation.[52] Despite the effort, Cuba remained diplomatically isolated, with only five nations recognizing the Grau government.[53]

In an another affront to U.S. interests, the Grau government left unclear its intention to pay back a public works loan made to the Machado government in its final months by Chase National Bank. It was widely believed that some of the money was used to fatten the wallets of Machado and his supporters rather than to build anything in Cuba. Payments on the $4.2 million remaining on the Chase loan were suspended by Grau, and while he did not flatly reject repayment, he certainly did not embrace a timetable. Wrangling over the Chase loan would go on for years between the United States and Cuba.

At times, the attacks on the United States and foreign capital left Welles indignant. On September 16, the ambassador asked Adolf Berle, a close adviser to Roosevelt, to speak to the student leaders "who have some slight grasp of economics" about Cuba's financial plight. "American companies, public utilities, importers and sugar mills, cannot and will not do business under present conditions," Welles wrote to Washington.[54] On the style of the revolutionary government and its propensity for decrees, Welles wrote on October 4 to Raymond Leslie Buell, director of the Foreign Policy Association: "[Grau] appears to feel that government consists in the promulgation of decrees, however ill thought out and impossible of fulfillment those decrees may be, and his mind seems to be suffering from the effects of an ill digested diet of such literature as Marx's 'Das Kapital' which he is given to quoting with great frequency."[55]

In another letter to Buell, Welles compared the Grau government to a "lunatic asylum." "The departments are filled with so-called committees of young men and boys removing old employees and appointing new ones, frequently effecting this change at the point of a revolver, with the very natural result that the administration of the executive branch of the Government has completely broken down." The American Chamber of Commerce of Cuba was equally unhappy with the revolutionary government. "Antagonistic to capital and business in general, [the government's] very existence has completely destroyed [the] confidence of the commercial, industrial and agricultural interests of the nation and produced almost complete paralyzation of these activities."[56]

It was precisely this attack on capital, foreign capital, and specifically U.S. capital that made the government revolutionary. It was the first time that a Cuban government fundamentally challenged U.S. economic and political domination of the island. By the time the government was finally overthrown by Batista and his allies, the revolution had altered the nature of the relationship between the two countries. It made the conflict between Cuban and U.S. economic interests a core domestic issue. In the aftermath of the revolution, the United States agreed to abrogate the Platt Amendment. The Cuban governments that followed the revolution did not rescind the far-reaching labor and social legislation. In fact, political debate for the next twenty years would focus on how to further the aims of the "revolution." The revolutionary government was derailed, but its ethos would serve as an example for the next generation of Cubans.

Nonetheless, the Revolution of 1933 was a missed opportunity. The well of

reforms was by no means dry when as a result of U.S. diplomatic intervention another Cuban popular movement was subverted. Among the measures
under consideration were a series of land reform plans aimed at distributing tracts to small cane growers and tenants.[57] A school of Cuban scholars
that compared U.S. intervention in the Revolution of 1933 with interference
in Cuba's War for Independence thirty-five years earlier soon emerged. These
nationalistic writings would fan the flames of anti-Americanism and bolster
the commitment of leaders a generation later to create a real revolution.[58]
The failure of 1933 remains a poignant symbol of the failure of a generation
of leaders who rose to power in the anti-Machado struggle. Even more than
did the overthrow of the Grau government in January 1934, the promise of
the Revolution of 1933 was squandered in the ensuing decades by the persistent corruption, violence, and decadence of the generation of political
leaders that led it.

Confrontation with the Communists

A lot of angry rhetoric was exchanged in the first weeks of the Grau government, but relatively little gunfire. That was about to change. On September
29, the government was faced with the first in a series of violent confrontations that would claim hundreds of lives in the coming months. The first
major clash occurred between the military and the Communists in the streets
of Havana. Initially, the Communists were granted permission to march
with the ashes of the martyred student leader Julio Antonio Mella to the Par-
que de la Fraternidad (Fraternity Park), adjacent to the Capitol, where they
were to be interred in a temporary monument. But as time for the march
drew near, Interior Minister Guiteras, perhaps fearing the Communists were
trying to create chaos and provoke U.S. intervention, rescinded approval.[59]
Soldiers were dispatched to the park and along the parade route, accompanied by members of several progovernment paramilitary groups. Undeterred,
the marchers proceeded with their plans and gathered on Reina Street. The
shooting began sometime around 1:30 p.m. as the march was about to begin.
As is often the case, the details about who fired first and when are clouded
in mystery and rhetoric. At some point, a hail of bullets was fired into the
crowd and most fled in panic, but some of the marchers returned fire and
there were several soldiers among the wounded. At least six people were
killed and twenty-seven injured, although some estimates range as high as
thirty dead and more than one hundred wounded.[60] Soldiers tried to capture Mella's ashes, but organizers of the march successfully whisked them
away, and they were kept in hiding for several decades.[61]

Even after the march was dispersed, the violence continued. The soldiers destroyed the monument to Mella and then proceeded to destroy the offices of the Anti-Imperialist League, an organization closely linked to the Communist Party, and to sack the offices of the Cuban National Confederation of Labor (Confederación Nacional Obrera de Cuba), a union organization controlled by the Communists. The bloody march was part of a widespread crackdown on the Communists that began prior to it and continued over the next several weeks and months, particularly in the countryside, as soldiers were sent into sugar plantations to break up strikes. Labor protests and strikes occurred at thirty-six sugar mills, and in six instances, at the minimum, the workers took control of the facilities and established "soviets." In at least one case in Oriente Province, the workers proceeded to trade sugar for shoes, clothing, and food; to distribute land to small farmers; to open schools; and to establish a free medical clinic. Left out of the government coalition from the start, the Communists and their sympathizers unleashed a barrage of labor actions across the island as they proclaimed Grau's government a "servant of the native exploiters and the Yankees."

Batista has traditionally borne the brunt of responsibility for the violence of September 29. Lionel Soto writes that Batista was "in agreement with Welles [on the need] to initiate a period of anti-worker and anti-communist terror on the road to toppling the Grau government and restoring the pre-existent oligarchical order." In his work on the Revolution of 1933, he goes on to charge Batista and the military with planning a "massacre" to send a clear message to the United States that Communism would not be tolerated.[62] Journalist Ruby Hart Phillips wrote on the day of the aborted march that it was Batista who decided to stop it. "Batista, in my opinion, is too ambitious to have radical leanings." Before the shooting, Phillips's husband, a *New York Times* reporter, spoke to a soldier heading to the march who told him it was "time a few of the communists were killed to put them in their places."[63]

Batista bears a large part of the responsibility for the bloody outcome of the march, but by no means does he stand alone in that regard. The crackdown at the rally was largely motivated by a desire on the part of the Grau government to challenge the United States's contention that the revolution was moving to the far left. There was a sense among some members of the government, including Guiteras, that the revolutionary government was the best option available to the working classes and that to seek a more radical solution would ultimately undermine labor reforms, create a climate for U.S intervention, and usher back into power the old *políticos*. "It is impossible for the masses to gain political control; thus instead of opposing this revolutionary government they should cooperate with it to obtain the satisfaction of the most immediate demands of the workers," Guiteras said in an interview two weeks prior to the march.[64] Guiteras was vying for control of labor, and the Communists were an impediment.

Batista opposed the march for his own reasons. By the middle of September, he was aggressively courting U.S. recognition. A government-authorized march by the Communists through the center of Havana was the last thing Batista wanted at a time when he was trying to convince the United States that the far left was not in control of the government. Welles was deeply concerned about Communist influence, noting on September 16 that "the communist wave is spreading with the utmost rapidity and facility throughout the country." At the same time, Batista was trying to create the perception of "order" throughout the island, a key prerequisite for recognition. He could not have been pleased with the bloody outcome of September 29, which was anything but orderly. Throughout the Communist crackdown, as he walked a tightrope between "order" and "violence," Batista urged his military commanders to break up Communist labor strikes "without bloodshed, if possible."[65]

In the aftermath, the Communists leveled blame on the entire government, particularly Grau and Guiteras. "With the unleashing of this bloody wave of terror, the government of Grau San Martín has removed its mask and displayed its horrible, cruel face more ferocious than the Ass with Claws [a nickname for Machado]," a Communist Party manifesto proclaimed several days after the shootings. They did not perceive Batista as the mastermind of the attack. Nor did Grau, or Guiteras, or anyone else in the government condemn Batista and the military for their actions; instead they defended them. For his part, Ambassador Welles, completely disillusioned with Grau and Guiteras, credited Batista for taking strong action against the Communists. "In the last analysis, I think the situation can only be saved, should Batista be willing to save it. His decided reaction against Communism and his apparent determination to maintain order will gain him the support of the commercial and financial interests here, and he will likewise have the support of the majority of the powerful political groups, provided he will agree to replace the present government with a government in which there can be some feeling of confidence." Welles's relationship with Grau was souring, and he had no relationship with Guiteras. The ambassador was predisposed to view any action favorable to the United States as emanating from Batista.[66]

Welles began to see Batista as the solution.

BATTLE OF THE HOTEL NACIONAL

The blood was barely dry from the aborted march when the government was faced with an even more fundamental challenge. The officers, barricaded at the Hotel Nacional since September 8, were still refusing to accept the government. The officers were armed and in open defiance, and they constituted a hostile camp in the center of Havana. They were overtly plotting with the ABC against the government and courting U.S. intervention by proposing to reestablish the Céspedes government inside the hotel, an offer rejected by the ousted president, because he wished to avoid bloodshed.[67]

The Hotel Nacional was an unlikely location for a siege. In 1933, it was the most modern and luxurious facility in the Caribbean. The most distinctive features were the two bell towers that sat atop the eight-story building. The bar and swimming pool on the northern portion of the property overlooked the Havana sea wall and the monument to the USS *Maine*. The entrance to Havana harbor was visible from the top floors of the hotel. The main entrance to the property was on the southern side, near the tennis courts. A number of commercial and residential buildings faced the hotel entrance, and several streetcar lines ran on both sides of the property.

Inside the hotel, Sanguily, feeling well enough by mid-September to assume command, turned it into a military outpost. Everything from cooking and cleaning to operating the elevators was assigned to the four hundred or so officers, a measure that became necessary when fearful workers refused to return to their jobs. For obvious reasons, tourists and business clients abandoned the hotel as well, leaving the officers as the only occupants. Sanguily, joined by Ferrer, the ousted war minister, and the military high command, plotted feverishly throughout September to find a way to defeat the soldiers who had stripped them of their commands. Ferrer unsuccessfully sought the support of Ambassador Welles for the actions taken by the officers. The officers then turned to the ABC as a potential ally. One plan called for a joint attack on the guardposts ringing the hotel. The idea was for the ABC civilian fighters to create a diversion while the officers stormed the guardposts, captured the weapons, and then marched on the Presidential Palace and took Grau prisoner. A second plan called for the ABC to smuggle two hundred rifles in to the officers, so they could lead an assault on the guardposts. Nothing ever came of either plan. The officers also sought to gain support from their former subordinates on the outside, an effort that failed miserably. In the end, the officers were friendless. Neither the ABC nor anyone else was willing to endorse and fight for their restorationist agenda.[68]

While the officers plotted in vain against the government, they were wise enough to develop a comprehensive defense plan. Even though they only had twenty-six rifles, four or five Thompson submachine guns, and a large number of shotguns, revolvers, and pistols with which to fight off the entire army, the officers crafted an inventive strategy. They placed their best marksmen on the balconies surrounding the hotel and each was given a rifle and about fifty rounds of ammunition. Their task was to pick off their enemies at a distance and take out the machine-gun emplacements around the hotel. In the terraces in front of the main entrance men were posted with shotguns and hunting rifles to pick off attackers at short range. In the lobby, four men were waiting with Thompson submachine guns in the event that the attackers broke through the first line of defense. Officers with pistols and revolvers were placed at each of the stairwells to prevent passage to the upper floors, while at the same time the elevators were to be disabled at the top floor of the hotel. There were several doctors among the officers, and they established a makeshift hospital on the sixth floor.

The officers were still hoping to gain popular support when the attack came unexpectedly in the early morning hours of October 2. Shortly after 5 a.m., several of the men inside the hotel noticed a massing of troops in and around the grounds, and a general alarm went throughout the building. Several minutes later, an armored vehicle was spotted from several blocks away driving toward the front entrance of the hotel. The vehicle entered the property, and quickly thereafter machine-gun fire opened up on the hotel from all directions. Soldiers poured from the vehicle, but they were quickly cut down by the marksmen posted on the balconies. The vehicle was forced to retreat. One by one, the marksmen picked off the soldiers manning the machine-gun nests around the hotel. Batista witnessed the beginning of the fighting from a vacant lot east of the hotel where thirty machine gunners were stationed. Within a few minutes about half of the gunners were dead, and Batista was forced to abandon the area as bullets struck his car.[69]

The opening salvo was a disaster for Batista and his men. The soldiers were forced to retreat out of range of the deadly rifle fire. Inside the hotel, the officers were buoyed by this promising beginning. "The sergeants had given them the opportunity to wash off with blood the offense they had received," Ferrer wrote in his memoirs. But the battle was about to enter a new phase. Shortly after the failed assault, at around 8:30 a.m., the soldiers unleashed a barrage of artillery fire against the hotel. One seventy-five-millimeter cannon fired point blank at the hotel from an adjacent street, while another cannon fired from the roof of the physics building at the nearby University of Havana. For good measure, the Cuban battle cruiser *Patria* lobbed shells at the hotel from the waterfront, although rough currents and inexperience on deck nullified the ship's effectiveness. Shells ripped through the walls of the hotel sending mortar and furnishings flying in all directions and making the air difficult to breathe. One shell burst a water pipe, and water began to pour into an adjacent elevator shaft hindering movement around the hotel. The hospital had to be moved from the sixth floor after a shell landed in a nearby hallway. Some of the shells obliterated the overhanging balconies attached to some of the rooms. Shrapnel from the shells wounded several of the officers. At the same time, the soldiers opened up with machine-gun fire from the surrounding buildings. A tank in the street also fired on the hotel.[70]

At approximately 12:30 p.m., the firing ceased, and several representatives of the Cuban Red Cross were seen walking with a white flag toward the front entrance of the hotel. The officers allowed them inside, and Víctor de Mendoza, the treasurer of the Red Cross, handed Sanguily and Ferrer a note from Batista setting forth surrender terms. The note specified that there would be a truce of one hour and that the officers' lives would be "respected" if they agreed to surrender. As part of the terms, the officers were to file out of the hotel, unarmed, in groups of five at ten-minute intervals. The officers asked for an extension of the truce until 3 p.m., which was granted, so that they could poll their men. During the truce, several women (wives of the officers) were allowed to leave the hotel, and the wounded on both sides were evacuated from the scene. The soldiers used the time to reposition the artillery, so that they could strike more effectively at the hotel.[71]

The officers received several bits of bad news during the truce. They operated a makeshift radio room inside the hotel by which they communicated with the ABC. At 1 p.m., they received a radio message from the secret society saying no help would be forthcoming. In addition, a review of the ammunition stores revealed that in the event of another assault they could hold out for only another fifteen minutes. The officers had miscalculated at every turn since September 4, and that pattern would continue even under these hopeless circumstances. Instead of accepting the terms of surrender, Ferrer went about drafting a counteroffer to Batista, in which the officers would be allowed to go free after their surrender with their sidearms. The polling of the officers took longer than expected, because many of the elevators were disabled. The vote was not complete when the soldiers promptly began firing at the hotel at 3 p.m. One of the officers, perhaps not aware the truce was over, looked out a window of the hotel and was shot dead. Another officer was killed by shrapnel from an exploding shell.[72]

The second barrage of artillery fire was by all accounts ferocious and broke the spirit of the officers. As shells landed from all sides, many of the officers abandoned the stairwells and hallways and sought safety in the basement. By 4 p.m., the officers manning defensive positions signaled their unwillingness to continue the fight. A white sheet was hung from the top floor of the hotel to indicate their surrender. After several minutes, a contingent of soldiers and civilians, led by Lieutenant Belisario Hernández, recently promoted from the rank of sergeant, made their way to the lobby entrance. Waiting for him in the lobby were Sanguily and Ferrer, who officially surrendered to Hernández.

The atmosphere was volatile and tense. The soldiers and paramilitary men surrounding the hotel suffered heavy losses, perhaps as many as one hundred dead and two hundred wounded. The officers lost only two men during the battle and suffered twelve casualties.[73] The civilians and some of the enlisted men began to cry out for vengeance. "Kill them. Kill them, right here," several shouted as Sanguily and Ferrer were escorted out. The process of transporting the officers from the hotel to prison took several hours because many trucks were required. In the interim, the officers were lined up in groups of two on the grounds of the hotel and were subjected to a tirade of insults by the soldiers and civilian fighters. There were only several dozen officers left on the hotel property when shooting erupted again. An eyewitness to the incident recalled a group of heavily armed civilians appearing near the tennis courts. The civilians opened fire on the unarmed officers with their revolvers and pistols. The soldiers assigned to safeguard the officers were none to quick to respond to the attack, and by the time they dispersed the crowd, eleven officers were dead and twenty-two wounded. The massacre was a serious blow to the officers, and they would never organize again as a cohesive fighting unit.[74]

As a military campaign, the battle of the Hotel Nacional was a near total fiasco for Batista and the army. Guiteras bears some responsibility for the outcome, because it was he who pushed for the attack and stayed by Batista's side most of the day coordinating it.[75] The initial assault was carried out before the artillery had an opportunity to soften up the officers' defensive positions. It is quite likely that a sustained and concentrated artillery barrage on the hotel would have broken the defenders' resistance with few, if any, casualties among the enlisted men. The machine-gun emplacements were poorly camouflaged and exposed to rifle fire from the hotel. More than anything else, poor planning and strategy contributed to excessive casualties. The army was embarrassed by the casualties inflicted by the officers and declined to give an official figure. As the death toll mounted, passions ran high among the soldiers and allied civilians and vengeance became the order of the day. One officer, who witnessed the slaughter of his unarmed colleagues, said Batista came onto the hotel property moments before the massacre and ordered the guards to "move away" from the prisoners, implying that he knew an attack by paramilitary groups was imminent. There is insufficient evidence to corroborate the story, but clearly, Batista, who directed the attack from a nearby underground garage, could have done more to safeguard the prisoners. He knew passions were running high and that some of the enlisted men "were understandably angry and upset" after seeing "their comrades shot like pigeons."[76]

In the aftermath of the attack, the government took great pains to divert attention from the massacre of the unarmed officers and to portray them as the aggressors. Batista maintained the officers attacked first on the morning of October 2, an unlikely story given the fact that several of their wives were inside the building at the time. The unexpected attack by the officers, rather than poor planning by the government, exposed civilians in nearby buildings to danger, since there was no time to evacuate them. At least one local resident, an American, was killed as he watched the battle from his balcony with binoculars. In the government's version of events, the officers ended the midday truce by firing on the enlisted men, another questionable tale given the fact the officers were low on ammunition. As for the massacre of the unarmed men, President Grau declared that was the result of several officers in the upper floors of the hotel opening fire on the soldiers and civilians below. "The besieging soldiers, seeing themselves attacked, answered in legitimate self-defense. That is why it has been said, mistakenly, that some officers were killed after they surrendered."[77] Journalist and Batista biographer Edmund Chester, in a version of events sympathetic to the government, wrote that he saw a civilian killed by an officer after the surrender. "There was a great deal of confusion at that time and I doubt that anyone could say exactly what happened. I am sure, however, that several enlisted men and one or two officers were killed by the fire from both sides after the officers had violated the white flag of surrender."[78]

Another explanation for the massacre was offered by U.S. military intelligence, which believed the guards fired into the air to keep back angry crowds. Some of the officers on the upper floors, believing the attack had resumed, fired at the soldiers, killing several of them. The guards and civilians then took vengeance on the unarmed officers. There is some evidence to suggest that the paramilitary groups wreaked the greatest havoc, and at least one wounded officer said he was saved by a soldier who carried him to safety. One journalist reported that the guards fired into the crowd to keep them from killing more officers.[79]

While it was a dubious military victory at best for Batista, politically it was a resounding success. The elimination of the old officer corps consolidated Batista's power within the military. A new officer corps, mostly loyal to him, was now in place. Furthermore, during the daylong battle not even one squadron came to the defense of their former superiors. The colonel from Banes was now the most powerful man in the country. He no longer needed the Student Directory to justify the army's takeover. They now needed him if they wished to retain their tenuous hold on power.

The Colonel and the Ambassador

With the victory at the Hotel Nacional, Batista's standing rose enormously in the eyes of Ambassador Welles, who saw in the colonel the means of disposing of the revolutionary government. The third meeting between Batista and Welles, just two days after the siege at the Hotel Nacional (October 4), marked a dramatic change in their relationship. For the first time, the ambassador put forth the scenario by which Batista could remove Grau and the students from power. After a discussion of the hotel attack, Welles began the process of massaging Batista's ego. The ambassador told Batista that "he himself was the only individual in Cuba who today represented authority." The commercial and financial interests supported the colonel because they are "looking for protections and can only find such protection in himself." Most of the political factions were in favor of his remaining as army chief of staff, Welles noted. The ambassador went on to observe that "the events of the National Hotel had diminished very materially that very small amount of popular support which the Grau San Martín regime may previously have possessed." And, in a clear warning to Batista, Welles said that "should the present government go down in disaster that disaster would necessarily inextricably involve not only himself but the safety of the Republic."

As if the underlying point of the conversation were not clear enough, Batista went right to the heart of the matter. Batista "expressed the belief that should any rapid change in the government be made it might be difficult to control his troops without further bloodshed which he desired at all hazards to avoid." After further discussion of the political situation, Batista requested regular meetings with Welles to "talk over conditions." The ambassador knew he had crossed the frontier in his dealings with Batista, so much so that he felt it essential to explain the relationship in the last paragraph of his dispatch. "The situation as regards my relations with Batista is, of course, anomalous. I feel it necessary to make plain, however, that there does not exist at the present time in Cuba any authority whatever except himself and that in the event of further disturbances which may endanger the lives and properties of Americans or foreigners in the Republic it seems to be essential that this relationship be maintained."[80]

Their bargaining positions had changed significantly from their most recent meeting, held on September 21, during which Batista expressed a desire to maintain the support of the Student Directory. At that earlier meeting, a proposal was made for the revolutionary government to present a list of "five non-political Cubans" to the political opposition for consideration as president. The political opposition was to select one of the five to replace Grau. The replacement was then "to appoint a neutral cabinet composed of individuals acceptable to all concerned." After the meeting Welles wrote: "[Batista] expressed the belief that [a] solution was imperative but that some solution must be found which would not result in open hostility on the part of the students and at the same time not result in open hostility on the part of the important groups and factions opposed to the present regime." Furthermore, Batista left the meeting with Welles promising to present the compromise to the students for consideration. There was no talk of imposing a solution on the students.[81]

All of that was before the siege at the Hotel Nacional. The power of Batista and the military to impose a solution on the civilians emerged ever so clearly after the defeat of the officers, aided further by the disunity among the political factions both inside and outside the revolutionary government. Welles simply pointed out the obvious to Batista in their meeting of October 4. Years later, Batista acknowledged that the meeting was an "important event" in his life. As Batista biographer Edmund Chester puts it, "It confirmed him, once and for all, as a man of international importance, the man who, in the opinion of the United States at least, controlled the destiny of Cuba." It also confirmed Batista's assessment that the revolutionary government must secure a wider base of internal support and U.S. recognition to survive. The two men struck an alliance of convenience. Batista wanted U.S. recognition, a stable government, and guarantees that the next president would keep him on as head of the army. Welles wanted to restore his reputation as a diplomat, which had been tarnished by the failure of the Céspedes government.[82]

Batista and Welles were in agreement that each would need to use the other to accomplish his goals; beyond that they could agree on little else. Welles clearly wanted the ouster of Grau, while Batista would accept any of a wide variety of presidential candidates, including Carlos Mendieta, the leader of the Nacionalistas; Miguel Mariano Gómez, the former mayor of Havana; or even Grau, as long as they accepted him as chief of the military. Batista's negotiating position was somewhat precarious, because in theory any new president had the right to appoint a new military chief. At times, Batista suspected that the political opposition was "using him and as soon as possible thereafter would get rid of him." So prior to installing a new president, the colonel wanted guarantees up front that he was to be retained. At one point in the negotiations with Mendieta, he demanded the appointment of Carbó as interior and war minister, a demand he later rescinded.[83]

The colonel and the ambassador were not particularly fond of each other, not surprising given their very different socioeconomic backgrounds and personal styles. Batista described Welles as *pesado* (a bore) and a man more concerned with diplomatic formalities than personal relations. Echoing Batista's observations, one Cuban journalist wrote that the ambassador "listened to everyone with a condescending smile." As was his nature, Welles was considerably more circumspect regarding his feelings toward Batista. Welles never criticized Batista publicly, but one writer noted that the ambassador did not "disguise his disdain whenever [Batista] was mentioned."[84]

The two men had to appease very different constituencies in order to maintain their respective positions. Welles needed to preserve his position as architect of the State Department's Cuba policy and more specifically its position of nonrecognition, which was constantly challenged by his superior, Secretary of State Hull. Batista needed to placate and satisfy his fellow sergeants, now commanding officers, before he made any move to change governments. A failure by Batista to secure consensus from his fellow commanders could lead to a military coup against him. After all, it was he who paved the way for such a scenario with his amazing rise to power. It is likely that many in the military thought of themselves as the "next Batista." Welles and Batista were also playing for radically different stakes. Welles was playing for his pride, while Batista was playing for his life. A mistake by Welles could lead to a bruised ego. A miscalculation by Batista could, and nearly did, lead to a firing squad. The difference in their relative stakes helps explain why Welles was adamant about ousting Grau, while Batista was more flexible about finding a political solution.

After the defeat of the officers at the Hotel Nacional, Secretary of State Hull, with whom Welles had a long and turbulent relationship, argued in favor of recognizing the Cuban government.[85] Welles countered that the defeat of the officers was a victory for Batista and the military, not the Grau government. Doubts about the Welles nonrecognition policy surfaced repeatedly in the North American and Cuban media. On October 17, Raymond Leslie Buell, research director of the Foreign Policy Association, questioned Welles privately about the policy. "Even if President Grau is a figurehead, the government under the immediate direction of Batista seems to be holding its own and I assume, in the absence of reports to the contrary, that it is in administrative control of the island." A bit later, Buell followed up with the following question: "Has the United States a right to demand the reorganization of the government as the price to recognition?" Welles responded on October 24 that the Grau government was not in administrative control of the island and that indeed much of the government was in "utter chaos." As for reorganizing the government, Welles wrote that "I feel we owe it to the Cuban people not to hamper their efforts to achieve a government in which they can have confidence, and from which they can obtain guaranties, both political and individual, by according recognition to a government which, as I pointed out to you in detail in a previous letter, is supported by a scant minority, and which, from every indication at the present moment, shows signs of becoming a low-grade military dictatorship."[86]

In November, the Cuban government stepped up its attacks on the ambassador. "The U.S. Embassy to Cuba must close or the United States must recognize the Grau Government," a Cuban government official told reporters. The official attributed the nonrecognition policy to Welles's "pride." Rumors of impending recognition by the United States were constantly in circulation, and Welles found it necessary to request a meeting with President Roosevelt to bolster his position. Roosevelt met with Welles on November 19 at Warm Springs, Georgia. The result of the meeting was the so-called Warm Springs Declaration, released on November 23, which amounted to a resounding victory for the Welles's policy of nonrecognition. Written by Welles, it repeated the now familiar theme. It read in part: "We have not believed that it would be a policy of friendship and of justice to the Cuban people as a whole to accord recognition to any provisional government in Cuba unless such government clearly possessed the support and the approval of the people of that Republic." President Roosevelt sided with Welles, his close personal friend, a page boy at his wedding, over Hull. The secretary of state would again privately challenge the policy at the Pan-American Conference in Uruguay, where he was pressed by some countries in Latin America to defend the nonrecognition policy. Reports appeared in several Uruguayan newspapers that Hull favored recognition, reports he denied. Welles won the internal State Department struggle over the question of recognition; however, he still needed the cooperation of his Cuban allies, principally Batista, to bring about the downfall of the government.[87]

Throughout October, Batista attended a series of meetings with the political opposition, most important those with Carlos Mendieta in an effort to convince him to assume the presidency. But, Mendieta proved to be an indecisive negotiating partner. A veteran of Cuban politics, Mendieta wanted to secure the support, or at least the acceptance, of the Student Directory before accepting the position. In addition, Mendieta was wary of Batista and rightly wondered whether the colonel might not engage in plots against him if it served his interests and whether he would in essence be nothing more than a prisoner of the man from Banes. As a result, Mendieta repeatedly changed his mind in the coming months about the wisdom of accepting the presidency. At the end of October and early November, Mendieta was on the verge of accepting Batista's invitation to power on several occasions, but each time he pulled back at the last minute.[88] Information about the Mendieta-Batista meetings began to circulate among the students and as early as October 5; the Student Directory began to consider an armed attack against Batista. In an effort to counter Batista's growing power, they sought an alliance with the ABC revolutionary movement, an overture that was ultimately rejected by the latter.[89]

These intrigues continued as Batista tried to further consolidate his position within the military. Formidable challenges remained. His rival, Pablo Rodríguez, was chief of Camp Columbia, the single most powerful military base in the country. At one point, several commanders began their own negotiations with Mendieta. There were rumblings of discontent among the sergeants who had not been promoted, and U.S. military intelligence speculated that some were "nursing a grudge." Troops in the provinces were often slow to respond to Batista's orders, and it occasionally became necessary to send a trusted ally to ensure that orders were obeyed. In one instance, the soldiers of a garrison in Guantanamo in eastern Oriente Province refused to accept Batista's choice of commander and sent him back to Havana. In an effort to establish discipline in Oriente, Batista appointed one of his closest advisers and a fellow conspirator, José Pedraza, as provincial commander. Pedraza's position as second in command was cemented in the same month with his promotion to lieutenant colonel and inspector general of the army.[90] Yet there was still danger for Batista within the military.

A Plot to Kill

The indecisiveness of Mendieta left Batista in a quandary. He was negotiating the removal of the president, yet he was unable to gain the acceptance of a successor. The negotiations went on for several weeks and everyone—friend and foe—was aware of them. It left him vulnerable to attack. The students were enraged by Batista's plan to oust Grau and replace him with Mendieta, thus ending their participation in the government. Several of the student leaders, joined by Interior Minister Guiteras, laid an ingenious trap to rid themselves of the colonel. Their efforts centered on a meeting scheduled for the evening of November 3 at the home of Batista's ally, Sergio Carbó.

Several days earlier, Batista called for a meeting of the revolutionary junta, the same group that established the revolutionary government two months earlier, to discuss the future of the Grau presidency. The goal of the session was to secure approval for a transfer of power to Mendieta; however, that became a moot point when Mendieta declined to accept the highest office. The junta agreed to meet again on November 3 ostensibly to discuss the future of the revolution.[91] The students, aware that Batista was plotting against them, met with Grau in the Presidential Palace on the morning of November 3 to map a strategy to confront Batista. The first plan was for Grau to resign and precipitate a crisis with the hope of catching Batista off-balance and gaining the advantage. However, later in the day, several students met with Guiteras and came up with an alternative plan, which entailed taking Batista prisoner at the meeting, trying him as a traitor, and executing him by early the next day. The students secured Grau's approval for the revised plan sometime in the early afternoon and proceeded to draft an arrest warrant, prepare for a summary court martial, and write an order of execution. They even sent delegates to the local newspapers to alert them to delay publication, so they would not miss the breaking news. As part of the trap, Guiteras went to visit several district commanders to secure their support, principally Pablo Rodríguez, who was to be named the new chief of the army. Guiteras posted armed men near Carbó's home and was prepared for a gun battle.[92] "Juridically speaking, at eight-thirty on the evening of the third of November, Mr. Batista was in the next world," one student leader recalled.[93]

As it turns out, Batista was made aware of a plot to "assassinate" him at the meeting by several sources, including an informant inside the palace. In an effort to safeguard his life, Batista, unbeknownst to the students, posted several soldiers outside Carbó's home and received assurances from a civilian member of the junta that he too would post armed men in the vicinity.[94] Student leader Juan Rubio Padilla remembers opening the door for Batista that night and as he closed it thinking the colonel had just entered "a rat trap." Batista's bodyguard was not allowed to enter the house, which was packed with government officials, military men, and students. Batista sensed danger from the moment he entered the house, he later told biographer Edmund Chester. A number of his enemies were present inside, and they were carrying submachine guns. When Batista entered, he moved toward a drawing room where Grau was speaking to several military commanders. Grau saw him approach and ordered him to wait outside until he called for him. The temporary banishment from a military meeting must have been humbling for him, but more humiliations were in store.[95]

After the military conference was concluded, Grau convened a meeting of the revolutionary junta, and Batista was allowed to take a seat adjacent to the president. Almost immediately, Grau accused Batista of being a traitor, of conspiring with Ambassador Welles, and warned him that he could be replaced. The president said he considered resigning as a result of the treachery.

Several members of the junta urged Grau to stay on and guide the revolution. Regarding the matter of replacing Batista, several members of the junta argued that the colonel was the "original source of the revolution and its soul." After some debate, Grau permitted Batista to speak. The colonel argued that under normal circumstances the president could replace the chief of the army but that these were not normal circumstances. Nevertheless, in an effort to find a way out of the difficult position in which he found himself, Batista apologized to Grau and promised to avoid compromising the president's position in the future. Juan Rubio Padilla remembered that Batista "let loose one of the most abject, most miserable, and most cowardly speeches that I have ever heard in my life. He exceeded himself in praising Grau." Batista recollected his address quite differently, describing it as "words of courtesy and respect for Dr. Grau." The apology, however it was worded, was intended to defuse the situation. Batista believed the students were waiting for him to react violently to Grau's suggestions, so that they could justify killing him.[96]

Shortly after Batista's remarks, Grau stunned the students by adjourning the meeting and allowing the colonel to leave with his position and his life. For the next few days, the students urged Grau to reverse his decision and arrest Batista. Grau told the students that as a result of the "scare we have given him, Batista will turn out to be the best choice." After repeated challenges over a period of days, Grau finally pulled rank: "The Directorio forgets that I am the President of the Republic and I give the orders here and Batista will continue as Chief of the Army." Despite Grau's decision, several students hatched a plan to go to Batista's home at Camp Columbia and abduct and execute him. The students never acted on the plan.[97]

A complex set of factors influenced Grau's decision to spare Batista. To begin with, the apprehension of Batista would likely have involved immediate bloodshed not only at the site of his arrest but throughout the island as his partisans became aware of his captivity and execution. Followers of Batista and Guiteras were poised for battle outside Carbó's home, and the colonel would not have gone quietly to his death. In addition, there was no assurance that Pablo Rodríguez, or anyone else for that matter, could placate the different factions within the military better than Batista. Assuming the government survived Batista's execution, there was no guarantee that the "new" Batista would not, in time, act against the government as well. Furthermore, Grau was fearful that with Batista out of the picture, Guiteras's power within the government and the military would grow enormously and perhaps endanger his own position. The move by Grau was designed to gain support from other sectors, including Batista and the military, because his main base of support, the Student Directory, was on the verge of collapse and in fact disbanded several days after the confrontation with Batista. In analyzing Grau's decision to spare Batista, it is important to consider the fact that he was a medical doctor, sworn to uphold life not take it. Violence was not a part of his nature.[98]

There were numerous lessons for Batista in this near-fatal confrontation with the students. It revealed his enemies. The threat posed by fellow conspirator Pablo Rodríguez and Interior Minister Antonio Guiteras, who was building a base of support in the navy, was becoming quite clear. In time, Batista would need to defeat both men if he wished to retain his grip on power. After the events of November 3, Batista curtailed his direct negotiations with Welles and the political opposition and preferred to act through intermediaries. He concentrated his efforts on consolidating his position in the military.

The unhappy alliance between students and soldiers, and among Grau, Guiteras, and Batista would hobble on for the time being, buffeted by one crisis after another. They would have to wait only a few days for their next major test.

CHAPTER 7

AN END TO
REVOLUTION

Reports of a possible military uprising began to reach Batista in early October. Intelligence indicated that segments of the military, including some of the newly promoted officers, were disgruntled with Batista and the course events had taken since September 4. Some felt the enlisted men had made a mistake in pushing out their former commanders (even though none had gone to the defense of the officers at the Hotel Nacional), while others felt continuing support of the Grau government was undermining military stability. And of course, there were always those passed over for promotion. On the civilian side, there was an element of the ABC revolutionary society, led by Carlos Saladrigas,[1] eager to strike against the government, although principal ABC leader Joaquín Martínez Sáenz was in exile and opposed to an attack.[2]

Unlike the previous high command that failed to heed reports of military conspiracies, Batista took the news very seriously. He fostered the development of an intelligence network in the military and paid careful attention to the information provided at all levels. Regular reports of suspicious movements and meetings among the officers and enlisted men made organizing a coup against Batista and Grau a formidable task. The conspirators later acknowledged that they frequently rescheduled meetings because they knew they were being monitored. Batista's intelligence network hampered efforts by the conspirators to disseminate vital information about the planned uprising.[3]

Besides his own spy network, Batista could rely on regular newspaper reports and frequent rumors to keep him informed about the status of his enemies. Weeks in advance of the uprising, key details leaked to the public and press. Ruby Hart Phillips wrote in her diary on October 19: "We are going to have a new revolution. While our information is not definite as yet it seems that the new revolt is to be headed by certain former officers of the Cuban army (those out of jail) and ABC members." Two weeks later, on November 1, she wrote even more specifically in her diary of the forthcoming uprising. "More information about the new revolution. There will be airplanes raining bombs, fighting in the streets, etc., etc."[4] The key question for Batista and Grau was: When?

The conspirators included officers and soldiers in the Aviation Corps, in the Presidential Guards, and at military installations throughout Havana, including the San Ambrosio barracks and arms supply depot and the Dragones military installation. There were conspirators within Camp Columbia itself. The conspirators included former Major Ciro Leonard, previously in charge of San Ambrosio and the supreme commander of the operation; Lieutenant José Barrientos of the Aviation Corps; Second Lieutenant Pedro Gener Núñez of the Presidential Guards; and perpetual revolutionary and self-designated Colonel Juan Blas Hernández, a guerrilla fighter against Machado, who only a few weeks earlier pledged his support to the Grau government. Some commanders, while refraining from an active role in the uprising, agreed to abstain from the fighting until it became clear which side would win. The information available indicates that a conspiracy against Batista and Grau had been in the works since the middle of September. Originally the uprising was to be a purely military affair, but the Saladrigas wing of the ABC learned of the plot and asked to be included. Some of the military men objected to participation by civilians, fearing that their lack of discipline and a scarcity of arms would hinder the operation. To overcome their doubts, Saladrigas promised to contribute a large cache of weapons from the ABC's stockpile and guaranteed that only armed supporters would be permitted to take part in the operation.[5]

The plan of attack was ingenious. The target day was November 8, a day when Batista was expected to be traveling outside Havana. It was to begin in the early morning hours with an aerial attack and bombardment of Camp Columbia, coupled with an uprising within the camp itself. With the government forces dazed and confused, the rebels were to seize military installations and police stations in and around Havana and march on Columbia. The imprisoned officers, defeated at the Hotel Nacional, were to be freed and assume command of the military forces. The conspirators hoped for a quick and decisive victory.

In the end, it was a spy, Corporal Ángel C. Fajardo, who gave away the conspiracy's timetable and eliminated any remaining element of surprise. After attending a meeting of plotters on the afternoon of November 7, Fajardo reported the details to Batista and his close adviser, Lieutenant Colonel Ignacio Galíndez. Batista ordered the immediate arrest of all those suspected of taking part in the planned uprising, particularly those at Camp Columbia. He ordered the placement of antiaircraft batteries around the base. Military discipline was already in disarray at some of the military installations in Havana, and Batista prepared for the inevitable uprising. To protect the identity of the spy, Fajardo was temporarily imprisoned with the other conspirators, but less than two weeks later, he was rewarded with a promotion to second lieutenant.

Fighting in the Streets

Batista knew that the air force was going to bomb Columbia, but he likely expected the attack to come around daybreak. The conspirators, realizing the plot was uncovered, decided to strike shortly after midnight. A strategy session between Batista and Guiteras, held at the colonel's home on the base, was just concluded when the bombs began to drop on Camp Columbia. One of the targets was Batista's home. Moments after Batista and several aides left the colonel's residence a bomb fell on the building adjacent to it, a school under construction, damaging a corner of the structure.[6]

The rebellion was in his midst. The attack planes were taking off from the military airfield located within the camp. As the air assault continued, Batista and aides dropped to the ground for cover. Noticing that one of the antiaircraft gunners was not firing, Batista, suspecting his loyalties lay elsewhere, ordered an aide, Captain Manuel Benítez, to force the man to fire. Benítez went behind the man, put a pistol to his back, and ordered him to fire at the attack planes. The gunner complied.[7] There were intense machine-gun duels between several of the pilots and the forces on the ground for about an hour.[8]

Ironically, Batista, his pregnant wife, and his daughter had moved to a home at Camp Columbia from their Toyo Street apartment after the Sergeants' Revolt, because of concerns about their safety. The move allowed Batista to stay close to the troops most loyal to him. Given its location on the outskirts of Havana, Batista believed Camp Columbia could be made "impregnable from attack."[9] The furnishings in the Batista home were modest, and their lifestyle was simple, so much so that one reporter described him at this time as the "Quaker Sergeant." One of the rooms was used as a study and resembled the "office of a professor of stenography."[10] There was no safe place on this night. His home became a rebel target. The colonel had taken steps to safeguard his family on the night of the attack, but because the air force attacked earlier than expected, his family was still at the base when the bombs fell. The plan was for his brother-in-law, Bausa, and a chauffeur to take his wife, Elisa; daughter, Mirta; and Pastora, Bausa's wife, to a safe house, where they would ride out the crisis. As they drove away, Elisa saw the bomb drop on the school next to their home. While her husband would be engaged in a difficult fight for the next forty-eight hours, she and the rest of her family were about to embark on their own difficult odyssey.[11]

The family went to the residence of a lieutenant loyal to Batista and the government, but it turned out that the loyalties of the home were divided.[12] After they arrived, Batista's family was ignored by the woman of the house. The atmosphere was tense. As the fighting spread throughout Havana, rumors began to circulate, fueled by reports from a rebel-controlled radio station, that Batista was dead, imprisoned, or in exile.[13] A relative of the homemaker, perhaps unaware of the identity of the guests in residence, cheered the news of Batista's death. Elisa remained silent, but her younger sister, Pastora, could not restrain herself and began to argue with her hosts. Despite the heated argument, the Batista family was allowed to remain at the home for what must have been a very long and uncomfortable day.

The air attack created chaos and confusion throughout Havana. The skies over Columbia and at the Presidential Palace, where Grau remained throughout the fighting, were lit up by flares, searchlights, and antiaircraft shells. But the perception of risk from the air was greater than the reality. The entire air attack consisted of three Corvair fighter planes, each carrying ten twenty-five-pound bombs. Only one of the pilots, Lieutenant José Barrientos, successfully dropped his payload. One of the other pilots did not release his bombs, while those dropped by another did not explode. A fourth pilot went up during the fighting carrying two 120-pound bombs, but he too decided not to drop his cargo. Barrientos returned to the military airfield to begin a second bombing run, but by that time Batista's forces were laying siege to the facility. They directed their machine-gun fire at the airplane hangars with the hope of damaging the planes within. A second airplane fitted with bombs was ready to go, but it was hit by gunfire as it left the hangar, and Barrientos was unable to take off. One of the rebel pilots flew north toward Key West and was picked up by a U.S ship. The two other pilots landed their airplanes, one forced down by enemy fire, in rural areas and made their escape.[14]

At the same time as the air attack was going on, the rebels were marching through the streets of Havana capturing government buildings and police stations at a rapid pace. Rebel supporters sped through the city in their automobiles giving predetermined signals to indicate that supporters were to take up positions at certain locations. As a sign of loyalty to the rebel cause, and as a means of identification, military men were to refrain from wearing their hats, while civilians wore green armbands.[15] By early morning they controlled much of Havana. The navy and its headquarters at the Castillo de la Punta (Castle at the Point), which sits near the entrance to Havana Harbor, remained loyal to the government, as did a contingent of seventy-five soldiers and police officers stationed at the Presidential Palace. The men at the palace were well armed and had a cannon and antiaircraft weapons at their disposal. The navy offered to evacuate President Grau to the Castillo de la Punta, but he decided to make a stand of it at the palace. With Grau were Guiteras, Carbó, and several military leaders, including Pablo Rodríguez. After capturing the nearby police headquarters, the rebels planned to launch a full-scale attack on the palace with the hope of capturing Grau.[16]

Shortly after the air attack began, Batista made his way to the military headquarters at the camp and prepared the counteroffensive. In the first hours of the rebellion, Batista thought he might lose the fight. Some of his forces fled into the neighborhoods surrounding Camp Columbia. Reports of rebel gains in Havana were coming in fast and furious. One eyewitness recalled that Batista considered handing power back to the officers.[17] The United States reportedly offered to allow him to take refuge aboard one of its battleships should he decide to flee.[18] But Batista hung on: the troops at Camp Columbia remained loyal to him.

Batista ordered a halt to all military flights across the island.[19] His soldiers encircled the military airfield sometime between 4 and 5 a.m. and began a grueling, four-hour attack on the facility. The rebels at the airfield were badly outgunned, and there was little place to take cover because of the flat terrain. There were originally more than one thousand rebels at the airfield, but most of them were poorly armed civilians. As the fighting went on, many of the civilians escaped to join their comrades in the city. The core of the rebel fighting force at the airfield consisted of eighty soldiers.[20] As the hours passed, the ring of fire grew tighter, and the government forces edged closer to the center of the airfield. By 9 a.m., the rebels had enough, and they surrendered. There were twenty corpses strewn across the battle zone and forty wounded. Batista's forces captured four hundred.[21]

But while Columbia was secure, Havana was in the hands of the rebels. At around the same time that the government took back control of the military airfield, the rebels were preparing for an all-out attack on the Presidential Palace. The rebels massed at Police Headquarters a few blocks south of the palace. Around 10 a.m., more than two thousand rebels, mostly civilians, marched on the building shouting, "To the palace! To the palace!"[22] As they marched, they fired a wide variety of small arms, rifles, and shotguns.

The rebels built a makeshift tank to lead the assault—a truck to which metal sheets were attached with holes cut out to provide a means for riflemen to shoot as the vehicle approached the palace. They gradually approached the edifice, but there was no return fire. One eyewitness thought the government troops would surrender without a fight.[23]

Inside the palace, President Grau, whose entire family was with him, comforted a young niece, while Guiteras sat on a sofa watching the approaching mob. As the rebels closed in, an officer told Grau that his men were ready to fire. The president reportedly ordered them to "fire in the air." The officer argued that they risked being overrun, but Grau insisted that they fire a warning shot. All at once machine guns and rifles were fired from every floor of the palace. For good measure, the antiaircraft weapons were fired and the noise sounded like "200 men were screaming at the same time." The palace shook with the intensity of the fire.[24] The rebels panicked and retreated down several of the streets leading away from the palace, abandoning the makeshift tank and dozens of rifles. Shortly thereafter, the rebels were forced to abandon Police Headquarters after that building was struck by antiaircraft missiles and cannon fire from the palace.

The attack on the palace widened the gulf of distrust between Grau and Batista. Earlier in the day, the president had asked Batista to send reinforcements to the palace to bolster his defense, but the additional troops never arrived. Grau believed the failure to send the reinforcements was a clear indication of Batista's lukewarm support for the government.[25] Cuba scholar Luis Aguilar notes that Batista only intervened in the struggle for Havana after victory became "inevitable."[26] It is unlikely Batista withheld reinforcements out of a desire to bring about Grau's demise. Grau's capture would have only left him more vulnerable. A new president installed by the rebels was less likely to accept him as chief of the army. A more plausible explanation can be found in the fact that Batista's forces were tied down at Columbia and he was unwilling to dispatch men to Havana until the situation there was under his control.

Furthermore, the loyalty of some of the government troops in Havana was suspect. A U.S. military intelligence report indicates that many of the government troops were prepared to join the rebels "if and when the latter's chances of success appeared assured."[27] Phillips noted the army's slow advance into Havana in her diary: "Either they couldn't decide who should come to town and do the fighting or they were waiting to see which side they should take—the government or the rebels."[28]

After securing Columbia, forces loyal to the government marched east on Havana and fought a series of battles with rebel soldiers, police officers, and civilians at the various police stations along the route. One of the first pitched battles came at the Tenth Precinct on the northern edge of Havana just across the Almendares River from Marianao, where rebels held student leader Rubén de León and Police Chief Gonzalo García Pedroso. After a fierce exchange of gunfire, the government troops positioned a cannon at a nearby cabaret and began lobbing shells into the building, a move that brought about a quick surrender. García Pedroso, de León, and several other hostages were freed unharmed.[29] Another tough battle was fought at the Eleventh Police Precinct in the Cerro neighborhood of north Havana, where fighting went on for several hours, wounding at least three and killing four, two soldiers and two police officers.[30]

The fighting went on all day in Havana, and the country was declared in a "state of war."[31] But by midafternoon the situation looked grim for the rebels. Soldiers were pouring into Havana. The rebels retreated east and south to escape government troops coming from the west; as they went, they vacated government buildings and the Dragones barracks. As part of a calculated strategy by Batista, the rebels were allowed to evacuate buildings and retreat.[32] After each retreat, some rebels abandoned the struggle and returned home. Some police officers and soldiers rejoined the government forces, hoping their dalliance with the rebels would go undetected.[33]

By late in the afternoon of November 8, the rebels were concentrated in two positions, the San Ambrosio arsenal, a block from Havana Bay, and Atarés, an eighteenth-century Spanish fortress overlooking Havana Bay from a high bluff. The two positions were separated by about ten city blocks, San Ambrosio located to the south of Atarés. Around 5 p.m., the battle cruiser *Cuba* began shelling San Ambrosio, blasting gaping holes into the building.[34] One of the cannon blasts blew the arm off a young ABC adherent, and he was rushed to the infirmary.[35] The rebels responded with heavy machine-gun fire, and with the aid of antiaircraft weapons from Atarés forced the cruiser to retreat out of firing range. At the same time as San Ambrosio was struck from the bay, government forces were taking positions around the building. They leveled blistering machine-gun fire at San Ambrosio for several hours. Photos from the period show the administrative offices of the building riddled with bullet holes.[36]

After an intense firefight, the rebels came to the conclusion that they could not withstand a long siege at San Ambrosio. Major Ciro Leonard ordered the retreat of the rebel forces to Atarés. Blas Hernández opposed the decision, arguing that they were duplicating the mistake made by the officers at the Hotel Nacional. Rather than concentrate their forces in one location, Hernández argued they should fight their way into the countryside, recruit more followers, and then stage another attack on Havana. But Leonard produced a telegram from a rebel commander in Las Villas Province, to the east of Havana, urging him to go to Atarés and promising that the commander would enter Havana with a force of five thousand newly recruited men. Based on that assurance, Hernández agreed to retreat to Atarés. In the aftermath of the revolt, one writer suggested that the telegram may have been part of a government trick to lure the rebels into one location.[37]

As part of a negotiated truce, the rebels were allowed to retreat to Atarés sometime after midnight on November 9.[38] With them, they took trucks full of ammunition, their retreat paving the way for one of the worst massacres of the revolution.

ATARÉS

Atarés was built on a high hill, about one hundred feet above the surrounding terrain, at the head of Havana Harbor. The heavy stones of the fortress were pushed into place by slaves between 1763 and 1767 as part of a series of new Spanish fortifications to protect the harbor from attacks by foreign powers.[39] Ships entering and leaving the port are visible from the south side of the fortress. Immediately below the imposing structure are a number of commercial piers. Residential neighborhoods face the fortress on the other three sides. To the southeast of Atarés lies Habana Vieja, the historic heart of the city, from where the rebels were retreating. To the north of the fortress lies El Cerro, one of the city's first suburbs, a wealthy neighborhood during the nineteenth century, but in decline by the 1930s. Atarés normally housed a garrison of about one hundred men, but on the morning of November 9, there were upwards of one thousand men and three women crammed into the fortress.[40]

It was a mix of poorly armed civilians and soldiers who streamed into Atarés in the early morning hours. There was a nervous tension inside the fortress, but the rebels believed Atarés could withstand the artillery bombardment everyone expected, because the stone ramparts were ten meters thick. "This is not the Hotel Nacional," was the optimistic phrase uttered by those inside.[41] The situation inside was chaotic; no one appeared to be in charge. Major Leonard tried to coordinate a plan of defense, but he was constantly interrupted by requests for additional firearms and suggestions by various people who filed in and out of his office. Unlike the disciplined officers at the Hotel Nacional, the rebels were a disorganized lot.[42] There was little food or water, and because of the overcrowding people slept on sacks inside the many rooms or roamed the parapets.

Throughout the night, Batista and his officers prepared for the attack. The rebels were allowed to retreat to Atarés, but they would not be allowed to leave without surrendering. The plan was to pummel the fortress from all sides with artillery fire. Several artillery pieces were moved to the "Loma del Burro" (Jackass Hill), a slope northwest of Atarés. A mortar was placed directly north of the fort near the intersection of Concha and Cristina streets, while another cannon was placed on the roof of a marketplace (the Mercado Único) northeast of the fortress. From the south, the battle cruisers *Cuba* and *Patria* were to lob shells into Atarés. Perhaps learning a lesson from the disastrous assault at the Hotel Nacional, Batista, knowing the rebels were well armed, did not order a land attack on the fortress. Instead, soldiers surrounded the fort at a safe distance from machine-gun fire and prepared to gradually tighten the circle around the defenders as their ability to fight diminished.

The artillery barrage began sometime around 8 a.m. The pounding was incessant in the first few hours, but ineffective, because those manning the artillery pieces had yet to perfect their targeting. They did so sometime around 11 a.m., and the old Spanish fortress became a death trap for the rebels. One shell fired from the Loma del Burro landed in the kitchen, decapitating the chef and wounding several others. Parts of the chef's body landed in a huge pot of rice and black beans. One eyewitness recalled that because of the shortage of food "we lifted the cook up and carried him out so no one would notice."[43] The eyewitness accounts tell the tale of a horrible slaughter. The constant pounding made the fortress shake. The dust stirred up by the bombardment made it nearly impossible to breathe. The mortar on Concha and Cristina had the most devastating impact on the rebels. Its shells were landing on a regular basis in the center courtyard where many of the rebels were huddled. One shell alone killed twenty men. "To get an idea how terrible the situation was there were places where to move one had to do so over corpses, many of them mutilated, without arms, headless."[44]

The rebels were ill-equipped to resist the artillery bombardment. They were well armed for a land attack on the fortress, but they could do little to stave off the artillery. The rebel machine-gun fire had no impact on the well-concealed government soldiers at the bottom of the hill. "No matter how hard I looked, I could find no one to shoot at. Our adversaries were well protected," one machine gunner recalled.[45] The rebels used their lone artillery piece to attack the battle cruisers in the bay and succeeded in forcing a retreat, but that artillery piece eventually broke down.[46] By early afternoon, the situation became desperate within the fortress. There was no evidence of reinforcements from the provinces coming to the rescue. Several rebels made a mad dash down the hill in an effort to escape the slaughter and were cut down by machine-gun fire. The fighting spirit of the rebels was broken, and most wanted to surrender. Disillusioned by the carnage, Major Leonard, sometime around 2 p.m., put a revolver to his head and committed suicide as an aide screamed, "Don't kill yourself, don't kill yourself."[47] Another of the organizers of the revolt, Pedro Gener Núñez lay inside the fortress dying of his wounds. Throughout the afternoon several other soldiers and civilians, anticipating a humiliating surrender, killed themselves. One of those committing suicide was a fifteen-year-old boy, the son of a journalist. The boy's last words were reportedly, "While I live I will not surrender, deliver me when I am dead."[48]

Some of the rebels wanted to fight on, including Blas Hernández and Captain Felipe Domínguez Aquino. They urged the rebels to resist the bombardment until nightfall, when they could fight their way out of the fortress and flee into the countryside. Some of the civilians supported the plan, but the remaining military men argued in favor of surrender.[49] There was confusion throughout the fortress as some began to mount white sheets and handkerchiefs on any visible structure to signal their defeat, while others screamed that the fight should continue to the death. A rumor spread that Blas Hernández shot someone trying to surrender.[50] Despite the pleas of those who wished to fight on, the trend toward surrender was unstoppable. Even after the white flags were posted, the shelling continued for some time, perhaps as long as thirty minutes.[51] By 4 p.m. the shelling stopped, and government forces stormed the hill to retake the fortress.

With the surrender, the fighting stopped but not the killing. According to eyewitness reports approximately twenty prisoners were marched down the hill, placed against a wall, and executed by government forces.[52] One of the prisoners fainted as the shooting began. "When I recovered consciousness I was lying on the ground with a body on top of me and covered with blood."[53] He moved the body aside and escaped while the soldiers were occupied elsewhere. Another group of prisoners was marched outside the gates of Atarés and reviewed by Captain Mario Hernández, one of the original conspirators of the Sergeants' Revolt. Mario Hernández asked for the whereabouts of Blas Hernández. Blas Hernández stepped forward and identified himself. According to several eyewitness accounts, Mario Hernández raised a pistol and shot the old guerrilla fighter, and then, as Blas Hernández lay on the ground, he shot him in the head.[54] Photos of Blas Hernández's dead body, published in the Cuban press, show his pockets turned inside out and his shoes removed.[55] One eyewitness reported that a soldier took Blas Hernández's hat and belt and began to mock the dead man by saying, "Look, I'm Blas Hernández now."[56]

Sources favorable to Batista treat the execution of Blas Hernández with varying degrees of denial. Franco Varona notes that Blas Hernández died "valiantly," but does not describe the circumstances.[57] The most shameful treatment of the execution comes from journalist and Batista biographer Edmund Chester, who fabricates a story to justify the death of Blas Hernández. "At the end, there was a great deal of hand-to-hand fighting at the gates of the fortress and Blas Hernández fell dead, a bullet through his chest. Old Blas had fought one too many battles. One report from Atarés was to the effect that Blas had been killed by an army officer after the surrender. It was one of those reports which could neither be confirmed or denied because the confusion following the surrender was so great," Chester wrote.[58] Batista never ordered an investigation into the death of Blas Hernández. As he would do countless times throughout his career, Batista chose to ignore the misdeeds of fellow officers to preserve army unity and his own position. Mario Hernández was the first to get away with murder under Batista's leadership, but he would not be the last.

Carteles condemned the murder of Blas Hernández, but not everyone was sympathetic to his plight. Journalist Enrique Lumen called the execution "repugnant," but added that the "nation has been liberated of a sentimental bandit, an enemy of peace and progress."[59] No one on the civilian side of the government protested the execution. When informed of it, Guiteras reportedly criticized the action, but excused it because Mario Hernández was a loyal revolutionary.[60] Blas Hernández's son, a military aide to his father and an eyewitness to his death, blamed Batista, Grau, and Guiteras in equal measure for his father's assassination.[61] Fidel Castro later listed the execution of Blas Hernández among Batista's many crimes, although he reserved comment on the role of Guiteras.[62]

Sporadic fighting would go on for several days throughout Havana and in the provinces, but the rebel insurrection was essentially over with the fall of Atarés. The death toll for the two days of fighting ranged between two hundred and five hundred, with hundreds more wounded.[63] It is probable that more than one hundred were killed in the shelling of Atarés alone.[64] Except for the explosion of a defective shell on the Loma del Burro that killed two soldiers and wounded three others, the government suffered no casualties during the siege of Atarés.[65] Most of the government casualties were caused in firefights at other locations or by snipers. As in the aftermath of the siege at the Hotel Nacional, the government refused to give out casualty figures for the armed forces, leading the U.S. military attaché to speculate that their losses were "very heavy."[66]

As a military campaign, the counterattack by government forces against the rebels throughout November 8 and 9 was far more effective than the earlier confrontation with the officers at the Hotel Nacional. Batista and his lieutenants were aided considerably by the confusion and lack of coordination among the rebel forces. Photos from the era show hundreds of unarmed civilians, many of them wearing jackets and ties, parading through the streets with enthusiasm. They were more a spectacle than a fighting force. In the early hours of the attack, they took over unoccupied or undefended government buildings and retreated as soon as they met organized military resistance. After the initial hand signals and occasional radio reports, there was little communication among the roaming bands of rebels, so they were often unsure where to mass their forces for an attack or when and where to retreat. "We were an armed group in the middle of the street, without orientation or purpose, vulnerable to attack at any moment by government forces. Our leader did not know where to go," one rebel later recalled.[67]

The most significant mistake on the part of the rebels was their failure to march on Camp Columbia in the early morning hours of November 8 when government forces were fighting to retake the military airfield.[68] Part of this failure can be attributed to the poor coordination between military and civilian forces. Another factor was the lack of seriousness among some of the rebels, who expected "the revolution of November 8 would be the same as the one of September 4: a revolution without shots or bloodshed."[69] A second critical error was the decision to mass rebel forces at Atarés where they could be subjected to the same sort of artillery bombardment that forced the surrender of the officers at the Hotel Nacional just five weeks earlier. Although many of the rebels thought Atarés was "not the Hotel Nacional," from a strategic standpoint it was. The decision by Batista to allow the rebels to retreat from one position to another within Havana was wise, because with each retreat their numbers dwindled. The emphasis on an artillery bombardment of Atarés, rather than a bloody land assault showed that the colonel had learned some lessons from the Hotel Nacional debacle.

The failure of the rebels to topple the government further strengthened Batista's hold on the military. In the short term, it united the disparate elements in the government against external forces, notwithstanding their internal struggle for control.

Mr. Caffery of Louisiana

Despite military victories by the government, the hostility of Ambassador Welles to the Grau regime never wavered. The Warm Springs Declaration in late November clearly vindicated Welles's position regarding nonrecognition, but at the same time President Roosevelt announced that the ambassador was to be recalled to Washington in December to oversee Latin America policy. From that point forward, Cubans, both inside and outside the government, knew his days were numbered, and some thought that perhaps the next ambassador might find the Grau government less objectionable. This political reality did not dissuade Welles, who worked feverishly until his final hours in Cuba trying to broker a deal to unseat Grau. Welles felt that if he left for Washington with Grau in power he would return "without the prestige of having accomplished anything."[70]

Welles half-heartedly backed efforts by Uruguayan Ambassador Benjamín Fernández Medina, who tried in late November and early December to negotiate a deal between Grau and the political opposition. After several weeks, Fernández Medina drafted a plan in which Grau would remain in power for a short time but with a cabinet composed of members of the political opposition. Welles told Grau he would do "everything possible" to support such a plan and then proceeded to undermine the negotiations by urging a Cuban political ally to accept the Medina plan only if Mendieta were named as president.[71] The talks collapsed on December 12, and Medina took the unusual step, for a diplomat, of publicly criticizing Welles for undermining the negotiations.[72]

By the time Welles left Cuba on December 13, nearly everyone was glad to see him go. Assistant Secretary of State William Phillips was "thankful to get him out of the Cuban mess for he was certainly making no helpful contribution."[73] Batista and Welles were no longer on speaking terms.[74] A *Miami Herald* editorial praised the decision to replace Welles. "The United States should not be concerned in what president the Cubans may choose, if law and order are established and maintained and if foreign obligations are recognized. The alleged activities of Ambassador Welles have aroused enmity and doubt in Cuba and Latin America and it would be for the best interests of our relationships that a change be made."[75] As a final testament to his diplomatic failure, Batista and several student leaders went to visit U.S. Chargé d'Affaires H. Freeman Matthews just hours after Welles's departure to urge recognition of the Grau government.[76]

President Roosevelt's "special representative" Jefferson Caffery of Louisiana arrived in Havana on December 18, and was left to sort out a political debacle of enormous proportions. The forty-seven-year-old Caffery could not rightly be called ambassador because Cuba and the United States did not have diplomatic relations. When Caffery arrived, Grau's hold on power was weak. The only force keeping him in the presidency was the military. Batista wanted U.S. recognition above all, and it was clear that could not be accomplished with Grau as president. Mendieta, the most likely candidate to succeed Grau, did not trust Batista. Batista did not trust Mendieta. Unable to come to an arrangement, the government and opposition debated an unending series of offers and counteroffers. Guiteras put pressure on all sides by trying to unite the political left into a viable force. Navigating this thicket of political confusion was Caffery's primary task.

The contrast between Caffery and Welles was clear from the onset. Caffery, whose father was a politician from the bayou country, did not let his social prejudices interfere with his sense of political pragmatism. While Welles spent hours trying to negotiate a political solution with the old Cuban political class, Caffery courted Batista and his fellow nouveau officers. Caffery distanced himself from the political negotiations and concentrated on establishing a relationship with the military. A bachelor, Caffery became one of the boys. He attended cockfights and bet on the outcomes, frequently winning. He went horseback riding at Camp Columbia with Batista. As Chester puts it, "Caffery and Batista became friends almost before Caffery had unpacked his bags."[77] Welles courted Batista but never felt comfortable with him.

One Cuban journalist described Welles as "elegant and enigmatic," yet that same reporter found Caffery anything but elegant: "[He] butchers Spanish and he does not even speak his own language properly. One realizes he is a diplomat by the fact that he blushes with ease. If he wore the clothes of Tom Mix [a star of Hollywood westerns in the 1930s], he would be a classic Texan."[78] Caffery stuttered, a debility that he turned into a strength, by learning to listen. A man of few words, when he did speak, he delivered an important message. Caffery's State Department dispatches reflect this clarity of vision. They were always short and to the point, unlike those of Welles, who could write pages and say little. Caffery nurtured relationships and confidences. Details revealed in confidence were kept in confidence, so much so that before his death Caffery destroyed nearly every piece of embarrassing correspondence spanning his lengthy diplomatic career.[79] He was careful not to give an assurance that he could not honor.[80]

Caffery and Batista could do business.

Incident at Sans Souci

Batista was a pariah to the middle and upper classes of Cuban society. He fit none of the ideal qualifications for leadership. Whatever his racial heritage, he certainly was not of white, European ancestry. He was not well educated, at least in the formal sense. He was not even from Havana. He was a poor country boy from eastern Cuba with questionable ancestry, yet he was the most powerful man on the island. Cuban high society viewed Batista as an "adventurer, an upstart and a despicable mulatto."[81] Student leader Justo Carrillo wrote that high society was "definitely against Grau and even more so against 'the nigger' (Batista) who had managed to climb to the highest military position in the country."[82] In his sudden ascent to power, Batista placed many Afro-Cubans into positions of greater prominence within the military. Among his personal bodyguards were several Afro-Cubans, and they accompanied him to all major events.[83]

Nothing better demonstrates high society's contempt for Batista than the events that occurred at the Sans Souci nightclub on New Year's Eve 1933. Built just after World War I, the Sans Souci club and casino was one of Cuba's premiere night spots. Located seven miles outside Havana in a rural area, the Sans Souci was made to resemble a Spanish villa. It offered indoor and outdoor live entertainment, featuring some of the most prominent North American and European entertainers of the era, including Eartha Kitt, Liberace, Marlene Dietrich, and Susan Hayward.[84] On the night of December 31, after a party at Camp Columbia, Batista, his wife, and a group of his top aides and their wives decided to go to the popular night spot. The Batista entourage, including Sergio Carbó, included six cars and a detachment of heavily armed bodyguards. Batista and the members of his party entered the club and were seated. After a few moments, the patrons gathered at the crowded nightclub noticed Batista and the other military men. Acting almost in unison, the upper classes decided to deal an insult to the colonel. As a group, perhaps led by the women, they got out of their seats and walked out of the nightclub. "The Colonel, his Indian face burning, his black eyes glittering with rage, sat stoically in his chair, as his aides somewhat nervously attempted to pick up the threads of a conversation," one eyewitness told a reporter.[85] Carbó's wife stood as the patrons were exiting and hurled insults at them.[86]

A proud man, Batista felt the sting of repudiation. In his friendly biography, Chester presented Batista's perspective of the incident when he described it as "one of the greatest acts of mass bad manners ever seen in Cuba or anywhere else."[87] It was the first of many social snubs directed against

Batista throughout his long political career. Several years later, a prominent social club in Matanzas Province, El Liceo, refused to honor the "mulatto sergeant."[88] In the years to come, the Batistas attempted to appease that high society, even try to become a part of it. Elisa Godínez was tutored in the social graces by several friends. Batista dressed in finely tailored clothes and shoes for every occasion. As was the custom among the wealthy political class, he bought a *finca* (farm) on the outskirts of Havana so he could meet and greet the social elite. He eventually divorced his wife, another product of poverty, and married a tall woman of Spanish descent. He grasped for acceptance, but never quite achieved it. The traditional elites would learn to tolerate him because he brought "order" to Cuban politics, and order was good for business. But the Batista of 1933 was a social undesirable in the eyes of the upper crust.

Despise him though they did, in December 1933 the traditional elite were in the unenviable position, from their perspective, of having to negotiate with Batista for political power. It is clear from the diplomatic correspondence that none of the old established politicians were eager to embrace Batista as a partner in power. Batista suspected that given the opportunity they would try to replace him.[89] Caffery played a key role in bridging the gap by holding firm in his support of Batista. The ambassador saw Batista as the key to order and stability on the island, and in his dealings with Cuban political leaders urged them to accept the colonel.[90]

Race in Cuba was never as black and white as it was in the United States. There was no legal segregation of schools or public facilities as there was in the U.S. South. In fact, Cubans could claim a long history of interracial cooperation. Interracial alliances and coalitions were common and necessary during the long thirty-year struggle for independence against Spain. Afro-Cubans fought and died in large numbers against the Spanish, as did Cubans of other racial and ethnic backgrounds. Cuban independence leader José Martí had advocated a racially egalitarian republic in which racial identities would be subsumed under the larger umbrella of a Cuban national identity (*Cubanidad*). As a result, powerful trends against racial discrimination simultaneously existed in Cuban society. U.S. influence in Cuba was a powerful force working against this ideal of racial harmony. Furthermore, Cuban elites fought hard to preserve the privileges that their race and class afforded them, so the issue of race was a deeply contested one, particularly during periods of crisis such as the early 1930s.[91]

The incident at Sans Souci contains elements of both racial and class snobbery. Carrillo points out that one of the leaders of the protest was the mother of an ousted officer and a grande dame of Cuban society. He attributes racial and class motives to the incident.[92] Batista's eldest son expresses the family's view: "Their [the nightclub patrons'] reaction was one of disdain [for] my father, whom they considered to belong to the lower classes. It was a statement of class superiority."[93] Superior though they may have felt, they could no longer rule Cuba without Batista.

ENDGAME

By early January 1934, it was clear that the political stalemate could not go on indefinitely. The United States would never recognize the Grau government, and without recognition the cycle of violence was destined to continue. Batista and his fellow commanders wanted a political solution, while maintaining their gains in the military. No longer a political novice, Batista's concept of the division of government power had evolved since the September 4 revolt. Batista now saw the role of the military as an "instrument of force and order" to bolster and support a civilian government.[94] Within that context, the armed forces were to stay out of the civilian political process as long as civilians did not impinge on military privilege. To Batista and his fellow officers, it was the military that ushered in revolutionary reforms. They were the spiritual leaders of the revolution and its guardians. The new ideology in the military was based, in part, on a desire to withdraw from the political process. But the arbitrary division of power along civilian and military lines guaranteed repeated military incursions into the civilian sphere. There was no neat and clean way to divide military and civilian power. It was subject to interpretation and reinterpretation each time a decision needed to be made.

Batista spoke more and more openly about the military's expanded role in government. "The army cannot be touched. The army, and this is what I have promised, will be the guarantor of whatever [political] arrangements we aspire to today," Batista told reporters in early December.[95] Batista was assertive in defining the military's newfound power. When a civilian court ordered the former officers released from military jails, Batista ignored the court and put forth a new set of legal arguments justifying their incarceration.[96] Even more controversial was Batista's refusal to turn over two military commanders to a civilian court for prosecution after they were implicated in the beating death of Mario Cadenas, a nineteen-year-old student, in December 1933. One of those implicated, Lieutenant Colonel Ignacio Galíndez, was by now the commander of the all-important Camp Columbia military base and a key supporter.

Concern over the role of the military in civilian affairs became a central theme of Cuban political life. The news magazine *Bohemia*, a vigorous opponent of Batista throughout his career, repeatedly warned of the growing power of the military. In response to Batista's comments about the military as "guarantor" of a political solution, one commentator questioned the qualifications of the colonel and his officers to serve as the arbiters of Cuba's future. "Have they sacrificed the most? Are they the most dignified? There is no doubt they are the strongest."[97] In an editorial on January 7, the magazine warned the public, "Of all the ills in the path of the Republic, at the beginning of the new year, none is as grave as the one represented by the preponderance of militarism. Militarism is a vine that has grown over the nation's territory in such proportions and under such circumstances that the features of a civil society have disappeared, erased by the shadows in which the omnipotent prestige of the Barracks grows."[98] In the same issue, the news magazine described Batista as a "Napoleonic Marshal" underneath a photo of the colonel dressed in a military overcoat and officer's hat.[99]

From the military's point of view, Grau was no longer serving their best interests. Rumors of new civilian uprisings were widespread, and the frequent confrontations and the resultant casualties were troubling to Batista and the military high command. As they saw it, stability was the key to solidifying the new military order. Two months earlier, Batista acted clumsily when he tried to remove Grau and was nearly outmaneuvered by Guiteras and the students. This time Batista paved the way for Grau's removal through a series of meetings with fellow officers throughout December and January.[100] In early January, Batista went to eastern Cuba to consult with Colonel Pedraza on the matter.[101] Batista attempted to get outright approval for a coup from Caffery in a meeting on January 10. The cagey diplomat, however, stopped short of condoning any particular action while sending a signal that something must be done. Caffery told Batista: "I will lay down no specific terms; the matter of your government is a Cuban matter and it is for you to decide what you will do about it."[102] By the middle of January, Batista knew precisely what he intended to do about it.

Grau could see the end coming. In December, he tried to retain power via the Medina plan. After that fell through, Grau signed a decree, in early January, calling for elections to a Constitutional Assembly by April 22. The purpose of the convention was not simply to redraw the Constitution of 1901 but to act as a legislative body until a regular schedule of congressional and presidential elections could be established. Originally, Grau was expected to stay on through the elections and up until May 20, 1934, but his thinking on this changed over a period of several days. At a cabinet meeting on January 8, Grau suggested that he resign and a new administration take power for the purpose of overseeing the elections.[103] Grau reiterated his willingness to resign in a meeting with Batista and Caffery on January 11.[104]

Grau may have been looking for an electoral mandate to reinvigorate his political career. To that end, efforts would soon be under way to organize Grau's civilian supporters into a political party that would come to be known as the Partido Revolucionario Cubano (Auténtico)—the Cuban Revolutionary Party (Authentic).[105] A plan to resign and then reemerge at some later date as a presidential candidate made sense from Grau's perspective. In early January, Grau was exceedingly unpopular, but over time it was reasonable to expect that his record of achievement would come to be seen in a more favorable light by the public. If Grau's party could gain substantial popular support in the Constitutional Assembly races, it would propel him into position for an elected term as president. Once elected, the United States would have little choice but to support and recognize his government. This made sense given the fact that constitutional elections were just three months away. The elections would give the new Constitutional Assembly moral and popular support against the military. An electoral scenario was preferable to the one Grau faced in the first month of 1934. Abandoned by many of his political supporters, he was in the uncomfortable position of relying on the military and Batista to maintain him in power. As provisional president, unrecognized by the United States and unable to gain support from the traditional political parties, his reliance on Batista made him a junior partner in power.

Batista decided to end the partnership after a January 13 meeting with Mendieta at a farm outside Havana.[106] At the meeting, Batista asked the ever-indecisive Mendieta to assume the position of provisional president. The colonel had reason to be optimistic this time because just nine days earlier, Mendieta, in a letter published widely in the Cuban press called on Grau to resign.[107] Behind the scenes, Caffery was urging Mendieta to accept the provisional presidency.[108] Batista recalled making the following proposition to Mendieta on January 13: "I am alone, almost alone, in this medley of turbulence and irresponsibility. I lack experience and have no historical background to support me in assuming the terrific task of solving the nation's problems alone. It is the duty of all of us to serve Cuba and your duty is greater than that of any other man at this time because of your political, revolutionary and patriotic standing."[109] Batista did not offer Mendieta total power but rather a power-sharing arrangement. His remarks made it clear that he too was "assuming" the challenge of solving the "nation's problems." The proposal, as Batista outlined it, was for him and Mendieta to work as equal partners. As a further condition, the colonel said he told Mendieta that revolutionary reforms must remain in place. The sixty-year-old Mendieta, perhaps uncertain about whether he might ever have another chance at the presidency, agreed to accept Batista's offer.[110]

Caffery, aware of Batista's intention to offer the presidency to Mendieta, fired off a series of diplomatic dispatches to Roosevelt seeking guarantees of U.S. recognition for a Mendieta government. The dispatches were sent even before Grau was informed of his pending removal. "I respectfully request at once authority to recognize Mendieta in the Presidency. If this is not (repeat not) done Batista will probably turn definitely to the left with definite disaster for all our interests here (or declare himself military dictator)."[111] Despite several pleas by Caffery, President Roosevelt declined to guarantee the advance recognition of a Mendieta government.[112] But, although Roosevelt declined prior recognition, every possible diplomatic signal was sent to ease the transition, including promises of a new reciprocal trade treaty and the annulment of the reviled Platt Amendment.

Mendieta's acceptance of the provisional presidency set into motion a rapid-fire sequence of events. The following afternoon (January 14), Batista and Mendieta asked Grau to meet with them.[113] At that gathering, Batista appealed to Grau to resign for the "good of the country." The colonel put forth as arguments the willingness of the United States to accept and recognize a Mendieta government and the likelihood that the Platt Amendment would be abrogated. Grau agreed to resign, but only to the revolutionary junta that had appointed him to the presidency in September.[114] The request by Grau may have been part of an effort to complicate matters for Batista and Mendieta. The junta had not officially met in months, and reorganizing them was no small feat. Furthermore, the junta, which included many former and current Grau supporters, was unlikely to rubber-stamp a Mendieta appointment.

Batista worked quickly to call together a civilian-military commission that resembled the revolutionary junta of September. Some of the original revolutionaries attended, but others were either unavailable or unaware of the meeting. Perhaps, Batista did not try particularly hard to reassemble the original junta, which included a number of his current enemies.[115] Whatever the case, the group that met at 2 a.m. on January 15 at Camp Columbia contained more military men and Batista allies than the earlier junta. At the junta meetings in September, Batista was the only voice for the military, whereas this meeting included substantial military representation, including both friends and foes of Batista. A substantial number of the members had ties to either Grau or Guiteras.

Batista began the meeting with a general statement about the decline in support for the Grau government and about Mendieta's willingness to step into the presidency. He concluded his opening remarks by praising the military's role in bringing about and preserving the revolution.[116] A furious debate immediately ensued. Student leader Rubén de León was the first to rise and attack Batista for "deserting the revolution" and challenged him to "remove his mask and frankly declare himself a military dictator."[117] At one point, de León threatened Batista by noting that "one can always find a bullet for a dictator." Angered by the remarks, Batista warned the student leader that he was surrounded by military men.[118] The meeting went on for several hours, and the fierceness of the attack by de León and several student colleagues derailed the plan to place Mendieta in power. Several key Batista supporters, including Carbó, abandoned Mendieta and sought a compromise candidate. Guiteras lobbied for the provisional presidency, and proclaimed to the media his willingness to accept the position.[119] However, no candidate was less acceptable to Batista and the army than Guiteras, and that draft movement went nowhere.

A key factor in derailing Mendieta was the opposition by the navy, perhaps spurred on by Guiteras. In the search for a compromise candidate, the name of Agriculture Minister Carlos Hevia surfaced.[120] Hevia was seen as ideal by some because of his participation in the Grau government and because of his ties to Washington. He was, in fact, a graduate of the U.S. Naval Academy at Annapolis and thought to be someone likely to garner support from Washington. Perhaps his background as a seaman made him an attractive candidate to the Cuban Navy. When several of Batista's allies backed away from Mendieta and threw their support to Hevia, he became the frontrunner for the provisional presidency.

The meeting adjourned with no decision at around 4:30 a.m. and reconvened ninety minutes later in Batista's home. During the recess, Batista reluctantly agreed to back Hevia. One commentator noted that Batista was hesitant to impose his will on the junta because he wanted the civilians to decide who would be the next president.[121] Student leader de León put it more sarcastically: "Colonel Batista, who fears nothing, is fearful of declaring himself a dictator . . ."[122] In spite of Batista's support for Hevia, or perhaps as a result of it, the junta remained deadlocked. A few student leaders, led by de León and backed by Commander Pablo Rodríguez, favored retaining Grau in power with a new cabinet. Some student leaders opposed Grau and suggested the appointment of someone unaffiliated with the government, such as a judge, to serve as provisional president.[123] The junta meeting broke up in the late morning with no agreement.

Each side left the reunion with the goal of garnering as much political support for their candidate as possible. Members of the Batista faction, including Carbó, went to meet with Mendieta to secure support for Hevia. Mendieta issued a statement backing Hevia, although his political party later rejected him. As a precautionary measure, Batista had his rival Pablo Rodríguez arrested, a precursor to his ultimate expulsion from the military a few days later.[124] In response to reports of a large pro-Grau demonstration at the palace, Batista dispatched troops and a tank there.

De León and his supporters went to the Presidential Palace to try to convince Grau to stay on as president. They found a president determined to resign. Grau spent the night waiting for a decision on his successor, and finally went to rest at 6 a.m.[125] Participants of the junta meeting began to trickle into the palace sometime around 7:30 a.m., and that trickle became a steady stream as the morning went on. Several noted the lack of support for Mendieta, and all asked Grau to remain as president. As Grau met with supporters inside the palace, the crowds began to grow outside, the number reaching several thousand by early afternoon. They chanted, "Grau don't go! Stay! Down with the politicians!" ("Que no se vaya Grau! Que se quede! Abajo los políticos!") Just before 10 a.m., Grau met with several journalists inside the palace and reiterated his intention of resigning. His words to the press reflect the weariness of four months of struggle and controversy. "I am satisfied with my actions. I have fulfilled my duties. Despite all the obstacles that have presented themselves, I have decreed laws of benefit to the nation. I have not bowed to foreign embassies. I have tried to benefit the public and acted firmly against the large businesses."[126]

Grau spent the next nine hours in meetings with supporters. A wide range of alternatives were presented to him. Some called on the departing president to replace Batista as chief of the army, a suggestion he rejected because of fears it would lead to a "civil war."[127] At one point supporters blocked the exits so that Grau's personal staff could not remove his belongings. Around 2 p.m., de León and Guiteras arrived and conferred with Grau as he was drafting his letter of resignation. In the midst of the impromptu conference, de León reportedly stood up and ripped up Grau's letter of resignation. "Grau is not quitting," de León told supporters as they cheered him on. One of Grau's cabinet ministers then rose and told the students that Grau was no longer acceptable to Batista and that they could not challenge the might of the military. The students shouted the cabinet minister down, but Grau remained resolute in his decision to resign.[128]

In an effort to placate the crowd outside the palace, Grau walked onto a balcony and made one of the noncommittal speeches for which he would become known throughout his career. "Fellow Cubans, you can feel secure in the fact that I will continue to defend your rights wherever I may be. Long live the Revolution."[129] The crowd drowned out the rest of his words, and he quickly went back inside.

In the midst of this confusion, Hevia sat in one of the presidential offices waiting to take power or withdraw, depending on the outcome. Shortly after his speech to the crowd, Grau met with his cabinet ministers, including Hevia, one last time. When Grau emerged from the cabinet meeting Hevia was by his side. The outgoing president introduced Hevia as his "substitute" and asked his supporters to back him. The transition of power was sealed with an embrace, and Grau prepared to depart the palace.

Photos of Grau on that day show a man weary with the weight of his responsibilities. His eyes appear swollen from lack of sleep. But eyewitness accounts attest to his calm amid the emotion of his final hours. Time and again, Grau proved to be one of the most cunning, calculating, and resilient politicians of the era. Not one to be swayed by emotions, Grau deduced that any challenge to the military could very well end in a bloodbath. He would live to challenge Batista on another day and under different circumstances.

At Camp Columbia, Batista was taking no chances regarding Grau's resignation. At 2 p.m. he ordered the troops assembled and informed them of Hevia's designation. Later in the day, he issued a statement to reporters offering the army's "enthusiastic" support for the Hevia government. He was careful to note that Grau's resignation was the result of his "free and spontaneous desires."[130] The troops Batista sent to the palace were under the command of a loyal captain, Belisario Hernández. Upon their arrival, they quickly formed into battle formation. Reports from the period suggest that the crowd began to move toward the Presidential Palace while chanting pro-Grau slogans. Hernández gave the order to fire, and chaos broke out in Zayas Park, across the street and north of the palace. Hundreds dropped to the ground for protection, while others ran in all directions. A second round of fire was unleashed on the crowd. When it was all over, three were dead and thirty-two wounded.[131] Minutes later the limousine of former President Ramón Grau San Martín left the palace.

"Presidente Relámpago"

Carlos Hevia y Reyes Gavilán was just thirty-four years old at the time of his appointment as provisional president.[132] The son of a prominent Cuban family, he served in the U.S. Navy in the Great War, the term used to describe World War I at the time. A graduate of Annapolis, he was one of the leaders of the failed, poorly executed Gibara invasion of 1931 that aimed to topple Machado. His father was a prominent member of Mendieta's Nacionalista Party, and perhaps he thought that connection might aid him in securing their support. At one time, he too was a Nacionalista, but then left the party to join the ABC. He later defected from the ABC and joined Grau's government, where he served as secretary of agriculture, industry, and commerce. It was under his leadership that the land reform policies of the Grau administration were inaugurated.

The most distinguishing feature of his presidency was its brevity. Hevia's tenure would last a little more than forty-eight hours, leading Cuban satirists to dub him "Presidente Relámpago" (the lightning president) and "Flor de un Día" (flower for a day).[133] His position was untenable from the start. He was closely associated with Grau, yet few of the former president's supporters were willing to back him. He was viewed by many as the military's candidate for the presidency, yet his support in the military was at best lukewarm. Although he had strong ties to the United States, it was clear he did not have the support of the embassy and would not receive recognition.[134]

The appointment of Hevia was a temporary measure to avoid a direct conflict between the different factions of the Grau government, particularly between the army and navy.[135] As he did so often throughout his career, Batista correctly read the political situation and banked on the inability of Hevia to gain the necessary political support to remain in power. With no political backing, the Hevia government would crumble, and the path would be clear for Mendieta. On January 16, the day after taking power, one group after another rejected Hevia's pleas to join the government.[136] As Hevia floundered, Batista ordered the removal from office of all mayors allied to Guiteras. The following day (January 17), the colonel suggested to several political leaders that they urge Hevia to resign.[137] Even more important, meetings were held between high-ranking army and navy officials to secure support for Mendieta. The navy had little choice but to shift their allegiance to Mendieta given Hevia's lack of political support. No doubt navy officials also realized that they could not win a fight with the army.[138]

Guiteras had his own reasons for initially backing Hevia. Tired of Grau and unable to gain the provisional presidency for himself, Guiteras saw Hevia as a candidate over whom he could exert influence. He played a critical role in securing Hevia's designation as provisional president. One writer in *Diario de la Marina* notes that "Guiteras could not win the battle but he could cause Mendieta to lose it."[139] When the outcome was still uncertain, Guiteras threatened to "fight against the army" if it did not accept Hevia as president.[140] No doubt Guiteras was counting on the support of the navy with which he had nurtured strong personal relations.[141] He went so far as to go onboard a Cuban battleship to exhort the navy to revolt, but rather than rise up in arms, the seamen escorted him off the ship.[142] As his support in the navy eroded, Guiteras tried desperately to organize a general strike to block the designation of Mendieta. When the call for a strike went largely unheeded, Guiteras went into hiding.

After a little over two days in power, Hevia submitted his resignation to Batista and to the revolutionary junta, a governing body that the scholar Lionel Soto notes "never selected him and which no longer existed."[143] He did so at 2 a.m. on January 18 and immediately left the Presidential Palace without waiting for his replacement. Cuba was effectively without a president. It would remain without a president until 6:30 a.m., when Secretary of State Manuel Márquez Sterling agreed to assume the job, at the urging of Batista, for the sole purpose of convening a cross-section of political leaders to pick a new president.[144]

The student leaders thought they saw an opportunity in the collapse of Hevia's presidency. In an effort to force Batista to declare himself a military dictator, many of the members of the revolutionary junta refused to meet.[145] It was obvious that Batista and the military wanted Mendieta, but with the refusal of the junta to meet there was no civilian process in place to select him. Batista did not want to impose a military solution on the problem of the provisional presidency, at least not publicly, because that would make him the central target of the new political opposition. With the resignation of Hevia, Batista had already taken part in the demise of three presidents, and he understood very well the value of having a civilian as the titular head of the government. The president served as a lightning rod for attacks from the political opposition, allowing Batista to remain in the background always ready and able to support the government—his government.

In search of a civilian solution to the succession dilemma, Batista argued to Márquez Sterling, now acting as president, that with the resignation of Hevia, and before him Grau, Mendieta was the only remaining candidate considered by the junta a few days earlier. Power should fall to him.[146] However, Mendieta and his followers rejected that suggestion, arguing that the military's fingerprints would be all over the selection process. Mendieta wanted to avoid the appearance that he was the military's candidate for fear it would undermine his legitimacy and weaken his administration. Taking these concerns into account, Márquez Sterling convened in the midmorning a meeting of Mendieta supporters and allies to ratify his selection as provisional president. The path was now clear for Mendieta to take over the atrophied office of provisional president.

In the days to come, Batista congratulated himself for avoiding a military dictatorship even though many had advised him of the "necessity" of one.[147] He lashed out at his former student allies who had supported the military revolt of September 4 that spawned the revolution, but who were now withholding their support of Mendieta because of "militarism." Some newspapers, including *Diario de la Marina*, praised Batista as a "born politician." The newspaper went on to commend him for refusing to use force to the "advantage" of the military and for his "preference and respect" for civilian power.[148]

CHAPTER 8

THE
MENDIETA YEARS

It was an odd sort of dictatorship. Batista was the strongman of a weak government. And, even though he was in a position of relative strength, there were enormous checks on his personal power throughout the two-year, provisional presidency of Carlos Mendieta Montefur (January 1934–December 1935). Some of the checks came from within the government, others from the political opposition that capitalized on the desperate economic conditions in Depression-era Cuba. Crippling strikes, political assassinations, indiscriminate bombing campaigns, and challenges of every conceivable sort to the government were part of everyday life. Newspapers and magazines of the period ran one editorial after another pleading for calm and a return to peaceful political discourse.[1] All to no avail. In the background hovered the shadow of U.S. Ambassador Jefferson Caffery. He tried to leave no fingerprints on the political advice he freely gave Mendieta and Batista. But in sleuthlike fashion, political opponents and allies detected Caffery's real or imagined involvement in every move by the Cuban government. Caffery became the face of imperialism for the political opposition. Some Cuban scholars have labeled it the "Caffery-Batista-Mendieta government" sarcastically naming the men in order of power and influence.[2]

From his position of strength within the army, Batista represented the strongest faction within a badly divided Cuban government. Batista was able to maintain power but little else. The government, by way of the army, could oppress the opposition, but it could not enact its own domestic political program. It scarcely had time to develop one. To the extent that there were triumphs in this period, they came in the foreign policy arena with the ample assistance of the United States. The most notable achievements were the abrogation of the Platt Amendment (May 1934) and the conclusion of a reciprocity treaty between the United States and Cuba (August 1934) that defined economic relations between the two countries for the next twenty-five years.

The civilian side of the Cuban government, led by the gray-haired Mendieta, consisted of a hodgepodge of political parties engaged in endless squabbles over patronage and power, even as the country was falling apart around them. Mendieta, a hero of Cuba's Independence War, was a man of enormous national and international prestige. Thirty years Batista's senior, Mendieta periodically followed his own political whims and dictates regardless of the colonel's opinions. From time to time, Mendieta made cabinet changes or signed decrees without consulting Batista at all. A dispute inevitably arose, and one of a host of mediators, among them Ambassador Caffery, interceded to patch up the relationship between the two men.

Other elements in the government challenged Batista as well. The judiciary regularly defied him by setting free civilians arrested by the army and national police. The Supreme Court indicted Batista for disregarding its orders and demanded that he testify before it, an invitation he ignored. Fellow military officers served as a restraint on his power as well. In making any decision, Batista needed to weigh the political implications for the armed services. Military conspiracies abounded throughout the period. The press, although some members received regular stipends from the government, periodically leveled their pens at Batista and the army.[3]

There were foreign constraints on the government as well. The United States exerted formidable economic pressure: without economic assistance from its powerful neighbor to the north, the Cuban government was hard pressed, at least in the short term, to sell its sugar crop, pay its employees, fund public works projects to employ the struggling masses, and meet its international financial obligations. Within the inner sanctum of the Cuban government, the United States was a powerful advocate for capital, particularly U.S. capital. Its defense of foreign capital at the expense of local business and labor made it a frequent target of nationalists and the growing labor movement. Any decree by the government favoring foreign business interests was sure to precipitate a new wave of confrontation with the political opposition.

Another significant check on government power was the labor movement, largely controlled by the political opposition—in this case Grau's Auténticos and the Communists. It launched one major strike after another, frequently paralyzing large sections of the country for extended periods of time. The general strike would become the political opposition's weapon of choice. It had crippled the Machado government, and the opposition thought it could do the same to Mendieta and Batista. They were not far from wrong. In March 1935, the labor movement nearly brought the government to its knees.

Batista employed brutality, charm, patronage, compromise, and guile to survive the next two years. He needed abundant amounts of all those ingredients to maintain and expand his power.

THE RELATIONSHIP WITH MENDIETA

In a peculiar way, Mendieta and Batista complemented each other.[4] Mendieta put a grandfatherly face on a regime that over time employed greater and greater brutality to stay in power. A man of impeccable honesty, he refused to give into the graft that seduced many of those around him. Plentiful are the stories of his personal integrity. On one occasion, when the president was strapped for cash, several advisers urged him to use "secret funds" to pay off a mortgage on a small farm he owned. Instead, Mendieta chose to cut back on his personal living expenses and pay the mortgage with his own money.[5] Typically described by historians as the first of Batista's "puppet presidents," the assessment is unjust. Mendieta genuinely struggled to retain civilian influence and control of the government.[6] As president, Mendieta frequently consulted with Batista on cabinet appointments but maintained the final say. A portion of the cabinet consisted of those loyal to Mendieta and the civilian politicians, while another portion was set aside for partisans of Batista and the military. Within the cabinet and the government there was a *civilista* (civilian) wing and a *militarista* (militarist) wing. There were also some cabinet positions set aside for "neutrals."[7]

Secret U.S. government records from the period and Caffery's personal correspondence detail an ongoing series of disputes between Mendieta and Batista.[8] Newspaper accounts frequently mention private meetings between the two, and others, as part of an effort to resolve various "crises" in the government.[9] In one case, Batista wanted an old friend and ally appointed to the cabinet, and urged this upon Mendieta. Despite Batista's lobbying, Mendieta rejected the appointment at the urging of another adviser.[10] The rejection by Mendieta caused Batista to lose face with his fellow military officers, and he "resented" it, although he grudgingly accepted the president's decision.[11] Another dispute flared up in December 1934, when Mendieta signed a decree disbanding Machado's Liberal Party, a decision he made against Batista's wishes.[12] "Batista is, of course, very displeased with Mendieta's action [regarding the Liberal Party] but, as usual, his good sense will prevail and he will not take any reprisals against Mendieta or the Government," Caffery wrote Welles.[13]

At times of crisis, Batista resented Mendieta's unwillingness to confront the political opposition, leaving the army to suppress striking workers and exposing it to public scorn.[14] After the army brutally put down the general strike of February–March 1935, Mendieta and his political associates began to fill the positions of the displaced workers with his party loyalists, a move opposed by Batista.[15] Still later, when Mendieta decided to cancel elections for a Constitutional Assembly and instead opted for presidential and congressional elections, Batista accepted the decision even though he disagreed with it.[16]

Time and again Batista tolerated Mendieta's streaks of independence. His tolerance can only be understood in the context of a Cuba in turmoil, a Cuba that had erupted in violence and already destroyed one dictator. The lessons of Machado's demise were not lost on Batista. He did not wish to become the face of the government by assuming the role of military dictator. Without the appearance of a fully functioning civilian government, the full wrath of the political opposition and the angry masses would be directed at Batista and the army. Mendieta was a useful lightning rod for all the criticism leveled at the government. Batista received some criticism, but the bulk of it fell on Mendieta and the discredited civilian politicians. Mendieta was a shield.

The appearance of civilian rule could not be achieved without some power sharing. In order to maintain appearances, Batista was forced to cede some authority to Mendieta and the political parties in the government coalition. Nonetheless, Batista kept his eye on Mendieta by naming a loyal confidant (Major Ulsiceno Franco Granero) as the head of the Presidential Guard. In addition to protecting Mendieta, Franco Granero quite likely spied on him as well.[17] The accusation gained some credence when in June 1934, Franco Granero came into conflict with Presidential Secretary Emeterio Santovenia. Several issues were in dispute, including Franco Granero's tendency to walk into cabinet meetings unannounced. A bell had been installed in the cabinet room, which he was supposed to ring before entering. The dispute, which included a fight over personnel and a clash over the arrest of several civilians, plunged the government into crisis for several days. Santovenia prevailed on the personnel matters, but the unannounced visits by Franco Granero continued.[18]

Relinquishing power did not come easy to Batista. Journalists, office seekers, businessmen, foreign visitors—all made the daily pilgrimage to Camp Columbia to visit or to solicit favors or to discuss world affairs with Batista.

One of those who came calling was famed sportswriter Damon Runyon of the Hearst newspaper syndicate. Runyon described the scene at Camp Columbia prior to his interview as follows: "If anyone doubts that Batista is the master of Cuba they need only spend several hours in his waiting room. One gets the impression that anyone who wants something in Cuba must see him."[19] Fellow journalist, Ruby Hart Phillips, echoed the observation when she wrote: "To call on Batista is something like trying to see the King of Siam or other potentate."[20]

These were heady times for the former cane cutter from Banes, and it must have taken all of his self-control to refrain from completely wresting power from the civilians. At times of greatest exasperation, Batista toyed with the idea of removing Mendieta from the presidency and fully taking the reins of power. The topic arose repeatedly in his conversations with Ambassador Caffery. Throughout the early months of their government, Batista was satisfied to leave Mendieta in power. Caffery in his frequent letters to Welles noted that Batista could "at any time install himself as Military Dictator."[21] However, Batista described Mendieta as a "pure" man because of his patriotism and integrity and expressed concern that the resignation of the president would bring "chaos."[22]

But as the months wore on, Batista began to give the matter more and more thought, particularly as Mendieta's shaky political coalition began to crumble in the face of repeated challenges by the political opposition. By the end of 1934, Mendieta and his allies were concerned that Batista would remove them from power, and Caffery found it necessary to repeatedly question Batista about his intentions. On October 16, 1934, Caffery reported that "Batista well knows that I believe (and he agrees) that it would be a great mistake for him (Batista) to set himself up either as President or as any sort of military dictator in this country."[23] Then again two weeks later, after a political dispute between Mendieta and Batista, Caffery wrote: "For the moment, at least, Batista still insists that he has no intention of removing Mendieta from the Presidency."[24] Batista came closest to declaring himself a military dictator during the general strikes that swept the island in February and March 1935. "President Mendieta has become considerably alarmed over the many street rumors that he is to be removed by Batista," Caffery wrote Welles on March 1.[25] In that instance, Mendieta asked Caffery to intercede with the colonel on his behalf. After discussing the subject with Batista, Caffery was less confident of his intentions. "While I still believe that Batista will not declare himself Dictator, or President, or Military Governor, or anything of the sort, I do believe that the matter has been occasionally flashing across his mind," Caffery wrote on March 6.[26] A month later, Caffery expressed concern that the constant praise showered on Batista by his supporters "may turn his head."[27]

The concept of a military governorship, as opposed to a military dictatorship, was suggested to Batista by his old friend in the Machado resistance, Carlos Manuel de la Cruz. One of Batista's principal advisers in this period, de la Cruz argued in February 1935, as strikes were sweeping the nation, that Batista and the military intervene in Cuban affairs and establish military supervision of the government until elections could be held. The model for this "intervention" was the appointment of Charles Magoon as provisional governor of Cuba from 1906 to 1909 by President Theodore Roosevelt. Magoon replaced Cuba's first president, Tomás Estrada Palma, after his government collapsed amidst a nationwide revolt. Caffery opposed the de la Cruz plan, and Batista evidently did not give it serious consideration.[28]

Ultimately, the notion of officially declaring himself military dictator held little appeal for Batista. Sometime in early 1935, he began to set his sights on the presidency. In April, Batista told Caffery that "many people are urging him to resign his position in the Army and run for President." Batista was careful to reassure Caffery that he had no intention of seeking election in the immediate future.[29] Still, the colonel put it on the record so the State Department could begin to consider the possibility of a President Batista. Future conversations with Caffery and others made it clear this was no passing fancy but a goal he aimed to achieve.

Perhaps Batista hesitated in removing Mendieta because, in most ways, he was a perfect fit. By the time he assumed the presidency, Mendieta, sixty at the time, was a thirty-year veteran of the Cuban political wars. His ambition was depleted. He liked the prestige of the presidency and its trappings, but he was not willing to wage a long, drawn-out struggle with Batista over real power. A dedicated family man, Mendieta liked returning every night to his wife and daughter at a reasonable hour. Furthermore, medical ailments (Mendieta suffered from diabetes) placed some restraints on his activities.[30] Even during the general strike of 1935, Mendieta left the Presidential Palace in the early afternoon to return home rather than monitor the state of the nation throughout the night.[31] He left the most disagreeable tasks to Batista, who frequently worked almost twenty hours a day. In his article, Runyon reported that Batista frequently woke up around 11 a.m. and worked until 6 or 7 a.m. the following day. To champion civilian rule, Mendieta would have had to work at least as hard as Batista, and it is uncertain that he could have triumphed even then.

Mendieta's vacillating personality also served to undermine his position within the government. Stories of his indecision are legendary. This is the same man who repeatedly changed his mind about accepting the presidency when it was offered to him by Batista on several occasions during the Grau administration. Caffery assessed Mendieta thus: "He is very kindly, friendly, cordial and without doubt means well; he is patriotic and honest, but he is indecisive, not very intelligent and not too morally courageous."[32] Documents from the period reveal a strong desire by Mendieta to avoid confrontation with political adversaries and friends alike. Even after it became politically expedient, Mendieta was reluctant to force the resignation of unpopular cabinet members. He belabored most important decisions to the point where confusion prevailed among all concerned. Mendieta changed his mind so frequently about when and how elections should be held that Caffery wrote almost daily updates on the situation.[33]

In fairness to Mendieta, he inherited a government with deep rifts. Within his government, the political parties waged nonstop warfare for political patronage jobs and cabinet positions. The civilian politicians were too busy squabbling among themselves to form any united front against Batista and the military. When Mendieta took power in January 1934, his government consisted primarily of a coalition of his Nacionalista Party, the ABC movement, led by Joaquín Martínez Sáenz, and the Partido Acción Republicana, a small political party led by Miguel Mariano Gómez. In June 1934, the ABC broke with Mendieta over the shooting deaths of several of its members at a political rally. A month later, Gómez, then the mayor of Havana, threatened to resign because he claimed that his supporters did not hold a sufficient number of cabinet positions. The Mendieta government received tepid support from the Conjunto Nacional Democrático, the party of former president Mario García Menocal, which agreed to accept patronage jobs from the government in return for not actively opposing it.

Arrayed against this none too formidable government coalition was a political opposition that, although disorganized as well, agreed Mendieta must fall. In addition to Grau and the Communists, the political opposition included former Interior Minister Antonio Guiteras, who in May 1934 founded a revolutionary organization by the name of Joven Cuba (Young Cuba), which advocated armed struggle against the government. These groups were later joined in the opposition by the ABC movement.[34] Mendieta was forced into a closer alliance with the military than he might have desired by the divisions within his own government coalition and the unrelenting attacks by the opposition. Commenting on the fragility of the government coalition, a supporter of the besieged Cuban president remarked to Caffery in October 1934 that his main bases of support were the "army and the American Embassy." In response to the remark, Caffery wrote to Welles: "Of course, this is not literally true, because he [Mendieta] is also supported by his own Nacionalista group; but I must sorrowfully admit that if Batista should withdraw the Palace guard I do not believe there would be many voices raised in protest, and certainly not a single hand raised to defend the Government."[35]

The provisional nature of the Mendieta government further undermined its legitimacy with the Cuban public. In fact, he was not President Mendieta but Provisional President Mendieta. No one, apart from a dozen or so civilians and military men, elected him to anything. Furthermore, the laws, the very underpinnings of any government, were all established by decree. There had been no legislative body since the fall of Machado. The Constitution, if one could call it that, was not the product of a national consensus reached at a constitutional convention but rather a decree set forth by Mendieta on February 3, 1934.[36] This constitutional statute, based on the Constitution of 1901, provided a wide range of individual liberties, including female suffrage, a prohibition against the death penalty, and greater protection for prisoners. However, the ink on the document was barely dry before constitutional guarantees were suspended the following month as a result of growing strike activity. Constitutional guarantees were suspended so often during the Mendieta administration that martial law was the rule rather than the exception.

Mendieta saw that the only way out of Cuba's political crisis was to hold elections for a Constitutional Assembly, but public disorder and political conflict led to the repeated postponement of elections. Prior to his fall from power, Grau set elections for a Constitutional Assembly for April 1934. The date for elections was pushed back until December 1934 by Mendieta. They were postponed several more times before the politicians finally decided against them and decided, instead, to hold presidential and congressional elections in January 1936. In the interim, Mendieta established a quasi-legislative body, known as the State Council (Consejo de Estado) in April 1934, consisting of fifteen or so political appointees.[37] The purpose of the council was to suggest laws to the president and cabinet, which then decided whether to issue those laws as decrees.

Regardless of these structural and personal weaknesses, Mendieta was the president of choice of the U.S. State Department, particularly Welles, now in charge of overall Latin America policy. Whenever Mendieta's star appeared on the decline, Welles would dictate a letter to Caffery urging his retention in the presidency. Caffery, who dealt with Mendieta on a day-to-day basis, was less enthusiastic in his support of Mendieta, whom he described as a "constant problem" for him and Batista.[38] Problem or not, Caffery delivered

Welles's message to Batista. Given the recent crisis over U.S. recognition, Batista had to weigh any move against Mendieta very carefully or risk his own demise.

Welles argued that Mendieta's vacillation may have been, if not intentional, then at least desirable. He described Mendieta as a man navigating between the extreme left and right of the Cuban political spectrum. "As it is, the Government, through what is considered in Cuba its own vacillation and weakness, has steered the middle course, has kept out of the pitfalls of anarchy and the equally dangerous alternative of dictatorship. I am not at all sure that Mendieta may not some day go down in history as the best President Cuba ever had and I hope some day to be able to tell him so."[39] Welles saw Mendieta as a check on Batista's power. Throughout 1934, Welles favored Mendieta's election to a full four-year term as president because of his refusal to accept "dictatorial methods."[40] His perspective changed after Mendieta's political support was eroded by the bitter strikes of 1935. However, even then, Welles wanted Mendieta retained as provisional president until elections were held. The idea of a Batista presidential candidacy "fills me with the most thorough-going pessimism," Welles wrote to Caffery in April 1935. His advice to Batista was to "postpone" his ambitions "until some future national election."[41]

For better or worse, Mendieta and Batista were stuck with each other for at least the next several years.

King Sugar

With the establishment of the Mendieta government, the United States acted quickly to try to stabilize the regime by granting it recognition five days after it took power. On January 23, 1934, Caffery, who was functioning as Roosevelt's "special representative" to Cuba, formally presented to President Mendieta the official recognition of the United States.[42] Most of Latin America and Europe followed suit. Crowds gathered along the Malecón in Havana to see the USS *Wyoming* fire a twenty-one gun salute to mark the occasion. Two days later (January 25), Batista made a courtesy call on Admiral Charles S. Freeman on board the *Wyoming*, and Freeman was in turn honored at a military review at Camp Columbia. The champagne and handshakes flowed freely, and all of it was captured in detail by the Cuban media. The message was clear. This government has the blessings of the United States.

Symbols were important, but behind the scenes the State Department, in the person of Assistant Secretary Welles, worked quickly to put together an economic-diplomatic assistance plan for the battered island. Ironically, the political turmoil, which was used by Welles to justify not recognizing the Grau government, did not subside during the Mendieta presidency. At times it was considerably worse. This, however, did not stop Welles from doing everything possible to keep the new Cuban government in power.

The urgency of the need for financial assistance was made clear in a January 24 internal State Department memo to Welles that recommended $5 million in immediate aid, of which $2 million should go for food to feed the hungry and $3 million to pay the salaries of government employees and veterans' pensions. An additional loan of $20 million was suggested to get Cuba through the immediate crisis. "It is believed that had such aid been extended in time the Céspedes Government would not have fallen, and it is practically certain that there will be a reaction against the Mendieta Government unless aid can be extended immediately."[43] The memo went on to suggest several other measures, including the suspension of foreign debt payments. In the following months, in rapid-fire succession, most of these measures and additional ones, were implemented. In April, the Cuban government suspended payment on some of its foreign debt for a two-year period. In the same month, the United States, through the Second Export-Import Bank, loaned the Cuban government $4 million to mint new coinage to pay its employees. Similar credits, totaling $11 million, were provided to Cuba in two installments the following year.[44]

Even more significant was the passage in May of the Jones-Costigan Act, which guaranteed Cuba a portion of the U.S. sugar market. Thereafter, Cuba was assigned, on an annual basis, a sugar quota based on the projected needs of the United States. Further economic assistance came in August when the United States and Cuba signed a comprehensive trade agreement, known as the Reciprocity Treaty. The treaty lowered the duty on Cuban sugar entering the United States. In addition it guaranteed Cuban tobacco growers a percentage of the U.S. market and provided benefits to producers of rum and fresh fruits and vegetables. In return, Cuban import duties on a wide range of U.S. finished goods were reduced. This gave the United States an enormous advantage over foreign competitors inside Cuba.

The result of these two major initiatives was to intimately intertwine the two economies for the next twenty-five years. In time, resentment grew in Cuba over the measures for a variety of reasons. The sugar quota ensured Cuba's dependence on one principal crop. Sugar monoculture was the scourge of the Cuban economy, and it remained so for the rest of the twentieth century. Sugar was king. When sugar prices were high on the world market, times were good on the island. When prices fell, times were bad. As long as Cuba relied on a single crop, it was extremely vulnerable to worldwide fluctuations in price. The proximity of the large U.S. market just ninety miles to the north was both a blessing and a curse. The quota guaranteed a stable market for Cuban sugar, but it also gave the United States extraordinary economic power over Cuba. That power was heightened by the fact that U.S. corporations controlled vast segments of the Cuban economy, including many of the sugar mills, the telephone and telegraph industry, and the railroads. It made for a skewed economy in which foreigners—Spaniards and Britons as well as Americans—essentially controlled private industry on the island. Cubans were economic outsiders in their own country. Boxed out of the private economy, Cubans turned to government as a money-making venture, which contributed to widespread corruption at all levels.[45] Foreign domination of the Cuban economy was and would remain a dominant theme of Cuban politics up through the Revolution of 1959. Efforts at diversifying the Cuban economy were vigorously debated throughout the years leading up to the revolution, but little progress was made in that regard.[46]

The advantage given to U.S. goods by the treaty further stymied the development of Cuban industry, ensuring that Cuba remained a source of raw materials and a purchaser of finished goods.[47] The fact that the trade agreement was made by a provisional government at a time when there was no legislative body to debate it was another sore point.[48] At the time, Grau attacked the Reciprocity Treaty for placing Cuba in a "submissive, dependent and enslaved" position vis-à-vis the United States.[49] Whatever the long-term implications of the trade initiative, the short-term result was a dramatic increase in Cuban exports to the United States and a boom in overall trade. Within a year, Cuban exports more than tripled, from $48 million in 1934 to $151 million in 1935. Exports to the United States grew by a whopping 213 percent, although most of this was from increased sugar sales. This translated into a dramatic increase in revenue for the Cuban government, whose budget increased from $42 million in 1933 to $65 million in 1935.[50]

On the political front, the United States was as eager as Cuba to be rid of the Platt Amendment, which only served to poison relations between the two nations and as a reminder to the rest of Latin America of repeated U.S. military intervention in the region. On the surface, the Good Neighbor policy emphasized a respect for the sovereignty of Latin America and the improvement of trade relations. The Platt Amendment, which allowed the United States to intervene militarily in Cuban affairs when its interests were endangered, was bad for business. From the Cuban perspective, the Platt Amendment was an affront to the nation. The United States had refused to accept its unilateral abrogation by Grau the previous year. However, with a friendly government in Havana, Washington was quick to seize the opportunity, and negotiations to rescind it began immediately. An agreement was reached in May, and the Platt Amendment was formally abrogated on May 29, 1934.

To mark the occasion, three days of celebration were declared throughout the island (June 9–11), and food and toys were distributed to needy families and children. A new monument was dedicated along the Malecón, and the Avenida del Puerto (Avenue of the Port) was renamed Avenida 29 de Mayo for the day the Platt Amendment was annulled. A special mass was celebrated at the Cathedral of Havana and was attended by President Mendieta and other dignitaries. Monuments throughout Havana, including the Presidential Palace were lit up in the evening to honor the event. Still, all in all, the celebrations were fairly subdued. There was a sense, reflected in the Cuban media, that its abrogation was long overdue and that the nation faced more serious challenges. The cover of the June 3, 1934, edition of *Bohemia* featured a cartoon of a winking Uncle Sam with a lengthy caption praising the "political liberation" of Cuba but acknowledging that the island was far from achieving "economic independence."[51] An editorial in *Carteles* called the abrogation a "great moral triumph" but called on the Mendieta government to move beyond it and undertake the "gigantic task of reconstructing the nation."[52] The *New York Times* saw the abrogation of the Platt Amendment as "more of a concession to the Latin temperament" than a fundamental change in the U.S. right to intervene to "protect its own nationals or their property."[53]

The abrogation of the Platt Amendment and the economic agreements with the United States, although subject to criticism, constituted real achievements for the Mendieta-Batista government, at least in the short term.[54] However, like everything else in the period, these accomplishments were overshadowed by unrelenting political violence. Bombs went off in Havana and other Cuban cities on a nightly basis. Just two weeks after the annulment of the Platt Amendment, on June 15, 1934, a bomb exploded as Mendieta spoke to a gathering of sailors at a naval facility near Havana. Two sailors standing directly behind the president were killed, and Mendieta was wounded in the hand. Three cabinet members were also injured by the blast, which was likely the work of Guiteras's supporters.[55] Just two days after the attempt against Mendieta, an ABC rally in Havana was fired on by political opponents, and fourteen died in the streets, including several of the attackers. Assassination attempts were a by-product of the era. On May 27, 1934, a Cuban soldier, guarding Ambassador Caffery's home, was killed when several men drove by in an automobile and opened fire on him and another guard.[56] Attempts were also made against Batista, Mendieta (a second time), Secretary of State Cosme de la Torriente, and a wide array of lesser public officials and journalists.

No amount of economic assistance could bring an end to the political violence in Cuban society. It was a struggle that the political forces that emerged in the aftermath of Machado would settle on the streets. In the next few years, the economic initiatives fostered a revival of the Cuban economy, but they had little impact on the growing political crisis. Some of the worst conflicts of the era were to follow, and a great deal more blood would be shed before Cuba achieved a measure of stability.

ARMY RELATIONS

The strongest element of the government coalition was clearly the army, but by no means was it a monolithic organization. Batista was at the top of the power pyramid; however, he did not rule the army alone. He relied on a number of key subordinates with whom he regularly consulted. Some of them had their own constituencies within the military and needed to be treated with due respect. A confrontation with any of them could plunge the country into crisis.

First among Batista's subordinates was Lieutenant Colonel José Eleuterio Pedraza, who emerged as second in command in the latter part of 1933. Pedraza, one of the original conspirators of the Sergeants' Revolt, was the antithesis of the smiling, joking Batista. A man of few words, Pedraza was not one for small talk and backslapping.[57] Pedraza was Batista's enforcer. A natural politician, Batista preferred the role of the smiling patriarch bestowing political favors and rewards on his allies and showering forgiveness on his political enemies. When heads needed to be smashed, Batista preferred to stay in the background and allow his subordinates to do the muscle work. Throughout his career, Batista appointed tough enforcers to key positions so that there was a certain distance between him and the ugly incidents that frequently occurred during his various periods in power. Pedraza was the first of these enforcers.

Time and again, Batista delegated the difficult, and violent, assignments to Pedraza. In 1933, when the loyalty of troops in eastern Cuba was in question and discipline needed to be imposed, Pedraza was assigned to do the job. When in April 1934, the labor movement emerged as the greatest challenge to the Mendieta-Batista government, Pedraza was named chief of the national police and placed in charge of putting down major strikes. In addition, he was also the inspector general of the army. The personal and professional ties between Batista and Pedraza were further strengthened in the mid-1930s, when Batista's brother-in-law (Heriberto Godínez) married Pedraza's sister.[58]

Pedraza was a man of violent temperament who preferred action to thought. One politician who knew him well, Santiago Rey Perna, a Menocalista in this period, described him as "a man of little intelligence but a great deal of character." In an interview, Rey added that Pedraza was "a very decisive man whose pulse never trembled for anything."[59] Pedraza inspired fear in many of his subordinates. "He is a cold-blooded, cruel and ruthless man, famous for his drastic methods of stamping out communists and terrorists," a U.S. military attaché observed in a 1937 report to Washington. The attaché went on to note: "He [Pedraza] rules with an iron hand, can shoot or hit with either hand and does not hesitate to do so. He is greatly feared and respected by all echelons of the Cuban nation."[60]

Even Batista, at times, may have felt intimidated by his fiery right-hand man. "Batista might be a little afraid of Pedraza in view of the fact that Pedraza stands very high indeed with the Army," Franco Granero told Ambassador Caffery on November 1, 1934. The head of the Presidential Guard went on to praise Pedraza as a "splendid organizer," while acknowledging that Batista was "a born leader but not such a good organizer as Pedraza."[61] The more than six thousand members of the National Police Force were known as "Pedraza's army," and he ran the organization with a great deal of autonomy.[62] U.S. military intelligence perceived Pedraza as a potential rival to Batista. In a 1937 report, the U.S. military attaché noted that if Batista were to "lose his grip or should his position become untenable, Pedraza will be ready and anxious to assume his heritage."[63] Batista was aware of Pedraza's separate base of support within the national police, and whenever he could, inserted men into it who were loyal primarily to him.[64]

In addition to Pedraza, there were several other key military men in this period, including Lieutenant Colonel Manuel López Migoya, Lieutenant Colonel Ignacio Galíndez, Lieutenant Colonel Francisco Tabernilla Dolz, and Lieutenant Colonel Mario Alfonso Hernández. Of lesser importance, but who had Batista's ear, were Major Jaime Mariné y Montes, his aide-de-camp; another assistant, Major Manuel Benítez y Valdez; and Major Arístides Sosa de Quesada, the intellectual voice of the military. Some of Batista's earlier friends and fellow conspirators, such as Urbano Soler and Ramón Cruz Vidal, remained in the military and achieved moderate success in their careers, but their influence on Batista was never very great. As we have seen, fellow conspirator Major Pablo Rodríguez was arrested in January 1934 for plotting against Batista and ultimately removed from the army. Rodríguez was arrested again in March and freed shortly thereafter. He gradually disappeared from public view.

After Batista and Pedraza, Galíndez held the most power in the army as a result of his position as chief of Camp Columbia and commander of the Sixth Army Regiment. It was Galíndez who was implicated in the beating death of student Mario Cadenas in December 1933. Subpoenaed by a civilian court to testify in the case, Galíndez never appeared. The question of his responsibility in the death of Cadenas was made moot by a general amnesty granted by President Mendieta in February 1934 for acts committed after the flight of Machado on August 12, 1933. With or without an amnesty, Batista would never have turned Galíndez in to the civilian authorities. Galíndez's leadership during the military uprising of November 1933 was crucial to Batista's survival in power. Loyalty to his subordinates, often to a fault, was a Batista trademark. As chief of Columbia, and in several other capacities, Galíndez remained in the Batista inner circle for the next decade.

Galíndez, a Spaniard by birth, emigrated to Cuba in 1920, at the age of seventeen. Shortly thereafter he enlisted in the cavalry and gradually worked his way up to sergeant major in 1929 (the same rank as Batista). Prior to the Sergeants' Revolt, Galíndez took a night course taught by Batista at one of the schools he worked at throughout Havana, so their friendship predated Batista's rise to power. As the godfather of Batista's oldest daughter, Mirta, Galíndez was virtually a member of the family in this period. Galíndez's foreign birth made him something of an outsider among some of his fellow officers, and he formed alliances with a small core of fellow Spanish officers in the Cuban Army. This group became known as the *Gallegos* (a nickname for the residents of the Spanish province of Galicia) or the *Españoles*.[65] U.S. military intelligence considered Galíndez one of the finest officers in the Cuban Army. "He is a great believer in training through competition, and the elements of his command are eternally engaged in some type of competition. His regiment, as reinforced by Cavalry, Field Artillery and Aviation, is head and shoulders above the rest of the Cuban Army in appearance, training and all around efficiency. He is not interested in military or civilian politics, devoting all his time to his command."[66]

López Migoya was an original conspirator of the Sergeants' Revolt and distinguished himself by his quiet loyalty to Batista. There was nothing flashy or controversial about him. Like Batista, Migoya, born in 1900, came from a poor rural family and never received more than a grade-school education. Like several other of his colleagues, he may have taken classes with Batista prior to their rise to power. Migoya, a lifelong bachelor, was a man known for his no-nonsense approach and professional manner. An efficient administrator, Batista appointed him as quartermaster general of the army, a position he held until 1941. "Colonel Migoya's work as Quartermaster General has been both honest and efficient, and he has kept the Cuban Army well fed, well clothed and well armed during the whole of his administration," according to a U.S. military intelligence report.[67] His loyalty to Batista would prove crucial in the struggles to come.

Tabernilla was another close confidant of Batista and one of the few officers (he was a second lieutenant on September 4, 1933) to join in the Sergeants' Revolt. He was one of the most polished officers in the Cuban Army and one of the few to graduate from the island's military academy. After the rise of the sergeants, Batista quickly took Tabernilla into his confidence, promoted him to lieutenant colonel, and made him commander of La Cabaña, the military fortress guarding the entrance to Havana Harbor. "He has been a standard for the Sergeant-Colonels to model after since the revolution," according to the assessment of U.S. military intelligence. U.S. military officials considered Tabernilla "100 percent loyal to Colonel Batista."[68] Tabernilla and Galíndez were fierce rivals and disliked each other immensely.[69] Twelve years older than Batista, Tabernilla remained one of his closest advisers until the end of his political career.

One of the most colorful personalities in Batista's inner circle was Jaime Mariné, who emigrated from Spain at an early age. He enlisted in the army in 1923, and like Galíndez and Migoya, may have taken a course with Batista. Mariné took part in the Sergeants' Revolt and became "the bottleneck through which all individuals desiring to see Colonel Batista must pass."[70] His appetite for corruption was legendary among Cubans of the period. "He was very intelligent but with few scruples," Rey, a political opponent, recollected years later.[71] "He greatly enjoyed the parties, the drinks, the women. For example, he would drive around Havana, in the period when he was its owner and master, along with Batista, in a brightly colored Cadillac, which was a shade of violet. In addition, he was known for the frequency of his relations with beautiful women," Rey said in an interview.[72]

U.S. military intelligence took a similar view of Mariné. "He works 16 hours a day furthering Colonel Batista's desires, with frequent time out to further his own. He has realized more financially than any of Batista's other close adherents, owning two big movie palaces and the fashionable Sans Souci dancing and gambling casino on the outskirts of Havana," according to a 1937 report.[73] The military attaché described him as "most intelligent, infernally clever and wields great influence on his Chief [Batista]." Pedraza showed little tolerance for the scheming Mariné and urged Batista to demote or replace him but to no avail. While Pedraza could not eliminate Mariné, he frequently checked his ambitions and made no effort to conceal his dislike of him.[74]

Batista tolerated Mariné because he relied on him, and men such as

Captain Belisario Hernández, to perform strong-arm tasks that were not of a strictly military nature. It was the opinion of U.S. military intelligence that Mariné and Hernández kept files on the personal lives of prominent politicians and journalists, the embarrassing particulars of which could be used against them if they proved uncooperative. More drastic measures, such as being forced to drink several bottles of laxative or a sound beating might follow. One U.S. military intelligence report claimed that Hernández "has been and is being used by Colonel Batista to modify and point out the error of their ways to various opponents of Colonel Batista, and on each occasion, with the aid of castor oil [a laxative] and other more drastic expedients, has performed his mission."[75]

Not everyone in Batista's military wore gloves of steel; the velvet ones were worn by Major Sosa de Quesada, a lawyer in his mid-twenties during this period. Handsome, tall, and slim, Sosa de Quesada spoke eloquently about the Batista reform agenda soon to be introduced to the nation. At the time of the Sergeants' Revolt, he was awaiting appointment to the officer corps. Sosa de Quesada sided with Batista in the uprising, despite the fact that a brother and uncle were commissioned officers, fought at the Hotel Nacional, and served time in prison. Whenever a respected public face was needed for a difficult task, Batista tapped Sosa de Quesada for the job. At the age of twenty-seven, he was appointed mayor of Havana, after the incumbent resigned in a scandal over misappropriated funds. Later, Batista named him to a series of high-profile posts, including chief of the military's judicial section, chief of the army's cultural section, and head of the oversight organization charged with bringing about education and sanitary improvements to rural Cuba. Throughout his career, Sosa de Quesada authored more than a dozen books on a wide variety of subjects, including the Cuban military and its reforms, education, and poetry.[76]

Another colorful member of the Batista entourage was Major Manuel Benítez, who for a short time in the late 1920s worked in Hollywood as a bit player in some early westerns. The rumor was that the actor Buck Jones taught him how to quick draw his pistol.[77] Benítez returned to Cuba shortly before the Sergeants' Revolt and received a commission as a second lieutenant. Like Tabernilla and Sosa de Quesada, he had the foresight to join the enlisted men in the uprising and quickly distinguished himself as a man of action. Batista frequently dispatched Benítez on dangerous missions, as he would do in August 1934 when revolt was threatened in the western province of Pinar del Río. Only twenty-five in 1934 (he was born on December 18, 1909), Benítez was one of the youngest members of Batista's inner circle. Over the years, the two men had a turbulent relationship, and Benítez's recklessness occasionally strayed into the criminal realm. He played an important role in Cuban politics for the next decade.[78]

Mario Hernández, like Pedraza, was a man of violent action. One of the original conspirators of the Sergeants' Revolt, he was the man who slammed his hand down on the table during the meeting between the enlisted men and officers on September 4 and urged Batista to speak more bluntly of their intentions. He was the man who shot Blas Hernández outside Atarés after his surrender and then for good measure put another bullet in his head as he lay on the ground. No steps were ever taken to discipline Mario Hernández. As a matter of fact, after the death of Blas Hernández, Mario Hernández was promoted to major and ultimately put in command of the Eighth Army Regiment in control of Pinar del Río Province in western Cuba. Command of provincial forces automatically elevated Hernández to the rank of lieutenant colonel.

However, there were indications early on that Hernández was not satisfied with the power-sharing arrangements that evolved after the triumph of the Sergeants' Revolt. Hernández thought command should rotate among the upper echelon officers and that Batista had usurped the power and authority of the others. Some assert that Hernández was secretly allied to Guiteras and was conspiring against Batista.[79] Clearly, Hernández was a man of great ambition, who was not overly impressed with Batista. His ambition and anger were his undoing.

THE CONSPIRACY OF MARIO HERNÁNDEZ

The downfall of Mario Hernández was not long in coming. Seeking to duplicate Batista's stunning rise to power, Hernández hatched a plan to kill the chief of the army on the first anniversary of the Sergeants Revolt (September 4, 1934) and, along with several others, assume control of the army and effective control of the nation. Many details of the coup, its subsequent failure, and the death of Mario Hernández were covered up by the army and may never be known. The army was not eager to publicize dissension within its ranks, and only cursory details of the events were released to the public. Some additional details can be gleaned from the diplomatic correspondence of the era and a few scattered personal accounts.

It is possible to trace the rough outlines of the conspiracy. At some point in August 1934, Hernández approached Pedraza and Migoya about the possibility of removing Batista from power. Hernández, not a man known for discretion, was overheard complaining to Migoya about Batista and the current power arrangements by at least one other officer. Frustrated by his supporting role, one junior officer reported that Hernández would strut in front of a map speaking of future conquests as if he were Napoleon and claimed that he would soon "ascend to the rank of general."[80] He was equally indiscreet in public, and several observers later reported that they overheard a drunken Hernández and a fellow conspirator talking about their plot at a popular establishment in Pinar del Río. Both Pedraza and Migoya reported Hernández's disloyalty to Batista. As was his custom, Batista did not act precipitously. He allowed Hernández to remain at large so that he could determine the full breadth of the conspiracy. As the days passed, another early Batista ally, Major Ángel Echevarría, was implicated in the conspiracy as well. Also involved was a captain in the Army Signal Corps, whose role was to send orders to military barracks throughout the island once the conspirators took power.

After gathering the information he needed, Batista pounced on his disloyal subordinate. At 4 a.m. on the morning of August 22, convinced of the serious nature of the conspiracy, Batista sent Major Benítez and a contingent of soldiers to Pinar del Río to arrest Hernández. What happened next is uncertain. In the official version of events given by the army, Hernández struck Benítez with his pistol after being informed of his arrest. He then tried to fire at the soldiers sent to arrest him. Hernández's pistol jammed, and he was unable to get off a shot. The soldiers fired back, seriously wounding Hernández. In an effort to save his life, the wounded lieutenant colonel was placed in an automobile for transport to the military hospital at Camp Columbia. The car carrying Hernández was reportedly driven at a high speed and crashed. Army officials maintained that it was the crash, not the bullet wounds, that killed Hernández. There is no way to definitively confirm or disprove the official account, although the actions of the military in the aftermath cast doubt on the story.[81] In a letter to a Havana newspaper, Hernandez's wife charged that her husband was shot and killed as he opened the door of their home. The widow alleged that the soldiers made no effort to arrest her husband and resorted to deadly force without provocation.[82]

The disposal of Hernández's body was kept from the public, and even his wife was not informed of the burial site. Some days after his death, some enterprising reporters found his unmarked grave in a cemetery on the outskirts of Havana. *Carteles* published a photo of the gravesite, piled high with stones.[83] The army may have wished to conceal its location in order to avoid its becoming a gathering spot for the political opposition, as had occurred in similar cases in the past. Certainly, Batista must have recollected how his own career was propelled by the delivery of a passionate eulogy at the graveside of another anti-government conspirator from the ranks of the military just a year earlier.[84]

By all accounts, the conspiracy was limited in scope and posed little real threat to Batista, particularly since Pedraza and Migoya remained loyal. Still, the betrayal by Hernández and Echevarría hit Batista hard. After the plot was crushed, Batista dictated a brief address that was read to the troops throughout the island on August 22. In it Batista said that he considered Hernández and Echevarría "family members" rather than subordinates. He alleged that the conspirators were abusing drugs and alcohol and cited that as a cause of their insubordination. In his conclusion, Batista called for army unity and "prayed" for the "elimination of traitors forever."[85] Echevarría and his fellow conspirator from the Army Signal Corps were arrested and immediately court-martialed. The military court, presided over by Tabernilla, convened at 5 a.m. on the morning of August 24 and sentenced the two men to death. Their lives were subsequently spared by President Mendieta, who refused to sign their death warrants.

There were other military conspiracies during the period. Just two months earlier, a plan was uncovered in the navy that led to the removal of the head of that branch of the armed forces and his replacement with a Batista ally. These plots served as a reminder to the chief of the army that his main constituency was the military. Batista knew he had to keep the soldiers and sailors and, most of all, their commanders, happy if he wanted to retain his grip on power. To that end, Batista initiated a major public works program in the armed forces aimed at upgrading military facilities throughout the island. By 1936, the military budget had risen to more than $14 million, slightly less than a quarter of the national budget.[86] This figure did not include an additional $2 million for the national police, which essentially served as an extension of the army. The military allocation dwarfed government expenditures to critical areas such as public works and agriculture. Even at the height of the Machado dictatorship, the military budget never exceeded 19 percent of the national budget. The ranks of the military and police swelled to more than twenty-two thousand by 1936, an increase of about eight thousand in a few short years—this in spite of the fact that Cuba had no foreign enemies.

In the process, Batista made sure to take care of himself, building a new home at Camp Columbia in 1934 to replace his modest sergeants' quarters. Some, like Caffery, saw it as ostentatious and "not in good taste. In fact, I can only describe its furnishings (in fact) as showy and gaudy."[87] When the issue of the residence was raised publicly by a political opponent, Batista claimed that the house, where he lived with his family, was in fact a new military headquarters. In a letter to the press, Batista wrote that he paid a monthly rent to the government for its use, although he did not specify the amount.[88]

In an effort to instill loyalty among the rank-and-file soldiers and sailors, Batista eliminated a host of petty distinctions between the officer corps and enlisted men. He permitted enlisted men to shop in military commissaries and buy merchandise at reduced prices, a privilege once reserved for officers. Differences in uniforms were minimized to emphasize the egalitarian nature of the new armed forces. At a promotion ceremony in April 1934, privates pinned medals on their new commanding officers.[89] Despite all his efforts to placate the soldiers and officers, new challengers did, from time to time, surface within the military. Mario Hernández was the first high-ranking army officer and confidante to betray Batista. He would not be the last. In striking a balance between military and civilian rule, Batista was mindful that the right alignment of military officers could oust him, whereas no immediate challenge by the civilians could bring about his demise.

Repressing *el Pueblo*

Keeping the Cuban Army from repressing the people (*el pueblo*) was no easy task. While Batista saw the wisdom of preserving a civilian facade to the government, even if that meant some limited power sharing, this wisdom was lost on some of his fellow officers and enlisted men. Attacks against civilians, principally political opponents and journalists, grew to alarming proportions in the years 1934 and 1935. Some incidents were almost comical, such as the case of a man arrested in June 1934 for claiming that Pedraza and the national police were torturing prisoners. Rather than investigating the allegations, the man was taken into custody for disparaging the police.[90]

On a regular basis, journalists critical of the government were whisked away at night by armed men and given what was known as the *palmacristi* treatment, *palmacristi* being the popular name for the laxative, castor oil.[91] Typically, the journalists were beaten and bullied before being forced to drink large amounts of castor oil. The victims would then be released and suffer several days' worth of severe stomach cramps, diarrhea, and dehydration. The attacks were not usually fatal, although one journalist did succumb.[92] Sometimes the attackers sought to conceal their identities, but other times they were more brazen. When police arrested former Cuban Ambassador Herminio Portell-Vilá, then working as a journalist, they warned him against criticizing the government and threatened him with the *palmacristi* treatment.[93] As an apparent show of media solidarity, Cuban newspapers and magazines typically ran stories on the victimization of competitors, thus preserving a rather detailed record of human rights violations against journalists. When the director of the news magazine *Bohemia*, Miguel A. Quevedo, was abducted, threatened, and forced to drink castor oil in October 1934, rival *Carteles* ran a story and photo on the incident and condemned the attack.[94]

Still, the harassment continued. One of the most violent attacks occurred in December 1934 against *Acción*, the newspaper of the ABC movement. To better place it in context, it is essential to understand the dramatic deterioration in relations between the ABC and the army throughout 1934. The roots of the conflict can be traced to the rejection by the ABC of the Sergeants' Revolt in August 1933, even though Batista, a member of the ABC at the time, offered it the lead role in a future government. The ABC leadership, made up primarily of middle-class and wealthy businessmen and professionals, could not conceive of the lower-class enlisted men unseating the officers. They backed the wrong side and were removed from power, along with President Céspedes, on September 4, 1933. Their hostility against the student/soldier government bubbled up most dramatically in the November 1933 revolt in which hundreds were killed. The ABC leaders ultimately regained a foothold in the government with Grau's ouster, but their mistrust of Batista and the army persisted. The ABC newspaper became a focal point for attacks against the army and its growing influence within the Mendieta government.

Relations reached their nadir on June 17, 1934, when political opponents of the movement fired on men and women marching through Havana during an ABC political rally attended by an estimated fifty thousand supporters.[95] Evidence indicates that the Communists and supporters of Guiteras were behind the attack, in which more than a dozen were killed, including some of the attackers, along with fifty wounded. Several eyewitnesses reported seeing members of the Cuban Navy and police force firing into the ABC masses.[96] The shootings led to a crisis in the government, and the ABC accused the army, specifically Batista and Pedraza, of purposely failing to provide proper protection for the rally. ABC President Martínez Sáenz, finance minister in the government, demanded the removal of Pedraza as chief of the national police, a reorganization of the navy, and the introduction of a parliamentary system to replace the provisional presidency.[97] When President Mendieta failed to comply with their demands, the ABC cabinet members resigned from the government and joined the political opposition.

In the coming months, Martínez Sáenz unleashed a ferocious series of political attacks against Batista culminating in a scathing public letter in August.[98] Among other things, Sáenz accused Batista of "cowardice," "misappropriation of public funds," and "bad taste" with regard to the construction of the home at Camp Columbia. Sáenz, then in exile in New York, went on to challenge Batista to a duel outside of Cuba. Over the next several years, Sáenz would periodically fling these and other charges at Batista. The colonel's typical response was to decry the growing tendency of Sáenz, and others in public life, to "destroy reputations" and to rely more on "scandal" than "patriotism" in their public discourse. The charge of "misappropriation of public funds" typically referred to the large expenditures on capital improvements at military facilities throughout the island. Batista defended the sums spent on the military, noting the service rendered by the soldiers and sailors to the nation and the employment the improvements provided to Cuban workers.

Sáenz expressed the organization's bitterness toward Batista and the army in a private meeting with Welles in Washington on October 15, 1934. At the meeting, Sáenz charged that the weapons used by the assailants on June 17 were provided by the military. Welles then wrote: "He [Sáenz] told me that he himself had asked Batista to give proper military protection both the night before the parade and the day of the parade and that he had been promised such protection but that the protection promised had been removed at Batista's own orders."[99] The ABC leader went on to assert that military leaders were trying to destabilize Cuba in order to justify a military dictatorship.[100]

The December 12, 1934, attack against *Acción* is not surprising given the contentious nature of the relationship between the ABC and the military; nevertheless, it was unique in its ferocity. On that evening, eight unidentified men with machine guns entered the newspaper's offices, ransacked them, and abducted six journalists. As was the norm in such cases, each of the journalists was made to ingest large amounts of castor oil. The abducted journalists reported that before they received the *palmacristi* treatment, the vehicle of their kidnappers was stopped by local police. It was allowed to continue after the kidnappers exhibited government identification. Coinciding with the attack, the government ordered the closing of the newspaper.[101] It was allowed to reopen several days later. From exile, Sáenz, once again lashed out at Batista and raised the specter of a military dictatorship. He urged his followers to show restraint so as not to give the army cause to crack down on all public dissent. The Caffery-Welles correspondence reveals a great deal about Batista's ambivalence and tacit approval of such attacks, as well as the State Department's tolerance of government-military violence.

In a December 15, 1934, letter to Caffery, Welles describes the castor oil incidents and the closing of *Acción* as "indefensible" and raises concern that the ABC would boycott future elections. In an effort to curtail similar attacks, Caffery and the embassy's First Secretary H. Freeman Matthews engaged Batista in a series of conversations over the next seven days, seeking guarantees against future *palmacristi* attacks. At no time during the conversations between Batista and the U.S. officials does the colonel deny prior knowledge of the assaults. Instead, Batista justifies them by repeatedly noting the "disquieting effect in the Army" of the negative publicity provided by *Acción*. "If, disturbed by stories of that kind, one *cuartel* [barracks] revolts, you can easily see what I may have to face," Batista reportedly told Caffery.[102]

Dissatisfied with Batista's lack of assurances regarding further *palmacristi* attacks, Caffery dispatched Matthews to meet with Batista to discuss the matter again. "I endeavored to impress upon him [Batista] the ammunition which such acts gave to the enemies both of the Cuban Government and of our Government in the United States," Matthews wrote in his memorandum of conversation dated December 18, 1934. Matthews expressed the State Department's hope that something could be done to "*suavizar*" (soften) the confrontational situation with the press. Batista expressed "regret" at the incident but again went on to justify the army's actions. "He [Batista] alluded again, however, to the difficulty of keeping his men in line in view of the daily bitter attacks on the army and wild and sensational reports published in *Acción*. He [Batista] said that, while he had no definite mode of procedure in mind, he would see what could be done to improve the situation and would do all in his power to prevent similar unfortunate occurrences in the future."[103]

Even though the attacks against the press were orchestrated by the army and national police, they were supported by the civilian members of the Mendieta-Batista government. There was no outcry or public denouncement of the incidents by President Mendieta or the members of his cabinet. Privately they offered the same excuses and justifications as Batista. In one conversation with Caffery, Mendieta challenged the attitude of the press toward the government. "He [Mendieta] believes it will be necessary to enact a law imposing fines on the papers when they publish stories that are false, as well as seditious."[104] Mendieta repeatedly gave the signal that political beatings were acceptable as a means of conducting government affairs. After an earlier set of attacks in October 1934, Mendieta met with a group of concerned journalists and promised to "address" their complaints but he urged the journalists to "cooperate" with the government.[105] Mendieta's message was clear: work with the government, or take your chances. Part of the government's ambivalence, in both the civilian and military wings, was perhaps in part due to the fact that dozens of journalists were on the government payroll. They were in essence being paid to, if not write favorably, then at least to curtail their criticism. The government did not take kindly to criticism from those to whom it was paying bribes. This of course is not to say that every journalist was on the government payroll. Many were not, but clearly the line between journalism and government service was somewhat blurred in this period. It was a peculiar perversion of the Cuban political system.[106]

In the end, the U.S. State Department concluded that if it applied too much pressure on Batista regarding the *palmacristi* attacks, it could undermine his position in the army and damage U.S. interests. The department determined that a unified Cuban Army with Batista at its head was essential to U.S. policy. In order to maintain the current situation, the United States turned a blind eye to some abuses. It is worth quoting Caffery's December 20, 1934, letter to Welles at length in this regard: "Of course, the authorities are going through the motions of looking for them [the perpetrators of the *Acción* attack], but I do not believe that they will find them. Feeling is so high in the Army against *Acción* that if the guilty individuals were found a very delicate situation might arise because probably the Army as a whole would place itself on the side of the accused and quite definitely against whoever attempted to punish them. Now to my mind, that would not be a pretty state of affairs. I need no argument to convince me that this is all wrong but, being on the job here, I must needs be very practical indeed, for if anything is done to break up the existing unity in the Army we can say good-bye once and for all to all the progress we have made, as well as to our present policy in this Island."[107]

Batista's reaction to the *palmacristi* attacks suggests a pattern of behavior dating back to the murder of Blas Hernández and the suspicious death of Mario Cadenas. His first line of defense was to distance himself from such assaults, either by claiming a lack of knowledge of the violent event or refusing to address the issue of prior knowledge. Sometimes a sham inquiry was conducted, but in the end hardly anyone in the military was ever punished for perpetrating violence against civilians. This pattern would repeat itself time and again over his several decades in power. The threat of a military uprising was, more often than not, privately given as the reason for tolerating abuses against civilians. That Batista faced formidable challenges from within the military, there is no doubt. Whether those threats serve as justification for the frequent violation of civil liberties by the military is a subject that scholars of the period will debate for decades. Clearly, when Batista considered it important enough he was able to impose his will on his subordinates and dispose of even his most formidable opponents within the military.

The political climate of the period was tolerant of attacks on political opponents, both verbal and physical. The political opposition employed violence against the government and journalists it considered unsympathetic to the revolutionary cause, as in the case of the Guiteras supporters who tried to murder the director of a conservative-leaning newspaper.[108] The government responded with its own brand of political violence. There were no human rights champions in the Mendieta-Batista government and few in the political opposition.

The political challenge for Batista throughout the 1930s was to walk a tightrope between allowing a measure of civilian control of the government, while at the same time maintaining the loyalty of his troops and allowing them to take part in the fruits of victory. Too much power for the military on the surface was sure to lead to further confrontation with the public and pressure from Washington. It was a balancing act that Batista performed for many years.

CHAPTER 9

LABOR UNREST

The Mendieta-Batista government spent a good deal of its time trying to suppress and oppress the Cuban labor movement. The labor movement spent a good deal of its time trying to topple the government. At least part of the labor movement's antagonism was based on the difficult economic conditions of Depression-era Cuba. Strikes were a by-product of these straitened circumstances and were endemic throughout the United States, Europe, and Latin America.[1] In this regard, Cuba was no different. What distinguished the Cuban situation, and made it more explosive than that of many other nations, was foreign control of the economy. Strikes in Cuba during the 1930s almost always had international implications. The largest employers were foreigners—U.S. corporations. Large strikes inevitably involved the United States and officials from the State Department, who were sworn to uphold U.S. rights and privileges on the island. Foreign involvement turned labor strikes into nationalistic movements aimed at challenging not only the Cuban government, but the United States.

As a result, the Mendieta-Batista government pledge to maintain "order" in a Cuban society wracked by violent revolutionary movements was automatically identified with foreign interests. The growing influence of U.S. Ambassador Jefferson Caffery further contributed to that perception. Caffery's public and private consultations with Cuban political and military officials intensified throughout 1935 and 1936, and he became an important power broker. Private correspondence between Caffery and Welles reveal that his role in Cuban politics was even more far-reaching than alleged by opposition newspapers and politicians. The opposition alleged a lot about

Caffery. The ambassador's visits to Camp Columbia and the Presidential Palace were front-page news and editorial fodder. Caffery's frequent horseback-riding trips with Batista were the subject of rumor and gossip by the Cuban press. But for all the speculation about Ambassador Caffery, the opposition and Cuban public were unaware of the pervasive nature of his interference in, and manipulation of, day-to-day Cuban affairs. Following in the tradition of previous powerful U.S. ambassadors, there was no piece of political minutiae in which Caffery did not involve himself. Enoch Crowder in the early 1920s virtually dictated the designation of the national cabinet. The importance of Sumner Welles in the removal of President Machado has been recounted in this work. However, in the wake of the Platt Amendment's abrogation, the role of the U.S. ambassador was supposed to be different. It was not. Caffery was the last ambassador to serve in Cuba while the Platt Amendment was still in force. Even though it was discarded by the two governments in May 1934, Caffery acted, and was treated, as if it were still in place. He would be the last U.S. ambassador to wield so much power and influence.

The combination of a volatile and politically active labor movement, a weak Cuban government, and a visible foreign presence made for social dynamite. The strikes of 1934 and 1935 were withering and incessant. The Mendieta-Batista government passed one antilabor law after another. In February 1934, it enacted a series of laws prohibiting sympathy strikes, requiring unions to give eight days notice before going on strike, and setting tough prison terms for union activists who defied the government. In addition, by law, a list of worker demands were to be submitted to the Ministry of Labor, which then appointed a commission to determine the legitimacy of the demands and whether a strike was justified. Unions that did not follow these guidelines could be disbanded by the government and replaced by unions more favorably disposed to the government. Following a corporatist model implemented in parts of South America, including Brazil, delegates to the Ministry of Labor were to be selected from each workplace and report on whether collective bargaining agreements were being enforced. All collective bargaining agreements were to be placed on file with the Ministry of Labor.[2]

The more the government tried to legislate control of the labor movement, the less control it had. The labor movement, allied in large part with Grau's Auténticos and the Communists, ignored the government's mandates. In March 1934, an ongoing strike by thirty thousand tobacco workers escalated into a nationwide general strike when dock workers at the port of Havana refused to load tobacco on incoming ships. The sympathy strike by the dock workers was followed by walkouts by doctors, bus and truck drivers, rail workers, sugar cane cutters, and employees of the electric, gas, water, and telephone companies. The number of strikers eventually reached two hundred thousand. This was a startling figure considering that the entire population of Cuba in 1934 was just over 4 million, a number that obviously included a large number of children, women working at home, and retired individuals. In order to survive, the government employed the national police, army, and navy to break the strikes. In what would become standard operating procedure, labor leaders and strikers were jailed by the dozens, the military and police were called onto operate basic services, and disobedient unions were disbanded. Strike breakers were brought in from the provinces by the army to operate the ports, and the stevedores were given a deadline to return to work or lose their jobs. The stevedores returned, and the national strike collapsed a bit at a time. The government prevailed.[3]

The warring sides barely released their death grips before they resumed the struggle. There were hundreds of strikes throughout 1934, and crises emerged again in August and October. In August, the workers from the Ministry of Communications, specifically postal and telegraph employees, went out on strike seeking economic relief in terms of matters like back pay, but also making some political demands, including a purge of former Machado supporters from the government. In the case of the communications workers, strike breakers were again used, and the resolve of the workers began to buckle. However, a determined campaign of sabotage and an inability to fill all the empty jobs led to a compromise in which the workers gained some concessions from the government. On October 8, the National Confederation of Cuban Labor (Confederación Nacional Obrera Cubana—CNOC), an umbrella labor organization controlled by the Communists, called for a one-day general strike to destabilize the government. The government was forced to mobilize troops and assume control of many vital services. To keep the buses and trolleys in Havana running, soldiers were assigned to ride on all the routes. The general strike met with mixed results because several rival unions refused to heed the call.[4]

These were pyrrhic victories at best for the civilian elements of the Cuban government. With each strike, it became more evident that President Mendieta and his political allies could not control the country without Batista and the army. The more Mendieta relied on Batista, the more he was shunned by the political opposition. The more he was shunned by the political opposition, the more he had to rely on force. The labor strife ultimately destroyed Mendieta's political career. Batista's power base in the army and police remained secure despite the ongoing struggles, although he would forever be tarnished by the brutality required to keep labor in check. In contrast,

Mendieta's power base was battered by the strikes. His authority as a political leader was based on something less tangible than the guns and grenades
of the army and police. It was based on his ability to persuade and convince
the different political groups to follow him. Failing that, all he could do was
oppress the opposition. Like Grau before him, Mendieta became a political
leader with few followers.

The strikes of 1934 were only a prelude to the largest labor strike in Cuban
history. The general strike of 1935 nearly paralyzed the country. For a few
days in March 1935, it was unclear whether the Mendieta-Batista government
would survive.

THE STRIKE OF 1935

What became a general strike involving some half a million workers evolved
gradually, over a period of a month, from a series of smaller labor disputes
that were primarily focused on securing economic gains and better working
conditions. These disparate labor strikes ultimately merged into a national
movement aimed at ousting the government. There were three major participants in the strike: the teachers and students at primary and secondary schools
across the island; the students and faculty at the University of Havana; and
the political opposition, principally Grau's Auténticos and the ABC revolutionary movement. The Communist labor unions and Guiteras's Joven Cuba
played a smaller role, joining the strike at a late date, because of a dispute
over strategy.[5]

The strike by primary and secondary schoolteachers and students gave the
labor movement its national character. Most of the larger towns and municipalities had a school of some sort, although this was not true of much of
rural Cuba, and the student/teacher walkouts brought national issues down
to the local and personal level. The students and faculty at the University
of Havana served as the organizers of the strike. They saw and seized the
opportunity to deal the Mendieta-Batista government a crippling blow. The
university students rarely attended classes in 1934 and 1935, as they remained
on a constant war footing against the government. Strikes were a part of
the curriculum. One dispute with the government was barely settled before
another began. It was their political vision and leadership that turned the
disjointed labor strikes into a referendum on the government. The third
major component was the political opposition, which joined the general strike
movement as it picked up momentum in late February and early March. As
it reached its peak, the opposition urged its loyal workers in the various
ministries of the national government to join the walkout. The participation

of government workers divided the administration against itself. Basic services were suspended, and the government was at a virtual standstill. For several days, with the exception of the military and police, virtually no one in Cuba worked.

These developments are clear in hindsight, but no one, least of all the government leadership, was prepared for the mass labor movement that emerged in March 1935. The beginnings can be traced back to a strike by primary school students in Havana in the middle of February. The students walked out of their classes in response to complaints by the faculty about a lack of teaching materials, inadequate classroom space, substandard school breakfasts, and the failure to receive back pay.[6] The action by the young adolescents was another manifestation of the political culture that dominated Cuba throughout the nineteenth and twentieth centuries in which, at an early age, students were taught to challenge authority and act as "revolutionaries." The notion of ten- and twelve-year-olds declaring a strike and then setting up committees to meet with government officials runs counter to the expectations of North Americans and the citizens of many parts of the world. But it was not extraordinary in the Cuba of the 1930s, where for generations the youth were accustomed to playing a leading role in revolutionary movements. Besides meeting with government officials, committees of grammar school students were sent to major Cuban newspapers and magazines to outline their position and demand a government response. Photos of the young strikers and a list of their names appeared in many of the publications.[7]

Students and teachers had good reason to be dismayed with educational conditions. Decay was evident at all levels of Cuban education. The system was in crisis. Political corruption and difficult economic times left the public school system often lacking even the bare essentials. Just days before the strike by primary school students, a powerful and influential civic and cultural organization, La Sociedad Económica de Amigos del País de La Habana, issued a scathing report on the state of Cuban education. In the report, the prestigious, nonpartisan organization alleged that three hundred and fifty thousand Cuban children received no education at all because of a lack of rural schools. The rural schools that did exist were little more than one-room straw huts. Students attending schools in Cuban cities and towns found severe overcrowding and inadequate materials, including a lack of books, pencils, and pens. The state of education on the island was so desperate, according to the report, that Cuban "civilization was in grave danger." The report went on to warn that "within a short period of time we are in danger of occupying the lowest cultural level of any people in this part of the world."[8]

The walkout by primary school students in Havana occurred at a time when tensions were already high between the government and students at the university and secondary levels. Days before the strike by primary students, university students concluded a successful strike against the government in which they secured additional funding for the institution and guarantees that jailed students were to be freed. Just days after returning to classes, however, there was talk of another university strike because of the delay in freeing imprisoned students. A similar confrontational approach to the government existed at the island's six provincial *institutos*. In the Cuban educational system an *instituto* was the equivalent of an advanced high school and early college learning center. Secondary school students frequently supported strikes by university students and faculty.

As the strike of primary school students was beginning to unfold, a tragic confrontation between the police and secondary school students in Havana exacerbated tensions and led to an expansion of the educational strike. On the evening of February 11, as students from the Instituto de La Habana were completing their classes, an accident involving three automobiles and a trolley car occurred in front of the school. Several hundred students went to the scene to observe the aftermath of the collision. Within a short time police arrived to find a crowd of some three hundred people at the crash site. Exactly what happened next is uncertain, but police reported that a shot was fired at them from the crowd. The police fired back, wounding a nineteen-year-old bystander, who died later that night. A second victim died the following day. Five others were wounded.[9] The police account of the shooting was widely disputed. The news magazine *Bohemia* declared that incidents of the sort are to be expected from a "government that has lost the support of the people" and must rely for its survival on the "guardians of order," the magazine's pejorative nickname for the military and police.[10]

The immediate result of the shooting was the declaration of a twenty-four-hour strike by the faculty and students at the *instituto*, which was then extended to seventy-two hours, and then indefinitely. The governing body of the *instituto*, on February 12, called on the government to "respect the lives of the [students]" and to render "justice [to those responsible] for the lamentable deeds."[11] As a condition of ending the strike, they demanded that the government guarantee the safety of the students.

University students wasted little time in calling a meeting of the University Strike Committee (Comité de Huelga Universitaria) to debate a response to the shooting. The committee met on February 13 and declared a seventy-two-hour strike. Another meeting was set for February 18, and that gathering developed into the first of several crucial turning points. Until then, there was no public talk of converting the strike into a nationwide political move-ment to oust the government. In addition to the educational strikes, a series of other ongoing, but unrelated, labor issues were occupying the govern-ment's attention, including a complaint by truck drivers over highway tariffs and tensions with doctors at municipal hospitals in Havana over salaries and working conditions.[12] Economic and workplace issues were of principal importance to these workers. The students and faculty at primary schools were also principally concerned with conditions in the schools.

The emphasis shifted away from workplace concerns on February 18, when the University Strike Committee voted to go on an "indefinite strike" and issued a series of demands directly challenging the Mendieta-Batista govern-ment and specifically the military. The demands included an end to special military courts for military personnel, termination of military supervision of the national police, a return of constitutional guarantees, the freeing of political prisoners, and the elimination of the Urgency Courts, which had been established to adjudicate acts of violence against the government. Eco-nomic demands, such as more funding for primary schools, especially those in rural areas, were tagged onto the end of the student manifesto.

By the time of the February 18 meeting, university students were clearly beginning to develop a national strategy to cripple the government. One student leader, Celestino Hernández, encapsulated the budding strategy when he noted that the government relied on the income provided by industry and business to survive. "The University as such does not constitute a source of production for the government, so the paralyzation of its educational activities will not motivate it. To win the demands and pressure Mendieta and Batista it is necessary for us to take our strike to the sources of pro-duction, the working sectors, undermining the government at its base and creating a problem for it."[13] The student, in a reference to U.S. economic power on the island, referred to Cuba as a "Yankee colony." Three days later, the faculty at the University of Havana, in an act of solidarity, voted to sup-port the student strike. The United States was a central topic of discussion at the faculty meeting as well, and a resolution to condemn Ambassador Caffery for "interference in national affairs" was debated, although ulti-mately rejected.[14] Sympathy strikes broke out at schools throughout Havana, and the movement quickly spread to the provinces. Soon the newspapers were littered with declarations from facilities across the island demanding justice and better conditions in the schools.[15] By the end of the month, edu-cation throughout Cuba was in a state of paralysis.

But educational paralysis was not the central goal of the university students. On February 22, the students called on all classes in society to support the

strike to secure a "Cuba based on a more just foundation."[16] In the following days, the students worked diligently to spread the strike to every industry on the island. It was in this period that the political opposition began to
mobilize in support of the strike. Grau's Auténticos issued a manifesto supporting the strike on February 21, while the ABC revolutionary movement
dispensed with public declarations and quietly backed the movement.[17] By
February 28, the university students declared they were no longer interested
in negotiating with a "reactionary and military regime which is carrying the
country into anarchy and disintegration."[18] The government itself must go.
The opposition news magazine *Bohemia*, in an editorial of February 24, spoke
of the strike's transformation from an educational protest to a national
antigovernment movement. The Mendieta-Batista government "does not care
whether the people can read, the schools are in miserable condition and the
teachers are indigent. The important point is that there should be enough
arms for its defense and soldiers to guard it." Only recently have the strikers seen the problem in "accurate terms," according to the editorial. "The
culture of Cuba will remain neglected as long as an anti-democratic imposition exists. Until the leaders of Cuba come from the people, they will not
feel the desire for improvement and a better life that the people feel."[19]

Although the strikers were probably unaware of it, their actions were ex-
acerbating deep divisions within the Mendieta-Batista government. The civilian and military wings of the government were in disagreement over how
to deal with the emerging crisis. Batista favored early intervention on the
part of the civilian government to avoid the inevitability of a clash between
the strikers and the military. To that end, the chief of the army wanted the
government to dock teachers' pay for the days missed. Initially, Mendieta
declined to heed this advice and tried to deal with each strike individually,
in some cases offering partial concessions. The president and his advisers
favored a strategy that called for splintering the strike movement by addressing the concerns of primary school students and teachers.[20] As the crisis
deepened, Batista became more and more exasperated with President Mendieta and considered removing him from power, a fact that emerged in the
form of rumor in the Cuban press.[21]

To make matters worse, two of the political parties with ties to the government, the Partido Acción Republicana, led by Miguel Mariano Gómez,
and the Conjunto Nacional Democrático, led by Mario García Menocal, initially refused to support the government against the strikers, perhaps waiting to see which side emerged standing from the fight. Another sign of the
divisions in the government were the resignations on February 22 of the ministers of education and commerce. Both men, professors at the University

of Havana, were threatened with the loss of their teaching positions at the institution if they did not resign from the administration. They chose the academy over the government.[22]

As the situation began to deteriorate, Batista quietly attempted to intervene in the matter with Minister of Justice Raúl de Cárdenas by questioning the government's "inertness" in meeting the "dangerous" challenge posed by the strikers. When nothing came of these efforts, Batista decided, on February 24, to ask Caffery to serve as an intermediary to President Mendieta. Batista prefaced his request by confiding to Caffery that elements within the military were urging him to take over as dictator in response to the threat posed by the strike. "As you know, it is the last thing I want to do, but the Government's inactivity and incapacity are only serving to furnish ammunition to the adherents of a dictatorship. I say this only to have you understand how hard it is for me to keep this job going and remain clear-headed," Caffery quoted Batista as saying. That very evening, Caffery sent word of Batista's concern to Mendieta. As a result, Mendieta met with Batista the following day (February 25) and tried to assure him that action would be taken.[23]

Yet several more days passed before a plan to dock teachers' salaries was announced by the government. In the interim, Batista remained dissatisfied with Mendieta and the civilian elements in the government, feeling certain that their failure "would result in probable disorders and bloodshed, for which the Army and Police would get the blame."[24] Furthermore, the talk of a military dictatorship continued, both inside and outside government circles. Laurence Duggan, a State Department official and confidante of Welles, visiting Havana at the time of the strike, wrote to Welles on February 28, that "propertied people are subtly suggesting" to Batista that he take the reins of power. Duggan believed that Batista was carefully considering his options in that regard. "My information indicates that he [Batista] is beginning to reach that stage of rationalization where to him the seizure of power seems to be the only way of ending the machinations of the politicians."[25]

There were sound reasons for President Mendieta and the civilian elements of the government to believe that their strategy of splitting the strike movement would work. Primary schoolteachers and students in their public declarations never voiced the same antagonism toward the government as their counterparts in higher education. Their emphasis, at least in public, was always on economic and workplace issues. They never made demands for a restructuring of the national government. In an effort to resolve the primary school strike, the government put out emergency bids for school materials on February 14. Two days later, the government began the process of distributing, across the island, seventy thousand blocks of paper, ten thousand pens, eight thousand pencils, and enough chalk for seven thousand classrooms. The government made several other concessions, including the approval of five thousand more school breakfasts and an increase in vacation time for the teachers.[26] The negotiations continued throughout late February and into early March, and on at least one occasion the government announced that an agreement was near.[27] The two sides ultimately deadlocked over economic issues in early March. Optimism about the possibility of reaching an agreement no doubt kept President Mendieta from docking teachers' salaries. As a result of the negotiating deadlock, however, the civilians finally gave in to Batista's wishes on February 28.

The strategy of splintering the strike movement failed. As it turned out, that failure had catastrophic consequences for President Mendieta and the civilian wing of the government, just as it did for the strikers and the political opposition. Within a few days, virtually all government power was transferred to the military. There had been a gradual erosion of civilian rule since September 4, 1933. The general strike created a landslide. It would be years before civilian politicians regained even the mediated power they wielded under President Mendieta.

Breaking the Strike

There was a lull in the conflict between the strikers and the government in early March. After having declared their desire to bring down the regime, the university leaders began negotiations with the political opposition to make it happen. The organization of the strike was facilitated by the fact that the University of Havana had been granted autonomy by the government, which meant that the military and police were forbidden from entering the grounds. This gave students and union organizers the ability to meet and plot strategy. It took several days to develop and implement a plan that called for the paralysis of transportation and commerce throughout Cuba. Unions in each workplace were approached individually, and they in turn needed to form strike committees to decide whether they wanted to join the national movement. There were as many reasons for joining the general strike as there were unions, and a definitive scholarly study on the general strike awaits an author.

The political opposition harbored divergent views about how to proceed against the government. Guiteras and the Communist labor leaders argued that an armed military movement was necessary to complement the efforts of the strikers. Armed units were necessary to fight the military and police. Without an armed movement, the strikers were vulnerable to attacks and intimidation. Guiteras, through his representatives, urged the strikers to hold off on a general strike until a fighting force was in place. He pledged to speed up his plans for an armed uprising in Santiago in eastern Cuba. The Communists were wary of a call for a general strike, because their own efforts in that regard had been put down by the government in October.[28] Grau's Auténticos and the ABC revolutionary movement were more enthusiastic about the prospects of success.[29] Both groups worked to mobilize their workers within the administration in a massive effort to plunge the government into the abyss. The Auténticos were a powerful voice in the trade union movement, and they put that muscle behind a strike. Despite concerns by the Guiteristas and the Communists, the strike movement steadily built up momentum throughout the first week of March. In the end, Guiteras and the Communist labor movement reluctantly supported the strike, although perhaps too late to do much good. Their decision to join the general strike derived from a desire to prevent reformist elements within the political opposition from exercising total control over the movement.

In the first days of March, the newspapers were filled with speculation about when the general strike would begin. The strike committee at the University of Havana worked to coordinate the many different unions joining the movement. Many of the unions wanted to strike immediately, but the students urged restraint until a critical mass could be reached. They wanted to deliver one swift and disabling blow to the government.[30] But instead of a knockout punch, the general strike resembled a series of waves crashing down on the administration. The first wave came on March 6, when several bombs went off at the Havana customshouse, injuring seven. The bombing heralded the intensification of the strike and served as a warning to government employees who opposed the walkout. The following day, workers at many of the government ministries never showed up. Over the next four days, the strike spread throughout the government workforce, as one strike committee after another approved of joining the walkout. A second wave broke on March 10 and 11, when many of the trade unions joined the work stoppage.

The list of industries and unions that took part in the general strike could fill pages. Most of the railroad unions participated, shutting down transportation across the island. Workers in virtually every ministry of the national government walked out, including education, commerce, labor, agriculture, justice, and sanitation—even the foreign ministry. Many municipal government workers, including those in Havana, Cienfuegos, and Cárdenas, refused to work. The national lottery was suspended for lack of a workforce. Trolley car and bus service in Havana was interrupted, as was truck traffic throughout Cuba. The few truckers who took to the roads found them laced with large quantities of nails. The lack of available transportation limited food and gasoline deliveries. Graphic artists went on strike, closing most of the nation's newspapers. Doctors, tobacco workers, barbers, soap and shoe factory workers, all refused to work. From March 7 to March 11, when the strike reached its maximum effectiveness, virtually no one worked at his or her job. If the military and police did not run it, it did not run.

The general strike produced its fair share of irony. One such moment occurred after the resignation, on March 5, of the second education minister in eleven days. When the third education minister was sworn in on March 7, he took his oath in a virtually abandoned building. As a reporter covering the event put it, "The employees and functionaries shined by their absence the entire day."[31] In many cases, soldiers and police officers were forced to run the trolleys that crisscrossed Havana, and the number of accidents increased dramatically. The New York *Daily News* ran a photograph of one of the accident scenes with the headline: "Guns Can't Run Cars."[32] Doctors from the military were assigned to civilian hospitals to treat the infirm and keep the facilities open. Soldiers ran the trains and buses. Sailors ran the customshouses at the ports.

Batista would not let the strikers win. At 1 a.m. on March 9, President Mendieta suspended all remaining constitutional guarantees, abolished university autonomy, and temporarily suspended the judiciary, essentially handing over all power to Batista and the military. A "state of war" was declared two days later. Mendieta had little choice. His political followers were few, and the bureaucracy so vital to the running of any government was on strike. The military was all he had left.

Batista was optimistic he could break the strike. "He [Batista] is convinced that if the Government maintains a firm stand the situation can be satisfactorily settled without bloodshed," wrote Caffery in one of several telegraphs he sent to Washington on March 7.[33] For every blow landed by the strikers, Batista answered with overwhelming force. When the bombs went off at the Havana customshouse on the morning of March 6, the army answered by encircling the University of Havana and searching those leaving the campus. The next morning the army occupied the university and closed its doors. A search of university grounds uncovered a cache of weapons. As the strike spread to most of the government ministries and the trade unions, Batista assigned military governors to all the provinces, naming Pedraza, his tough right-hand man, as the military governor of Havana. A 9 p.m. curfew was established in Havana, unauthorized meetings were forbidden, and groups of three or more were not allowed to walk the streets. Government employees were authorized by law to use deadly force against those trying to keep them from work. Hundreds of union activists and university students were jailed, with some estimates of the incarcerated exceeding one thousand.

The death penalty was established for those engaging in sabotage or firing on members of the military and police. Impatient at the judicial process inherent in a death penalty proceeding, some members of the military and police took matters into their own hands. The bullet-riddled bodies of political opponents began to appear in empty lots in and around Havana. One of the best-known victims was Enrique Fernández, a former subsecretary in the interior ministry under Guiteras, who was taken into custody by Major Mariné. Fernández's wife went to the police station pleading to see her husband, but the authorities did not allow her to speak with him, and she went home in the early morning hours of March 11. Not even the fact she knew of her husband's detention was sufficient to save his life.[34]

The public disposal of the bodies was clearly a message of terror directed at opponents of the government. This sort of desecration became a trademark of Batista regimes under extreme pressure, and the tactic was employed with great frequency in the late 1950s as the revolutionary movement against the Batista government gained momentum. Batista cannot be linked directly to the murder of political opponents and the public exposure of their bodies; however, the pattern, under his leadership, is unmistakable. At times of crisis, the dead bodies of his political opponents frequently turned up in public parks and vacant lots.

It is of historical importance to clarify the issue of brutality and murder during the general strike of 1935 and in its immediate aftermath. That the strike was brutally suppressed there can be no doubt. The number of people killed during the height of the strike, March 6 to March 11, ranges between ten and fifteen, figures that include several soldiers and policemen killed in fighting. In Havana, there were nightly gun battles between authorities and revolutionaries. When the sun went down, bombs went off throughout the city. Similar outbreaks of violence occurred in various locations throughout the island, including Santiago and Cárdenas. An attempt was made on the life of a close Batista ally, Liberal Party leader Ramón Vasconcelos, on March 6. Vasconcelos was wounded in the arm and recovered, but one of his bodyguards was killed. A plan to assassinate Batista by detonating explosives as his car passed was uncovered and foiled.[35] Pacifists were in short supply on all sides of the conflict.

As so often happens during violent political upheavals, each side stretches the facts to make its arguments more convincing. Lying and disinformation can be powerful weapons in a political struggle to the death. Such was the case of an accusation made by former Cuban President Carlos Hevia, a member of the Auténtico Party who fled Cuba on March 12, landed in Miami, and proceeded to tell the U.S. media that between March 9 and the day of his arrival "200 persons have been massacred." The front-page headline in the New York *Daily News* read: "Cubans Kill 200 in Riots."[36]

This distortion, and worse, would be repeated for generations to come in some of the most important historical works on the period, including the monumental study, *Cuba: The Pursuit of Freedom* by Hugh Thomas, and the books by revolutionary historian José Tabares del Real.[37] Contemporary Cuban sources of the period, including an opposition newspaper, estimated the death toll at ten, with fifteen wounded.[38] U.S. military intelligence estimated between ten and thirteen were killed, a figure revised downward several days later.[39] Even after Batista left power for the first time in 1944, no evidence of larger massacres during the general strike surfaced, despite the fact that his enemies in the media were legion. In the future, the death toll may be revised upward when comprehensive studies on the impact of the general strike outside Havana are completed. But, as it stands now, there is no historical evidence to suggest a death toll even remotely approaching the hundreds.

For most of the eighteen months since the uprising of September 4, Batista had preferred to work in the background. Occasionally he surfaced, issued a statement, and then retreated to Camp Columbia, where he conducted his government business. The man from Banes generally left center stage to the president of the republic. But, during the general strike, his leadership became transparently obvious. Batista entered the Cuban political spotlight and never fully relinquished it again. After the general strike, he began attending public functions, political banquets, and ribbon-cutting ceremonies, and he started to greet civilian dignitaries from foreign nations, in short, acting as the head of state.[40] Within a year, he would announce his own social and educational program for Cuba. All these trends became more pronounced in the months after the general strike, but their beginnings can be found in his handling of that event. The transformation from Colonel Batista to Batista the political leader had begun.

During the strike, Batista ran a virtual shadow government from Camp Columbia. On a daily basis, government ministers flocked to his headquarters to consult with him on the ongoing actions. Sometimes they liked what they heard and sometimes they did not. Upon leaving a meeting with the chief of the army, the finance minister was asked to comment on the outcome. "I do not know a word about anything and I do not want to know anything. On the other hand, he [Batista] knows everything. Go there and ask him."[41] Batista issued two statements to the nation during the height of the general strike, communicating the tough stand he intended to take against labor and the political opposition. In the first, issued March 6, Batista said that when strikes arise from "supreme need" and make "logical and humane demands we should be the first to aid them." In contrast, he claimed, the current strike was driven by "sectarian" interests and would only result in a "greater evil." He went on to comment that "it would be imprudent for the Government and ourselves, the Constitutional Armed Forces, to shirk responsibilities and not put an end to what for our country represents a disgrace and a blot as a civilized nation." The army chief concluded by stating that the government and army were capable of and willing to use "the instruments of order at our disposal."[42]

If Batista's first message to the strikers was not clear enough, he was even more strident on March 8, after government employees joined the general strike. "We can assure you that the strike will totally fail and it is the firm proposition of this government to be invariable in these plans, along with the Armed Forces, which completely seconds them." The strikers should not expect that the work stoppage will lead to "another 12th of August [date of Machado's ouster] or a 4th of September [date of Céspedes' removal]," Batista warned. Those who believe "this [government] will fall are "mistaken" and "stupid."[43] In his statement, Batista outlined a series of new measures aimed at curtailing the strike, including plans to replace striking government workers if they did not return by March 11. New appointments were proceeding, he said, and those replaced would not be allowed back into government service. Strike organizers would be permanently removed from their positions regardless of whether they returned to work or not.

A visit to a government minister on March 10 by a delegation of ABC members, Auténticos, and university professors was one of the first indications that the strike movement was in trouble. In that meeting, later reported to Ambassador Caffery, the strike leaders said they were "disposed to support Batista and make agreement with him on sole condition apparently of his changing Mendieta for another president."[44] Gone was the talk of ousting the military. The strikers, apparently to save face, were willing to settle for the political head of the nearly powerless President Mendieta. The proposed deal went nowhere. As the tide turned, the parties affiliated with Menocal and Gómez, on March 10, following their habit of supporting the winning side, came out in support of the government.

The strike leaders had good reason to be concerned about the movement. Within the next forty-eight hours, the strike began to unravel as government employees trickled back to work on March 12. Apart from military and police brutality, the threat to permanently replace government workers played an important role in breaking the strike. The government began to selectively replace government workers from lists of interested applicants compiled during the strike. Striking customs workers were among the first targeted for replacement.[45] Replacement workers were escorted to their jobs under heavy military and police escort. In Depression-era Cuba, there were plenty of unemployed and poorly paid workers coveting government jobs. So many people applied for education positions that the government had to announce that no more were available.[46] Their willingness to cross a picket line in search of economic opportunity was key to ending the strike.

Another fatal blow to the strike was the decision by the two unions representing primary school teachers, whose complaints were the original impetus for the strike, to begin negotiations with the government to save their jobs. Union leaders asked for an extension of time, beyond the March 11 deadline, to confer with their members nationwide. The extension was granted, and the teachers agreed to return to work on March 14, having secured no major concessions from the government. Most of the teachers at the other levels of the Cuban educational system returned to work as well. Their defeat was complete. In the coming days and weeks, dozens of teachers were fired across the island. Some school districts were reorganized; others were eliminated. The director of the Instituto de La Habana, scene of the tragic trolley car accident a month earlier, was summarily dismissed.[47] A similar fate befell workers at many government ministries, whose posts were taken by loyalists of Mendieta's Nacionalista Party. The failure of the strike gave the government the perfect excuse to cull employees with hostile political affiliations.[48]

As the workers began to return, political opposition leaders, like Carlos Hevia and dozens of others, began to depart for exile in the United States. No effort was made to block their departure. "Batista says also that he is perfectly willing for various leaders of the subversive movement, who are now in hiding, to leave the country: he does not want to shoot people and will be only happy if the leaders get out of the country as quickly as possible," Caffery wrote Welles.[49]

By March 14, the general strike was over. For the second time in just over a year, the government had suppressed a nationwide walkout. For decades, Cuban revolutionaries debated the ingredients required to topple a government, and while a general strike was considered an important weapon, most strategists came to believe that it alone could not accomplish the task. This theory would be tested against Batista again in the 1950s. Fidel Castro, a boy of eight at this time, would remember the lessons of 1935 when he waged his own struggle against the man from Banes.

Death of Guiteras

The defeat of the general strike further reinforced Antonio Guiteras's conviction that only an armed revolutionary movement battling against the army and police could topple the Mendieta-Batista government. He died trying to create such a movement.

After the Grau government fell in January 1934, the former interior minister declared his hostility to the new regime and went into hiding. Except for a brief period in August 1934, when he was imprisoned, Guiteras spent the last sixteen months of his life incognito in and around Havana. To evade authorities, he moved from apartment to apartment every few days. It was his custom to walk the streets of Havana in disguise, typically wearing sunglasses and a hat. His followers were careful to frequently change the automobiles used to transport him around the city. (Guiteras did not know how to drive.) The less he was seen, the more he captured the Cuban imagination. Some considered him a gangster—the Dillinger of Cuba. In fact, the U.S. State Department branded him "Cuba's Public Enemy No. 1."[50] Others saw him as a brave revolutionary struggling to free the nation from the grip of a military dictatorship.[51]

The goal of his organization, Joven Cuba (Young Cuba), was the creation of a "revolutionary dictatorship," to guide the island to greater social justice. As Guiteras and his followers saw it, the principal problem for Cuba was its "colonial state." This lack of national sovereignty was responsible for a Cuban "economic structure" that "does not serve collective needs from inside but produces income calculated by and for those from outside."[52] Once in power, Guiteras wanted to implement large-scale land reform, nationalize public service companies (most of these owned by U.S. investors), confiscate and nationalize all industries that did not provide their workers with a living wage, dramatically increase education spending, and initiate a literacy campaign. All of these programs were to be part of the first phase of a socialist revolution.

His methods were controversial. During his months in hiding, Joven Cuba took part in a series of assassination attempts, bank robberies, and kidnappings, all aimed at promoting a revolutionary uprising. These acts served two primary purposes: some, such as the June 15, 1934, attempt on President Mendieta's life, were intended to destabilize the government, while others, such as the $50,000 in protection money extorted from a sugar plantation owner in late 1934, were to pay and train a revolutionary army. An entire wing of Joven Cuba (La Comisión Nacional de Acción) was dedicated to planning and executing attacks on the government and raising funds for the uprising. Another wing of the organization (La Comisión Nacional Técnica

Insurreccional) was responsible for recruiting and training members for the revolutionary army. Prospective recruits were required to fill out enlistment forms detailing their knowledge of firearms and explosives. One of these forms was obtained by U.S. military intelligence and passed on to Batista.[53]

Guiteras's audacity and willingness to shoot it out with the military and police made him a figure of awe. One political associate remembered the enormous daring with which Guiteras handled a police roadblock. As the police officer approached the vehicle in which Guiteras was riding, he pulled out his pistol. When the officer looked inside the vehicle, Guiteras pointed the pistol at him and asked, "Who are you looking for? For me?" The nervous guard waved the car on, assuring Guiteras that he was not the one being sought. Whether true or not, the story reveals a great deal about the image of a fearless revolutionary that he and, after his death, his followers worked so hard to promote.[54]

The events surrounding his capture in August 1934, illustrate again Guiteras's penchant for risk taking. On the afternoon of August 8, acting on a tip, police entered a home in the Vedado section of Havana where Guiteras was hiding. When he became aware of the raid, Guiteras tried to use a sheet to climb down from a second story window, but he slipped and fell, fracturing an ankle. Although he was in great pain, he limped for a block before he was apprehended by police. Guiteras was then taken to a hospital emergency room under heavy police guard. Several of his followers organized an armed rescue operation, but they were dissuaded by the heavy police presence in and around the hospital, and they feared their leader might die in a shoot-out. Guiteras was charged with conspiracy against the government and the unlawful possession of a firearm. The charges were dismissed by the courts, and he was released from custody on August 15, 1934.

One of Joven Cuba's most brazen acts was the kidnapping of Eutimio Falla Bonet on April 3, 1935, just a few weeks after the failure of the general strike.[55] "Operation Falla" was personally approved by Guiteras as part of his grand plan to finance a military uprising. The daily habits and movements of the twenty-eight-year-old target, the son of a wealthy and prominent Cuban family, were carefully observed for a period of several weeks until his routine was fairly well established. On most evenings, Falla Bonet visited his brother-in-law's Havana home and usually departed the residence around 9 p.m. A decision was made to seize him after his visit of April 3. Guiteras reasoned that because this visit was typically Falla Bonet's last stop of the day, no one would be suspicious of his disappearance for several hours.

Falla Bonet entered his chauffeur-driven Packard shortly after 9 p.m. on the designated evening, and it was followed by two cars containing five armed men from Joven Cuba. When Falla Bonet's car reached a quiet street en route to his hotel, the first Joven Cuba car pulled up alongside it, and forced it to the right side of the road. The driver quickly exited the vehicle and pointed a pistol at the chauffeur. The second Joven Cuba vehicle pulled up behind Falla Bonet's car, and four men carrying machine guns came out and surrounded the Packard. Falla Bonet and his chauffeur were taken to one of the vehicles and transported to a home rented especially for the purpose of housing him. The chauffeur was kept in a room above the garage, while the wealthy businessman was taken to the dining room. After a short while, a member of Joven Cuba told Falla Bonet he was in the custody of a group of revolutionaries and that a "contribution" to the cause was required.[56]

The cost of his freedom would be $300,000. When Falla Bonet protested that he did not have sufficient funds, the kidnappers displayed an intricate knowledge of his finances, obtained through their research, and assured him that he indeed did have that much. Falla Bonet then signed a letter authorizing his attorney to hand over the money to a representative of Joven Cuba in one-hundred-dollar bills at a public location. Upon receipt of the money, Falla Bonet was released. Guiteras was ecstatic over the success of the operation. Looking at the money laid out on a bed, he told a follower, "Here we have the revolution in our hands."[57]

The kidnapping caused a sensation in Cuba. The ransom was one of the largest ever paid, and it brought increased pressure on the Cuban government to apprehend Guiteras. A quick exit for Guiteras and Falla Bonet's money were now essential in order to usher in the next phase of the revolutionary struggle. The goal was to smuggle both into Mexico. There the revolutionaries expected to receive sympathetic treatment from President Lázaro Cárdenas, a leader of Mexico's own revolutionary struggle and a frequent critic of the United States. In Mexico, Guiteras hoped to organize a force of trained revolutionaries to land in Oriente Province in eastern Cuba and wage an armed struggle against the Mendieta-Batista government.

Throughout April 1935, Guiteras considered a variety of escape plans, including traveling as a passenger on a commercial steamer. Ultimately, he chose to depart from nearby Matanzas Province from a small colonial-era fort, known as El Morrillo, built in the eighteenth century to discourage attacks on the city of Matanzas. The scheme called for Guiteras and about fifteen close followers, including two women, to meet on the grounds of the old fortress on the evening of May 7, 1935. There they would board a rented yacht and depart for Mexico. In order for the plan to work, Guiteras needed the cooperation of supporters in the Cuban Navy, which he had heavily courted during his tenure as interior minister.

The key to the plan was Captain Carmelo González Arias, the commander of the Third Marine Company, headquartered in the city of Matanzas. At one time, El Morrillo served as the headquarters of the company, but they had recently relocated, and only a small garrison was kept at the fort. As it turns out, Captain González was a boyhood friend of Guiteras, and efforts were made to bring him into Joven Cuba. Overtures were made to the captain, and he expressed his willingness to aid the revolutionary organization. Although some doubted his sincerity, González was taken on several occasions to meet Guiteras, who made the final decision to bring the captain in on the escape plan. The decision to trust González cost Guiteras his life. An ambitious man, González informed the Chief of the Cuban Navy Ángel Aurelio González of his contacts with Guiteras, who in turn informed Batista. A trap was set.

In the closing days of April, some of Guiteras's followers began making their way to Matanzas to prepare for their departure. On May 2, members of Joven Cuba reported to Guiteras that raids by the military were increasing in Matanzas, and some were worried about the escape operation. Guiteras pushed aside those concerns and decided to proceed with the plan. In this same time period, perhaps in an effort to gain intelligence about the government, Guiteras asked a friend to contact Lieutenant Colonel Ignacio Galíndez and request a meeting. Galíndez informed Batista of the proposal, and the army chief approved of the reunion. Batista instructed Galíndez to offer Guiteras a cabinet-level position in the government in return for his support. As part of the script, Galíndez was to inform Guiteras of the government's general knowledge of his escape plans, although not the specifics. The Galíndez-Guiteras meeting was set for 1 p.m. on May 6 at a Havana rooming house.

Galíndez arrived first and was shown into the living room, where he was introduced to several members of Joven Cuba. Shortly thereafter, Guiteras arrived, and the two men were directed to an upstairs room where they spoke for approximately two hours, all the time Guiteras holding a newspaper with a pistol wrapped inside of it. There were apparently no eyewitnesses to the meeting, so what we know of it comes from a letter written by Galíndez in 1946 and published in *Bohemia* and from secondhand accounts by Guiteras's followers.[58] As per Batista's plan, Galíndez offered Guiteras a cabinet position, an offer Guiteras rejected because of his dissatisfaction with government policies. As the meeting neared its conclusion, Galíndez applied political pressure on Guiteras by informing him that Batista was aware of his plan to rent a yacht and sail from the coast of northern Cuba.[59] Guiteras denied he was planning to go into exile and promised to hold another meeting with Galíndez in the near future.

Lost in history's shadows are the reasons why Guiteras chose not to heed Galíndez's warning. Guiteras told one follower that he thought Batista wanted him to stay in Cuba, so they could continue negotiating his possible participation in the government. Overconfidence may have been his undoing. Shortly after the Galíndez meeting, one follower remembered him remarking, "Many times they have said they were going to catch me and nothing ever happens."[60] The following morning (May 7), doubts about his safety and that of his followers began to trouble him. A member of Joven Cuba visited Guiteras and reported that during a bus ride an acquaintance told him that the "whole world knew" of the revolutionary leader's imminent departure from Cuba.[61] Despite these warnings, Guiteras moved ahead with the escape plan.

Guiteras left Havana bound for El Morrillo around 5:30 p.m. on May 7. He wore a white suit, sunglasses, and a finely woven straw hat bent low to cover his face. To complete the ensemble, Guiteras sported a machine gun and carried $4,000 of the Falla Bonet kidnapping money. Another $18,500 was concealed in the false bottom of a typewriter. These funds were to be used to cover the group's expenses while in Mexico.[62] The car trip to the old Spanish fort took about two and a half hours. El Morrillo, with its single tower, overlooks the western side of the Bay of Matanzas.[63] The small fort is two stories high, with gun emplacements every few feet on the first floor. The wooden roof is covered with orange tiles in the Spanish style. When Guiteras arrived, he entered the fort to find his colleagues dining on roast pork, beer, and *yuca* (a popular Caribbean root plant).

The first concern of Guiteras and his followers was the whereabouts of the yacht, which had not been sighted. Captain González, who was present at the fort for much of the evening and early morning, periodically went out into the bay with a small boat in search of the vessel. As it turns out, the yacht was detained in and around Havana because of heightened naval activity and was many hours behind schedule. The boat would, in fact, never arrive. After eight hours of waiting, several members of the party suggested the trip be postponed. Guiteras rejected those suggestions and decided instead to send out two parties, each consisting of two men, on separate missions. The first pair was to secure more weapons in the event that a defense of El Morrillo became necessary. The other two were sent back to Havana to check on the status of the rented yacht. Both left the old fort around 4 a.m. on the morning of May 8, 1935. They did not have to travel very far before they noticed a growing military presence on the roads leading to El Morrillo. They became suspicious, and a messenger was sent to warn Guiteras of impending danger. He would arrive too late. At about this time, Captain González made one last trip on his boat in search of the yacht and never returned.

The attack commenced two hours later, shortly after 6 a.m. One member of the Guiteras party noticed the lights of several trucks, filled with soldiers, approaching the fort. The word went out throughout El Morrillo, and Guiteras and the other startled members of Joven Cuba congregated on the first floor. One with military experience, Carlos Aponte, a Venezuelan who had fought with Augusto Sandino in Nicaragua, took charge of the situation and ordered them to exit by a side door and venture into the woods. One can quite easily picture the chaotic nature of the retreat as they filed out of the fort into the semidarkness. Three members of the Guiteras party ran into the woods and escaped. The remaining members marched through the underbrush as the soldiers began to pursue them. Catching a glimpse of them, one of the soldiers opened fire. The attack dispersed them into even smaller groups. One member of Joven Cuba decided to make a stand and opened fire on the soldiers with his machine gun. In the exchange of gunfire he was wounded and taken prisoner, along with several other members of the group.

Guiteras, Aponte, and two others avoided capture and continued their efforts to break the army's encirclement. The four eventually reached the banks of the Canímar River and walked alongside it until they found a cave with several fishermen plying their trade. At gunpoint, Aponte ordered one of the fishermen to transport them away from the area. As they were preparing to leave, the soldiers approached, and one member of Guiteras's party opened fire on them. Guiteras and Aponte retreated again and soon found themselves on the banks of a dry stream. The soldiers chased them and fired at them again. One bullet entered Guiteras's heart and killed him instantly. After a gun battle in which one soldier was killed and several wounded, Aponte was shot in the head and died moments later. The remaining members of Joven Cuba were arrested.

Within a few weeks of Guiteras's death, the North American author and journalist Carleton Beals made the following prophetic observation about the dead revolutionary: "Now if they could, but in the not distant future, the Cuban people will burn Ambassador Jefferson Caffery and Colonel Fulgencio Batista in effigy; but they will write songs about Antonio, they will build monuments to him. Some day his statue will stand on the Malecón beside the monument to the *Maine* and the statue of the great Antonio Maceo. There will be no statue for Batista. There will be only bitter memories of Caffery."[64]

Beals could have been talking about post-1959 Cuba, where Guiteras is firmly ensconced in the revolutionary pantheon of martyrs. Every act of his short life (he died at the age of twenty-eight) has been chronicled in great detail in articles and books. Revolutionary scholarship has produced no biographies of Batista, Grau, or many of the other important figures of the period. But there is a thriving Cuban scholarship on the life of Guiteras, with a new book released every few years. In the introduction to a recent work, a prominent Cuban government official wrote that Guiteras and Fidel Castro are the two most significant Cuban political figures of the twentieth century and that there is an ideological and political "thread" that binds them.[65] A colleague of mine remarked several years ago that symbolically "Guiteras is Fidel."[66]

With this in mind, any assessment of his life must come face to face with the power of Guiteras the symbol. The Guiteras myth overshadows Guiteras the man. Several more generations may need to pass before a critical assessment of his career can be made. Just as some of the revolutionary works tend to romanticize his violence, so did earlier assessments dismiss him as merely a thug and gangster. Assessments such as the following by Batista biographer Edmund Chester were typical: "He was always on the side of disorder and terrorism, a leader of the militantly disgruntled minority." In the same section, Chester describes Guiteras as a "dime-novel personality who led a group of malcontents into a campaign of terrorism."[67] The director of *Diario de la Marina*, whom Guiteras had tried to assassinate the prior year, wrote a few days after the events at El Morrillo that "Guiterismo [Guiteras's political thought] was and is like a Creole rage that bites to the right and left, and never established roots in the heart of the people."[68]

New inquiries about Guiteras need to assess his political career from the perspective of his accomplishments. While Guiteras has often been compared to Fidel Castro, he is clearly not Fidel. They are similar in that they both favored armed struggle as a revolutionary tool and they both sought to establish insurgencies in eastern Cuba by training a revolutionary force in Mexico. But the similarities end there. Guiteras's track record of building and holding together political coalitions is unspectacular at best. In early 1934, he broke with Grau and the Auténticos and established his own political organization, one that never even came close to gaining the leadership of the opposition. After he died, Joven Cuba gradually eroded, and most of the remaining members eventually rejoined the Auténticos in 1937, so clearly the institutional framework he established was unable to survive his personalistic leadership. Guiteras's ongoing conflict with the Communist leadership and his suppression of them as interior minister in the Grau government needs to be explored further. Given the nature of the Communist government in Cuba, this is not a topic that is likely to be championed there any time in the near future. In any future assessment of Guiteras, his callous attitude toward human life, such as in the case of the execution of Juan Blas Hernández, needs to be placed alongside his obvious bravery and willingness to die for his ideals. Just as in the past he was treated with too much disdain, today he is treated with too much reverence.

In the scholarly literature, the Guiteras-Batista relationship is frequently portrayed as a life-and-death struggle between two sworn enemies. There is considerable evidence to support this interpretation. Guiteras, after all, hatched a plot to arrest and execute Batista in November 1933, a plot that nearly cost the colonel his life. Batista's handling of Guiteras at El Morrillo differs greatly from the treatment he extended to other members of the political opposition, whom he allowed to flee into exile after the failed general strike. Batista, who knew the specifics of the planned escape, could have allowed Guiteras to sail away into exile. Instead, he made the decision to detain him, knowing it might cost Guiteras his life. Batista did not make a public statement on the death of Guiteras, but his aide Major Jaime Mariné made the following remarks: "The elimination of Guiteras represents a great benefit for Cuba. Not only does it remove a perturbing factor from the country's life but it may save many youths who might have been misguided enough to join Guiteras's cause."[69]

CHAPTER 10

THE ELECTIONS

OF 1936

President Mendieta's political career died during the general strike; all that was left was to wait for the interment. That came nine months later, in December 1935, when he resigned in a squabble over upcoming elections. During his last nine months in office, Mendieta was forced to preside over an electoral process largely dictated to him by Ambassador Caffery and Colonel Batista. He continued to serve as the lightning rod for most public criticism. The civilian politicians taking part in what remained of the political process were, for the most part, unwilling or unable to attack Batista or Caffery. They settled, instead, for using President Mendieta as a punching bag. Gone were the private suggestions from Washington or Camp Columbia that Mendieta should seek an elected term of office and serve for another four years. As far as Caffery and Batista were concerned, the only remaining role for Mendieta was to sit in the presidential hot seat until it could be handed over to an elected president. One political opponent, in exile in Mexico, described Mendieta in the waning months of his presidency as "Mister Nobody" (Don Nadie).[1]

TIME FOR AN ELECTION

In 1935, the central goal of U.S. foreign policy toward Cuba was to push forward with a plan for presidential and congressional elections. Welles and Caffery, the architects of the post-Machado policy, were in the uncomfortable position of having to defend the removal of one dictator (Machado) and his replacement by another (Batista). Elections were intended to dispel that unsightly image at home in the United States and abroad in Cuba and Latin America. One of the most eloquent critics of U.S. Cuba policy was Leslie Buell, president of the Foreign Policy Association, who maintained a heated private correspondence with Welles throughout the year. "Sooner or later critics inevitably will point out that the Roosevelt administration intervened to rid Cuba of one dictatorship only to create a more terrible one," Buell wrote Welles in a letter dated May 27, 1935. In the same letter, Buell discounted the State Department's assertion of nonintervention in Cuban affairs. "It seems to me impossible to deny that during the last two years the State Department has consistently attempted to choke off the possibility of real revolution in Cuba, both political and social, hoping to divert developments into 'Constitutional' channels."[2]

Of course, Welles publicly denied any U.S. interference in Cuban affairs, and he did so privately, to Buell, as well. "I wish again to affirm, however, that at no time has this Government, either directly or indirectly, attempted to 'choke off the possibility of real revolution' or otherwise interfered. I have no doubt that our policy has been misinterpreted in some quarters, but this does not alter the true facts of the matter."[3] Few believed Welles at the time, and scholars and journalists have written volumes about U.S. interference in Cuban internal affairs. One might be able to excuse Welles's assertions about noninterference as the typical rationalizations of a powerful man trying to justify difficult decisions. Perhaps, one could argue, that at least Welles believed these assertions—that is, were it not for the overwhelming evidence in his own private papers. Even the most skeptical observers of U.S. Cuba policy could not have imagined the level of interference documented in minute detail by Welles and Caffery in their private correspondence. On a daily basis, Ambassador Caffery dispensed wisdom on political alliances, electoral formulas, and campaign strategies, whether he was asked for his opinion or not. Caffery put it to Welles this way in one of his letters: "The hardest nut to crack is, of course, this matter of the elections because it has required and still requires my constant daily hammering."[4]

Caffery and Welles wanted an election, but they wanted a certain type of election—one that guaranteed that Batista would continue to operate in the background as a stabilizing force. They willingly accepted Batista and the army's dominant role in Cuban politics, which is what motivated the army chief to allow elections in the first place. Any presidential candidate must come to a "perfectly sincere, frank, understanding with Batista," Welles pointed out in a July 11, 1935, letter to Caffery. Welles, the chief Latin America policymaker for the Roosevelt administration, opposed the formation of a revolutionary opposition party and its participation in the elections. "In all probability, the army would get highly exercised as to the nature of the campaign before many weeks had passed and, on the plea that these political leaders were inciting to rebellion, undertake repressive measures which would vitiate the freedom of the campaign and make the holding of anything approaching honest elections almost impossible."[5] In short, the U.S. State Department wanted an election with a moderate opposition and an outcome it could control. These Cuban elections were a Washington confection.

Carlos Mendieta was one name the State Department did not want to see on the ballot in the presidential elections, scheduled for December 1935. Mendieta had become a divisive figure in Cuban politics, and no major political party would agree to participate in elections if he was a candidate. Of course, most of the center-left political opposition was in no position to take part in elections because their leaders were either in exile, in prison, or dead. This did not concern Washington policymakers like Welles and Caffery, who could not care less whether the Auténticos, Communists, or Joven Cuba took part in the elections. For the sake of legitimacy, however, they needed Cuban conservatives, now organized under the banner of the Conjunto Nacional Democrático to participate in the elections. The Conjunto, headed by former President Mario García Menocal, who served from 1913 to 1921, was opposed to a Mendieta candidacy.[6] At sixty-nine, despite a series of infirmities, General Menocal, a leader of Cuba's independence struggle, was a key political figure and remained so until his death in 1941. The rivalry between Menocal and Mendieta dated back several decades, and their dislike for each other surfaced as a major issue later in the electoral process.

The Conjunto was a powerful political party with a viable organization in every province and major city and town on the island. As a result of shrewd political maneuvering on the part of Menocal and party leaders, it had survived the Machado era and the subsequent years of violence. If it took part in elections, it would provide a formidable challenge to Mendieta's Nacionalista Party and several smaller allied parties. In fact, in an electoral census conducted prior to the elections, in October 1935, the Conjunto registered by far the most members—419,000 of a total 1.1 million registered voters. That figure was one hundred thousand more than Mendieta's Nacionalistas, which registered the second-most members. Of course, the largest political party may have been Grau's Auténticos, which did not take part in the electoral process. Given the abstention of the Auténticos, the participation of the Conjunto was essential. If Mendieta was on the ballot, the Conjunto would not be, so Mendieta had to go.

Easing Mendieta Out

It was in the best interests of Cuba, according to Welles, if Mendieta accepted "that his task is to see his country through the provisional period and to turn over the government to whomever the people may freely elect."[7] The first person that needed convincing of this was Mendieta, and Caffery quickly set about that task. When on April 22, Mendieta asked Caffery for advice on a future presidential run, the ambassador counseled against it.[8] The following month, when Mendieta expressed a lingering desire to enter the campaign, Welles urged Caffery to be more direct in his discussions with the president. "I wonder, however, in view of the gravity of the situation, if you could not at an early moment see the President at his country place alone and talk the problem over with him in a personal way."[9] Caffery expressed optimism that Mendieta would do whatever they wanted him to do. "I am convinced that, at an intimation from us that he should not run, he would no longer consider doing so: in other words, he will gladly follow any advice we give him on the subject."[10]

To further nudge the process along, Caffery expressed his doubts about a Mendieta candidacy to Batista, who up until late May viewed a run by Mendieta in a favorable light. On May 23, Caffery met with the colonel to discuss plans for the December elections. At the meeting, Caffery reported that Batista was willing to back away from a Mendieta presidential candidacy "if I thought that unwise." Perhaps feeling a little guilty about double-crossing Mendieta, Batista asked Caffery to break the news to the president. The issue reached a climax over the course of the next week when Mendieta realized that his political options were narrowing. On May 26, the president met with Batista and agreed to issue a statement on June 1 saying that he would not seek the presidency. Caffery described Mendieta's attitude to being forced into early retirement as "splendid" and "very positive."[11]

But the coming months would prove that Mendieta's agreeableness was a facade. He would go to considerable lengths to delay and sabotage the upcoming presidential and legislative elections. One way he tried to block Caffery and Batista was to withhold support for a political coalition they were trying to build, behind-the-scenes, to assure the victory of a candidate acceptable to them. In September, Caffery wrote to Welles that Mendieta's forced withdrawal from the race was "still a source of bitter grievance to the President."[12] Regarding Mendieta's procrastination in supporting the Caffery-Batista political coalition, the ambassador wrote in October: "It is of course, very hard for Mendieta to agree to any combination which definitely leaves him out of the [Presidential] Palace next May."[13]

As might be expected, the Mendieta-Batista relationship soured. The president refused to appoint a Batista ally to a key cabinet position and declined to replace the chief of the Cuban Navy, who was creating a public spectacle by gambling away large sums at the casinos.[14] At one point, President Mendieta contemplated a showdown with Batista by calling for the resignations of Lieutenant Colonel Pedraza as chief of police and five militarily allied cabinet ministers.[15] Open confrontation, however, was not Mendieta's way, and he decided against such a drastic plan. He preferred passive resistance and benign neglect. As the head of the Nacionalista Party, Mendieta's cooperation was crucial in crafting a political coalition for the upcoming elections. This required Batista to meet with Mendieta frequently in the months prior to the election to secure his support. Inevitably, Mendieta would happily agree to Batista's proposals and then do nothing to implement them. Batista was able to obtain from Mendieta "only fair words and no appropriate action."[16]

The fact that Batista could not exercise force against Mendieta provided the president with a powerful weapon, because to do so would place the colonel, rather than Mendieta, at the epicenter of national politics. For Batista, there were still great advantages to working in the shadows, and the president knew this. Even though Batista had begun his metamorphosis from military leader to politico, the time was not right for a public admission of his political influence. Caffery served as a crucial mediator between Batista and Mendieta and kept their conflict in check. It took constant badgering on the part of Caffery to get Mendieta to move in the desired direction. Caffery expressed his frustration to Welles in an October 26 letter: "You cannot possibly realize how I had to hammer at him, often day by day, and how many times I have had to get him to undo things that he has done."[17] In the end, however reluctantly, Mendieta generally complied with the wishes of Caffery and Batista.

With Mendieta soon to be out of the presidential equation, Batista and Caffery needed a candidate with whom they could work. This was a tricky issue, because Batista did not want a Menocal victory out of concern that the old general would prove too independent. If Menocal and the Conjunto learned of Batista's aversion to them they could pull out of the elections, completely discrediting them.[18] Defeating the Conjunto required Batista to deeply engage himself in the political process and in the job of building a coalition among the three remaining political parties. "He [Batista] definitely wants to get together a political combination that can easily win the elections by a comfortable majority, and I believe that he will succeed in getting such a combination together," Caffery reported to Welles.[19] This was no easy task, because the Conjunto, with 419,000 registered members, represented just over 37 percent of the eligible voters. In second place were the Nacionalistas with 317,000, followed by the discredited Liberal Party of Machado with 244,000 members, and the party of former Havana Mayor Miguel Mariano Gómez with 140,000 members. The math was simple: if the Conjunto made an alliance with any of the three other parties, it would almost assuredly win the presidency and control of the Cuban Senate and House of Representatives.

Miguel Mariano Gómez was the man around whom Batista and Caffery chose to build a political coalition.[20] There were a lot of reasons for choosing Gómez. His Partido Acción Republicana was small, accounting for only about 13 percent of eligible voters, but it provided a base upon which to build. Mendieta, the Nacionalista standard bearer, was out of the question, and no candidate from the Liberal Party, discredited by its association with Machado, could hope to win the presidency. In fact, the Liberal Party was disbanded by law at the end of 1934, only to be legalized again several months later, at Batista's private urging, so they could take part in the elections. Beyond his party affiliation, Gómez had other strengths, including his family's traditional ties with the Liberal Party. His father, José Miguel Gómez, was the country's second president and a wildly popular figure. The younger Gómez broke with the Liberals during the Machado dictatorship, so he had the advantage of having Liberal Party ties without being a Liberal. As mayor of Havana, he gained executive experience and managed city affairs capably. And, Gómez had the blessing of Sumner Welles and the United States. "It just happens that Gómez unites the conditions of availability with the qualities of Liberal origin and 'revolutionary' antecedents together with his demonstrated ability as Alcalde [mayor] of Habana," Welles wrote Caffery in October.[21]

This is not to suggest that the process of selecting Gómez was a linear one. There were many twists and turns along the path to Gómez's selection as the presidential candidate for a three-party coalition that included the Nacionalistas, Liberals, and Acción Republicana. Recounting all the wheeling and dealing, backstabbing, and political chicanery would entail a book in itself. At one point Batista favored an alliance between the Conjunto and the Nacionalistas, the two largest parties, but that plan was nixed when it became obvious that General Menocal would not surrender the presidential nomination to another candidate. Then there was the problem of President Mendieta's intransigence and the desire of other Nacionalista leaders to nominate a candidate from their own party.[22] The Liberal Party was also split. Batista loyalists favored Gómez, while another faction favored Batista's long-time friend, soon-to-be foe, Carlos Manuel de la Cruz.

The first attempt at a three-party alliance, with Gómez as the standard bearer, collapsed in late June, only to be revived again in September. An agreement between the Nacionalistas and Acción Republicana to make Gómez their presidential candidate was not reached until early October, barely two months before the election. These two parties were not strong enough to assure a victory over the Conjunto, so Batista and Caffery still needed to get Liberal Party support for Gómez. Their efforts were complicated by Cruz, who refused to withdraw his candidacy. Liberal Party members were placed in the awkward position of rejecting someone from their own party in order to back an outsider, Gómez. The National Assembly of the Liberal Party could not agree on a candidate, so Provincial Assemblies were called, and the delegates to those assemblies voted to back Gómez. It took until the middle of November, with the election just a month away, to establish the Tripartite Coalition (Coalición Tripartita), as it came to be known.

Cruz would not go down without a fight. His supporters appealed the decision of the Liberal Provincial Assemblies to Cuba's Superior Electoral Tribunal, charging that Liberal delegates could not back Gómez over Cruz. In what appeared to be a death blow to the Caffery-Batista political coalition, the electoral tribunal voted on November 19 to side with Cruz and void Liberal participation in the alliance. The primary beneficiary of the ruling was Menocal and the Conjunto, who knew that without Liberal Party support Gómez could not win.[23]

The elections were now in jeopardy. A decision by President Mendieta and the cabinet to amend the electoral tribunal's ruling could lead to the withdrawal of Menocal and the Conjunto from the race. If the government did nothing, they would likely end up on the losing end. Menocal would be elected president, and there would be dissension in the army. In his political meetings, Batista maintained that he would accept Menocal as president, but his actions indicate that he was willing to do whatever he could to prevent that scenario. Caffery noted that Batista was "very much disturbed [by the electoral tribunal's decision] but determined to find some satisfactory way out."[24]

AN ELECTORAL EXPERT

The way out was soon charted by Welles, sitting in Washington, who in late November began two days of negotiations with a Conjunto representative. This, of course, fits the Cuban political pattern of the time. Rather than accept the decision of its own official body, the Superior Electoral Tribunal, Cuban political leaders sought guidance in Washington. Conjunto leaders had nothing to gain by sending a representative to Washington to meet with Welles, yet years of conditioning caused them to do just that. The State Department, with its own agenda, was quite willing to offer its "impartial" advice, knowing it would further its aims. Three State Department memorandums detail the conversations between Welles and Conjunto representative Pedro Cué on November 25 and 26. They reveal, once again, the pervasive nature of U.S. interference in the Cuban electoral process. The conversations followed a now predictable trajectory. After declarations of impartiality by Welles, the assistant secretary of state applied his special brand of pressure, always careful not to say too much, yet to say enough to impart his meaning.

At the first meeting, on the afternoon of November 25, "[Welles] said that it would not, of course, be proper for him to propose any solution [to the electoral impasse], but that he did wish to inform Dr. Cué in all sincerity that he thought it essential that the Government and the interested parties in Cuba get together and arrive at some satisfactory basis for procedure." Then Welles emphasized Washington's recent economic assistance and the trade agreement with Cuba and noted "that the vast majority of the Cuban people would not knowingly take action which might eventually affect their continuance." Cué noted that it was not in the best interests of the Conjunto to reach an agreement with the other parties. Rather than address that issue directly, Welles repeated his mantra of impartiality and said Washington was interested in removing all impediments to elections, no matter which party had a grievance. The conversation concluded when Welles told Cué that he was confident Conjunto leaders would be willing to negotiate a solution once they "recognized the gravity of the situation."[25]

At the second meeting, on the morning of November 26, Welles came forward with a proposal aimed at solving the electoral impasse. He proposed the appointment of a U.S. electoral expert to "study" the Cuban Superior Electoral Tribunal's decision and "make recommendations" of a nonbinding nature. Cué requested time to relay the proposal back to Conjunto party leaders. By the time Cué returned in the afternoon, Welles had what he wanted: an agreement by the Conjunto to accept an electoral expert selected by Washington.[26] Even though the electoral adviser's recommendations would not be binding, Welles must have known those recommendations would provide justification for proceeding with the elections.

The State Department's first choice of an electoral adviser was Howard Lee McBain, dean of the graduate school at Columbia University. Several years earlier, McBain helped draft an electoral code for Cuba, but he declined this latest assignment, out of fear that his decision would be used to further the candidacy of a candidate favorable to the State Department and

Batista.[27] The State Department's second choice, Professor Harold Willis Dodds, president of Princeton University, accepted the invitation to serve as an expert in the Cuban electoral debacle. The timetable called for Dodds to issue his findings in early December. The controversy forced Cuban officials to postpone presidential and congressional elections until January 1936.

No seer was needed to determine Dodds' ultimate findings.[28] The way the mission was constructed predetermined its outcome. In briefing Dodds, Welles made it clear that the "sole interest of this government lies in the restoration of the political stability of Cuba and that, in our judgment, such restoration depends inevitably on the holding of fair elections in which no undue pressure is brought to bear and in which all of the parties participate." While Dodds's stated job was to review the decision of the Superior Electoral Tribunal, his real job was to save the elections. He was well aware that if he did not circumvent the decision of the electoral tribunal, the three government parties would withdraw, and there would be no election. The State Department tried hard to publicly distance itself from the Dodds mission, even though Welles and Caffery briefed him extensively. "But, I do feel that his usefulness will be greatly increased if he deliberately creates the impression that he is operating independently of the Embassy and will be guided in his decisions solely by his own estimate of the situation," Welles wrote to Caffery in late November.[29]

Dodds informed Ambassador Caffery of his decision two days before he made it public. In a December 4 letter to Welles, Caffery noted that Dodds would refrain from attacking the decision by the Superior Electoral Tribunal, but "he will attempt to find a solution by suggesting that the [Cuban] Government issue a decree which, in democratic fashion, will allow the Liberals to support whatever candidate they desire to support."[30] This was just what Caffery, Welles, and Batista wanted: a recommendation by Dodds that would ensure victory for their handpicked president by allowing the Liberal Party to support Miguel Mariano Gómez. Of course, the idea of allowing the elections to proceed with three candidates—Gómez, Menocal, and Cruz—was never considered a real option, because it did not fit the outcome carefully constructed by Batista and the U.S. State Department. As soon as Dodds's decision was made public on December 6, Mendieta and the Cuban government acted quickly to enact a decree-law codifying his recommendation. Victory for the Caffery-Batista political coalition was once again assured.

But there was still one major hurdle to be surmounted before the twisted and tortured elections could take place, and that was to assure the participation of a political opposition. Menocal and Conjunto party leaders were well aware that the election was stolen from them. Even prior to the revocation of the electoral tribunal's decision, Menocal became cognizant of the far-reaching interference of Batista and Caffery in molding the three-party coalition against him.[31] In mid-November, Menocal considered withdrawing the Conjunto from the race. The unexpected decision by the electoral tribunal, disqualifying Liberal Party participation in the alliance, breathed new life into the party. Dodds's decision took that electoral life away. For a little over a week, Menocal pondered his options. A draft document withdrawing all Conjunto candidates from the election was drafted, and Menocal considered going into exile in the United States.[32]

In the end, however, Menocal and Conjunto Party leaders decided to stay in the race. Decades later, one party member attributed the decision to Menocal's "great feelings of love for Cuba."[33] Patronage probably had as much to do with the decision as patriotism. From a pragmatic standpoint, it was better to gain a share of power than no power at all. Menocal was a veteran of the crooked politics of Cuba, having stolen his own presidential election in 1916.[34] Even in a losing cause, the Conjunto was likely to win a fair number of congressional seats and mayoralties throughout the island. These positions translated into power and patronage, the lifeblood of any political party. Menocal also feared that a decision to withdraw from the elections might split his party, with some dissident factions remaining in the race.[35]

The wily elder statesman of Cuban politics demanded a price for remaining in the election, and that was the resignation of President Mendieta. Rather than attack Batista and the army or Caffery and the State Department, Menocal targeted his old political rival. In an interview in *Bohemia*, Menocal declared that he no longer had "confidence" in President Mendieta's "impartiality."[36] As a face-saving measure, the attack on Mendieta made sense, since any political party wishing to participate in the government would need the cooperation of Batista and Caffery. President Mendieta was the easy target. On December 11, 1935, bowing to pressure from Menocal and the Conjunto, Provisional President Mendieta resigned. Secretary of State José Barnet y Vinageras, a colorless, career diplomat was sworn in to replace him. The ABC, in its underground newspaper, noted that Menocal merely succeeded in removing "the puppet from the scene." The puppet show orchestrated from Camp Columbia and the United States Embassy would continue.[37]

Although Mendieta was an affable and congenial man, his twenty-three months in power were typified by brutality and bloodshed. Upon entering office, Mendieta, who had a preference for white cotton suits, pledged that his attire would never be soiled by the "blood of the people." Remembering his remark, one journalist remarked that upon his departure, Mendieta's suit bore "many red stains."[38] For all his shortcomings, Mendieta wielded a measure of power as president and served as a small check on Batista's power. Civilian power and authority reached a low ebb in the next few years, and Mendieta's successors found themselves totally eclipsed by Batista.

President Mendieta returned to the life of a private citizen. He never realized his dream of an elected presidential term. His role was now to play the elder statesman, periodically emerging to voice an opinion on a political or policy matter. For a time, he retained some influence within his party, but over the next five years that dissipated as well. He lived to age eighty-seven, dying in 1960, a year after the triumph of the Cuban Revolution. He was one old soldier who did fade away.

Election Results

The legitimacy of the election was questioned both inside and outside of Cuba. Critics were unaware of the extensive interference by Caffery and Batista; however, they criticized the race on the grounds that it excluded a large portion of the Cuban electorate, particularly the Auténticos. During the campaign, the opposition news magazine, *Bohemia*, ran weekly editorials lambasting the exclusion of revolutionary segments from the electoral process. In articles and cartoons they frequently compared the elections to a "conga line" with the same worn-out politicians and political ideas going around and around. Their political cartoons were particularly biting. In one, a blind man rejoices because he cannot see what is going on around him. In another, a man wakes up after being asleep for more than three years. Based on initial news reports, he believes the dictator Machado is still in power. In still another, the presidential candidates appear at a theater, and a member of the public asks them about the current show. The candidates respond in unison that they "do not know, because they have no program." The political satire went on for months. Only Batista and the military were spared insult and rebuke, probably out of a sense of self-preservation. The news magazine indicated as much in a cryptic political cartoon of Batista, drawn with exaggerated Afro-Cuban features, in which the caption simply reads, "*Tabú*" (Taboo).[39]

The race lacked the spirited debates and intensive campaigning of prior elections. There was little excitement in the electorate, and in fact only 60 percent of the eligible voters cast ballots, despite the fact that these were the first elections in nearly eight years. In an editorial on December 1, *Bohemia* noted the strangeness of the campaign: "Today no one speaks, everyone is silent; [the politicians] have no defined programs, and regardless, they are incapable of even making vague allusions to their programs."[40] The conservative-leaning *Diario de la Marina* belatedly echoed similar sentiments.[41] There was a lifeless quality to the campaign because there was in fact little difference between the two main candidates, Gómez and Menocal, who both were members of the old political establishment. As a result of illness, Menocal did not campaign aggressively, and Gómez was the only candidate to tour the island. As a further disincentive to vigorous campaigning, Menocal knew he was going to lose no matter what he did.

Even a political figure like Cosme de la Torriente, a close ally of the United States and a former cabinet member under President Mendieta, repeatedly complained privately to Welles of U.S. interference in the electoral process. In a November 5, 1935, letter, Torriente noted that "out of every ten people, eight say that Miguel Mariano [Gómez] is the candidate being imposed by Batista, Caffery and yourself." Seven weeks later, Torriente, who did not make his critique publicly, described Dodds's electoral plan as a "monstrosity." The result of the electoral machinations, Torriente wrote, was to create a "repulsion" among the public toward the elections and to ensure that the

Criticizing Batista could be dangerous business. *Bohemia* published this political cartoon by an anonymous artist on August 11, 1935. Its caption simply says, "*Tabú*" (Taboo).

life of the next government would be "precarious." He concluded his letter of December 21 1935, by accusing Caffery and Dodds of "meddling in our electoral problems."[42]

In the United States, the Foreign Policy Association vocalized in public the concerns raised in private by its president to Sumner Welles several months earlier. On the eve of the election it released a blistering commentary on the Cuban elections. "The campaign has thus come to be substantially a contest between the two old parties—Conservatives and Liberals—while the groups which sought a New Deal are outlawed. Their leaders have lost faith in democratic processes and plan armed revolution." In the same article, the author, Charles A. Thomson, noted that elections in Cuba were important to the U.S. administration because President Roosevelt was himself up for election in November and he did not want it to appear as if the "United States had employed its influence to overthrow one dictatorship—that of Machado— only to have it succeeded by another."[43]

There was never any doubt about the outcome of the elections held on January 10, 1936. Miguel Mariano Gómez's victory had been secured weeks before by political chicanery, intervention by Washington, and impressive coalition building by Batista and Caffery. The Tripartite Coalition swept to an easy victory in the congressional races as well as winning all 24 Senate seats (4 seats for each of the six provinces) and 90 of the 160 seats in the Cuban House of Representatives. Always thinking ahead, Batista, in his growing role as political kingpin, worked behind the scenes to secure twelve minority Senate seats for the losers. In order to do so, the Constitution was retroactively amended to increase the size of the Senate to thirty-six members. The seats were irrelevant in terms of overall control of Congress, but Batista knew that by doling out the patronage, he was buying a measure of loyalty or at the very least minimizing the chances of a future confrontation. "[Batista] feels that if something of this kind is not done, members of the Conjunto will eventually align themselves with the Auténticos and start trouble," Caffery wrote to Welles. Assistant Secretary Welles initially objected to the modification of the Cuban Constitution for these purposes but ultimately backed down.[44]

Caffery and Batista got their man—the forty-six-year-old Gómez was scheduled to be sworn in on May 20, 1936. The question was, would he remain their man or become his own?

CHAPTER 11

IN THE SHADOW
OF BATISTA

The year 1936 marks an unheralded watershed in the history of the Cuban Republic and the career of Fulgencio Batista. The period of revolutionary turmoil was at an end. The general strike of 1935 was the last gasp of revolutionary forces seeking to redefine the core of Cuban society. As historian Robert Whitney puts it, Batista had succeeded "in disciplining the masses."[1] The venue for political struggle now shifted from the battlefield of the streets to the halls of government and the backrooms where political deals were made. Reform, not revolution, would typify the next fifteen years of Cuban history.

Batista evolved with the times. Since September 4, 1933, he had been the unrivaled leader of the Cuban military, and that constituency remained a key element of his support throughout his entire public life. But the sword proved to be double-edged. The more Batista used it, the more reliant he became on his hierarchy of lieutenant colonels who administered regiments in every province of the island. Individually, they were no match for him, but if several were ever to ally against him, they could pose a significant and, perhaps fatal, threat. There were other disadvantages to the use of brute force to settle political disputes. Violence created instability throughout Cuban society, and instability was bad for business. As long as order was maintained, business could function more or less normally, and the United States would look the other way as Batista charted the island's destiny.

Although only thirty-five in 1936, Batista understood power and the many forms in which it manifests itself. Besides the power that the armed forces provided with the bayonet, the military also served Batista as a base from which to dispense lucrative public works contracts across the island. He had secured a blank check from President Mendieta to make improvements to military facilities without the prior approval of the cabinet or the president. Military facilities were largely neglected in the years after independence, but in the mid 1930s, Batista initiated an enormous reconstruction program throughout the nation. The squalid old wooden barracks were replaced with new structures of bricks and mortar. He lavished money on Camp Columbia, the name of which was changed to Ciudad Militar (Military City), building a host of new medical, recreational, and housing facilities there. Libraries, social clubs, theaters, and swimming facilities were built at every major military installation on the island.[2]

Even more important, Batista used his power base in the military to nudge and push his way into the civilian political arena. At first, he tiptoed onto the political stage, but later he became the main attraction. His first major foray into the world of elective politics came with his efforts to construct a winning coalition for the elections of 1936. After securing a presidential term for Miguel Mariano Gómez, Batista spent the next four years trying to build a winning coalition for himself. As one of the principal architects of the Tripartite Coalition, along with Ambassador Caffery, Batista became one of its most influential political leaders. Although the coalition eventually disintegrated, Batista, over the next four years, cobbled together some of the remnants into a political coalition with himself as its standard bearer.

Violence was no longer the first weapon employed against disagreeable political opponents. Batista wielded the civilian politicians' own system, of which they were the alleged masters, against them. When President Gómez proved uncooperative, Batista employed his political allies against him, rather than a battalion of soldiers. Political disputes were now to be settled in the political arena. Gradually, the revolutionary parties came to accept the fact that Batista-backed governments could not be ousted by force, and that the electoral process was their best avenue to power. The Auténticos; the Communists, operating through a front party known as the Partido Unión Revolucionaria (Union Revolutionary Party);[3] and the ABC revolutionary movement rejoined the electoral process in the late 1930s. Former President Ramón Grau San Martín, leader of the Auténticos, emerged as Batista's most formidable rival, and the two waged a series of masterful political duels over the course of the next decade.

For Batista to succeed as a political leader, he needed a social agenda. The first move in that direction came in February 1936, when he established an army program to bring education to rural Cuba. Batista, who saw the army as part of the Revolution of 1933, not apart from it, developed a plan to hire sergeant-teachers and assign them to rural areas ignored by the existing public education system. This proved a controversial undertaking and led to one of the defining moments of his early political career. The rural schools program was part of a comprehensive set of reforms, modeled on New Deal initiatives in the United States. Batista followed up these achievements with a sweeping national program, introduced in 1937, and known as the Triennial Plan, which dealt with everything from forest conservation to guaranteeing a percentage of the sugar cane sales to small growers, known as *colonos*.

The Batista of the late 1930s was engaged in the tricky process of extricating himself from his own military success. He sought to transform himself into a civilian politician while still maintaining control of the military, and he began to prefer business suits to army uniforms. But his enemies never saw him as anything but a military man, and they sought to constantly remind the public of the origins and foundations of his power.

President of the Banquet Circuit

Provisional President José A. Barnet Vinageras would scarcely merit more than a footnote in Cuban history were it not for the fact that his passivity and political inexperience paved the way for an enormous expansion in the power of the military and its chief. For all his weaknesses, Mendieta repeatedly stalled, delayed, and resisted Batista's efforts to expand military power at the expense of civilian authority. Barnet, a career diplomat, lacked Mendieta's stature and prestige. He had none of his predecessor's credentials as an independence fighter and revolutionary leader.

A tall man of regal bearing, Barnet was a virtual unknown to the Cuban public when he was sworn into office on December 13, 1935, after Mendieta's resignation. He belonged to the world of diplomatic functions and protocol, having served twenty-eight years in Cuba's foreign service.[4] Barnet, seventy-one at the time, had spent much of his adult life outside of Cuba in various diplomatic posts from Beijing to Paris with stops along the way in Liverpool and Rio de Janeiro. As if to make the alienation between provisional president and public complete, Barnet was not even born in Cuba, but rather Barcelona, Spain, and his wife, whom he met while stationed in Paris, was French.

Barnet was more comfortable holding a cocktail napkin than the reigns of power. He was completely out of his element in the brutal, bloody politics of 1930s Cuba. In his five months in office, December 11, 1935, to May 20, 1936, Barnet distinguished himself for the exquisite banquets he hosted at the Presidential Palace. One North American reporter wrote that Barnet "lived quietly in the Presidential Palace, entertaining with dinners which were culinary triumphs. He performed his traditional presidential duties with correctness and an eye to protocol. The public was hardly conscious that a president lived in the palace."[5] Cuban historian Portell-Vilá, a political opponent of the provisional government, said Barnet carried out his official functions with "aplomb" but never strayed into questions of public policy and politics.[6] One of Batista's closest military advisers, Major Arístides Sosa de Quesada, reflecting on Barnet fifty years after his presidency, acknowledged that "he did not have much power. He did not seek power, either. [Barnet] was not interested in government matters, or anything related, because the problems were very difficult."[7]

President Barnet became the object of ridicule and mockery by the opposition press. The news magazine *Bohemia* missed few opportunities to poke fun at his invisible role in the government. One political cartoon depicted three young boys pretending to be members of the government. One boy tells another to play the role of president. The second boy says with some trepidation that "he does not know what to do." The first boy reassures him that he can learn the part quickly, "by doing all that he is told."[8] *Bohemia* saved its most stinging commentary for the transition period when Barnet handed over power to Gómez. In its edition of May 24, 1936, the magazine ran an enormous photo of a bespectacled Barnet with a short caption summarizing his presidency that read, in part: "He retires from his office leaving in his wake insipidness and incomprehension. And, while the nation has confronted the most grave of problems, President Barnet, in an interminable succession of feasts, receptions and banquets, has taken glory from ostentation in bitter contrast with the poverty and lack of resources of our people. His passage through the Presidency marks an era of superficiality which results in a dignified finishing touch to his entire life."[9]

Batista seized on Barnet's inexperience and the power vacuum created by the lengthy transition period between Mendieta and Gómez to push through the State Council a series of bold initiatives that transformed the armed forces into the largest social-service provider on the island. On February 27, 1936, the Civic-Military Rural Schools (Escuelas Rurales Civico-Militares) program was established, allowing the army to construct, run, and maintain schools throughout the Cuban countryside. In the days that followed, the provisional government passed a virtual grab bag of additional public service programs, all of them to be administered by Batista and the army. Time was of the essence, because the newly elected Congress was scheduled to take office in April, and passing additional legislation would prove more cumbersome and subject to public scrutiny. On March 30, the National Corporation for Public Assistance was established with the aim of assisting poor families receive medical care and other social services by distributing profits from the national lottery. The Technical Public Health Service was established on the same day. It was responsible for establishing and regulating a uniform code of sanitary law, keeping vital health statistics, research on infectious diseases, and oversight of food and water quality. The next day, the State Council created the National Tuberculosis Council, a program near and dear to Batista because of his brother's death from the disease years earlier. The tuberculosis council was charged with improving treatment facilities throughout the island, building additional facilities where necessary, and establishing a national, state-of-the-art sanatorium for treating the most serious cases. Also established, in separate legislation, was the Civic-Military Institute, which was to construct and oversee orphanages for children who had lost parents in work-related accidents. It was to serve the children of civilian workers as well as those of military and police personnel. A certain number of international scholarships to children from throughout Latin America were awarded to these schools. All of these ambitious programs were placed under a supervisory agency, established and administered by Batista, known as the Corporative Council of Education, Sanitation, and Charity.[10]

Ambassador Caffery virtually ignored President Barnet during his five-month occupancy of the Presidential Palace, a pattern dating back to when Barnet served as Mendieta's secretary of state. While functioning as Cuba's chief diplomat, Barnet complained privately that Caffery, going against all diplomatic protocol, "paid him no attention" and spoke directly to Batista when he wished to resolve a problem of state.[11] Caffery seldom mentioned President Barnet in his diplomatic correspondence and dispatches, while, at the same time, devoting a great deal of space to recounting meetings with Batista and President-Elect Gómez, among other political leaders. Although Caffery paid lip service to concerns about growing military power, there are no indications that he objected to the army's encroachment in civilian affairs. This is noteworthy, given Caffery's extensive meddling in other matters during this period, particularly labor legislation aimed at reducing the number of American professionals working in Cuba.[12]

This surge of social welfare legislation was a power grab by Batista, who wished to position himself as Cuba's benefactor. In the coming months, Batista campaigned vigorously across the island to garner public support for these programs. Improving the image of the army as a whole was another important theme and toward that end, Batista utilized radio, movies, pamphlets, and books. One reporter called it "one of the great publicity campaigns of island history."[13] With his deep and booming voice, Batista readily admitted at political rallies and dinners that he was the author of these social reform measures, often citing his impoverished youth in Banes as the inspiration. "Wherever there is pain I will always try and mitigate it," Batista told a February gathering of businessmen in Camagüey.[14]

There were early indications that President-Elect Gómez planned to make the curtailment of military power a central goal of his administration, and these social welfare laws were a preemptive strike against any such effort. Despite the fact that Batista was largely responsible for Gómez's electoral triumph, the two did little socializing in the weeks after the election. Early on, Batista felt Gómez was snubbing him. "The only cloud that I can see on the political horizon at this juncture is due to the fact that Batista feels Miguel Mariano to be unappreciative of all that he has done for him," Caffery wrote to Welles on March 20, 1936. "Miguel Mariano apparently finds it very difficult to express appreciation."[15]

President-Elect Gómez looked with dismay on unfolding developments. At one point, he met with Barnet to complain about the social legislation, which would "tie the hands of the succeeding administration." At the meeting, Barnet said the legislation had been an "imposition by the military authorities."[16] The growing role of the military was the chief concern raised by President-Elect Gómez in a preinaugural visit to Washington in April 1936, which included a meeting with President Roosevelt. During a lengthy conversation with Sumner Welles, Gómez declared that it was "imperative that free, democratic institutions should once more obtain and that Army influence should be limited to those spheres with which it was properly concerned." Batista's future role in the Cuban government was a central topic of conversation. The President-Elect told Welles that "Batista should realize what the functions and prerogatives of the Constitutional President are, and that he was prepared to recognize what the rights and prerogatives of the Commanding Officer of the Army should be."[17]

Gómez did not intend to play the figurehead role as perfected by Barnet. Even though Batista was largely responsible for his election, Gómez took seriously the notion, that he, and not the army chief, was to lead Cuba for the next four years.

GÓMEZ AND BATISTA: THE CLASH

Miguel Mariano Gómez was one of the most colorful politicians of the prerevolutionary era. A man of diminutive stature, he probably was no more than five-feet, four-inches tall, a fact that did not stop him from engaging in a series of duels throughout his political career, including one over an insulting newspaper article regarding his father.[18] The public bestowed several nicknames upon him, including "88 Caliber," for the disproportionately large sidearm he was fond of carrying, and the "Prince of Jíbaro," because Jíbaro was where the Gómez family had its country estate. Gómez, often referred to in the press simply as Miguel Mariano, was a favorite of Cuban caricaturists, who focused on his small physical stature; his jet black hair, usually parted straight down the middle; his black-rimmed glasses; and his thin, oval face. Gómez's colorful career provided endless ammunition for political satire. Known as a political deal maker, his propensity to make and break alliances lent itself to *chistes*, humorous little stories popular in Cuban society. One political cartoon in *Bohemia* on this subject depicts a man weighed down by several heavy valises. An observer tells a friend: "That man is obsessed with keeping track of all the political deals made by Miguel Mariano."[19]

Despite all the jokes about Miguel Mariano Gómez, he was a man of intense pride and the scion of a politically influential and wealthy family. His father, José Miguel Gómez, was a founder of the Liberal Party and the nation's second president (1909–1913). José Miguel was an intensely popular political leader, even though his administration was plagued by corruption and scandal. As so often was the case in Cuban politics, if José Miguel, nicknamed *Tiburón* (the Shark), was not wealthy before entering office, he was upon leaving, accumulating a fortune estimated by some at $8 million.[20] Among his dubious achievements were the institutionalization of regular government payments to the Cuban press in return for favorable coverage and the establishment of a national lottery, which would line the pockets of corrupt Cuban politicians for decades.

As a result, José Miguel's only son, Miguel Mariano, educated in private schools in Europe and the United States, entered adulthood a rich man.[21] In his youth, he gained a reputation as a playboy and a man hesitant to turn down a party invitation. Still, from an early age he was groomed for political life, frequently appearing with his father at political functions and banquets. During his father's administration, he was elected to the Cuban House of Representatives. Later on, in 1917, he conspired, alongside his father, to lead a rebellion to contest the fraudulent elections of 1916. Father and son were captured, served time in prison, and were eventually released by the Menocal government (1913–1921). When his father died in 1921, he assumed a leadership role in the Liberal Party and in 1926 was elected mayor of Havana, arguably the second-most important political office in Cuba, after the presidency. As a result of his popularity, Machado forced Gómez out of his position in 1928, and eventually into exile, from where he campaigned against the dictator. His anti-Machado credentials and his return as mayor of Havana in 1934 were springboards to his emergence as a compromise candidate of the Tripartite Coalition in the elections of 1936.

There could hardly have been two more dissimilar men in Cuban politics than Miguel Mariano Gómez and Fulgencio Batista. Gómez was a member of the wealthy upper class, while Batista grew up in a house with a dirt
floor. Gómez was groomed for the world of politics and public life; Batista
was a self-made man who emerged from the power vacuum created by the
flight of Machado in August 1933. The two had little in common, and there
is little indication that either wanted that to change. Photographs of the two
men rarely show them smiling or at ease with each other.[22] The two families were uncomfortable with each other as well, probably because of class
differences. Santiago Rey Perna, a Menocalista politician who had extensive
dealings with both men, was told by one cabinet minister that the two families "cannot get along well; they are different types of people."[23]

Meetings between Gómez and Batista were frequently awkward and uncomfortable, and they found it difficult to communicate. Illustrative of this
point was a series of meetings in late November 1936 aimed at patching up
the relationship between the president and army chief. Batista initiated the
get-togethers by communicating to Ambassador Caffery his "ardent desire
to get along with President Gómez." In a December 11 letter to Welles, Caffery recollects the events and paraphrases Batista as follows: "If I am doing
anything which the President doesn't approve, let him tell me, but please
have him desist from unwise public declarations in my regard when he hasn't
yet said anything to me."[24] Caffery passed the remark on to President Gómez,
who decided to invite Batista to dinner to discuss their differences. "He
[Gómez] *did* invite Batista to dinner but, to the latter's surprise, gave him
no opportunity of talking of affairs of interest," Caffery writes. The defense
minister, an ally of the army chief, explained to the president that Batista
was "surprised" that matters of substance had not been discussed. "Thereafter Gómez invited Batista again to the Palace for an evening of conversation, but again made no mention of any matter of particular importance."[25]
This pattern of miscommunication and noncommunication typified the relationship between the two.

The Gómez-Batista marriage of political convenience was bereft of a hon-
eymoon. The bad feelings began in the preinaugural period and continued
through the constitutional crisis of late December 1936, which would again
reveal the true source of power in Cuba. On the night before Gómez's inauguration, Batista received the first of many surprises. President-Elect Gómez
announced his cabinet appointments to the Cuban press before consulting
with him.[26] The president-elect did give Batista the option of approving the
defense minister, who at least in name was to be the army chief's direct
supervisor.[27]

This perceived snub of Batista was followed by Gómez's inaugural address before Congress, which, in several parts, addressed the issue of "spheres" of government authority and mentioned the importance of reclaiming the sphere of the president. Gómez praised the army for "upholding law and order" but said it was now time to return to "a normal political situation." Near the end of his speech, he observed: "Without a show of force which is respected, order is vain, and this is generally admitted; the moral pedestal of the Republic is the Army, it is its effective and physical support and its material and practical base. It is absolutely indispensable for the defense of the State, facing commotions and disturbances, which interrupt the rhythm of its functioning; but a precarious force if not animated and directed by reason and justice."[28]

In a working democracy there would be nothing unusual about the president's failing to inform the chief of the army of his political appointments or about his setting forth plans for the military. But, this was no democracy. One *New York Times* reporter described the government as "three-fourths constitutional."[29] Regardless of their public declarations, Caffery and Welles knew it too. In the coming months, they would twist constitutional logic in every direction to try to explain the peculiar brand of Cuban democracy they had helped bring into being. Privately, they expected Gómez to work with Batista with the understanding that there would be a gradual return of civilian privilege and authority. They spent hour upon hour trying to convince President Gómez to give Batista his due "*consideración*."[30]

As the United States saw it, Gómez was to have mediated presidential powers. He was to share executive authority with Batista. Welles and the State Department expected Batista to gradually transfer power to President Gómez as part of the "new situation" arising from the recent elections, but they were unwilling to set a timetable for him.[31] Welles, the architect of U.S. policy toward Cuba, laid out for Caffery the essential blueprint in a series of private letters over the course of 1936. The crux of the policy was to steer a middle course between the civilian aspirations championed by President Gómez and the military wing of the government led by Colonel Batista.

The United States would not tolerate an open military dictatorship in Cuba. The removal of President Gómez by Batista would trigger a strong response from Washington, a point Welles made very clear to Caffery. Economic and diplomatic sanctions were to be the weapons of choice in the event of a military takeover. "Intervene we will not," Welles wrote Caffery on June 18, 1936. "But I think we would be entirely justified, without waiting for the pressure of public opinion through the Congress, in terminating the Trade Agreement, in taking such action under such sugar legislation as might then exist as we could take in the direction of limiting Cuban sugar advantages in this market, and finally, in suspending diplomatic relations on the ground that while we would not intervene by force, nevertheless, we could not stand by and see the establishment in Cuba of a government which deprived the Cuban people of their right of self-government. . ." Welles urged Caffery to relay that message to the "responsible military leaders before any plan for military domination crystallized."[32]

The following month, Welles found it necessary to deliver a similar warning in response to growing military discontent with President Gómez. The anger was precipitated by Gómez's decision to lay off several thousand government employees, many of them military reservists who had replaced striking workers during the labor stoppages of the previous year. At least some of the departed reservists were replaced by political appointees, a fact that upset Batista,. "At the risk of their lives and with great loyalty these reserves defended the spirit of civilization and our national institutions, " Batista declared publicly in response to the dismissals.[33] Reflecting on the possibility of a military coup, Welles wrote Caffery: "If the Cuban army wishes to take the quickest way to self destruction, and, incidentally the destruction of Cuba as it now is, that is the course to pursue."[34]

But U.S. opposition to a military dictatorship did not translate into an open embrace of civilian rule. Batista was in a position of power, and Gómez would have to negotiate with him. No one in the State Department expected, or wanted, Batista to disappear. In response to rumors in September that the United States planned to oust the Cuban military chief after its own November elections, Welles urged Caffery to give Batista the names of those spreading the gossip. "He may think it desirable to see the gentlemen in question in order that he may tell them to try and behave themselves a little more like sensible human beings and less like morons."[35]

After a series of politically motivated attacks carried out by the police in October 1936, including the beating of a member of the Cuban House of Representatives, President Gómez dispatched a messenger to Welles to express his indignation and seek advice. Welles urged moderation on the angry Gómez. "It seemed to me that there was only one of two alternatives before President Gómez—the first, an open and definite rupture with Colonel Batista and with the Army, and that this was an alternative which no friend of Cuba and of Dr. Gómez could possibly desire; the other, a policy of cooperation with Colonel Batista and a policy of placing confidence in him in those matters which come within his legitimate jurisdiction."[36]

No matter how often this message was given to President Gómez, he refused to accept it. In his speeches, press interviews, and meetings, Gómez repeatedly spoke of protecting civilian prerogatives and keeping Batista in his place. "I am absolutely sure of this: the days of dictatorship in Cuba have passed. Now everyone has his place and no more than his place," President Gómez told a *New York Times* reporter, in describing his relationship with Batista and the army.[37] There was never an acknowledgment by the president in his public declarations that he must in fact negotiate with Batista. In the same *New York Times* article, Gómez intimated that he was considering cuts to the military budget, a suggestion that could only have angered the colonel. Even in private, Gómez resisted negotiations with Batista. In their private meetings, the president and army chief seemed to get along well, but their conversations frequently lacked substance. Everyone left feeling better, but Gómez and Batista immediately went back to acting independently of each other.[38] This independence of action served to undermine President Gómez because it revealed the extent to which executive power had been transferred to Batista and the army since the Sergeants' Revolt of September 1933. It was quite clear that Batista did not need the approval of Gómez to proceed with his plans for the nation.

The images in the Cuban press of the day are stark: the barnstorming Batista promoting his social agenda across the island, contrasted with the embattled Gómez closeted away in the Presidential Palace, appearing ineffective and weak. Batista received rare praise from the opposition press, including *Bohemia*, which lauded him for his efforts at addressing Cuba's social ills.[39] His travels through the countryside were covered in great detail, including a trip to the mountains of Las Villas in June to select a site for the nation's premiere tuberculosis sanatorium and another in December to Pinar del Río to promote his social agenda. More and more, Batista was treated like a head of state, not only by the media, but by foreign governments. In the spring, Batista was honored with a medal from the Spanish government and a few months later was awarded the Order of Merit by the Chilean ambassador. Batista's wife, Elisa Godínez, began to receive awards and news coverage normally accorded a first lady. In October, she was honored by the Cuban Red Cross, along with the wife of former President Mendieta. Her birthday celebration in December was hosted by the defense minister at his ranch and attended by political dignitaries, not President Gómez, and covered by the media.

In contrast, the president's political bumbling, inaction, and fits of temper were the subject of countless articles and editorials in Cuban newspapers and magazines. As usual, the most biting satire came from *Bohemia*, which leveled a flurry of attacks on Gómez. In one political cartoon, from September 1936, two businessmen gather on the street to talk. One mentions that he has a vacancy in his office and inquires of the other whether he knows of someone "that is not doing anything?" The other responds: "Yes sir: Miguel Mariano." In another cartoon, a visitor to the Presidential Palace asks a seated President Gómez why he has a handkerchief with a knot on top of his desk. Gómez replies: "So I can remind myself that I am the President." The assault continued week after week. In one satirical article, *Bohemia* praised Gómez for his many accomplishments, including learning to "blow smoke from his nose" by the age of fifteen. In a political cartoon from December, President Gómez describes to a friend some recent advice from his doctor urging him not to "smoke while working." The friend responds: "So then you are not smoking," to which Gomez replies, "No, I am not working."[40] Both *Bohemia* and the more conservative *Diario de la Marina* attacked the government for failing to address the nation's problems.[41]

—Doctor, ¿qué significa ese nudo en el pañuelo?
—Nada, compadre, es para acordarme que yo soy el Presidente.

The magazine *Bohemia* published this political cartoon on December 13, 1936. Here, a comical-looking President Gómez is conversing with another man who asks him "the significance of the knot in the handkerchief" that lies on the desk before him. Gómez replies, "It is to remember that I am the President." Taunting Gómez became great sport during his brief administration.

Even the anti-Batista press acknowledged what Gómez could not: That he would have to negotiate for power with the colonel. *Bohemia* columnist Miguel Coyula called for "harmonious equilibrium" between the civilian and military wings of the government. "Now more than ever it is indispensable for Cuba to have an equilibrium of powers," wrote Coyula, an opponent of military rule. In unusually candid language, Coyula noted that if the military's influence over government had dramatically increased in recent years and if Fulgencio Batista was frequently the subject of "hyperbolic praise" it was because of civilian politicians who have been "indifferent, accommodating, weak and inept." As Coyula saw it, President Gómez needed to restore public confidence in civilian institutions before he could expect to regain lost power and authority. He concluded the editorial by noting that "when a government of laws fails, government is imposed by the sword."[42]

Privately, Ambassador Caffery also advocated a gradual shift of power away from the military to civil authorities and repeatedly lamented, in his dispatches and private correspondence, Gómez's failure to understand political realities. Chief among his blind spots, according to Caffery, was his inability to see that "Dr. Gómez was elected for the sole reason that I insisted on it and Batista carried it out."[43] The second political truth that evaded Gómez was that change in the balance of power must occur incrementally. Five weeks before his inauguration, Caffery described the president-elect's handling of the military as "the all important factor." In assessing a future Gómez administration, Caffery wrote Welles on April 14, 1936, that civilian "accomplishments must be achieved little by little; normal conditions can be restored only gradually."[44] This was advice that Caffery repeatedly gave President Gómez, who, in turn, repeatedly ignored it.

Was it a political mistake on the part of Gómez to accept the presidency under these circumstances? Certainly, he must have known that Batista and Caffery were largely responsible for putting him in power, and, as a lifelong politician, must have realized that their support came with a price. How is it then that he failed to accept the reality of his position? Part of the answer lies in his miscalculation of support from Washington. Gómez calculated that in any power struggle between a duly elected president and a military dictator, the United States would be forced, by public opinion, to back him. At times, Caffery thought the perception of U.S. support emboldened the Gómez government and led it to take a more confrontational approach with Batista and the military. In a letter to Welles, dated July 9, 1936, the ambassador, perhaps referring to the recent dismissal of military reservists, wrote that "one of the reasons why members of the Government have committed so many '*barbaridades*' [barbarities] recently is that they feel that the Embassy will be able to prevail upon Batista not to throw out Dr. Gómez."[45] Indeed, President Gómez failed to comprehend the tepid nature of U.S. support for "democracy" in Cuba. With war looming on the world horizon as a result of the expansionist designs of Nazi Germany and imperial Japan, the State Department was more than content to allow the gradual evolution to democracy guided by Colonel Batista, who up to that point had proven a reliable ally. Cuba was no longer front and center in the U.S. media, as it had been several years earlier during the Machado dictatorship and the subsequent revolution. Gómez's failure to understand the precarious nature of his hold on the presidency and the limited extent to which the United States was willing to back him contributed mightily to his political downfall.

Central to this misunderstanding between President Gómez and the U.S. State Department was the question of Batista's role, what Welles had described as his "legitimate jurisdiction." The power of the army chief of staff had grown exponentially in recent years at the expense of the presidency. Welles and Caffery were willing to accept the balance of power as it existed in the spring of 1936 when Gómez was sworn in as president. Negotiations for augmenting civilian power were to proceed from that point forward, whereas Gómez wanted an immediate reversal of some of Batista's recent power gains. By the time Gómez took power, Batista had contacts and influence in virtually every government department, a strong base of support in Congress, authority over the military and police, and control of 25 percent of the national government's budget. Gómez was faced with the unenviable task of serving a four-year term as Batista's junior partner. With patience, the president might have been able to negotiate, bargain for, and grasp additional powers, but it would be a slow process, and one to which Gómez was unwilling to submit.

Of course, there were other important factors accounting for Gómez's political failures, most important his inability to build a coalition in the Cuban Congress, where he was almost universally reviled. Part of this dilemma lay in the fact that the Tripartite Coalition was cobbled together for the sole purpose of winning the elections of 1936. There was no ideological fabric to bind the three parties (Nacionalistas, Liberals, and Acción Republicana) together. They were little more than a conglomeration of independent office-seekers vying for political power and the payola that came with it. As a result, the Tripartite Coalition, with 24 of 36 senators and 90 of 162 representatives, controlled the Cuban Congress in name only. The defeated Conjunto of Mario Menocal, with 12 senators and 70 representatives, was in fact the largest single voting bloc. The lack of ideological cohesion within

the Tripartite Coalition was compounded by Gómez's complete misman-
agement of political affairs, both among the parties allied with him and in
regards to relations with the political opposition.

The largest congressional voting bloc within the Tripartite Coalition belonged to the Liberal Party (ten senators and thirty-five representatives), but
it was under the influence of Batista. As a result, Gómez needed to court the
army chief in order to gain support from this faction, a concession he was
unwilling to make. The second-largest contingent belonged to the Nacionalistas (nine senators and thirty representatives). The Nacionalistas were
dominant during the Mendieta presidency and were eager for another opportunity to hold power. Many within the party hoped that Gómez would self-
destruct, so that he could be replaced by either Mendieta or Vice President
Federico Laredo Brú, another Nacionalista.[46] Dissatisfied with the amount of
patronage given to party members by Gómez, the Nacionalistas became his
intractable enemies. Efforts to divide political posts among members of the
Tripartite Coalition bedeviled Gómez throughout his brief presidency and
contributed mightily to his lack of popularity in Congress. Coalition members criticized the president for showing favoritism to his own party and for
vacillating for months on the selection of administration officials, particularly at the subsecretary level.[47] The president's own party, with five senators and twenty-five representatives, was the smallest in congress and needed
allies if Gómez hoped to advance his own agenda and challenge Batista.

As for the political opposition, Menocal and many of the other Conjunto
leaders were long-time adversaries of President Gómez, as they had been of
his late father, and were unlikely to offer him much support under any circumstance. However, he exacerbated old antagonisms by refusing to certify
Conjunto electoral victories in various municipalities, even when they were
the clear winners. For months, the president kept Conjunto municipal office-
holders from assuming their posts. In contrast, Batista had courted the Conjunto by pushing for the establishment of twelve minority senatorships for
the party after it failed to win even one in the general election. The legislation, deridingly dubbed by some as the "Gift Law" (Ley Regalo), was originally intended to derail a potential alliance between the Conjunto and Grau
and the Auténticos.[48] As it turned out, the move created lasting good will
between the Conjunto and the military chief. It paid off for Batista in the
near term during the showdown with President Gómez and in the long
term, when he decided to openly seek the presidency.

Perhaps, if Gómez had succeeded in building a political coalition in Congress, he might have been able to force himself into a position of greater
power vis-à-vis Batista. But that was not the case, and Gomez was politically

isolated for almost every minute of his seven months in power. His political isolation was so complete that within a month of taking office the possibility of impeachment was already under consideration by some members of Congress. Impeachment was one way of circumventing Washington's, and particularly Welles's, objections to a military coup. "I must say again that Miguel Mariano is a very hard man to maintain in the Presidency, and especially in view of the fact that were it not for us he would be removed from the Presidency without much delay," Caffery wrote Welles on June 22, 1936. "(Incidentally, this could be done of course in perfectly legal fashion because Congress would take the necessary steps)."[49]

Batista's Social Agenda

Batista was never more popular than during the period between 1936 and 1940. For the first time, and perhaps the last, he had a clear vision of how he wanted to remake Cuban society. He was the most powerful man in Cuba and probably the most popular, although there were more than a few detractors. A pragmatic man of action, Batista began in 1936 to reveal an expansive political and social vision for the country. The Batista of this period can best be described as a corporatist dictator with a populist agenda.[50]

"Corporatist" seems an appropriate term to describe Batista, because he espoused a central role for government in organizing, supervising, and mediating competing interests within society. Nowhere was state mediation more important than in managing disputes between labor and capital. It was, after all, a general strike that finished off Machado in 1933 and nearly did the same to him two years later. It was incumbent on the state to reconcile differences for the greater good of society. Justice and profits could only be ensured when labor and capital worked together for their mutual benefit, a credo Batista espoused in frequent speeches to workers and businessmen. Both sides must maintain "social discipline" so that their conflicts do not plunge the nation into crisis.[51]

A dictator he clearly was, although Batista saw himself as a benevolent one, and he certainly never possessed the overwhelming kind of power that Trujillo brought to bear in the Dominican Republic.[52] In one dispatch to Washington, the U.S. military attaché described Batista as a "semi-dictator" who exerted his power "mildly."[53] At first, Batista eschewed the "dictator" label, but with time, particularly after the downfall of President Gómez, Batista grudgingly accepted it, adding the caveat that he was a "democratic dictator."[54] On one occasion when asked about his autocratic powers, Batista compared himself to Simón Bolivar, the great Latin American independence leader of the nineteenth century, who was charged with the same offense. "Later we have seen it demonstrated how posterity has vindicated him [Bolivar], the hero of America, and that has given me comfort," Batista responded. On another occasion, he noted that his influence was based on history, which has "projected me in front of the public."[55]

As the most powerful man in Cuba, Batista saw himself as the ultimate guarantor and mediator of order and stability. Conscious of the worldwide contest between fascism and communism, Batista made it clear that he was not beholden to either ideology. "I am an evolutionist," he said in response to a reporter's question. "I believe in and try to work for the progress of my country."[56] While trying to steer a middle course, as a good mediator should, Batista flirted with both ends of the political spectrum. He periodically expressed admiration for Mussolini and Italian fascism, but this was at most a passing fancy.[57] As the 1930s progressed, he leaned more to the political left, extolling the virtues of the Mexican Revolution and President Lázaro Cárdenas, a heralded revolutionary leader. His swing to the left was capped by his political alliance with Cuban Communists in 1938, a move that greatly troubled U.S. policymakers.

Populism was embedded in all his social programs, as he sought to appeal to the masses, both to derail potential revolutionary movements against him and to build a base of support for a future presidential run. Although he began his career as a revolutionary, Batista was uncomfortable with the tumultuous change created by revolution and clearly favored a reformist approach. His reputation as a right-wing dictator not withstanding, the Batista of this era saw that Cuban society, with its many class inequities, needed to be reformed, and he set about trying to reform it. The centerpiece of his early reform agenda was the rural education program, which was originally envisioned as a campaign against illiteracy. It, however, evolved into a comprehensive educational and health program that reached into virtually every abandoned corner of rural Cuba.[58] That it needed to be done, there can be no doubt. One generation after another of civilian politicians had ignored Cuba's rural population.

Living conditions in rural Cuba were the subject of periodic exposés by the Cuban press, but after a few days the headlines faded from memory and so did recognition of the problems. One such report was published by *Bohemia* in its edition of June 21, 1936, focusing on the prevalence of substandard housing, the lack of sanitary facilities, and the failure to distribute land to Cuba's peasants (*guajiros*). The author, América Ana Cuervo, writes: "Life in a country home is synonymous with misery. There is no appreciable difference between the Creole *bohío* and the housing encountered by the discoverers when they arrived at our island."[59] She went on to note that no housing code governed the construction of homes in the rural districts, that safe drinking water was a rare commodity, and that water supplies were frequently contaminated by sewage and feces. As a result, the countryside was frequently ravaged by epidemics of typhoid, malaria, and intestinal parasites. Another conclusion of the article was that land distribution was necessary to create a class of small landholders in rural Cuba. "Certainly these disgraces have been recognized by our government officials, but it is a certainty that they have lacked the courage to resolve the problem."[60]

The conditions of rural Cuba did not escape the attention of the outside world. A commission of prominent North American scholars issued a comprehensive 523-page report in 1935 entitled *Problems of the New Cuba*, in which they cited rural conditions, specifically the lack of educational facilities, public-health resources, and social welfare programs as one of the major challenges facing the island.[61] "Schools in Cuba are failing entirely to meet the needs of the rural population. This is a situation not at all unique to Cuba, but has existed there so long and been so aggravated that the effects are now scarcely less than a national calamity."[62] Health conditions were abominable in the Cuban countryside, and residents suffered from higher rates of malaria, infantile diarrhea, and infant mortality than did their urban counterparts. The numbers did not completely tell the story, because many patients traveled to Havana (as Juan Batista had years earlier), because it was the only place on the island with adequate health facilities. As a result, the death rate in Havana was inflated by those traveling to the city from the outlying regions. Poor sanitary conditions in rural areas and little recognition by the population of public-health issues contributed mightily to the spread of disease. In the case of tuberculosis, the Commission on Cuban Affairs noted that treatment clinics "in the interior are meager, and methods of control are unsatisfactory and incomplete."[63] Housing in rural areas and small towns was inadequate, and residents of country districts were provided with few social services.[64]

Batista came from the countryside and therefore was intimately familiar with conditions in rural Cuba. When he spoke on the subject, he did so with great passion and delivered some of his finest speeches. Fighting to defend his civic-military schools from attacks by President Gómez and his supporters, Batista delivered one of his most eloquent speeches to a packed banquet hall in Pinar del Río, the island's westernmost province, on December 16, 1936.[65] He was in the province to retrace the march of independence leader Antonio Maceo forty years earlier during the war with Spain, but at every stop his social agenda, at that moment being debated by Congress, was a main topic of discussion. In the first part of the speech, before a civilian audience, he declared himself the "father" of the revolution of September 4, 1933, a revolution that was made possible by "beliefs of conscience." Justifying his actions, and those of his followers, since the revolution, Batista declared: "It is the condition of men to think, in every action of their lives, what the repercussions on public opinion will be of their actions. For me, the man of beliefs does not gear his conduct in any way to the state of public opinion that at any given moment shapes the environment or the circumstances. Rather, the man of convictions acts at every critical moment in accordance with the necessities demanded by the environment, no matter what the criticisms, good or bad, the state of opinion might produce."

Easing into the topic of his social agenda, Batista joked with the audience about his involvement in issues beyond the normal scope of the military. "Magnificent is the position I find myself in, two stars on my collar and three on each shoulder [indicating his rank], young, powerful, and loved, at least by the army which I command." ("By the people as well," shouted several interrupting his speech). A few sentences later, after noting that he could live comfortably without involving himself in social issues, Batista raised several questions frequently posed to him. "Why if this does not pertain to you, do you do this or that? Why do you assume powers that you do not have?" He said the answer was simple: "Because there is conscience and there are convictions."

Batista posed a similar question to the audience about his proposals for rural education. "Why did this idea germinate in me?" He answered the question near the end of his speech, stating that the rural education program "does not only provide instruction, does not only pretend to teach the alphabet, to read, to write, to add and subtract; rather, it proposes to educate, to teach, to prevent [disease], to shape the mind of the ignorant men, women and children." And why should this effort not be championed by the army? Batista responded with another question: "Why must the army be only an instrument of war—and not a symbol of peace—rather than a symbol of extermination?"

That Batista had ulterior motives for his rural education program, such as the expansion of military power and a desire to build a platform for his own presidential run, there can be no doubt. But he could have chosen any number of other causes to champion, such as labor reform, economic development, higher education, or road construction, to name just a few. In one way or another, Batista would ultimately address all of those issues, but his first major effort to reform Cuban society was centered on rural education. He fought for this program like few other causes in his career. Batista's deeply felt convictions on the subject, coupled with the report by the Commission on Cuban Affairs, inspired him to develop a comprehensive plan of action.[66] The army chief announced his intention to expand rural education in late September 1935. On February 27, 1936, Provisional President Barnet and the State Council provided Batista and the army with the legal authorization to establish and maintain the program. It took off quickly, and by the end of the year more than seven hundred new schools were in operation, serving thirty-five thousand elementary school children and twenty thousand adults. Ultimately, the army would create 1,070 new schools throughout rural Cuba.[67]

Under Batista's plan, sergeant-teachers, after a two-month training period, were dispatched to isolated areas of the Cuban countryside with the primary mission of establishing a school. Upon arrival, the sergeants were to make contact with local residents and rally the community behind the project. No funds were allocated in the military budget for school construction, so sergeants were expected to secure a parcel of land, preferably through a charitable donation. A school was then constructed by local residents using donated materials. As a result, the quality and size of the schools varied greatly from location to location. In some cases, local farmers allowed the sergeant-teachers to use vacant buildings on their property to house the new schools, so some of the first classes were held in old stables, storage buildings, and abandoned houses. Sergeant-teacher Rogelio Jiménez Capote, assigned to Las Villas Province in central Cuba, taught his first classes in an old barracks used to store sugar cane carts. The school had a dirt floor, a roof of zinc, and before long, 118 students.[68]

Sergeant-teacher Emilio Carrillo found no school building waiting for him when he arrived in rural Camagüey Province in the late summer of 1936. Carrillo was told that if he did not convince the residents to construct a school, he would be unemployed in short order. He felt "demoralized and confused" upon seeing that the area for his proposed school consisted of "marshy land covered by grass." After an uneasy first night, Carrillo recalled years later, he was greeted by a group of local residents who assured him that a school would be built. Local residents organized a parents and neighbors association, and the following Saturday was set aside for construction. On the designated day, the group of volunteers was divided into three work teams: the first to cut down the grass and dig drainage channels to carry water away from the property, the second to gather stones and dirt to fill in the site, and the third to go to a nearby forest to cut down the trees that would be used to build the school. The school was completed within a week.[69]

In the first academic year, 1936–1937, given the rapid growth of the schools,

Batista as a railroad brakeman, probably around 1919, which would make him about eighteen years old in this photo. He later was seriously injured and nearly killed working on the railroad.

Batista at about age eighteen at a formal sitting in Camagüey. He later told family members that "everything he owned at the time" was in the photo.

Batista, Elisa, and baby Mirta in the late 1920s, before his rise to fame. The sergeant's stripes on Batista's right shoulder indicate his rank.

The recently promoted Colonel Batista. The photo dates from shortly after September 4, 1933. Batista has only the colonel's stars and one medal on his uniform.

8 de sep. de 1933
BaTisTa - CORONEL

Camp Columbia under attack on November 8, 1933. Rebel airmen attempted to drop a bomb on Batista's home but missed and hit the adjacent building.

Batista with archenemy Antonio Guiteras sometime in 1933. At the time, Guiteras, minister of war, was technically Batista's superior. Guiteras would die in a shoot-out with the army less than two years later.

Batista receiving a medal from President Carlos Mendieta Montefur sometime in 1934 or 1935. Standing at strict attention, third from left, is José Pedraza, Batista's second-in-command.

Batista (in the center) and some of his closest military advisers in a casual photo at Camp Columbia in the mid 1930s. Colonel Francisco Tabernilla is the second from left. Colonel Pedraza is fourth from the right. Major Manuel Benítez is second from the right. Chief political aide Jaime Mariné is on the far right.

President Miguel Mariano Gómez and Batista in a rare photo, taken sometime in 1936, in which both men are smiling. By the end of the year, Batista would ensure President Gómez's impeachment.

Batista and his soldiers on horseback in central Cuba in search of a site for a tuberculosis sanatorium. The photo probably dates to 1936.

An avid horseman in the 1930s, Batista appears to be preparing his horse for a ride. Batista frequently went horseback riding with U.S. Ambassador Jefferson Caffery as a prelude to conducting state business.

Batista with daughter Mirta and son Rubén Fulgencio at Camp Columbia in the mid-1930s.

Assistant Secretary of State Sumner Welles exchanging words with Batista during his November 1938 visit to Washington, D.C. Welles and Batista had a long, rocky relationship. Colonel Francisco Tabernilla looks on.

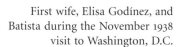

First wife, Elisa Godínez, and Batista during the November 1938 visit to Washington, D.C.

President Federico Laredo Brú chats with Batista in a photo from the late 1930s. Brú was considered one of Batista's most compliant presidents.

Another family shot from the late 1930s.

Former President and political king maker Mario García Menocal meeting with Batista during the 1940 presidential campaign. Menocal's support was crucial in guaranteeing Batista the victory.

Campaign van decorated by Batista partisans for the 1940 presidential campaign.

Formal portrait from the October 1940 inauguration.

the curriculum was largely transplanted from the island's urban schools to the rural settings, without much effort to customize it. Much of the initial class time was spent on the basics of reading and writing, in keeping with the original goal of combating illiteracy in the countryside. From late morning to midafternoon (usually 11 a.m. to 4 p.m.), the school was used by school-age children, from grades 1 to 6. Two nights a week were reserved for adult education courses. There were typically no classes in the early mornings during prime agricultural seasons, so that children could work on area farms and plantations. Of course, class plans, curriculum, and hours of operation varied greatly from region to region, and probably from school to school.

The army's philosophy toward the rural schools evolved over time. Physical education was originally intended to serve the same role in the rural schools as it did in the military, that is to instill a "sense of discipline and patriotism," rather than as simply a form of recreation.[70] "The school-day starts at 7:00 a.m., with setting-up exercises, followed by singing of the National Anthem, the Fourth of September Anthem and a credo dealing with the better life and ending with a eulogy to Colonel Batista," observed one U.S. military official who visited a school in the late fall of 1936.[71] The emphasis on discipline through physical education was eliminated after the first year, perhaps as a result of criticism. Still, there was no doubt about the army's role in administering the schools. The sergeant-teachers wore military uniforms in the classroom, a practice that continued after the first year, and they frequently rode on horseback throughout the community, compelling, when necessary, parents to send their children to school. There were certain practical advantages to army administration of the schools, including the fact that sergeant-teachers were assigned to certain rural districts and forced to live there until their enlistment period was complete. One of the major obstacles to establishing schools in rural Cuba had always been the inability to attract civilian teachers to remote regions. In the past, "most [civilian] teachers assigned to such districts frequently had sufficient political influence to get themselves transferred to a more urban district," Batista told a visiting U.S. educator.[72]

As the program evolved, greater emphasis was placed on agricultural subjects and vocational training, and a curriculum geared specifically to a rural environment was developed. Each school was supposed to have a community garden, and agricultural techniques were to be learned through practical application. The boys were taught vocational skills such as carpentry, mechanics, stone masonry, and painting, while the girls were schooled in the domestic arts, such as cooking, weaving, sewing, and vegetable canning. The mission of the schools greatly expanded over time, and the sergeant-teachers were expected to teach children and adults better sanitary practices and take blood samples from sick children, so that they could be sent to an army laboratory for analysis.

In keeping with the broad mission, each school was to serve as a community club for area residents. On weekends and evenings, the school was transformed into a community center for dances, fund-raising activities, and community gatherings. Each school was supplied with a radio receiving set, so that students and residents could get information of the outside world. The army censored the broadcasts. The radio programming was to include lectures, recitals, and concerts, so as Batista saw it, the "spirit shall be stimulated and the farmer be taught in the way that is proper for his simple life, but with the tendency of forming in him a strong conception of civic citizenship."[73] Occasionally movies, or as they were called by some at the time, "moving pictures," were sent to the schools, so that they could be viewed by area residents.

In an effort to support this ambitious agenda, the island was divided into forty zones, and each was provided with a traveling mission of six or seven experts in varying fields, including nursing, agronomy, veterinary medicine, dentistry, domestic science, and tradesmen of all sorts. These experts rotated through the different schools in their assigned zones complementing and enhancing the efforts of the sergeant-teachers. They typically delivered specific lectures or programs to adults and children on a wide variety of subjects from personal hygiene and sanitation to disease prevention and child-rearing skills. Eventually special boarding schools (Hogares Infantiles Campesinos) were established in each zone for particularly gifted students. Mobile health units traveled to the various schools in each zone.[74]

The work was quite demanding, according to Mireya LaFuente, a home economics expert assigned to rural Camagüey Province in 1936. LaFuente recalled having to travel to the different schools, either on horseback, or on an ox or sugar cane cart. Some areas were so inaccessible that she had to walk for miles to get to the school. Once she arrived in an area, she was at the mercy of area residents in terms of sleeping accommodations. She often slept on the floor or in the same bed with several children. On one occasion, she remembered sleeping in a rat-infested corn storage shed. "I had heard it said that the rats were dangerous and it was the same to them whether they ate a big toe on your foot or your nose, that while they gnawed they blew [into the wound] and as a result the victim felt no pain," LaFuente wrote years later. "I was well covered but I was afraid that the same way they made holes in the sacks [of corn], they could also penetrate my clothes. So, my aim was to stay on the defensive and not sleep."[75]

There was a strong paternalistic undercurrent to Batista's rural education program and an element of social control. The former impoverished boy from Banes wanted to lift the Cuban *guajiro* out of physical and mental impoverishment. And, Batista had a very clear vision of what the new *guajiro* should be like. "The day will arrive when the laggardness and timid aspects of our peasants, which makes the hard task of agriculture so sterile, shall be converted, through this strenuous effort and through the multiplication of the example, into lucidity and a source of energy for the individual and for the Nation," Batista wrote in a memorandum summarizing the goals of the program. He also expected the schools to impart a certain "discipline" that would serve to shield the "country people [from] obnoxious teachings which guide the adult and the child, whether male or female, through paths of perdition for themselves and for their country."[76]

Apart from his social aims, Batista wanted to change the image and reputation of the Cuban Army, a point alluded to in his Pinar del Río speech, from the well-earned perception that it was an agent of oppression to the softer image of a revolutionary force conducting good works throughout the island. There is little doubt that he achieved some success in this regard. The army's administration of the rural education program and its other social outreach programs "is having a most beneficent effect upon the popularity of Colonel Batista and the Army at large—In sharp contrast are the poorly managed governmental departments with their frequently changed, inefficient, futile and costly politically-appointed personnel," wrote a U.S. military official in an assessment to Washington. "This contrast extends to the Congress where legislative activity is neglected in the mad scramble for patronage and personal financial gain. The comparison is odious and the deductions to be drawn by the Cuban masses are most clear."[77] As part of the public relations campaign, one gifted child from each rural school was awarded the Flor Martiana (the Flower of José Martí, in honor of the Cuban independence leader) and brought to Havana for a parade in front of the Presidential Palace. The army even sponsored a song-writing contest on the theme of rural education, and the winning *Himno a la Educación* (Hymn to Education) was selected in December 1936.[78]

Rural education and the other social-service programs required a different sort of soldier—one who was well educated and idealistic. Hundreds of teachers and other professionals were recruited into the ranks of the army to help administer the rural education program. Sergeant-teachers and mission experts needed a degree in teaching, agriculture, law, medicine, dentistry, or a related field before they could enlist in the army. A new branch was established to administer the program, known as the Cultural Section (Sección de

Cultura). Batista assigned the soldier/lawyer/poet, Arístides Sosa de Quesada, the softer face of the new army, the task of organizing the Cultural Section, and promoted him to Lt. Colonel.[79] Members of the corps were identified by a special insignia on their uniform—a crossed saber and pen with a book in the center. Like their students, the sergeant-teachers were periodically brought to Havana to be showcased in parades and other public ceremonies.

The two monthly military journals, *El Ejército Constitucional* and *Cultura Militar y Naval,* dedicated a good deal of space to rural education and the other social-service programs administered by the army. The transformation of Cuba by the army and its members was a central theme of many of the articles. In one edition of *El Ejército Constitucional,* the editors published a one-act play entitled *La escuela rural* (*The Rural School*), in which the main characters are Cirilo, a drunken and abusive farmer; his deferring wife, Candelaria; their children; and the sergeant-teacher assigned to run the rural school. As the play opens, we meet the surly, drunken father, who rules over his family like a tyrant. Cirilo sees no value in education, and as a result, no one in the family can read. Near the end of the first scene they are visited by the sergeant-teacher, who emphasizes to them the importance of education. When the father resists efforts to enroll his children in the school, the sergeant becomes assertive and demands that not only the children attend but also the father. "But, I will save you, because for that purpose I have placed that labor on my shoulders," the sergeant-teacher notes at the end of the first scene.[80]

The second scene takes place three years later. When we again meet the family, their lives have been transformed by the rural school. The formerly drunken father is now administering one of the largest farms in the region. He addresses his wife with more respect, and the children love to read and are busily going about their studies. As the play ends, the young students and adults provide testimonies on the wonders of the school. The father proclaims to the sergeant-teacher, and the assembled group, how he has emerged from ignorance to embrace learning. He hugs his family members and speaks of the "grandiose work" of the Civic-Military Rural Schools. There is substantial evidence to suggest that the reality of Batista's rural education program fell short of the happy ending depicted by the play, although one writer favorable to Batista claims that eighty thousand students learned to read in these rural institutions.[81] Batista claimed the national illiteracy rate dropped to 39 percent in 1937, falling from 48 percent five years earlier.[82] In his study, Gerald Read praises as a "tremendous accomplishment" the army's ability to construct a rural school system virtually overnight, but doubted whether many of the substantive goals, such as reducing illiteracy, were accomplished.[83] Lowry Nelson, in his classic sociological work, *Rural Cuba*, published in 1950, identifies many of the same problems noted by the Commission on Cuban Affairs in 1935, including high rates of illiteracy, a shortage of schools, an inadequate number of teachers, substandard housing, and poor sanitation. Nelson's study concludes that the literacy rate in rural Cuba did not increase as a result of the rural schools program, although there is some evidence to suggest that there was an increase in literacy while the army controlled the schools but a subsequent decline once they were turned over to the civilian government in 1940.[84]

To just say that the rural education program fell short of its goals misses a great deal of the point. It was the first ambitious effort to change the living conditions in rural Cuba. What impact did it have on future efforts to reshape the countryside? Did the rural education program of the late 1930s influence the work of revolutionaries in the 1960s? Was the Literacy Campaign of 1961, an achievement touted by the Castro government, an adaptation of the earlier literacy effort? On the surface at least, there are some striking similarities between the two programs. The origins of both can be traced to the army. Both programs were organized on a military model, and in both cases civilians were commissioned to go into the countryside and teach. And, borrowing a phrase from the title of the classic work by Richard Fagen, Batista in the 1930s, like Castro in the 1960s, was seeking to "transform the political culture" of the Cuban peasantry.[85]

The connections have yet to be drawn between the two rural education programs. The program of the 1930s, like much of Cuban history prior to 1959, has been overlooked by scholars. There are ample studies on education and health care in postrevolutionary Cuba, but in the rush to write about the Revolution of 1959, scholars have failed to address what came before it.[86] The rural civic-military schools are another example of the scholarly abandonment of the prerevolutionary period (1902–1959).

Impeachment

As 1936 came to a close, Batista had every reason to be satisfied with his efforts to bring education to rural Cuba. By all accounts, the program and his other social reforms were popular with the public. "It is just to confess that the work the army is carrying out, by the initiative of its chief, in the area of education, harms no one. On the contrary it benefits our country folk, left as is commonly said, in the hand of God. It does not take away prerogatives from the Civilian Government, rather it cooperates with it for the betterment of the country, which is in the end, what should preoccupy us the most," one editorial proclaimed in *Bohemia*.[87] Seldom did Batista receive such praise from Cuba's most important weekly news magazine, which for years championed the opposition against him. A "work of indisputable merit" was how a writer for the more conservative news magazine *Carteles* described the rural education program."[88]

In addition to public and media support, Batista believed that President Gómez, despite their rocky relationship, also supported the rural education program. In early September, the two men attended a ceremony honoring seven hundred sergeant-teachers preparing to start the new school year. As late as the middle of November, Batista told a U.S. State Department official that the program had the backing of the civilian government.[89] On the political surface everything appeared calm. But, the financial and political equation began to change in mid-November, once it became apparent that the army would be unable to continue funding the program without additional monies. A cash infusion of between $1.5 million and $2 million was required to keep the program afloat. In order to save it, Batista proposed a nine-cent tax on every 325-pound bag of sugar produced on the island.[90] The colonel sought and ultimately secured the backing of the *hacendados*, the large sugar mill owners, and the *colonos*, the small sugar planters, for the proposed tax. Some opponents charged that these endorsements were more the result of army pressure than a belief in the merits of the law.[91] In early December, the bill was approved by the Cuban Senate and appeared destined for quick approval in the House. Anticipating swift passage of the legislation, Batista departed on a fifteen-day tour of Pinar del Río Province on December 5.

For weeks, President Gómez maintained public silence on the issue. In keeping with their usual mode of communication, neither Gómez or Batista broached the subject of the nine-cent tax with the other. Four days after Batista's departure, on December 9, President Gómez made clear his decision to fight the legislation. On that day, the president met with several congressional leaders at the Presidential Palace and urged them to vote against it. In the event it passed, he vowed to veto the bill. The president's opposition soon became front-page news. "The President knows also that this is a matter very close to Batista's heart," Caffery wrote to Welles.[92]

For Batista, this latest, unexpected move by President Gómez was almost more than he could stand. Informed of Gómez's opposition the following day, Batista threatened to return immediately to Havana even though it could precipitate a crisis.[93] His supporters in the military pressured him to remove Gómez by force and to dismiss Congress. Batista decided against such drastic measures, knowing they would antagonize the State Department and endanger economic and trade agreements with the United States.

Batista was not one to act precipitously, especially in a crisis. In repeated messages to Ambassador Caffery, the colonel assured him that violence would not be used against President Gómez and the civilian politicians.[94] Instead, Batista opted to oust the president through constitutional means. The final showdown between the two men took place in the halls of Congress.

Batista immediately mobilized his political forces. A campaign to pass the sugar legislation and remove the president was orchestrated by Batista from a distance, so as to avoid the appearance that he was "imposing" a military solution. The first step was to get the legislation passed in the House. In anticipation of a House vote on the nine-cent tax bill, the army's political office at Camp Columbia, directed by Major Jaime Mariné, sent out tele-grams inviting congressional members to the military base out of "urgent necessity."[95] Once they were assembled at the base, Mariné emphasized to each member the importance to Colonel Batista of passing the legislation. Mariné was a master at applying political pressure, both subtle and overt. During this crisis, and on other occasions, he offered some legislators a car-rot in the form of patronage; on others, he utilized a stick in the form of economic threats against their private businesses.[96] As if the point were not clear enough, Mariné sent letters to members of the House, reminding them of the crucial vote on the tax legislation scheduled for December 18. In the letter, he noted Batista's "sincere demonstrations of affection" for their sup-port.[97] It was at times like this that Mariné earned his keep. His official title was aide-de-camp of the colonel chief of the army, but he acted as a sort of political chief of staff to Batista. Mariné was disliked by many in the military hierarchy, including number-two man Pedraza, but no one could deliver in the political arena like he could, so Batista kept him around for years.

There is evidence to suggest that Batista met with several legislators at his temporary headquarters in Pinar del Río to further drive home the agenda. At the meeting, Batista told one senator that he had spent "enough time on the fence" and that he must now decide whether he was "with Batista or with Gómez." The senator finally declared himself in the colonel's corner. In the course of the conversation, Batista reportedly suggested to the legislators that they vote to impeach the president so the "Congress will not have to be dissolved."[98]

For his part, President Gómez tried to rally support in Congress against the legislation but found that even some members of his own party refused to go along with him. Menocal's Conjunto Party members were almost unan-imous in their opposition to the president, while the Liberals and Nacio-nalistas, were equally divided. In frustration, the president lashed out at Congress. It was yet another display of bad politics on the part of Gómez, directed against the members of a body that would soon be called on to decide his political fate. An effort to strike a legislative compromise, one establishing a juvenile court (something the president favored) if Gómez dropped his opposition to the nine-cent tax, went nowhere.

The president's central argument against the tax bill was that it encroached further on civilian power. Gómez was quoted in the newspapers by his supporters as vowing to "jealously guard" the authority of the executive branch of government. He would not interfere in the functioning of Congress, the judiciary, or the army and did not expect those branches of government to impede his authority. Some of the president's followers began to use the word "fascist" to describe the rural education program, although Gómez initially refrained from using the word. "Behind this law there is an attempt to establish a fascist government," Congressman Eduardo Suárez Rivas, declared during floor debate. "There is an effort to take away from the Executive branch its most important powers."[99] As expected, on the morning of December 19, the Cuban House of Representatives voted overwhelmingly, 106–43, to support the nine-cent tax.

Having quietly returned to Camp Columbia, Batista, suffering from a severe bout of influenza, conducted a bedside interview with reporters praising the "meritorious work" of the House of Representatives.[100] As for President Gómez, the humiliating legislative defeat was the least of his problems. The lopsided vote indicated there were probably sufficient votes to impeach him. Cuban constitutional statutes at the time required a two-thirds vote of the House to impeach the president, in this case 108 votes. A simple majority was required in the Senate to convict and remove the president. Talk of impeachment began to take hold in the House. The president was to be charged with "interfering" in the work of the legislative body and "threatening" members with reprisal if they did not vote his way. The charges were a cynical farce given the army's involvement in the legislative process. From the beginning of the crisis, Mariné beseeched legislators to find a "constitutional" way to resolve the crisis, constitutional being a code word for impeachment.[101]

True to his word, the president, vetoed the nine-cent tax bill on December 21, even though he knew it would not stand. In his veto message, Gómez acknowledged the "high aim of diffusing culture in our country and eradicating illiteracy." But, the military was the wrong agency to undertake the task. "I must state in a categorical manner that it is the Department of Education and not military institutions that should assume charge of this work. Military education is convenient for those who desire a military career and is indispensable for development of the severe discipline necessary in the

forces created for the purpose of defending the nation, but for the formation of the citizen who is later to exercise the rights devolving on him in a
democracy, civil instruction by a teacher who is not of the army is necessary because it is peace and the exercise of citizenship that should be in-
stilled into the spirit of the child."

Pressure was mounting. There were rumors that a delegation from the
army was set to go to the Presidential Palace and ask for Gómez's resignation. The army delegation never appeared, but some prankster sent over
eight large moving vans. Needing no help from the unsolicited movers,
Gómez and his family began to remove their personal belongings from the
Presidential Palace. The president met with supporters again and vowed to
resist to the bitter end. "They will have to kill me or remove me," Gómez
told one follower. Several of his loyalists discussed the possibility of going
into exile, but the president argued against such a drastic move.[102] There was
some slight hope that, perhaps, the advocates of impeachment might not
be able to muster the required two-thirds majority in the House. But that
hope was dashed, just after 2 a.m. on December 22, when the House voted,
111–45, to impeach the president. A committee of three House members was
selected to prosecute the president at the Senate trial scheduled to start the
following day.

Gomez's political prospects were bleak and looking bleaker by the hour.
The press now put its full weight behind the impeachment effort. In assessing media coverage of the crisis, it is important to note that attacks against
Batista and proclamations supporting the president were seldom published
by the large newspapers, perhaps out of fear of army reprisal. In one case,
a group of students from the University of Havana, still closed after twenty-
one months, issued a manifesto backing Gómez but could find no one to
publish it. After issuing the manifesto, the students promptly went into hiding.[103] Nonetheless, the editorial support for impeachment is noteworthy. The
largest and most influential newspapers in Cuba, including *Diario de la Marina, El País*, and *El Avance* called on the president to resign his office and
spare the nation the painful spectacle of his removal. The powerful publisher
of *Diario de la Marina*, José Rivero, praised the man but attacked his politics, specifically his inability to work with the army. Gómez understood the
"theory" of governance but not the reality. The president is a "man of laws
and, as a result, predisposed to not recognize other realities, but those written on paper," Rivero observed. Resignation would be an "elegant gesture."[104]

Throughout the crisis there was a flurry of diplomatic activity. In the days
immediately after Gómez came out against the legislation, Caffery searched
for a compromise between the two men that would preserve the president in

power. The ambassador was pessimistic. "It is difficult to perceive the possibility of any satisfactory way out of the impasse," Caffery wrote in a December 17 dispatch to Washington. President Gómez took the position that "if it must fall—let the Republic fall." Batista told the ambassador candidly that he feared a military revolt against him if he wavered in his campaign against Gómez. The army officers "are almost hysterical in their opposition to him [Gómez], Caffery observed. There were rumors of a military conspiracy to topple Batista. In an effort to calm tensions, Batista met with his lieutenant colonels to assure them that Gómez would not remain in power much longer. In the end, the best Caffery could secure was a delay in any move to oust the president, until the conclusion of the Inter-American Conference for the Maintenance of Peace, already under way in Buenos Aires, but set to wrap up business on December 23.[105]

Caffery's failure to secure a guarantee that Gómez would remain in power raised a number of policy questions that could only be resolved by President Roosevelt. The matter was further exacerbated by a desperate appeal from the Gómez government. On December 19, the Cuban ambassador to Washington, Guillermo Patterson, warned Roosevelt of a "military dictatorship" and the "consequent impairment of democratic and constitutional government" if Gómez were impeached and removed from office. The diplomatic note made no specific request of Roosevelt, but the underlying message was a plea for intervention.[106] Two days later, Roosevelt made a decision regarding the Cuba crisis. He decided to do nothing. The only suggestion Roosevelt made was to urge Caffery to "point out to the appropriate persons that what President Gomez had done in calling in legislative leaders to lay before them his attitude with regard to the sugar tax bill, was exactly what he and other presidents in democracies had frequently done and that this action was not considered in other countries to give grounds for the charge of infringement of legislative prerogatives."[107]

No political life preserver from Washington was forthcoming for the embattled Cuban president. The next day, December 22, the State Department prepared a memorandum declaring that the issue of U.S. recognition would not "arise" if President Gómez were impeached. "This Government would merely continue relations with the Cuban Government," read the last line of the memorandum.[108]

The Gómez presidency was nearly at an end. At 4 p.m. on December 23, the Cuban Senate convened as a tribunal and conducted one of the fastest political trials on record. Gómez refused to appear before the hearing but sent a brief statement challenging the constitutionality of the proceedings and noting that the charges were the result of "pressures from known sources."[109]

Knowing the outcome, he left the Presidential Palace shortly before midnight, accompanied by a group of friends and political supporters. Just after 1 a.m., on Christmas Eve, Gómez was convicted of the charges and formally removed from office. Hours after his ouster, the former president issued a "Manifesto to the People of Cuba," lashing out at Batista and the army. In the document, which was not published in the Cuban press, he openly used the word "fascist" to describe the policies of the military. Referring to Batista as the "reformist apostle of the new epoch," the former president questioned whether it would not be more "frank and sincere" to "install" the colonel as president. Near the end of the manifesto, mimeograph copies of which were circulated through the streets of Havana, Gómez declared that his "sin consisted of [the fact] that I came here to be in effect the President of the Republic and not an echo and figurehead for anybody."[110]

At noon, on December 24, Federico Laredo Brú was sworn in as president of Cuba. He was Cuba's tenth chief executive in less than four years.[111] Within days, Batista would deny that there were any plans to remove him.[112]

CHAPTER 12

CUBAN
STRONGMAN

The impeachment of President Gómez cleared away any remaining artifice. Fulgencio Batista was in charge of Cuba. Presidents served at his pleasure. In the hours and days after Federico Laredo Brú was sworn in as Cuba's latest chief executive, it was unclear whether his tenure would be short or long.[1] There were persistent rumors that Batista would install his close personal friend, Foreign Minister Rafael Montalvo, in the presidency. But the military chief took a liking to the sixty-one-year-old Brú, and in a statement to the nation two days after the impeachment spectacle, Batista declared that the new president was a man with whom he could work. "I have faith, and my hope is well founded. Colonel Laredo Brú has my full support, soul and body, muscle and energies, which I put with frankness at his entire disposition. I am fortunate to be able to say that seldom have my presentiments deceived me."[2]

He was certainly not deceived by Laredo Brú. What followed was a four-year political alliance that proved to be one of the most important of Batista's career and paved the way for his own presidential run in 1940. At first, Brú was little more than window dressing when it came to the business of the island. The president attended all the important state functions, of course, but always at his side was the youthful Batista. When there were important policy initiatives to unveil, it was Batista who did the unveiling. When the Roosevelt administration issued an invitation to visit Washington, it was sent to Batista not Brú. But over time their political relationship would evolve into one of trust, and when international and national political currents pushed Batista toward democratic elections, it was Brú whom the military chief entrusted to negotiate the path to a new constitution and presidential elections with his political opponents. A reserved and quiet man, Laredo Brú was content to serve as a junior partner to Batista and enact programs devised by the colonel and his advisers. In unassuming fashion, he gradually made himself indispensable to the army leader—so much so that Brú, the puppet of 1937 and 1938, became something of a power broker in 1939 and 1940.

The tumultuous political climate of the late 1930s served as the backdrop for this unusual political evolution. Batista emerged from the impeachment struggle with Gómez the undisputed strongman of Cuba, and for the next eighteen months he proceeded to impose his social and political agenda on the citizens of the island. In 1937, Batista announced, with great fanfare, an ambitious blueprint for social reform, known as the Triennial Plan, in which he set forth the legislative agenda for Congress and the provincial governments for the next three years. However well-intentioned, the plan was at its core undemocratic, relying on the corrupt political institutions of the provisional government, distorted by military influence, for its review and implementation.

By 1938, after five years of quasi-military rule, the outcry for political reform in Cuba became deafening. The political process excluded vast segments of the population. The establishment of a new constitution was the stated goal of all the provisional governments since 1933, but after years of excuses, the jails were still filled with political prisoners, opposition parties were outlawed, and there was no electoral code in place to elect a constitutional assembly. An astute politician, Batista knew that these aspirations could be suppressed for just so long.

On the international scene, Hitler and Mussolini were on the verge of plunging Europe into another world war. The Spanish Civil War raged, and before the decade was over, General Francisco Franco would crush the Spanish Republic with the help of Nazi Germany. Many in the U.S. media found it difficult to discern an ideological difference between Batista and these other dictators, despite his frequent declarations that he was neither fascist nor socialist. Clearly, there was a difference in magnitude. Cuba was certainly no threat to world peace, and the oppression on the island was tame in comparison to what was unfolding in the Third Reich. Still, for those following world events, the image of Batista in full dress uniform, with high black boots, standing above frequent military parades in the Caribbean sun was not reassuring. Beyond image, the removal of President Gómez, although technically legal, clearly amounted to little more than a coup d'état. Periodic beatings of reporters and the occasional discovery of the corpse of a political opponent with a bullet in the head made it even clearer how far Cuba was from anything resembling democracy.

The Roosevelt administration remained committed to Batista, but with the understanding that he would pave the way for a new and democratic constitution. Any move in the direction of open dictatorship was sure to meet with harsh retaliation from the United States and, quite likely, internal revolt, so in essence there was only one way for Batista to go—toward reform and a reopening of the Cuban political process. Batista made his move in mid-1938, when he suspended further deliberation of the Triennial Plan and pledged again to hold elections for a constitutional assembly. From that point forward, his days as a military man were numbered. Batista did not intend to surrender power, but in order to retain it, he now needed to make the delicate transition from army chief to presidential candidate and then win a national election. A new constitution would mean the end of the provisional and quasi-legal governments that Batista used to wield power. In any new constitution, real authority would be vested in the president and Congress.

One of Batista's greatest challenges of the period was to attract a constituency beyond the corrupt politicians who supported him and the military. The colonel could claim revolutionary credentials because of his wide-ranging social agenda, but the bulk of his political support came from the government parties, which for years put on an impressive show of incompetence and corruption. So, to better compete for the presidency, Batista moved to the political left with the hope of gaining a portion of the "revolutionary" vote. His search for friends led him in 1938 to the Cuban Communists and a stunning political alliance that lasted for years.

Inevitably, Batista's leftward drift created friction with Washington, and during the election campaigns of 1939 and 1940, Batista frequently attacked U.S. foreign policy toward Cuba and advocated measures detrimental to foreign investors. His attacks were in keeping with the principles of the Revolution of 1933, which was, at least in part, about establishing greater independence from the United States. Much of the revolutionary legislation enacted by Grau and supported by Batista was aimed at doing just that, but in his presidential quest, the colonel made his criticisms of the United States public and pointed in a way that he rarely had before. In private, he waged a bitter diplomatic struggle with his sometimes friend, sometimes nemesis, U.S. Assistant Secretary of State Sumner Welles, over the payment of Cuba's foreign debt. The reassignment of U.S. Ambassador Jefferson Caffery in March 1937 contributed to the tension between the two nations. Ever since his arrival in December 1933, Caffery served as a buffer between Welles and Batista, easing friction between them. Caffery's replacement, Joshua Butler Wright, did not form a close bond with Batista, and the result was a diminished role for the U.S. ambassador in Cuban affairs.[3] Batista further tweaked the United States by remaining neutral in the struggle between Mexico and Washington over Mexico's expropriation of foreign oil interests in 1938. The colonel went so far as to visit Mexico in February 1939 and lavish praise on President Lázaro Cárdenas, leading some in the U.S. State Department to worry that he would follow Mexico's example and expropriate American sugar properties in Cuba.

As the world prepared for war, democracy in Cuba experienced a resurgence. Cuba was in the process of building democratic institutions, and Colonel Batista was in the final stages of his evolution from military man to presidential candidate.

A Compliant President

For the most part, President Federico Laredo Brú is portrayed in the scholarly literature as the consummate puppet. As Hugh Thomas put it, "he was pleased to surrender his soul completely to Batista."[4] There is some truth in this assessment, but it is far from the entire story. Historical records, newspaper articles, and personal accounts from the period reveal a much more complex political relationship between Colonel Batista and President Brú, particularly as it evolved over time.

Brú entered the presidency precariously. As vice president he was the constitutional successor to the impeached Gómez. But he was not the first choice of the military.[5] In addition, there was concern that the new president would side with the departed Gómez in the struggle over the tax for rural education. In no mood for further challenges, Batista imposed a cabinet on Brú sprinkled with his allies and confidantes with the idea of placing the new president in a "straitjacket."[6] Two days after Brú's inauguration, Batista took it upon himself to announce the government's short-term agenda, which consisted of two items: final passage by the Senate of the nine-cent tax on sugar to fund rural education, a measure that was passed within a few days, and elections for a constitutional assembly. "With the [Brú] administration and Congress identified with these two promising proposals and with the armed forces complying with and enforcing the laws, the people of Cuba are to be congratulated," Batista told the nation.[7]

Rather than react angrily to the constraints placed on him by the military, one of the new president's first acts was to praise the military and ask for its support. Brú possessed a certain pragmatism that allowed him to recognize the political realities of his position. Unlike Gómez, he did not spend time lamenting the overwhelming influence of the military in government. He recognized it and worked within those boundaries.[8] Brú quickly declared his support for Batista's rural education plan, and six days after his inauguration (December 30, 1936) the controversial sugar tax bill went into effect. And, while Batista was unveiling the government's program, President Brú set about administrative tasks such as outlining employment practices in the new government. The tone of the Batista-Brú governing partnership was set in the first few days of the new administration. For the next four years (1937–1940), Batista served as a sort of spiritual guide for the government, unveiling and campaigning for a series of social and economic reforms, while Brú acted as a business administrator, promoting and implementing the agenda. It was also left to Brú to slog through the daily mud of Cuban politics.

During this same period, Batista went about the task of building a political coalition to secure his own election. In line with his political agenda, he decided to come out from the shadows. His intervention in the Gómez affair publicly exposed him to an even greater extent than his earlier government interventions. With his power and influence now out in the open, Batista decided to put himself on an equal level with the president at official functions, so that at virtually every major public event, the military chief and president sat at the same table, along with their wives. Colonel and president traveled across the island together unveiling public works projects, cutting ribbons, and addressing parades. Seldom was the president given an award without the same tribute being given to Batista. For reasons of protocol the president was given a prominent place at national events, but no one was confused about who held real power.

U.S. Military Attaché E. W. Timberlake accompanied Colonel Batista and President Brú on one of their trips to the eastern province of Camagüey in early April 1937, and after a parade consisting of some military units and about ten thousand school children, he described the following scene: "This obviously prepared demonstration was followed by an impromptu parade by a mob of at least 15,000 wildly enthusiastic 'sons of the soil' from Camaguey and Oriente, who milled by hysterically shouting the praises of Colonel Batista, and utterly ignoring the President. The police at first tried to stop this demonstration, but upon the orders of Colonel Batista, allowed it to proceed for more than an hour." The demonstration was followed by a four-hour banquet in which all the preliminary speakers "were drowned out by cries for Batista, who eventually promised '*dos palabras*' [two words] and then talked enthusiastically and well, without notes, for 45 minutes."[9] Even some political leaders in the government coalition did not take President Brú very seriously. At a meeting to debate electoral reform held at Batista's farm on the outskirts of Havana in late November 1937, a reunion at which several cabinet members were present, Brú disagreed with one of the speakers, and the "President was informed of his true [puppet] status in no uncertain terms by a politician present." According to U.S. military intelligence, Brú threatened to resign over the incident, but Batista, after "smoothing out his ruffled feathers," convinced the president to stay on.[10]

The opposition press hammered away mercilessly at President Brú on the issue of his lack of authority. It was dangerous to attack Batista or the military directly, so Brú became a surrogate target. The political cartoon was among the sharpest knives in the media arsenal. In an April 1937 *Bohemia* caricature, one man is desperately trying to convince another about some startling news regarding Laredo Brú. The first man says: "May I see my children in poverty if it is not the truth." The second man remains unconvinced about the disclosure, still unknown to the reader. The cartoon concludes, when in an effort to enhance his credibility, the first man raises the stakes and wishes for the "worst luck to befall me," if the news about Laredo Brú being president is untrue. Two months later, the authority theme was used

This jibe was first published in the newspaper *Avance* and then republished by the magazine *Bohemia* on June 5, 1938. A self-satisfied President Brú (whose nickname was Fico) stands on a scale labeled *gobierno* (government) and wonders "how can there still be those who doubt that I carry weight in this government." Unbeknown to the president, an apelike Batista is pressing his foot down on the scale, clearly reflecting the cartoonist's view of who was in charge of the Cuban government.

in another political cartoon. In the panel, a seemingly bored Laredo Brú stands by a balcony at the Presidential Palace tapping his fingers, while two men converse by his desk. The first man points at a whistle lying on the desk and asks the other: "Is that the whistle Laredo uses (when he wants something)." The second man responds: "No sir, he doesn't blow any whistles." In another jab at Brú, and at Batista as well, *Bohemia* ran a political cartoon the following year of the president standing on a scale named "*Gobierno*" (government). As he sees the needle go up on the scale, a smiling Brú declares proudly, "And, there are still those who doubt that I carry weight in this government." Unbeknownst to the president, an apelike figure in a military uniform resembling Batista has a heavy foot on the scale.[11]

Political cartoons ridiculing Batista were rare, but *Bohemia* occasionally took the risk. Sometimes the magazine poked fun at Batista in such a way as to maintain plausible deniability about what it was doing. One such instance occurred shortly before the discredited midterm congressional elections of March 1938, when the magazine ran a front-page cartoon depicting various political billboards with a picture of the candidates on them. One of the billboards contained a picture of a brutish figure with certain facial characteristics resembling Batista. Under the billboard of the fictitious candidate was the name "José Bruto y Travieso" (José Dumb and Mischievous).[12]

There were good reasons for the opposition press to hide its true intentions. Journalists critical of the government, and particularly the military, still faced the threat of a beating and the forced feeding of massive amounts of laxatives. These attacks declined as the political process opened up, but as late as May 1938, the publisher of a weekly news magazine, after criticizing the government, was kidnapped and forced to drink castor oil.[13] On numerous occasions, the government shut down publications or radio stations for "violating the law." The opposition newspaper *La Prensa* was closed on two occasions, once in September 1938, for writing about the possible dissolution of Congress, and again, from February to April 1939. Radio Station CMQ and the news magazine *Zig-Zag* were also targeted by the government.[14] Harsh criticism of Batista and the military was still taboo in this period, so the vast majority of ridicule was heaped on Brú and members of Congress. This was particularly true during the first two years of Brú's presidency. Batista became a less dangerous target for political satire by early 1939, as his entrance into civilian politics appeared imminent.

Many political figures would not have accepted the presidency under these conditions. Laredo Brú did and went further. He became a champion of the Batista social agenda, even going so far as to suggest on one occasion that Batista was outside the law because of his guiding role in the Revolution of 1933. Brú's remark, made in September 1939, came in response to a political attack by former President Mario Menocal calling on him to show greater independence from Batista and the army. Menocal further demanded that the members of the cabinet respond to the orders of the president rather than the commands of the army chief. Brú's answer was remarkably candid, and it read in part: "I cannot put any obstacles in the way of Colonel Batista, who is the Chief of the Revolution of the Fourth of September, and who has been responsible for all the governments which we have had since that time." The president described his government as the "culmination of a revolutionary process" and the direct result of Batista's "intervention in the political, social and economic activities of the Nation." Brú went on to say that he was confident that Batista and the army would remain neutral in the upcoming constitutional assembly elections scheduled for November 15, 1939.[15] It was a clear public admission by Brú of his inability to control Batista.[16]

This cartoon ran on the front page of the magazine *Bohemia* on February 27, 1938. Journalists had to be careful of military reprisal if they attacked Batista or the military directly, but sometimes they targeted Batista in a way that provided them with plausible deniability. In this image, which ran prior to the discredited congressional elections of 1938, the campaign poster on the bottom right suspiciously resembles Batista, and the candidate's name is "José Bruto y Travieso" (José Dumb and Mischievous).

The reference by President Brú to Batista as the "chief" of the Revolution of 1933 was no accident. It was part of a larger political and public relations campaign by Batista and his supporters to wrest away the mantle of revolutionary leadership from Grau. Both sides attempted to lay claim to the accomplishments of the Revolution of 1933 in the period leading up to the elections of 1939 and 1940. Batista political adviser and confidante Juan J. Remos set forth the case most clearly in a June 1938 article in *Bohemia*: "He [Batista] sowed the seeds of the Revolution; he made the Revolution of September 4; the Revolution did not make him."[17] In his speeches, Batista was not shy about declaring himself the "soul and leader of the Cuban Revolution of 1933" and listing its achievements as his own.[18] For their part, Grau and his supporters argued that they were the ideological descendants of José Martí and the liberators of Cuba. The very name of the party—Partido Revolucionario Cubano (Auténticos)—Cuban Revolutionary Party (Authentics)—suggested that they were the real revolutionaries and that Batista and his supporters were the impostors. Many of the former student leaders, such as Eduardo Chibás, were members of the party and regular contributors to the Cuban press.[19] This debate between Batistianos and Auténticos raged on for years in Cuba and continues to this day in Miami among the dying remnants of those two political movements.

So the government's message was clear: Batista was the leader of a revolution, Brú an administrative caretaker. So why did Federico Laredo Brú accept such a compromised presidency and the ridicule that went with it? Any answer to that question must be in large part speculative, since he never publicly addressed the issue. But one need only read the Cuban newspapers and magazines of the period to see that there was a great yearning to create civilian institutions capable of governing the nation. There was a strong strain in Cuban political thought in the late 1930s that argued that the military must be gradually eased out of its dominant position in government. Civilian institutions must be rebuilt. A new, sovereign constitution, unlike the 1901 version imposed on Cuba by the United States, was perceived as the solution. Democratic institutions to keep the military in check would flow from that new constitution. The disproportionate influence of the military was seen as an outgrowth of the post-Machado chaos; some even justified the military's role because it brought "order" to a fragmented society. The restoration of "order" was an accomplishment frequently cited by supporters of Batista and the military.[20] However, with the return of stability, many argued, it was time to put the military back under civilian administration, as it had been for much of the postindependence era, prior to 1933. The opposition should be brought back into the political process to counterbalance the government, but there was also a cry for patriotic Cubans to fight for *La Patria* from inside the government.[21] President Brú embraced this latter role. Publicly and privately, he justified his actions by arguing that he was working for a constitutional assembly that would "be an expression of the free will of the people, without interference either from the armed forces or the government."[22]

There was nothing inevitable about the establishment of democratic institutions in Cuba. Even after Batista committed himself to a constitutional assembly, he considered pulling back from democratic reforms. On at least two occasions, once in May 1937 and again in April 1939, Batista gave serious thought to disbanding Congress.[23] He was faced with a dilemma: if he chose to remain as island strongman, history indicated that Cuban society would eventually explode around him. This was the lesson of Machado. If he chose to move toward democracy, Batista would need to sacrifice a great deal of power, because a freely elected president would share power with Congress and an independent judiciary. The military could no longer be used, at least not as openly, to exert pressure on uncooperative public officials. Batista chose the latter course, but he tried to control the political process so that the end result would be his selection-election as president.

It is in directing this process that President Brú played an important role. Batista came to trust the older man's political judgment and counsel. As early as August 1937, U.S. military intelligence recognized Brú as an influential political adviser to Batista. "The fact is becoming increasingly evident that the President's experience, political training and general sagacity is daily growing more valuable to Batista," the U.S. military attaché wrote in a dispatch to Washington.[24] Batista had good reason to trust Brú's political skills. Brú was the epitome of the traditional Cuban politician. A veteran of Cuba's second Independence War (1895–1898), he had risen to the rank of colonel in the Liberation Army. An accomplished lawyer, after independence he served as secretary to the Audiencia (the principal court) in Las Villas Province in central Cuba and later as an assistant prosecutor for the Supreme Court. He served as interior minister under the elder President Gómez, retiring from politics in 1913 to practice law in the port city of Cienfuegos. In the 1920s, he was active in the opposition to the corrupt government of President Alfredo Zayas and helped organize the Veterans' and Patriots' Movement. Brú was one of the principal leaders of an armed uprising against the Zayas government in 1923, a revolt quickly put down. (At that time, Batista was assigned to guard the country home of Zayas). Brú resurfaced again in 1933 as a cabinet member in Céspedes's short-lived government, brought to an end by the Sergeants' Revolt. As a founding member of the Nacionalista

Party and a confidante of former President Mendieta, he was deemed a suitable candidate for the vice-presidential post under the younger Gómez in the January 1936 elections. So by the time Brú assumed the presidency, he was well versed in the intrigue of Cuban politics.

With his experience, Brú proved invaluable to Batista and his presidential aspirations, while at the same time working to nudge Cuba toward democratic reform. When negotiations between Batista and the political opposition, led by Grau, reached an impasse over the conditions for presidential elections in 1940, it was Brú who interceded and helped forge a compromise. The three men met privately for hours, on several occasions, at the president's summer home and were eventually able to fashion a deal. The president's public persona was one of a taciturn and humorless politician, although friends, who referred to him as "Fico," frequently commented on his dry, understated sense of humor and the endless stream of anecdotes that he used to break the tension during heated discussions.[25] Brú's decision to accept an extension of his presidential term from May 1940 until October 1940 was crucial to securing the participation of the political opposition in presidential elections, because it allowed the parties enough time to organize a national campaign against Batista.[26] And, while Brú protected Batista's right to seek the presidency, he was also able to secure concessions from the colonel, including his resignation from the army in December 1939.[27]

This evolution in Brú's status was facilitated by the fact that the government could not possibly claim neutrality in the constitutional assembly and presidential elections, if one of the candidates, namely Batista, was perceived to be running the government machinery. So as the elections of 1939 and 1940 approached, Batista was forced to distance himself more and more from the government. Brú's freedom to act grew as Batista's direct involvement diminished. Some signs of greater independence were visible by the middle of 1938, when Brú reshuffled his cabinet to weed out some Batista supporters and appoint those loyal to him.[28] By the following year, Batista and Brú were publicly expressing differences on social policy, and on one occasion the president, in the closing days of the constitutional assembly elections, vetoed social legislation strongly supported by the army chief.[29] Brú also objected to Batista's campaign attacks against the United States, which he feared would hurt economic relations between the two countries.[30] In frequent dispatches and letters, U.S. officials took note of Batista's declining power and influence. A State Department memo, dated January 17, 1939, noted that the Cuban "House [of Representatives] would not pass legislation merely because Batista wanted it." The same memo expressed the view that President Brú "is not inclined to go along with Batista merely because the latter wants him to."[31] Ambassador Wright commented, in an April 1939 letter to Welles, that "President Laredo Brú has grown in stature during the time I have been here: he has shown spirit and courage in some of his veto messages, and does not seem quite such a puppet as before."[32]

For his efforts to bring about a democratic transition in Cuba, President Brú earned the praise of members of the opposition, like historian Portell-Vilá and Congressman Eduardo Suárez Rivas. Portell-Vilá described Brú as an "astute" and "masterful" politician who combined "concessions with opportunistic affirmations" of civilian power.[33] In his autobiographical work, Suárez Rivas credits President Brú with resisting military pressure and working to establish "civilian power and respect for the law."[34] In assessing Laredo Brú's political legacy, his deference to Batista must be weighed against his commitment to bring about democratic change.

THE "BELIEVE IT OR NOT" CONGRESS

Illegitimate since birth, the morally challenged Congress remained an unpredictable factor in the unsteady march toward Cuban democracy. Made up entirely of political parties that struck a deal with Batista and the military, there was no legitimate revolutionary voice in the legislative branch of government. Its independence was called into question time and time again, most spectacularly during the impeachment hearings and trial. Many observed that Congress existed simply so that the members could collect a paycheck at the taxpayers' expense.[35] Members were frequently absent, and it was often difficult to achieve a quorum to vote on legislation. When Congress did act, it was often to line the pockets of its members. Media reports of scandalous behavior were commonplace. When considering a political amnesty to pave the way for democratic elections, it was alleged that some of those included in the list were criminals who paid bribes to influential members.[36] When a bill to pay off a portion of Cuba's foreign debt passed Congress, it allegedly included $10 million extra in bonds for kickbacks to legislators and members of the military. For years, congressmen suspected of taking part in the scheme were given the nickname "*bono*" (bond).[37] Congress provided the nation with an ongoing display of expensive comic theater. Each scandal and betrayal of public trust was more unbelievable than the next, leading the news magazine *Bohemia* to speculate that in the future people would marvel at some of those serving in Congress in 1937 and be forced to cite the famous phrase from Ripley, "Believe It or Not."[38] While many were indignant, there was a high tolerance level for corruption in Cuba's political culture. "They [the crooked politicians] were known. They were criticized. But, they were also admired because they had the ability to act as criminals with impunity," wrote historian Portell-Vilá, reflecting on the period.[39]

To be fair, members of Congress were not the only ones implicated in political corruption. Military commanders throughout the island served as regional lords bestowing favors on area residents for a cost.[40] In rural areas, soldiers and officers peddled their influence as a commodity. "If a *guajiro* desires to insure himself of justice before a primary court, he first presents a pig to the Sergeant in command of the village in which the court is located. If a merchant desires to receive some special favor from the Executive, he first interviews an influential Army officer. If an individual has a doubtful suit against a bank or a large business concern, he insures victory by first seeing the local regimental commander," reported the U.S. military attaché.[41] There was also an extensive illegal gambling network, sanctioned by the army, in the Cuban countryside that threatened the economic livelihood of the rural poor. "This includes all types of games of chance, in addition to the daily '*bolito*' (an offshoot of the weekly lottery), and frequent 'contributions' by the workers for fiestas glorifying the military."[42] In Havana, Lieutenant Colonel Pedraza and Major Mariné were frequently mentioned in connection with illegal gambling activities.[43] And then of course, there was the improving financial well-being of Batista, whom some speculated was already a millionaire. Although his personal wealth multiplied exponentially in the years to come, by this time Batista was already profiting from inflated government contracts and gambling proceeds. With a lovely new home at Military City and a ranch in the countryside, Batista was no longer the modest Quaker Sergeant of 1933—although not quite the very wealthy man he later became.[44] The rest of the executive branch of government was not without sin. In September 1937, news that officials in the treasury and agriculture ministries were attempting to monopolize rice imports and pass on higher prices to consumers came to light.[45] And, of course, when finances forced government layoffs, the first to go were competent employees with no political connections. Still, the Congress, because of its public nature, was the most visible embodiment of corruption on the island.

A cautionary note on Cuban corruption is appropriate at this point. Much has been written about Cuban decadence and dishonesty, particularly during the Batista dictatorship of the 1950s, but little effort has been made to put that corruption into context. Similar patterns of fraud can be found throughout Latin America, so there is a great need for comparative studies to put the Cuban case in its proper context. The existing scholarly and periodical literature on the subject emphasizes the revolutionary interpretation that corruption was a key factor leading to the overthrow of Batista in 1959.[46]

Returning to the issue of corruption in the Cuban Congress, for better or worse, it was with this morally compromised, semilegitimate legislative body that Batista and Brú needed to work to secure their evolving agenda. In 1937 and the first months of 1938, colonel and president were most interested in getting the Congress to pass legislation enacting social reforms laid out in the Triennial Plan. Later on, they pressured Congress to legislate itself out of existence in favor of a constitutional assembly. The attitude in Congress to these pressures ranged from stiff resistance to malaise to a willingness to negotiate.

Batista demonstrated his great power over Congress during the impeachment struggle, but once that was over and the colonel's influence was out in the open, the members began to treat him as they would any chief executive. In return for passing Batista's legislative program they expected to be rewarded with patronage, payola, and public works projects in their provinces. Disputes over these issues frequently led legislators to withdraw their support for legislation or, even worse, fail to show up for work. This attitude exasperated Batista and led him to privately threaten the dissolution of Congress in the spring of 1937. On that occasion, Defense Minister Remos, at Batista's request, called congressional leaders into a meeting and warned them that they had only "a matter of hours" to begin work on a legislative agenda. At first, congressional leaders threatened to call the colonel's bluff, but in the end they blinked and agreed to meet on a regular basis.[47] Batista publicly denied that threats were made to do away with Congress. "I am not a lover of tyranny and those who thought the Congress would disappear and that immediately a dictatorship would emerge were mistaken. [I] never considered that idea," Batista said.[48]

The threat to dissolve Congress could not be used every day. Sooner or later the members were bound to defy him, and then Batista would be faced with a lose-lose scenario. The colonel could dissolve Congress and face intense international economic and political pressure or, in the alternative, he could allow Congress to remain in session and show weakness. Either scenario was likely to lead to internal instability. The cagey Batista needed to utilize just the right combination of terror and reward to bend the Congress to his will.

Terror came in the form of unexpected visits by military and police enforcers to the homes of outspoken critics and disagreeable legislators. The case of House Speaker Carlos Márquez Sterling serves as a useful example in this regard.[49] Márquez Sterling was from a prominent and wealthy political family. His late father, Manuel Márquez Sterling, served as president for several hours during the transfer of power from Hevia to Mendieta in 1934.

As secretary of state, the elder Márquez Sterling later negotiated the treaty abrogating the Platt Amendment. His son, following in his father's political footsteps, won a seat in the Cuban House of Representatives in the 1936 elections and was chosen by the members to be president of that legislative body. His major misfortune was that he backed President Gómez in the impeachment struggle.[50] Although Márquez Sterling was out of the country on a diplomatic mission at the time of the ouster, Batista and the military were not about to allow him to remain in his high-profile position.

Upon his return to Cuba in January 1937, Márquez Sterling conferred with the impeached Gómez and informed him that he planned to resign as House leader, because he was confident of the army's ability to "find the votes" to remove him. To Márquez Sterling's surprise, after he informed his opponents of his impending resignation, they decided to formally remove him anyway. This additional humiliation was evidently orchestrated by the army and Batista political adviser Major Mariné. Angered by the move, Márquez Sterling took part in a bitter nine-hour debate on the floor of the House on February 2, 1937, during which he declared that while "Colonel Batista [in the past] brought order, today he has been transformed into Cuba's primary destabilizing force."[51] At the end of the debate, Márquez Sterling was stripped of his leadership position.

The matter did not end there. Márquez Sterling's criticism of Batista during the floor debate earned him a 3 a.m. telephone call from Major Mariné with a demand that he come to see Colonel Batista immediately at Military City. A car was sent to transport the congressman to the base, but his wife explained that he was not home. The next day, Márquez Sterling attended the House session and during floor debate brought up the subject of declining civilian authority in government. That evening, while dining with an aide at his home, the congressman was visited by Batista's "strong-arm man," Captain Belisario Hernández, wearing civilian clothes rather than a military uniform.[52] A visit by Captain Hernández, a former New York City cab driver who spoke broken English, was usually the prelude to a beating or worse. The six-foot, two-inch Hernández was reportedly "lightning quick in his actions and has a blazing temper." His missions of "persuasion" were directed at civilian political opponents and disobedient officers. U.S. military intelligence made the following observation about Hernández: "He has great physical strength and endurance, but is below the average in intelligence. He has to date invariably gotten results, as he is absolutely devoid of personal fear. He has been wounded four times and decorated at least a dozen times."[53]

Fearing for his life, Márquez Sterling and his wife briefly conferred, and she then began calling fellow legislators to inform them of the threat to her husband. In the meantime, Márquez Sterling went to the living room and asked the waiting Hernández about the "purpose of his visit." The captain replied that his "orders" were to take him to see Batista. The congressman replied that the hour (10 p.m.) was late and that he would prefer to see the colonel the following day. Hernández answered that "tomorrow would be too late." In an effort to buy time, Márquez Sterling told Hernández, he wanted to go upstairs to change his clothes, but to his surprise as he began walking up the stairs, the captain followed in close pursuit. While this tense scene played out inside, soldiers surrounded the home. As the congressman changed his clothes, the captain sat in an adjoining office waiting for him. In those uneasy moments, Márquez Sterling decided that under no circumstances would he leave his residence with Captain Hernández. At about the same time that he finished changing, a fellow legislator, Congressman Carlos Frayle Goldarás, arrived to offer moral support in the confrontation. Within a few minutes, the house was filled with legislators and family friends, and Hernández backed down and left, along with his fellow soldiers.

In the next few days, Senator José Manuel Casanova, aligned with the government, inquired of Batista about the safety of Congressman Márquez Sterling and the significance of the Belisario Hernández visit. The answer was vintage Batista. The colonel said he could not "respond to the reactions of his friends and partisans." Batista, however, let the senator know that Márquez Sterling could "relax" and that nothing else was likely to occur. Nevertheless, the message had been delivered.

Reward—the other component of Batista's modus operandi—came in the form of patronage, kickbacks, contracts, and salary. As long as Batista allowed the Congress to operate, members were able to tack their pet projects on to key legislation. Congress was slow to adopt legislation on electoral reform, a political amnesty, and guidelines for a constitutional assembly, but it could be a model of haste and efficiency when voting on contracts and other financially beneficial projects. On one occasion, in September 1937, it passed 350 laws in a marathon twenty-eight-hour session. This rash of public works legislation was motivated, at least in part, by the expectation of a Supreme Court ruling forcing half the House members to stand for reelection the following year.[54]

By the use of his veto power, President Brú served as another check on Congress. However, unlike his predecessor, Brú took a hands-off attitude toward the legislative body. He declined to lobby Congress for or against pending legislation. It was clear from his public statements that he supported the Batista social agenda and that anything undercutting it was likely to receive a presidential veto. Legislation aimed at limiting Batista's presidential aspirations was also sure to meet with his disapproval. But he was never politically aggressive in his advocacy. Brú left the convincing and persuading to Batista and the military. Politically, this approach made sense, because it protected him from the same sort of charges that led to Gómez's impeachment.[55]

These were the tools Batista, with the help of the president, utilized to motivate Congress, but the task was further complicated by a series of other factors. For one, the impeachment struggle had sharply divided Congress, and an antimilitary opposition emerged in the House of Representatives, known as the Frente Parlamentario Democrático (Democratic Parliamentary Front). This minority coalition transcended party affiliations and consisted of members from all the major political parties in Congress at the time, including the Liberal Party, which had the closest links to Batista. No similar coalition emerged in the Senate, although a handful of members in the upper house were frequent critics of the military. Although the group received little attention from the Cuban press, members of the front spoke out frequently about the excesses of the military in government.[56]

The composition of the front underscored another challenge facing Batista. This coalition consisted of members from several parties, because with the exception of the Communists, Cuba's political parties were ideologically weak. Typically, what united members of a political party were personal ties to the leader and the access that gave them to patronage. The lack of a unifying ideology undermined party discipline and unity. The practical result of this was that Batista and his political allies were often in the unenviable position of having to negotiate with individual members or blocs of members rather than three or four party leaders, who could be relied on to secure the necessary votes. Furthermore, as time went on, the government parties began to fragment over a variety of issues—everything from patronage to the drafting of a strategy for the elections of 1939 and 1940. Even some of Batista's allies in the Liberal Party questioned whether they would fare better if they broke with the government. Despite protestations from Batista, some party leaders distanced themselves from the government, although they stopped short of a formal break.[57]

All in all, Congress presented Batista with an untidy set of political issues. He would have to weave his way through this fractious, ever-changing jigsaw puzzle of political alliances, if he was to achieve his personal and political goals.

TRIENNIAL PLAN

The Triennial Plan, unveiled in June 1937, was one of the oddest and most ambitious blueprints for social reform ever produced in Cuba. It was a logical extension of the Batista reform agenda of the prior year. At some points, the twenty-page document reads like a shopping list of desired programs and results for the nation, with no formula to achieve the stated goals. Other portions are quite specific, such as the section regarding sugar, in which the text outlines legislation to regulate the island's most important industry and protect the rights of the small sugar producers, or *colonos*. Critics referred to it as the "three-hundred-year plan," and, in fact, it would probably have taken that long to implement all of the suggestions included therein.[58] Among the recommendations were the following:[59]

- Distribution of state lands to the rural poor
- Health insurance for working mothers
- Promotion and development of a national fishing industry
- An extensive program of reforestation
- Establishment of provincial agrarian markets
- A housing program for the elderly poor
- Regulations for sexual education
- Establishment of a national banking system
- A credit program to assist workers in building homes
- Paid national holidays for workers
- Creation of a national aquarium
- Development of a standardized curriculum for the mentally handicapped
- Free schooling for the poor
- Establishment of a school for the fine arts in each of the six provinces
- Government publication and distribution of Cuban scholarly and literary works

It was a document of youthful idealism, produced by the thirty-six-year-old Batista after months of consultations with civilian experts from many different professions. He unveiled many of the details during a lengthy interview with the owner of the island's most important newspaper, *Diario de la Marina*, which ran a lengthy story on the plan. In the right-hand corner of the front page was a large photo, taken during the interview, of the owner, José I. Rivero, and Batista, wearing a white sports jacket. His decision to wear civilian clothes, rather than an army uniform, appeared to be part of his ongoing effort to reshape his political image.[60] "There are many that want to ignore that I am the leader of a constructive revolutionary movement," Batista told Rivero. "Others want to see in me a simple guardian of order. But what do they understand by order? Because, I view this more as a concept of architecture rather than police work."[61]

Batista's career would take many a jaded turn in the years to come, but there is little of the cynical to be found in the Triennial Plan. In it are contained his fondest dreams for Cuba. It was hopelessly impractical, and most of it never came to fruition. In its failure, one can find the apex of Batista's career. It was a document full of ideas, some inarticulate and imprecise to be sure, but still it burst forth with concepts. In the 1950s, Batista papered over his dictatorial practices with mind-numbing statistics about endless public works projects, all intended to obfuscate his grasp for power. At least the Batista of the late 1930s was in search of ideas at the same time he was grasping for power.

Perhaps the most impractical aspect of the plan was the way Batista envisioned its implementation. It was to be a model of corporatist consultation. After its unveiling in June 1937, and after Batista secured President Brú's strong support, Interior Minister Emiliano Amiell Ginori was charged with traveling to each of Cuba's six provinces and formally presenting it to the provincial legislatures. He did this throughout the summer and autumn of 1937. From there the plan was to make its way to the municipalities and the local governing councils and down the government path to ward bosses and neighborhood councils. At each step, officials were to comment on the plan and make suggestions for its implementation and improvement. After this extensive review process, all the suggestions were to be encapsulated by the Interior Ministry and presented to the president. The chief executive was then charged with proposing appropriate legislation to Congress. Given the wide scope of the original plan, one could have envisioned dozens of pieces of legislation emerging from this nationwide, soul-searching process.

This extensive national consultation was never completed. Time was against the Triennial Plan. Pressure to move toward a constitutional assembly grew. Critics saw the Triennial Plan as a subversion of the democratic process, because it was to be implemented by the discredited government in power. The fundamental issues raised by the plan were more appropriate for consideration by a newly elected constitutional assembly and the government that emerged from that process, critics charged. A few weeks after the unveiling, a magazine columnist noted the "contradiction" between the Triennial Plan and the deliberations under way for a constitutional assembly to restructure Cuban government and society.[62] Raymond Leslie Buell, the influential president of the Foreign Policy Association, congratulated Batista for presenting a plan to address Cuba's "social problems." However, Buell warned that such reforms should not be undertaken by a "fascist dictatorship," but rather by a "democratic government, with its origins in a Constitutional Convention."[63]

Despite the criticisms, Batista pushed ahead with the program through the winter of 1937 and the spring of 1938. On November 20, 1937, before a

crowd of one hundred thousand packed into Tropical Stadium, on the outskirts of Havana, Batista spoke in passionate terms of the Triennial Plan. For
those critics who charged that such a plan could not be implemented by an
undemocratic government, Batista responded that "there has never been a
democratic government" in Cuba since the establishment of the republic in
1902. "We are willing, even with our [military] uniforms on, to remain within
the boundaries of respect for citizens' rights; with our uniforms on we plan
to behave ourselves within the framework of democracy." The advocates of
a constitutional assembly would prefer the patient to die rather than administer "first aid" in the form of the Triennial Plan, he claimed. Batista's speech,
broadcast by radio to the nation, capped a day of activities throughout
Havana as up to one hundred fifty thousand people were bussed from across
the island to take part in ceremonies and parades.[64]

Despite the impressive mobilization of November, by early spring it was
clear that momentum for the plan was sputtering. Events overtook it. In January 1937, Congress passed a law reopening and reorganizing the University
of Havana and the nation's secondary schools after a two-year shutdown. A
broad amnesty was passed at the end of December 1937, granting even the
hated Machado absolution for his political crimes, but the ex-dictator, already
ill, would die in exile. The amnesty paved the way for a wide-ranging dialogue between the government and the opposition, and over the next few
months opponents started returning from exile. The Triennial Plan, drafted
without their input, was seen as an obstacle.

Deteriorating economic conditions also contributed to the demise of the
plan, which called for the distribution of some thirty-three thousand acres
of state-owned land to some fifty thousand rural poor.[65] As part of this
modest land reform measure, which passed Congress in December 1937, the
government was to provide funds for seeds, livestock, and farming equipment.
The measure was widely criticized as inadequate to deal with the problem.
It was said that "Batista distributes land, but in paper bags" ("Batista reparte
la tierra, pero en bolsas de papel").[66] A decline in worldwide sugar prices
and the resultant drop in state revenues made it impossible for the government to provide the promised assistance. More successful was the passage of
health insurance legislation for working mothers, which among other things
covered hospitalizations.[67]

The most important component of the Triennial Plan was the legislation
regulating the sugar industry, which was introduced in Congress in July 1937
and passed at the end of August. The Sugar Coordination Law (Ley de Coor-
dinación Azucarera) established a government agency to arbitrate disputes
between large sugar estates and small sugar producers. Under the law, the
small producers, for the first time were guaranteed a minimum quota and

price for their sugar. Equally important, *colonos*, who leased their land from the large sugar mills, were now protected from arbitrary eviction. The Cuban government agreed to guarantee their leases in perpetuity, and maximum rents were established. The legislation further attacked the mills' economic domination of rural areas by mandating that small businesses, independent of the mill, be allowed to operate on mill property. It also set minimum wages for cane cutters and permanent employees during the harvest (*zafra*) and the dead season (*tiempo muerto*).[68]

For Batista, the former sugar cane cutter from Banes, the legislation must have been deeply satisfying. He knew firsthand that small cane growers, particularly those leasing their lands, were subject to terrible exploitation. *Colonos* were at a big disadvantage when bargaining with the mills, because although they could grow and harvest the cane, they could not process it into sugar. Frequently they had no way to transport their crop to the mill, except by using rail systems owned by the mills. This was the case in Banes, where the United Fruit Company dominated economic relations in the region, and a similar dynamic existed throughout much of the rest of the island, particularly in the east.[69] The new sugar legislation capped the amount the large sugar mills could charge small producers for transportation costs. Agriculture Minister Amadeo López Castro, a personal friend of Batista, was the architect of the legislation, which fundamentally altered rural economic conditions. It provided economic stability for the small planters, and it encouraged the growth of small businesses throughout the countryside.

While the sugar legislation was a major accomplishment, most of the Triennial Plan went unfulfilled. Batista withdrew it from consideration in May 1938, clearing another obstacle in the path of constitutional assembly elections. The decision was a "difficult step" for Batista, who "believed his future glory would be derived" from the plan, Cuban Ambassador to the United States Pedro Martínez Fraga told Welles. In remarks to the nation, the colonel questioned the wisdom of delaying "urgent and substantive reforms for which the different classes are insistently clamoring," but said he was doing so because of requests by the political opposition.[70] He did not abandon the principles of the plan but rather converted them into a campaign platform for the presidential elections of 1940. The protections granted the *colonos*, coupled with his ongoing rural education program, gave Batista the credentials to battle Grau for leadership of the "revolution." The end of deliberations over the Triennial Plan marked the beginning of two years of campaigning, electioneering, and backroom negotiations to establish the rules for Cuba's new democracy.

CHAPTER 13

ROAD TO DEMOCRACY

Cuban politics was not for the meek. During their careers, political figures could expect to spend considerable amounts of time in exile or jail. Grau, Menocal, Miguel Mariano Gómez, Mendieta, Sáenz—all of the major Cuban political leaders of the era experienced one or both. Then there was the violence, always just under the surface, ready to erupt. Sometimes political scores were settled in a hail of bullets. Political assassinations, although less frequent in the late 1930s and early 1940s than in earlier periods, were hardly rare occurrences. The mayor of Marianao, a suburb west of Havana, was assassinated by someone whom he picked up in his car one morning in January 1939. In October of the same year, two members of Joven Cuba were found dead on a street in the Vedado section of Havana. Near their bodies was a placard that read, in part: "The revolution purifies its following for the national liberation." In Camagüey, the following year, a victorious congressional candidate was gunned down in an apparent electoral dispute. Former Secretary of State Orestes Ferrara, an old Machado ally, was wounded, and his chauffeur was killed, during an assassination attempt in March 1940. A year later, a congressman from Oriente was murdered in the vestibule of a hotel. Over the years, Batista, Grau, Mendieta, and many other prominent political leaders were the targets of assassination. The use of violence as a political tool would increase in the coming decade.[1]

If the risks were great, so were the rewards. There were, of course, financial benefits for any capable politician, but even beyond that there was the adulation of followers, who relied on party leaders for their livelihood. This financial link was a powerful bond. The leader that could provide for the economic well-being of his followers was a beloved person indeed. When that ability diminished, so did the political prospects of the leader. As a result, political alliances were elastic and subject to reconsideration on a regular basis. Few politicians remained in the same party their entire career and most shifted allegiances periodically, so that to be successful, a Cuban politician needed to get used to working with former enemies and attacking former friends.

Fulgencio Batista was a natural politician. No past insult was too great that it could not be overlooked at a time of political necessity. In the campaigns of 1939 and 1940, as he would throughout his career, Batista appealed to friends and foes alike in his efforts to build a winning political coalition.

POLITICAL ALLIANCES

In 1938, there were three major political movements in Cuba. There were, of course, the government parties (Nacionalistas and Liberals), and now most recently the Conjunto, as a result of a split between Menocal and some of the party leadership. In the eyes of many, these parties were discredited by their contemporary ties to Batista and the military, and in the case of the Liberals, their past links to Machado. These factors not withstanding, they still maintained a loyal core of supporters, if for no other reason than the fact that they controlled government patronage. This coalition, with some exceptions, backed Batista.

The second major political force was the Cuban Revolutionary Party (Auténticos) led by former President Grau San Martín. His every declaration and pronouncement was reported by the Cuban press. He and his followers spoke with great passion of the accomplishments of the Revolution of 1933 and their plans to continue the renovation of Cuban society, if they could regain power. Grau, who left office in January 1934 with almost no political support, had succeeded in recreating himself as a sort of idealistic mystic forced into Miami Beach exile because of his principles. Their electoral strength was as yet unproven, but their visibility inside and outside Cuba suggested that they were a force with which to be reckoned. Auténtico political rallies were well attended, and Grau was a celebrity. Many political insiders believed that in a one-on-one presidential race between Grau and Batista, the former president would emerge triumphant.[2]

The followers of former President Menocal constituted the third major political force on the island. The ultimate political survivor, Menocal, now seventy-two, had reshaped the remnants of the old Conservative Party, yet again, into another powerful organization, this time named the Partido

Demócrata-Republicano (Democrat-Republican Party). The decision to form a new party was forced on Menocal by some leaders of the Conjunto, who after the impeachment proceedings decided to join the government coalition rather than remain in the opposition. In response to their act of defiance, Menocal resigned from the Conjunto in May 1937 and over the course of the next few years bled its membership, in addition to attracting new followers, so that by election time, the Conjunto, the largest single receiver of votes in 1936, was little more than a second-tier party.[3]

Several smaller political movements factored into the electoral equation. The party of impeached President Miguel Mariano Gómez, Acción Republicana, a fringe party in the 1936 elections, was destined to remain so. At one time part of the government coalition, the party was firmly in the anti-Batista camp and seeking an alliance with the Auténticos. The ABC revolutionary society, in the vanguard of the struggle against Machado, was now a shell of its former self. Interparty squabbles had decimated the organization, and many of its members abandoned the movement. Joaquín Martínez Sáenz, a cofounder of the movement, presided over the crumbling remains. Like Gómez, Sáenz was solidly in the anti-Batista camp and seeking an alliance with the Auténticos. Finally, there were the Communists, split into two separate political organizations, a front party known as the Partido Unión Revolucionaria (United Revolutionary Party), established in 1937, and the official party, operating illegally. As part of an international "Popular Front" strategy to combat the spread of fascism, the Cuban Communists were in search of allies on the left. In the case of Cuba, the fascist threat was perceived to be Batista and the military, and so the Communists repeatedly sought an alliance with the Auténticos in the years from 1936 through 1938. Grau rejected the offers, perhaps, remembering their fierce attacks against him during his presidency, thus leaving the Communists without a political dance partner.[4]

This was the political landscape Batista found as he entered the electoral arena. The military chief could not stand pat and expect the government parties to lead him to victory. If he hoped to become Cuba's next president, he needed to add allies and divide enemies. He found allies in the most unlikely of partners. Well aware of the Auténticos reticence to ally themselves with the Communists, Batista made tentative steps in their direction by allowing them to form their front party in 1937. In July of the same year, Communist Party officials met again with Grau and other elements of the Cuban left in an effort to form a Revolutionary Popular Front against Batista, but no agreement was reached.

Several months later, in early 1938, Batista made his first serious overture to Communist leaders, using Mexican diplomat Octavio Reyes Spíndola as an intermediary. The use of a trusted diplomat was a typical modus operandi for Batista, who in the past used Caffery (or Caffery used him, depending on the perspective) to deliver messages to political friends and foes. Unlike Caffery, U.S. Ambassador Wright was hesitant to immerse himself in the spider web of Cuban politics. At least once, Batista asked Wright to lobby Cuban politicians, as Caffery had done, but the ambassador declined, saying "any such intrusion into the affairs of the Legislative Power was absolutely contrary" to his announced policy.[5]

Reyes Spíndola was a logical choice to serve as an intermediary with the Communists, because he was a close friend of Batista's dating back to September 1933, and on good terms with Communist Party officials.[6] From a Mexican standpoint, the mediating role made sense, as it strengthened relations between the two nations at a time when Mexico was locked in a bitter struggle with the United States over the expropriation of oil properties.[7] In the late 1930s, Reyes Spíndola and the Mexican government went out of their way to curry favor with Batista. Mexican President Lázaro Cárdenas gave Batista a thoroughbred horse and awarded him the Aztec Order of the Eagle in December 1938. This burst of Mexican generosity culminated with an official invitation to Batista to visit Mexico City the following year.[8]

Aided by Reyes Spíndola, some initial meetings between Batista and two members of the Communist Party politburo, Chairman Blas Roca[9] and Joaquín Ordoqui, were held as early as mid-January 1938.[10] Spurned by the Auténticos, the Communists began to consider the possibility of an alliance with Batista. The colonel was, after all, in a position to grant the party immediate concessions. In another peacemaking gesture, Batista allowed the Communists to establish a daily newspaper, *Noticias de Hoy*, in May 1938. Details of a formal alliance between the Communists and Batista were hammered out at a meeting in July 1938 at Military City. The outline of the deal was as follows: Batista would allow the Communists to establish a legal party and permit them to create a national labor organization. In return, the Communists would back Batista's presidential aspirations. Legalization of the Communist Party occurred in September 1938, and four months later the Confederación de Trabajadores de Cuba (Confederation of Cuban Workers) was founded. By 1939, the Communists were firmly in the Batista camp.[11]

The alliance illustrates the fluidity of Cuban politics. Two years earlier, at a Communist Party meeting, Roca declared Batista an assassin, responsible for the death of Guiteras and other revolutionary leaders.[12] By 1938, however, Batista was making "progressive steps," including his development of the rural education program and the recent legislation protecting the *colonos*.

Batista had found the path to democracy, Communist leaders declared, and this was a form of government they were, for the time being, willing to support.[13] The alliance required party members to make a gymnastic mental leap. Batista, the assassin of yesterday, was now the progressive reformer of a new era. It was a leap that some party members were unwilling to make and several bolted the party.[14]

The alliance entailed risks for Batista. Some political allies publicly questioned the merits of such a coalition. Senator Santiago Verdeja, a member of the Conjunto and a Batista ally, chastised the colonel for striking such an alliance, arguing that it could "separate (him) from victory" in the presidential election. In a public letter to Batista, Verdeja equated communism with "misery, bureaucracy and blood." Responding to the senator, Batista set forth his reasons for the alliance in practical terms. "We know that [the party's] final objective is Marxism," Batista acknowledged, but the alliance is "rooted in a democratic regime" committed to upholding a new constitution.[15]

The move to the left strained relations with the United States. Batista's ties to the Communists were the subject of countless reports by U.S. military intelligence, the State Department, and the F.B.I. throughout the late 1930s and early 1940s.[16] Whenever Batista publicly attacked the United States, Communist influence was frequently cited as a factor.[17] In a November 1939 dispatch, Ambassador Wright complained about Batista's support of the Communist Party, which "consists of contributions of funds, the appointment of communist leaders to positions of trust, and participation through representatives of the army, in communist manifestations. As a result of this official protection, the Communist Party has grown in numbers and in strength." Wright was further peeved that at the same time Batista was supporting the Communists, they were disseminating literature throughout Cuba defending the Soviet Union and attacking U.S. imperialism.[18] U.S. officials carefully monitored Batista's public and private statements regarding the party. Most of the intelligence reports expressed concern about Batista's "leftist" tendencies, but a few verged on the hysterical and linked him to international Communist conspiracies of all sorts. A U.S. military intelligence report from the mid-1940s suggested that Batista wanted to retain power in Cuba "so that he can better serve the Communists, and that he is planning to become a power not only among Cuban Communists, but also in the Communist organizations of other Latin American countries. His scheming, self-confident, and unscrupulous character does not decrease the possibility of such an ambition on his part. His hatred of the United States and Americans in general spells added trouble in the future."[19]

Batista played a double game with the United States when it came to his relations with the Communists. In meetings with U.S. officials Batista down-played the importance of the alliance, while at the same time, he used the language of social reform, which Washington faithfully interpreted as social-ism, to pressure his powerful northern neighbor and increase his political independence. For the rest of his career, he would either minimize or accen-tuate his relationship with the Communists depending on the audience.[20]

In a November 1938 visit to the United States, Batista met privately with Under Secretary of State Welles (promoted from assistant secretary the year prior) on two occasions, and in one of the reunions the legalization of the Communist Party was discussed. In his justification to Welles, the colonel noted that the party's legalization was part of his "political maneuvering." Batista told Welles that he wanted to legalize the Communist Party and other "extreme left elements" to "bring these groups out into the sunlight and would show to the entire country how limited in number their sup-porters really were." Before moving onto the next subject, Batista told Welles that he believed that "communism would never make any formidable show-ing in Cuba."[21] In an April 1939 meeting with Ambassador Wright, the colo-nel again minimized the importance of the alliance. At that time, Batista "admitted that he intended to avail himself of their [Communists'] support, but he rather contemptuously waved aside any intimation (not from me, but from those who criticize his actions) that he was reflecting their policies."[22] While he was making these reassuring statements to U.S. officials, he was courting Communist support across the island, and their presence at his campaign rallies and other public events was obvious and duly noted by U.S. officials and other observers.[23]

As part of his double game, Batista also sought to understate the intimacy of his ties with the Mexican government, which, at the time, the United States equated with socialism. When Mexico invited Batista for an official visit, the Cuban ambassador in Washington declared that the colonel had declined it.[24] Four months later, in February 1939, Batista was dining with President Cárdenas in Mexico City and addressing the Mexican Congress. Batista also attempted to downplay the influence of Mexican social policy on his own reforms, particularly the rural education program.[25] Washington feared that the Mexican example of expropriating oil properties might be applied by Cuba to the U.S.-dominated sugar industry, and Batista was none too quick about reassuring his northern neighbor. A close aide to Batista admitted to a U.S. Embassy informant that the expropriation of sugar properties was an economic weapon the colonel was willing to employ in the event relations with Washington soured.[26] Of course the constant championing of Mexican independence from the United States by the Cuban Communist daily news-paper served to fan the flames of distrust.[27]

Batista was no Communist. The alliance was more a testament to pragmatism than to ideology. Time and again throughout his long political career, Batista showed an enormous capacity to overlook past insult and treachery, and current ideological differences, in order to strike a political deal. The fact that for years the Communists had reviled him as a dictator and assassin was irrelevant to the political realities of the late 1930s. The Communists could help him secure the presidency, and that was what mattered to him.

Batista's political deal making did not end with the Communist alliance. It was merely the first of several blows struck against Grau and the Auténticos. At the same time he was negotiating with the Communists, Batista was working diligently to sow seeds of dissent among the Auténticos. Not that the Auténticos needed much help in that regard. The former student leaders were a quarrelsome bunch and were forever fighting over matters of principle and splitting the Auténtico coalition. In late 1937, a segment of the party, led by Carlos Prío Socarrás broke away from Grau because of his decision to take part in the political process leading to a constitutional assembly. The rebels opted for the path of ongoing insurrection and formed the Organización Insurrecional Auténtica (Authentic Insurrectional Organization).[28]

Another division occurred among the remaining party members over the best political strategy to use in dealing with Batista and the military. One segment of the party, including Grau and the popular Eduardo Chibás, favored constant oratorical attacks against the armed forces as a way of distinguishing the Auténticos from other political parties. This group came to be known as the *civilistas*, for their defense of civilian prerogatives in government. Their opponents, labeled, not so flatteringly, the *militaristas*, argued in favor of a more diplomatic approach to the armed forces. One of the leaders of the *militaristas*, ironically enough, was Rubén de León, the former student leader who as Grau was being removed from office in 1934, threatened Batista by observing that "one can always find a bullet for a dictator."[29]

It was this disagreement over strategy that Batista used to drive a wedge between the two groups. Once again, the colonel used Reyes Spíndola to act as the go-between. In the late summer of 1938, Spíndola requested a meeting with León.[30] After receiving Grau's blessing, León and others met with the diplomat, who told the former student leader that Batista was considering "drastic" action against President Laredo Brú and that he was seeking Auténtico support for his plans. Spíndola suggested that León meet with Batista at Military City. León declined the offer and reported the conversation to Grau, who approved of the decision to forgo a meeting with Batista. Within days, Spíndola contacted León again, and a second meeting with the diplomat was arranged, again with Grau's blessing. At this second meeting, Spíndola was much more blunt in his assessment of President Laredo Brú.

The president and Congress were "obstacles" to Batista's revolutionary plans, Spíndola told León, assuring him that the colonel wanted to put differences with Grau aside and seek an alliance with the Auténticos. The possibility of a "revolutionary coup" to oust the president was put on the negotiating table. Grau and Batista could rule jointly, as they had in 1933, according to the offer suggested by Spíndola.[31]

León looked on the proposal favorably and saw it as an "opportunity to impose [Auténtico] revolutionary ideology on the prevailing chaos."[32] The participants in the meeting flew to Miami to inform Grau of the news, and a debate ensued. While eager to regain power, Grau and the Auténticos were wary of yet another Batista coup, realizing that they themselves had been the victim of such a maneuver. There was no guarantee that Batista, in the future, would not make a similar deal with another political party or coalition and depose them yet again. Despite these reservations, the majority sentiment was to move ahead cautiously. Grau, fearing that he was being set up for embarrassment by Batista, decided that the negotiations with the colonel must not involve party officials. Grau ordered León to refrain from meeting with Batista, an order he disobeyed upon returning to the island.[33]

As so often was the case with the Auténticos, everyone fancied himself a leader, and León and three others broke with party discipline and met with Batista at the home of a friend. At the meeting, León recalled, Batista greeted them "effusively," despite the fact that they had been rivals for four years.[34] Batista set forth his plan. He asked the Auténticos to stage a rally with fifty thousand participants in front of the Capitol calling for the ouster of the president and Congress. Batista guaranteed them that the police would make no effort to disperse the crowd. The colonel pledged that the Auténticos would be permitted to appoint the members of the new provisional government. The party delegates agreed with the plan. All that was left was to secure Grau's approval and set the date for action.

When informed of the meeting, Grau chastised León, noting that with "Batista nothing is ever certain." Sure enough, a few days later, Batista sprang his trap. Information about the meeting with León was leaked to the Cuban press. Batista made a great show of public unity with Brú and members of Congress. In a statement to the press, Batista declared: "I have unshakable faith in the present Government which is presided over by Colonel Laredo Brú, as much for its honor as for its integrity; I swear this on my honor."

Batista's political chicanery continued when the government shut down an opposition newspaper, *La Prensa*, for accurately publishing news of the supposed plot. The government closure order declared that the newspaper published "false, insidious, calumnious and unpatriotic" information.[35] As a result of the embarrassing revelations, the Auténticos distanced themselves from the negotiations and from León and his allies, including former pentarch Sergio Carbó. Shortly thereafter, León and several others were stripped of their positions on the party's National Executive Committee. Angered by his demotion, León and a core group of supporters broke with Grau and formed a small splinter party that would become known as the Realistas (Realists) for their pragmatic approach to politics. The Auténticos expended their energies attacking each other, and León even considered the possibility that rivals within the party leaked the information about the Batista meeting to the press. The bickering made Batista stronger.[36] With no place left to turn, León and his Realistas eventually backed the army chief in the upcoming elections.

Batista never had any intention of toppling President Laredo Brú and installing his archrival Grau. In one of his Washington meetings with Welles in November 1938, Batista alluded to his efforts to divide the Auténticos. "He [Batista] told me that by a patient policy pursued over a long period he had succeeded in dividing the Auténtico Party into two parts, one of which was now represented in the present government and which comprised the abler and more common-sense leaders of the party," Welles reported in a State Department memorandum of conversation.[37] All of this political subterfuge occurred before the opposition political parties were even allowed to officially organize inside Cuba, a process that began in the closing days of 1938.

RETURN OF THE EXILE

Cuba's most celebrated exile, Ramón Grau San Martín, returned from Miami Beach on December 9, 1938, in a public relations move of exquisite timing. In the weeks leading up to the event, the island was aflutter over Batista's sixteen-day official visit to Washington, his meeting with President Roosevelt, his attendance at Armistice Day ceremonies at Arlington National Cemetery, and speculation that Cuba's powerful northern neighbor was about to lend it $50 million for public works projects across the island. Batista was hailed in the Cuban press as "El Mensajero de la Prosperidad" (messenger of prosperity). In contrast to the pomposity of Batista's Washington visit and homecoming, Grau returned to Cuba on a Pan-American Airways clipper plane, a service running regular tourist flights from Florida to Havana. No public statement was issued beforehand announcing his return. He just showed up at the airport outside Havana at around 10 a.m. on an overcast morning, four years after his departure, and waited for the news to spread throughout the nation. Spread it did. Newspapers rushed special editions to press announcing his return. Enthusiastic supporters rushed to the airport to greet him. The most serious threat to Batista's presidential aspirations was now back in Cuba. The political contest could now begin in earnest.[38] Grau wasted little time in mounting a formidable challenge to Batista and the government. The former president gathered fellow opposition leaders, Menocal, Sáenz, and Miguel Mariano Gómez, at his home for a much publicized meeting on January 5, 1939, to pressure the government to recognize all political parties and adopt an electoral code for a constitutional assembly. For Batista, the political implications of the meeting were significant. A Grau-Menocal alliance could only mean trouble for his presidential aspirations. Batista, with his alliance of three government parties, the Communists, and the Realistas, could likely defeat either Grau or Menocal, but probably not both.[39]

Despite the emerging alliance, the opposition faced a difficult task. Batista and his political and military associates were uniquely positioned to extract campaign "contributions" from the wealthy and the business community. On occasion, Batista appealed directly for funds at private meetings with important businessmen. The suggested contribution hovered around $5,000 but could rise dramatically depending on the circumstances. One American sugar company donated $60,000 to Batista's campaign coffers.[40] The general attitude of most businessmen was to contribute rather than risk the "retaliations or reprisals that might occur toward those who did not respond," Ambassador Wright wrote, paraphrasing the opinion of a prominent American businessman.[41] When appeals failed to secure a contribution, terror was an option, at least that was the perception of some businessmen. In a confidential memorandum to the U.S. State Department, one informant claimed that Batista was overheard stating that "if business interferes in my plans, business men will be found scattered throughout the repartos [neighborhoods] with ants crawling from their mouths."[42] In some cases, companies were asked to appeal to their workers to vote for Batista and his allies.[43]

If coercion were not advantage enough, Batista had at his disposal the military bureaucracy with its extensive network of connections across the island, as well as the contacts of the parties in power. Batista's supporters were not shy about dipping into government accounts to subsidize political activities, including the costs associated with registering their followers for the elections. Intense pressure was applied on employees and their families to register with one of the government parties. Uncooperative employees were frequently shown the door.[44]

In contrast, the national organizations of the opposition parties, particularly the Auténticos and the ABC, were in disarray after four years in exile, during which they were forced to operate clandestinely. The opposition packed little clout in Congress. The Auténticos and the ABC had abstained from the 1936 general elections and the 1938 midterm campaign and therefore had no members in the legislative body. Gómez's strength was minuscule, and Menocal's influence greatly diminished in the governing body after the break with the Conjunto. As a result, their ability to shape the debate over electoral legislation setting the terms of the constitutional assembly and general elections was minimal. Abstention was the only sword the opposition held over the government, but it was a powerful weapon. Without their participation, the elections would be considered a farce, both nationally and internationally. The opposition wielded this weapon to great effect, securing concessions from Batista and the government on numerous occasions.

As noted earlier, Batista's influence over Congress was on the wane as well. As a candidate, he was unable to exert the same degree of pressure on a recalcitrant legislative body. From its perspective, the Congress was faced with the unenviable task of legislating itself out of existence. Much of 1939 was spent trying to craft a political formula by which members of Congress would retain their jobs and influence, while at the same time a constitutional assembly would be elected to debate the very nature and existence of the executive, legislative, and judicial branches. As the uncertainty over elections dragged on, Cuba inched closer to crisis. The terms of half the members of Congress and President Laredo Brú were set to expire in the spring of 1940, which would leave the country with no chief executive and only half the legislative body intact.

Batista grew exasperated with the legislative process and drafted an emergency plan in April 1939 to dissolve Congress either by force or by presidential decree. Under the plan, President Laredo Brú would set a date for a constitutional assembly. Once elected and convened, the assembly would then designate a provisional president, who would rule until general elections were held. Although supposedly secret, elements of the plan were debated in the Cuban press. The news magazine *Carteles*, frustrated with congressional machinations, urged Batista to use "authoritarian" means, if necessary, to bring about a constitutional assembly.[45] For its part, the opposition feared that Batista would manipulate the assembly to secure the provisional presidency for himself. There are indications that he toyed with the idea.[46] Ultimately, he rejected the notion, no doubt surmising that the tenure of any provisional president appointed by the constitutional assembly was likely to be brief. In response to charges that he was seeking a backdoor entry to the presidency, Batista told reporters: "Let my adversaries, or those who confound my morals with their own, or their intentions with mine, note that I have no such intentions, nor am I impatient to get there [the presidency] in a hurry."[47] As in the past, Washington exerted economic and diplomatic pressure on Batista to dissuade him from drastic action.[48]

A general framework for elections was finally agreed on in the spring of 1939, after several electoral codes were passed and amended. The elections were to be held in close proximity to each other, the constitutional assembly elections in the fall (November 15, 1939) followed in late winter (February 28, 1940) by the presidential and congressional elections. There was an underlying contradiction in the scheduling of the two elections so close together. How could a new Congress and president be elected for multiyear terms while a constitutional assembly was debating the nature of Cuba's government? Such an election, before a new constitution was in place, would undermine the purpose of drafting such a document. Cuba's political leaders have "lost their mental clarity" by arranging the elections in such a fashion, declared the news magazine *Carteles*. In another editorial the magazine called the linking of the two elections an "inexcusable marriage" that would allow politicians to interfere with and undermine the sovereignty of the constitutional assembly.[49] With this contradiction in place, Cuba lurched toward elections.

Batista's campaign strategy was to veer to the left in an effort to undercut Grau and the Auténticos. In the weeks leading up to the constitutional assembly election, Batista made a series of speeches infuriating U.S. officials. On the sixth anniversary of the September 4 Revolution, Batista made mention of "absorbing monopolies" and "unequal treaties" in a reference to the Reciprocity Treaty with the United States. On the issue of Pan-American solidarity in the face of a new world war (Great Britain and France declared war on Germany the day before the speech), Batista remarked that unity would depend on whether the smaller nations were treated with "respect and consideration."[50] Ambassador Wright, displeased with the tenor of the speech, felt it singled out the United States for criticism. "All in all, the speech had little encouragement for those who are fearful that Colonel Batista's present policies constitute the greatest threat to Cuba," Wright wrote in a dispatch to Washington.[51]

One policy that concerned the United States was Batista's advocacy of a debt reduction plan decreasing the amount Cuban borrowers would have to pay to foreign banks and creditors. This issue dated back to 1933 when, in the midst of the worldwide Depression, the Cuban government declared a moratorium on mortgage payments, a measure set to expire in July 1939. With the lifting of the moratorium, many Cubans were afraid of losing their properties. The new debt reduction plan was a nationalistic measure, with obvious appeal to the political left, aimed at protecting eighty thousand

Cuban property owners, small and large, from foreclosure. It was of particular benefit to Cuban sugar companies, many of which owed substantial sums to foreign and national creditors.[52] The United States vigorously opposed the measure arguing that it would hurt Cuba's international credit.

Despite U.S. opposition, Batista campaigned on the issue across Cuba. One of his most forceful defenses came during a speech in front of one hundred thousand in the city of Matanzas ten days before the constitutional assembly elections. The speech, full of double entendres and compliments immediately followed by criticism, infuriated Ambassador Wright. As an example, Batista emphasized the importance of the relationship with the United States, while at the same time dubiously praising Cuba's powerful northern neighbor for helping the island achieve "half liberty." On the question of the Reciprocity Treaty with the United States, Batista observed that "the only thing reciprocal about the treaty is its name." As for the debt reduction plan, Batista argued that such a measure was the only way to protect Cuban property from falling into foreign hands. In a dispatch to Washington, Wright declared the speech "full of insinuation and innuendo." The ambassador also saw it as a "direct public warning to the United States not to intervene in Cuba's internal affairs . . ."[53] As part of Batista's ongoing double game, political apologists for the colonel soon arrived at the U.S. Embassy to assuage bruised feelings and assert that the speech was merely for "local consumption."[54]

While Batista campaigned across the island, the opposition was forced by a lack of resources and organization to conduct a more modest campaign. The role of the military in government and Batista in particular was their central issue. But what the opposition parties lacked in contacts and money they made up for with cunning and guile. Instead of running lesser-known candidates against the government parties in some of the more difficult races, the opposition placed the names of their leaders on the ballot in multiple provinces. Grau's name was on the ballot in all six provinces, as was the case with Menocal. Gómez ran in three of the six provinces. The high name recognition and popularity of these leaders made up for some of the opposition's other disadvantages. Among the three of them, they were elected to thirteen seats in the seventy-six-member constitutional assembly. The maneuver, approved by the electoral tribunal, made all the difference in what was to be an extremely tight election.[55]

The opposition, which received 541,914 votes, compared with 538,090 for the government parties, squeaked out an upset victory. They gained a six-seat edge (forty-one out of seventy-six seats) in the new constitutional assembly.[56] Many of Batista's supporters decried the results and wanted him to challenge the election. But he made a tactical decision to accept the results rather than engage the opposition in a time-consuming political struggle. He would, however, use the threat of a challenge as a bargaining chip in subsequent negotiations with the opposition.[57] The decision to accept the results must be understood in the context of an ongoing political campaign. The presidential election was less than four months away. To concentrate on the lost election, through a lengthy legal squabble, would hinder efforts in the next election. There was another battle to be fought, and ultimately for Batista, the presidential election, rather than the composition of the constitutional assembly, was the priority.

Even in defeat, there was some good news for the Batista camp. The colonel gained enormous national and international credibility for his acceptance of the election results. Just as important was the way the election was conducted. True to his word, Batista kept the military in the barracks on election day, and he was lavishly praised for it. The news magazine *Carteles* joined in the "national tribute to Coronel Batista for the irreproachable attitude of the Armed Forces" during the constitutional assembly elections. "Instead of pressuring the citizen as on other occasions to vote for government candidates, and impeding with threats, beatings and detentions the free suffrage of the oppositionist, the Army and the National Police generously guaranteed the democratic rights of the people."[58] Military noninterference in a national election was a singular accomplishment in Cuban history up to that point. Since the beginning of the Cuban Republic in 1902, the armed forces had played a crucial role in rigging virtually every national election. This election was different, and there was great hope throughout Cuba that the presidential elections would be carried out in a similar fashion.

For the sake of the historical record, let it be noted that there is some evidence to suggest that Batista, once it became clear that the elections were lost, tried to rig the vote tally in Las Villas Province in central Cuba, where the government won seven seats to the opposition's nine. Batista reportedly inquired "whether or not the results could be altered to show a government victory." Nothing came of the effort when several close political supporters of the colonel declined to take part in such an effort.[59] Despite these allegations, the elections were the fairest in Cuban history.

The defeat left Batista with an important decision: whether or not to continue with his presidential campaign. There was some speculation that he would withdraw from the presidential election.[60] Defeat led to recriminations within the government camp. Several prominent supporters blamed Batista for the electoral defeat and called on him to quit the race. At a Liberal Party meeting in late November, one senator told Batista that it was his "unpopularity" that cost the government parties the election. Batista responded angrily that poor political leadership was responsible for their defeat. He declared his intent to take control of the government parties and direct the presidential campaign himself.[61] This was not something he could do in a colonel's uniform.

ARMY RESIGNATION

The decision to resign from the army on December 6, 1939, was the logical extension of Batista's presidential aspirations going back as far as 1934 when the presidency of Carlos Mendieta teetered on collapse. Congress paved the way in late November by passing legislation allowing Batista to retire early with full pension and the ability to enter the presidential race, despite the fact that the electoral code required that members of the military retire a year before seeking elective office. The legislation got around this technicality by making an exception when a military officer retires as the result of "public necessity."[62] The move was a calculated risk for Batista. By resigning as military chief of staff, he was handing the most powerful position in the nation to his second-in-command, Lieutenant Colonel José Eleuterio Pedraza. Would Pedraza remain loyal? Many observers believed Pedraza would demand of a future president, Batista or anyone else, the same predominant role in government affairs exercised by his predecessor. This arrangement would reduce Batista, even if he won the election, to a quasi figurehead. U.S. Military Attaché Henry A. Barber Jr. thought Batista's power would be "decidedly limited" should he succeed to the presidency. "It is the opinion of the Military Attache that when Colonel Pedraza is indifferent to Colonel Batista's recommendations, or favorable to them, he will cooperate, but that should any difference of opinion arise between the two men, Colonel Pedraza will most decidedly do what he himself thinks best."[63] The issue surfaced in the U.S. media as well in a *Saturday Evening Post* article that intimated that Pedraza might betray Batista given the opportunity. The writer, J. P. McEvoy, referred to Pedraza as a "dark horse" whom the public would be "hearing from." McEvoy went on to observe: "Those who know him [Pedraza] say he is not so smart as Batista but craftier—not so dynamic but deadlier."[64] The article infuriated Batista, and he complained bitterly to Ambassador Wright for having introduced him to the reporter.[65]

The precarious nature of the situation was compounded by the fact that Batista was not resigning to assume the presidency. He was resigning to become a candidate for the presidency in elections that were not to be held for several months. So at the same time Batista was running a national campaign he would have to keep tabs on the military and ensure his base of support there. In a showdown between Batista and Pedraza, with whom would the military side? It was a question that would eventually require an answer.

Batista was banking on loyalty in the period after his resignation, something he had invested heavily in throughout his military career. Always loathe to punish an officer, no matter the transgression, Batista was accustomed to looking the other way when allegations were made. The most recent case of bad behavior on the part of a high-ranking officer occurred in the summer of 1939 when the chauffeur of Lieutenant Colonel Benítez allegedly killed a store owner in the city of Pinar del Río in western Cuba for failing to buy lottery tickets from his boss. The killing purportedly occurred at the instigation of Benítez, who was recalled to Havana, dressed down by Batista, and then told that he would be forced to retire from the army. Several weeks passed, and Batista reconsidered the matter, deciding instead to transfer Benítez to Matanzas and to appoint him chief of the military academy. The incident created temporary friction between Batista and Benítez, but before long they were back on good terms with no negative impact on Benítez's upward mobility. No public board of inquiry was ever convened. Such was the price of loyalty.[66]

Batista's departure from the army marked a fundamental turning point in his life. He entered in 1921, as a country boy from Banes with a lot of smarts, but no power and no influence. He left the army the most powerful man in Cuba and a figure on the international scene. The bittersweet nature of the event for Batista and the troops was captured in the press photos of the day. In one photograph, published in *Bohemia*, Batista and Pedraza are seated side by side at a banquet table, and their eyes appear to be moist. The Batista children—there were two by his wife at the time, Mirta, twelve, and Rubén, six—still remembered the day with great emotion many years later. Everyone in the family felt great sadness knowing that "things would never be the same," Rubén recalled. One observer noted that the young boy had tears in his eyes, but Rubén denied it, saying "the sun was bothering him." But, as if to sum up the feelings of the crowd, one speaker made mention of the boy's efforts to conceal his tears in his farewell speech.[67]

Batista's last day in the military began with a formal ceremony at Military City in which he pinned the insignia of army chief on Pedraza's lapel. Batista's resignation created a chain reaction of promotions within the army. Lieutenant Colonel López Migoya assumed one of Pedraza's roles as inspector general of the army, a position that essentially made him second-in-command. Migoya's low-key nature served him well in this instance, because more powerful personalities such as Lieutenant Colonel Galíndez and Lieutenant

Colonel Tabernilla were passed over for this key position. Selected as the new national police chief was Major Bernardo García Domínguez, a close ally of the new army chief, who was promoted to lieutenant colonel. As part of the revamping, Major Mariné was promoted to lieutenant colonel and shortly thereafter retired from the army, to join Batista as a political aide in the presidential campaign.

After all the insignias, medals, and promotions were awarded, Batista gave an emotional speech to the troops: "If [my] spirit was not accustomed to the difficult struggle that the Revolution has set before us in the last six years, this day would be very difficult for us. My heart is weighed down by emotion and suffers intensely this farewell moment. I feel optimistic and sad; and at the same time happy, because we are always sure that Cubans must struggle for the well-being and exaltation of our nation. Today I leave the ranks of an institution in which I have spent a great part, and the best part, of my youth. I leave the armed forces that gave days of unforgettable glory and tranquillity to the Republic," Batista told the troops in his opening remarks.[68]

Later in the speech, Batista addressed his critics: "Now I am citizen Fulgencio Batista, and as such I am going to claim my rights and fulfill my duties. Now no one can say, not even the most recalcitrant enemies, that Batista interferes with the Powers of the Public; now no one can indicate that [I] retain powers that do not belong to me." The now-retired colonel concluded the speech by praising Pedraza and predicting more "days of glory" for the armed forces.[69] After long and emotional applause, a wave of soldiers hoisted Batista and Pedraza on their backs and carried them into the banquet hall for lunch. The entire day was a series of banquets and speeches as Batista bid farewell to each branch of the armed forces and the national police in separate ceremonies. Shortly after the pomp and circumstance, Batista moved his family to a small house in Miramar, a suburb west of Havana, and the former colonel plunged into the day-to-day struggles of a presidential campaign. He never wore a military uniform again.[70]

ELECTIONS OF 1940

Managing the presidential campaign consumed Batista's energies for the next eight months, as the opposition waged a vigorous campaign to thwart his presidential aspirations. In control of the constitutional assembly, opposition members contemplated raising the minimum age for election to the presidency to forty-five, a move that would automatically disqualify the thirty-nine-year-old Batista. More important, the opposition forces, fresh from their victory, demanded the postponement of elections for several months, until the middle of 1940. Sensing Batista was slipping, the opposition hoped the delay would give them enough time to organize a winning national campaign. If the government refused to accede to a postponement, the opposition threatened to boycott the elections, a move that would turn them into a mockery. Although humbled by his recent defeat, Batista still had moves to make in this complex political chess match. The Congress, never eager about relinquishing control to the constitutional assembly, refused to pass a budget for the newly elected body. A nudge by Batista could move the budget process along. In addition, President Brú, who worked to mediate the dispute, steadfastly defended Batista's right to seek the presidency. Moreover, Batista and his supporters refused to drop a potential challenge to the constitutional assembly based on the election of opposition party leaders to multiple seats. Weeks of hard-nosed negotiations lay ahead of the two sides.

President Brú used the threat of resignation, a move that would have plunged the island into crisis, to pressure the government parties and the opposition to reach a compromise. From his unique position of leverage, the president drafted a compromise plan, the general outlines of which were ultimately accepted by all sides. The opposition received the postponement it sought until July 14, 1940. The constitutional assembly received a budget and was given several months to draw up a blueprint for government but, as part of the deal, was to make no effort to legislate. It would remain in session from February 9 to June 18, 1940. Batista was permitted to seek the presidency. Brú agreed to stay on past the expiration of his term in May, although the terms of half the members of Congress were allowed to lapse. Equally important was a procedural concession made by Grau and the opposition that prohibited voters from splitting their ballots. In the 1940 elections, Cuban voters would have to cast a straight ballot for one political party ticket or another. This provision favored Batista, who was the candidate for six political parties, while Grau was the candidate for three. Loyal party members, displeased with Batista, would have to vote for him nonetheless, if they wanted the rest of their party's slate of candidates to get their votes.[71]

Once the general parameters of the compromise were in place, Grau and Batista made an enormous show of unity on April 5 by driving together (in Batista's car) to the Presidential Palace and beseeching President Brú to stay in office. The two bitter opponents went out of their way to blow political kisses at one another, each man wishing the other good fortune in the upcoming race. Batista told reporters that if his opponent were to win, "I shall probably be the first citizen to offer him my sincere congratulations." Grau went a bit further. When asked by a reporter to predict the winner, the old professor replied, "No matter which of us wins, the Republic will triumph."[72]

Photo opportunities aside, it was apparent to Batista after his recent electoral defeat that he could not win the presidential race unless the political
geography changed dramatically. Batista had two options: coax the defection
of a major group away from the opposition or utilize the military to secure
victory for his coalition. Historical evidence indicates Batista chose to do
both to varying degrees. This was an election Batista was unwilling to lose.

The constitutional assembly election results pointed to some striking ideological differences in the two opposing political camps. Grau, the darling
of the Cuban political left, was working side by side with Menocal, the ultra-
conservative political boss of an earlier generation. Batista, the symbol of
bourgeois order, was in alliance with the Communists. There was no ideological cohesiveness in the two political camps. These were alliances of political convenience. While Batista narrowly lost the constitutional assembly race,
an analysis of the electoral results shows that parties of the right and center dominated at the polls, garnering 65 percent of the vote.[73] Looking at the
election results in ideological terms, there was great potential for shifting
coalitions. Menocal, the epitome of traditional politicians, was clearly out
of place in the Grau-led opposition, which sought to identify itself as revolutionary. Likewise, the Communists were an odd fit in the Batista coalition,
which had effectively been ruling the country with military backing for six
years. Ideologically, at least, Menocal and his supporters seemed better suited
in the Batista coalition, while the Communists were more in line with Grau.
As noted earlier, personal enmity between Grau and the Communists pre-
vented a political deal between them. Although they were adversaries, there
was no open hostility between Batista and Menocal.[74]

In the recent election, Menocal's Democrat-Republican Party was the
third-highest vote-getter, after the Auténticos and Liberals, pulling in about
16 percent of the vote. In addition, Menocal held the balance of power at the
constitutional assembly, if he and his fifteen delegates defected to Batista,
control of the body would shift. The opposition had narrowly defeated
Batista with Menocal's support, so it stood to reason that it could ill-afford
his defection. On the other hand, if Batista could strike a political deal with
Menocal, his election to the presidency seemed assured. All these political
insights were well known to Grau, Batista, and Menocal. In the end it would
come down to who was willing to offer the aging patriarch of Cuban politics the best deal. Well-versed in the art of political negotiation, Menocal's
support would not come cheaply.

As early as mid-January 1940, negotiations between Menocal and Batista
began through intermediaries.[75] For the next two months, Menocal and his
surrogates carried on separate, ongoing negotiations with Grau and Batista
seeking to extract the best deal from both sides. There was a small element

within Menocal's coalition that favored going to the elections without any alliance, but the numbers showed that while Menocal might be able to pick the next president—either Grau or Batista—neither he nor one of his followers was likely to be the next president. This did not stop him from trying. At one point in the negotiations with the Batista camp the suggestion was made that Batista step aside as the presidential candidate and designate one of Menocal's closest supporters as the chosen one. Menocal even urged the United States to "suggest" to Batista that he withdraw from the race.[76] For obvious reasons, the offer held little appeal for Batista. The political negotiations were further complicated by an internal struggle within the Menocal coalition. Members of the party were evenly split on whether to join forces with Grau or Batista. Those who objected to Batista were particularly uncomfortable with his embrace of the Communists and demanded that he dump them from the coalition, a concession Batista was unwilling to make. Some, arguing in favor of an alliance with Batista, contended that the army would not allow its former boss to lose the presidential election. An alliance with Batista was the only way to ensure Menocal and his supporters access to power and positions, they argued.[77]

In the end, Batista came across with the best deal, and Menocal accepted in mid-March. Under the Batista plan, Menocal would be allowed to pick the candidates for vice president, the mayor of Havana (always an important political plum), three of six provincial governorships, and twelve Senate seats. The deal was marginally better than the one offered by Grau, but patronage cannot entirely explain the Batista-Menocal agreement. Grau and his supporters bungled the negotiations by treating their counterparts in the Menocal camp with "considerable disdain." Batista vigorously pursued the alliance with Menocal, while Grau offered concessions reluctantly and only after similar moves were first made by his opponent.[78] Batista, young enough to be Menocal's son, played on the old general's vanity. In the early stages of the negotiations, Batista made a visit to Menocal's home to argue for the alliance, a show of respect and deference that impressed the old man.[79] This was a courtesy visit Grau was unwilling to make. Once the alliance with Batista was approved by Menocal, it was presented to the party's National Committee, which debated it for two days, and was narrowly accepted.

The news of a Batista-Menocal alliance shook Cuba. Within days, Grau offered to resign as president of the constitutional assembly in recognition of the fact he no longer had the votes to maintain the position.[80] Batista and Menocal issued a manifesto to the nation on March 31, arguing their alliance was motivated by a desire to perform a "national service." The manifesto claimed that the alliance offered the hope of a national consensus by bringing together a "large majority of voters" under one political umbrella. This majority could go forward to strengthen republican institutions and build "a generous understanding without clouds between the governing and the governed."[81]

On the face of it, the alliance with Menocal seemed to assure Batista's election to the presidency, but, taking nothing for granted, he campaigned as if he were trailing badly. The former military man poured considerable amounts of his own money into an elaborate media campaign and toured the island for eighteen days by rail in June on a self-proclaimed "Train of Victory."[82] As the train pulled into stops across the island, loudspeakers played festive Cuban music. Campaign workers began to distribute food and other consumer items to those at the station. A doctor traveled with Batista and was on hand to provide medical care and supplies to needy families.[83] At times attendance was poor, and Batista reportedly paid the separate rail fare of nine thousand supporters to greet the train at one stop in Camagüey Province.[84] Batista was a tireless campaigner, and as he went from event to event, he was forever being offered food. It was his practice to never turn down a meal for fear of insulting a potential voter. Even in cases where he was concerned about sanitary conditions, he ate what was given, but he developed the practice of going to a private area and expelling the food by inducing vomiting. It was a dietary practice he maintained till the end of his life.[85] *New York Times* reporter Ruby Hart Phillips called it the "most extensive and expensive campaign" in the island's history. "Thousands of printed circulars, pamphlets, photographs, novelties, banners, electric signs, posters, sound trucks, moving pictures, campaign songs, speeches on the radio, telephone calls, and other propaganda devices were utilized," she wrote.[86] In comparison, the underfunded Grau settled for radio and print interviews and more modest campaign travels.

Batista's win-at-all-costs attitude manifested itself within the armed forces. The shadow of the army hung over this election in a way that it did not in the prior campaign. Across the island, members of the opposition complained of a systematic campaign of intimidation and coercion against its supporters. On July 2, the opposition parties submitted a fourteen-page report to President Brú, detailing dozens of acts of electoral interference. Opposition supporters were subjected to beatings, threats, and jailings. Radio stations sympathetic to the opposition were closed or threatened with closure. The report cited efforts by the military to monopolize transportation on election day, so that only Batista supporters would be able to get to the polls. Abuses were most pronounced in Matanzas and Camagüey Provinces. In response to the report, the Superior Electoral Tribunal requested the transfer of the provincial commander in Camagüey, a move that was agreed to by Pedraza after that officer came down with a convenient and sudden illness.[87] Batista supporters submitted their own countercharges, which amounted to little more than an effort to divert attention away from the issue of military interference.

As if intimidation and a lack of resources were not challenge enough for the Grau campaign, the opposition forces were riven by internecine political strife over patronage. The struggle became so fractious that Grau withdrew from the presidential race for several days at the end of April to give his supporters time to contemplate a presidential election without him at the top of the ticket. The ploy temporarily quelled the rancor among his supporters, and Grau quickly reentered the campaign. The professor's coalition was further divided by his decision to select a relative unknown, Carlos E. de la Cruz, as his vice presidential candidate, despite intense lobbying for the position by ABC leader Sáenz. As a result of this perceived snub, ABC voters were advised to leave the vice presidential portion of the ballot blank. These quarrels boded ill for the Grau campaign.[88]

After nearly two years of political surprises, betrayals, and negotiations, election day was anticlimactic. By Cuban standards the elections were orderly, with the press reporting six dead and forty wounded in scattered incidents across the island. The opposition claimed widespread military interference in the elections. The polls had barely closed when Batista declared himself the winner and pledged in a national address to serve as the "President of all Cubans."[89] In the coming weeks, election results proved the accuracy of his claim to the presidency. The opposition waged a bitter fight against his inauguration, challenging every questionable ballot to the Superior Electoral Tribunal. Opposition leaders such as Eduardo Chibás charged that the military's actions amounted to nothing less than a "coup." In one article, he insisted that the "butt end of a rifle, after falling on the chest of the *campesino* [country person] broke the ballot box." Defending the delaying tactics of the opposition, Chibás charged that the responsibility for the possible postponement of the inauguration "falls entirely" on those who "violated the electoral process."[90]

The opposition strategy was working. Challenges bogged down the national electoral machinery to the point that Batista's inauguration, scheduled for October 10, 1940, was in jeopardy. As he had done so many times in the past, President Brú broke the impasse. Five days before the inauguration, he ordered the Superior Electoral Tribunal to immediately decide on the validity of the challenges. The president argued for the declaration of Batista as the winner, noting that even if all the challenges were found to be valid, it would not change the outcome of the race. In response to the president's order, the review process was accelerated, and Batista was finally declared the winner. In a last-ditch effort to spoil the inauguration, the opposition filed a petition with the Supreme Court challenging the acceleration order issued by President Brú. On October 9, the Supreme Court rejected the petition, and the way was at last cleared for Batista's inauguration.

The final vote count was not particularly close: 805,125 for Batista and 573,526 for Grau.[91] However, the involvement of the military tainted the results. One could easily argue that given all the factors in his favor, Batista would have won decisively without military coercion and intimidation. However, the former colonel was unwilling or unable to control the enthusiasm of his military supporters, and the fingerprints of their illicit involvement are everywhere. Despite the overwhelming odds in his favor, particularly after the alliance with Menocal, Batista did not clamp down on military involvement as he had in the constitutional assembly election. Losing was not something he would permit. U.S. officials posted to the embassy and working for military intelligence believed the Cuban army played a crucial, if not decisive, role in the elections, and this belief was reflected in countless dispatches to Washington. "Coercion by the Army was, of course, an important factor in Colonel Batista's victory," wrote an embassy official several days after the election.[92]

Batista would be president.

Epilogue

The inauguration took place in the Hall of Mirrors at the Presidential Palace to a standing-room-only audience of Batista supporters and diplomats from thirty foreign nations. Wearing a black tuxedo and tails, the former cane cutter from Banes was sworn in as president of Cuba by the chief justice of the Supreme Court before a battery of radio microphones transmitting the event across the seven hundred-mile long island. There was the hope that this election, controversial though it was, marked a fundamental turning point in the life of the nation. The dream of democracy, if not the reality, was being played out on the national stage. Cuba was experimenting with democracy. But was Batista, a man accustomed to being obeyed, the right man to lead that experiment? Would he ultimately turn on his imperfect creation and destroy it? These fears would dominate the next decade of Cuban history, whether Batista was in power or out.

For Batista, the presidency was the fulfillment of a dream. Although the elections were tainted, it was the only time in his career that he could claim victory in a democratic election that was broadly recognized as legitimate.[93] For the next four years, Batista ruled openly as a democratic leader with a contentious Congress blocking many of his most ambitious initiatives. As Batista stood before the microphones on inauguration day, his wife standing nearby, pregnant with their third child, it is tempting to speculate about what he planned for himself and the nation. Danger, a staple of his long career, was in his midst in the form of the very military system that he had catapulted into preeminence. A showdown with Pedraza for ultimate power was in the offing. There was also another woman in his life, a twenty-year-old, fair-skinned, green-eyed beauty, the daughter of Spanish immigrants, whom he had met three years earlier when his military motorcade nearly ran her down as she rode her bicycle.[94] By the time of his inauguration, Marta Fernández Miranda was living in a private home provided by Batista and would soon also be pregnant with his child.[95] The strength of that relationship grew throughout his presidency.

At the same time, in the foothills of Oriente Province another young boy, this one born to a wealthy landowner and his common-law wife, lived a life of relative privilege. The fourteen-year-old Fidel Castro Ruz would shortly enter the exclusive Colegio Belén in Havana, where he would excel in sports and academics. For the next twelve years, he witnessed and participated firsthand in Cuba's democratic experiment. He came to reject that experiment.[96]

The greatest tempest lay ahead for Cuba and Batista.

NOTES

CHAPTER 1. END AND BEGINNING

1. For Batista's version of events, see Fulgencio Batista Zaldívar, *Respuesta* (Mexico City; Manuel Leon Sánchez, 1960), 119–138.

2. After the fall of Batista, several hundred of his officials and supporters were executed by the revolutionary government; see Hugh Thomas, *Cuba: The Pursuit of Freedom* (New York: Harper and Row, 1971), 1,074–1,075, for an account of the trials. He estimates that 207, mostly low-ranking officials of Batista's government, were executed.

3. The Batista children, interview by author, tape recording, Coral Gables, Fla., April 24, 1998.

4. Interior Minister Santiago Rey Perna, interview by author, Miami, March 28, 1997.

5. Pedraza, related to Batista's first wife by marriage, would flee with his family several hours later.

6. Most accounts agree on this date, but one revolutionary historian, José Tabares del Real, gives Batista's date of birth as September 12, 1899, although he provides no explanation of the discrepancy; see *La Revolución del 30: Sus dos últimos años* (Havana: Editorial de Ciencias Sociales, 1973), 186. Tabares del Real told me the confusion stems from the different dates Batista used when he applied to enter the army in an effort to circumvent the age requirements.

7. Emil Ludwig, *Biografía de una isla* (Mexico City: Editorial Centauro, 1948), 336, provides the information about the selection of Batista's name. Rubén Darío (1867–1916) was at the height of his popularity with the publication in 1896 of *Prosas profanas*. Saint Fulgentius died in 633, and his saint day is celebrated on January 16. He was the bishop of Écija in Andalusia, Spain. The information on Saint Fulgentius comes from the Catholic Community Forum Web site; http://www.catholic-forum.com/saints/saintfov.htm.

8. Questions have been raised about whether Belisario Batista recognized the future president as his son. The doubts center on his 1921 army enlistment papers, in which only his mother's name appears. It was most likely the result of a clerical error and was in fact corrected in 1923 when he reenlisted. One exponent of the Batista as illegitimate child theory is Rafael Fermoselle; see *The Evolution of the Cuban Military: 1492–1986* (Miami: Ediciones Universal, 1987), 152n2.

9. Batista's eldest son and daughter provide much of the information about their grandparents. A much less sympathetic source is Raúl Acosta Rubio, a former personal secretary of the president in the 1940s and 1950s.

10. Mirta Batista Ponsdomenech, interview by author, tape recording, Miami, March 27, 1997.

11. This piece of information comes from Raúl Acosta Rubio, *Cuba: Todos culpables (Relato de un testigo: Lo que no se sabe del dictador Batista y su época)* (Miami: Ediciones Universal, 1977), 145. Acosta Rubio's information needs to be looked at very carefully. In the 1940s, while on Batista's payroll, he wrote a glowing biography of the then president. He became disillusioned with his former patron after Batista abandoned him in Cuba, and his second biographical work, in many places, contradicts the information in the first. There are also some very obvious errors in the second work, including Batista's birthday and the birth order of Batista's siblings. Acosta Rubio's earlier work is *Ensayo biográfico Batista: Reportaje histórico* (Havana: Benito García Rameau, 1943).

12. Batista always carried a photo of his mother in his wallet; Fulgencio Rubén Batista Godínez, correspondence to author, March 10, 1999.

13. Fulgencio Rubén Batista Godínez, interview by author, tape recording, Coral Gables, Fla., April 30, 1998.

14. The Batista family is uncertain of the year in which Juan Batista was born. They estimate between 1902 and 1905. The range of years was provided by Fulgencio Rubén Batista Godínez, correspondence to author, March 10, 1999. However, President Batista, in a speech he gave in 1954, said there was a five-year age difference between him and Juan. The speech, dedicating a tuberculosis sanatorium, was published in its entirety in *Una historia en dos discursos y un artículo* (Havana: Editorial Echevarría, 1955). Given that Hermelindo was born in 1906, it is likely that Juan was born in the middle months of 1905.

15. Hermelindo's son, Ramón, had a love affair with his uncle Francisco's wife, which created a scandal in Cuban society in the early 1950s; Acosta Rubio, *Cuba: Todos culpables*, 166.

16. Santiago Rey recalls that on one occasion Batista asked him to intervene with an allied politician who was criticizing his brother. As Rey tells it, the president was protective of his brother, even if he thought him to be mistaken; Santiago Rey Perna, interview by author, tape recording, Miami, April 29, 1998.

17. Messersmith to Welles, June 10, 1940, Sumner Welles Papers, Office Correspondence, 1920–1943, Franklin Delano Roosevelt Library, Hyde Park, N.Y.

18. Military Intelligence Division, Correspondence and Record Cards, 1918–1941, Cuba, file 2012-132, record group (hereafter RG) 165, National Archives, Washington, D.C.

19. Messersmith to Welles, June 10, 1940, Welles Papers, Office Correspondence, 1920–43.

20. Edmund A. Chester, *A Sergeant Named Batista* (New York: Henry Holt, 1954),

76, provides an overview of the disputes regarding Batista's heritage. Chester wrote the classic "great man" hagiography, so prevalent in the Unied States and Latin America during the period. Chester received Batista's blessing to write the book and so it provides an account of events from Batista's prespective.

21. For a classic work on the definition of race in Latin America, see Richard Graham, ed., *The Idea of Race in Latin America, 1870–1940* (Austin: University of Texas Press, 1990).

22. Fulgencio Rubén Batista Godínez, interview by author, tape recording, Coral Gables, Fla., April 30, 1998.

23. Gimperling described Batista as *achinado* in a report dated September 5, 1933. His revised racial-ethnic analysis was made on October 24, 1933; Lt. Col. T. N. Gimperling, military attaché, Cuba, G-2 Report, September 5, 1933, file 2012-168, RG 165; and Cuba (Combat), "Batista's Control of Troops," G-2 Report, October 24, 1933, file 2012-133, RG 165.

24. Alan Knight writes on this subject in "Racism, Revolution and Indigenismo: Mexico, 1910–1940," in *The Idea of Race* (see note 21, above). Richard Slatta discovers a similar phenomena relating to the Gauchos of Argentina in *Gauchos and the Vanishing Frontier* (Lincoln: University of Nebraska Press, 1983).

25. R. Hart Phillips, *Cuban Sideshow* (Havana: Cuban Press, 1935), 305–306. Phillips writes: "All sorts of stories concerning his [Batista's] parentage are flying around Cuba, even one that his grandfather is a Chinaman. I was raised among North American Indians and the Asiatic cast of his face is Indian not Chinese. However, the Colonel states firmly that his parents were Cubans. He won't go beyond that although I asked him."

26. Fulgencio Rubén Batista Godínez, interview by author, tape recording, Coral Gables, Fla., April 30, 1998.

27. Even though Banes had a distinct regional identity, it was attached to the city of Gibara, a little over forty miles to the north, until 1910, when it was declared a separate municipality. The classic work on Banes was written by Ricardo Varona Pupo (1885–1945), a local educator, who witnessed the transformation of the town at the end of the nineteenth century and beginning of the twentieth; see *Banes: Crónicas*: (Santiago: Imprenta Rex, 1930), 92–94. The authors of the classic Marxist study *United Fruit Company: Un caso del dominio imperialista en Cuba* (Havana: Editorial de Ciencias Sociales, 1978) drew heavily from Varona Pupo's work, as do I. Another important source is Victor Amat Osorio, who grew up in Banes in the 1940s. In exile in Miami, Osorio wrote a sentimental history of the town; *Banes (1513–1958): Estampas de mi tierra y de mi sol* (Miami: New Ideas Printing, 1981).

28. Batista's oldest son says his grandparents owned the *bohío*, but Chester makes no mention of ownership; Fulgencio Rubén Batista Godínez, interview by author, tape recording, Coral Gables, Fla., April 30, 1998. In 1937, the older Batista gave a brief account of his childhood home and living conditions in Banes to a visiting educator from the United States. A summary of that account was included in a State Department dispatch by H. Freeman Matthews, chargé d'affaires, on January 30, 1937, a copy of which was also provided to U.S. military intelligence; Military Intelligence Division, regional file, 1922–1944, Cuba—Pre-1940, folder 2520, RG 165.

29. Varona Pupo, *Banes*, 73.

30. *United Fruit Company*, 303.

31. Amat Osorio, *Banes*, 251.

32. Fulgencio Rubén Batista Godínez, interview by author, tape recording, Coral Gables, Fla., April 30, 1998.

33. For a detailed account of the methods used by United Fruit to acquire its land, see *United Fruit Company*, 56–63.

34. Ibid., 286. Frederick Upham Adams, *Conquest of the Tropics* (Garden City, N.Y.: Doubleday, Page and Co., 1914), 250, estimates that in 1913, United Fruit's rail system consisted of 110 miles of track, nineteen locomotives, and eight hundred freight cars.

35. Chester, *A Sergeant Named Batista*, 6.

36. *United Fruit Company*, 113.

37. Amat Osorio, *Banes*, 586.

38. Chester, *A Sergeant Named Batista*, 3.

39. There is some confusion regarding the number of years that Batista attended the Quaker school. Chester, *A Sergeant Named Batista*, 7, asserts that he began attending the school at the age of eight, in 1909, as part of a deal with his parents. Hiram H. Hilty, *Friends in Cuba* (Richmond, Ind. Friends United Press, 1977), 60, writes that Batista began attending the school in 1911 during the "excitement over the new [school] building." He was a graduate of the class of 1912–1913, according to Hilty, 60n.42. Hilty's sources are far stronger, and he is the more reliable source.

40. Acosta Rubio, *Cuba: Todos culpables*, 145.

41. Chester, *A Sergeant Named Batista*, 7, writes of his early love of reading. As Chester tells it, Batista occasionally played the national lottery and on one occasion after winning a small sum, spent it on books; *A Sergeant Named Batista*, 8. Ulpiano Vega Cobiellas, *Batista y Cuba: Crónica política y realizaciones* (Havana: Cultural, 1955), 17.

42. His reputation as a teacher was so great that Varona Pupo, in his history of Banes, dedicates a short chapter to his work and accomplishments; *Banes*, 206–207.

43. Juana M. Pérez Durand, interview by author, Banes, Cuba, April 21, 1999. Pérez Durand was Fernández's daughter-in-law. Fernández was born on June 1, 1862, and died September 21, 1946. He was a teacher in Banes for seventy years.

44. Although Fernández is identified as a director of the school by Cuban sources, the mission records kept at Earlham College in Richmond, Indiana, contain no information about him; Ellen Stanley, assistant archivist, correspondence to author, February 23, 1999.

45. Cuban Field Committee, Martin to Tebbets, January 9, 1911, Correspondence, Lilly Library, Earlham College. The pattern of missionaries following large corporations into Latin America is part of a neocolonial pattern replicated throughout the continent. Missionaries viewed themselves as part of a "civilizing" mission, which complemented neocolonial governments like the United States and their corporations, which argued that they were "developing" these nations rather than exploiting them. For the pattern in Cuba, see Louis A. Pérez Jr., "North American Protestant Missionaries in Cuba and the Culture of Hegemony, 1898–1920," in his *Essays on Cuban History: Historiography and Research* (Gainesville: University Press of Florida, 1995).

46. The description of the school comes from Hilty, *Friends in Cuba*, 59–60.

47. Mirta Batista Ponsdomenech, interview by author, tape recording, Miami, March 27, 1997. A newspaper report in 1933, shortly after the removal of a U.S.-backed government from power, described him as a "Quaker Sergeant" for the simplicity of his home. The article in *La Mañana*, October 15, 1933, was translated into English

and sent to Washington; Welles to Secty. of State, October 18, 1933, Dept. of State, decimal file, 1930–1939, file 837.00/4258 RG 59.

48. Acosta Rubio, *Cuba: Todos culpables*, 151.

49. Frequently described as the "Race War of 1912," there is a growing body of scholarly literature seeking to identify the social and economic factors fueling the uprising. The role of the peasantry is another area of expanding research. A good place to start is with Louis A. Pérez Jr., "Politics, Peasants, and People of Color: The 1912 'Race War' in Cuba Reconsidered," *Hispanic American Historical Review* 66, no. 3 (August 1986).

50. For information on the Jamaican migration to Cuba, see Elizabeth McLean Petras, *Jamaican Labor Migration: White Capital and Black Labor, 1850–1930* (Boulder, Colo.: Westview Press, 1988).

51. Varona Pupo identifies the five men as Manuel Díaz, Simeón Varona, a man nicknamed "Sun Sun," Dimas Robainas, and Ignacio Vaillant. He notes that there may have been at least one other victim; *Banes*, 114–118. Amat Osorio repeats much of the same information; *Banes*, 573–574.

52. The news magazine *Bohemia* printed some photos of Batista as a boy as part of a short biography it published when he left office as president in 1944. The photos depict him working as a carpenter and tailor; "Una vida extraordinaria: Fulgencio Batista y Zaldívar, el Guajirito de Banes," *Bohemia*, October 8, 1944.

53. Acosta Rubio, *Cuba: Todos culpables*, 145–146. An article published in *La Mañana*, October 15, 1933, says the tailor shop was owned by a Tomás Gómez; Welles to Secty. of State, October 18, 1933, Dept. of State, decimal file, 1930–1939, file 837.00/4258 RG 59.

54. Fulgencio Batista Zaldívar to Enrique Pizzi de Porras, March 24, 1967, private collection of Carmen Pizzi Santurio, Miami. The letter is one of the few recollections of Batista's childhood written in his own hand. The original reads:

> Para mi mente de entonces, todo resultaba novedoso: la espuma que formaban las aguas al romper con violencia en los bajíos arenosos; el ruido de las olas, murmurantes unas veces, quejumbrosas otras; las mareas, los rompientes, los arrecifes amenazadores . . . todo me encantaba, hasta la imprevista turbonada que nos obligaba a remar con fuerza hacia tierra, y el arcoiris, alrededor del cual mi padre cuajaba leyendas. Y en el centro de aquellos fenómenos se destaca en mi memoria la figura menuda, bonita, tierna y bondadosa de mi madre, sus compotas de hicaco, sus guisados a la marinera y la jigüera de campaña en la que daba el café carretero a mi padre.
>
> Allí la veo, jovencita—joven murió, al cumplir 29—plantada a la orilla, nerviosa y feliz a la vez esperando con ansiedad el arribo del hijo sobre las recias espaldas del papá-nadador, que zambullendo intentaba asustarla al dejar al garete el bote y flotando los remos.

55. Most historical accounts identify 1915 as the date of her death, but her tombstone indicates that she died in 1916. Batista's eldest son, Fulgencio Rubén Batista Godínez, correspondence to author, June 17, 1999, notes that the tombstone may be mistaken. Despite the eldest son's reservations, I have chosen to go with the date on the tombstone because it best fits the chronology of events. If one accepts the 1915 date, then one must account for an additional year in Batista's life. The sketchy details of the next five years make more sense with the 1916 date of death. This conclusion is

also based on my assessment of the elder Batista's relationship with his mother. By all accounts he was a loving son, so if the date on his mother's tombstone were incorrect, why would he not change it? Vega Cobiellas, *Batista y Cuba*, 18, writes that Batista left home at the age of sixteen, which would place his departure sometime in 1917.

56. Fulgencio Rubén Batista Godínez, interview by author, tape recording, Coral Gables, Fla., April 30, 1998.

57. Hilario Martínez, *Biografía del Coronel Fulgencio Batista y Zaldívar* (Havana, 1938), 23. A second source for this information is an official biography of Fulgencio Batista on file at the Biblioteca Nacional José Martí in Havana, which dates back to the early 1940s; see folleto 923.17291.

58. Acosta Rubio, *Cuba: Todos culpables*, 84, recounts the story of his father's willingness to let his son explore the world. Ludwig, *Biografía de una isla*, 336–337, provides the contrasting story. There must be some truth in the Ludwig account because Batista provides excerpts of it in his book *Paradojismo: Cuba, víctima de las contradicciones internacionales* (Mexico City: Ediciones Botas, 1964), 30.

CHAPTER 2. RESTLESS ADOLESCENCE

1. Fulgencio Rubén Batista Godínez, interview by author, tape recording, Coral Gables, Fla., April 30, 1998.

2. The two major sources for this period of Batista's life are Edmund Chester and Raúl Acosta Rubio, both of whom wrote official biographies. They are in agreement on the basic chronology for the years between 1916 and 1921, although they differ on some details. See *A Sergeant Named Batista*, 10; and *Ensayo biográfico Batista*, 84. For a more negative perspective, see Acosta Rubio's *Cuba: Todos culpables*.

3. Fulgencio Rubén Batista Godínez, interview by author, tape recording, Coral Gables, Fla., April 30, 1998.

4. Chester, *A Sergeant Named Batista*, 11; and Acosta Rubio, *Ensayo biográfico Batista*, 84.

5. The photo album was the work of Félix J. Castro and Pantaleón Ramos Camuzo, supporters of Batista, who traveled to Banes in 1934 or 1935 to prepare an album honoring Batista for his patriotism after the Revolution of 1933. It contains many important photographs from the period; see Biblioteca Nacional, Batista Photo Album Collection, album #12. The woman is most likely Francisco's godmother, known to the family as "Fefa"; Fulgencio Rubén Batista Godínez, correspondence to author, June 17, 1999.

6. San Germán was renamed Urbano Noris by the revolutionary government.

7. For a history of the Cuban railroads, see Oscar Zanetti and Alejandro García, *Caminos para el azúcar* (Havana: Editorial de Ciencias Sociales, 1987). The connection to Antilla was completed in the period between 1900 and 1910.

8. Dumois has since been renamed Herrera.

9. Chester, *A Sergeant Named Batista*, 12; and Acosta Rubio, *Ensayo biográfico Batista*, 84–85.

10. Acosta Rubio, *Ensayo biográfico Batista*, 87.

11. Ibid. See also *United Fruit Company*, 244.

12. Chester, *A Sergeant Named Batista*, 14; and Acosta Rubio, *Ensayo biográfico Batista*, 87.

13. The account of Batista as a strikebreaker comes from Acosta Rubio, *Cuba: Todos culpables*, 146.

14. Chester, *A Sergeant Named Batista*, 14.

15. *United Fruit Company*, 243.

16. Zanetti and García, *Caminos para el azúcar*, 252. For an overview of the boom and bust cycles of Cuban sugar, see *United Fruit Company*, 161–165 and 242–243. Another excellent source on the sugar industry's economic boom and decline in the period from 1900 to 1929 is Thomas, *Cuba: Pursuit of Freedom*, 536–563.

17. Cándida Zaldívar died on October 8, 1940.

18. Fulgencio Rubén Batista Godínez, interview by author, tape recording, Coral Gables, Fla., April 30, 1998.

19. See Ricardo Adam y Silva, *La gran mentira: 4 de septiembre de 1933* (Havana: Editorial Lex, 1947), 99–100. Adam y Silva was an officer displaced by Batista in the aftermath of the Revolution of 1933. Hugh Thomas tells the story somewhat differently. He writes that Batista worked with the army during the Antilla rail strike; *Cuba: Pursuit of Freedom*, 636.

20. Ramón Grau San Martín was rumored to be gay. Another rumor claimed that he had slept with his brother's wife and impregnated her, which lead to the brother's suicide. Neither of the rumors was ever substantiated.

21. Fulgencio Rubén Batista Godínez, interview by author, tape recording, Coral Gables, Fla., April 30, 1998. Batista was told this by a boyhood friend of his father's, Pedro Díaz Carballosa.

22. Acosta Rubio, *Cuba: Todos culpables*, 146. This account would be suspect if the author did not provide specific detail, such as the street where he lived with the prostitute.

23. Mirta Batista Ponsdomenech, correspondence to author, June 11, 1999.

24. Acosta Rubio, *Ensayo biográfico Batista*, 90.

25. Ibid. Chester also makes note of Batista's reading habits in *A Sergeant Named Batista*,16.

26. The best account of this accident is contained in Acosta Rubio, *Ensayo biográfico Batista*, 89–90. Chester provides a very sketchy account in *A Sergeant Named Batista*, 16. My April 30, 1998, interview with Fulgencio Rubén Batista Godínez provides additional details on the accident's aftermath. Batista's oldest daughter remembers that it was his right leg that was injured; Mirta Batista Ponsdomenech, correspondence to author, June 11, 1999.

27. Fulgencio Rubén Batista Godínez, interview by author, tape recording, Coral Gables, Fla., April 30, 1998.

28. A boyhood friend of Batista's told his son years later that his father had been hospitalized for several weeks in Camagüey. This seems unlikely because Holguín is adjacent to Cacocum, and Batista would most likely have been taken to a hospital or clinic nearby and then later taken to Camagüey to recuperate; interview by author, tape recording, Coral Gables, Fla., April 30, 1998.

29. Fulgencio Rubén Batista Godínez, interview by author, tape recording, Coral Gables, Fla., April 30, 1998.

30. For a detailed overview of the labor struggles of the period, see Zanetti and García, *Caminos para el azúcar*, 289–309.

31. If he had played any role at all, he would have used that involvement to curry favor with the powerful Cuban labor movement.

32. Fulgencio Rubén Batista Godínez, correspondence to author, March 10, 1999.

33. Batista's oldest son said that in their conversations his father always emphasized the professional and academic opportunities offered by the army, not finances; Fulgencio Rubén Batista Godínez, correspondence to author, June 17, 1999.

34. Chester, *A Sergeant Named Batista*, 17; and Acosta Rubio, *Ensayo biográfico Batista*, 93.

35. Chester, *A Sergeant Named Batista*, 19; and Acosta Rubio, *Ensayo biográfico Batista*, 93–95.

36. Acosta Rubio, *Cuba: Todos culpables*, 147.

37. Adam y Silva brings up the issue without offering an opinion on Batista's birth status. He even goes so far as to reprint the military document in which his name was corrected in 1923 to include the name Batista; *La gran mentira*, 99–100. Fermoselle states the case for Batista as an illegitimate child more directly; *Evolution of the Cuban Military*, 152n2.

38. Adam y Silva, *La gran mentira*, 100.

39. As fate would have it, on the train ride to Havana, Batista had a chance encounter with a man whose destiny would be intertwined with his own for decades. A future political ally, Andrés Rivero Agüero, was then going to Havana to study law. He would be elected president in November 1958 and would flee the country along with Batista a little over a month later; Fulgencio Rubén Batista Godínez, interview by author, tape recording, Coral Gables, Fla., May 19, 1998.

CHAPTER 3. SERGEANT STENOGRAPHER

1. The 1919 Cuban Census estimates the population of Cuba at 2,889,004 and the population of the city of Havana at 363,506. The suburbs immediately surrounding Havana at the time had about 100,000 residents; see *Census of the Republic of Cuba* (Havana: Maza, Arroyo y Caso, 1919), 284–288.

2. For an overview of Cuba's tourism industry, see Rosalie Schwartz, *Pleasure Island: Tourism and Temptation in Cuba* (Lincoln: University of Nebraska Press, 1997).

3. For a working-class perspective of the city in the late 1910s and early 1920s, see Miguel Barnet, *Gallego* (Madrid: Ediciones Alfaguara, 1981). The work is a fictional account of a Spanish immigrant who arrives in the city in 1916, but it is based on historical research.

4. Acosta Rubio, *Ensayo biográfico Batista*, 104. Fulgencio Rubén Batista Godínez, correspondence to author, August 4, 1999.

5. His elder daughter and son remember viewing the latest movies in the Presidential Palace, where they were shown in a large drawing room on the second floor facing the inner courtyard or on a covered terrace on the third floor. A screening area was also set aside at their home in Camp Columbia; Fulgencio Rubén Batista Godínez, correspondence to author, August 4, 1999; and Mirta Batista Ponsdomenech, correspondence to author, August 3, 1999. John Dorschner and Roberto Fabricio note in *The Winds of December* (New York: Coward, McCann and Geohegan, 1980), 67, that the movies frequently began after midnight.

6. Chester, *A Sergeant Named Batista*, 18. Acosta Rubio, *Ensayo biográfico Batista*, 94.

7. Fermoselle, *Evolution of the Cuban Military*, 139.

8. For an excellent class analysis of the Cuban Army prior to the Revolution of 1933, see Lionel Soto, *La Revolución del 33*, 3 vols. (Havana: Editorial Pueblo y Educación, 1985), 3:68–76.

9. Chester, *A Sergeant Named Batista*, 17 and 101–102.

10. While arguing against the "Sergeants' Revolt" of September 4, 1933, Adam y Silva, nonetheless, eloquently enumerates the complaints of the enlisted men; see *La gran mentira*, 55–57 and 104–109. While still a sergeant, Batista took a fellow enlisted man to eat at the officer's club in La Cabaña but became miffed because of the lack of a tablecloth and demanded that one be placed on the table. The administrator of the club complied with Batista's wishes; Fulgencio Rubén Batista Godínez, interview by author, tape recording, Coral Gables, Fla., May 19, 1998.

11. Chester, *A Sergeant Named Batista*, 57. Adam y Silva notes that the domestic service was voluntary and greatly desired; *La gran mentira*, 105. Thomas argues that the class distinctions were actually less stark in the Cuban Army than in the armed forces of other Latin American countries; see *Cuba: Pursuit of Freedom*, 583.

12. This was prevalent in the early 1930s but may have been standard practice even earlier; Chester, *A Sergeant Named Batista*, 57. The U.S. military attaché believed the troop counts were inflated; Lt. Col. T. N. Gimperling, military attaché, "Military Establishment," G-2 Report, October 3, 1933, file 2012-100 RG165.

13. Adam y Silva, *La gran mentira*, 57. The Cuban currency in this period and up until today is the peso. In the period covered by this work, the dollar and peso were roughly equivalent in value. As a result, often writers in the United States or Cuba are not specific about which currency they are quoting when giving prices for items. Adam y Silva does not specify dollars or pesos in this citation. For the purposes of this work, all prices are in U.S. dollars.

14. Thomas, *Cuba: Pursuit of Freedom*, 547. Carleton Beals, in a polemical exposé against Cuban corruption and U.S. involvement, *The Crime of Cuba* (Philadelphia: J. B. Lippincott, 1934), 225–227, notes that the United States looked the other way when it came to Cuban electoral fraud.

15. Thomas, *Cuba: Pursuit of Freedom*, 555–556. Beals offers the $2 million to $14 million estimate, although he defends Zayas for stealing less than his predecessor, General Mario Menocal; *The Crime of Cuba*, 232–236. Louis A. Pérez Jr. provides a laundry list of additional corruption schemes in *Cuba: Between Reform and Revolution* (New York: Oxford University Press, 1988), 234.

16. Alfredo Zayas y Alfonso (1861–1934) and his administration have been largely ignored by historians and other scholars. He is seen as a transition figure between President Menocal and the dictatorship of Gerardo Machado. For an overview of his career, minus the corruption and controversy, one of the best sources is a speech delivered to the Cuban History Academy by its president on the first anniversary of Zayas's death; "Elogio del Dr. Alfredo Zayas y Alfonso Individuo de Número, leído por el Dr. Tomas de Justiz y Del Valle, Presidente de la Academia, en la sesión solemne celebrada en la noche del 11 de abril de 1935" (Havana: Imp. El Siglo XX). Perhaps the best analysis of the Zayas government is contained in the classic political history by Herminio Portell-Vilá, *Nueva historia de la República de Cuba (1898–1979)* (Miami: La Moderna Poesia, 1986), 252–316. Thomas provides a short summary of the Zayas administration in *Cuba: Pursuit of Freedom*, 564–568.

17. Early biographies of Batista emphasize his studious nature as the reason that

he often did not retire to bed at the specified time; see Chester, *A Sergeant Named Batista*, 18; and Acosta Rubio, *Ensayo biográfico Batista*, 94.

18. Chester and Acosta Rubio tell the story of a youthful Batista warning an abusive sergeant to treat him with respect. It is difficult to know whether such stories, which clearly pander to Batista and which both authors sprinkle throughout their works (often they are identical), have any merit; see *A Sergeant Named Batista*, 18–19; and *Ensayo biográfico Batista*, 94–95.

19. The invention of tape recorders has greatly reduced the demand for shorthand, but at the time it was an essential skill for most offices; see Robert L. Grubbs and Estelle Popham, *Gregg Shorthand for Colleges, Speed Building* (New York: McGraw-Hill, 1976).

20. Hilario Martínez wrote a short biography of Batista propounding the importance of stenography to the "development and betterment of the individual"; *Biografía del Coronel Fulgencio Batista y Zaldívar*, 8. He was profiled in the Spanish-language professional journal, *El Taquígrafo Gregg* in 1939; see Roberto J. Madan, "La obra educacional del Coronel Batista," *El Taquígrafo Gregg* (Havana), no. 66 (January 1939): 841–843. In 1957, he was the honorary president of the fourth Hispano-Americano-Filipino Stenography Congress; see the proceedings of the *IV Congreso Hispano-Americano-Filipino de Taquigrafía* held in Vitoria, Spain, July 17–23, 1957. Years later, Ángel V. Fernández wrote about the pride Cuban stenographers felt in having "un Presidente Taquígrafo"; *Memorias de un taquígrafo* (Miami: Ediciones Universal, 1993), 60–61. Fernández worked as a government stenographer, and his book is a reminiscence of the different events he attended in that capacity.

21. Excerpts from Batista's diary, provided by the family, indicate that he also took courses in typing and commercial stenography at the Escuela Moderna in Marianao in May 1921 and typing and grammar courses at the Colegio Santa Teresa in Havana in early 1922. The family has restricted access to the diary, which chronicles his early army life throughout the 1920s and early 1930s, but has provided the author with some excerpts.

22. Fulgencio Rubén Batista Godínez, telephone conversation, August 3, 1999. Fernández, *Memorias de un taquígrafo*, 61, remembers that before one speech in 1942, Batista showed members of the stenography crew the shorthand notes for the speech.

23. Acosta Rubio, *Cuba: Todos culpables*, 148.

24. Few of the articles have survived. The circulation was probably limited, primarily to students and teachers at the school.

25. Acosta Rubio reprinted the entire text of the story in *Ensayo biográfico Batista*, 105.

26. Acosta Rubio, *Ensayo biográfico Batista*, 97. Chester, *A Sergeant Named Batista*, 20–21.

27. Fulgencio Batista y Zaldívar, *Sombras de América: Problemas económicos y sociales* (Mexico City: E.D.I.A.P.S.A, 1946), 12, provides information about his early writings.

28. Another clear indication that the article had not attracted the attention of his army superiors.

29. Acosta Rubio, *Ensayo biográfico Batista*, 101. Chester, *A Sergeant Named Batista*, 22.

30. Her given name was María Elisa, although everyone addressed her by her middle name.

31. The story about the first meeting and formal introduction comes from Batista's oldest son, Fulgencio Rubén Batista Godínez, correspondence to author, July 27, 2005. Also, Fulgencio Rubén Batista Godínez, interview by author, tape recording, Coral Gables Fla., April 30, 1998.

32. Batista would serve as a witness at the wedding; Fulgencio Rubén Batista Godínez, correspondence to author, August 4, 1999.

33. Mirta Batista Ponsdomenech, interview by author, tape recording, Miami, May 20, 1998.

34. The Batista children, interview by author, tape recording, Coral Gables, Fla., April 24, 1998.

35. Mirta Batista Ponsdomenech, interview by author, tape recording, Miami, March 27, 1997.

36. Fulgencio Rubén Batista Godínez says he had a close and loving relationship with his half-brother, Félix Valdespino; Fulgencio Rubén Batista Godínez, correspondence to author, August 4, 1999.

37. Mirta Batista Ponsdomenech, correspondence to author, August 3, 1999.

38. Mirta Batista Ponsdomenech, interview by author, tape recording, Miami, May 20, 1998. As a young girl she questioned, "Why did marriage have to be like this?"

39. The definitive work on women and social/sexual relationships for the early republican period has yet to be written. The role of women after the Cuban Revolution of 1959 has been studied to some degree, but a great deal more scholarship is needed in that area as well.

40. I owe these insights to Mirta Batista Ponsdomenech, who spoke candidly of the family's pain over the divorce. She recalls her mother receiving the divorce papers sometime in April 1945, around the time her first child was born; interview by author, tape recording, Miami, May 20, 1998.

41. Diary of Fulgencio Batista, excerpts provided by the family. The diary excerpt states that Juan Batista came from Camagüey, but in a 1954 speech dedicating a tuberculosis sanatorium, President Batista said his brother was living in Banes when he contracted the disease. The speech is reprinted in its entirety in *Una historia en dos discursos y un artículo* (Havana: Editorial Echevarría, 1955).

42. *Una historia*, 19.

43. There has been little written about tuberculosis and treatment options in Cuba and other Caribbean islands. For an overview of the U.S. historical literature on tuberculosis, see Barbara Gutmann Rosenkrantz, ed., *From Consumption to Tuberculosis: A Documentary History* (New York: Garland Publishing, 1994).

44. *Una historia*, 19.

45. At the time, there were six hospitals in Cuba dedicated to patients who had contracted tuberculosis and cancer; see *Census of the Republic of Cuba 1919*, 250–251.

46. The best statistics available are from the 1919 census, 259.

47. *Una historia*, 19.

48. Fulgencio Rubén Batista Godínez, correspondence to author, August 16, 1999.

49. Chester says there were forty-two other applicants; *A Sergeant Named Batista*, 22. Acosta Rubio gives no number; *Ensayo biográfico Batista*, 102. An article published in *La Mañana*, October 15, 1933, says Batista surpassed fourteen other candidates; Welles to Secty. of State, October 18, 1933, Dept. of State, decimal file, 1930–1939, file 837.00/4258 RG 59.

50. The phrasing is from Chester, *A Sergeant Named Batista*, 23. Acosta Rubio gives an almost identical account in *Ensayo biográfico Batista*, 103.

51. Ruiz was subsequently appointed by Machado as military supervisor of Havana Province and remained so until the lifting of martial law in July 1933. He was forced out of the army in August of the same year because of his close ties to Machado; Lt. Col. T. N. Gimperling, military attaché, Havana, "Important Problems and Issues Requiring Governmental Recognition and Action," G-2, July 27, 1933, file 2657-330 (195), RG 165. Ortega refused to accept the "Sergeants' Revolt" of September 1933 and was discharged from the army.

52. Acosta Rubio reprints a large portion of Batista's letter requesting the school; *Ensayo biográfico Batista*, 115–116. Chester makes no mention of it.

53. After his rise to power, Batista handed over management of the farm to his brother-in-law, Antonio Bausa; Fulgencio Rubén Batista Godínez, interview by author, tape recording, Coral Gables, Fla., April 30, 1998. Acosta Rubio says he also sold coal and eggs; *Ensayo biográfico Batista*, 120–121. He also worked as freelance stenographer for at least one local law firm; Fulgencio Rubén Batista Godínez, interview by author, tape recording, Coral Gables, Fla., May 19, 1998.

54. Luis Rodolfo Miranda, *Reminiscencias cubanas: De la guerra y de la paz* (Havana: Imp. P. Fernandez y Cía, 1941), 223–226. The book consists of a series of recollections of life in Cuba. The farm in question was owned by Miranda, who never identified the persons behind the charges against one Leonides Fernández.

55. The salary information comes from the Office of the Military Attaché, Maj. William H. Shutan, G-2 Report, March 2, 1926, RG 165. His oldest son, Fulgencio Rubén Batista Godínez, recalls that his father still owned the car in the late 1930s, after his rise to power; Fulgencio Rubén Batista Godínez, interview by author, tape recording, Coral Gables, Fla., April 30, 1998. Adam y Silva uses the fact that Batista owned a car to argue that conditions in the Cuban Army could not have been so bad; *La gran mentira*, 128. Acosta Rubio says he bought a used car, living-room furniture, and clothes for his wife when he won third place in the Cuban National Lottery; *Cuba: Todos culpables*, 148.

56. The best work on the Cuban military in the prerevolutionary period remains Louis A. Pérez Jr.'s *Army Politics in Cuba, 1898–1958* (Pittsburgh, Pa.: University of Pittsburgh Press, 1976). Fermoselle's *Evolution of the Cuban Military* utilizes a wide variety of sources, although it is often difficult to follow and has no coherent thesis. The legacy of Spanish colonial rule, the history of dependent development, and the importance of foreign capital are traditionally cited as reasons for the expanded role of the military in Latin America. Much of the literature focuses on the southern cone states of Argentina, Brazil, and Chile. The classic work by John Johnson, *The Military and Society in Latin America* (Stanford, Calif.: Stanford University Press, 1964) is now a bit dated. For Argentina, see the works of Robert Potash, *The Army and Politics in Argentina 1928–1945: Yrigoyen to Peron* (Stanford, Calif.; Stanford University Press, 1969); and *The Army and Politics in Argentina 1945–1962: Peron to Frondizi* (Stanford, Calif.: Stanford University Press, 1980). For Brazil, see Thomas Skidmore, *The Politics of Military Rule in Brazil* (New York: Oxford University Press, 1988).

57. It is unclear from the diary excerpt provided by the family whether his father was already dead by the time he recovered from his own illness. Fulgencio Rubén Batista Godínez repeats the story in my interview with him; Fulgencio Rubén Batista Godínez, interview by author, tape recording, Coral Gables, Fla., April 30, 1998.

58. Chester gives the date as sometime around August 1931; *A Sergeant Named Batista*, 26–27. Acosta Rubio offers no specific time frame for Batista's entry into the ABC.

CHAPTER 4. *MACHADATO*

1. It would later evolve into the preferred strategy of workers and students seeking political and economic reforms.

2. Portell-Vilá, *Nueva historia*, 360. In Spanish the citation reads: "Los cubanos nunca más volverían a ser la misma gente de una repentina explosión de rabia para luego ser olvidadizos e inclinados a perdonar; iban a aprender a odiar, a tomar venganza, a practicar cualquier violencia o a justificarla en nombre de la lucha política." (Translation mine).

3. Ibid., 324–332. Portell-Vilá dedicates an entire chapter to Machado's public works campaign.

4. Louis A. Pérez Jr. argues that because of U.S. domination of Cuba's major industries during the prerevolutionary period (1902–1959), politics was the primary outlet for ambitious middle-class Cubans seeking to increase their wealth; *Cuba: Between Reform and Revolution*, 213–224. This view was espoused by the ABC movement in the early 1930s. It was seen as a major institutional flaw hindering the development of a normal democratic process in Cuba; *El ABC al pueblo de Cuba: Manifesto-Programa* (Havana, 1932), 21–22, in Sumner Welles Papers, Latin America files, 1933–1943, Cuba, general. Pérez has written extensively on the era and the unsavory impact of U.S. domination and intervention on Cuban political structures. See also his *Cuba and the United States: Ties of Singular Intimacy* (Athens: University of Georgia Press, 1990); and *Cuba under the Platt Amendment, 1902–1934* (Pittsburgh, Pa.: University of Pittsburgh Press, 1986).

5. Portell-Vilá, *Nueva historia*, 341.

6. The so-called Chadbourne Plan.

7. Pérez, *Cuba: Between Reform and Revolution*, 248–256, outlines the general economic woes of the island. Thomas, *Cuba: Pursuit of Freedom*, 557–563, devotes a chapter to the decline of the Cuban sugar industry. Portell-Vilá, *Nueva historia*, 351–352, provides the aforementioned statistics.

8. Thomas, *Cuba: Pursuit of Freedom*, 580–581.

9. Lt. Col. T. N. Gimperling, military attaché, Havana, "Loyalty of the Cuban Army," G-2 Report, August 21, 1933, file 2012-133(7), RG 165.

10. Portell-Vilá, *Nueva historia*, 322–323. Thomas, *Cuba: Pursuit of Freedom*, 574, says André was murdered for implying that Machado's daughter was a lesbian.

11. Portell-Vilá, *Nueva historia*, 343.

12. Mella would join the growing pantheon of political martyrs whose deaths would be celebrated on an annual basis as the embodiment of Cuban nationalism and sacrifice. The strain of martyrdom runs deep in Cuban political culture, dating back to the Independence Wars, in which most of the Cuban leadership, including José Martí and Antonio Maceo, died in battle. In the Cuban national anthem, taken from a poem by José Martí, is the line "Morir por la Patria es vivir" (To die for the country is to live).

13. Robert J. Alexander, *Communism in Latin America* (New Brunswick, N.J.:

Rutgers University Press, 1957), 271, suggests several possibilities as to who killed Mella, including a double agent for the Communists and Machado. Portell-Vilá, *Nueva historia*, 347–348, suggests that Mella was murdered by former Comintern (Communist International) colleagues because he was moving away from revolutionary Marxism toward mainstream politics.

14. Portell-Vilá outlines the evolution of the Guggenheim-Machado negotiations in *Nueva historia*, 360–370.

15. This was the so-called Root interpretation of the Platt Amendment, named for Elihu Root, U.S. secretary of war at the time of Cuban independence. Guggenheim believed this impartiality was mistaken for support of Machado. He outlines the policy goals of his ambassadorship in his book *The United States and Cuba: A Study in International Relations* (New York: Macmillan, 1934).

16. Guggenheim's work is sprinkled with racist commentary about the inferiority of Cubans and other Latin Americans when compared with Anglo-Saxons. On the issue of political compromise, the Cuban opposition was, in his opinion, imbued with a "gambling instinct" to gain power and viewed Machado's willingness to compromise as weakness; *United States and Cuba*, 170–171.

17. Fidel Castro would do the same in 1956 in his struggle against the Batista government.

18. Batista's involvement in the clandestine radio station is not widely known. Dr. Luis Pérez Moreno, former owner of the radio station, which came out of hiding after the fall of Machado, mentions Batista in passing in the epilogue to his book on caring for the blind; *Cómo cuidar y atender a los ciegos* (N.p., 1983), 97. Acosta Rubio, *Ensayo biográfico Batista*, 125, lists several reporters to whom Batista fed information.

19. Acosta Rubio identifies one such tract as *Pro esto pro patria*, which argued in defense of charges against Eduardo Chibás Guerra, a prominent Cuban engineer, and the father of Eduardo Chibás Ribas, who would become one of Batista's fiercest political opponents; *Ensayo biográfico Batista*, 123.

20. It is important to note that this group was not the exact same group that planned the overthrow of the military in September 1933. Cruz Vidal states that Batista and he slowly recruited more members to the group over time, but he may be overstating his role; Cruz Vidal to Antolín Gonzalez del Valle, November 8, 1983, Fulgencio Batista Zaldívar Papers, private collection of Fulgencio Rubén Batista Godínez, Coral Gables, Fla.

21. Fulgencio Rubén Batista Godínez, interview by author, tape recording, Coral Gables, Fla., May 19, 1998.

22. Chester, *A Sergeant Named Batista*, 101–102.

23. His friend Urbano Soler was also assigned to the case.

24. Acosta Rubio, *Ensayo biográfico Batista*, 122–123. The other two defense lawyers were Pedro Cue and Ricardo Dolz. Acosta Rubio states that Batista had a prior relationship with Cue as well. Chester implies that Batista knew Dolz too; *A Sergeant Named Batista*, 28.

25. Andrés Rivero Agüero, who supported Batista in the 1950s, was a lawyer in de la Cruz's law firm in the late 1920s and remembered Batista doing work for the firm; Fulgencio Rubén Batista Godínez, interview by author, tape recording, Coral Gables, Fla., May 19, 1998.

26. Acosta Rubio, *Ensayo biográfico Batista*, 124–125. Chester writes of the confrontation, although he does not mention the possibility of drawing a gun; *A Sergeant Named Batista*, 28.

27. Acosta Rubio, *Ensayo biográfico Batista*, 124, writes of Batista's and Soler's efforts to protect de la Cruz. Mario Riera Hernández, *Un presidente constructivo* (Miami, 1966), 3, makes a similar assertion. Vega Cobiellas, *General Fulgencio Batista Zaldívar*, 30–31, published excerpts from a letter de la Cruz sent to the Cuban newspapers praising Batista and Soler for accompanying him and Gonzalo Freyre de Andrade to court every morning.

28. Acosta Rubio, *Ensayo biográfico Batista*, 125–126, writes of the potential arrest. Chester makes no mention of it.

29. Portell-Vilá, *Nueva historia*, 373. The information on the bullet wounds comes from U.S. embassy employee Edward Reed; Reed to Secty. of State, September 27, 1932, file 2637-330(173), RG 165.

30. Machado denied any involvement in the murder of the Freyre de Andrade brothers, blaming it on Vázquez Bello's supporters and an "atmosphere of vengeance"; Gerardo Machado y Morales, *Ocho años de lucha* (Miami: Ediciones Históricas Cubanas, 1982), 50.

31. Acosta Rubio, *Ensayo biográfico Batista*, 126–128.

32. Fulgencio Rubén Batista Godínez, interview by author, tape recording, Coral Gables, Fla., May 19, 1998. Andrés Rivero Agüero was with de la Cruz at the time and retold the story years later.

33. The conversation in which Batista asked Soler to remove incriminating documents from his apartment was held with his wife present in the residence but "in such a way that she should not take notice"; Acosta Rubio, *Ensayo biográfico Batista*, 125–126.

34. Fulgencio Rubén Batista Godínez, interview by author, tape recording, Coral Gables, Fla., May 19, 1998.

35. Ramón Cruz Vidal said that Batista was very "cautious and distrusting" and hesitant to include others in the conspiracy, and that it was he who recruited many of the later conspirators; Cruz Vidal to Gonzalez del Valle, November 8, 1983, Fulgencio Batista Zaldívar Papers, private collection of Fulgencio Rubén Batista Godínez, Coral Gables, Fla.

36. In 1971, when Cruz Vidal was collecting information for his memoirs, Batista wrote to him and told him that there were more people involved in the army uprising than he suspected, pointing out that in any revolutionary movement "discretion" is vital to "avoid errors created by impatience"; Batista to Cruz Vidal, June 3, 1971, Fulgencio Batista Zaldívar Papers, private collection of Fulgencio Rubén Batista Godínez, Coral Gables, Fla.

37. Panchín's health scare was related to me in a letter from his nephew; Fulgencio Rubén Batista Godínez, correspondence to author, September 17, 1999.

38. Mirta Batista Ponsdomenech, interview by author, tape recording, Miami, May 20, 1998. I owe many of the observations on the relationship between the two brothers to her.

39. Portell-Vilá, *Nueva historia*, 377.

40. Ibid.

41. Tom Pettey, "Cuban Misery Groans under Iron-Fist Rule," *New York Herald Tribune*, January 25, 1933. Russell Porter, "Machado Says Foes Stir Cuban Unrest," *New York Times*, January 31, 1933.

42. One of the best works on the Good Neighbor policy in general and on Cuba, specifically, is Irwin F. Gellman's *Roosevelt and Batista: Good Neighbor Diplomacy in Cuba, 1933–1945* (Albuquerque: University of New Mexico Press, 1973).

43. Welles had served as assistant secretary of state under Woodrow Wilson, but with the exception of a few, select missions, held no position under the Republican administrations of Coolidge and Hoover.

44. Sumner Welles Papers, Latin America files, 1933–1943, Cuba, essentials, 1933.

45. For some examples of the coverage, see "Un público numeroso se congrego para saludar al embajador americano," *Diario de la Marina*, May 8, 1933; "Sumner Welles," *El Mundo*, May 7, 1933; and "Sumner Welles Takes Up Task as U.S. Envoy," *Havana Evening Telegram*, May 8, 1933.

46. The accommodations were made for Welles by Edward L. Reed, a legal adviser with the U.S. embassy in Havana; Welles to Reed, April 26, 1933, Welles Papers, Latin America files, 1933–1943, Cuba, 1933, R-W.

47. *El País*, July 21, 1933; *Información*, July 6, 11, 12, 17, and 22, 1933; *Diario de la Marina*, July 17, 1933.

48. Machado's observations are contained in a memoir written by the former president and published by his great-grandson nearly fifty years after his ouster from power; Machado, *Ocho años de lucha*, 67.

49. *Denuncia*, April 26, 1933.

50. Machado, *Ocho años de lucha*, 71.

51. Memo of May 12, 1933, Sumner Welles Papers, Latin America files, 1933–1943, Cuba, conversations, 1933–1934.

52. Welles was taken aback by Ferrara's statement. "It is worthy of emphasis in this regard that of his own initiative, without the slightest intimation to that effect from me, he (Ferrara) stated that the President, if the matter were put up to him in the proper manner by political leaders both of his party and of the Opposition, would be willing to agree to a program of conciliation and cooperation for the benefit of Cuba and to resign his office. I did not consider that this was a particularly appropriate occasion to discuss this question in any great detail with him and I made no comment"; memo of May 12, 1933.

53. Welles outlines his formula in several different places but perhaps most clearly in a June 3, 1933, letter to Congressman Hamilton Fish; Welles to Fish, June 3, 1933, Welles Papers, Latin America files, 1933–1943, Cuba, 1933.

54. Welles to Jefferson Caffery, May 30, 1933, Welles Papers, Latin America files, 1933–1943, Cuba, 1933. See also letter from Welles to Raymond Buell, July 13, 1933, Welles Papers, Office Correspondence, 1920–1943, Buell, Raymond L., 1933–1934.

55. Welles to Fish, June 3, 1933.

56. Welles specifically wanted to return in time to attend the Pan-American Conference scheduled for December in Montevideo, Uruguay. Among those he told were Raymond Buell, editor of *Foreign Policy Reports*, a publication produced by the Foreign Policy Association; see Welles to Buell, July 13, 1933.

57. *Información*, July 31, 1933.

58. The meeting was held on July 25, 1933. Cintas said that Roosevelt told him that Welles should be advising and counseling each party to the negotiations, not imposing

solutions on the Cuban government. Machado made the erroneous assumption that Welles did not have Roosevelt's full support; Machado, *Ocho años de lucha*, 89.

59. Hamilton Fish had warned Welles that Machado would not go easily. In a handwritten addendum to a letter dated July 19, 1933, Fish writes, "Don't let the old fox trick you. He is sparring for time"; Fish to Welles, July 19, 1933, Welles Papers, Latin America files, 1933–1943, Cuba, 1933.

60. Welles to Secty. of State, July 8, 1933, Welles Papers, "1933 Revolution," copies of SW Papers, 1915–1943.

61. Machado, *Ocho años de lucha*, 100.

62. Phillips, *Cuban Sideshow*, 45.

63. *Diario de la Marina*, August 3, 1933.

64. Welles to Secty. of State, August 7, 1933, Dept. of State, decimal file, 1930–1939, file 837.00/3594.

65. Both Welles and Machado agreed on the figure of seventeen dead. Phillips and Portell-Vilá estimate that twenty died in the confrontation; see Welles to Secty. of State, August 7, 1933, Dept. of State, decimal file, 1930–1939, file 837.00/3609; Machado, *Ocho años de lucha*, 102; Phillips, *Cuban Sideshow*, 53; and Portell-Vilá, *Nueva historia*, 391.

66. Machado, *Ocho años de lucha*, 110. Welles to Secty. of State, August 9, 1933, Dept. of State, decimal file, 1930–1939, file 837.00/3622.

67. Machado, *Ocho años de lucha*, 105–109. Machado adviser Alberto Lamar Schweyer makes a similar claim in his *Como cayó el Presidente Machado* (Madrid: Espasa-Calpe, 1934), 172.

68. In years to come, the pact with Machado would be a stain on the revolutionary credentials of the Communist Party.

69. In a dispatch to the State Department on August 11, Welles writes, "Some of the more violent members of the opposition are bitterly opposed to this solution. The more responsible leaders of the opposition, however, have determined to accept this solution as a patriotic necessity in order to insure protection of the elements which have been supporting the present Government"; Welles to Secty. of State, August 14, 1933, Dept. of State, decimal file, 1930–1939, file 837.00/3641.

70. Machado, *Ocho años de lucha*, 116. Machado is not alone in the belief that Welles orchestrated the appointment of Céspedes. Portell-Vilá describes Welles as "obstinate" in his support of Céspedes, an old friend of the ambassador's; *Nueva historia*, 395–396.

71. Machado, *Ocho años de lucha*, 123.

72. *El ABC al pueblo de Cuba: Manifesto-Programa*, 23–28.

CHAPTER 5. SERGEANTS' REVOLT

1. Carlos Manuel de Céspedes (1871–1939) was the son of Cuba's first president-in-arms during the Ten Years War (1868–1878). He was a veteran of the War for Independence. After his provisional government was toppled, he retired from public life. Ironically, he died a few days before Machado.

2. The wives of the two men were friendly, and they corresponded with each other for years; autobiography of Mathilda Welles, unpublished manuscript, Welles Papers, Personal Business Correspondence, 1909–1950.

3. This was the recollection of Mathilda Welles; autobiography of Mathilda

Welles, unpublished manuscript, Welles Papers, Personal Business Correspondence, 1909–1950.

4. This grim story and many others were told to *New York Times* reporter Ruby Hart Phillips; *Cuban Sideshow*, 67.

5. Autobiography of Mathilda Welles, unpublished manuscript, Welles Papers, Personal Business Correspondence, 1909–1950.

6. This sort of coverage was fairly typical of the period. For a typical example, see *Carteles*, August 20 and 27, 1933.

7. Phillips, *Cuban Sideshow*, 68–69.

8. "Carteleras," *Carteles*, 27 August 1933. The magazine declared that the violence was a "safety valve" for the public.

9. Horacio Ferrer, *Con el rifle al hombro* (Havana: El Siglo XX, 1950), 341.

10. Both figures come from Soto, *Revolución del 33*, 3:11. Soto probably takes the numbers from Adam y Silva, *La gran mentira*, 71. U.S. Military Attaché T. N. Gimperling estimated that thirty officers had been arrested; Lt. Col. T. N. Gimperling, military attaché, Havana, Cuba, "Cuba (political) (combat)," G-2 Report, August 25, 1933, file 2657-q-330 (199), RG 165.

11. Adam y Silva argues that Batista and his fellow conspirators manipulated these rumors to spur on the enlisted men to revolt; *La gran mentira*, 111–117. Ferrer heard of the rumors and tried to calm the fears of the enlisted men by issuing a memo a day before the revolt; *Con el rifle al hombro*, 347.

12. Ferrer, *Con el rifle al hombro*, 295–297. Welles concurred in this assessment; Welles to Secty. of State, August 24, 1933, Dept. of State, decimal file, 1930–1939, file 837.00/3706, RG59. Arístides Sosa de Quesada, awaiting appointment to the officer corps. at the time, and who would later rise to the rank of general under Batista, remembered that the "army was without leaders"; Arístides Sosa de Quesada, interview by author, tape recording, Miami, May 18, 1998.

13. According to Ferrer, Sanguily suffered from peritonitis as the result of a burst ulcer; *Con el rifle al hombro*, 338.

14. Generational struggle is a common theme in Cuban historiography. The Generation of 1933 would argue that the earlier generation had betrayed revolutionary values and principles. This same argument would be made by the Generation of 1953 against their fathers. Underlying this interpretive framework is a competition for political and economic power among generations.

15. Soto emphasizes class as a motivating factor in the army revolt that brought Batista to power. He argues against Adam y Silva and others who see the events of September 4, 1933, as a pure power grab by Batista and his fellow sergeants; *Revolución del 33*, 3:73–74.

16. In addition to the twenty-year rule, the enlisted man was required to serve at least eight years as sergeant before being appointed as a second lieutenant. Adam y Silva discusses the law in great detail as part of his attack on the enlisted men; *La gran mentira*, 17–23. Ferrer also cites the law as a contentious issue; *Con el rifle al hombro*, 340.

17. Vega Cobiellas, *Batista y Cuba*, 22. Portell-Vilá, *Nueva historia*, 378–379 and 387–389, provides background on the formation of the ABC. Thomas, *Cuba: Pursuit of Freedom*, 594–595, writes about the cell structure of the organization.

18. Adam y Silva eloquently describes the chaos as follows: "En aquellos días

azarosos, el Estado Mayor de tal no tenía sino el nombre, donde cada cual hizo y dispuso segun su grado de apasionamiento, y mas bien parecia un comité revolucionario, al que tenía acceso cualquiera, pues a nadie se preguntaba quién era o de dónde venía, bastado simplemente alegar que se era revolucionario"; *La gran mentira*, 124.

19. Capt. Mario Torres Menier, who attended one of the meetings, writes about the numerous conspiracies in the officer corps in a memoir published the following year; "Mi Diario," *Bohemia*, February 25, 1934. Ferrer thought this was part of a plot by Menocal, because the meetings were held at the home of Gustavo Cuervo Rubio, a close friend and ally of the former president. But the principal participants were members of the Student Directory; *Con el rifle al hombro*, 342.

20. The information comes from M. Franco Varona, a journalist of the period, and one of the first to write a history of the Revolution of 1933. He estimates in *La Revolución del 4 de septiembre* (Havana, 1934), 31–32, that 107 officers had met with Menocal to discuss the overthrow, a number that seems exaggerated. Soto believes a Menocal conspiracy was in the works, although no definitive proof exists; *Revolución del 33*, 3:8–9. Welles believed Menocal was "intriguing with a number of officers of the army to bring about the resignation of President Césepdes and his replacement by a candidate selected by himself"; Welles to Hamilton Fish, October 20, 1933, Welles Papers, Latin America files, 1933–1943, Cuba, 1933, E. Perez, *Army Politics in Cuba*, 81, also notes the disunity in the military in the aftermath of Machado's fall from power.

21. Franco Varona holds this view. "No tenía entonces [mid-August] el sargento Batista idea precisa sobre lo que seria el movimiento. Era necesario—pensaba—hacer algo en pro del Ejército y a ello tendio todo su interes"; *Revolución del 4 de septiembre*, 24.

22. Macau was the owner of Academia Milanés where Batista briefly taught stenography. Macau and Batista conspired together as members of the ABC, and it is likely that the former had some knowledge of the military conspiracy. Batista asked Macau to try to secure support for the movement from the ABC; Acosta Rubio, *Ensayo biográfico Batista*, 136.

23. One of the earliest meetings of the conspirators took place in the home of del Busto, a lawyer, who at the time was a civilian. He later joined the army, was promoted to captain, and named judge advocate by Batista. They would remain friends for many years. Del Busto would die in exile in Florida. Franco Varona briefly mentions the meeting in del Busto's home; *Revolución del 4 de septiembre*, 26. Details of the long friendship between del Busto and Batista were related to me by Batista's son; Fulgencio Rubén Batista Godínez, correspondence to author, March 23, 2000.

24. Some lists do not include Soler in the original group of conspirators, although this is unlikely, given his close friendship with Batista and their history of joint conspiracies. For example, Soto omits Soler in his list of original conspirators; *Revolución del 33*, 3:14–15.

25. Soto's list of eight original conspirators is as follows: Batista, Rodríguez, Pedraza, Lopez Migoya, Mario Hernández, Ángel Echevarría Salas, Cruz Vidal, and Maymir; *Revolución del 33*, 3:14–15. Soto may draw his list from the one offered by deposed Capt. Ricardo Adam y Silva; *La gran mentira*, 101–102. Both Adam y Silva and Soto omit Mariné, but he was clearly present at many of the early meetings.

Silva notes Mariné's presence at a meeting of conspirators in late August; *La gran mentira*, 103. Cruz Vidal identifies ten original conspirators. He omits Maymir but adds Sgts. Belisario Hernández and Urbano Soler and soldier Jorge Powell Pedroso; Cruz Vidal to Antolín González del Valle, November 8, 1983, Fulgencio Batista Zaldívar Papers, private collection of Fulgencio Rubén Batista Godínez, Coral Gables, Fla. There are numerous variations, most with the same core members with one or two additions or subtractions. Riera Hernández, *Un presidente constructivo*, 6, starts off by identifying the following eight: Sgts. Maymir, Pedroso, Pablo Rodríguez, Pedraza, Lopez Migoya, and Galíndez, and Cpls. Ángel Hechevearría and Juan Capote Fiallo. However, in the next sentence he expands the eight to fifteen by adding Cruz Vidal, Mario Hernández, Heriberto Marchena, Gregorio Querejeta, Belisario Hernández, Nicolás Cartaya, and Mariano Gajate. Batista never provided a complete listing of his fellow conspirators.

26. The banquet took place on October 10, 1930, and Rodríguez was on the organizing committee; Adam y Silva, *La gran mentira*, 58–59.

27. Adam y Silva, *La gran mentira*, 101. His dislike of Batista is such that he claims, although he provides no proof, that Batista actually collaborated with Machado; *La gran mentira*, 125. Adam y Silva takes this theme from student leaders, who after they were ousted from power by Batista, tried to label him as a Machado collaborator. Justo Carrillo, a member of the Student Directory, argued in his 1994 book, written in exile in Miami, that Batista was a "privileged stenographer" who "enjoyed great preferential treatment within the Machado regime, to the point of being sinful"; *Cuba 1933: Students, Yankees and Soldiers*, English ed. (New Brunswick, N.J.: Transaction Publishers, 1994), 66–67. Tabares del Real, *Revolución del 30*, 140–141, describes Batista as the "administrative secretary" of the movement. Phillips, *Cuban Sideshow*, 166–167, also believes that Rodríguez was the original leader.

28. José Tabares del Real cites Rodríguez as a source in his biography of Antonio Guiteras; *Guiteras* (Havana, Editorial de Ciencias Sociales, 1973). Adam y Silva, *La gran mentira*, also cites Rodríguez as a source in his bibliography.

29. Fulgencio Rubén Batista Godínez, interview by author, tape recording, Coral Gables, Fla., May 19, 1998.

30. Cruz Vidal to Fulgencio Rubén Batista Godínez, October 5, 1990, Fulgencio Batista Zaldívar Papers, private collection of Fulgencio Rubén Batista Godínez, Coral Gables, Fla. Riera Hernández, *Un presidente constructivo*, 55, also makes a spirited defense of Batista's leadership, describing Rodríguez as "*incoloro*" (colorless).

31. There is no written account of the first meeting between Rodríguez and Batista.

32. Miguel Ángel Hernández y Rodríguez (1906–1933), a member of the Engineering Corps, belonged to an ABC cell that consisted primarily of military men, although some civilians were members. More aggressive than Batista in his opposition to Machado, Hernández constructed and placed bombs for the ABC. It is probable that Hernández and Batista knew each other given that they were both sergeants and belonged to the same branch of the ABC. They probably did not conspire together, and Batista never mentioned him as a fellow conspirator. With Hernández's emergence as a hero, Batista would have been eager to promote such an association had one existed. A member of his ABC cell, Justo González, wrote a short biography of Hernández, published in 1937; *Sargento Miguel Ángel Hernández* (Havana: Cultural, 1937).

33. After Hernández was apprehended, *New York Times* reporter Phil Phillips (Ruby Hart Phillips's husband) tried to intercede with Ambassador Welles to get him released, but he did not take up the cause; Ruby Hart Phillips, *Cuban Sideshow*, 96.

34. There is great confusion over the date of the Hernández burial, some of it tied to the intense and angry debate over Batista's historical role in the events of 1933. The newspapers of the period clearly indicate the burial of the three leaders took place on August 19, 1933. As an example, see "El sepelio del estudiante Alpízar, el obrero Iglesias y el soldado Hernández," *Diario de la Marina*, August 20, 1933. Carrillo also gets the date right; *Cuba 1933*, 63. Chester mistakenly gives the date of Hernández's burial as August 18, the date his body was found; *A Sergeant Named Batista*, 35. Thomas makes the same error; *Cuba: Pursuit of Freedom*, 631. Adam y Silva gives August 25 as the burial date. Soto, perhaps relying on Adam y Silva, makes the same mistake.

35. The reflection comes from Capt. Mario Torres Menier; "Mi diario," *Bohemia*, February 25, 1934.

36. There is no complete transcript of the funeral oration. The excerpt comes from Acosta Rubio, *Ensayo biográfico Batista*, 135–136. Important details of the speech are also contained in Chester, *A Sergeant Named Batista*, 35–36.

37. Chester, *A Sergeant Named Batista*, 35.

38. Capt. Torres Menier, who attended the funeral, told his superiors of Batista's speech, according to Adam y Silva; *La gran mentira*, 125. Curiously, Torres Menier makes no mention of this in his published memoir.

39. Sergeant Bernardo Luna and Corporal Oscar Díaz recalled Carbó attending the burial. Carbó, publisher of a popular weekly, *La Semana*, would play an extraordinarily important role in the coming weeks. Luna and Díaz shared their memories of the burial years later with Batista's son; Fulgencio Rubén Batista Godínez, interview by author, tape recording, Coral Gables, Fla., May 19, 1998. Acosta Rubio provides details of the burials scene; *Ensayo biográfico Batista*, 136. A few months later, Batista told a reporter that he made important civilian contacts at the burial. The article was published in *La Mañana*, October 15, 1933. See also Welles to Secty. of State, October 18, 1933, Dept. of State, decimal file, 1930–1939, file 837.00/4258 RG 59.

40. The August 26, 1933, edition of *La Semana* would frequently be cited in years to come as both prophetic and proof that Carbó was attempting to broaden support for his own conspiracies beyond the students with whom he was associated at the time. Fulgencio Batista, *The Growth and Decline of the Cuban Republic* (New York: Devin-Adair, 1964), 11, cited the importance of Carbó's newspaper and that particular edition.

41. Batista told Chester that Carbó was crucial to gaining civilian support and without him the chances of success would have "greatly diminished"; *A Sergeant Named Batista*, 38–39. There is near unanimity on Carbó's importance to the movement. Soto writes of Carbó, "se convertía en el eslabon enlazador de la conspiración de los alistados y de los fermentos estudiantiles no ya tan solo en privado, sino publicamente"; *Revolución del 33*, 3:19–21.

42. Adam y Silva maintains that the conspirators did not begin to meet until August 26 or 27, but this clashes with information provided by Franco Varona that indicates that the meetings began before the Hernández funeral; *La gran mentira*, 102. Franco Varona writes that the conspirators tried to get Carbó to publish the

manifesto in his August 26 edition, clearly indicating that the meetings took place at least several days prior; *Revolución del 4 de septiembre*, 26–27.

43. Franco Varona provides the most detailed account of the early days of the conspiracy; *Revolución del 4 de septiembre*, 24–27.

44. Franco Varona, *Revolución del 4 de septiembre*, 26. Cruz Vidal says they all resigned together; Cruz Vidal to Antolín González del Valle, November 8, 1983, Fulgencio Batista Zaldívar Papers, private collection of Fulgencio Rubén Batista Godínez, Coral Gables, Fla. Acosta Rubio disputes the resignation account, noting that after Batista gained power, he sent emissaries to the ABC to seek an alliance by declaring himself an "abecedario." He writes that Batista went with a civilian, Ramón Macau, to meet with cell leader Manuel Martí Escasena. When Batista failed to garner support from the ABC, he began to seek out contact with the student movement; *Ensayo biográfico Batista*, 136–138.

45. José Augustín Fernández, a vice president at the telephone company, declined to broadcast the manifesto, arguing that it would hurt the cause of the enlisted men; Chester, *A Sergeant Named Batista*, 38. Franco Varona relates the story about Carbó; *Revolución del 4 de septiembre*, 26–27.

46. The appointment of Montes had an unsettling effect on the armed forces, according to Adam y Silva; *La gran mentira*, 111–113. Franco Varona identifies the appointment of Montes as a key factor in Batista's decision to topple the military leadership; *Revolución del 4 de septiembre*, 23.

47. Batista made the remark several weeks after the successful revolt, in *La Mañana*, October 15, 1933. See also Welles to Secty. of State, October 18, 1933, Dept. of State, decimal file, 1930–1939, file 837.00/4258 RG 59.

48. Ibid., 121. Adam y Silva speculates that Carbó encouraged the ouster of the officers to further his own revolutionary plans, perhaps realizing that once the conspirators ousted their superiors they would have to topple the government to prevent their reinstatement. Franco Varona notes the evolution as well; *Revolución del 4 de septiembre*, 27.

49. This is what he told Chester; *A Sergeant Named Batista*, 39–40.

50. The date comes from Franco Varona; *Revolución del 4 de septiembre*, 31. Soto argues that no definitive proof of a Menocal conspiracy exists, but there is enough circumstantial evidence to make it plausible; *Revolución del 33*, 3:8–9.

51. Welles to Secty. of State, August 24, 1933, Dept. of State, decimal file, 1930–1939, file 837.00/3706, RG 59. Phillips, *Cuban Sideshow*, 165–166, likewise suspected a Menocal conspiracy.

52. The U.S. military attaché had Batista's interview in *La Mañana*, October 15, 1933, translated and sent to Washington; Lt. Col. T. N. Gimperling, military attaché, "Stability of Government Armed Revolutionary Movements," G-2 Report, November 1, 1933, file 2657-330 RG 165.

53. Adam y Silva dedicates part of a chapter to the influence of the Masons on the movement. He declares that masonry strayed "far from the principles of brotherhood" by fostering the conspiracy. The particular Mason's lodge in question had a high percentage of military men as members; *La gran mentira*, 83–86. Cruz Vidal said that Grand Venerable Teacher Carlito Piñeiro allowed the conspirators to meet at the lodge at Avenida Carlos III; Cruz Vidal to Antolín González del Valle, November 8, 1983, Fulgencio Batista Zaldívar Papers, private collection of Fulgencio Rubén Batista Godínez, Coral Gables, Fla.

54. Vega Cobiellas, *General Fulgencio Batista Zaldívar*, 32. The quote from Batista reads as follows: "Escogí un hombre de cada puesto o compañía y luego otro en quien pudiera confiar y así sucesivamente hasta que sólo fuera menester dar la señal de que la hora determinada había llegado."

55. Batista told this story to Chester; *A Sergeant Named Batista*, 41.

56. Franco Varona claims that sergeants, corporals, and enlisted men throughout the island had prior knowledge of the revolt, but this is unlikely, particularly in the eastern provinces; *Revolución del 4 de septiembre*, 28. In later years, some of the sergeants said they were surprised when they received orders from Batista to take over the installations. As an example, Abelardo Gómez Gómez, the sergeant who took command of a squadron in Holguín, did not know of the conspiracy until he received a cablegram on September 4; Fulgencio Rubén Batista Godínez, interview by author, tape recording, May 19, 1998. In an interview published in the Cuban newspaper *La Mañana*, October 15, 1933, Batista says the conspirators were "lacking" in Oriente and Pinar del Río Provinces; Welles to Secty. of State, October 15, 1933, Dept. of State, decimal file, 1930–1939, file 837.00/4258 RG 59.

57. Both instances were reported by Adam y Silva. The first was a discussion between Lt. Tomás Regalado and Lt. Col. Héctor de Quesada; *La gran mentira*, 95–97.

58. Lt. Col. T. N. Gimperling, military attaché, "Stability of Government Armed Revolutionary Movements," G-2 Report, November 1, 1933, file 2657-330 RG 165.

59. Ferrer, *Con el rifle al hombro*, 345. The edict included meetings among the officers as well.

60. Ibid., 347.

61. This according to Chester, *A Sergeant Named Batista*, 40–43.

62. Ibid., 41–42.

63. The best sources for the events of that morning are the accounts by Torres Menier, "Mi diario," *Bohemia*, February 25, 1934; Batista, *Respuesta*, 393–405; and Chester, *A Sergeant Named Batista*, 42–50. In his book, Batista gave the official stamp of approval for his version to Chester, and in *Respuesta* he quotes Chester almost verbatim for eight pages. However, in some spots, Batista corrects or augments the version of events offered by his biographer.

64. The best account of this exchange comes from Batista, *Respuesta*, 398–400. Chester wrongly identifies the blundering conspirator as José Capote; *A Sergeant Named Batista*, 43. Chester refrains from mentioning the part where Batista asks Capote to consider shooting himself, perhaps because this conflicts with Chester's heroic narrative. There may be a little more to the story than either Batista or Chester recount. In an undated article in *Diario de la Marina*, by Gustavo Herrero, Batista said that Capote let slip information about the conspiracy to members of the air corps, and that one of them, evidently a cook, asked Torres Menier to join the conspiracy.

65. Chester, *A Sergeant Named Batista*, 43–44.

66. Torres Menier, "Mi diario," *Bohemia*, February 25, 1934; and Chester, *A Sergeant Named Batista*, 45–46. Chester declares that by entering the club, Torres Menier was "walking into a trap" set by Batista. Cruz Vidal also remembers Batista "sweating profusely" and "nervously touching his hair"; Cruz Vidal to Antolín González del Valle, November 8, 1983, Fulgencio Batista Zaldívar Papers, private collection of Fulgencio Rubén Batista Godínez, Coral Gables, Fla.

67. Chester. *A Sergeant Named Batista*, 46.

68. Adam y Silva, *La gran mentira*, 136–144. Obviously, Adam y Silva did not perceive the threat either, because he too failed to act decisively.

69. My account is essentially a synthesis of recollections provided by Torres Menier and Batista. The two accounts are fundamentally in agreement. In Batista's version of events, Torres Menier addressed the crowd first.

70. Chester emphasizes the "dignity" theme; *A Sergeant Named Batista*, 48.

71. This is the recollection of Adam y Silva; *La gran mentira*, 138. Neither Torres Menier nor Chester provide that detail.

72. Adam y Silva, *La gran mentira*, 139. Hernández was one of the more colorful of the original conspirators. A year later he would plot to oust Batista from power. Cruz Vidal remembers the Hernández incident as well; Fulgencio Rubén Batista Godínez, interview by author, tape recording, Coral Gables, Fla., May 19, 1998.

73. Adam y Silva, *La gran mentira*, 139.

74. Adam y Silva reaches this same conclusion; *La gran mentira*, 142–144.

75. Ferrer wrote of the events of September 4 in his memoir; *Con el rifle al hombro*, 349–356.

76. Ibid., 351.

77. Adam y Silva, *La gran mentira*, 150.

78. Lt. Col. T. N. Gimperling, military attaché, Cuba (Combat) (Loyalty), "Summary of Army Mutiny of September 4–5, 1933," G-2 Report, September 26, 1933, file 2012-133 RG 165.

79. Adam y Silva, *La gran mentira*, 143. He mistakenly identifies Oscar Díaz as Tomás Díaz. Chester provides additional details of the meeting; *A Sergeant Named Batista*, 59–60.

80. Chester mentions the Carbó meeting; *A Sergeant Named Batista*, 60. Adam y Silva notes the meeting with Blas Hernández; *La gran mentira*, 144. Blas Hernández (1879–1933) remains one of the most neglected historical figures of the period. Nearly forgotten today, he was a prominent folk hero of the era with ties to Col. Mendieta. The opposition newspaper, *Oposición*, the mouthpiece of Mendieta's political party, Asociación Unión Nacionalista, ran a profile of him in its June 1933 edition, a copy of which was retained by Sumner Welles in his files. The paper's correspondent foreshadows Herbert Matthews's visit to Fidel Castro in the Sierra Maestra by visiting Blas Hernández at his secret camp and traveling with him. As Matthews would do years later, the unnamed reporter visiting Hernández would grossly overestimate the number of men under his command, which he placed at six hundred; "Uno del Consejo de la Dirección Corresponsal en Campaña," *Oposición*, June 1933, in Welles Papers, Latin America files, 1933–1943, Cuba, political. For a biographical sketch of Blas Hernández, see Ángel Aparicio Laurencio, *Blas Hernández y la Revolución de 1933* (Miami: Ediciones Universal, 1994).

81. Fulgencio Rubén Batista Godínez, interview by author, tape recording, Coral Gables, Fla., April 30, 1998. In the future, the amethyst ring would become a symbol of identification for Batista's inner circle. He would frequently present such a ring, surrounded by small diamonds, to close friends. It was a clear symbol to anyone in government that the person wearing the ring had a special relationship with Batista. The original ring was evidently a gift from a stenography student who could not afford to pay for her classes.

82. Céspedes did not learn of the revolt until about 3 a.m. on September 5, when

he was informed by several cabinet ministers of the uprising; Franco Varona, *Revolución del 4 de septiembre*, 69–70.

83. Ferrer, *Con el rifle al hombro*, 352.

84. Adam y Silva, *La gran mentira*, 148; and Torres Menier, "Mi diario," *Bohemia*, February 25, 1934.

85. I owe this account to Adam y Silva, who quotes an eyewitness to the event; *La gran mentira*, 158–164. Chester's account, on most points, closely mirrors the details provided by Adam y Silva; *A Sergeant Named Batista*, 60–63.

86. This observation belongs to José M. Irisarri, one of the soon-to-be named pentarchs, in "Cómo nació y cómo murió la Comisión Ejecutiva," *Bohemia*, August 26, 1934.

87. Franco Varona, *Revolución del 4 de septiembre*, 63–65.

88. Ibid., 49–50. Sgt. Pedro Rodríguez Ochoa, stationed at La Cabaña, said Soler was not flatly rejected by the troops. They elected someone else, before Soler showed up; Fulgencio Rubén Batista Godínez, interview by author, tape recording, Coral Gables, Fla., May 19, 1998.

89. This testimony comes from Cpl. Luis Robaina Piedra, who remembered elections at the officers' training school. Years later, Batista's oldest son married Robaina's daughter. He was eventually promoted to general; Fulgencio Rubén Batista Godínez, interview by author, tape recording, Coral Gables, Fla., May 19, 1998.

90. Soto provides an overview of the navy's participation; *Revolución del 33*, 3:29–31. Franco Varona writes that the navy "immediately adhered" to the movement; *Revolución del 4 de septiembre*, 53–55. U.S. Military Attaché T. N. Gimperling received regular reports from the Cuban military on the number of personnel in the different branches of Cuba's armed forces. The report for July 31, 1933, estimates Cuban army strength at between 10,345 and 10,928. No explanation is provided for the discrepancy; Lt. Col. T. N. Gimperling, military attaché, "Cuba (Combat)," G-2 Report, September 21, 1933, file 2012-100 RG 165. The navy estimate comes from "Cuba (Combat)," G-2 Report, April 24, 1933, file 2012-119 RG 165. The police estimate is from "Cuba (Combat)," G-2 Report, June 29, 1933, file 2012-119 RG 165.

91. Ferrer, *Con el rifle al hombro*, 352–353.

92. The Foreign Policy Association, which conducted a detailed study of the events leading up to the revolution, concluded that Batista and his allies had not "foreseen that their coup might involve a change in the civil government"; Charles A. Thomson, "The Cuban Revolution: Reform and Reaction," *Foreign Policy Reports*, January 1, 1936, 262. Chester would have us believe that Batista came out against the Céspedes government at the 8 p.m. meeting, but this is clearly an effort to enhance Batista's revolutionary credentials. According to Chester, "He berated the American influence which had created the Céspedes government." No other source corroborates this version of events; *A Sergeant Named Batista*, 61. Pérez, *Army Politics*, 82, argues that the takeover of Camp Columbia and the detention of the officers "were measures designed to enhance the negotiating position" of the conspirators. He maintains that the enlisted men thought their grievances would be resolved quickly and that they would return command to the officers.

93. The details were provided to Adam y Silva by several eyewitnesses, including Sergeants Pablo Rodríguez and López Migoya; *La gran mentira*, 178–179.

94. Padilla recounted his version of events to fellow Directory member Justo

Carrillo; *Cuba 1933*, 143–144; and Emilio Laurent, *De oficial a revoluciónario* (Havana: Imp. Ucar, García y Cía., 1941), 130.

95. Batista, *Respuesta*, 407, writes that he would have preferred a single leader and that consideration for the presidency was given to university professor Carlos de la Torre, who could not accept the position for "family and health reasons."

96. Among the other groups taking part were Pro Ley y Justicia, represented by Ramiro Valdés Daussá, and the ABC Radical, represented by Oscar de la Torre.

97. Ramón Grau San Martín (1887–1969) would wage a running battle with Batista for the next twenty-five years. Toppled as president in 1934, he would return to power after defeating Batista's hand-picked successor in the 1944 presidential election. After Castro came to power, he remained in Cuba, where he died.

98. Carlos Prío Socarrás (1903–1977) succeeded Grau as president from 1948 to 1952. He was overthrown on March 10, 1952, by a military conspiracy led by Batista. He backed Castro in the struggle against the Batista dictatorship, but went into exile in Miami when the revolution veered toward Communism. Prío committed suicide.

99. The proclamation is reprinted in Soto, *Revolución del 33*, 3:35–36.

100. Quoted in Carrillo, *Cuba 1933*, 148.

101. José M. Irisarri, "Cómo nació y cómo murió la Comisión Ejecutiva," *Bohemia*, August 26, 1934.

102. Ibid. For Batista's reaction, see Chester, *A Sergeant Named Batista*, 67 and 165; Acosta Rubio, *Ensayo biográfico Batista*, 142–143; and Vega Cobiellas, *Batista y Cuba*, 26.

103. General Order No. 1 was reprinted by Soto; *Revolución del 33*, 3:28; and Varona, *Revolución del 4 de septiembre*, 41–42. On Rodríguez's initial displeasure, see Adam y Silva, *La gran mentira*, 170.

104. Rubio Padilla retold the story to Justo Carrillo; *Cuba 1933*, 151–152.

105. The dialogue between Céspedes and Grau has been recounted, with minor variation, by any number of sources. See Enrique Lumen, *La Revolución cubana 1902–1934: Crónica de nuestro tiempo* (Mexico City: Ediciones Botas, 1934), 95–97. Céspedes's farewell remarks were recorded by Franco Varona; *Revolución del 4 de septiembre*, 71–72.

CHAPTER 6. REVOLUTION OF 1933

1. In the Hispanic Caribbean, the term *negro*, literally meaning "black man," can be endearing or profane depending on intent and context. Batista's enemies would have used it as a racial slur. Herminio Portell-Vilá, historian and journalist, recalls the term frequently applied to Batista during this period; *Nueva historia*, 405. Welles also makes a point of Batista's race. After their first meeting on September 5, 1933, Welles describes him as a "mulatto with an admixture of Chinese blood"; Welles to Secty. of State, September 5, 1933, Dept. of State, decimal file, 1930–1939, file 837.00/3750 RG 59.

2. On August 25, 1933, Gimperling writes; "Although there have been rumors in Havana of a possible military 'coup,' I feel very sure that nothing of the sort will be attempted. I base my estimate on several reasons, the principal reason being that no officer in the Army (except Sanguily who is dangerously ill) is capable of successfully undertaking a military 'coup'"; Lt. Col. T. N. Gimperling, military attaché, Cuba (Political) (Combat), "Stability of Government. Loyalty of the Army," G-2 Report, August 25, 1933, file 2657-330 (199) RG 165.

3. Lt. Col. T. N. Gimperling, military attaché, Cuba (Political), "Stability of Government. Armed Revolutionary Movement," G-2 Report, September 5, 1933, file 2657-330 (201) RG 165. Welles to Secty. of State, September 5, 1933, Dept. of State, decimal file, 1930–1939, file 837.00/3747 RG 59. Sergio Carbó published the cartoon in *La Semana*, September 1933. The cartoon is reproduced in Phillips, *Cuban Sideshow*, 117.

4. Jefferson Caffery to Welles, September 14, 1933, Dept. of State, decimal file, 1930–1939, file 837.00/3747 RG 59.

5. Welles to Secty. of State, September 5, 1933, Dept. of State, decimal file, 1930–1939, file 837.00/3750 RG 59.

6. Welles to Secty. of State, September 5, 1933, Dept. of State, decimal file, 1930–1939, file 837.00/3756 RG 59.

7. Bernardo Luna to Fulgencio Rubén Batista Godínez, September 14, 1984, Fulgencio Batista Zaldívar Papers, private collection of Fulgencio Rubén Batista Godínez, Coral Gables, Fla. Luna writes to Batista's oldest son: "Para mí que estuve a su lado las interminables horas, fue la transformación de un hombre que asumía cada vez mayor potencia material y espiritual y era un ejemplo de magnificencia humana."

8. Soto, *Revolución del 33*, 3:45. Later in his book, he analyzes in great depth Batista's role as a "counterrevolutionary under imperialistic direction," 348–357. One of the most influential scholars on the period, Luis E. Aguilar, also attributes great significance to the first meeting between Batista and Welles; *Cuba 1933: Prologue to Revolution* (Ithaca, N.Y.: Cornell University Press, 1972) 210–211. Adam y Silva cites Pablo Rodríguez as the source for the anecdote about the frosty reception received by Batista at the U.S. Embassy; *La gran mentira*, 187. Military Attaché Gimperling was also in attendance and reported on the atmosphere; Lt. Col. T. N. Gimperling, military attaché, Cuba (Combat) (Loyalty), "Summary of Army Mutiny of September 4–5, 1933," G-2 Report, September 26, 1933, file 2012-133 RG 165.

9. Batista, *Growth and Decline of the Cuban Republic*, 8–10, writes of the discussion. This conversation could have occurred at the first meeting between Welles and Batista, when security was the key issue for the ambassador, or even later in September. Batista's account appears credible in light of Welles's early reaction to the Sergeants' Revolt. It is curious that Welles makes no mention of this discussion with Batista in his diplomatic dispatches, but he perhaps considered it an exploratory topic, not worthy of mention. *Growth and Decline of the Cuban Republic* is in fact an English translation of Batista's earlier work, *Piedras y leyes* (Mexico City: Ediciones Botas, 1961). A similar account of the conversation with Welles can be found on pages 12–16 of that work.

10. Carlos Mendieta (1873–1960) would eventually replace Grau as part of a U.S.-brokered arrangement with Batista. Known as the first of the "puppet presidents" under Batista, he retained considerably more control than those who would follow him. Batista showed a good deal of respect for Mendieta, a veteran of Cuba's Independence War, who rose to the rank of colonel.

11. The strategy clearly emerges in a series of dispatches Welles sent to Washington throughout September 5. On his plan for a coalition government, Welles states his objective clearly in a letter to Congressman Hamilton Fish in response to a speech critical of Cuba policy. "Consequently, if I understand your address correctly when you state that what Cuba requires is a concentration government, I am

not only in accord with you, but I have been doing my utmost since the 4th of September, against very material odds both here and in the United States, to accomplish this very end"; Welles to Fish, October 20, 1933, Welles Papers, Latin America files, 1933–1943, Cuba, 1933, E–F.

12. The excerpt from Batista's first speech comes from *Diario de la Marina*, September 6, 1933.

13. The AP report was picked up by *Diario de la Marina*, September 5, 1933. Vega Cobiellas, *Batista y Cuba*, 26–27, makes a similar point about Batista's intentions.

14. This is the view expressed by Adam y Silva; *La gran mentira*, 244.

15. The figures come from Franco Varona, *Revolución del 4 de septiembre*, 77–78. Soto is in agreement; *Revolución del 33*, 3:60–61. By early 1934, the number of former officers who had returned fell to 106, according to a detailed report prepared by U.S. Military Attaché T. N. Gimperling. The report, dated February 16, 1934, lists 633 officers by name, including the 106 officers who remained in the military after September 4, 1933; Cuba (Combat), "Personnel: Commissioned Officers," G-2 Report, February 16, 1934, file 2012-133 (60) RG 165.

16. Torres Menier, "Mi Diario," *Bohemia*, February 25, 1934. An excerpt of the circular was reprinted by Adam y Silva; *La gran mentira*, 224.

17. Grau alludes to this effort to persuade lower-ranking officers to support the government in his first meeting with Welles; Welles to Secty. of State, September 5, 1933, Dept. of State, decimal file, 1930–1939, file 837.00/3756 RG 59.

18. By far the most detailed account of the negotiations comes from Adam y Silva; *La gran mentira*, 226–241.

19. The observation was made by student leader Juan Rubio Padilla; see Carrillo, *Cuba 1933*, 154–155.

20. Ferrer, *Con el rifle al hombro*, 366–367. Adam y Silva notes that there was some willingness on the part of the officers to accept this offer. However, when one lieutenant agreed, Carbó immediately placed another obstacle in his path; *La gran mentira*, 231.

21. The direct quote from Batista reads as follows: "La cuestión sería fácil si todos los oficiales fueran decentes, como lo es Ud., pero el problema está en que como los alistados confían en mí, y yo les he traído a esto, ¿cómo van a ser mandados de nuevo por quienes no están en su caso?"; Adam y Silva, *La gran mentira*, 238. Luna, an aide to Batista, remembered only five people present during the negotiations— two representatives of the officer corps, Capt. Luis Lois and Capt. César Celorio; Carbó; Batista; and himself; Bernardo Luna to Fulgencio Rubén Batista Godínez, September 14, 1984, Fulgencio Batista Zaldívar Papers, private collection of Fulgencio Rubén Batista Godínez, Coral Gables, Fla.

22. Adam y Silva, *La gran mentira*, 239.

23. The students saw no alternative but to promote Batista, according to Justo Carrillo and Juan Rubio Padilla; *Cuba 1933*, 162–163. Sergio Carbó, *Prensa Libre*, December 10, 1944; in Adam y Silva, *La gran mentira*, 234.

24. The issue of an appropriate rank was discussed by Batista and several of his followers at a meeting prior to his arrival at the palace. His followers agreed that colonel was most appropriate; Bernardo Luna to Fulgencio Rubén Batista Godínez, September 14, 1984, Fulgencio Batista Zaldívar Papers, private collection of Fulgencio Rubén Batista Godínez, Coral Gables, Fla.

25. Among those promoted in the first wave were Pablo Rodríguez, José Pedraza, and Manuel López Migoya to the rank of captain; Ángel Echevarría and Mario Hernández to first lieutenant; Ignacio Galíndez and Oscar Díaz to second lieutenant; see Adam y Silva, *La gran mentira*, 493. The overall figure comes from Acosta Rubio, *Ensayo biográfico Batista*, 153. Riera Hernández, *Un presidente constructivo*, 9, differs only slightly from Acosta Rubio, writing that 532 were promoted. Welles speculated about a "mutiny" if other enlisted men were not promoted; Welles to Secty. of State, September 10, 1933, Dept. of State, decimal file, 1930–1939, file 837.00/3803 RG 59.

26. Chester, *A Sergeant Named Batista*, 74. Vega Cobiellas, *Batista y Cuba*, 25, uses similar language to make the same point. Twenty years earlier, Franco Varona drew the same conclusion; *Revolución del 4 de septiembre*, 78–80.

27. Batista, *Growth and Decline of the Cuban Republic*, 6.

28. This is the explanation given by Adam y Silva and others for the decision by the officers to congregate at the Hotel Nacional. It is just as likely that some of them were there as part of a plan to induce U.S. intervention. Adam y Silva dedicates an entire chapter to the topic; *La gran mentira*, 281–290. Ferrer concurs with Adam y Silva; *Con el rifle al hombro*, 378. Capt. Tomás R. Yanes said the hotel was one of the few locations large enough to accommodate the officers who wanted to "exchange impressions" and plot a joint strategy; "Los psychoses del Hotel Nacional," *Carteles*, December 17, 1933.

29. This observation was made by student leader Rubén de León in a series of articles he wrote for *Bohemia* describing the rise and fall of the revolutionary government; Rubén de León, "La verdad de lo ocurrido desde el cuatro de septiembre," *Bohemia*, February 4, 1934. Portell-Vilá notes that Franca felt uncomfortable with the students and their proposals, while Portela was envious of the influence Grau, Carbó, and Irisarri had with the students; *Nueva historia*, 409. The demand to eliminate the pentarchy was made by Menocal and the political parties that had taken part in the mediation proceedings, according to Rubio Padilla; Carrillo, *Cuba 1933*, 163.

30. Grau voiced no objection.

31. Eduardo Chibás, *Prensa Libre*, May 24, 1944; in Adam y Silva, *La gran mentira*, 272–274. Carbó arrived at the same conclusion as Grau about the reticence of the United States to land troops.

32. Eduardo Chibás (1907–1951) became one of Batista's fiercest opponents. He eventually broke with Grau, established the Orthodox Party (Partido Ortodoxo), and waged a vigorous campaign against political corruption. He became a mentor to Fidel Castro in the late 1940s. As part of a warning about the state of Cuban democracy, he shot himself during a radio broadcast in August 1951 and died ten days later.

33. Welles to Secty. of State, September 10, 1933, Dept. of State, decimal file, 1930–1939, file 837.00/3803 RG 59.

34. Rubio Padilla provides a detailed account of events to Justo Carrillo; *Cuba 1933*, 165–175. Chibás provides a similar account of the selection of Grau in a 1944 newspaper story. However, Rubio Padilla claims that Chibás did not attend that meeting. Chibás wrote that he had nominated Grau, while Rubio Padilla took credit for the Grau nomination; Chibás, *Prensa Libre*, May 24, 1944, in Adam y Silva, *La gran mentira*, 276–277.

35. Welles to Secty. of State, September 7, 1933, Dept. of State, decimal file, 1930–1939, file 837.00/3781 RG 59. The offer to Céspedes was reported by Adam y Silva; *La*

gran mentira, 183–184. Batista biographer Edmund Chester provides details on the United Fruit offer. He notes that during that period U.S. Consul Gen. Frederick Dumont inquired of United Fruit whether it would be possible to "divert" one of their steamers to Cuba to "pick up Batista"; *A Sergeant Named Batista*, 88–90.

36. Welles to Secty. of State, September 9, 1933, Dept. of State, decimal file, 1930–1939, file 837.00/3807 RG 59.

37. Antonio Guiteras Holmes (1906–1935), a fiery social revolutionary, emerged as a formidable opponent to Batista. After the fall of the Grau government, he organized an armed revolutionary movement against the Batista-backed government, known as Joven Cuba. He died in a shoot-out with the army two years later and became an important political symbol in the early years of the Castro government. The most comprehensive account of his life is the already cited work by Tabares del Real, *Guiteras*. Other useful works include Newton Briones Montoto, *Aquella decisión callada* (Havana: Editorial de Ciencias Sociales, 1998); Calixta Guiteras, *Biografía de Antonio Guiteras* (Havana: Cooperativa Obrera de Publicidad, 1960), a short memoir written by his sister; Olga Cabrera, *Guiteras: La época, el hombre* (Havana: Editorial de Arte y Literatura, 1974); and by the same author, *Guiteras: Su pensamiento revolucionario* (Havana: Editorial de Ciencias Sociales, 1974).

38. Perhaps the best analysis of this political struggle can be found in Soto's *Revolución del 33*, 3:100–110. Soto aligns the factions as follows: Grau with the reformist-centrists, Guiteras with the revolutionary-leftists, and Batista with the proimperialist-rightists. The analysis forms part of the prevailing revolutionary interpretation. Soto overstates Batista's sympathy for the right wing at this point in his career. Aguilar describes the three as a "strange triumvirate, the dramatis personae around whom events and decisions were to revolve"; *Cuba 1933: Prologue to Revolution*, 170.

39. Among the biographical works on Grau are G. Rodríguez Morejón, *Grau San Martín* 2nd ed. (Havana: Úcar, García y Compañía, 1944); Antonio Lancís, *Grau: Estadista y político (Cincuenta años de la historia de Cuba)* (Miami: Ediciones Universal, 1985); and Miguel Hernández-Bauzá, *Biografía de una emoción popular: El Dr. Grau* (Miami: Ediciones Universal, 1987).

40. Aguilar, *Cuba 1933: Prologue to Revolution*, 173.

41. Hugh Thomas writes that Batista was not "really a military man at all: rather he was a civilian in uniform who owed his rise to political finesse"; *Cuba: Pursuit of Freedom*, 680.

42. Guiteras, *Biografía de Antonio Guiteras*, 12. Antonio Guiteras, "Septembrismo," *Bohemia*, April 1, 1934.

43. Thomas, *Cuba: Pursuit of Freedom*, 650, takes note of the nickname.

44. Phillips, *Cuban Sideshow*, 275, provides a useful description of Guiteras.

45. Carrillo says that Guiteras ordered the dispersal of a Communist march on September 29, which resulted in many deaths; *Cuba 1933*, 230–231. Soto blames Batista, the army, and the civilian militias for the attack on Communist marchers, but he notes that Guiteras never condemned the attack; *Revolución del 33*, 3:174–175. Calixta Guiteras claims that her brother presented his resignation as a result of the shootings, but it was rejected; *Biografía de Antonio Guiteras*, 11.

46. Carrillo discusses Guiteras's efforts in the navy and the plot to arrest Batista; *Cuba 1933*, 313–314 and 244–261. On the Revolutionary Guard, see Soto, *Revolución del 33*, 3:127.

47. The unsuccessful attempt occurred on October 26, 1933. Tabares del Real, *Guiteras*, 197.

48. Guiteras, *Biografía de Antonio Guiteras*, 10.

49. Batista proclaimed his coup on March 10, 1952, toppling a constitutionally elected government, as a revolution.

50. A list of proposed reforms was circulated to the troops by Batista on September 22, and they were reproduced by Gimperling in a report to his superiors; Lt. Col. T. N. Gimperling, military attaché, Cuba (Combat), "Military Policy. Influences Affecting Policy and Military System," G-2 Report, September 23, 1933, file 2012-146 RG 165.

51. The legislation worsened anti-immigrant sentiments, already heightened by the economic crisis. As a result, thousands of Haitian and Jamaican workers were forcibly repatriated, losing the few assets they had amassed. The repatriations were also fueled by racism; Soto, *Revolución del 33*, 3:199–201.

52. Soto provides a detailed overview of the conference; *Revolución del 33*, 3:288–301. The annexation remark was made by Herminio Portell-Vilá, a delegate to the conference. U.S. Secretary of State Cordell Hull voted for the nonintervention resolution citing the commitment of the Roosevelt administration to the Good Neighbor policy, but raised concerns about the lack of a definition for what constitutes intervention. Gellman provides insights into Hull's negotiations with the Cuban delegation; *Roosevelt and Batista*, 74–76.

53. The five nations were Mexico, Peru, Uruguay, Panama, and Spain.

54. Welles to Secty. of State, September 16, 1933, Dept. of State, decimal file, 1930–1939, file 837.00/3915 RG 59.

55. Welles to Buell, October 4, 1933, Welles Papers, Latin America files, 1933–1943, Cuba, 1933, B.

56. Welles to Buell, October 24, 1933, Welles Papers, Latin America files, 1933–1943, Cuba, 1933, B. The Chamber of Commerce's view was expressed by its president, Maurice T. McGovern; McGovern to Welles, November 15, 1933, Welles Papers, Latin American files, 1933–1943, Cuba, 1933, E–F.

57. The plan was for the government to get first preference in buying foreign sugar properties that were for sale and distributing them to local tenants; Carrillo, *Cuba 1933*, 322–325. Soto sees the decree setting forth the government's right as an attack on the big *latifundios* (large landed estates); *Revolución del 33*, 3:257–259.

58. Robert Freeman Smith chronicles the development of this scholarly tradition in "Twentieth-Century Cuban Historiography," *Hispanic American Historical Review* 44 (February 1964): 44–73. Louis A. Pérez Jr. continues the theme in "In the Service of the Revolution: Two Decades of Cuban Historiography, 1959–1979," *Hispanic American Historical Review* 60 (February 1980): 79–89.

59. Soto argues that Guiteras thought the Communists and workers influenced by them were providing a pretext for U.S. intervention; *Revolución del 33*, 3:149–150. Carrillo agrees; *Cuba 1933*, 231.

60. The lower estimate comes from Phillips, *Cuban Sideshow*, 151; and Portell-Vilá, *Nueva historia*, 415. Soto claims the death and casualty tolls were much higher; *Revolución del 33*, 3:166.

61. The ashes were kept in private homes for many years until they were turned over to the Central Committee of the Communist Party in the 1960s, according to Juan Marinello as quoted in Soto, *Revolución del 33*, 3:166n101.

62. Ibid., 3:168–173. The Communist Party blamed the Grau government and did not single out Batista, but Soto argues that they did not perceive the extent of the colonel's power.

63. Phillips, *Cuban Sideshow*, 151.

64. *El País*, September 16, 1933, in Aguilar, *Cuba 1933: Prologue to Revolution*, 185.

65. Welles to Secty. of State, September 16, 1933, Dept. of State, decimal file, 1930–1939, file 837.00/3915 RG 59. Lt. Abelardo Gómez Gómez, in charge of the military district in Holguín, said that Batista contacted him on or about September 25, 1933, and told him to act quickly against the Communists who had taken control of several sugar processing plants in the region. Batista ordered him to "dislodge the workers without violence, if possible" ("Batista le ordenó que los desaloje sin derramamiento de sangre, si es posible"); Fulgencio Rubén Batista Godínez, interview by author, tape recording, Coral Gables, Fla., May 19, 1998.

66. *Suplemento de Bandera Roja*, October 3, 1933, in Soto, *Revolución del 33*, 3:171. Welles to Buell, October 4, 1933, Welles Papers, Latin America files, 1933–1943, Cuba, 1933, B.

67. Ferrer lays out the plan to bring back Céspedes in a detailed letter he sent to Grau on September 13. He reprints the letter in its entirety in *Con el rifle al hombro*, 379–381. Sumner Welles, often accused of urging the officers to take a stand against the government, wrote on September 10 that he received a visit from Ferrer, who on behalf of the army officers "petitioned" him to "have a sufficient force of American marines landed to disarm the soldiers and the innumerable civilians who are armed and that should I agree they would at once proclaim that President Céspedes was the sole legitimated President of Cuba and undertake the recruiting and training of a new army." Welles declined to receive the petition; Welles to Secty. of State, September 10, 1933, Dept. of State, decimal file, 1930–1939, file 837.00/3810 RG 59. At the time, there was widespread belief that Welles was backing the officers. Among those making that claim were student leader, Carrillo; *Cuba 1933*, 233; and Franco Varona, *Revolución del 4 de septiembre*, 80.

68. I draw much of my account of events at the Hotel Nacional from eyewitness reports, particularly the statements of Ferrer, Torres Menier, Adam y Silva, and Yanes. See Ferrer, *Con el rifle al hombro*, 375–403; Torres Menier, "Mi diario—La toma del Hotel Nacional, " *Bohemia*, March 4, 1934; Adam y Silva, *La gran mentira*, 291–320; and Yanes, "Los psychoses del Hotel Nacional," *Carteles*, December 17, 1933. For recountings of events more sympathetic to Batista and the government, see Chester, *A Sergeant Named Batista*, 101–118; and Franco Varona, *Revolución del 4 de septiembre*, 77–89.

69. The story about Batista comes from Chester, *A Sergeant Named Batista*, 107. Lt. Pedro Rodriguez Ochoa remembered that Batista was nearly shot in the area around the *Maine* Monument while inspecting the troops; Fulgencio Rubén Batista Godínez, interview by author, tape recording, Coral Gables, Fla., May 19, 1998.

70. Ferrer, *Con el rifle al hombro*, 390. The Cuban government wanted to ensure that U.S. citizens were not inside the hotel before it unleashed the artillery barrage, which probably began after they received assurances from Welles; Welles to Secty. of State, October 2, 1933, Dept. of State, decimal file, 1930–1939, file 837.00/4107 RG 59.

71. The complete text of the surrender note was published in Ferrer, *Con el rifle al hombro*, 397; and Chester, *A Sergeant Named Batista*, 109–110.

72. Soto provides the best analysis of the ABC's decision to reject an alliance with the officers, attributing it to ongoing negotiations between the secret society and the government in which they hoped to join the ruling coalition; *Revolución del 33*, 3:136.

73. This is the figure provided by Phillips, *Cuban Sideshow*, 160, but estimates vary slightly; Welles estimated eighty dead and two hundred wounded; Welles to Secty. of State, October 3, 1933, Dept. of State, decimal file, 1930–1939, file 837.00/4119 RG 59.

74. Ferrer remembered the shouts calling for his death; *Con el rifle al hombro*, 400. Adam y Silva was an eyewitness to the massacre and retells it in *La gran mentira*, 310–312.

75. In a meeting the day before the attack, Guiteras was the strongest advocate of an assault on the Hotel Nacional; Soto, *Revolución del 33*, 3:130. After Sanguily and Ferrer were taken prisoner, they were brought to a makeshift headquarters where both Batista and Guiteras were present. They were told earlier in the day that Batista and Guiteras were coordinating the attack; Ferrer, *Con el rifle al hombro*, 398–400.

76. Phillips says she tried to get an official figure, but the army would not provide one; *Cuban Sideshow*, 160. Adam y Silva, *La gran mentira*, 310, remembers Batista on the grounds of the Hotel Nacional shortly before the massacre. Batista's remarks were related to Chester, *A Sergeant Named Batista*, 112. Riera Hernández, *Un presidente constructivo*, 9, says two paramilitary groups were present during the attack on the hotel and its aftermath—Pro Ley y Justicia (For Law and Justice), commanded by Santiaguito Alvárez and Mario Labourdette, and the ABC Radical, led by Oscar de la Torre.

77. Grau made the statement to a Mexican publication after he went into exile and many months after the battle at the Hotel Nacional. By then, he would have had time to reflect on the events; Franco Varona, *Revolución del 4 de septiembre*, 88.

78. Chester, *A Sergeant Named Batista*, 112.

79. This version of events was pieced together by Gimperling through his personal contacts; Lt. Col. T. N. Gimperling, military attaché, Cuba (Combat), "Capture of Officers in National Hotel," G-2 Report, October 3, 1933, file 2012-133 RG 165. He repeated this assertion three days later. Yanes, "Los psychoses del Hotel Nacional," *Carteles*, December 17, 1933, wounded twice during the massacre, credits a soldier with saving his life. Phillips, *Cuban Sideshow*, 162–163, writes that twenty were killed when the soldiers fired into the crowd.

80. Welles to Secty. of State, October 4, 1933, Dept. of State, decimal file, 1930–1939, file 837.00/4131 RG 59.

81. Welles to Secty. of State, September 21, 1933, Dept. of State, decimal file, 1930–1939, file 837.00/3982 RG 59.

82. Chester, *A Sergeant Named Batista*, 115.

83. The observation regarding Batista's apprehension comes from T. N. Gimperling, U.S. military attaché, in Cuba (Political), "Stability of Present Administration," G-2 Report, December 12, 1933, file 2657-330 (244) RG 165. On Batista's desire to appoint Carbó, see Welles to Secty. of State, October 27, 1933, Dept. of State, decimal file, 1930–1939, file 837.00/4292 RG 59.

84. The "*pesado*" remark was made to Chester, *A Sergeant Named Batista*, 150. The journalistic observation was made Ramón Vasconcelos, "El amigo Ben," *El País*, December 13, 1933. Adam y Silva makes the observation about Welles's disdain for

Batista in *La gran mentira*, 358. Years later, however, Welles described Batista as "extraordinarily brilliant and able" in his book *The Time for Decision* (New York: Harper and Brothers, 1944), 197.

85. Welles's son, Benjamin Welles, chronicles the turbulent relationship and details Hull's successful campaign to force him out of the State Department. Hull threatened to make public accusations that Welles had requested sexual favors from several Pullman employees during a 1940 train ride; Benjamin Welles, *Sumner Welles: FDR's Global Strategist* (New York: St. Martin's Press, 1997), 1–3 and 341–354.

86. Gellman, *Roosevelt and Batista*, 63–64, reviews the policy dispute between Hull and Welles. Buell to Welles, October 17, 1933, Welles Papers, Latin America files, 1933–1943, Cuba, 1933, B. Welles to Buell, October 24, 1933, Welles Papers, Latin America files, 1933–1943, Cuba, 1933, B.

87. The statement made by Herminio Portell-Vilá, a Cuban delegate to the Pan-American Conference was published in the *Havana Post* and other newspapers on November 21, 1933. For the text of the Warm Springs Declaration, see Dept. of State, decimal file, 1930–1939, November 24, 1933, file 837.00/4258 RG 59. Gellman, *Roosevelt and Batista*, 75, provides details on the issues facing Hull in Uruguay.

88. Welles provides a fairly good synopsis of the back-and-forth negotiations between Batista and Mendieta in his dispatches of October 27 through November 3; Welles to Secty. of State, decimal file, 1930–1939, files 837.00/4292, 837.00/4301, 837.00/4321, 837.00/4322, and 837.00/4331, RG 59. Military Attaché T. N. Gimperling provides an overview of Mendieta's concerns about Batista in Cuba (Political), "Stability of Present Administration," G-2 Report, December 12, 1933, file 2657-330 (244) RG 165.

89. Carrillo, *Cuba 1933*, 243–244, discusses the gradual way in which the students became aware of Batista's negotiations with the political opposition. And, in Welles to Secty. of State, October 6, 1933, Dept. of State, decimal file, 1930–1939, file 837.00/4140 RG 59, Welles discusses the possibility of an attack by the Directory against Batista and of a possible student alliance with the ABC.

90. Military Attaché T. N. Gimperling wrote a series of reports in October 1933 on the loyalty of the Cuban military and the challenges facing Batista; see Cuba (Combat), "Strength and Composition," G-2 Report, October 17, 1933, file 2012-133 (20) RG 165; Cuba (Combat), "Loyalty and Discipline," G-2 Report, October 19, 1933, file 2012-133 (23) RG 165; Cuba (Combat), "Strength and Composition," G-2 Report, October 24, 1933, file 2012-133 (26) RG 165; Cuba (Combat), "Loyalty," G-2 Report, October 30, 1933, file 2012-133 (27) RG 165. Welles observes that other Cuban military leaders were negotiating with Mendieta but did not name them. Even if they were acting on behalf of Batista, the possibility for mischief was present. Welles writes that "unless a solution is rapidly found the army will disintegrate"; Welles to Secty. of State, October 31, 1933, Dept. of State, decimal file, 1930–1939, file 837.00/4321 RG 59.

91. There are numerous interpretations concerning the purpose of the meeting. Thomas, *Cuba: Pursuit of Freedom*, 664, notes that it was convened to deal with the threat of U.S. intervention and uneasiness in the military. Adam y Silva, *La gran mentira*, 360–361, argues the meeting was convened by Carbó as part of an effort to "renovate" the revolution and that one of the issues to be discussed was the replacement of Grau. Carrillo, *Cuba, 1933*, 246–250, writes that the meeting was called to spring a trap on Batista. It is likely that all these motives were operating in tandem.

92. Tabares del Real, *Guiteras*, 203–204, relates events from Guiteras's perspective. Besides Pablo Rodríguez, Tabares del Real asserts that Captain Mario Hernández was opposed to Batista's continued leadership.

93. Carrillo, *Cuba 1933*, 244–254, provides the most detailed account of the events of November 3, based on an account provided by Juan Rubio Padilla.

94. Batista's suspicions may account for his decision to forgo a meeting at the Presidential Palace on the night of November 2, when he was "summoned" by Grau; Welles to Secty. of State, November 3, 1933, Dept. of State, decimal file, 1930–1939, file 837.00/4331 RG 59. Batista recounted his version of the events of November 3 in letters to his eldest son, excerpts of which have been provided to the author; Fulgencio Batista Zaldívar to Fulgencio Rubén Batista Godínez, October 27 and 28, 1972, Fulgencio Batista Zaldívar Papers, private collection of Fulgencio Rubén Batista Godínez, Coral Gables, Fla.

95. Padilla's observation can be found in Carrillo, *Cuba 1933*, 250. Chester, *A Sergeant Named Batista*, 125, writes of Batista's apprehension.

96. Fulgencio Batista Zaldívar to Fulgencio Rubén Batista Godínez, October 27 and 28, 1972, Fulgencio Batista Zaldívar Papers, private collection of Fulgencio Rubén Batista Godínez, Coral Gables, Fla. Carrillo, *Cuba 1933*, 253–258, writes about the efforts to get Grau to reverse his decision. Lumen, *Revolución cubana*, 216–217, writes of Batista's apology to Grau, but says nothing about the various intrigues surrounding the meeting.

97. Carrillo, *Cuba 1933*, 253–256.

98. The observation about Grau's concern about Guiteras's growing influence was made to Batista's eldest son by Grau's niece; Fulgencio Rubén Batista Godínez, correspondence to author, February 2, 2001.

CHAPTER 7. AN END TO REVOLUTION

1. Carlos Saladrigas Zayas (1900–1957), the nephew of former President Alfredo Zayas, would emerge as one of Batista's closest allies in the years to come. He was selected by Batista to run for the presidency in the elections of 1944 but was defeated by Grau. Saladrigas went on to serve as a cabinet minister under Batista in the 1950s.

2. The most complete account of the conspiracy can be found in Adam y Silva, *La gran mentira*, 321–332. Chester, *A Sergeant Named Batista*, 129–131, provides information about the intelligence reports received by Batista. Franco Varona, *Revolución del 4 de septiembre*, 96, attributes anger over promotions as a key factor for the uprising. U.S. Military Attaché T. N. Gimperling reported many of these same factors, including dissatisfaction over promotions and displeasure with the Grau government; Cuba (Combat), "Loyalty," G-2 Report, October 30, 1933, file 2012-133 (27) RG 165.

3. Adam y Silva, *La gran mentira*, 322–328, notes on several occasions how the conspiracy was disrupted by spies.

4. Phillips, *Cuban Sideshow*, 183–187.

5. Adam y Silva, *La gran mentira*, 324–326, indicates that elements of Artillery Battalion No. 1 at the Máximo Gómez Barracks were also involved in the conspiracy. He also relates the deal made by the military leaders and Saladrigas.

6. There is some discrepancy among the sources over the precise time of the air attack. Chester, *A Sergeant Named Batista*, 131, writes the attack began at 1:30

a.m. Franco Varona, *Revolución del 4 de septiembre*, suggests a 2 a.m. start. Adam y Silva, *La gran mentira*, 333, places it at midnight. What is clear is that the attack was moved up.

7. Chester, *A Sergeant Named Batista*, 134, provides these details.

8. Franco Varona, *Revolución del 4 de septiembre*, 105, was an eyewitness to the machine-gun exchanges.

9. In the past, army headquarters was at the Castillo de la Fuerza in Habana Vieja (Old Havana). U.S. Military Attaché T. N. Gimperling summarizes Batista's decision to relocate army headquarters in a dispatch to Washington; Cuba (Combat), G-2 Report, December 15, 1933, file 2012-133 RG 165.

10. The description of Batista's home comes from an article in *La Mañana*, October 15, 1933; Welles to Secty. of State, October 18, 1933, Dept. of State, decimal file, 1930–1939, file 837.00/4258 RG 59.

11. Fulgencio Rubén Batista Godínez, interview by author, tape recording, Coral Gables, Fla., April 30, 1998. The story was related to him by his mother, Elisa.

12. The Batista family could not recall the name of the lieutenant.

13. Among other things, the ABC-controlled station also broadcast the death of Grau and Guiteras and the landing of U.S. troops; see Morejón, *Grau San Martín*, 80–81.

14. Adam y Silva, *La gran mentira*, 335, provides details of the air attack and the actions of the various pilots. *Carteles* ran a page of photos on the air attack, and one of the captions indicates that one plane suffered damage from enemy fire and crash-landed in Matanzas Province; "El Bombardeo de Columbia," *Carteles*, December 17, 1933. See also, Phillips, *Cuban Sideshow*, 200–201.

15. I owe these details to Phillips, *Cuban Sideshow*, 212; and Franco Varona, *Revolución del 4 de septiembre*, 152.

16. Lumen, a journalist present inside the palace during the attack, provides the best account of it; *Revolución cubana*, 129–141. He identifies the cabinet ministers present with Grau and estimates the number of defenders.

17. Adam y Silva, *La gran mentira*, 334.

18. Phillips, *Cuban Sideshow*, 202, writes: "Colonel Batista was so bewildered that the American government offered to take him aboard one of the battleships in the bay, if worst came to worst."

19. Franco Varona, *Revolución del 4 de septiembre*, 105.

20. The figure comes from Phillips, *Cuban Sideshow*, 202.

21. There is uniformity among the sources on the number of dead, wounded, and captured at the military airfield, unlike the figures provided for the other phases of the uprising. See Adam y Silva, *La gran mentira*, 337; and Franco Varona, *Revolución del 4 de septiembre*, 106–107.

22. Lumen, *Revolución cubana*, 137. Adam y Silva, *La gran mentira*, 338–339, estimates 10 a.m. as the time of attack.

23. Chester, *A Sergeant Named Batista*, 137, was an eyewitness to the battle at the palace. He described the tank as a "queer-looking vehicle."

24. I owe these details to Lumen, *Revolución cubana*, 137–139. A similar account was related by Morejón, *Grau San Martín*, 81–83.

25. Grau related this to his nephew, who was in the palace at the time of the attack; Ramón Grau Alsina, interview by author, tape recording, Miami, May 19,

1998. Lumen, *Revolución cubana*, 137, notes Batista's failure to comply with Grau's order.

26. Aguilar, *Cuba 1933: Prologue to Revolution*, 195. Chester, *A Sergeant Named Batista*, 137, ignores the issue except to say that the soldiers at the palace were part of "Batista's forces."

27. Lt. Col. T. N. Gimperling, military attaché, Cuba (Combat), "Loyalty," G-2 Report, November 15, 1933, file 2012-133 (30) RG 165.

28. Phillips, *Cuban Sideshow*, 202.

29. Franco Varona, *Revolución del 4 de septiembre*, 119–120, provides some details of the battle at the Tenth Precinct. Adam y Silva, *La gran mentira*, 339, gives a similar account.

30. Franco Varona, *Revolución del 4 de septiembre*, 118–119, provides details on the dead and wounded at the Eleventh Precinct. Adam y Silva, *La gran mentira*, 339, again gives a similar account.

31. Soto reprints the declaration of a state of war from *La gaceta oficial*, November 8, 1933; *Revolución del 33*, 3:230n181.

32. Chester, *A Sergeant Named Batista*, 139, outlines this strategy. Soto, *Revolución del 33*, 3:229–230, notes the large number of desertions after every retreat.

33. Adam y Silva, *La gran mentira*, 338.

34. "San Ambrosio por la Revolución," *Carteles*, December 17, 1933, indicates that the cruiser attacked at 5 p.m. Soto, *Revolución del 33*, 3:231, estimates the time of attack at 3 p.m.

35. Franco Varona, *Revolución del 4 de septiembre*, 120–132, chronicles the experiences of a young boy who took part in the defense of San Ambrosio and later Atarés. He excerpted the story from another little-known publication, entitled *La Mujer*. The boy helped carry the wounded ABC member to the infirmary.

36. "San Ambrosio por la Revolución," *Carteles*, December 17, 1933, published several photos of the damage.

37. Adam y Silva, *La gran mentira*, 345, suggests there may have been trickery involved.

38. Welles said this retreat was part of a "concerted arrangement" between the rebels and the government. He estimates the time of retreat as 3 a.m.; Welles to Secty. of State, November 9, 1933, Dept. of State, decimal file, 1930–1939, file 837.00/4354 RG 59.

39. As of 2001, Atarés was being used as a police station by the Cuban government.

40. Most estimates agree on a figure of about one thousand, the number reported by one rebel in an anonymous article, "Atarés: El relato de un combatiente," *Carteles*, December 17, 1933. A soldier held prisoner by the rebels, Agustín Gutiérrez García, estimates 1,500 in Franco Varona, *Revolución del 4 de septiembre*, 112. Adam y Silva, *La gran mentira*, 345, puts the figure at "1,000 or more." Lumen, *Revolución cubana*, 142, estimates three thousand.

41. "Atarés: El relato de un combatiente," *Carteles*, December 17, 1933. This observation was made by the anonymous rebel. Franco Varona, *Revolución del 4 de septiembre*, 117, also notes that the rebels thought the fortress was impregnable.

42. "Atarés: El relato de un combatiente," *Carteles*, December 17, 1933. This observation was also made by a young eyewitness, whose story was related to Franco Varona; *Revolución del 4 de septiembre*, 128–129.

43. Phillips, *Cuban Sideshow*, 214, provides the most detailed account of the unfortunate chef's fate. A less graphic account was published in "Atarés: El relato de un combatiente," *Carteles*, December 17, 1933.

44. Franco Varona, *Revolución del 4 de septiembre*, 115. He attributes this quote to Gutiérrez García. An even more grisly account of the carnage at Atarés is provided by Lumen, *Revolución cubana*, 167–169. The soldiers manning the deadly mortar were profiled in "El mortero que dejó insostenible la defensa de Atarés," *Bohemia*, November 19, 1933.

45. "Atarés: El relato de un combatiente," *Carteles*, December 17, 1933.

46. Adam y Silva, *La gran mentira*, 346, mentions the retreat of one battle cruiser and the breakdown of the artillery piece.

47. "Atarés: El relato de un combatiente," *Carteles*, December 17, 1933. In the aftermath of the battle, a short biography of Ciro Leonard, a veteran of the War of Independence, was published in *Bohemia*, November 19, 1933.

48. An eyewitness related this to Phillips, *Cuban Sideshow*, 216. The boy was Enrique Pizzi, son of Cuban journalist Enrique Pizzi de Porras.

49. "Atarés: El relato de un combatiente," *Carteles*, December 17, 1933. Domínguez Aquino reportedly addressed the rebels, putting forth his credentials as a capable leader and "guaranteed" the rebels that their efforts at breaking out of the encirclement would succeed; Franco Varona, *Revolución del 4 de septiembre*, 114. Adam y Silva, *La gran mentira*, 346–347, tells a similar story.

50. Franco Varona, *Revolución del 4 de septiembre*, 131.

51. Phillips, *Cuban Sideshow*, 205. Welles also notes that government forces continued to fire on Atarés after the surrender; Welles to Secty. of State, November 9, 1933, Dept. of State, decimal file, 1930–1939, file 837.00/4362 RG 59.

52. Phillips, *Cuban Sideshow*, 205, was given that figure by an eyewitness. Adam y Silva, *La gran mentira*, 347, writes that twenty-seven were executed. Welles received a report that fourteen were executed; Welles to Secty. of State, November 9, 1933, Dept. of State, decimal file, 1930–1939, file 837.00/4361 RG 59. Tabares del Real, *Revolución del 30*, 150, puts the number executed at fifty.

53. Phillips, *Cuban Sideshow*, 206, retells the story.

54. Phillips, *Cuban Sideshow*, 206–207 and 216–217. Adam y Silva, *La gran mentira*, 347, gives a similar account. Newton Briones Montoto, *Aquella decisión callada* (Havana: Editorial de Ciencias Sociales, 1998), 210, writes that Blas Hernández was already wounded in the leg when Mario Hernández shot him.

55. "La muerte de Blas Hernández," *Carteles*, December 17, 1933. The publication ran several photos of Blas Hernández, including two of his corpse.

56. Phillips, *Cuban Sideshow*, 217.

57. Franco Varona, *Revolución del 4 de septiembre*, 100. He does note that the prisoners were in danger and that they were threatened, 132.

58. Chester, *A Sergeant Named Batista*, 140.

59. Lumen, *Revolución cubana*, 144.

60. Briones Montoto, *Aquella decisión callada*, 210. Tabares del Real, *Guiteras*, 209–210, notes that Guiteras met with Mario Hernández "thirty minutes after the fall of Atarés," but mentions nothing of the execution of Blas Hernández.

61. Ironically, Blas Hernández's son was named Mario; Aparicio Laurencio, *Blas Hernández*, 59–75.

62. Fidel Castro, *History Will Absolve Me* (Secaucus, N.J.: Lyle Stuart, 1961), 48. Castro made the charge while on trial for trying to overthrow the Batista dictatorship in October 1953. His silence regarding Guiteras's culpability may have to do with the fact that by the time of his trial, Guiteras was seen by some as a revolutionary martyr.

63. On the low end, Tabares del Real, *Revolución del 30*, 150, estimates one hundred dead and two hundred wounded. On the other extreme, Franco Varona, *Revolución del 4 de septiembre*, 100, writes of two thousand dead and wounded. Chester, *A Sergeant Named Batista*, 140, gives a figure of five hundred dead and hundreds wounded, as does Soto, *Revolución del 33*, 3:234.

64. Phillips, *Cuban Sideshow*, 204, thinks there were between 150 and 200 dead and 200 wounded at Atarés. The author of the *Carteles* article writes that there were two hundred dead and wounded inside the fortress; "Atarés: El relato de un combatiente," *Carteles*, December 17, 1933.

65. Franco Varona, *Revolución del 4 de septiembre*, 118, provides the information on the faulty shell.

66. Lt. Col. T. N. Gimperling, military attaché, Cuba (Political), "Armed Revolutionary Movements," G-2 Report, November 13, 1933, file 2657-330 (226) RG 165.

67. "Atarés: El relato de un combatiente," *Carteles*, December 17, 1933.

68. This is the assessment of Adam y Silva, *La gran mentira*, 335–338.

69. This observation comes from the anonymous rebel; "Atarés: El relato de un combatiente," *Carteles*, December 17, 1933.

70. This was the assessment of Assistant Secretary of State William Phillips; Gellman, *Roosevelt and Batista*, 73–74.

71. Welles to Secty. of State, December 7, 1933, Dept. of State, decimal file, 1930–1939, file 837.00/4480 RG 59. In the very same dispatch Welles writes of his understanding with Grau and of his efforts to subvert that very same arrangement.

72. Medina's criticisms were published in newspapers in Cuba and the United States. For a sampling, see Tom Pettey, "Welles Blamed as Conciliation in Cuba Fails," *New York Herald Tribune*, December 12, 1933; and "Government Expected to Adopt More Radical Steps in Future Action," *Havana Post*, December 12, 1933.

73. Gellman, *Roosevelt and Batista*, 74.

74. Philip F. Dur, *Jefferson Caffery of Louisiana: Ambassador of Revolutions; An Outline of His Career*, rev. ed. (Lafayette: University of Southwestern Louisiana, 1998), 16.

75. "Well, Welles," *Miami Herald*, November 26, 1933.

76. Matthews to Secty. of State, December 14, 1933, Dept. of State, decimal file, 1930–1939, files 837.00/4521 RG 59 and 837.00/4522.

77. Caffery described his cockfighting and horseback riding exploits in his unpublished autobiography; Jefferson Caffery, *Adventure in Diplomacy*, unpub. manuscript, Caffery Papers, University of Southwestern Louisiana, Lafayette, La. Caffery biographer and close personal friend, Philip Dur, says that Caffery told him he frequently beat Pedraza at the cockfights; Philip F. Dur, interview by author, notes, Lafayette, La., April 1998. Chester, *A Sergeant Named Batista*, 150.

78. Lumen, *Revolución cubana*, 187–190. The quote in Spanish reads as follows: "Chapurrea el español y no habla correctamente ni su propio idioma. Su condición de diplomático se descubre en que se sonroja con facilidad. Con el atavío de Tom Mix, haría un texano clásico."

79. Caffery (1886–1974) destroyed so many of his documents that his personal papers border on the irrelevant. The best insights into Caffery can be found in his correspondence to others.

80. I owe many of these insights into Caffery's personality to Philip Dur.

81. Lumen, *Revolución cubana*, 195.

82. Carrillo, *Cuba 1933*, 317.

83. Alejandro de la Fuente, *A Nation for All: Race, Inequality, and Politics in Twentieth-Century Cuba* (Chapel Hill: University of North Carolina Press, 2001), 134–137, provides a short overview of the opportunities for advancement in the military for Afro-Cubans in the years after the fall of Machado.

84. I draw much of the historical information about Sans Souci from a document found at the Cuban Information Archives Web site; "Sans Souci: Havana Night Club and Casino," http://www.cuban-exile.com/doc_176-200/doc0193.html.

85. The incident was not widely reported in the Cuban media, perhaps because of censorship restrictions or fear. The best account of it comes from Phillips, *Cuban Sideshow*, 258–259. It is from her that I take the eyewitness account. Chester, *A Sergeant Named Batista*, 75, mentions the incident briefly, as does Carrillo, *Cuba 1933*, 317, although he writes that it occurred on December 19. It went largely unnoticed in the U.S. media.

86. This detail comes from information given to me by Batista's eldest son; Fulgencio Rubén Batista Godínez, correspondence to author, September 17, 1999.

87. Chester, *A Sergeant Named Batista*, 100.

88. De la Fuente, *Nation for All*, 199.

89. Lt. Col. T. N. Gimperling, military attaché, summarizes the mutual distrust in his dispatch of December 12, 1933; Cuba (Political), "Stability of Present Administration," G-2 Report, December 12, 1933, file 2657-330 (244) RG 165.

90. Others making this point include Lumen, *Revolución cubana*, 194–195; and Gellman, *Roosevelt and Batista*, 156.

91. The best work on the subject is the previously cited book by De la Fuente. Other important works include Tomás Fernández Robaina, *El negro en Cuba, 1902–1958: Apuntes para la historia de la lucha contra la discriminación racial* (Havana: Editorial de Ciencias Sociales, 1994); and Aline Helg, *Our Rightful Share: The Afro-Cuban Struggle for Equality, 1886–1912* (Chapel Hill: University of North Carolina Press, 1995).

92. Carrillo, *Cuba 1933*, 317 and 358n5.

93. Fulgencio Rubén Batista Godínez, correspondence to author, September 17, 1999.

94. This evolution in Batista's philosophy is explained and placed in its best light by Acosta Rubio, *Ensayo biográfico Batista*, 165–176, and Franco Varona, *Revolución del 4 de septiembre*, 161–180. The specific quote comes from Acosta Rubio, 170. Acosta Rubio explains that Batista tried to instill a sense of loyalty for military interests above personal and other political interests. "A crear, y esto muy especialmente, dentro de la clase militar, una conciencia desligada de los sectores políticos. Procuraba el nuevo líder crear una casta que defendiera en un momento, no los intereses personales, sino los principios de una clase" (168).

95. "Batista no abandonara a los alistados que le secundaron en la jornada del día cuatro," *Diario de la Marina*, December 4, 1933. The newspaper reprinted an interview originally published in the newspaper *Información*.

96. Adam y Silva, *La gran mentira*, 403–405, discusses the legal arguments surrounding the case of the officers.

97. Miguel Ángel Quevedo, "Glosando las declaraciones de un coronel," *Bohemia*, December 10, 1933.

98. "Dolorosas realidades," *Bohemia*, January 7, 1934.

99. Ibid.

100. Guiteras reports that the leaders of the military districts met on numerous occasions at Camp Columbia to discuss Grau's fate; Antonio Guiteras, "Septembrismo," *Bohemia*, April 1, 1934. Adam y Silva, *La gran mentira*, 369, writes of numerous meetings as well. He notes that the decision to oust Grau was made at a meeting at the end of December. Tabares del Real, *Guiteras*, 217, identifies military meetings on January 13 and 14, 1934.

101. Tabares del Real, *Guiteras*, 217.

102. Caffery to Secty. of State, January 13, 1934, Dept. of State, decimal file, 1930–1939, file 837.00/4605 RG 59.

103. Tabares del Real, *Guiteras*, 217.

104. In his discussion with Caffery, Grau said he would be willing "to give place to a non-political successor to be chosen by me from a panel of three names to be selected by the opposition on condition that one of the names at least must be acceptable to me"; Caffery to Secty. of State, January 11, 1934, Dept. of State, decimal file, 1930–1939, file 837.00/4596 RG 59.

105. The party was formally established in February 1934 and would serve as the main opposition group in the years to come.

106. Batista met with Mendieta to discuss Grau's departure on January 11, although at that time they considered two other men for the presidency; Caffery to Secty. of State, January 13, 1934, Dept. of State, decimal file, 1930–1939, file 837.00/4605 RG 59.

107. Mendieta's letter of January 4, 1934, and Grau's letter of response on January 5, 1934, have been reprinted in a number of sources, including Lumen, *Revolución cubana*, 207–212; and Tabares del Real, *Guiteras*, 215–217.

108. Gellman, *Roosevelt and Batista*, 79.

109. The remarks are from shorthand notes taken by Batista shortly after the meeting with Mendieta. Batista shared the notes with biographer Edmund Chester; *A Sergeant Named Batista*, 154.

110. There is no written account by Mendieta of the January 13 meeting. Vega Cobiellas, *Batista y Cuba*, 35, quotes Batista on the issue of securing a pledge from Mendieta to respect revolutionary reforms. Phillips, *Cuban Sideshow*, 264, notes that Mendieta was torn over whether to be "provisional president or become a candidate for president in the next elections." Several Batista supporters maintain that the colonel offered his resignation to Mendieta, but that is so unlikely that it hardly merits serious debate; Franco Varona, *Revolución del 4 de septiembre*, 165; and Acosta Rubio, *Ensayo biográfico Batista*, 170.

111. Caffery's first dispatch requesting recognition was sent to Washington at 3 a.m. on January 14. Batista would not inform Grau of his decision until much later in the day; Caffery to Secty. of State, January 14, 1934, Dept. of State, decimal file, 1930–1939, file 837.00/4606 RG 59.

112. Phillips to Caffery, January 14, 1934, Dept. of State, decimal file, 1930–1939, file

837.00/4609 RG 59. In part, Roosevelt replied, "It is of course impossible to pledge recognition of any individual or group before certain conditions are an accomplished fact."

113. There is some dispute over the date of the meeting. Grau, interviewed a few days after the meeting, recalled that it occurred on January 14, but Batista told Chester the meeting occurred on January 13—the same day as his earlier meeting with Mendieta. I have chosen January 14 as the likely date of the meeting because Grau's recollection was closer to the date of the actual reunion. Caffery's State Department dispatches indicate that as late as 1 p.m. on January 14, Grau knew nothing of his ouster. It also seems unlikely that Batista and Mendieta could have arranged a meeting with Grau so hastily, that is, within hours of their own meeting. For sources favoring the January 14 date, see "Detalles de cómo se produjo la sustitución del ex presidente Dr. Ramón Grau San Martín," *Diario de la Marina*, January 16, 1934; Caffery to Secty. of State, January 14, 1934, Dept. of State, decimal file, 1930–1939, file 837.00/4608 RG 59; and Phillips, *Cuban Sideshow*, 275. For Batista's version of events, see Chester, *A Sergeant Named Batista*, 155–157.

114. The accounts of this meeting are largely in agreement; Chester, *A Sergeant Named Batista*, 155–157; and Adam y Silva, *La gran mentira*, 375–376.

115. Adam y Silva, *La gran mentira*, 379, provides a list of twenty-four people in attendance at the junta meeting, including several government ministers. Among the students were Rubén de León, Eduardo Chibás, Lincoln Rodon, and Segundo Curti. The allies of Batista included Sergio Carbó, Lucilo de la Peña, and Lt. Col. Manuel López Migoya. The navy was represented by Capt. Ángel A. González.

116. Adam y Silva, *La gran mentira*, 380–381, offers a lengthy excerpt from Batista's opening statement, which he took from an article in the newspaper *Ahora* of January 15, 1934. Vega Cobiellas, *Batista y Cuba*, 31, provides some details of this meeting.

117. Rubén de León, "Últimos días del gobierno de Grau San Martín," *Carteles*, March 11, 1934. Vega Cobiellas, *General Fulgencio Batista Zaldívar*, 48–51, provides a similar version of events leading up to the selection of Mendieta as provisional president.

118. Chester, *A Sergeant Named Batista*, 155–156.

119. On the morning of the junta meeting, Guiteras told reporters he would accept the provisional presidency if selected by the group; see "Ha renunciado la presidencia de la república, Grau San Martín," *Diario de la Marina*, January 15, 1934. Guiteras did not attend the junta meeting, according to Tabares del Real, *Guiteras*, 218.

120. The navy was crucial in steering the deliberations toward Hevia. In an analysis piece in *Diario de la Marina*, "La situación en trazos," January 16, 1934, a commentator observed that Guiteras, unable to secure the presidency for himself, threw his support behind Hevia. Sources include Phillips, *Cuban Sideshow*, 277; Soto, *Revolución del 33*, 3:322–323; and Carrillo, *Cuba 1933*, 343.

121. This is the observation of Levi Marrero, who would go on to become one of Cuba's most distinguished historians; Levi Marrero, "Cuatro horas sin presidente," *Bohemia*, January 28, 1934.

122. Soto, *Revolución del 33*, 3:321, quotes the newspaper *Ahora*, January 15, 1934.

123. Several student leaders issued a proclamation to this effect; "Mantiene el Coronel Mendieta su ofrecido apoyo al Sr. Hevia," *Diario de la Marina*, January 16, 1934. Carrillo, *Cuba 1933*, 341–343, restated his position.

124. There were rumors that Grau might try to strip Batista of his command and replace him with Rodríguez. He was released later that morning at the request of the navy. Tabares del Real, *Guiteras*, 218, writes that Guiteras ordered Rodríguez to go to Camp Columbia and relieve Batista of his command. Information on the arrest of Rodríguez was published in "El último día del Presidente Grau en Palacio," *Bohemia*, January 21, 1934.

125. I draw much of my information on events at the Presidential Palace from two eyewitness accounts: "El último día del Presidente Grau en el Palacio," *Bohemia*, January 21, 1934; and Phillips, *Cuban Sideshow*, 281–283.

126. "Declaraciones del Dr. Grau S. Martín," *Diario de la Marina*, January 16, 1934.

127. "El último día del Presidente Grau en el Palacio," *Bohemia*, January 21, 1934.

128. The story comes from Phillips, *Cuban Sideshow*, 281.

129. "El último día del Presidente Grau en el Palacio," *Bohemia*, January 21, 1934.

130. "Declaraciones del Jefe del E.M. del Ejército," *Diario de la Marina*, January 16, 1934.

131. There is general agreement on the number of dead, although there is quite a variation in the number of wounded: "Tres muertos y treinta y dos heridos frente a Palacio ayer," *Diario de la Marina*, January 16, 1934, puts the figure at three dead and thirty-two wounded. Phillips, *Cuban Sideshow*, 279, estimates four dead and fourteen wounded. Adam y Silva, *La gran mentira*, 383, suggests it was four dead and ten wounded.

132. Carlos Hevia (1904–1964) would go on to become a cofounder of the Partido Revolucionario Cubano (Auténtico) in February 1934. He would later serve in the cabinet of President Carlos Prío Socarrás. He was designated by the Auténticos to run in the 1952 elections, which were derailed by the Batista coup of March 10, 1952. After Castro triumphed, he went into exile, where he died several years later.

133. *Bohemia* bestowed upon him the first nickname in its edition of January 21, 1934; The second has been used by many writers including Soto, *La Revolución del 33*, 3:331.

134. "Muy lejano el reconocimiento," *Diario de la Marina*, January 17, 1934. The article states that an unidentified source in the U.S. Embassy saw little difference between a Grau administration and a Hevia administration.

135. A short report on the front page of the January 17, 1934, *Diario de la Marina* ran an excerpt of a competitor's article stating that Batista had told his commanders that his support of Hevia was "transitory."

136. This process of rejection is carefully detailed by Soto, *Revolución del 33*, 3:327–330; and Adam y Silva, *La gran mentira*, 383–385.

137. Franco Varona, *Revolución del 4 de septiembre*, 175. Adam y Silva, *La gran mentira*, 385, notes that two prominent political leaders who urged Hevia to resign were Secretary of State Manuel Márquez Sterling and Nacionalista leader Cosme de la Torriente.

138. Caffery's dispatches to Washington throughout January 17 make it clear that avoiding a confrontation with the navy was a priority for Batista; Caffery to Secty. of State, January 17, 1934, Dept. of State, decimal file, 1930–1939, files 837.00/4626, 837.00/4628, 837.00/4630, 837.00/4633 RG 59. Other sources include Soto, *Revolución del 33*, 3:330; Tabares del Real, *Guiteras*, 218–219, which notes the navy's reluctance to challenge the army; Phillips, *Cuban Sideshow*, 278; and Carrillo, *Cuba 1933*, 343–344. None of the sources identifies those in attendance at the army-navy meetings.

139. "La situación en trazos," *Diario de la Marina*, January 16, 1934. There is no byline on the article.

140. "Ha renunciado la presidencia de la república, Grau San Martín," *Diario de la Marina*, January 15, 1934.

141. Tabares del Real, *Guiteras*, 199–202, details Guiteras's efforts with the navy.

142. "En la casa del Coronel Batista," *Diario de la Marina*, January 18, 1934.

143. Soto, *Revolución del 33*, 3:331.

144. The process leading up to Márquez Sterling's assumption of power is detailed by Levi Marrero, "Cuatro horas sin presidente." Phillips, *Cuban Sideshow*, 286–290, provides another eyewitness account of events.

145. Marrero makes this point in "Cuatro horas sin presidente." A similar observation is made by Adam y Silva, *La gran mentira*, 386; and Franco Varona, *Revolución del 4 de septiembre*, 178.

146. Levi Marrero, "Cuatro horas sin presidente."

147. See Batista's remarks to the nation in "Alocución," *Diario de la Marina*, January 19, 1934.

148. Vega Cobiellas, *General Fulgencio Batista Zaldívar*, 52, produces an extensive excerpt of Batista's statement to the nation, including his critique of his former allies. Gustavo E. Urrutia, "Armonías," *Diario de la Marina*, January 24, 1934.

CHAPTER 8. THE MENDIETA YEARS

1. *Carteles* emphasized this time and again throughout the period. For examples, see "Regresión barbárica," April 15, 1934; "¿Quién tiene la palabra?" September 2, 1934; and "Paz y justicia," September 9, 1934.

2. Tabares del Real, *Revolución del 30*, 157–158, makes this a central theme of his work. Carleton Beals goes even further when he writes that Mendieta was "Caffery's office boy and Batista his top sergeant." This dismissal of Mendieta and Batista by Beals strikes of North American arrogance, implying that the two Cubans were simply flunkies of the ambassador without their own thoughts; see Carleton Beals and Clifford Odets, *Rifle Rule in Cuba* (New York: Provisional Committee for Cuba, 1935), 6.

3. Caffery estimated that as many as eighty journalists were on the government payroll at one time; Caffery to Welles, March 1, 1935, Welles Papers, "Major Correspondents, 1920–1950," Jefferson Caffery, February–March 1935.

4. Gellman, *Roosevelt and Batista*, 98, describes the relationship as "symbiotic."

5. In a private letter to Welles, Caffery reports that "some of his [cabinet] secretaries are said to be stealing in shameless fashion"; Caffery to Welles, September 14, 1934, Welles Papers, "Major Correspondents, 1920–1950," Jefferson Caffery, September–October 1934. For the story of Mendieta's personal honesty, see Caffery to Secty. of State, November 26, 1934, decimal file, 1930–1939, file 837.001/Mendieta, Carlos/17, RG 59.

6. Among those using the "puppet" designation for Mendieta are Hugh Thomas, *Cuba: Pursuit of Freedom*, 691–705; and Herminio Portell-Vilá, *Nueva historia*, 429–431. Portell-Vilá also describes Mendieta as a "decorative figure." However, he gives Mendieta credit for preserving a civilian role in government and preventing a long-term military dictatorship (455).

7. I owe this insight to Portell-Vilá, *Nueva historia*, 430–431. He goes onto to identify some of the *civilista* members of Mendieta's first cabinet as Joaquín Martínez Sáenz (minister of hacienda), Jorge Mañach (minister of education), and Emeterio Santovenia (presidential secretary). Some of the *militaristas* were Félix Granados (minister of the interior), Gabriel Landa (minister of communications), and Carlos de la Rionda (minister of agriculture).

8. As mentioned in an earlier note (see chap. 7, n. 79), Caffery destroyed most of his personal documents. However, his ally and mentor, Sumner Welles, unlike Caffery, seems to have saved every letter ever written to him. Welles kept up a comprehensive and ongoing correspondence with Caffery for many years. It reveals the unofficial side of U.S. diplomacy in Cuba and details with great specificity the gritty particulars of U.S. influence. The correspondence, part of the Sumner Welles collection at the Franklin D. Roosevelt Presidential Library, is invaluable for Cuban scholars and diplomatic historians interested in Caffery's career. Among other things, it chronicles with careful thoroughness the relationship between Batista and Mendieta.

9. For some examples, see "La actualidad nacional," *Carteles*, July 8, 1934; and "La actualidad nacional," December 30, 1934.

10. Secretary of State Cosme de la Torriente opposed the appointment of Carlos Manuel de la Cruz, one of the lawyers with whom Batista collaborated in the struggle against Machado.

11. Caffery to Welles, October 30, 1934, Welles Papers, "Major Correspondents, 1920–1950," Jefferson Caffery, September–October 1934.

12. Caffery was not informed of the decree prior to Mendieta's approval; Caffery to Welles, December 3 and 5, 1934, Welles Papers, "Major Correspondents, 1920–1950," Jefferson Caffery, November–December 1934.

13. Caffery to Welles, December 5, 1934, Welles Papers, "Major Correspondents, 1920–1950," Jefferson Caffery, November–December 1934.

14. On September 5, 1934, Caffery wrote to Welles, regarding a strike against the Cuban Telephone Company, that "Batista feels very strongly in this connection that the Government puts him in the position of taking all the blame for not allowing the strikers to return to work"; Caffery to Welles, September 5, 1934, Welles Papers, "Major Correspondents, 1920–1950," Jefferson Caffery, July–September 1934. Again, on February 25, 1935, with the threat of a nationwide strike growing, Caffery wrote Welles that "Batista demonstrated yesterday [February 24], I believe, more anger and disgust with the Government for its inertness than have ever seen him show. He said that the Government had done absolutely nothing to meet this very dangerous student strike situation"; Caffery to Welles, February 25, 1935, Welles Papers, "Major Correspondents, 1920–1950" Jefferson Caffery, February–March 1935.

15. "Batista is very much annoyed with the Nacionalistas' political antics in re filling strikers' jobs in Government Departments"; Caffery to Welles, March 16, 1935, Welles Papers, "Major Correspondents, 1920–1950," Jefferson Caffery, February–March 1935.

16. The electoral code was amended for that purpose on July 2, 1935.

17. Adam y Silva, *La gran mentira*, 405–406, identifies Franco Granero as a Batista spy. He writes that Franco Granero frequently attended government meetings uninvited. President Mendieta allegedly had a special bell installed so that Franco Granero could signal before he entered the presidential chambers. Portell-Vilá, *Nueva*

historia, 437, likewise writes that Batista had Mendieta under surveillance, although he does not identify those conducting the surveillance.

18. For a synopsis of the crisis, see "El Dr. Santovenia renunció su cartera por haberse ordenado el traslado del Capitán Aragón, Ayudante Presidencial," *Diario de la Marina*, June 3, 1934; and Miguel de Marcos, "La chicharra de Ulsiceno," *Bohemia*, June 10, 1934.

19. Runyon's article, which originally appeared in the *New York American* on February 5, 1934, was translated into Spanish and reprinted in *Carteles*; Damon Runyon, "Batista, el 'Amo' de Cuba," February 18, 1934.

20. Phillips, *Cuban Sideshow*, 303. This corresponds to her diary entry of February 2, 1934.

21. Caffery capitalized the words "Military Dictator"; Caffery to Welles, June 4, 1934, Welles Papers, "Major Correspondents, 1920–1950," Jefferson Caffery, January–June 1934.

22. Caffery to Welles, July 21, 1934, Welles Papers, "Major Correspondents, 1920–1950," Jefferson Caffery, July–September 1934. Vega Cobiellas, *General Fulgencio Batista Zaldívar*, 57, quotes at length a statement by Batista denying a newspaper report by *El Crisol* that he planned to seek election to the presidency.

23. Caffery to Welles, October 16, 1934, Welles Papers, "Major Correspondents, 1920–1950," Jefferson Caffery, September–October 1934.

24. Caffery to Welles, October 31, 1934, Welles Papers, "Major Correspondents, 1920–1950," Jefferson Caffery, September–October 1934.

25. Caffery to Welles, March 1, 1935, Welles Papers, "Major Correspondents, 1920–1950," Jefferson Caffery, February–March 1935.

26. Caffery made liberal use of capital letters in his original; Caffery to Welles, March 6, 1935, Welles Papers, "Major Correspondents, 1920–1950," Jefferson Caffery, February–March 1935.

27. Caffery to Welles, April 16, 1935, Welles Papers, "Major Correspondents, 1920–1950," Jefferson Caffery, April–June 1935.

28. The first mention of such a plan in Caffery's correspondence came on February 18, 1935. The plan was brought to Caffery's attention by another Batista adviser, Félix Granados. "He [Granados] told me that he has heard that Carlos Manuel [de La Cruz] has been recently attempting to persuade Batista to form what he calls an Intervención Cubana, that is, that Batista take over the Government as a Military Governor of the type of Magoon, to remain in office only during the elections. I told Granados that I disapproved highly of the plan"; Caffery to Welles, February 18, 1935, Welles Papers, "Major Correspondents, 1920–1950," Jefferson Caffery, January–February 1935.

29. Caffery to Welles, April 13, 1935, Welles Papers, "Major Correspondents, 1920–1950," Jefferson Caffery, April–June 1935.

30. Portell-Vilá, *Nueva historia*, 429, claims that Mendieta had diabetes. The information is reliable given that the historian knew the president.

31. Caffery wrote Welles that "Most of the days when the [strike] movement was going on, President Mendieta left the Palace early in the afternoon for his Finca, where he remained until after nightfall. I believe that possibly as a result of some observations of my own, he did not go to the Finca [ranch] during the last two days of the strikes"; Caffery to Welles, March 15, 1935, Welles Papers, "Major Correspondents, 1920–1950," Jefferson Caffery, February–March 1935.

32. Caffery to Welles, July 21, 1934, Welles Papers, "Major Correspondents, 1920–1950," Jefferson Caffery, July–September 1934. Gellman, *Roosevelt and Batista*, 85–86, writes of Mendieta: "His greatest weakness, however, came from his own personality. The new president suffered from an inability to make firm decisions, compounded by an almost obsessive desire to win sympathy from every segment of the divided Cuban society."

33. On Mendieta's position regarding corruption in his cabinet, Caffery writes in a letter to Welles: "Mendieta is, of course, not inclined to believe these reports or to do anything about them"; Caffery to Welles, September 14, 1934, Welles Papers, "Major Correspondents, 1920–1950," Jefferson Caffery, September–October 1934. Caffery's 1935 correspondence is bursting with information about the political maneuvering regarding elections. Mendieta's indecision about how to handle the matter is a recurring theme. See Caffery to Welles, March 1 and 4, 1935.

34. After June 1934, the ABC movement began to fragment. The largest segment, led by Sáenz, joined the opposition to the Mendieta government. However, another segment, that led by Saladrigas, stayed in the government coalition. This was the beginning of the end of the ABC as a powerful national movement. It would gradually disintegrate, and by the end of the decade, it was almost irrelevant.

35. Caffery to Welles, October 16, 1934, Welles Papers, "Major Correspondents, 1920–1950," Jefferson Caffery, September–October 1934.

36. The Constitution of 1901 had been greatly discredited by the amendments made by Machado supporters in 1928, which extended his term of office. It was never recognized by the Grau government, leaving the country in a sort of constitutional limbo. The abrogation of the Platt Amendment in May 1934 paved the way for the reestablishment of the 1901 Constitution until the adoption of a new one in 1940.

37. The constitutional statute decreed by Mendieta on February 3, 1934, called for the State Council to consist of between fifty and eighty members, but it never approached that number.

38. Caffery to Welles, October 11, 1934, Welles Papers, "Major Correspondents, 1920–1950," Jefferson Caffery, September–October 1934.

39. Welles to Caffery, October 12, 1934, Welles Papers, "Major Correspondents, 1920–1950," Jefferson Caffery, September–October 1934.

40. Welles to Caffery, December 3, 1934, Welles Papers, "Major Correspondents, 1920–1950," Jefferson Caffery, November–December 1934.

41. Welles to Caffery, April 15, 1935, Welles Papers, "Major Correspondents, 1920–1950," Jefferson Caffery, April–June 1935.

42. Two months later, Caffery was named U.S. Ambassador to Cuba.

43. J. H. Edwards to Welles, January 24, 1934, Welles Papers, Latin America Files, 1933–1943, Cuba, Financial Aid. The claim that economic aid might have saved the Céspedes government is dubious given the fact that the government lasted only three weeks, hardly enough time to develop and implement an assistance plan. Welles outlined part of the plan to Cuban Secretary of State Cosme de la Torriente the following day. Some disagreements between the two governments over the distribution of $2 million in food aid may have derailed that part of the program; Welles to Torriente, January 25 and February 13, 1934, Welles Papers, Office Correspondence, 1920–1943, Torriente, Cosme de la, 1933–1934.

44. The details of the first transaction were announced to the public in a press release on April 30, 1934; Welles Papers, Latin America files, 1933–1943, Cuba, Financial

Aid. The $4 million was be used to coin $10 million in Cuban pesos. A brief over-view of U.S. financial assistance to Cuba is provided by Charles A. Thomson, "The Cuban Revolution: Reform and Reaction," *Foreign Policy Reports*, January 1, 1936.

45. This is one of the principal arguments of Louis Pérez Jr. in *Cuba: Between Reform and Revolution*. Batista was well aware of the dangers of Cuba's sugar mono-culture and its dependence on the United States; *Sombras de América*, 379–383.

46. U.S. dominance of the sugar industry was a central point raised by the ABC in its 1932 manifesto against Machado; *El ABC: Al pueblo de Cuba; Manifiesto-Programa*, November 1932, 13–14 and 21–22. Even today (2006), sugar remains the dominant crop, although the Cuban government has tried to diversify the economy by developing the tourism and biotechnology sectors, among others.

47. Tabares del Real goes into some detail on the detrimental impact of these trade arrangements; *Guiteras*, 231–234. Gellman, *Roosevelt and Batista*, 114–115, notes that the treaty, although "highly beneficial" to Cuba in the short term, "allowed United States products to drive native goods off the market, making diversification even more difficult than before."

48. Portell-Vilá, *Nueva historia*, 432, makes this observation.

49. The article was published on the front page of *El País Información* on Novem-ber 7, 1934. Welles kept a copy of it in his files; Welles Papers, Latin America files, 1933–1943, Cuba, 1934, G.

50. Thomson, "The Cuban Revolution," 273. Gellman, *Roosevelt and Batista*, 129, provides slightly different numbers, although they are similarly upbeat.

51. *Bohemia*, June 3, 1934.

52. "La derogación de la Enmienda Platt," *Carteles*, June 17, 1934.

53. "New Cuban Treaty," *New York Times*, May 31, 1934.

54. All of these initiatives were part of a blueprint created by Welles in early 1933 to strengthen relations between the two countries. They had been placed on hold during the Grau administration when all efforts were directed at ousting a govern-ment viewed as dangerous to U.S. interests.

55. Tabares del Real, *Guiteras*, 261–262, attributes to Guiteras the assassination attempt against Mendieta. "El atentado a Mendieta," *Bohemia*, June 17, 1934, provides an overview of the assassination attempt.

56. T. N. Gimperling gave an account of the attack against Caffery and another incident aimed at H. Freeman Matthews, First Secretary of the U.S. Embassy, to his superiors; Lt. Col. T. N. Gimperling, military attaché, Cuba (Political), "Diplomatic and Consular Representatives Accredited from Foreign Countries," G-2 Report, May 28, 1934, file 2657-330 (280) RG 165.

57. "Había que sacarle las palabras," Santiago Rey Perna recalls; interview by author, tape recording, Miami, April 29, 1998.

58. I owe this information to Batista's oldest son; Fulgencio Rubén Batista Godínez, interview by author, tape recording, Coral Gables, Fla., April 30, 1998. Later on, in the early 1950s, Batista's stepson, Félix Valdespino, would marry Pedraza's daughter. However, this occurred after the rupture in relations between Batista and Pedraza.

59. Santiago Rey Perna, interview by author, tape recording, Miami, April 29, 1998. His exact words are: "Era un hombre de pocas luces, pero de mucho carácter" and "Era un hombre muy decidido, que no le temblaba el pulso para nada."

60. Maj. E. W. Timberlake, military attaché, Cuba (Population and Social), "Police System," G-2 Report, March 31, 1937, file 2012-137 (15) RG 165.

61. Caffery to Welles, November 1, 1934, Welles Papers, "Major Correspondents, 1920–1950," Jefferson Caffery, November–December 1934.

62. It is important to note that in 1934–1935 the National Police Force numbered about 3,700 men. It was reorganized in 1936 to include the provincial police departments, swelling the numbers to over six thousand.

63. Maj. E. W. Timberlake, military attaché, Cuba (Population and Social), "Police System," G-2 Report, March 31, 1937, file 2012-137 (15) RG 165.

64. Once again, I owe this observation to Timberlake, who makes it in his report of March 31, 1937.

65. This observation was made by Fulgencio Rubén Batista Godínez, interview by author, tape recording, Coral Gables, Fla., May 19, 1998. Galíndez's relationship to the family was expanded on by Fulgencio Rubén Batista Godínez in correspondence to author, June 6, 2002.

66. The assessment was made by U.S. Military Attaché E.W. Timberlake on June 15, 1937; Cuba (Combat-Army), "Who's Who on Commissioned Personnel," G-2 Report, June 15 1937, file 2012-168 (5) RG 165. Timberlake gives Galíndez's birth date as February 6, 1903.

67. These observations come from Col. Henry A. Barber Jr., military attaché, Cuba, "Who's Who," G-2 Report, February 10, 1941, file 2012-168 (27) RG 165. Batista's oldest son, Fulgencio Rubén, remembers him as a "discreet" and "very quiet man"; correspondence to author, June 6, 2002..

68. Maj. E. W. Timberlake, military attaché, Cuba (Combat-Army), "Who's Who on Commissioned Personnel," G-2 Report, June 16, 1937, file 2012-168 (7) RG 165. Timberlake gives Tabernilla's date of birth as April 13, 1889.

69. This insight comes from Fulgencio Rubén Batista Godínez, correspondence to author, June 6, 2002.

70. Again, the assessment comes from Timberlake; Cuba (Combat-Army), "Who's Who on Commissioned Personnel," G-2 Report, June 17, 1937, file 2012-168 (9) RG 165. According to Timberlake, Mariné was born in Munguia, Spain, on July 24, 1904.

71. "Muy inteligente y de pocos escrúpulos" was how Rey put it; interview by author, tape recording, Miami, April 29, 1998.

72. "Le gustaba mucho las fiestas, los tragos, las mujeres. Por ejemplo, se paseaba por La Habana, en el período que era dueño y señor junto a Batista, en un automóvil Cadillac, de colores llamativos, violeta o alguna otra cosa así. Además se le conocía por la frecuencia de sus relaciones con mujeres bellas"; Santiago Rey Perna, interview by author, tape recording, Miami, April 29, 1998.

73. Maj. E. W. Timberlake, military attaché, Cuba (Combat-Army), "Who's Who on Commissioned Personnel," G-2 Report, June 17, 1937, file 2012-168 (9) RG 165.

74. This observation was made by both Santiago Rey and by Military Attaché Timberlake.

75. Maj. E. W. Timberlake, military attaché, Cuba (Combat-Army), "Who's Who on Commissioned Personnel," G-2 Report, June 2, 1937, file 2012-168 (1) RG 165. Timberlake connects the activities of Mariné and Hernández in file 2012-168 (9). U.S. military intelligence was not alone in connecting Mariné and Hernández to political acts of violence; see Adam y Silva, *La gran mentira*, 435–442.

76. Sosa de Quesada (1908–2000) died in exile in Miami. Much of the information about him comes from my oral history interview, newspaper accounts of his activities, and his writing. In his last letter to me, a few days before his death, Sosa de Quesada enclosed two recent poems; Arístides Sosa de Quesada, correspondence to author, April 13, 2000.

77. Maj. E. W. Timberlake, military attaché, Cuba (Combat-Army), "Who's Who on Commissioned Personnel," G-2 Report, June 10, 1937, file 2012-168 (3) RG 165. Timberlake provides the Hollywood tidbits.

78. Benítez's career would take many twists and turns over the years. In 1944, President Batista fired him as chief of the national police, shortly before leaving office. He would later join Grau's Auténticos and serve in the Cuban Congress. After the Revolution of 1959, he went into exile in Miami. As of 2002, in his early nineties, he still hosted a popular radio show in Miami. Benítez died in 2003.

79. The chief advocate of this assertion is Tabares del Real, who makes the claim in *Guiteras*, 196.

80. The remarks were made to Batista's eldest son in 1990 by Fernando Neugart, an officer in the army's legal division who served under Mario Hernández. It was also Neugart who overheard the conversation between Hernández and Migoya; Fulgencio Rubén Batista Godínez, interview by author, tape recording, Coral Gables, Fla., May 19, 1998.

81. The official army account was published in the Cuban daily newspapers; see, for example, "Altos Jefes del Ejército conocían lo que tramaban Hernández, Erice y Echevarría," *Diario de la Marina*, August 23, 1934. Accounts of the conspiracy were summarized by Freeman Matthews in a series of dispatches to Washington throughout August 22 and 23; Matthews to Secty. of State, August 23, 1934, decimal file, 1930–1939, file 837.00/5380, RG 59.

82. Her allegations are made in a letter to Batista published in the opposition newspaper, *Acción*. However, copies of the newspaper are rare in Cuba and the United States. *Carteles*, September 2, 1934, summarizes her accusations. Tabares del Real, *Guiteras*, 292–293, reproduces excerpts of the letter.

83. "¡Esta es la tumba del Teniente Coronel Mario Hernández!" *Carteles*, September 2, 1934.

84. See chapter 5 for details on Batista's eulogy at the grave of Sgt. Miguel Ángel Hernández.

85. A copy of Batista's written statement to the troops was published in most of the nation's daily newspapers; "Circular del Coronel Batista," *Diario de la Marina*, August 23, 1934.

86. Thomson, "The Cuban Revolution," 274–275. Phillips, *Cuban Sideshow*, 312, says the military accounted for a third of the national budget, but Thomson provides precise figures.

87. Caffery to Welles, October 19, 1934, Welles Papers, "Major Correspondents, 1920–1950," Jefferson Caffery, September–October 1934.

88. Excerpts from the letter were published in *Diario de la Marina*; "El Jefe del Ejército hace unas declaraciones en relación con las del Dr. J. Martínez Sáenz," December 16, 1934.

89. T. N. Gimperling, military attaché, reported on these efforts by Batista in several dispatches to Washington; Cuba (Combat), "Loyalty and Discipline," G-2 Report,

March 26, 1934, file 2012-146 (4) RG 165; and Cuba (Political), "Armed Revolution-ary Movements," G-2 Report, April 9, 1934, file 2012-133 (67) RG 165.

90. "Un nuevo Atarés?" *Carteles*, June 10, 1934.

91. Castor oil is also known as *aceite de ricino*.

92. Carlos Garrido, the editor of the newspaper *La Voz*, died after receiving the *palmacristi* treatment.

93. Portell-Vilá, *Nueva historia*, 442.

94. "Atropello al Director de 'Bohemia,' " *Carteles*, October 14, 1934.

95. In a report to Washington, T. N. Gimperling reports that estimates of the crowd ranged between thirty thousand and seventy thousand. He favored the lower esti-mate; Lt. Col. T. N. Gimperling, military attaché, Cuba (Social), "Public Order and Safety," G-2 Report, June 19, 1934, file 2657-330 (287) RG 165.

96. Portell-Vilá, *Nueva historia*, 435–456; and Tabares del Real, *Guiteras*, 261–262, among others, cite Guiteras's Joven Cuba organization and members of the Com-munist Party as responsible for the attacks. Gimperling reports witnessing police officers firing revolvers and gas bombs into the crowd. He also claims that "snipers" from the Cuban Navy fired at the crowd at another location; Lt. Col. T. N. Gimper-ling, military attaché, Cuba (Social), "Public Order and Safety," G-2 Report, June 19, 1934, file 2657-330 (287) RG 165.

97. There were differing reports concerning what exactly the ABC demanded of the government. However, the removal of Pedraza and the establishment of a par-liamentary system were mentioned in all the accounts. For a short summary of the political crisis, see "Una semana de crisis política," *Carteles*, June 30, 1934.

98. It is difficult to find copies of the August 14, 1934, letter by Sáenz, or even excerpts, because many Cuban newspapers declined to publish it. *Diario de la Marina* and *Bohemia* cited concerns about public calm in explanation of their deci-sions to withhold publication. They may have been under pressure by the government and the military to refrain from publishing the letter; "¡Por los sagrados intereses patrios!" *Diario de la Marina*, August 15, 1934; and "Siluetas actuales," *Bohemia*, August 19, 1934. U.S. Assistant Military Attaché L.V.H. Durfee provided his superi-ors with a synopsis of the two letters in an August 16, 1934, dispatch to Washington; Cuba (Combat), "Military Policy," G-2 Report, file 2012-133 (72) RG 165.

99. Welles, State Dept. memo, October 15, 1934, Welles Papers, Latin America files, 1933–1943, Cuba, 1934, Ma.

100. Ibid.

101. The accusation by the abducted journalists was included in an article in the *New York Times* but omitted by *Diario de la Marina*; "Castor Oil Forced on Cuban Editors," *New York Times*, December 13, 1934; and "El Dr. Joaquín Martínez Sáenz hace unas declaraciones a los periodistas de los E. Unidos," *Diario de la Marina*, December 14, 1934.

102. Caffery to Welles, December 17, 1934, Welles Papers, "Major Correspondents, 1920–1950," Jefferson Caffery, November–December 1934.

103. Freeman Matthews, December 18, 1934, memorandum of conversation, Welles Papers, "Major Correspondents, 1920–1950," Jefferson Caffery, November–December 1934.

104. Caffery to Welles, December 19, 1934, Welles Papers, "Major Correspondents, 1920–1950," Jefferson Caffery, November–December 1934. When Caffery addressed

the matter to Cuban Secretary of State Cosme de la Torriente, the secretary offered to speak with the editor of *Acción* and "advise him to discontinue the publication of alarming and misleading news calculated to damage the Government and Army"; Caffery to Welles, December 18, 1934.

105. "Los periodistas protestan ante el presidente," *Carteles*, October 28, 1934.

106. There is clearly a need for a scholarly review of press relations in the prerevolutionary period, a topic that is well beyond the focus of this study.

107. Caffery to Welles, December 20, 1934, Welles Papers, "Major Correspondents, 1920–1950," Jefferson Caffery, November–December 1934.

108. In March 1934, Guiteras's supporters unsuccessfully tried to assassinate José Ignacio Rivero; Tabares del Real, *Guiteras*, 287.

CHAPTER 9. LABOR UNREST

1. For the United States, see Irving Bernstein, *Turbulent Years: A History of the American Worker, 1933–1941* (Boston: Houghton Mifflin, 1970); James R. Green, *The World of the Worker: Labor in Twentieth-Century America* (New York: Hill and Wang, 1980); and Roger Keeran, *The Communist Party and the Auto Workers Unions* (Bloomington: Indiana University Press, 1980). For Europe, see Wolfgang Abendroth, *A Short History of the European Working Class*, trans. Nicholas Jacobs and Brian Trench (New York: Monthly Review Press, 1972). For Latin America, see Ruth Berins Collier and David Collier, *Shaping the Political Arena: Critical Junctures, the Labor Movement, and Regime Dynamics in Latin America* (Princeton, N.J.: Princeton University Press, 1991).

2. Tabares del Real, *Guiteras*, 236–241, provides a nice overview of the antilabor legislation of the Mendieta-Batista government.

3. Tabares del Real, *Guiteras*, 251–256, offers a fairly detailed account of the March 1934 strike and other labor activism during that year. Also useful are Gellman, *Roosevelt and Batista*, 90–91; and Ruby Hart Phillips, *Cuba: Island of Paradox* (New York: McDowell, Obolensky, 1959), 161. This book by Phillips follows up on her earlier work, *Cuban Sideshow*. Both works are essentially diary entries of her thirty years in Havana, most of them as a correspondent for the *New York Times*. The racist language and condescending tone were cleaned up for the second book to reflect the thinking of a different era. I have decided to use both works as sources in this biography.

4. For a brief overview of the strike, see "La huelga del lunes," *Carteles*, October 14, 1934.

5. For a discussion of strategy, see Tabares del Real, *Guiteras*, 263–265.

6. "La Unión Nacional de Maestros se queja de la preterición de que hacen víctima al educador," *Diario de la Marina*, February 10, 1935.

7. "Los huelgistas escolares no han pedido más que materiales para trabajar y mejor desayuno," *Diario de la Marina*, February 13, 1935, provides some information on how the preadolescents organized their committees. The February 24, 1935, edition of *Bohemia* ran a photograph of one such committee.

8. The February 1, 1935, report was published in its entirety by *Diario de la Marina*; "Señala la Sociedad Económica pautas para contener la decadencia cultural en Cuba," February 6, 1935.

9. I draw my account of events from *Diario de la Marina* and *Bohemia*. See

"Perdió la vida anoche un estudiante en una alteración del orden en Monte y Zulueta," *Diario de la Marina*, February 12, 1935; and "En las orillas del abismo," *Bohemia*, February 17, 1935. Ironically, the nineteen-year-old was not a student, but the faculty and students felt the attack by the police was directed at them.

10. "En las orillas del abismo," *Bohemia*, February 17, 1935.

11. The text of a declaration by the governing body was published in its entirety in *Diario de la Marina*; "Ampliado a 72 horas el paro en el Instituto y la declaración de protesta del consejo del plantel," February 13, 1935.

12. For information on the medical strikes, see "El comité de huelga médica se reunirá hoy con el Dr. Raúl de Cárdenas para terminar el paro," *Diario de la Marina*, January 18, 1935.

13. The quote comes from an article in *El Mundo* in its February 19 edition. The article was sent back to Washington by H. Freeman Matthews to the Secty. of State, February 19, 1935, decimal file, 1930–1939, file 837.00/6026 RG 59.

14. The faculty meeting occurred on February 21; "Claustro Universitario, por medio de una comisión, propondrá soluciones inmediatas," *Diario de la Marina*, February 22, 1935.

15. A partial list of the school districts involved can be found in "Se generaliza la huelga en el Magisterio," *Diario de la Marina*, 21 February 1935.

16. "Los últimos manifestos de los universitarios," *Diario de la Marina*, February 23, 1935.

17. As late as February 24, Batista was unsure whether the ABC movement was supporting the strike, although he thought they "probably" were; Caffery to Welles, February 25, 1935, Welles Papers, "Major Correspondents, 1920–1950," Jefferson Caffery, February–March 1935. By early March, it was clear the ABC was sympathetic to the strike movement, and its newspaper, *Acción*, reflected that point of view.

18. "President Defends Action to Better School Conditions," *Havana Post*, March 1, 1935.

19. "El problema escolar," *Bohemia*, February 24, 1935.

20. Interim Education Minister Pelayo Cuervo Navarro told Caffery that the government was trying to drive a "wedge" between the university students and the primary school teachers; Caffery to Welles, February 27, 1935, Welles Papers, "Major Correspondents, 1920–1950," Jefferson Caffery, February–March 1935.

21. See the following: "En la reunión de Columbia no se trató anoche de cambios en el Gobierno, sino de las medidas necesarias para evitar desórdenes por la huelga," *Diario de la Marina*, March 1, 1935; "No existen motivos por el momento para esperar una violenta agresión del Ejército en asuntos políticos," *El Mundo*, March 2, 1935; "President Defends Action to Better School Conditions," *Havana Post*, March 1, 1935.

22. The decision to resign is explained in "Se cree posible que el doctor Julio Quintana ocupe el puesto que dejó vacante el Dr. Capote," *Diario de la Marina*, February 23, 1935.

23. The details in this paragraph were laid out in a February 25, 1935, letter from Caffery to Welles; Welles Papers, "Major Correspondents, 1920–1950," Jefferson Caffery, February–March 1935.

24. Caffery to the Secty. of State, memorandum of conversation, February 27, 1935, decimal file, 1930–1939, file 837.00/6063 RG 59.

25. Duggan to Welles, February 28, 1935, Welles Papers, Office Correspondence, 1920–1943, Duggan, Laurence, 1933–1935.

26. "Está llegando al almacén de la Secretaría de Educación el material gastable de escuelas," *Diario de la Marina*, February 17, 1935.

27. For information on the negotiations, see "Cree Pelayo Cuervo que la huelga del magisterio quede solucionada mañana viernes," *Diario de la Marina*, February 28, 1935; "La huelga de maestros," *Diario de la Marina*, March 1, 1935; and "Confía que volverán a sus aulas el lunes," *El Mundo*, March 1, 1935.

28. I owe most of my insights on strategy to Tabares del Real, *Guiteras*, 263–264 and 298–300.

29. Duggan to Welles, March 5, 1935, Welles Papers, Office Correspondence, 1920–1943, Duggan, Laurence, 1933–1935. In his letter, Duggan writes: "I have just been informed by a person who is reliable, though definitely sympathetic to a labor movement, that the leaders in the effort to bring about a general strike are confident of success."

30. Duggan to Welles, March 6, 1933, Welles Papers, Office Correspondence, 1920–1943, Duggan, Laurence, 1933–1935. In his letter, Duggan outlined the role of the University Strike Committee as related to him by one of its members, Eduardo Chibás.

31. "Toma posesión Anaya Murillo," *Diario de la Marina*, March 8, 1935.

32. "Guns Can't Run Cars," *Daily News*, March 13, 1935.

33. Caffery to Secty. of State, March 7, 1935, decimal file, 1930–1939, file 837.00/6123, RG 59.

34. This horrible story is related in some detail by Adam y Silva, *La gran mentira*, 435–436. Adam y Silva bases his account on information given to him by one Enrique C. Henríquez. A virtually identical version of this story can be found in Luis Conte Agüero, *Eduardo Chibás: El adalid de Cuba* (Miami: La Moderna Poesía, 1987), 218.

35. Acosta Rubio, *Ensayo biográfico Batista*, 189–190, mentions the plot against Batista. It was not widely reported in the media. For information on some of the gun battles and bombings, see "Durante las primeras horas de la noche se registraron varios intensos tiroteos en La Habana," *Diario de la Marina*, March 13, 1935; "Lanzaron una bomba sobre un ómnibus en Monte y Pila: Seis personas resultaron lesionados," *Diario de la Marina*, March 12, 1935; and "Cinco bombas estallaron en Cárdenas ayer," *Diario de la Marina*, March 8, 1935. Phillips, *Cuba: Island of Paradox*, 164–166, provides a firsthand account of life in Havana during the general strike.

36. The *Daily News* article was based on a story by the Associated Press wire service, "Cuba Massacres 200"; *Daily News*, March 12, 1935.

37. Thomas, *Cuba: Pursuit of Freedom*, 699, writes that "the numbers shot by the police and army could not have been less than a hundred." Tabares del Real, *Guiteras*, 261, writes: "Después de derrotar la huelga de marzo, el Gobierno clausuró todos los planteles, separó de sus cargos a cientos de profesores y maestros, asesinó a miles de estudiantes."

38. The news clipping from the March 15, 1935, edition of *El Crisol* was transmitted to Washington in a State Department dispatch by H. Freeman Matthews; Matthews to Secty. of State, March 15, 1935, decimal file, 1930–1939, file 837.00/6192, RG 59.

39. Capt. L.V.H. Durfee, assistant military attaché, Cuba (Social), "Strikes," G-2 Report, March 12, 1935, file 2657-330 (336) RG 165. Durfee made the initial estimate.

Four days later, his supervisor, T. N. Gimperling, revised the death toll downward; Lt. Col. T. N. Gimperling, military attaché, Cuba (Social), "Public Order and Safety," G-2 Report, March 16, 1935, file 2657-330 (340) RG 165.

40. These events were reported on by, among others, *Bohemia*, which in its edition of June 9, 1935, ran a photo of Batista attending the inauguration of a new hospital emergency room. In the same edition, the magazine ran a photo of a luncheon held by Batista at Camp Columbia for visiting members of the Rockefeller Foundation.

41. "'Las dictaduras de grupos no pueden continuar agitando al país,' declara el Cor. Batista," *Diario de la Marina*, March 7, 1935. This article provides a good overview of activity at Camp Columbia during the general strike.

42. "Declaraciones del Coronel Batista," *Diario de la Marina*, March 7, 1935.

43. With most of the newspapers closed as a result of the general strike, Batista called in a reporter from *Diario de la Marina* to make the statement; "Los huelguistas están equivocados y fracasarán totalmente, afirma el Cor. Batista," *Diario de la Marina*, March 9, 1935.

44. Caffery to Secty. of State, March 10, 1935, decimal file, 1930–1939, file 837.00/6142, RG 59.

45. Caffery sent dispatches every few hours throughout the general strike reporting on efforts to get workers to return to their posts; Caffery to Secty. of State, March 9, 1935, decimal file, 1930–1939, file 837.00/6137, RG 59.

46. "No hay plazas vacantes," *Diario de la Marina*, March 14, 1935.

47. "Se prepara el decreto que crea institutos y universidades libres," *Diario de la Marina*, March 19, 1935, provides a good overview of some of the changes enacted by the government less than a week after the strike was broken.

48. Caffery reported on the political firings in several personal letters to Welles. In one, Caffery writes that "President Mendieta continues to assure everyone concerned that he is opposed to Justo Luis [Pozo]'s present tactics of filling available jobs with Nationalists, Justo Luis goes merrily ahead and fills the jobs with Nationalists just the same"; Caffery to Welles, March 19, 1935, Welles Papers, "Major Correspondents, 1920–1950," Jefferson Caffery, February–March 1935.

49. Caffery to Welles, March 16, 1935, Welles Papers, "Major Correspondents, 1920–1950," Jefferson Caffery, February–March 1935.

50. Matthews to Secty. of State, May 9, 1935, decimal file, 1930–1939, file 837.00/6295, RG 59.

51. I owe most of the details in this section to Jose Tabares del Real's well-researched biography of Guiteras. See specifically the section on the closing days of his life, 266–325.

52. Tabares del Real, *Guiteras*, 277–280, quotes extensively from Joven Cuba's Revolutionary Program and lists many of its policy initiatives.

53. Lt. Col. T. N. Gimperling, military attaché, Cuba (Social), "Public Order and Safety," G-2 Report, November 6, 1934, file 2657-361 (12) RG 165.

54. Tabares del Real, *Guiteras*, 269.

55. There are at least two well-documented accounts of the Falla Bonet kidnapping, and although they differ on some minor points, they are very similar; Tabares del Real, *Guiteras*, 288–290; and Briones Montoto, *Aquella decisión callada*, 4–11. The contemporary account by U.S. military intelligence contains some obvious errors, such as the length of Falla Bonet's captivity, which raises some doubt about its

reliability; Lt. Col. T. N. Gimperling, military attaché, Cuba (Social), "Public Order and Safety," G-2 Report, April 18, 1935, file 2657-361 (15) RG 165.

56. The word "contribution" is from Tabares del Real, *Guiteras*, 289. Briones Montoto, *Aquella decisión callada*, 8, writes that the revolutionaries assured Falla Bonet that he would be paid back upon the triumph of the revolution.

57. Briones Montoto, *Aquella decisión callada*, 10.

58. Galíndez wrote the letter to *Bohemia* journalist Jorge Quintana for his multipart series on the death of Guiteras. Unfortunately, copies of the *Bohemia* edition containing Galíndez's letter are rare. A search in Cuba and the United States for the Galíndez letter proved unsuccessful. For the Guiterista perspective on the Galíndez meeting, see Tabares del Real, *Guiteras*, 317–318; and Briones Montoto, *Aquella decisión callada*, 18–19. Both Tabares del Real and Briones Montoto draw heavily from the *Bohemia* articles.

59. Batista's oldest son provides a different version and interpretation of events, based on a conversation he had with Galíndez in December 1993. Galíndez, near the end of his life, reportedly told him that the purpose of the meeting with Guiteras was to warn him that he should flee. Batista's oldest son argues it is highly improbable that his father would have offered a cabinet position to Guiteras at that time, given the controversy engendered by his urban guerrilla campaign; Fulgencio Rubén Batista Godínez, interview by author, tape recording, Coral Gables, Fla., May 19, 1998.

60. Guiteras gave his opinion about possible future negotiations to enter into the government to follower Juan Febles Secretal; Jorge Quintana, "La muerte de Antonio Guiteras," *Bohemia*, September 29, 1946. Briones Montoto, *Aquella decisión callada*, 19, relates the remark about his propensity for avoiding capture.

61. Tabares del Real, *Guiteras*, 319.

62. I owe these details to Tabares del Real, *Guiteras*, 319. Tabares del Real asserts that the $22,500 in Falla Bonet ransom money was stolen by members of the military after Guiteras's followers were apprehended.

63. As of 2002, the fort was being used as a museum to house Amerindian artifacts and exhibits on Guiteras's life and death.

64. Carleton Beals, "Cuba's John Brown," *Common Sense*, July 1935, 6.

65. One of the most recent works is the work by Reinaldo Suárez Suárez, *Un insurrecional en dos épocas* (Havana: Editorial de Ciencias Sociales, 2001), which argues that the struggle waged by Guiteras in the 1930s was continued by Castro in the 1950s. The prologue was written by Armando Hart Dávalos.

66. Humberto García Muñiz, an associate researcher at the University of Puerto Rico, made this observation to me on several occasions during the spring of 2001, as I was writing this book. At the time, he was teaching at Rutgers University as a visiting professor.

67. Chester, *A Sergeant Named Batista*, 158–159.

68. J.I.R., "Impresiones," *Diario de la Marina*, May 11, 1935. In Spanish the excerpt reads: "El guiterismo, que era y es algo así como una rabia criolla que muerde a derecha y a izquierda, no echó jamás raíces en el corazón del pueblo."

69. J. D. Phillips, "Guiteras Is Slain in Battle in Cuba," *New York Times*, May 9, 1935. Chester, who knew Batista quite well, writes that the two men were involved in a "long feud"; *A Sergeant Named Batista*, 159.

CHAPTER 10. THE ELECTIONS OF 1936

1. A typewritten copy of the article by José M. Irisarri, a former pentarch, published in *Karikato* on July 14, 1935, is in Welles Papers, Latin American files, 1933–1943, Cuba, Political (Pers. and Conf.). Irisarri described Caffery, Batista, and Mendieta as the "Diabolical Trinity." Individually, Irisarri labeled Caffery as the "Procónsul," Batista as the "Lackey," and Mendieta as "Don Nadie."

2. Buell to Welles, May 27, 1935, Welles Papers, "Buell Correspondence—disagreements."

3. Welles to Buell, June 13, 1935, Welles Papers, "Buell Correspondence—disagreements."

4. Caffery to Welles, October 17, 1935, Welles Papers, "Major Correspondents, 1920–1950," Jefferson Caffery, July–October 1935.

5. Welles to Caffery, July 11, 1935, Welles Papers, "Major Correspondents, 1920–1950," Jefferson Caffery, May–December 1935.

6. Mario García Menocal (1866–1941) was a dominant figure in Cuban politics for more than forty years, running for president for the first time in 1908. Menocal remained a key player on the political scene until the day he died. Like many other figures of the early twentieth century, he has been largely ignored by scholars. There is a vital need for a scholarly biography of Menocal.

7. Welles to Caffery, April 15, 1935, Welles Papers, "Major Correspondents, 1920–1950," Jefferson Caffery, April–June 1935.

8. Caffery to Welles, April 23, 1935, Welles Papers, "Major Correspondents, 1920–1950," Jefferson Caffery, April–June 1935.

9. Welles to Caffery, May 22, 1935, Welles Papers, "Major Correspondents, 1920–1950," Jefferson Caffery, May–December 1935.

10. Caffery to Welles, May 22, 1935, Welles Papers, "Major Correspondents, 1920–1950," Jefferson Caffery, April–June 1935.

11. Caffery to Welles, May 27, 1935, Welles Papers, "Major Correspondents, 1920–1950," Jefferson Caffery, April–June 1935.

12. Caffery to Welles, September 14, 1935, Welles Papers, "Major Correspondents, 1920–1950," Jefferson Caffery, July–October 1935.

13. Caffery to Welles, October 3, 1935, Welles Papers, "Major Correspondents, 1920–1950," Jefferson Caffery, July–October 1935.

14. Batista wanted Mendieta to appoint Manuel Despaigne as minister of defense, but Caffery noted, "for some reason or other, Mendieta doesn't seem to want to do so." According to Caffery, Batista was "disgusted with the way González, the Chief of the Navy, is carrying on, particularly with his frequent gambling at the Casino"; Caffery to Welles, July 12, September 28 and October 17, 1935, Welles Papers, "Major Correspondents, 1920–1950," Jefferson Caffery, July–October 1935.

15. Caffery to Welles, July 27, 1935, Welles Papers, "Major Correspondents, 1920–1950," Jefferson Caffery, July–October 1935.

16. This is how Caffery put it to Welles in an August 13, 1935, letter; Welles Papers, "Major Correspondents, 1920–1950," Jefferson Caffery, July–October 1935.

17. Caffery to Welles, October 26, 1935, Welles Papers, "Major Correspondents, 1920–1950," Jefferson Caffery, July–October 1935.

18. Batista would have been agreeable to a Conjunto victory, if Menocal were not the presidential candidate. However, once he decided to seek the presidency, Batista began to work on crafting an alliance of the three other participating parties. Batista believed that if Menocal won, "the country will be faced with a very difficult situation"; Caffery to Welles, October 12, 1935, Welles Papers, "Major Correspondents, 1920–1950," Jefferson Caffery, July–October 1935.

19. Caffery to Welles, September 21, 1935, Welles Papers, "Major Correspondents, 1920–1950," Jefferson Caffery, July–October 1935.

20. Miguel Mariano Gómez (1890–1950) is another forgotten political figure of the republican era. As the son of José Miguel Gómez, he was the heir to a political and financial dynasty. His political involvement dated back to the 1920s, when he was elected to the Cuban House of Representatives. He died as the result of a jeep accident on his ranch in October 1950. He was flown to New York City for surgery and died there.

21. Welles to Caffery, October 14, 1935, Welles Papers, "Major Correspondents, 1920–1950," Jefferson Caffery, May–December 1935.

22. Caffery wrote to Welles about the tensions within the Nacionalista Party on numerous occasions, including June 25 and 29, 1935; Welles Papers, "Major Correspondents, 1920–1950," Jefferson Caffery, April–June 1935. As late as November, a month before the election, some Nacionalista leaders were still considering reinstating Mendieta as a candidate, Caffery wrote to Welles on November 20, 1935.

23. The decision of the Superior Electoral Tribunal was published in its entirety by *Diario de la Marina*; "El Tribunal Superior Electoral dicta importante fallo en relación con la Coalición en La Habana," November 20, 1935.

24. Caffery to Welles, November 21, 1935, Welles Papers, "Major Correspondents, 1920–1950." Jefferson Caffery, November–December 1935.

25. All of these excerpts come from a U.S. State Dept. memorandum of conversation dated November 25, 1935; Welles Papers, Latin America files, 1933–43, Cuba, Political, "Electoral Reform"—Pedro Cué. There is no extant account from Cué's perspective. It is unlikely that there are any Cuban Government records on the meeting either, since Cué was not a member of the government at the time.

26. U.S. State Dept., memorandums of conversation, November 26, 1935, Welles Papers, Latin America files, 1933–1943, Cuba, Political, "Electoral Reform"—Pedro Cué.

27. This was the impression Welles gained after discussing the matter with McBain, who initially was interested in the assignment; Welles to Caffery, November 29, 1935, Welles Papers, "Major Correspondents, 1920–1950," Jefferson Caffery, May–December 1935.

28. A full scholarly investigation of Dodds's handling of the assignment and the factors leading to his decision has yet to be conducted.

29. The quotations in this paragraph are taken from a letter Welles wrote to Caffery on November 29, 1935; Welles Papers, "Major Correspondents, 1920–1950," Jefferson Caffery, May–December 1935.

30. Caffery to Welles, December 4, 1935, Welles Papers, "Major Correspondents, 1920–1950," Jefferson Caffery, November–December 1935. For the full text of Dodds's decision, see "Texto íntegro del informe de Mr. Dodds," *Diario de la Marina*, December 7, 1935.

31. In a letter to Caffery, Welles makes the following observation: "The Menocalista leaders are perfectly cognizant of every phase of the activity which Batista has displayed in working for an alliance and unified organization among the Nacionalistas, the Marianistas, and the Liberal Party. His [Batista's] statement to Menocal in his last interview, that the only advice he had given to the Liberal leaders was that they should join forces with some other major party without specifying which party, is not credited"; Welles to Caffery, November 13, 1935, Welles Papers, "Major Correspondents, 1920–1950," Jefferson Caffery, May–December 1935. Caffery makes reference to plans by some Conjunto leaders to blame the State Department for political meddling in a letter to Welles dated November 15, 1935.

32. A copy of the draft letter was given to Batista by a spy inside the Conjunto camp. Batista, in turn, gave a copy to Caffery. Batista also handed the ambassador a one-page intelligence report, dated December 8, 1935, outlining Menocal's proposed strategy in the wake of Dodds's decision; Caffery to Welles, December 9, 1935, Welles Papers, "Major Correspondents, 1920–1950," Jefferson Caffery, November–December 1935.

33. Santiago Rey Perna, interview by author, tape recording, Miami, April 29, 1998.

34. For an overview of the 1916 electoral shenanigans and some history on the Menocal-Mendieta rivalry, see Thomas, *Cuba: Pursuit of Freedom*, 525–535.

35. Ironically, one of those considered likely to bolt the party if it withdrew from the elections, was Santiago Rey Perna. The information on Rey Perna was included in the December 8 intelligence report given by Batista to Caffery.

36. "Bohemia entrevista al Gral Menocal," *Bohemia*, December 15, 1935. See also "Menocal Retires from Cuban Race," *New York Times*, December 8, 1935.

37. "El proceso electoral," *ABC*, December 1935. The underground newspaper was kept by Welles in his files; Welles Papers, Office Correspondence, Cuban Political Situation, 1934–1935. For the full text of Mendieta's resignation speech, see "Manifiesto del Coronel Mendieta al Pueblo," *Diario de la Marina*, December 11, 1935.

38. Phillips, *Cuba: Island of Paradox*, 159, made the observation.

39. The conga reference was a consistent thread in *Bohemia*'s coverage. For a good example, see the editorial "La 'conga' vuelve," June 30, 1935. The cartoon about the blind man, "En la calle," ran on September 15. The caricature of the man asleep for more than three years, "Catalepsia," appeared in the July 28 edition. The clueless presidential candidates, "A la puerta del cine," were featured on November 10. The "Tabú" cartoon on Batista was published on August 11. "Tabú" was the name of a popular song composed by Margarita Lecuona. It achieved commercial success in the United States in 1935.

40. "Le verdad y nada más que la verdad," *Bohemia*, December 1, 1935. A similar observation is made by Russell H. Fitzgibbon and H. Max Healey, "The Cuban Elections of 1936," *American Political Science Review* 30 (August 1936): 724–735.

41. The newspaper was not particularly critical during the election campaign, but once Gómez was in power, it criticized the government for engaging in petty political squabbles and not addressing the major issues of the nation. Although the government was elected "without national enthusiasm because of a lack of specific programs," the public still placed confidence in the elected officials to carry out the

nation's business, according to one editorial; "No hacer es deshacer," *Diario de la Marina*, July 10, 1936.

42. Torriente to Welles, November 5 and December 21, 1935, Welles Papers, Office Correspondence, 1920–1943, Torriente, Cosme de la, 1935–1936.

43. Thomson, "The Cuban Revolution," 275–276.

44. Caffery to Welles, January 13, 1936, Welles Papers, "Major Correspondents, 1920–1950," Jefferson Caffery, January–June 1936. Welles voiced his concerns to Caffery in letters dated January 14 and 16. In the letter of January 14, Welles writes: "Once this precedent is created, there is obviously no limit to the demands that might be made on the part of one or the other of the defeated parties, and the result would be, in my considered judgment, to nullify the whole salutary effect of the elections themselves."

CHAPTER 11. IN THE SHADOW OF BATISTA

1. Everyone writing on the period owes a debt to Robert Whitney for being one of the first scholars to look beyond the dictator Batista and critically analyze and dissect his political thought and ideology. I have borrowed liberally from his insights in this chapter. In addition to his well-received book, *State and Revolution in Cuba: Mass Mobilization and Political Change, 1920–1940* (Chapel Hill: University of North Carolina Press, 2001), Whitney has written several articles touching on the subject, including "The Architect of the Cuban State: Fulgencio Batista and Populism in Cuba, 1937–1940," *Journal of Latin American Studies* 32 (May 2000): 435–459; and "History or Teleology? Recent Scholarship on Cuba before 1959," *Latin American Research Review* 36 (2001): 220–236. In his book, he devotes an entire chapter (pp. 122–148) to Batista's efforts at "disciplining" the Cuban masses and his subsequent efforts at restructuring Cuban society and political culture.

2. *Diario de la Marina* ran a full page of photos on some of the improvements made to Camp Columbia/Ciudad Militar as part of a supplement to the newspaper; "Ciudad Militar," December 12, 1935. President Mendieta approved a provision allowing the army to spend money for needed construction projects without going out for public bid for the fiscal years 1933–1935. Batista, *Growth and Decline*, 233, briefly describes the improvements made to military facilities. See also Adam y Silva, *La gran mentira*, 437–438; and Vega Cobiellas, *Batista y Cuba*, 44–45.

3. In 1939, the party, by then allied to Batista, changed its name to the Partido Unión Revolucionaria Comunista.

4. Little has been written about Barnet (1864–1945), except to note his subservient posture to Batista. One of the most detailed articles about his career prior to assuming the presidency was published by *Diario de la Marina* at the time of Mendieta's resignation; "Tiene un historial brillante el nuevo Presidente interino," December 12, 1935.

5. Phillips, *Cuba: Island of Paradox*, 173. This perception of Barnet was widely held. Another author, Regino Díaz Robainas, makes a similar observation in a short biographical pamphlet he wrote about Colonel Batista shortly after his death in 1973; *Cuba, Batista y la historia* (Guatemala City: Cultural Centroamericana, 1973), 12.

6. Portell-Vilá, *Nueva historia*, 456.

7. Arístides Sosa de Quesada, interview by author, Miami, May 18, 1998.

8. "Juegos infantiles," *Bohemia*, March 29, 1936.

9. "Dr. José A. Barnet," *Bohemia*, May 24, 1936. In Spanish the citation reads: "Abandona el cargo dejando una estela de anodinismo, de incomprensión. Y mientras el país ha confrontado los más graves problemas, el Presidente Barnet, en una interminable sucesión de fiestas, recepciones y banquetes, ha hecho gala de una ostentación que contrastaba amargamente con la pobreza y faltas de recursos de nuestro pueblo. Su paso por la Presidencia marca una etapa de superficialidad que resulta digno colofón de toda su existencia." The conservative newspaper, *Diario de la Marina*, was much kinder in its assessment, calling him the "President Diplomat, the President Conciliator." In a farewell article, the newspaper noted that his "benevolent and gentle smile" was often enough to resolve conflicts; "El Presidente que cesa y el Presidente que comienza," *Diario de la Marina*, May 20, 1936.

10. Acosta Rubio, *Ensayo biográfico Batista*, 201–206, provides a nice summary of the programs and their organization. Another useful source for understanding the structure of the various organizations is the army's monthly magazine, *Ejército Constitucional*. The June 1937 edition is of particular interest. Also useful is Vega Cobiellas, *Batista y Cuba*, 50–54.

11. Barnet made this observation to previous Secretary of State Cosme de la Torriente; Torriente to Welles, June 8, 1936, Welles Papers, Office correspondence, 1920–1943, Torriente, Cosme de la, 1935–1936.

12. Caffery outlines some of the objectionable, from his perspective, legislation in a February 26, 1936, letter to Welles; Welles Papers, "Major Correspondents, 1920–1950," Jefferson Caffery, January–October 1936.

13. Phillips, *Cuba: Island of Paradox*, 177.

14. Vega Cobiellas, *General Fulgencio Batista Zaldívar*, 61–62, provides excerpts of two of his speeches from the period.

15. In the letter, Caffery pouts that he too is underappreciated by Gómez. "In my own case I did not expect nor did I want him to do or say anything, but with Batista it is different"; Caffery to Welles, March 20, 1936, Welles Papers, "Major Correspondents, 1920–1950," Jefferson Caffery, January–October 1936. Portell-Vilá, *Nueva historia*, 462, notes that Gómez kept his social contact with Batista to a minimum.

16. Welles to Caffery, April 23, 1936, Welles Papers, "Major Correspondents, 1920–1950," Jefferson Caffery, January–October 1936.

17. Welles to Caffery, April 23, 1936, Welles Papers, "Major Correspondents, 1920–1950," Jefferson Caffery, January–October 1936.

18. Phillips, *Cuba: Island of Paradox*, 174; and Portell-Vilá, *Nueva historia*, 460.

19. "Monomanía," *Bohemia*, September 29, 1935.

20. Beals, *Crime of Cuba*, 212–218, chronicles some of the abuses and provides the $8 million estimate. Thomas, *Cuba: Pursuit of Freedom*, 504–513, details several of Gómez's money-making schemes.

21. Miguel Mariano had four siblings, all sisters.

22. One of the best examples is a photo published by *Bohemia* in its edition of October 18, 1936, with a caption entitled "La reunión trascendental." The picture captures Batista, Gómez, and Defense Minister Montalvo at a reunion at the Presidential Palace. No one is smiling, and none of the participants is making eye contact with the others. They all look decidedly uncomfortable.

23. Santiago Rey Perna, interview by author, Miami, April 29, 1998. Treasury

Secretary Articus Cruz made the following comment to Rey: "Chico, él [Miguel Mariano Gómez] tiene conflictos por razones familiares. No se pueden llevar bien, porque son grupos humanos diferentes."

24. Caffery to Welles, December 11, 1936, Welles Papers, "Major Correspondents, 1920–1950," Jefferson Caffery, November–December 1936. Caffery later included this letter in an official State Department dispatch; Caffery to Secty. of State, December 18, 1936, Dept. of State, decimal file, 1930–1939, file 837.00/7763 RG 59.

25. Caffery to Welles, December 11, 1936, Welles Papers, "Major Correspondents, 1920–1950," Jefferson Caffery, November–December 1936 (emphasis is Caffery's). Caffery does not specify the meeting dates, only saying that they began a "couple of weeks ago."

26. Caffery, who would repeatedly side with Batista in the coming months, describes President-Elect Gómez's failure to consult with Batista "a mistake"; Caffery to Welles, May 22, 1936, Welles Papers, "Major Correspondents, 1920–1950," Jefferson Caffery, January–June 1936. Gómez also failed to inform some of his closest supporters until the day before his inauguration, a slight that would be remembered later when his impeachment was debated in Congress; "Sensacional," El País, December 22, 1936.

27. Batista favored Domingo Morales y Castillo for the job but agreed to allow the president to select retired General Rafael Montalvo; Caffery to Welles, May 25, 1936, Welles Papers, "Major Correspondents, 1920–1950," Jefferson Caffery, January–June 1936.

28. Col. T. N. Gimperling, military attaché, Cuba, (Political), "Present Executive," G-2 Report, May 21, 1936, file 2657-363 (26) RG 165. Gimperling sent an English-language version of the president's address to Washington, excerpts of which I have quoted.

29. Russell Porter, "Freed Cuba Comes to Test of People," New York Times, July 6, 1936.

30. In a July 16, 1936, letter to Welles, Caffery notes Gómez's unwillingness to show Batista any "consideración." A few days later, Caffery met with Gómez and urged him to show Batista "consideración"; Caffery to Welles, July 16 and 25, 1936, Welles Papers, "Major Correspondents, 1920–1950," Jefferson Caffery, July–August 1936.

31. Welles to Caffery, April 23, 1936, Welles Papers, "Major Correspondents, 1920–1950," Jefferson Caffery, January–October 1936.

32. Welles to Caffery, June 18, 1936, Welles Papers, "Major Correspondents, 1920–1950," Jefferson Caffery, January–October 1936.

33. The Batista quote comes from Phillips, Cuba: Island of Paradox, 175. Caffery wrote to Welles on July 3, 1936: "The Army, of course, is again furious with Miguel Mariano"; Welles Papers, "Major Correspondents, 1920–1950," Jefferson Caffery, July–August 1936.

34. Welles to Caffery, July 8, 1936, Welles Papers, "Major Correspondents, 1920–1950," Jefferson Caffery, January–October 1936. Caffery made the U.S. position clear on numerous occasions, including a September meeting with Defense Minister Montalvo, in which the latter expressed a desire to change "the system" after the U.S. elections in November. "I told him positively and plainly that any attempt to destroy the democratic system in this country would not redound to Cuba's benefit"; Caffery to Welles, September 21, 1936.

35. Welles to Caffery, September 3, 1936, Welles Papers, "Major Correspondents, 1920–1950," Jefferson Caffery, January–October 1936.

36. The intermediary sent by President Gómez was José Gómez Mena, who spoke to Welles on a variety of other matters. The excerpt comes from an October 22, 1936, letter from Welles to Caffery, in which he relates the details of the meeting; Welles Papers, "Major Correspondents, 1920–1950," Jefferson Caffery, January–October 1936.

37. Russell Porter, "Gomez Promises Freedom in Cuba," *New York Times*, July 4, 1936.

38. Caffery's letters are bursting with positive reports about meetings between Batista and Gómez, only to be followed by evidence of bad relations a few days later. On June 30, Caffery writes that Batista's "attitude to the President is a changed one for the better." Four days later, the army is "again furious with Miguel Mariano." On July 16, Batista was "more indignant than ever with Miguel Mariano," but a day later, after a meeting between the two men, things were now "*bastante satisfactoria*"; Caffery to Welles, June 30 and July 3, 16, and 17, 1936, Welles Papers, "Major Correspondents, 1920–1950," Jefferson Caffery, January–August 1936.

39. "Cómo ha organizado el Ejército de Cuba la educación cívico-militar," *Bohemia*, September 6, 1936.

40. The untitled cartoon featuring the two businessmen ran in *Bohemia* on September 13, 1936. The cartoon about the handkerchief also ran, without a title, in *Bohemia* on December 13, 1936. For the article on Gómez's smoke-blowing abilities, see "Hombres célebres contemporáneos: Miguel Mariano Gómez," *Bohemia*, December 20, 1936. The cartoon on Gomez's medical advice ran under the headline "Truco viejo," *Bohemia*, December 20, 1936.

41. "No hacer es deshacer," *Diario de la Marina*, July 10, 1936; and in an untitled editorial, *Bohemia*, June 14, 1936.

42. Miguel Coyula, "El equilibrio de los poderes," *Bohemia*, June 28, 1936. The final sentence of the column reads as follows: "No olviden lo que dijo uno de nuestros grandes: cuando falla el gobierno de las leyes, se impone el gobierno de la espada."

43. Caffery to Welles, April 27, 1936, Welles Papers, "Major Correspondents, 1920–1950," Jefferson Caffery, January–June 1936.

44. Caffery to Welles, April 14, 1936, Welles Papers, "Major Correspondents, 1920–1950," Jefferson Caffery, January–June 1936. Caffery made similar statements in letters to Welles on April 13 and 27 and July 21, 1936. In the July 21 letter, Caffery writes that the president "while surrendering no presidential privileges and prerogatives, [must] have Batista understand that he is not making a fight on him." He goes on to inform Welles that he will be dining with President Gómez in the next few days and "may get an opportunity to say something pertinent."

45. Caffery to Welles, July 9, 1936, Welles Papers, "Major Correspondents, 1920–1950," Jefferson Caffery, July–August 1936.

46. Caffery writes of Nacionalista efforts to secure the presidency for Brú or Mendieta in a July 16, 1936, letter to Welles; Welles Papers, "Major Correspondents, 1920–1950," Jefferson Caffery, July–August 1936.

47. The issue of government appointments and the manner in which they were doled out was a recurrent theme and led to great bitterness against Gómez. His failure to resolve this issue was the subject of numerous letters between Caffery and

Welles. Of particular interest are a letter by Caffery to Welles, August 28, 1936, Welles Papers, "Major Correspondents, 1920–1950," Jefferson Caffery, July–August 1936; and Welles's response of the following day. Columnist Miguel Coyula, "Ambiente de confusión," *Bohemia*, June 14, 1936, criticizes Gómez for delays in filling key government posts. Santiago Rey Perna makes a similar observation; interview by author, Miami, April 29, 1998.

48. Eduardo Suárez Rivas, *Un pueblo crucificado* (Miami: Service Offset Printers, 1964), 100, was one of those to refer to the bill as "Ley Regalo." He was elected to the House of Representatives as a member of the Liberal Party and was one of the few to oppose the impeachment of President Gómez.

49. Caffery's letter was in response to Welles's warning about tough action in the event of a military coup; Caffery to Welles, June 22, 1936, Welles Papers, "Major Correspondents, 1920–1950," Jefferson Caffery, January–June 1936.

50. Whitney, *State and Revolution in Cuba*, 149–176, emphasizes many of these same points.

51. For some examples of Batista's thoughts in this period regarding the relationship between labor and capital, see Porter, "Dual Cuban Regime Denied by Batista," *New York Times*, July 5, 1936; "Batista opina sobre los problemas nacionales," *Carteles*, November 8, 1936; Whitney, *State and Revolution in Cuba*, 161, which provides an excerpt from a speech Batista delivered to the Cuban Chamber of Commerce in New York in 1938; and Phillips, *Cuba: Island of Paradox*, 188–189, who quotes Batista from a speech given in February 1939 after a visit to Mexico to see President Lázaro Cárdenas.

52. The classic work on Trujillo remains Robert Crassweller's, *Trujillo: The Life and Times of a Caribbean Dictator* (New York: Macmillan, 1966). For an overview of U.S foreign policy toward the Dominican Republic during the Roosevelt administration, see Eric Paul Roorda, *The Dictator Next Door: The Good Neighbor Policy and the Trujillo Regime in the Dominican Republic, 1930–1945* (Durham, N.C.: Duke University Press, 1998). For an account of Trujillo's final days, see Bernard Diederich, *Trujillo: The Death of the Dictator* (Princeton, N.J.: Markus Wiener, 1998).

53. Col. T. N. Gimperling, military attaché, Cuba (Political), "Stability of Present Administration," G-2 Report, January 27, 1937, file 2657-330 (383) RG 165.

54. Phillips, *Cuba: Island of Paradox*, 190.

55. Acosta Rubio, *Ensayo biográfico Batista*, 214–215 and 222.

56. "Batista Host to U.S. Press," *Havana Post*, October 8, 1936.

57. He singled out Italian fascism for praise in remarks to a United Press reporter in November 1936, although he again declared that he was a proponent of neither fascism or communism. The story ran in newspapers throughout the United States. See also " 'Si es necesario seré dictador'—declara Batista," *La Prensa*, November 7, 1936. Phillips, *Cuba: Island of Paradox*, 190, notes that at "one time" he was an admirer of Mussolini.

58. Gerald H. Read, "Civic-Military Rural Education of Cuba: Eleven Eventful Years (1936–1946)" (Ph.D. diss., Ohio State University, 1950), 182, notes that the original goal of reducing illiteracy was far too limited to address the complex set of problems facing rural Cuba. It is a sad testament to the lack of scholarship on the subject that this unpublished dissertation remains, more than fifty years after its completion, one of the most comprehensive studies of Batista's rural education

programs. The best contemporary work on the subject, although favorable to the government, was written by Lt. Col. Arístides Sosa de Quesada, president of the council overseeing Batista's reform agenda; *El Consejo Corporativo de Educación, Sanidad y Beneficencia y sus instituciones filiales* (Havana: Instituto Cívico-Militar, 1937).

59. América Ana Cuervo, "Mejoramiento de la vivienda campesina," *Bohemia*, June 21, 1936. The excerpt reads as follows: "La vida en el hogar campesino es sinónimo de miseria. Ninguna diferencia apreciable existe entre el bohío criollo y aquél encontrado por los descubridores al llegar a nuestra Isla."

60. Ibid. In Spanish the excerpt reads: "Ciertamente que tales desgracias no han sido desconocidas por nuestros gobernantes, pero es un hecho cierto que les ha faltado el valor para resolver el problema."

61. Commission on Cuban Affairs, *Problems of the New Cuba: Report of the Commission on Cuban Affairs* (New York: Foreign Policy Association, 1935). The report, commissioned by President Mendieta, was extraordinarily influential and was used extensively by future governments and the political opposition in framing political debates over education, health care, and social-service programs. Cubans were initially supposed to serve on the commission, but because of the volatile political climate of the period, a decision was ultimately made to exclude them (vi). The exclusion of Cubans gave the commission's work a greater sense of impartiality, which ultimately contributed to its prestige. The chairman of the commission, known officially as the Commission on Cuban Affairs, was Welles's antagonist, Raymond Leslie Buell, president of the Foreign Policy Association.

62. Ibid., 137. La Sociedad Económica de Amigos del País de la Habana issued similar findings on February 1, 1935. The report by the prestigious civic organization was published in its entirety in *Diario de la Marina*; "Señala la Sociedad Económica pautas para contener la decadencia cultural en Cuba," February 6, 1935.

63. Commission on Cuban Affairs, *Problems of the New Cuba*, 95–128, provides a detailed overview of public-health conditions throughout the island.

64. Ibid., 159–181, summarizes social welfare programs in Cuba at the time.

65. The speech was broadcast by radio to the nation. It was published in its entirety in the daily newspaper, *El País*; " 'La Ley del Azúcar quita al que puede unos centavos para dárselos al que por desgracia los necesita,' dijo Batista," December 19, 1936. The excerpts used in the next few paragraphs read in Spanish as follows; "Es condición del hombre pensar en cada acto, la repercusión que ha de tener en la opinión pública con motivo de su gesto. Para mí el hombre de convicciones no responde con su conducta en manera alguna a un estado de opinión que en determinado momento forma el ambiente o la circunstancia, sino que el hombre de convicciones actúa en cada momento crítico de acuerdo con la necesidad que el ambiente exige, sean cuales fueren las críticas que un estado de opinión enferma o sana, pueda producir." "Magnífica posición la mía, dos estrellas en el cuello y tres en cada hombro, joven, poderoso y querido por lo menos por el Ejército que mando." "¿Por qué si no te corresponde tú haces esto o haces aquéllo? ¿Por qué te abrogas facultades que no tienes?" ". . . Porque hay conciencia y hay convicciones."

On the idea of rural education: "¿Por qué germinó esa idea en mí?" The program "no solamente da instrucción, que no solamente pretende enseñar el alfabeto, a leer, a escribir, a sacar cuentas; sino que pretende educar, enseñar, a prevenirse, formar la mentalidad de los hombres, de las mujeres y de los niños ignorantes."

On the army and its role: "¿Por qué el Ejército sólo ha de ser instrumento de guerra y no símbolo de paz más que símbolo de exterminio?"

66. Read, "Civic-Military Rural Education," 168–175, cites the report as a key factor leading to the establishment of the schools. He also cites Batista's childhood experiences and the writings of José Martí as instrumental. I find little evidence to support the assertion that Martí's political thought was a major factor. There is a tendency in Cuban history to attribute every important program, one way or another, to Martí.

67. In 1940, the schools were turned over by the army to the Ministry of Education. At the time there were about fifty-seven thousand students attending the schools; Read, "Civic-Military Rural Education," 392–396. The army claimed to have established more than 1,300 schools, but Read writes that military officials were "padding statistics" (211n10). Originally, Batista estimated that between 2,700 and 3,000 schools would be needed (184). The 3,000 figure comes from Phillips, *Cuba: Island of Paradox*, 178–179. Fulgencio Batista Zaldívar, *Paradojas* (Mexico City: Ediciones Botas, 1963), 61, claims to have established 2,710 schools between 1936 and 1944. Gellman, *Roosevelt and Batista*, 147, provides the enrollment figures for the first year of the rural education program.

68. Rogelio Jiménez Capote to Emilio Carrillo, May 20, 1985; Fulgencio Batista Zaldívar Papers, private collection of Fulgencio Rubén Batista Godínez, Coral Gables, Fla. Batista's eldest son provided it to the author, along with two other accounts, one by Emilio Carrillo, undated, and the other by Mireya LaFuente, undated. At one time, Carrillo, in exile in South Florida, considered writing a book on the subject of the civic-military schools, and he deserves all the credit for compiling the three written accounts used in this section. Sosa de Quesada, *Consejo Corporativo*, 37–75, provides what appears to be a complete listing of all the rural schools established in the first year, the teachers assigned, and the locations of the schools. Capote taught at a school in the Caracas neighborhood on a farm known as Dos Hermanos (Two Brothers), 61.

69. Emilio Carrillo, undated account, Fulgencio Batista Zaldívar papers, private collection of Fulgencio Rubén Batista Godínez, Coral Gables, Fla. Read, "Civic-Military Rural Education," 213–222, describes in further detail the process of school site selection and efforts by the sergeant-teachers to get the community involved. Sosa de Quesada, *Consejo Corporativo*, 50, identifies an Enrique J. Carrillo assigned to rural Camagüey in the Magarabomba neighborhood on a farm known as Las Mercedes. The account provided by Batista Godínez matches up with the location identified in Sosa de Quesada's book.

70. Read, "Civic-Military Rural Education," 245–259, writes about the curriculum at the various stages of development, from grades 1 to 6. He mentions physical education on 248.

71. Col. Gimperling made the observation and it was passed on to Washington by his successor; Maj. E. W. Timberlake, military attaché, Cuba (Combat-Army), "Army Policy," G-2 Report, June 3, 1937, file 2277-17 (2) RG 165.

72. Matthews to Secty. of State, January 30, 1937, Military Intelligence Division, regional file, 1922–1944, Cuba—Pre-1940, folder 2520, RG 165.

73. Batista set forth his ideas on this and many other aspects of the rural schools in a five-page memo to diplomat H. Freeman Matthews. A copy of the memo was

provided to U.S. military intelligence, which in turn sent it to Washington; Matthews to Secty. of State, November 17, 1936, Military Intelligence Division, regional file, 1922–1944, Cuba—pre-1940, folder 2520, RG 165. The programming for the rural schools was provided by another new agency established by Batista—the Radio Transmission Cultural Service (El Servicio Cultural de Radiodifusión); Vega Cobiellas, *Batista y Cuba*, 50.

74. Batista outlined the various mission specialists in the November 17, 1936, memo to Matthews. Batista, *Growth and Decline*, 77–79, briefly reviews the organization of the rural schools. Read, "Civic-Military Rural Education," 276–312, notes that the types of mission specialists evolved over time. They also served other functions, including providing additional training to the sergeant-teachers and inspecting the programs provided by the schools. Chester, *A Sergeant Named Batista*, 168–169, describes the specialists assigned to the rural zones. I owe special thanks to Arístides Sosa de Quesada, onetime director of the rural schools, for his insights; interview by author, Miami, May 18, 1998. Vega Cobiellas, *General Fulgencio Batista Zaldívar*, 129–135, provides a wealth information on the structure of the rural education program.

75. Mireya LaFuente to Emilio Carrillo, undated account, Fulgencio Batista Zaldívar papers, private collection of Fulgencio Rubén Batista Godínez, Coral Gables, Fla. In Spanish the excerpt reads as follows: "Yo había oído decir que las ratas eran peligrosas y que lo mismo se comían el dedo gordo de un pie que la nariz, que mientras roían iban soplando y por ello el paciente no sentía ningún dolor. Yo estaba bien cubierta pero temía que al igual que le hacían agujeros a los sacos, también pudieran taladar mi ropa y la cosa era estar a la defensiva, no dormir."

76. This quote also comes from Batista's November 17, 1936, memo.

77. Maj. E. W. Timberlake, military attaché, Cuba (Combat-Army), "Army Policy," G-2 Report, June 7, 1937, file 2277-17 (3) RG 165. Pérez, *Army Politics*, 113, agrees that the programs lessened hostility toward the military.

78. Sosa de Quesada, *Consejo Corporativo*, 22–24, describes in detail the Flor Martiana ceremony and its significance. The winning musical composition was written and composed by Andrés DePiedra-Bueno and Buenaventura Yañez, 94–95. The first chorus goes as follows:

Para abrir los futuros caminos
y en los yernos propicios sembrar
y encender aurorales destinos:
educar! educar! educar!

79. Sosa de Quesada not only wrote and assembled the materials for *Consejo Corporativo*, but later authored a pedagogical work for the sergeant-teachers; *Motivaciones escolares: Libro de lectura para alumnos de 20., 30., y 40. grados de orientación para los maestros rurales* (Havana: P. Fernández y Cía, 1939).

80. Santiago Torra, *La escuela rural*, in *El Ejército Constitucional*, June 1937, 11–15.

81. Vega Cobiellas, *Batista y Cuba*, 49, makes the claim.

82. Batista, *Sombras de América*, 399.

83. Read, "Civic-Military Rural Education," 454–471, summarizes his conclusions.

84. Lowry Nelson, *Rural Cuba* (Minneapolis: University of Minnesota Press, 1950), 220–256, summarizes his findings on education and conditions in the Cuban

countryside. His statistics on literacy can be found on 239–244. For data on the gradual reduction of illiteracy through 1938 and its subsequent upswing, see Samuel Bowles, "Cuban Education and the Revolutionary Ideology," *Harvard Educational Review* 41 (1971): 472–500; and Richard Jolly, "Education—the Pre-Revolutionary Background," in Dudley Seers, ed., *Cuba: The Economic and Social Revolution* (Chapel Hill: University of North Carolina Press, 1964), 161–280.

85. Richard Fagen, *The Transformation of Political Culture in Cuba* (Stanford, Calif.: Stanford University Press, 1969), 33–68, describes in some detail the organization of the Literacy Campaign. For another perspective, see Jonathan Kozol, *Children of the Revolution: A Yankee Teacher in the Cuban Schools* (New York: Delacorte Press, 1978).

86. In addition to those already cited, other interesting works on education in Cuba, particularly in the post-1959 period, include Max Figueroa Esteva, Abel Prieto and Raúl Gutiérrez, *The Basic Secondary School in the Country: An Educational Innovation in Cuba* (Paris: Unesco Press, 1974); Carl J. Dahlman, *The Nation-Wide Learning System of Cuba* (Princeton, N.J.: Research Program in Economic Development, Woodrow Wilson School, Princeton University, 1973); Karen Wald, *Children of Che: Childcare and Education in Cuba* (Palo Alto, Calif.: Ramparts Press, 1978); and Lisandro Pérez, "The Demographical Dimensions of the Educational Problems in Socialist Cuba," *Cuban Studies/Estudios Cubanos* 7 (January 1977): 33–57. In regards to health care, again the research has focused primarily on the revolutionary period. Some useful works include Sergio Díaz-Briquets, *The Health Revolution in Cuba* (Austin: University of Texas Press, 1983); Nelson P. Valdes, "Health and Revolution in Cuba," *Science & Society* 35 (Fall 1971): 311–335; Ross Danielson, *Cuban Medicine* (New Brunswick, N.J.: Transaction Books, 1979); and Julie M. Feinsilver, *Healing the Masses: Cuban Health Politics at Home and Abroad* (Berkeley: University of California Press, 1993).

87. "Cómo ha organizado el Ejército de Cuba, la educación cívico-militar," *Bohemia*, September 6, 1936. The passage in Spanish reads: "Justo es confesar que la obra que lleva a cabo el Ejército, por iniciativa de su Jefe, en el campo de la enseñanza, ni perjudica a nadie, sino por el contrario beneficia a nuestro campesino, dejado como es dicho vulgar, de la mano de Dios, ni le quita atribuciones al Gobierno Civil, sino que coopera con él al mejoramiento del país que es al fin y al cabo lo que debe preocuparnos más."

88. "Una labor de positivo mérito," *Carteles*, November 22, 1936.

89. Matthews to Secty. of State, November 17, 1936, Military Intelligence Division, regional file, 1922–1944, Cuba—pre-1940, folder 2520, RG 165.

90. Batista, *Respuesta*, 411–412, notes that the nine cents was to be paid for every 325 pounds of sugar, although he does not say how that figure was arrived at.

91. The *colonos* association declared their support for the nine-cent tax on December 16. A letter made public by the association was published in *Diario de la Marina*; "Grata al colonato la Ley azucarera de los 9 centavos," December 17, 1936. One of those charging that the army pressured the *hacendados* and *colonos* was Congressman Raúl de Cárdenas during House debate. A copy of his speech was kept on file at the U.S. State Dept., decimal file, 1930–1939, file 837.001, Gomez., Miguel M./24 ½ RG 59.

92. Caffery to Welles, December 12, 1936, Welles Papers, "Major Correspondents, 1920–1950," Jefferson Caffery, November–December 1936.

93. Caffery to Welles, December 11, 1936, Welles Papers, "Major Correspondents, 1920–1950," Jefferson Caffery, November–December 1936. In this three-page letter, Caffery provides a brief summary of the events leading up to Gómez's impeachment.

94. Caffery to Welles, December 14 and 16, 1936, Welles Papers, "Major Correspondents, 1920–1950," Jefferson Caffery, November–December 1936.

95. The remark about "imposing" comes from Caffery to Welles, December 17, 1936, Welles Papers, "Major Correspondents, 1920–1950," Jefferson Caffery, November–December 1936. Copies of Mariné's telegram to legislators were included in a voluminous book, apparently compiled by supporters of President Gómez, and sent to the U.S. State Department. The undated book is entitled *Copia de documentos: Relativos a la destitución del Presidente de la República de Cuba Dr. Miguel Mariano Gómez*; Dept. of State, decimal file, 1930–39, file 837.001, Gomez, Miguel M./24 ½ RG 59.

96. Mariné offered Congressman Suárez Rivas a leadership position in the House in exchange for his vote. He declined the position; *Un pueblo crucificado*, 101–102. Suárez Rivas provides important insights (97) into how Batista's political operation worked and how Mariné ran it. Details of the economic threats made against House and Senate members were given in an anonymous memo dropped off at the U.S. State Department. The author may have been Sen. Ramón Zaydín M. Sterling, a supporter of President Gómez, who according to a handwritten note, attached to the memo, brought it into the State Department. Welles kept the undated memo in his files; Welles Papers, Latin America files, 1933–1943, "Cuba 1936–1937."

97. Mariné's reminder letter was also included in the book about Gómez's ouster; Dept. of State, decimal file, 1930–1939, file 837.001, Gomez, Miguel M./24 ½ RG 59.

98. The information about the meeting between Batista and several legislators comes from the undated memo; Welles Papers, Latin America files, 1933–1943, "Cuba 1936–1937." The charge that Batista met with legislators to ask them to oust the president was repeated in a diplomatic message by the Cuban Ambassador to President Roosevelt; Laurence Duggan, memorandum of conversation, December 19, 1936, Dept. of State, decimal file, 1930–39, file 837.00/7802 RG 59.

99. Suárez Rivas, *Un pueblo crucificado*, 102–103. The translated excerpt reads in Spanish as follows: "Aquí, tras esta ley, hay un intento de gobierno fascista. Se está tratando de quitarle al Poder Ejecutivo sus máximas facultades."

100. " 'En nombre del pueblo debemos estar todos prestos a testimoniar nuestro agradecimiento al Poder Legislativo,' " *El País*, December 19, 1936.

101. Caffery reported on Mariné's activity in a State Department dispatch. Caffery to Secty. of State, December 17, 1936, Dept. of State, decimal file, 1930–39, file 837.00/7760 RG 59.

102. The president's statements regarding his refusal to resign and his advice to his supporters against exile were made in the presence of Suárez Rivas, *Un pueblo crucificado*, 104. Some members of Congress, who sided with Gómez, requested and were granted a leave of absence, so they could travel to the United States until tensions eased. At least one Gómez defender left for Miami the day the president was ousted; J. D. Phillips, "Gomez to Defend Acts in Cuba Today at Trial in Senate," *New*

York Times, December 23, 1936; and by the same author, "Cuba Inducts Laredo Bru: He Sees an Era of Progress," *New York Times*, December 25, 1936.

103. J. D. Phillips, "Gomez Impeached, 111–45: Ouster in Cuba Held Sure as Senate Overrides Veto," *New York Times*, December 22, 1936. Throughout the crisis, Phillips notes several occasions of self-censorship by the Cuban media. See also "Sugar Tax Passed by House in Cuba," *New York Times*, December 19, 1936.

104. J.I.R, "Impresiones," *Diario de la Marina*, December 22, 1936; "Horas decisivas," *El Avance*, December 21, 1936.

105. The events are well chronicled in the Welles-Caffery correspondence and the ambassador's State Department dispatches. Of particular note are Caffery to Welles, December 11, 12, and 14, 1936, Welles Papers, "Major Correspondents, 1920–1950," Jefferson Caffery, November–December 1936; and Caffery to Secty. of State, December 17 and 18, 1936, Dept. of State, decimal file, 1930–1939, files 837.00/7760 and 7764 RG 59. The U.S. military attaché reported rumors of a conspiracy against Batista. Col. T. N. Gimperling, military attaché, Cuba (Political), "Stability of Present Administration," G-2 Report, December 17, 1936, file 2657-330 (375) RG 165.

106. Laurence Duggan, memorandum of conversation, December 19, 1936, Dept. of State, decimal file, 1930–1939, file 837.00/7802 RG 59.

107. Laurence Duggan, memorandum of conversation, December 21, 1936, Dept. of State, decimal file, 1930–39, file 837.00/7787 RG 59.

108. Laurence Duggan, memorandum, "Presidential Succession in Cuba, 1933–1936," December 22, 1936, Dept. of State, decimal file, 1930–1939, file 837.00/7816 RG 59.

109. Gómez's defense statement was published in its entirety in the *New York Times*; "The Defense Statement by Gomez," December 24, 1936.

110. The manifesto was distributed in the form of a flyer throughout parts of Cuba. Caffery sent a copy of it to Welles; "Manifiesto al Pueblo de Cuba," Welles Papers, "Major Correspondents, 1920–1950," Jefferson Caffery, 1937. U.S. military intelligence translated the document into English and sent it to Washington; military attaché, "Farewell Address of Miguel Mariano Gomez," January 21, 1937, file 2657-330 (383) RG 165. The official sentence by the Senate was published in the *Gaceta oficial*, December 24, 1936.

111. In this list I include Machado, General Herrera (who served for a couple of hours), Céspedes, Grau, Hevia, Márquez Sterling (also in power for just a few hours), Mendieta, Barnet, and Gómez.

112. Caffery to Secty. of State, December 28, 1936, Dept. of State, decimal file, 1930–1939, file 837.00/7800 RG 59.

CHAPTER 12. CUBAN STRONGMAN

1. Laredo Brú (1875–1946) was the last of the so-called puppet presidents under Batista, and his role in the transition from dictatorship to democracy in the 1930s has been largely ignored.

2. J. D. Phillips, "Batista Gives Aim of Cuban Regime," *New York Times*, December 27, 1936.

3. Caffery was the last ambassador to gain appointment under the Platt Amendment, and his departure signaled a significant diminution in the traditional power of the U.S. ambassador to Cuba. Once considered the second-most powerful position,

after the Cuban president, and at times, arguably the most powerful, the U.S. ambassador's post, although still important, would never regain that influence after Caffery's departure. Caffery was named ambassador to Brazil, and his replacement, Joshua Butler Wright, arrived in August 1937. The new ambassador seldom used his first name, preferring just the first initial, so in the media, and in State Department records, he was almost always addressed as J. Butler Wright. Gellman, *Roosevelt and Batista*, 154–158, assesses Caffery's tenure in Cuba.

4. Thomas, *Cuba: Pursuit of Freedom*, 705.

5. The fact that Batista and the military were considering replacing Brú with Montalvo was common knowledge; J. D. Phillips, "Cuba Inducts Laredo Bru; He sees an Era of Progress," *New York Times*, December 25, 1936; "New Regime in Cuba," *New York Times*, December 27, 1936; and Portell-Vilá, *Nueva historia*, 474–475.

6. Portell-Vilá writes that the "straitjacket" analogy was used by several Batista supporters to describe the imposition of a cabinet on Brú; *Nueva historia*, 476.

7. J. D. Phillips, "Batista Gives Aim of Cuban Regime," *New York Times*, December 27, 1936.

8. Whatever opinion one holds of Brú's legacy, few doubt his political acumen. Pérez, *Army Politics*, 111, makes this point. So do Portell-Vilá, *Nueva historia*, 475–476; and Suárez Rivas, *Un pueblo crucificado*, 109.

9. Maj. E. W. Timberlake, military attaché, Cuba (Political), "Loyalty of Local Governments to Central Government," G-2 Report, April 15, 1937, file 2657-330 (385) RG 165.

10. The account comes from Maj. E. W. Timberlake, military attaché, to Assistant Chief of Staff, "Reported Resignation of President Laredo Bru," November 26 and 27, 1937, files 2657-330 (393) and 2657-330 (394). Timberlake does not provide the name of the offending politician.

11. All the cartoons ran in *Bohemia*. The one about the man who doubts that Laredo Brú is president appeared on April 18, 1937, under the headline "Cohetes" (Firecrackers). The cartoon with the whistle was published on June 6, 1937, also under the headline "Cohetes." The "Cohetes" page was set aside by the magazine for political and social satire. The one featuring the scale ran with no headline on June 5, 1938.

12. *Bohemia*, February 27, 1938.

13. Phillips, *Cuba: Island of Paradox*, 187, writes that on May 4, 1938, Felipe Rivero, publisher of *Jorobemos*, was kidnapped and forced to drink castor oil. The prior year, the vice rector of the University of Havana, Rodolfo Méndez Peñate, a vocal critic of the government, received similar treatment. The attack against Peñate was mentioned by Juan Reporter, "12 meses de actualidad política," *Bohemia*, January 9, 1938.

14. Phillips, *Cuba: Island of Paradox*, 187, speculates that articles on the possible dissolution of Congress were the cause of the first *La Prensa* closure. Vega Cobiellas, *General Fulgencio Batista Zaldívar*, 90–91, writes that the closure was the result of "audacious, unwholesome and sensationalist" coverage. The real reason the newspaper was closed was probably because it leaked news of negotiations between Batista and several Auténtico leaders to oust President Brú. The closure is reviewed more thoroughly in chapter 13 of this work. The September 1938 closure led to widespread condemnation by the political opposition. *Bohemia* ran a critical editorial on September 11, 1938, and followed it up with four pages of interviews on the closure

the following week; "Bohemia pregunta: ¿Qué opina usted del decreto que restringe la libertad de la prensa?" September 18, 1938. *Carteles* editorialized against the second closure of *La Prensa* and the action taken against *Zig-Zag*; "A confesión de parte . . . ," May 7, 1939. *Zig-Zag* may have been closed because of a political cartoon run by the magazine that the Cuban ambassador to the United States, Pedro Martínez Fraga, found highly insulting; Edward P. Lawton to Secty. of State, March 25, 1939, Confidential U.S. Diplomatic Post Records: Cuba, Part 1, 1930–1939, microfiche, University Publications of America, Frederick, Md.

15. Copies of Menocal's manifesto are rare, because only one Cuban newspaper, *Acción*, published it. In contrast, Brú's response to Menocal widely published, including in *Diario de la Marina*; "Manifestaciones del Presidente de la República," September 15, 1939. The quoted paragraph from Brú's response reads in Spanish as follows: "Con plena responsibilidad de mis palabras, no puede obstaculizarse al Jefe del Ejército Coronel Batista, que a su vez es el Jefe de la Revolución del 4 de Septiembre, de la cual han sido consecuencia directa todos los Gobiernos que hemos tenido hasta hoy, su intervención en las actividades políticas, económicas y sociales de la Nación a quien ha sido y es el factor determinante de todo el proceso revolucionario del cual es culminación este Gobierno." A copy of Menocal's manifesto was sent in a dispatch to Washington by the first secretary of the embassy; Willard L. Beaulac to Secty. of State, September 6, 1939, Dept. of State, decimal file, 1930–1939, file 837.00/8533 RG 59. U.S. Military Attaché Maj. Henry A. Barber sent a dispatch twelve days later summarizing the Menocal manifesto and Brú's response to it; Cuba (Political), "Exercise of Governmental Power," September 18, 1939, file 2657-330 (417).

16. Menocal expressed his dissatisfaction with President Brú to U.S. Ambassador J. Butler Wright during a private meeting on November 2, 1939. Wright wrote to Welles of Menocal's reaction in the following terms: "He [Menocal] observed that the President was wrong when he publicly stated that he considered Colonel Batista to be 'beyond the law' because he was the author of the Revolution of 1933, whereas Menocal described him [Batista] as a by-product of the Revolution, but in no sense the author"; Wright to Welles, November 3, 1939, Welles Papers, Office Correspondence, 1920–1943, Wright, J. Butler, September–November 1939. Vega Cobiellas, *General Fulgencio Batista Zaldívar*, 73–75, gives more examples of Brú's deferential ways.

17. Juan J. Remos, "La Gestión Personal del Coronel Batista," *Bohemia*, June 5, 1938. The quote in Spanish reads: "él había sembrado la Revolución; él había hecho la Revolución del 4 de septiembre; la Revolución no lo había hecho a él." Remos was one of Batista's closest political advisers. He worked with Batista on the establishment of the rural education program and also served in the cabinet of President Brú, first as defense minister and then as foreign minister. Vega Cobiellas, *General Fulgencio Batista Zaldívar*, 79–80, provides another example of Remos's image building.

18. Batista's remarks about being the "soul and leader" of the revolution were made before a joint session of the Mexican Congress on February 10, 1939. The U.S. military attaché's office in Havana sent a brief summary of Batista's remarks to Washington; Cuba (Political), "Stability of Present Administration," February 21, 1939, file 2657-330 (403). Every year on the anniversary of September 4, 1933, Batista delivered a speech marking the event and listing the accomplishments of the revolution. A compilation of these speeches was published in 1944; Fulgencio Batista, *Revolución social o política reformista: Once aniversarios* (Havana: Prensa Indoamericana,

1944). The speech from 1939 is particularly useful as a summary of revolutionary accomplishments, 109–135.

19. Some examples of pro-Auténtico articles from the period include Guillermo Martínez Márquez, "Cordialidad sin presupuesto," *Bohemia*, September 11, 1938; Martínez Márquez, "Universitario a ídolo popular," *Bohemia*, September 18, 1938; Eddy Chibás, "Los gobiernos de Cuba: Grau San Martín (1933–1934)," *Bohemia*, June 5, 1938; and Chibás, "Varias horas con Grau San Martín," *Bohemia*, September 26, 1937.

20. A good example are the remarks made by Foreign Minister Montalvo in February 1937 to *Diario de la Marina*; " 'Hace falta en Cuba una democracia sincera que tenga autoridad y que excluye a la política de oficio para dar paso a la de sentimiento y utilidad pública,' " February 11, 1937. The search for order and stability was one of the main reasons "business and industry and the conservative elements of Cuban society rallied behind Batista," according to lawyer and author, Mario Lazo, *Dagger in the Heart: American Policy Failures in Cuba* (New York: Funk and Wagnalls, 1968), 50–52.

21. The already cited column by Miguel Coyula, "El equilibrio de los poderes," *Bohemia*, June 28, 1936, is a good example of a journalistic commentary that seeks to explain the rise of military power and set forth a path to greater civilian authority in the government. The debate over military versus civilian power dominated the Cuban press throughout the late 1930s, as did the conditions required for a constitutional assembly. What follows is not intended to be an exhaustive compilation of relevant articles but merely a sampling: "La realidad del momento político," *Carteles*, January 3, 1937, examines the causes for the increase in military power; "La unión por la doctrina," *Carteles*, March 7, 1937; and Juan Reporter, "La nota política de la semana: A la deriva," *Bohemia*, July 18, 1937. Coyula particularly calls for patriotism from within the government and outside of it to bring about a constitutional assembly in his column, "Movimiento de opinión," *Bohemia*, July 18, 1937. See also Juan Reporter, "La nota política de la semana: Constituyente soberana o farsa Machadista," October 24, 1937. Coyula writes of having "*fé*" (faith) in President Brú and his ability to place his civilian government on a stronger footing in "Sobre terreno firme," *Bohemia*, August 14, 1938. The call for patriotism from all in bringing about a constitutional assembly was made again in a *Bohemia* editorial, February 5, 1939. In the days immediately preceding the constitutional assembly elections, *Carteles* called for all Cubans to participate in a process that would bring about the end of the provisional governments; "Deber y responsabilidad de la ciudadania," November 12, 1939; and "La fórmula liberadora," November 19, 1939. In the aftermath of the constitutional assembly elections, a *Carteles* editorial praised the government, specifically the military, for not interfering in the vote; "Interrogación trascendente," November 26, 1939.

22. *Diario de la Marina*, "Manifestaciones del Presidente de la República," September 15, 1939.

23. Batista considered dissolving Congress in May 1937 because of frustration over the legislative body's failure to meet on a regular basis to consider reform legislation. In April 1939, Batista was upset with Congress for failing to pass amendments to the electoral code that would permit him to seek the presidency. U.S. Military Attaché Maj. E. W. Timberlake sent two dispatches to Washington on Batista's threat to disband Congress in May 1937; Timberlake to Assistant Chief of Staff, "Rumors as to

Instability of Present Government," G-2 Report, May 31, 1937, file 2657-330 (388). He followed it up with "Resumed Legislative Activity and Adoption of Minimum Program," G-2 Report, June 2, 1937, file 2657-330 (389). The events of April 1939 were detailed in a series of four letters between Ambassador Wright and Assistant Secretary Welles; Wright to Welles, April 18 and 19, 1939, Welles Papers, Office Correspondence, 1920–1943, Wright, J. Butler, April–June 1939; and Welles to Wright, April 21 and 22, 1939.

24. Maj. E. W. Timberlake, military attaché, Cuba (Political), "Present Members of Advisory Councils," August 11, 1937, file 2657-384 (1). Portell-Vilá, *Nueva historia*, 501, among others credits Brú as one of Batista's key political advisers.

25. I owe the observations about his humor and how he employed it during negotiations to Portell-Vilá, *Nueva historia*, 501; Phillips, *Cuba: Island of Paradox*, 182, notes his "dry sense of humor."

26. Brú's participation in these negotiations was widely covered by the press and noted by U.S. diplomatic dispatches. For a press account, see Teodorico Raposo, "Grau y Batista llegaron juntos," *Bohemia*, April 14, 1940. U.S. Chargé d'Affaires Willard L. Beaulac summarizes the importance of Brú's mediating role in a January 11, 1940, dispatch to Secretary of State Cordell Hull; Welles Papers, Office Correspondence, 1920–1943, Beaulac, William, 1940.

27. Information about Brú's role in these negotiations can be found in various sources, including Portell-Vilá, *Nueva historia*, 500–501; and Gellman, *Roosevelt and Batista*, 177–178. Suárez Rivas, *Un pueblo crucificado*, 127–128, highlights the benefits to Batista of the negotiations. See also Jorge García Montes and Antonio Alonso Avila, *Historia del Partido Comunista de Cuba* (Miami: Ediciones Universal, 1970), 216–217.

28. Portell-Vilá, *Nueva historia*, 489, makes this observation about the cabinet changes made in August 1938. Columnist Miguel Coyula sees the cabinet reshuffling as a positive step; "Sobre terreno firme," *Bohemia*, August 14, 1938.

29. The bill in question was the so-called Mortgage Reevaluation Law or Mortgage Moratorium, which would have reduced the mortgage debt of property owners throughout the island. The United States strongly opposed the legislation because of the impact it would have on U.S. lenders. The State Department was suspicious of Batista's motives for supporting the legislation, fearing it was part of his growing hostility to the United States; Wright to Welles, October 20, 24, and 31, 1939, Welles Papers, Office Correspondence, 1920–1943, Wright, J. Butler, September–November 1939. *Carteles* published an editorial siding with the president on the mortgage issue; "El veto del Ejecutivo," October 29, 1939.

30. Brú favored a more conciliatory approach than Batista in negotiations with the United States over a supplemental trade agreement. A State Department dispatch on the subject was kept on file by Welles; Wright to Secty. of State, September 2, 1939, Welles Papers, Office Correspondence, 1920–1943, Wright, J. Butler, September–November 1939. The president objected to several of Batista's campaign speeches, particularly one delivered in the city of Matanzas on November 5, 1939, which Ambassador Wright described as "swash-buckling" and critical of U.S. economic policy toward Cuba; Wright to Secty. of State, November 9, 1939, Welles Papers, Office Correspondence, 1920–1943, Wright, J. Butler, September–November 1939; and Wright to Welles, November 7, 1939, Welles Papers, Office Correspondence, 1920–1943, Wright, J. Butler, September–November 1939.

31. Welles kept a copy of the unsigned memo in his personal records; U.S. Dept. of State, memorandum, January 17, 1939, Welles Papers, Office Correspondence, 1920–1943, Wright, J. Butler, January–March, 1939. Wright speculated on Batista's diminished influence on legislators in a letter to Welles in August; Wright to Welles, August 24, 1939, Welles Papers, Office Correspondence, 1920–1943, Wright, J. Butler, July–August 1939.

32. Wright to Welles, April 18, 1939, Welles Papers, Office Correspondence, 1920–1943, Wright, J. Butler, April–June 1939. Wright goes on to note: "On the other hand, you will have observed that Batista is making almost weekly announcements of his withdrawal from certain political questions." Three months earlier, a State Department memo, dated January 17, 1939, indicated that "Batista's strength [in congress and with President Brú] has lessened rather than increased"; Welles Papers, Office Correspondence, 1920–1943, Wright, J. Butler, January–March 1939.

33. Portell-Vilá, *Nueva historia*, 475–476.

34. Suárez Rivas, *Un pueblo crucificado*, 109. A similar observation is made by García Montes and Alonso Avila, *Partido Comunista*, 216–217. Carlos Márquez Sterling, a member of the House of Representatives in the period and a critic of the military, credits Brú, in his history of Cuba, with helping to pave the way for a constitutional assembly. The book was coauthored with his son Manuel Márquez Sterling; *Historia de la isla de Cuba* (Miami: Books and Mas, 1996), 218.

35. Juan Reporter, "La nota política de la semana: A la deriva," *Bohemia*, July 18, 1937.

36. The amnesty for dollars controversy was written about in an editorial in *Bohemia*, May 30, 1937. The subject of those included in the amnesty legislation came up again in an article by Juan Reporter; "La nota política de la semana: Amnistía a plazos," *Bohemia*, September 12, 1937.

37. Portell-Vilá, *Nueva historia*, 487–489, provides details on the bonds.

38. *Bohemia*, July 11, 1937.

39. Portell-Vilá, *Nueva historia*, 489. The quote in Spanish reads: "Se les conocía, se le criticaba, pero también se les admiraba porque habían tenido la habilidad de ser criminales impunes."

40. Adam y Silva, *La gran mentira*, 449–461, attempts to summarize the extensive network of army corruption. Perez, *Army Politics*, 105–106, argues that Batista was aware of the corruption and used it to build loyalty.

41. Maj. E. W. Timberlake, military attaché, Cuba (Combat-Army), "Army Policy," G-2 Report, October 13, 1937, file 2012-133 (82).

42. Maj. E. W. Timberlake, military attaché, Cuba (Combat-Army), "Army Policy," G-2 Report, April 20, 1938, file 2012-133 (87).

43. This was a frequent charge made against the two military leaders. Timberlake claims Pedraza and Mariné were "constantly at swords point over the proceeds from gambling"; Cuba (Political), "Political Issues and Problems," G-2 Report, March 24, 1938, file 2657-330 (399). Menocal told Ambassador Wright that Pedraza was involved in the "collection of money which he obtained from gambling and from the protection of gambling activities"; Wright to Welles, November 3, 1939, Welles Papers, Office Correspondence, 1920–1943, Wright, J. Butler, September–November 1939. Pérez, *Army Politics*, 106, implicates both in gambling kickbacks. Adam y Silva, *La gran mentira*, 457–458, writes about Mariné's abuses. It is clear that he is writing about Mariné, although he does not give his name.

44. Portell-Vilá, *Nueva historia*, 437–438 and 478, comments on army corruption in general and Batista, specifically. Thomas, *Cuba: Pursuit of Freedom*, 692, writes that Batista profited from the inflated costs of uniform sales to the armed forces.

45. The details of this elaborate malfeasance were detailed in a *Bohemia* editorial on September 5, 1937.

46. Among the works favoring the revolutionary government's interpretation of corruption and its role in the events of 1959 are E. Vignier and G. Alonso, *La corrupción política administrativa en Cuba, 1944–1952* (Havana: Editorial de Ciencias Sociales, Instituto Cubano del Libro, 1973); Pedro Luis Padrón, *¡Qué república era aquella!* (Havana: Editorial de Ciencias Sociales, 1986); and Raúl Aguiar Rodríguez, *El bonchismo y el gansterismo en Cuba* (Havana: Editorial de Ciencias Sociales, 2000). For a general overview of corruption as a social issue, see Michael Clarke, ed., *Corruption: Causes, Consequences and Control* (New York: St. Martin's Press, 1983).

47. U.S. military intelligence reported on the crisis in a series of already cited dispatches of May 31 and June 2, 1937. See note 23 above.

48. Acosta Rubio, *Ensayo biográfico Batista*, 222, writes that the remarks were made in a speech on January 10, 1938. In Spanish the quote reads as follows: "No soy amante de la tiranía y en ello se han equivocado los que pensaron que el Congreso iba a desaparecer y que inmediatamente surgiría una dictadura. . . . Jamás abrigué esa idea."

49. Stories about the resignation of House President Carlos Márquez Sterling ran in the Cuban media in February 1938, but they do not even hint at the terrifying series of events that led to his departure. Fortunately, Sumner Welles preserved a detailed, four-page letter from Márquez Sterling recounting the events. The document is invaluable in evoking a sense of the political terror of the period. My account of the events comes largely from the letter; Carlos Márquez Sterling to Welles, February 8, 1937, Welles Papers, Latin America files, 1919–1943, Cuba, 1936–1937. Márquez Sterling (1898–1991), an active member of Congress throughout the Batista era, makes no mention of the incident in his book. After the fall of Batista, he went into exile in the United States, where he died.

50. They were not members of the same political party. Márquez Sterling was in the Liberal Party at the time.

51. The translation is not a literal one, but rather attempts to capture the overall meaning of Márquez Sterling's letter. The full sentence, with the quoted phrase, reads: "En el curso de una de estas interrupciones, declare que yo habia admirado al Coronel Batista por sus condiciones personales, pues se habia sabido hacer de abajo-arriba, que siendo hombre de extraccion humilde, habia sabido llegar muy alto, pero que esta admiracion habia desaparecido, porque en realidad, si el Coronel Batista habia conseguido el orden, hoy estaba convertido en el primer pertubardor de Cuba." (Márquez Sterling did not use accents in the letter to Welles.)

52. This is how Maj. E. W. Timberlake, military attaché, described Captain Hernández; Cuba (Political), "Present Members of Advisory Councils," August 11, 1937, file 2657-384 (1).

53. The information on Hernández's life comes from a short biography written by Maj. E. W. Timberlake, military attaché, Cuba (Combat-Army), "Who's Who on Commissioned Personnel," G-2 Report, June 2, 1937, file 2012-168 (1). In November 1937, Hernández was reportedly sent to Oriente Province to discipline a disobedient lieutenant colonel. In the process, Hernández may have shot the colonel in the leg;

Cuba (Combat-Army), "Loyalty, Discipline and Morale," G-2 Report, November 19, 1937, file 2012-133 (83). Adam y Silva, *La gran mentira*, 442, comments on Hernández's unsavory reputation and his visit to see Márquez Sterling. The political opposition would have loved to get their hands on Hernández. On one occasion, Hernández was attacked by four Auténticos in Miami, while en route to West Point; Caffery to State Department, June 10, 1935, Confidential U.S. Diplomatic Post Records: Cuba, Part 1, 1930–1939.

54. Juan Reporter, "El 'Adiós a la vida' de la Cámara," *Bohemia*, September 26, 1937; and Juan Reporter, "12 meses de actualidad política," *Bohemia*, January 9, 1938.

55. Emilio Núñez Portuondo, a member of Brú's cabinet, described the president's congressional strategy to Ambassador Wright; Wright to Welles, October 31, 1939, Welles Papers, Office Correspondence, 1920–1943, Wright, J. Butler, September–November 1939.

56. Suárez-Rivas, *Un pueblo crucificado*, 109–131, details the struggles of the antimilitary opposition.

57. The divisions in the Liberal Party are laid out in great clarity in a series of letters and memorandums received by Welles in the spring of 1937; Matthews to Welles, March 31, 1937, Welles Papers, Office Correspondence, 1920–1943, Matthews, H. Freeman, 1937. Included in this letter from Matthews is a two-page memo by Liberal Senator José Manuel Casanova. Also of great insight is an eight-page, undated, memorandum written by another Liberal Senator, Manuel B. Capestany; in Office Correspondence, 1920–1943, Godoy, Raul, 1937.

58. Phillips, *Cuba: Island of Paradox*, 183, makes reference to the "three hundred-year plan."

59. The Interior Ministry of the Cuban government published a 415-page book that included the Triennial Plan and transcripts of many government meetings debating it; *Líneas básicas del programa del Plan Trienal* (Havana: Carasa y Cía, 1937).

60. J.I.R., "El Coronel Batista expone al Dr. José I. Rivero, en una transcendental entrevista, un vasto plan, ya en marcha, de amplia reconstrucción y de equilibrio social," *Diario de la Marina*, June 20, 1937.

61. The quote comes from the already cited article. In Spanish Batista's quote reads: "Hay muchos que quieren ignorar que yo soy el jefe de un movimiento revolucionario constructivo. Otros quieren ver en mí simple cancerbero del orden. Pero ¿que entienden por el orden? Porque de éste yo poseo un concepto más propio de la arquitectura que de la gendarmería."

62. Miguel Coyula, "Movimiento de opinión," *Bohemia*, July 18, 1937. Others expressing similar sentiments were sometime ally, sometime foe, Sergio Carbó, "La oposición opina sobre las últimas declaraciones del Coronel Batista," *Bohemia*, May 15, 1938; and Alejandro Vergara, "Mis puntos de vista sobre las declaraciones del Cnel. Batista," *Bohemia*, May 22, 1938.

63. Raymond Leslie Buell, "El Plan Batista," *Bohemia*, August 15, 1937.

64. Batista's speech was published verbatim in *Diario de la Marina*, " 'En nuestro plan no hay fascismo ni comunismo; Es cubano-nacionalista,' dijo el Cnel. Batista," November 21, 1937. The quoted excerpt in Spanish reads: "Nosotros estamos queriendo, aun con el uniforme puesto, mantenernos en el plano del respeto y del derecho ciudadanos; con el uniforme puesto mantenernos y desenvolvernos dentro del cuadro democrático."

65. Cuban Ambassador Pedro Martínez Fraga told Welles that finances were

central to the withdrawal of the Triennial Plan. A memorandum of conversation, dated May 5, 1938, makes the following observation: "The Ambassador said that the financial and economic situation of Cuba, however, was such that there simply was not money enough available to go ahead with the plan and that under these conditions it had necessarily been the wisest policy to make it known that nothing further would be done with the plan for the time being"; U.S. State Dept., memorandum of conversation, May 5, 1938, Welles Papers, Latin America files, 1919–1943, Cuba, January–September 1938. Maj. E. W. Timberlake, military attaché, likewise writes that economics were a major factor in the shelving of the Triennial Plan; Cuba (Political), "Political Issues and Problems," G-2 Report, May 11, 1938, file 2657-330 (400) RG 165.

66. Whitney, *State and Revolution in Cuba*, 157–165, provides an overview of the land reform measure and the sugar legislation, which were central components of the Triennial Plan. Portell-Vilá, *Nueva historia*, 478, makes note of the popular saying regarding Batista's land reform measure.

67. Nearly seventy years later, this form of health-care coverage is not guaranteed in many nations of the world, including the United States.

68. The text of the bill was published in the *Gaceta oficial*, September 3, 1937, 3,794–3,803.

69. There are many fine works on the Cuban sugar industry and on economic relations between the *colonos* and mills. See Ramiro Guerra, *Azúcar y población en las Antillas* (Havana: Editorial de Ciencias Sociales, 1970); Fernando Ortiz Fernández, *Cuban Counterpoint: Tobacco and Sugar* (New York: Alfred A. Knopf, 1947); and Juan Martínez-Alier and Verena Martínez-Alier, *Cuba: Economía y sociedad* (Paris: Editorial Ruedo Ibérico, 1972). For a more recent work, see Antonio Santamaría García, *Sin azúcar no hay país: La industria azucarera y la economía cubana (1919–1939)* (Seville: Secretariado de Publicaciones de la Universidad de Sevilla, 2001).

70. The observation from Ambassador Fraga comes from the U.S. State Dept., memorandum of conversation, May 5, 1938, Welles Papers, Latin America files, 1919–1943, Cuba, January–September 1938. Vega Cobiellas, *General Fulgencio Batista Zaldívar*, 85–86, includes a lengthy excerpt of Batista's comments given on May 14, 1938.

CHAPTER 13. ROAD TO DEMOCRACY

1. *Bohemia* ran three pages of stories and photos on the assassination of Marianao Mayor Pedro Acosta; "El asesinato de Pedro Acosta," January 29, 1939. Details of the murder of the two Joven Cuba members were sent to Washington in a dispatch by embassy First Secretary Willard L. Beaulac; Beaulac to Secty. of State, November 2, 1939, Dept. of State, decimal file, 1930–1939, file 837.00/8569 RG 59. Modesto Maidique was gunned down, evidently as a result of an electoral dispute, on January 13, 1941. Congressman Gilberto Pardo Machado was killed on June 26, 1941. Mario Riera Hernández, *Cuba política, 1899–1955* (Havana: Impresora Modelo, 1955), 487–488, provides information on both killings. I have noted throughout this work the numerous attempts to assassinate Batista, including the plot by Guiteras in November 1933. Threats were made against his life prior to the delivery of his speech at the Tropical Stadium in support of the Triennial Plan in November 1937. Batista made note of the threat in his speech; *Diario de la Marina*, " 'En nuestro plan

no hay fascismo ni comunismo,' dijo el Cnel. Batista," November 21, 1937. Assassination would become a political art form in the 1940s and 1950s as *gansterismo* flourished on the island. Each political party supported political action groups at the University of Havana that regularly killed members of the opposition.

2. U.S. Ambassador George S. Messersmith, who replaced Butler Wright after his unexpected death in December 1939, made this assertion on many occasions in his private correspondence and in his diplomatic dispatches; Messersmith to Secty. of State, July 9, 1940, Dept. of State, decimal file, 1940–1944, file 837.00/8802 RG 59; also, Messersmith to Welles, July 6, 1940, Welles Papers, Office Correspondence, 1920–1943, Messersmith, G., July 1940. On several occasions, Caffery had made similar observations about Grau's enormous electoral appeal. In an October 22, 1934, letter to Welles, Caffery observed that had a presidential election been held on any day since Grau's removal from office in January 1934 "without question Grau would have won them by colossal majorities"; Caffery to Welles, October 22, 1934, Welles Papers, "Major Correspondents, 1920–1950," Jefferson Caffery, September–October 1934.

3. "He renunciado al CND para considerarme patriótica y legalmente en absoluta libertad," *Bohemia*, May 9, 1937. In this article Menocal explains his reasons for resigning from the Conjunto.

4. Others have reached the conclusion that the lingering bitterness between Grau and the Communists hindered the possibility of a political alliance; see Whitney, *State and Revolution in Cuba*, 167.

5. The difference in style between Caffery and Wright is substantial and evident in their respective correspondence with Welles. Caffery acted as he saw fit and in line with his interpretation of U.S. interests. Rarely did he seek guidance from Welles. Wright, on the other hand, repeatedly sought Welles's permission to act, and in many of his discussions with Batista he made it clear that he was simply a conduit of information for Welles. The report of the conversation on lobbying Cuban legislators comes from Wright to Welles, March 17, 1939, Welles Papers, Office Correspondence, 1920–1943, Wright, J. Butler, January–March 1939. In the letter, Wright went on to say that he would do some quiet lobbying "through reliable third parties."

6. When Caffery first arrived in Cuba, it was Reyes Spíndola who introduced him to Batista. The three men went for occasional horseback rides together in the countryside; Philip F. Dur, "Conditions for Recognition," *Foreign Service Journal* 62 (September 1985): 45. Reyes Spíndola and the activities of the Mexican diplomatic delegation were prominently featured in the pages of *Noticias de Hoy*, the Communist Party newspaper that Batista allowed to open as negotiations were under way on May 16, 1938.

7. There are a number of excellent works on the expropriation of the oil properties by the Cárdenas government. One of the classic studies belongs to Lorenzo Meyer, *Mexico and the United States in the Oil Controversy, 1917–1942*, trans. Muriel Vasconcellos (Austin: University of Texas Press, 1977). For a more recent work, see Jonathan C. Brown, *Oil and Revolution in Mexico* (Berkeley: University of California Press, 1993).

8. "This is a continuation of the effort to win Batista to Mexico and away from the United States," the U.S. military attaché reported in a December 14, 1938, dispatch to Washington. "No opportunity is lost"; Maj. Henry A. Barber Jr., Cuba (Comments on Current Events), "Cuban-Mexican Relations," file 2056-250 (1). Rubén de León,

El origen del mal: Cuba, un ejemplo (Coral Gables, Fla.: Service Offset Printers, 1964), 312–313, states that President Cárdenas denied a request by the Auténticos for weapons and refused to allow them to establish a military camp in the state of Quintana Roo. U.S. Ambassador Wright took particular notice of a framed and autographed photo of President Cárdenas in Batista's office and suggested to the military attaché that the colonel should be provided one of Roosevelt as well; Wright to Barber, November 8, 1938, Confidential U.S. Diplomatic Post Records: Cuba, Part 1, 1930–1939, University Publications of America, Frederick, Md.

9. Born Francisco Calderío, Blas Roca (1908–1987), would later change his name. The longtime chairman of the Cuban Communist Party would survive well into the Castro era. He remained a member of the Party's Politburo and Central Committee until a year before his death.

10. Whitney, *State and Revolution in Cuba*, 169, says the first meeting between Batista and the two Communists may have occurred as early as January 15, 1938. This is significantly earlier than originally thought. Robert J. Alexander, *Communism in Latin America* (New Brunswick, N.J.: Rutgers University Press, 1957), 278, writes that an invitation by Batista to the two Communist leaders did not occur until July 1938. It is possible to reconcile the two dates if one considers the possibility that earlier secret meetings were held to pave the way for the July 1938 meeting in which the parameters of the alliance were formalized. García Montes and Alonso Avila, *Partido Comunista*, 196–208, are vague when it comes to providing exact dates for the meetings, although they cite Reyes Spíndola as a key go-between, 196. Suárez Rivas, *Un pueblo crucificado*, 148, notes the importance of the Mexican diplomat in fostering the negotiations. The issue of dates underlines the need for a thorough scholarly study of the issue.

11. The alliance between Batista and the Communists is a politically inconvenient one, both for the Cuban Revolution and for members of the Cuban exile community who considered themselves *batistianos*. As a result, it has been largely ignored in the historiography. Cuban scholarship would greatly benefit from an in-depth study of the alliance.

12. García Montes and Alonso Avila, *Partido Comunista*, 179, write that Roca made the remarks in 1936 at a plenum of the Central Committee.

13. García Montes and Alonso Avila, *Partido Comunista*, 198–201, discuss the language used by the party to justify an alliance with Batista.

14. García Montes and Alonso Avila, *Partido Comunista*, 201, give the names of several party defectors.

15. Acosta Rubio, *Ensayo biográfico Batista*, 238–240, duplicates substantial portions of the correspondence. Verdeja, a senator from Matanzas Province, led the Conjunto revolt against Menocal's leadership.

16. There are dozens of reports on Communist activities in Cuba during the period from 1938 through 1944. Batista's interactions with Communist Party leaders were closely monitored, and informants occasionally obtained correspondence between the two parties and sent it on to the FBI. See, for example, John Edgar Hoover to Brig. Gen. Sherman Miles, Military Intelligence Division, September 5, 1940, file 2657-330 (437-A), RG 165; and Hoover to Adolf A. Berle Jr., Military Intelligence Division, February 10, 1941, file 2657-330 (431), RG 165.

17. One such case was his November 5, 1939, speech in the city of Matanzas.

Ambassador Wright noted that Batista supporters blamed the colonel's desire to garner electoral support for the Communists for the harsh anti-U.S. tone of the speech; Wright to Secty. of State, November 7, 1939, Dept. of State, decimal file, 1930–1939, file 837.00/8576 RG 59.

18. Wright to Secty. of State, November 10, 1939, Dept. of State, decimal file, 1930–1939, file 837.00/8580 RG 59.

19. Col. Egon R. Tausch, military attaché, "Growing Power of Communism in Cuba," February 23, 1944, folder 000.1 Cuba, RG 319.

20. Batista, *Piedras y leyes*, 54–55 and 424–425, argues the alliance with the Communists was the result of a worldwide effort to unite against the Axis powers. He notes that the United States was allied with the Soviet Union. He makes a similar argument in *Paradojas*, 35.

21. U.S. Dept. of State, memorandum of conversation, November 10, 1938, Welles Papers, Latin America files, 1919–1943, Cuba, November–December 1938.

22. Wright to Welles, April 18, 1939, Welles Papers, Office Correspondence, 1920–1943, Wright, J. Butler, April–June 1939.

23. U.S. Naval Attaché Ross E. Rowell took note of the large numbers of Communists present at a Batista campaign rally in November 1939. "The largest group in the parade, which was nearly as large as the rest of the entire parade put together, was that of the Communist Party." Rowell concluded his dispatch by noting: "Unless Colonel Batista checks the growing activities of the Communists it is considered likely that he will soon find a very delicate and serious labor situation on his hands"; Rowell, naval attaché, Cuba (Political), "Political Forces," November 10, 1939, Military Intelligence Division, regional file, 1922–1944, folder 3000-Cuba, RG 165. Many others took note of the high visibility of the Communists at Batista rallies, including Acosta Rubio, *Ensayo biográfico Batista*, 231; and García Montes and Alonso Avila, *Partido Comunista*, 222.

24. U.S. Dept, of State, memorandum of conversation, October 18, 1938, Welles Papers, Latin America files, 1919–1943, Cuba, October–November 1938. Cuban Ambassador Pedro Martínez Fraga told Welles that Batista had declined the invitation.

25. Read, "Civic-Military Rural Education," 183–184.

26. Ambassador Wright does not reveal the name of the informant in his dispatch to Washington; Wright to Secty. of State, September 2, 1939, Welles Papers, Office Correspondence, 1920–1943, Wright, J. Butler, September–November 1939. The chief of Mexico's cultural mission to Cuba suggested the expropriation of sugar properties in June 1938; Portell-Vilá, *Nueva historia*, 491–492, discusses the issue. The issue of possible expropriations was also raised in the North American media; see, for example, J. P. McEvoy, "Not All Rum and Rumba," *Saturday Evening Post*, May 20, 1939. Vega Cobiellas, *Batista y Cuba*, 40–41, clearly sees Batista's trip to Mexico as a sign of Cuba's growing independence from the United States.

27. Scarcely a day went by when *Noticias de Hoy* did not run a glowing article about some aspect of the Mexican government, President Cárdenas, or Mexican culture; see, for example, Juan Marinello, "Comentario: Otro ejemplo mexicano," May 16, 1938; or "El gesto de México señala el principio de la libertad económica de la América," May 17, 1938.

28. I draw much of my information on the Auténticos in this period from León, *Origen del mal*. For information on the Grau-Prío split, see 314–315.

29. The León-Batista confrontation is recounted in this work, Chapter 7. The *civilista-militarista* conflict is chronicled in León, *Origen del mal*, 317–319.

30. In his work, León, perhaps writing from memory, states that the negotiations took place in December 1938. The negotiations with Spíndola occurred in the summer of 1938. Contemporary accounts of events make the timetable clear. In November 1938, when Batista visits Washington, he alludes to the split among the Auténticos. León also notes that the negotiations occurred while Grau was still in exile. Grau returned in early December 1938. For a contemporary account, see Miguel Coyula, "La voz de Grau San Martín," *Bohemia*, September 11, 1938.

31. León, *Origen del mal*, 320–324, details the Spíndola meetings.

32. León, *Origen del mal*, 324, writes of his favorable impression of the proposed deal. A third meeting with Spíndola and a committee of party members was held so that the diplomat could repeat the offer of an alliance with the Auténticos. Those present at the third meeting included Sergio Carbó, Enrique de la Hoza, Oscar de la Torre, Rodolfo Méndez Peñate, and Félix Hurtado.

33. León, *Origen del mal*, 324–325.

34. León, *Origen del mal*, 326, states that the other party members in attendance were Carbó, Oscar de la Torre, and Armando Roda.

35. Batista's remarks to the press and some of the circumstances surrounding the closure of *La Prensa* were detailed in two State Department dispatches by Willard L. Beaulac, chargé d'affaires ad interim; Beaulac to Secty. of State, September 2 and 3, 1938, Confidential U.S. Diplomatic Post Records: Cuba, Part 1, 1930–1939, University Publications of America, Frederick, Md.

36. León, *Origen del mal*, 325–331.

37. U.S. Dept. of State, memorandum of conversation, November 10, 1938, Welles Papers, Latin America files, 1919–1943, Cuba, November–December 1938.

38. For more on Grau's return, see Guillermo Martínez Márquez, "La Habana 1938–1939," *Bohemia*, February 5, 1939. There was a practical reason for Grau's return as well. The electoral census legislation required eligible voters to register by December 12, 1938. Batista's Washington trip dominated the news for several weeks, including the *Bohemia* editions of November 20 and 27 and December 4, 1938.

39. The meeting was widely publicized and commented on; see "Cuatro líderes nacionales en trascendental acuerdo, piden la convocatoria a Constituyente," *Bohemia*, January 8, 1939; and "Editorial," *Bohemia*, January 15, 1939.

40. Gellman, *Roosevelt and Batista*, 182.

41. Ambassador Wright cites several sources of information in his letter to Welles, including prominent American businessman Dayton Hedges and Frank Mahoney, a representative of the Compañía Cubana de Electricidad (Cuban Electric Company); Wright to Welles, April 28, 1939, Welles Papers, Office Correspondence, 1920–1943, Wright, J. Butler, April–June 1939.

42. The informant was Antonio Acosta Rendueles who made the observations about ants and businessmen to American Consul General Coert du Bois. Ambassador Wright forwarded the information to Welles; Wright to Welles, July 27, 1939, Welles Papers, Office Correspondence, 1920–1943, Wright, J. Butler, July–August, 1939.

43. Gellman, *Roosevelt and Batista*, 182.

44. "Habladurías: Volcado el censo electoral en las afiliaciones políticas," *Carteles*, July 30, 1939.

45. "La buena senda," *Carteles*, May 21, 1939.

46. Ambassador Wright clearly thought that Batista was seeking selection to the presidency via the constitutional assembly. "I hardly think that many Cubans give much thought as to whether Batista's election by the Constituent Assembly will be regular or irregular, but almost all of them are convinced that he is going to be elected by some means or other"; Wright to Welles, June 1, 1939, Welles Papers, Office Correspondence, 1920–1943, Wright, J. Butler, April–June 1939. In the same letter, Wright details a conversation with one of Batista's closest civilian advisers, Juan J. Remos, who expressed similar concerns.

47. The Batista press conference was held on April 20, 1939. A partial translation of his comments was sent by Ambassador Wright in a dispatch to Washington and by private letter to Welles; Wright to Secty. of State, April 21, 1939, Welles Papers, Office Correspondence, 1920–1943, Wright, J. Butler, April–June 1939. The quoted remark by Batista was originally made on April 2, 1939, and reiterated at the press conference.

48. Welles could not have been clearer in an April 22, 1939, letter to Wright. "I can only hope that notwithstanding the serious difficulties which have been created for him, Colonel Batista will clearly see that both in his interests and in the interests of Cuba it is imperative that nothing in the nature of a coup d'etat take place. A move of this kind in my judgment would be playing in the hands of his opponents and would inevitably create a situation here which would make it quite impossible for this Government to continue to cooperate in any effective way with the Cuban Government during these coming months when effective cooperation from us is so peculiarly necessary"; Welles to Wright, April 22, 1939, Welles Papers, Office Correspondence, 1920–1943, Wright, J. Butler, April–June 1939. Wright translated the text of Welles's letter on April 24. Confirmation of the delivery of the message was made by Wright in an April 25 letter to Welles.

49. "La pérdida de claridad mental," *Carteles*, May 7, 1939; and "Pobre Constituyente," *Carteles*, August 20, 1939.

50. Batista, *Revolución social*, 131–135. The offending remarks were relatively mild, but Washington was particularly sensitive to criticism from Cuba. In Spanish, the comment on monopolies and unequal treaties, reads as follows: "Vibra el sufrimiento y la desigualdad, cuando el Estado marcha sin rumbo fijo, sin una economía bien organizada, y la industria, desorientada, carece de estímulos, asfixada por los monopolios absorbentes y los tratados desiguales." On the issue of Pan-American solidarity, Batista said: "La unión entre nosotros sólo depende del respeto y de la consideración que nos tengamos. Ni fuertes ni débiles, ni grandes ni pequeños: las naciones son iguales ante el derecho propio."

51. Wright to Secty. of State, September 5, 1939, Dept. of State, decimal file, 1930–1939, file 837.00/8532 RG 59.

52. The debt reduction plan was known variously as the mortgage revaluation, mortgage revalorization, or the mortgage moratorium issue. Working with civilian advisers, Batista drafted a plan in 1938 to address the complicated debt issue. One of the best explanations of the plan was offered by Batista in a series of interviews published in the newspaper *El País* in November 1938 and written by the journalist Enrique Pizzi de Porras. Copies of the newspaper are rare, but Batista gave translated copies of the interview to Welles at the time of his November 1938 Washington

visit; Welles to Ellis Briggs, November 15, 1938, Welles Papers, Latin America files, 1919–1943, Cuba, October–November 1938.

53. What exactly Batista said in the Matanzas speech may never be known with precision. Anticipating a strong response from the United States, official versions of the speech were revised before they were given to the Cuban press for publication; *Carteles*, "El discurso del Coronel Batista," 19 November 1939. Batista's remark about the lack of reciprocity in the Reciprocity Treaty was reported in this editorial ; Wright and other U.S. officials reported at length on the Matanzas speech. Wright's summary of the Matanzas speech comes from Wright to Secty. of State, November 9, 1939, Dept. of State, decimal file, 1930–1939, file 837.00/8579 RG 59. The "half-liberty" reference was made by Military Attaché Henry A. Barber Jr., Cuba (Political), "Foreign Relations,"G-2 Report, file 2657-352 (3).

54. Wright to Secty. of State, November 7, 1939, Dept. of State, decimal file, 1930–1939, file 837.00/8576 RG 59.

55. Grau won seats in Havana, Matanzas, Las Villas, and Oriente, while Menocal won in Pinar del Río, Havana, Las Villas, and Oriente. Gómez won in Havana, Las Villas, and Oriente; "Candidatos a la Constituyente que se estiman electos en las seis provincias," *Diario de la Marina*, November 21, 1939. Suárez Rivas, *Un pueblo crucificado*, 124–125, argues that the placement of opposition leaders on multiple ballots was crucial to their victory. Ultimately, the party leaders each took one seat at the assembly, but the other seats they had secured were doled out to their party members.

56. Riera Hernández, *Cuba política*, 476–482, provides the most comprehensive electoral results.

57. Acosta Rubio, *Ensayo biográfico Batista*, 236–237. Chester, *A Sergeant Named Batista*, 176–177, writes that Batista made the following magnanimous statement: "The elections have been lost. Perhaps that was a good thing. The ballot boxes have been honored and the people have responded, giving a greater number of votes to the opposition. It is true, as has been argued logically by some of our leaders, that the names of national leaders of the opposition, some of them Presidential candidates, were carried on the ballots in six provinces. While this is irregular, to say the least, such an eventuality should have been anticipated in the electoral laws. The laws, in the end, will have to resolve that problem. But the fact is, we've lost the elections." Chester may be overstating Batista's magnanimity. There is no record of such a statement in any of the Cuban newspapers and magazines reviewed for this work. Even *Diario de la Marina*, which was fond of publishing verbatim texts of speeches made no mention of the above remarks. The closest Batista came to conceding defeat was a written statement issued November 23, 1939, in which he praised the troops. In that speech, Batista noted that the election was a victory for the country. "We should not speak of the victorious or the vanquished"; "Cuba anhela una Carta Magna humana, que permita una legislación," *Diario de la Marina*, November 24, 1939.

58. "Nos adherimos," *Carteles*, November 26, 1939. Likewise, *Bohemia* took note of the impartial attitude of the military, although more reserved in its praise; "Editorial," November 26, 1939. *Diario de la Marina*, "Honestidad comicial," November 17, 1939, lauded the honesty of the election. The wire services reported on the orderly nature of the elections. As an example, see "Orderliness of Poll Pleases All Cubans," *New York Times*, November 17, 1939.

59. This alleged attempt at vote tampering is reported by Ambassador Wright in a dispatch to Washington; Wright to Secty. of State, November 24, 1939, Dept. of State, decimal file, 1930–1939, file 837.00/8589 RG 59.

60. R. Hart Phillips, "Batista Men Lose in Cuban Election for New Assembly," *New York Times*, November 20, 1939.

61. Aspects of this meeting were detailed in a dispatch to Washington by Willard L. Beaulac, first secretary of embassy; Beaulac to Secty. of State, November 24, 1939, Dept. of State, decimal file, 1930–1939, file 837.00/8589 RG 59.

62. The legislation was first introduced in the Cuban House in July but stalled there for several months. Final passage in both houses of Congress was completed on November 28, 1939; "Se reformará el retiro de los militares," *El Mundo*, July 26, 1939. *Diario de la Marina* published the full text of the new law on November 29. Portell-Vilá, *Nueva historia*, 496, discusses the law.

63. Maj. Henry A. Barber Jr., military attaché, Cuba (Political), "Pre-Election Activities," August 16, 1939, file 2657-330 (410).

64. McEvoy, "Not All Rum and Rumba," *Saturday Evening Post*, May 20, 1939.

65. Batista to Wright, May 8, 1939, Welles Papers, Office Correspondence, 1920–1943, Wright, J. Butler, April–June 1939. Batista was provided advance copies of the article. The letter from Batista was enclosed with another letter from Wright to Welles, dated May 16, 1939, describing the incident. Like Barber, Menocal thought Batista would lose control of the army if he resigned to run for the presidency. Menocal relayed this belief to a visiting U.S. official; Wright to Welles, August 24, 1939, Welles Papers, Office Correspondence, 1920–1943, Wright, J. Butler, July–August 1939.

66. Some details of the murder of the storekeeper are provided by the U.S. Embassy and the military attaché's office in a series of dispatches to Washington; Beaulac to Secty. of State, August 9, 1939, Dept. of State, decimal file, 1930–1939, file 837.20/143 RG 59. See also Col. Henry A. Barber Jr., military attaché, Cuba (Who's Who), "Who's Who on Lt. Col. Manuel Benítez y Valdez, Chief of Police," May 16, 1941, file 2012-168 (3); and Barber, Cuba (Comments on Current Events), "Changes in Regimental Commanders," July 28, 1939, file 2056-250 (7).

67. Fulgencio Rubén Batista Godínez, correspondence to author, October 11, 2003.

68. "Discurso del Coronel Batista," *Diario de la Marina*, December 7, 1939.

69. Ibid.

70. Batista's eldest son, Fulgencio Rubén, writes that he never saw his father in uniform after his retirement from the army. "Cuando mi padre dejó el ejército, no volvió a usar uniforme nunca más"; Fulgencio Rubén Batista Godínez, correspondence to author, October 11, 2003. His father did keep and frame two pairs of his sergeant stripes, one of which he always kept in his study. Batista's eldest daughter made a similar observation. "Mi padre jamás volvió a usar un uniforme después que se retiró y menos tenerlo en su closet"; Mirta Batista Ponsdomenech, correspondence to author, October 22, 2003.

71. Beaulac laid out the details of Brú's plan in a January 11, 1940, letter to Welles in which he attached a State Department dispatch of the same date; Welles Papers, Office Correspondence, 1920–1943, Beaulac, William, 1940. The status of the political negotiations was a frequent topic in the private correspondence between U.S. Ambassador George Messersmith, who replaced Butler Wright after his death in December 1939, and Under Secretary Welles. Of particular value are Messersmith's

letters to Welles of April 2, 4, and 9, 1940, Welles Papers, Office Correspondence, 1920–1943, Messersmith, G., March–April 1940. The importance of the prohibition against ballot splitting cannot be overstated; see Suárez Rivas, *Un pueblo crucificado*, 127–128; and Portell-Vilá, *Nueva historia*, 499.

72. "Cordialidad y buenas palabras," *Carteles*, April 14, 1940. For another perspective, see Teodorico Raposo, "Grau y Batista llegaron juntos," *Bohemia*, April 14, 1940. Some of the final details had been worked out by Grau, Batista, and Brú at a private meeting held two days earlier; Messersmith to Secty. of State, April 4, 1940, Confidential U.S. Post Records: Cuba, Part 1, 1930–1939, University Publications of America, Frederick, Md. Batista's quote to the press comes from a follow-up dispatch by Messersmith on April 6, 1940.

73. An article in *Carteles* noted that the government parties (Liberals, Nacionalistas, and the Conjunto), plus the parties of Menocal and Gómez, and a small splinter party (the Populares) received 608,997 votes, while the left-of-center parties (revolucionarios), the Auténticos, the Communists, the ABC, Realistas, and the tiny Agrarian Party received 399,781 votes. There is considerable room for debate over which party falls into which category, but clearly the results indicate a conservative majority; "Las elecciones constituyentes," November 26, 1939.

74. As noted in chapter 10, Batista engineered a deal in 1936 granting Menocal's party minority representation in the Senate, despite the fact it had lost every Senate race.

75. U.S. Chargé d'Affaires Willard Beaulac informed Welles of the negotiations between Menocal and Batista in a letter dated January 19, 1940. The information was relayed to Welles at the request of the Cuban Ambassador to the United States, Pedro Martínez Fraga; Welles Papers, Office Correspondence, 1920–1943, Beaulac, Willard, 1940.

76. Menocal's efforts to get the United States to pressure Batista to resign were detailed in numerous State Department dispatches; Messersmith to Secty. of State, March 9, 1940, Dept. of State, decimal file, 1940–1944, file 837.00/8695 RG 59; and Beaulac to Secty. of State, March 11, 1940, Dept. of State, decimal file, 1940–1944, file 837.00/8697 RG 59.

77. The internal party debates were related in great detail by two prominent party leaders, Gustavo Cuervo Rubio and Antonio Acosta, to U.S. Consul General Coert du Bois and relayed to the embassy in memorandums dated March 6 and 13, 1940. The two memorandums were in turn forwarded to Washington by the ambassador; Messersmith to Secty. of State, March 14, 1940, Dept. of State, decimal file, 1940–1944, file 837.00/8699 RG 59.

78. These observations by prominent Menocal supporters were cited in the aforementioned memorandums of Coert du Bois.

79. Suárez Rivas, *Un pueblo crucificado*, 125–126, notes the importance of the visit. He writes that the terms of the alliance were negotiated over various meetings at the home of Batista political adviser Jaime Mariné.

80. As a courtesy, the Batista-Menocal delegates allowed Grau to stay on as president of the constitutional assembly. He formally stepped down some weeks later to dedicate himself to the presidential campaign.

81. The manifesto was published in its entirety by *Diario de la Marina*, March 31, 1940.

82. Messersmith claimed that Batista "bitterly" resented having to use his own personal funds and was angry that requests for loans from American banks to fund his campaign were rejected; Messersmith to Welles, July 12, 1940, Messersmith Papers, University of Delaware, Newark, Del., item 1390.

83. Acosta Rubio, *Ensayo biográfico Batista*, 243–244, provides the anecdotes on the "Train of Victory."

84. This information was provided by a North American railroad executive to U.S. Naval and Air Attaché Hayne D. Boyden and passed onto the embassy in a July 6, 1940 report; Dept. of State, decimal file, 1940–1944, file 837.00/8827 RG 59.

85. The anecdote about Batista's eating habits comes from his son Jorge Batista Fernández; interview and notes by author, New York City, July 23 and 25, 2001.

86. Phillips, *Cuba: Island of Paradox*, 198.

87. A copy of the report was provided to Ambassador Messersmith, who relayed it to Washington; Messersmith to Secty. of State, July 9, 1940, Dept. of State, decimal file, 1940–1944, file 837.00/8802.

88. Portell-Vilá, *Nueva historia*, 500, cites the squabbling and Grau's selection of a vice presidential candidates as key factors in his defeat. "Martínez Sáenz en la Vice," *Bohemia*, March 31, 1940, provides a brief overview of the vice presidential candidates considered by Grau.

89. R. Hart Phillips, "Col. Batista Claims Cuban Presidency; Clashes Mar Vote," *New York Times*, July 15, 1940.

90. Eddy Chibás, "La brava, los recursos y la toma de posesión," *Luz*, September 25, 1940. A copy of this article was included in a dispatch by Beaulac to Secty. of State, September 26, 1940, Dept. of State, decimal file, 1940–1944, file 837.00/8849 RG 59.

91. Riera Hernández, *Cuba política*, 491–512, provides the results for every race on the island.

92. Beaulac to Secty. of State, July 20, 1940, Dept. of State, decimal file, 1940–1944, file 837.00/8809 RG 59. Military Attaché Maj. Henry A. Barber Jr. writes in a July 17 report to the War Department: "In general, however, the army succeeded in aiding the Batista machine, partly by intimidation, partly by persuasion, and partly by preventing opposition candidates from getting to the polls"; Cuba (Pre-Election Activities), "Activities Prior to Presidential Election," file 2657-330 (425).

93. Batista would claim victory in presidential elections in 1954 and 1958, but those campaigns were in the midst of the Cuban Revolution, during which much of the body politic abstained in dissent.

94. The story of their first meeting was widely told and retold in Cuba. Jorge Batista Fernández, the eldest child of Fulgencio Batista and Marta Fernández, believes it to be an accurate account; Jorge Batista Fernández, interview and notes by author, New York City, July 23 and 25, 2001. Chester, *A Sergeant Named Batista*, 23–24, was evidently given this same account by Fulgencio Batista.

95. Jorge Batista Fernández says his mother had a miscarriage in 1941, a year before he was born; interview and notes by author, New York City, July 23 and 25, 2001. Mirta Batista Ponsdomenech says she learned of the affair between her father and Marta Fernández in 1938 or 1939; interview by author, tape recording, Miami, May 20, 1998.

96. There are any number of accounts of Castro's early life. One of the best is contained in the biography by Robert Quirk, *Fidel Castro* (New York: W. W. Norton, 1993), 3–30. See also Tad Szulc, *Fidel: A Critical Portrait* (New York: Morrow, 1986); and Lionel Martin, *The Early Fidel: Roots of Castro's Communism* (Secaucus, N.J.: Lyle Stuart, 1978).

BIBLIOGRAPHY

ARCHIVES

Batista Photo Album Collection. Biblioteca Nacional José Martí, Havana, Cuba.

Caffery, Jefferson. Papers. University of Southwestern Louisiana, Lafayette, La.

Cuban Field Committee. Lilly Library, Earlham College, Richmond, Ind.

Grau de Agüero, Polita. Papers. Cuban Heritage Collection, University of Miami, Coral Gables, Fla.

Messersmith, George. Papers. University of Delaware Library, Newark, Del.

Roosevelt, Franklin D. Presidential Papers. Presidential Library, Hyde Park, N.Y.

U.S. Department of State. Decimal File, 1930-1939. Record Group 59. Washington, D.C.: National Archives.

U.S. Diplomatic Post Records. *Cuba, Part I, 1930-1939.* Frederick, Md.: University Publications of America, Microfilm.

U.S. Military Intelligence Division. Correspondence and Record Cards, 1918-1941. Record Group 165. Washington, D.C.: National Archives.

GOVERNMENT PUBLICATIONS

Cuba. *Census of the Republic of Cuba, 1919.* Havana, Maza, Arroyo y Caso, S en C.

———. *Constitution of 1940.* Library of Congress, Washington D.C.

———. *Gaceta Oficial de la República de Cuba, 1933-1940.* New York Public Library, New York.

———. *Líneas básicas del programa del Plan Trienal.* Havana, Carasa y Cía, 1937.

U.S. Department of Foreign Relations. *Foreign Relations of the United States, 1933.* Diplomatic Papers. The American Republics, vol. 5. Washington, D.C.: Government Printing Office, 1952.

———. *Foreign Relations of the United States, 1934.* Diplomatic Papers. The American Republics, vol. 5. Washington, D.C.: Government Printing Office, 1952.

―――. *Foreign Relations of the United States, 1935.* Diplomatic Papers. The American Republics, vol. 4. Washington, D.C.: Government Printing Office, 1953.

―――. *Foreign Relations of the United States, 1938.* Diplomatic Papers. The American Republics, vol. 5. Washington, D.C.: Government Printing Office, 1956.

―――. *Foreign Relations of the United States, 1939.* Diplomatic Papers. The American Republics, vol. 5. Washington, D.C.: Government Printing Office, 1957.

―――. *Foreign Relations of the United States, 1940.* Diplomatic Papers. The American Republics, vol. 5. Washington, D.C.: Government Printing Office, 1961.

INTERVIEWS

Batista Fernández, Robert, Elisa Aleida Batista Godínez, and Fulgencio Rubén Batista Godínez. Interview by author. Tape recording. Coral Gables, Fla., 23 April 1998.

Dur, Philip F. Interview by author. Notes. Lafayette, La., 4 and 5 April 1998.

Durand, Juana Pérez. Interview by author. Notes. Banes, Cuba, 21 April 1999.

Fernández, Jorge Batista. Interview by author. Notes. New York, N.Y., 23 and 25 July 2001.

Godínez, Fulgencio Rubén Batista. "The Young Batista." Interview by author. Tape recording. Coral Gables, Fla., 30 April 1998.

―――."The Military Speaks." Interview by author. Tape recording. Coral Gables, Fla., 19 May 1998.

Perna, Santiago Rey. Interview by author. Tape recording. Miami, Fla., 28 March 1997.

―――. Interview by author. Tape recording. Miami, Fla., 29 April 1998.

Ponsdomenech, Mirta Batista. Interview by author. Tape recording. Miami, Fla., 27 March 1997.

―――. Interview by author. Tape recording. Miami, Fla., 20 May 1998.

de Quesada, Arístides Sosa. Interview by author. Tape recording. Miami, Fla., 18 May 1998.

NEWSPAPERS AND MAGAZINES

Bohemia

"El mortero que dejó insostenible la defensa de Atarés," November 19, 1933.

Miguel Angel Quevedo. "Glosando las declaraciones de un coronel," December 10, 1933.

"Dolorosas realidades," January 7, 1934.

"El último día del Presidente Grau en Palacio," January 21, 1934.

Levi Marrero. "Cuatro horas sin presidente," January 28, 1934.

Rubén de León. "La verdad de lo ocurrido desde el cuatro de septiembre," February 4, 1934.

Mario Torres Menier. "Mi Diario," February 25, 1934.

―――. "Mi Diario―La Toma del Hotel Nacional," March 4, 1934.

Antonio Guiteras. "Septembrismo," April 1, 1934.

Miguel de Marcos. "La chicharra de Ulsiceno," June 10 1934.

José M. Irisarri. "Cómo nació y cómo murió la Comisión Ejecutiva," August 26, 1934.

"En las orillas del abismo," February 17, 1935.

"El problema escolar," February 24, 1935.

"La verdad y nada más que la verdad," December 1, 1935.

América Ana Cuervo. "Mejoramiento de la vivienda campesina," June 21, 1936.

Miguel Coyula. "El equilibrio de los poderes," June 28, 1936.

"Cómo ha organizado el Ejército de Cuba la educación cívico-militar," September 6, 1936.

Sergio Carbó. "La oposición opina sobre las últimas declaraciones del Coronel Batista," May 15,1938.

Juan J. Remos. "La Gestión Personal del Coronel Batista," June 5, 1938.

Eddy Chibás. "Los gobiernos de Cuba: Grau San Martín (1933–1934)," June 5, 1938.

Guillermo Martínez Márquez. "Cordialidad sin presupuesto," September 11, 1938.

Teodorico Raposo. "Grau y Batista llegaron juntos," April 14, 1940.

Jorge Quintana. "La muerte de Antonio Guiteras," September 29, 1946.

Carteles

"Carteleras," August 27, 1933.

Tomás Yanes. "Los psychoses del Hotel Nacional," December 17, 1933.

"El bombardeo de Columbia," December 17, 1933.

"San Ambrosio por la Revolución," December 17, 1933.

"Atarés: El relato de un combatiente," December 17, 1933.

"La muerte de Blas Hernández," December 17, 1933.

Damon Runyon. "Batista, el 'Amo' de Cuba," February 18, 1934.

Rubén de León. "Ultimos días del gobierno de Grau San Martín," March 11, 1934

"Regresión barbárica," April 15, 1934.

"La derogación de la Enmienda Platt," June 17, 1934.

"Paz y justicia," September 9, 1934.

"Atropello al Director de 'Bohemia,'" October 14, 1934.

"La huelga del lunes," October 14, 1934.

"Una labor de positive mérito," November 22, 1936.

"La union por la doctrina," March 7, 1937.

"Pobre Constituyente," August 20, 1939.

"El veto del Ejecutivo," October 29, 1939.

"Deber y responsibilidad de la ciudadania," November 12, 1939.

"El discurso del Coronel Batista," November 19, 1939.

"Interrogación trascendente," November 26, 1939.

"Las elecciones constituyentes," November 26, 1939.

Denuncia
April 26, 1933.

Diario de la Marina

"Un público numeroso se congrego para saludar al embajador americano," May 8, 1933.

"El sepelio del estudiante Alpízar, el obrero Iglesias y el soldado Hernández," August 20, 1933.

"Ha renunciado la presidencia de la república, Grau San Martín," January 15, 1934.

"Detalles de cómo se produjo la sustitución del ex presidente Dr. Ramón Grau San Martín," January 16, 1934.

"Muy lejano el reconocimiento," January 17, 1934.

"Altos Jefes del Ejército conocían lo que tramaban Hernández, Erice y Echevarría," Auguest 23, 1934.

"El Dr. Joaquín Martínez Sáenz hace unas declaraciones a los periodistas de los E. Unidos," December 14, 1934.

"El Jefe del Ejército hace unas declaraciones en relación con las del Dr. J. Martínez Sáenz," December 16, 1934.

"Señala la Sociedad Económica pautas para contener la decadencia cultural en Cuba," February 6, 1935.

"La Unión Nacional de Maestros se queja de la preterición de que hacen victima al educador," February 10, 1935.

"Perdió la vida anoche un estudiante en una alteración del orden en Monte y Zulueta," February 12, 1935.

"Los huelgistas escolares no han pedido más que materiales para trabajar y mejor desayuno," February 13, 1935.

"Se generaliza la huelga en el Magisterio," February 21, 1935.

"Cree Pelayo Cuervo que la huelga del magisterio quede solucionada mañana viernes," February 28, 1935.

"'Las dictaduras de grupos no pueden continuar agitando al país,' declara el Cor. Batista," March 7, 1935.

"Los huelgistas están equivocados y fracasarán totalmente, afirma el Cor. Batista," March 9,1935.

"Se prepara el decreto que crea institutos y universidades libres," March 19, 1935.

"El Tribunal Superior Electoral dicta importante fallo en relación con la Coalición en La Habana," November 20, 1935.

"Manifiesto del Coronel Mendieta al Pueblo," December 11, 1935.

"Tiene un historial brillante el nuevo Presidente interino," December 12, 1935.

"El Presidente que cesa y el Presidente que comienza," May 20, 1936.

"No hacer es deshacer," July 10, 1936.

J.I.R., "El Coronel Batista expone as Dr. José I. Rivero, en una transcendental entrevista, un vasto plan, ya en marcha, de amplia reconstrucción y de equilibrio social," June 20, 1937.

"'En nuestro plan no hay fascismo ni comunismo; es cubano-nacionalista,' dijo el Cnel. Batista," November 21, 1937.

"Manifestaciones del Presidente de la República," September 15, 1939.

"Honestidad comicial," November 17, 1939.

"Candidatos a la Constituyente que se estiman electos en las seis provincias," November 21, 1939.

"Cuba anhela una Carta Magna humana, que permita une legislación," November 24, 1939.

El Ejército Constitucional
Santiago Torra. "La escuela rural," June 1937.

The Havana Evening Telegram
"Sumner Welles Takes Up Task as U.S. Envoy," May 8, 1933.

The Havana Post
"Government Expected to Adopt More Radical Steps in Future Action," December 12, 1933.
"President Defends Action to Better School Conditions," March 1, 1935.
"Batista Host to U.S. Press," October 8, 1936.

Luz
Chibás, Eddy. "La brava, los recursos y la toma de posesión." September 25, 1940.

Miami Herald
"Well, Welles," November 26, 1933.

El Mundo
"Sumner Welles," May 7, 1933.
"Confía que volverán a sus aulas el lunes," March 1, 1935.
"No existen motivos por el momento para esperar una violenta agresión del Ejército en asuntos políticos," March 2, 1935.

New York Daily News
"Cuba Massacres 200," March 12, 1935
"Guns Can't Run Cars," March 13, 1935.

New York Herald Tribune
Tom Pettey. "Cuban Misery Groans under Iron-Fist Rule," January 25, 1933.
———. "Welles Blamed as Conciliation in Cuba Fail," December 12, 1933.

New York Times
Russell Porter. "Machado Says Foes Stir Cuban Unrest," January 31, 1933.
"New Cuban Treaty," May 31, 1934.
"Castor Oil Forced on Cuban Editors," December 13, 1934.
J. D. Phillips. "Guiteras Is Slain in Battle in Cuba," May 9, 1935.
"Menocal Retires from Cuban Race," December 8, 1935.
Russell Porter. "Gomez Promises Freedom in Cuba," July 4, 1936.
———. "Dual Cuban Regime Denied by Batista," July 5, 1936.
———. "Freed Cuba Comes to Test of People," July 6, 1936.
J. D. Phillips. "Gomez Impeached, 111–45: Ouster in Cuba Held Sure as Senate Overrides Veto," December 22, 1936.
———. "Gomez to Defend Acts in Cuba Today at Trial in Senate," December 23, 1936.
———. "Cuba Inducts Laredo Bru: He Sees an Era of Progress," December 25, 1936.
———. "Batista Gives Aim of Cuban Regime," December 27, 1936.
"Orderliness of Poll Pleases All Cubans," November 17, 1939.
R. Hart Phillips. "Batista Men Lose in Cuban Election for New Assembly," November 20, 1939.
———. "Col. Batista Claims Cuban Presidency; Clashes Mar Vote," July 15, 1940.

Noticias de Hoy
Juan Marinello. "Comentario: Otro ejemplo mexicano," May 16, 1938.

"El gesto de México señala el principio de la libertad económica de la América," May 17, 1938.

Oposición
"Uno del consejo de la Direccíon Corresponsal en Campaña," June 1933.

El País
Ramón Vasconcelos. "El Amigo Ben," December 13, 1933.
"'La Ley del Azúcar quita al que puede unos centavos para dárselos al que por desgracia losnecesita,' dijo Batista," December 19, 1936.
"Sensacional," December 22, 1936.

La Prensa
"'Si es necesario sere dictador'—declara Batista," November 7, 1936.

Saturday Evening Post
"Not All Rum and Rumba," May 20, 1939.

BOOKS AND PERIODICALS

Abendroth, Wolfgang. *A Short History of the European Working Class*. Translated by Nicholas Jacobs and Brian Trench. New York: Monthly Review Press, 1972.
Acosta Rubio, Raoul [Raúl]. *Batista ante la historia: Relato de un civilista*. Havana: Imprenta "La Milagrosa," 1938.
———. *Cuba: Todos culpables (Relato de un testigo: Lo que no se sabe del dictador Batista y su época)*. Miami: Ediciones Universal, 1977.
———. *Ensayo biográfico Batista: Reportaje histórico*. Havana: Ucar García y Cía., 1943.
Adam y Silva, Ricardo. *La gran mentira: 4 de septiembre de 1933*. Havana: Editorial Lex, 1947.
Aguilar, Luis E. *Cuba 1933 Prologue to Revolution*. Ithaca, N.Y.: Cornell University Press, 1972.
Aguiar Rodríguez, Raúl. *El bonchismo y el gansterismo en Cuba*. Havana: Editorial deCiencias Sociales, 2000.
Alba, Víctor. *Historia del frente popular: Análisis de una táctica política*. Mexico City: Libro Mex, 1959.
Alexander, Robert. *Communism in Latin America*. New Brunswick, N.J.: Rutgers University Press, 1957.
———. *A History of Organized Labor in Cuba*. Westport, Conn.: Praeger, 2002.
Alvarez, Vladimir. *Batista: Padre del comunismo*. Havana: Impresora "Daleleña," 1959.
Amat Osorio, Víctor. *Banes (1513–1958): Estampas de mi tierra y de mi sol*. Miami: New Ideas Printing, 1981.
Aparicio Laurencio, Ángel. *Blas Hernández y la Revolución Cubana de 1933*. Miami: Ediciones Universal, 1994.
Argote-Freyre, Frank. "The Political Afterlife of Eduardo Chibás: Evolution of a Symbol, 1951–1991." *Cuban Studies* 32 (2001): 74–97
———. "In Search of Fulgencio Batista: A Reexamination of Prerevolutionary Cuban Historiography." *Revista Mexicana del Caribe* 11 (2001): 193–228

Barnet, Miguel. *Gallego*. Madrid: Ediciones Alfaguara, 1981.

Batista y Godínez, Fulgencio Rubén. *La Revolución del 4 de septiembre de 1933: Síntesis de su proceso histórico, 1933–1944*. Pamphlet. Miami, Fl.: 2003.

Batista y Zaldívar, Fulgencio. *Cuba Betrayed*. New York: Vantage Press, 1962.

———. *Una historia en dos discursos y un artículo*. Two speeches. Havana: Editorial Echevarría.

———. *The Growth and Decline of the Cuban Republic*. Translated by Blas M. Rocafort. New York: The Devin-Adair Company, 1964.

———. *Paradojas*. Mexico City: Ediciones Botas, 1963.

———. *Paradojismo: Cuba, victima de las contradicciones internacionales*, 2nd ed. Mexico City: Ediciones Botas, 1964.

———. *Piedras y leyes: Balance sobre Cuba*. Madrid: Servicio Exterior del Libro Actual, 1963.

———. *Respuesta*. Mexico City: Imp. "Manuel Leon Sanchez," 1960.

———. *Revolución social o política reformista*. Havana: Prensa Indoamericans, 1944.

———. *Sombras de America; problemas económicos y socials*. Mexico City: E.D.I.A.P.S.A., 1946.

Beals, Carleton. *The Crime of Cuba*. Philadelphia: J. B. Lippincott Company, 1934.

———. "Cuba's John Brown." *Common Sense*, July 1935: 6–8.

———. and Clifford Odets. *Rifle Rule in Cuba*. New York: Provisional Committee for Cuba, 1935.

Beaulac, Willard L. *Career Ambassador*. New York: The MacMillan Company, 1951.

Benjamin, Jules Robert. *The United States and Cuba: Hegemony and Dependent Development, 1880-1934*. Pittsburgh: University of Pittsburgh Press, 1977.

Bernstein, Irving. *Turbulent Years: A History of the American Worker, 1933–1941*. Boston: Houghton Mifflin, 1970.

Bowles, Samuel. "Cuban Education and the Revolutionary Ideal." *Harvard Educational Review* 41 (November 1971): 472–500.

Briggs, Ellis. *Farewell to Foggy Bottom: The Recollections of a Career Diplomat*. New York: David McKay Company, Inc., 1964.

Briones Montoto, Newton. *Aquella decisión callada*. Havana: Editorial de Ciencias Sociales, 1998.

Brock, Lisa and Castañeda Fuertes, Digna, eds., *African-Americans and Cuban before the Cuban Revolution*. Philadelphia: Temple University Press, 1998.

Brown, Jonathan C. *Oil and Revolution in Mexico*. Berkeley: University of California Press, 1993.

Buch, Luis. *Un insurrecional en dos épocas: Con Antonio Guiteras y con Fidel Castro*. Interview by Reinaldo Suárez Suárez. Havana: Editorial de Ciencias Sociales, 2001.+

Cabrera, Olga. *Guiteras: La época, el hombre*. Havana: Editorial de Arte y Literatura, 1974.

———. *Guiteras: Su pensamiento revolucionario*. Havana: Editorial de Ciencias Sociales, 1974.

Cairo Ballester, Ana. *La Revolución del 30 en la narrativa y el testimonio cubanos*. Havana: Editorial Letras Cubanas, 1993.

Carrillo, Justo. *Cuba 1933: Students, Yankees and Soldiers*. New Brunswick, N.J.: Transaction Publishers, 1994.

Castro, Fidel. *History Will Absolve Me*. Secaucus, N.J.: Lyle Stuart, 1961.

Chester, Edmund A. *A Sergeant Named Batista*. New York: Henry Holt and Company, 1954.

Cisneros, Rubén. *Biográfia en Poesias del Mayor General Fulgencio Batista: Último Presidente de Cuba Republicana*. Pamphlet, n.d.

Clarke, Michael. *Corruption: Causes, Consequences and Control*. New York: St. Martin's Press, 1983.

Collier, Ruth Berins and David Collier. *Shaping the Political Arena: Critical Junctures, the Labor Movement, and Regime Dynamics in Latin America*. Princeton: Princeton University Press, 1991.

Commission on Cuban Affairs. *Problems of the New Cuba: Report of the Commission on Cuban Affairs*. New York: Foreign Policy Association, 1935.

Conte Agüero, Luis. *Eduardo Chibás: El adalid de Cuba*. Miami: La Moderna Poesía, 1987.

Córdova, Efrén. *Clase trabajadora y movimiento sindical en Cuba (1819–1959)*, vol. 1. Miami: Ediciones Universal, 1995.

Dahlman, Carl. "The Nation-wide Learning System of Cuba," Discussion paper no. 38, Research Program in Economic Development, Woodrow Wilson School, Princeton University, 1973.

Danielson, Ross. *Cuban Medicine*. New Brunswick, N.J.: Transaction Publishers, 1979.

De la Fuente, Alejandro. *A Nation for All. Race, Inequality, and Politics in Twentieth-Century Cuba*. Chapel Hill, N.C.: The University of North Carolina Press, 2001.

De León, Rubén. *El origen del mal: Cuba, un ejemplo*. Coral Gables, Fla.: Service Offset Printers, Inc., 1964.

Díaz-Riquets, Sergio. *The Health Revolution in Cuba*. Austin, Tex.: University of Texas Press, 1983.

Díaz Robainas, Regino. *Cuba, Batista y La Historia*. Guatemala City: Cultural Centroamericana, 1973.

Domínguez, Jorge I. "The Batista Regime in Cuba." In *Sultanistic Regimes*, edited by H. E. Chehabi and Juan J. Linz. Baltimore: Johns Hopkins University Press, 1998.

———. *Cuba: Order and Revolution*. Cambridge, Mass.: The Belknap Press of Harvard University Press, 1978.

Dorschner, John and Robert Fabricio. *The Winds of December*. New York: Coward, McCann & Geohegan, 1980.

Duarte Oropesa, José. *Historiología Cubana: Desde 1898 hasta 1944*. Miami: Ediciones Universal, 1974.

Dur, Philip F. "Conditions for Recognition." *Foreign Service Journal* 62 (September 1985): 45.

———. *Jefferson Caffery of Louisiana: Ambassador of Revolutions: An Outline of His Career*. Rev. ed. Lafayette, La.: University of Southwestern Louisiana, 1998.

El ABC al Pueblo de Cuba: Manifesto-Programa. Found in Sumner Welles Papers. November 1932.

Esteva, Max Figueroa, Abel Prieto, and Raúl Gutiérrez. *The Basic Secondary School in the Country: an Educational Innovation in Cuba*. Experiments and innovations in education, no. 7. Paris: Unesco Press, 1974.

Fagen, Richard. *The Transformation of Political Culture in Cuba*. Stanford: Stanford University Press, 1969.

Feinsilver, Julie M. *Healing the Masses: Cuban Health Politics at Home and Abroad*. Berkeley: University of California Press, 1993.

Fermoselle, Rafael. *The Evolution of the Cuban Military: 1492-1986*. Miami: Ediciones Universal, 1987.

Fernández, Angel V. *Memorias de un taquígrafo*. Miami: Ediciones Universal, 1993.

Fernández, Damián J. *Cuba and the Politics of Passion*. Austin, Tex.: University of Texas Press, 2000.

Fernández Miranda, Roberto. *Mis relaciones con el general Batista*. Miami: Ediciones Universal, 1999.

Fernández Robaina, Tomás. *El negro en Cuba, 1902-1958: Apuntes para la historia de la lucha contra la discriminación racial*. Havana: Editorial de Ciencias Sociales, 1994.

Ferrer, Horacio. *Con el rifle al hombro*. Havana: "El Siglo XX," 1950.

Fitzgibbon, Russell H. and H. Max Healey, "The Cuban Elections of 1936," *The American Political Science Review* 30 (August 1936): 724–735.

Franco Varona, M. *La Revolución del 4 de septiembre*. Havana: n.p., 1934.

Freeman Smith, Robert, ed., *Background to Revolution: The Development of Modern Cuba*. New York: Alfred A. Knopf, 1966.

———. *The United States and Cuba: Business and Diplomacy, 1917–1960*. New York: Bookman Associates, 1960.

García Montes, Jorge and Antonio Alonso Avila. *Historia del Partido Comunista de Cuba*. Miami: Ediciones Universal, 1970.

Gellman, Irwin F. *Roosevelt and Batista: Good Neighbor Diplomacy in Cuba, 1933–1945*. Albuquerque, N. Mex: University of New Mexico Press, 1973.

González Jiménez, Emeterio M. *Cuba y Batista*. Miami: Talleres de Ahora Printing, 1989.

González, Justo. *Sargento Miguel Angel Hernández* .Havana: Cultural, 1937.

González Palacios, Carlos. *Revolución y seudo-revolución en Cuba*. Havana: Editorial Lex., 1948.

Graham, Richard, ed. *The Idea of Race in Latin America, 1870–1940*, with an introduction by Richard Graham. Austin: University of Texas Press, 1990.

Green, James R. *The World of the Worker: Labor in Twentieth-Century America*. New York: Hill and Wang, 1980.

Grubbs, Robert L. and Estelle Popham. *Gregg Shorthand for Colleges, Speed Building*. New York: Gregg Division/McGraw-Hill, 1976.

Guerra y Sanchez, Ramiro. *Azucar y población en las Antillas*. Havana: Instituto Cubano del Libro, Editorial de Ciencias Sociales, 1970.

Guggenheim, Harry F. *The United States and Cuba: A Study in International Relations*. New York: The Macmillan Company, 1934.

Guiteras, Calixta. *Biografía de Antonio Guiteras*. Havana: Cooperativa Obrera de Publicidad, 1960.

Gunther, John. *Inside Latin America*. New York: Harper & Brothers, 1941.

Gutmann Rosenkrantz, Barbara, ed. *From Consumption to Tuberculosis: A Documentary History*. New York: Garland Publishing, Inc., 1994.

Helg, Aline. *Our Rightful Share: The Afro-Cuban Struggle for Equality, 1886–1912*. Chapel Hill, N.C.: University of North Carolina Press, 1995.

Hernández-Bauzá, Miguel. *Biografía de una emoción popular: El Dr. Grau*. Miami: Ediciones Universal, 1987.

Hilty, Hiram H. *Friends in Cuba*. Richmond, Ind.: Friends United Press, 1977.

Ibarra, Jorge. *Prologue to Revolution: Cuba, 1898-1958*. Translated by Marjorie Moore. Boulder, Colo.: Lynne Rienner Publishers, 1998.

Johnson, John J. *The Military and Society in Latin America*. Stanford: Stanford University Press, 1964.

Johnston, Laurie. "Education, National Identity and Citizenship in Pre-revolutionary Cuba, 1902–1958." Paper presented at the Association of Caribbean Historians, XXXI Conference, Havana, Cuba 12–16 April 1999.

Justiz y Del Valle, Tomás. *Elogio del Dr. Alfredo Zayas y Alfonso Individuo de Número*. Havana: Imp. El Siglo XX, 1935.

Keeran, Roger. *The Communist Party and the Auto Workers Unions*. Bloomington, Ind.: Indiana University Press, 1980.

Knight, Alan. "Racism, Revolution and Indigenismo: Mexico, 1910–1940." In *The Idea of Race*, edited by Richard Graham, Austin, Tex.: University of Texas Press, 1990.

Kozol, Jonathan. *Children of the Revolution: A Yankee Teacher in the Cuban Schools*. New York: Delacorte Press, 1978.

Lancís, Antonio. *Grau: Estadista y político: Cincuenta años de la historia de Cuba*. Miami: Ediciones Universal, 1985.

Laurent, Emilio. *De oficial a revolucionario*. Havana: Imp. Ucar, García y Cía., 1941.

Lazo, Mario. *Dagger in the Heart: American Policy Failures in Cuba*. New York: Funk & Wagnalls, 1968.

López Vilaboy, José. *Motivos y culpables de la destrucción de Cuba*. San Juan, Puerto Rico: Editora de Libros, 1973.

Ludwig, Emil. *Biografia de una Isla*. Mexico City: Editorial Centauro, 1948.

Lumen, Enrique. *La Revolución Cubana 1902-1934: Crónica de nuestro tiempo*. Mexico City: Ediciones Botas, 1934.

MacGaffey, Wyatt, and Clifford R. Barnett. *Twentieth-Century Cuba: The Background of the Castro Revolution*. Garden City, N.Y.: Anchor Books, Inc., 1965.

Machado y Morales, Gerardo. *Ocho años de lucha*. Miami: Ediciones Históricas Cubanas, 1982.

Madan, Robert J. "La obra educacional del Coronel Batista," *El taquígrafo Gregg*. January 1939: 841–843.

Márquez Sterling, Carlos and Manuel Márquez Sterling. *Historia de la isla de Cuba*. Miami: Books & Mas, Inc., 1996.

Martin, Lionel. *The Early Fidel: Roots of Castro's Communism*. Secaucus, N.J.: Lyle Stuart Inc., 1978.

Martínez, Hilario. *Biografía del Coronel Fulgencio Batista y Zaldívar*. Havana: n.p., 1938.

Martínez-Alier, Juan and Verena Martínez-Alier. *Cuba: Economía y sociedad*. Paris: Editorial Ruedo Ibérico, 1972.

Martínez-Fernández, Luis, D. H. Figueredo, Louis A. Pérez, and Luis González. *Encyclopedia of Cuba: People, History, Culture*. Westport, Conn.: Greenwood Press, 2003.

McLean Petras, Elizabeth. *Jamaican Labor Migration: White Capital and Black Labor, 1850–1930*. Boulder, Colo.: Westview Press, Inc., 1988.

Meyer, Lorenzo. *Mexico and the United States in the Oil Controversy, 1917–1942*. Translated by Muriel Vasconcelos. Austin, Tex.: University of Texas Press, 1977.

Montaner, Carlos Alberto. "Cómo y por qué la historia de Cuba desembocó en la revolución." *Encuentro de la Cultura Cubana* 19 (2000-2001): 65–78.

Ordoqui, Joaquín. *Elementos para la historia del movimiento obrero en Cuba*. Havana: Comisión Nacional de Escuelas de Instrucción Revolucionaria, 1961.

Ortiz Fernández, Fernando. *Cuban Counterpoint*. New York: Alfred A. Knopf, 1947.

Osa, Enrique de la. *Cronica del Año 33*. Havana: Editorial de Ciencias Sociales, 1989.

Padrón, Pedro Luis. *Qué república era aquella!* Havana: Editorial de Ciencias Sociales, 1986.

Pérez, Lisandro. "The Demographical Dimensions of the Educational Problems in Socialist Cuba." *Cuban Studies/Estudios Cubanos*. 7 (January 1977): 33-57.

Pérez, Louis A., Jr. *Army Politics in Cuba, 1898-1958*. Pittsburgh: University of Pittsburgh Press, 1976.

———. *Cuba: Between Reform and Revolution*, 2nd ed. New York: Oxford University Press, 1995.

———. *Cuba and the United States: Ties of Singular Intimacy*. Athens, Ga.: The University of Georgia Press, 1990.

———. *Cuba Under the Platt Amendment, 1902-1934*. Pittsburgh: University of Pittsburgh Press, 1986.

———. "North American Protestant Missionaries in Cuba and the Culture of Hegemony, 1898–1920." In *Essays on Cuban History: Historiography and Research*, 53–72. Gainesville, Fla.: University Press of Florida, 1995.

———. "Politics, Peasants and People of Color: The 1912 'Race' War in Cuba Reconsidered." *HAHR*. 66 (1986): 509–539.

———. "In the Service of the Revolution: Two Decades of Cuban Historiography, 1959–1979." *HAHR*. 60 (February 1980): 79–89.

Pérez Moreno, Luis. *Cómo cuidar y atender a los ciegos*. Miami[?]: n.p., 1983.

Pérez-Stable, Marifeli. *The Cuban Revolution: Origins, Course and Legacy*, 2nd ed. New York: Oxford University Press, 1999.

Phillips, R. Hart. *Cuban Sideshow*. Havana: Cuban Press, 1935.

———. *Cuba, Island of Paradox*. New York: McDowell, Obolensky, 1959.

Pichardo, Hortensia. *Documentos para la historia de Cuba*. Havana: Editorial de Ciencias Sociales, 1980.

Pino-Santos, Oscar. *Historia de Cuba: Aspectos fundamentales*, 2nd ed. Havana: Editorial Nacional de Cuba, 1964.

Pío Elizalde, Leopoldo. *Difamación*. Mexico City: Publicaciones de Defensa Institucional Cubana, 1961.

Portell-Vilá, Herminio. *Nueva historia de la República de Cuba, 1898-1979*. Miami: La Moderna Poesía, 1986.

Potash, Robert. *The Army & Politics in Argentina 1928-1945: Yrigoyen to Peron*. Stanford: Stanford University Press, 1969.

———. *The Army & Politics in Argentina 1945-62: Peron to Frondizi*. Stanford: Stanford University Press, 1980.

Proceedings of the IV Congreso Hispano-Americano-Filipino de Taquigrafia. Stenographer Notes. Vitoria, Spain: 17–23 July 1957.

Quirk, Robert. *Fidel Castro*. New York: W.W. Norton & Company, 1993.

Read, Gerald H. "Civic-Military Rural Education of Cuba: Eleven Eventful Years (1936–1946)." Ph.D. diss., Ohio State University, 1950.

————. "The Cuban Revolutionary Offensive in Education." *Comparative Education Review.* 14 (June 1970): 131–143.

Riera Hernández, Mario. "Un presidente cordial: Carlos Prío Socarrás, 1927–1964." Unpublished manuscript.

————. *Cuba política, 1899–1955.* Havana: Impresora Modelo, 1955.

————. *Un Presidente Constructivo.* Unpublished excerpt from *Presidentes cubanos.* Miami, 1966.

Rito, Esteban. *Lucha de clases y movimiento obrero.* Havana: Impr. Nacional de Cuba, 1961.

Riverend, Julio Le. *Historia de Cuba.* Havana: Imp. "Federico Engels," 1975.

Rodolfo Miranda, Luis. *Reminiscencias cubanas: De la guerra y de la paz.* Havana: Imp. P. Fernandez y Cía, 1941.

Rodríguez Morejón, G. *Grau San Martín.* Havana: Ediciones el Mirador, 1944.

Roorda, Eric Paul. *The Dictator Next Door: The Good Neighbor Policy and the Trujillo Regime in the Dominican Republic, 1930-1945.* Durham, N.C.: Duke University Press, 1998.

Rouse, Irving. *The Tainos: Rise & Decline of the People Who Greeted Columbus.* New Haven, Conn.: Yale University Press, 1992.

Ruiz, Ramón Eduardo. *Cuba: The Making of a Revolution.* New York: W.W. Norton & Company, 1968.

Sandoval, José Enrique. *Indice cronológico de la legislación social cubana.* Havana: Rambla, Bouza, 1935.

Santamaría García, Antonio. *Sin azúcar no hay país: la industria azucarera y la economía cubana (1919–1939).* Seville: Secretariado de Publicaciones de la Universidad de Sevilla, 2001.

Santovenia, Emeterio S. *José Miguel Gómez: Contribución biográfica a la conmemoración del primer centenario de su nacimiento.* Havana: Academia de la Historia de Cuba, 1958.

Santovenia, Emeterio S. and Raul M. Shelton. *Cuba y su historia.* 2nd ed., 3 Vols. Miami: Rema Press, 1965.

Schweyer, Alberto Lamar. *Como cayó el Presidente Machado.* Madrid: Espasa-Calpe, 1934.

Schwartz, Rosalie. *Pleasure Island: Tourism and Temptation in Cuba.* Lincoln: University of Nebraska Press, 1997.

Sims, Harold D. "Cuban Labor and the Communist Party, 1937-1958." *Cuban Studies/Estudios Cubanos.* 15 (1985): 43–58.

Skidmore, Thomas. *The Politics of Military Rule in Brazil.* New York: Oxford University Press, 1988.

Slatta, Richard. *Gauchos and the Vanishing Frontier.* Lincoln: University of Nebraska Press, 1983.

Smith, Robert Freeman. "Twentieth Century Cuban Historiography." *HAHR.* 44 (February 1964): 44–73.

Sosa de Quesada, Arístides. *Brasas en la nieve: poemas.* Miami: Ediciones Universal, 1971.

————. *El Consejo Corporativo de Educación, Sanidad y Beneficencia y sus Instituciones Filiales.* Havana: Instituto Civico-Militar, 1937.

————. *Motivaciones escolares; libro de lectura para alumnos de 2o., 3o., y 4o. grados y de orientación para los maestros rurales.* Havana: P. Fernández y Cía, 1939.

Soto, Lionel. *La Revolución del 33*, 3 Vols. Havana: Editorial Pueblo y Educación, 1985.

Suárez Rivas, Eduardo. *Un pueblo crucificado* (Miami, Service Offset Printers, 1964).

Szulc, Tad. *Fidel: A Critical Portrait*. New York: Morrow, 1986.

Tabares del Real, José. *Guiteras*. Havana: Editorial de Ciencias Sociales, 1990.

———. *La Revolución del 30: Sus dos últimos años*. Havana: Editorial de Ciencias Sociales, 1973.

Tellería, Evelio. *Los congresos obreros en Cuba*. Havana: Editorial de Ciencias Sociales, 1984.

Thomas, Hugh. *Cuba: The Pursuit of Freedom*. New York: Harper & Row, 1971.

Thomson, Charles A. "The Cuban Revolution: Fall of Machado." *Foreign Policy Reports* (18 December 1935): 248–260.

———. "The Cuban Revolution: Reform and Reaction." *Foreign Policy Reports* (1 January 1936): 261-276.

Torriente, Cosme de la. *Cuarenta años de mi vida, 1898-1938*. Havana: "El Siglo XX," 1939.

Tremols, Jose J. *El 4 de septiembre en la Marina cubana*. Havana: Imprenta Siglo XX, 1935.

Upham Adams, Frederick. *Conquest of the Tropics*. Garden City, N.Y.: Doubleday, Page & Company, 1914.

Valdés, Nelson P. "Health and Revolution in Cuba." *Science and Society* 35 (Fall 1971): 311–331.

Varona Pupo, Ricardo. *Banes: Crónicas*. Santiago: Imprenta Rex, 1930.

Vega Cobiellas, Ulpiano. *Batista y Cuba: Crónica política y realizaciones*. Havana: Publicaciones Cultural, S.A., 1955.

———. *La personalidad y la obra del General Fulgencio Batista Zaldívar*. Havana: Cultural, S.A., 1943.

Vignier, E. and G. Alonso. *La corrupción política administrativa en Cuba*. Havana: Editorial de Ciencias Sociales, Instituto Cubano del Libro, 1973.

Wald, Karen. *Children of Che: Childcare and Education in Cuba*. Palo Alto: Ramparts Press, 1978.

Welles, Benjamin. *Sumner Welles: FDR's Global Strategist*. New York: St. Martin's Press, 1997.

Welles, Sumner. *The Time for Decision*. New York: Harper & Brothers Publishers, 1944.

Whitney, Robert. "The Architect of the Cuban State: Fulgencio Batista and Populism in Cuba, 1937–1940." *Journal of Latin American Studies* 32 (May 2000): 435–459.

———. "History or Teleology? Recent Scholarship on Cuba before 1959." *LARR* 36 (2001): 220–236.

———. *State and Revolution in Cuba: Mass Mobilization and Political Change, 1920–1940*. Chapel Hill, N.C.: The University of North Carolina Press, 2001.

Zanetti, Oscar and Alejandro García. *Caminos para el azúcar*. Havana: Editorial de Ciencias Sociales, 1987.

———, et al. *United Fruit: Un caso del dominio imperialista en Cuba*. Havana: Editorial de Ciencias Sociales, 1976.

INDEX

ABOUT THE AUTHOR

Frank Argote-Freyre teaches history at Kean University as well as working as an activist in the Latino community. The flight of his family from Cuba in the late 1950s and early 1960s led him to explore the period prior to the Cuban Revolution and drew him to the subject of Batista. Prior to embarking on an academic career, Argote-Freyre worked as a journalist for ten years and served three years as a congressional press secretary. He lives in New Jersey with his wife, Caridad, and two children, Amanda and Andrew.